DATA STRUCTURES AND ALGORITHMS USING

JAVA™

William McAllister
St. Joseph's College

JONES AND BARTLETT PUBLISHERS
Sudbury, Massachusetts
BOSTON   TORONTO   LONDON   SINGAPORE

World Headquarters

Jones and Bartlett Publishers
40 Tall Pine Drive
Sudbury, MA 01776
978-443-5000
info@jbpub.com
www.jbpub.com

Jones and Bartlett Publishers
Canada
6339 Ormindale Way
Mississauga, Ontario L5V 1J2
Canada

Jones and Bartlett Publishers
International
Barb House, Barb Mews
London W6 7PA
United Kingdom

Jones and Bartlett's books and products are available through most bookstores and online booksellers. To contact Jones and Bartlett Publishers directly, call 800-832-0034, fax 978-443-8000, or visit our website www.jbpub.com.

Substantial discounts on bulk quantities of Jones and Bartlett's publications are available to corporations, professional associations, and other qualified organizations. For details and specific discount information, contact the special sales department at Jones and Bartlett via the above contact information or send an email to specialsales@jbpub.com.

Production Credits
Publisher: David Pallai
Acquisitions Editor: Timothy Anderson
Editorial Assistant: Melissa Potter
Production Director: Amy Rose
Production Editor: Katherine Macdonald
Senior Marketing Manager: Andrea DeFronzo
V.P., Manufacturing and Inventory Control: Therese Connell
Composition: Northeast Compositors, Inc. and International Typesetting and Composition
Cover Design: Kristin E. Parker
Cover Image: © Vitezslav Halamka/ShutterStock, Inc.
Printing and Binding: Malloy, Inc.
Cover Printing: Malloy, Inc.

Library of Congress Cataloging-in-Publication Data
McAllister, William (William James)
  Data structures and algorithms using Java / William McAllister. —
1st ed.
      p. cm.
  Includes index.
  ISBN-13: 978-0-7637-5756-4 (pbk.)
  ISBN-10: 0-7637-5756-X (pbk.)
1. Computer algorithms. 2. Data structures (Computer science)
3. Java (Computer program language) I. Title.
  QA76.9.A43M373 2008
  005.13'3—dc22
                                    2008013120

6048
Printed in the United States of America
12 11 10 09 08   10 9 8 7 6 5 4 3 2 1

Dedication

To my best friend and wife, Gretchen (a.k.a Maggie),
who supplied endless encouragement and hundreds of commas

Contents

Preface   xi

Chapter 1   Overview and Java Review   1

  1.1   Data Structures   2
      1.1.1   What Is Data?   2
      1.1.2   What Is a Data Structure?   5
  1.2   Selecting a Data Structure   6
      1.2.1   The Data Structure's Impact on Performance   6
      1.2.2   Determining the Performance of a Data Structure   8
      1.2.3   The Trade-Off Process   9
  1.3   Fundamental Concepts   11
      1.3.1   Terminology   11
      1.3.2   Access Modes   13
      1.3.3   Linear Lists   13
      1.3.4   Data Structure Operations   13
      1.3.5   Implementing a Programmer-Defined
               Data Structure   15
      1.3.6   Procedural Abstractions and Abstract Data
               Types (ADTs)   17
      1.3.7   Encapsulation   18

v

1.4   Calculating Speed (Time Complexity)   19
      1.4.1   Big-O Analysis (O Standing for Order of Magnitude)   20
      1.4.2   Algorithm Speed   22
      1.4.3   Relative Speed of Algorithms   23
      1.4.4   Absolute Speed of an Algorithm   26
      1.4.5   Data Structure Speed   29
1.5   Calculating Memory Overhead (Space Complexity)   31
1.6   Java Review   33
      1.6.1   Arrays of Primitive Variables   33
      1.6.2   Definition of a Class   35
      1.6.3   Declaration of an Object   37
      1.6.4   Accessing Objects   39
      1.6.5   Standard Method Name Prefixes   40
      1.6.6   Shallow and Deep Copies   41
      1.6.7   Declaration of an Array of Objects   44
      1.6.8   Objects that Contain Objects as Data Members   45
      1.6.9   Classes that Extend Classes, Inheritance   47
      1.6.10 Parent and Child References   48
      1.6.11 Generic Types   49
Knowledge Exercises   53
Programming Exercises   55

Chapter 2   Array-Based Structures   59
2.1   The Built-in Structure Array   60
      2.1.1   Multidimensional Arrays   63
2.2   Programmer-Defined Array Structures   65
      2.2.1   Unsorted Array   66
      2.2.2   Sorted Array   73
      2.2.3   Unsorted-Optimized Array   79
      2.2.4   Error Checking   84
2.3   Implementation of the Unsorted-Optimized Array
      Structure   88
      2.3.1   Baseline Implementation   88
      2.3.2   Utility Methods   101
2.4   Expandable Array-Based Structures   105
2.5   Generic Data Structures   106
      2.5.1   Design Considerations   107
      2.5.2   Generic Implementation of the Unsorted-Optimized
              Array   109
      2.5.3   Client-Side Use of Generic Structures   115
      2.5.4   Heterogeneous Generic Data Structures   117
2.6   Java's ArrayList Class   118
Knowledge Exercises   120
Programming Exercises   121

Chapter 3   Restricted Structures   125

    3.1   Restricted Structures   126
    3.2   Stack   129
         3.2.1   Stack Operations, Terminology, and Error Conditions   129
         3.2.2   Classical Model of a Stack   130
         3.2.3   A Stack Application: Evaluation of Arithmetic Expressions   144
         3.2.4   Expanded Model of a Stack   146
    3.3   Queue   148
         3.3.1   Queue Operations, Terminology, and Error Conditions   148
         3.3.2   Classical Model of a Queue   150
         3.3.3   Queue Applications   161
         3.3.4   Expanded Model of a Queue   162
    3.4   Generic Implementation of the Classic Stack, a Methodized Approach   164
         3.4.1   Generic Conversion Methodology   164
    3.5   Priority Queues   168
    3.6   Java's `Stack` Class   168
    Knowledge Exercises   170
    Programming Exercises   171

Chapter 4   Linked Lists and Iterators   173

    4.1   Noncontiguous Structures   174
    4.2   Linked Lists   176
    4.3   Singly Linked Lists   177
         4.3.1   Basic Operation Algorithms   178
         4.3.2   Implementation   188
         4.3.3   Performance of the Singly Linked List   191
         4.3.4   A Stack Implemented as a Singly Linked List   194
    4.4   Other Types of Linked Lists   200
         4.4.1   Circular Singly Linked List   202
         4.4.2   Double-Ended Singly Linked List   202
         4.4.3   Sorted Singly Linked List   204
         4.4.4   Doubly Linked List   205
         4.4.5   Multilinked List   207
    4.5   Iterators   210
         4.5.1   Implementation of an Iterator   212
         4.5.2   Multiple Iterators   217
    4.6   Java's `LinkedList` Class and `ListIterator` Interface   223
    Knowledge Exercises   226
    Programming Exercises   228

Chapter 5   Hashed Data Structures   231

    5.1   Hashed Data Structures   232
    5.2   Hashing Access Algorithms   232
         5.2.1   A Hashing Example   235

5.3   Perfect Hashed Data Structures   237
      5.3.1   Direct Hashed Structure   238
5.4   Nonperfect Hashed Structures   246
      5.4.1   Primary Storage Area Size   252
      5.4.2   Preprocessing Algorithms   259
      5.4.3   Hashing Functions   262
      5.4.4   Collision Algorithms   263
      5.4.5   The Linear Quotient (LQHashed) Data Structure
              Implementation   276
      5.4.6   Dynamic Hashed Structures   290
Knowledge Exercises   298
Programming Exercises   301

Chapter 6   Recursion   303

6.1   What Is Recursion?   304
6.2   Understanding Recursive Algorithms   305
      6.2.1   *n* Factorial   306
      6.2.2   The Code of a Recursive Algorithm   307
      6.2.3   Tracing a Recursive Method's Execution
              Path   308
6.3   Formulating a Recursive Algorithm   313
      6.3.1   Definitions   313
      6.3.2   Methodology   314
      6.3.3   Practice Problems   317
6.4   Problems with Recursion   325
      6.4.1   Dynamic Programming Applied to Recursion   327
6.5   Backtracking, an Application of Recursion   328
      6.5.1   A Generalized Backtracking Algorithm   333
      6.5.2   Algorithm Adaptation Methodology   335
Knowledge Exercises   346
Programming Exercises   347

Chapter 7   Trees   351

7.1   Trees   352
      7.1.1   Graphics and Terminology of Trees   352
7.2   Binary Trees   356
      7.2.1   Terminology   356
      7.2.2   Mathematics   358
7.3   Binary Search Trees   360
      7.3.1   Basic Operation Algorithms   364
      7.3.2   Performance   380
      7.3.3   Implementation   392

7.3.4   Standard Tree Traversals   398
7.3.5   Balanced Search Trees   406
7.3.6   Array Implementation of a Binary
          Search Tree   413
7.3.7   Performance   419
7.3.8   Java's `TreeMap` Data Structure   423
Knowledge Exercises   427
Programming Exercises   429

Chapter 8   Sorting   431

8.1   Sorting   432
8.2   Sorting Algorithm Speed   434
      8.2.1   Minimum Sort Effort   435
      8.2.2   An Implementation Issue Affecting
              Algorithm Speed   436
8.3   Sorting Algorithms   436
      8.3.1   The Binary Tree Sort   437
      8.3.2   The Bubble Sort   442
      8.3.3   The Heap Sort   449
      8.3.4   The Merge Sort   458
      8.3.5   Quicksort   465
Knowledge Exercises   473
Programming Exercises   475

Chapter 9   Graphs   477

9.1   Introduction   478
      9.1.1   Graphics and Terminology of Graphs   480
9.2   Representing Graphs   484
      9.2.1   Representing Vertices   484
      9.2.2   Representing Edges   485
9.3   Operations Performed on Graphs   491
9.4   Implementing Graphs in the Vertex Number Mode   493
9.5   Traversing Graphs   494
      9.5.1   Depth-First Traversal   497
      9.5.2   Breadth-First Traversal   503
9.6   Connectivity and Paths   503
      9.6.1   Connectivity of Undirected Graphs   506
      9.6.2   Connectivity of Directed Graphs   506
      9.6.3   Spanning Trees   509
      9.6.4   Shortest Paths   518
Knowledge Exercises   530
Programming Exercises   534

Appendices   537

Appendix A   ASCII Table   537

Appendix B   Derivation of the Average Search Length of a Nondirect
Hashed Data Structure   541

Appendix C   Proof That If an Integer, P, Is Not Evenly Divisible by an Integer Less
Than the Square Root of P, It Is a Prime Number   545

Appendix D   Calculations to Show That $(n + 1) (\log_2(n + 1) - 2)$ Is the Minimum
Sort Effort for the Binary Tree Sort   547

Glossary   549

Index   563

Preface

Introduction

Data Structures and Algorithms Using Java is an undergraduate-level textbook for a computer science curriculum. It covers the entire syllabus of the Association of Computing Machinery standard curriculum courses CS103i and CS103o, "Data Structures and Algorithms" (CS2001 evolutions of the traditional CS2 course). As such, it is intended to be used as the primary text for these courses. The book is built upon my academic and industry experience, combining the pedagogical techniques I've developed and refined during 29 years of teaching with my practical knowledge of the computer field acquired during 28 years in the industry. The resulting integration of theory and application will help students at all levels to understand core concepts that will enhance their success in later courses, and ultimately, in their careers.

Why Another Data Structures Book

My primary reason for writing this book was to produce a text that was more readable, engaging, and instructive than those currently in print without compromising the scope of the ACM CS103 course material.

I wanted the text to engage students outside the classroom in the process of investigative discovery. The motivation for this was based partially on the findings from two National Science Foundation grants my colleagues and I received, whose purpose was to investigate ways of attracting students into technical areas of national need (including computer professionals) and retaining them through graduation. "Data Structures and Algorithms," a sophomore-level course, is usually the "make-or-break" course for computer science majors. As a co-principal investigator on both of these grants, I realized that a highly accessible Data Structures and Algorithms text, with improved pedagogy, would help retain students majoring in computer science.

Advantages of This Text

I've endeavored to present the minimal amount of Java code necessary to illustrate the implementation of the learned concepts. This minimal code set leaves plenty of room for meaningful programming assignments, while being thorough enough that a computer professional could use the text as a source code reference book.

The book is more comprehensive in some topic areas than current books in print, which makes it more appealing to highly capable students. The clearer language, simple examples, and abundance of instructional figures, including nearly 300 illustrations and more than 50 tables, make it more accessible to the majority of students who might otherwise struggle to grasp these and other, more challenging, concepts.

The text is aimed at both the computer scientist who implements, refines, or improves the classic data structures and the software engineer who selects and integrates library implementations of these data structures into particular applications. From the computer scientist's viewpoint, the design of each of the classic data structures is discussed and their algorithms' pseudocode developed and implemented. In addition, the characteristics of each structure that give rise to its speed and space complexity advantages (or disadvantages) are examined. From the software engineer's viewpoint, the text presents the relative merits of the classic data structures to the extent that an optimum choice could be made for a particular application. This is accomplished by deriving the speed and memory requirements of each of the classic data structures in a quantified manner, with the performance of each structure compared in a summary table at the end of each chapter. In addition, multivariable graphs are presented to demonstrate how to locate optimum design points from a memory requirement point of view. Finally, the use of the Java API implementation of the data structures is demonstrated.

Other significant advantages of this book are: a methodized approach to recursive algorithm development aimed at teaching students to "think" recursively; an introduction to the techniques and benefits of dynamic programming; and line-by-line discussions of the significant portions of the implementation code, which include the techniques for encapsulating data within a structure and the techniques for implementing generic structures.

Programming Language Background

The implementation language used in the text is Java, but since the first chapter includes a review of objects and the Java constructs and syntax necessary to understand the book's code examples, students with a programming background in other high-level languages should find the book approachable. The Java review guides students through an understanding of the fundamental concepts essential to data structures that are particular to object-oriented languages, such as Java's use of reference variables, its memory allocation model, arrays of objects, shallow and deep object copies, parent-to-child references, composition (containership), and generic features of Java 1.4.

Organization

The text employs a unique, student-friendly pedagogical approach and organizational structure. The chapters that present the classic data structures (Chapters 2, 3, 4, 5, 7, and 9) use a common template, rooted in the object paradigm, as the organizational basis of each chapter. The use of this template, embellished with topics particular to each structure, permits the student to "anticipate" the material presented in each chapter, which in turn makes the text more readable. The template begins by stating the shortcomings of the structures studied to that point and identifies the ways in which the new structure addresses some of these shortcomings. Then the structure is visually introduced, and its initialization and operation algorithms are developed in pseudocode. These algorithms are then fully implemented in Java as an encapsulated homogenous structure, and the structure's use is then demonstrated in a telephone information request application. Next, the performance of the structure is quantified, discussed, and compared to the performance of the previously studied structures. Finally, the use of the Java API implementation of the structure is discussed and demonstrated.

Chapter 1 is an introduction to the basic concepts of data structures and a review of Java. The first part of the chapter introduces the student to the concept of a data structure and its impact on the performance of a software product. The terminology and fundamental concepts common to all data structures are discussed, including encapsulation, abstraction, and algorithm performance. This section concludes with a discussion of speed complexity, space complexity, and Big-O analysis. The second part of the chapter is a review of the Java concepts and constructs necessary to understanding the implementations presented in the text. The topics include array declarations, class definitions and objects, containership, inheritance, shallow and deep copies, and the use of the generic features of Java 1.4 to write generic methods and classes.

Chapter 2 discusses the implementation of the built-in structure array and presents three programmer-defined, array-based structures. A major pedagogical advantage of this chapter is that it utilizes the simplicity of arrays and the students' familiarity with them to facilitate a discussion of the concepts common to all data structures. In the first part of the chapter, the student is encouraged to view arrays from a new perspective: a data structures perspective. Once viewed from that perspective, they can be used as a case study to illustrate the techniques of memory modeling and performance trade-offs that were employed in their design. The second part of the chapter begins the book's study of *programmer-defined* data structures by presenting three data structures built upon arrays. The simplicity of these structures allows the student to focus on learning the concepts common to all data structures. Then, having gained an early understanding of these concepts, students are free to concentrate on the more complicated conceptual details of the structures presented in subsequent chapters. The chapter also presents techniques for expanding arrays at run-time and for converting the array-based implementation developed in the chapter to a fully generic data structure using the generic features of Java 1.4. It concludes with a discussion of the use of the ArrayList class included in the Java API.

Chapter 3 presents the restricted structures Stack and Queue. The first part of the chapter discusses what they have in common with other data structures and encourages the student to consider what about them is restricted. Thus the student understands that Stack and Queue are part of the broader data structure landscape, rather than two isolated computer science topics. The second part of the chapter presents the details of Stack and Queue, including a full implementation of each structure. The Queue implementation is used as the basis of presenting a methodized approach to converting a data structure class to a fully generic class using the generic features of Java 1.4. The chapter concludes with a discussion of priority queues and the use of the Stack class included in the Java API.

Chapter 4 introduces the student to linked lists, their use in the implementation of a stack, and iterators. The first part of the chapter discusses singly linked lists and their implementation. It also includes a discussion of several variations of a singly linked list, doubly linked lists, and multi-linked lists. The second part of the chapter introduces the concept of an iterator, a discussion of the advantages of its use, and a full implementation of an iterator class. As part of this implementation, the concept of an inner class is introduced, which includes a discussion of why classes are coded as inner classes. The chapter concludes with a discussion of the use of the LinkedList and ListIterator classes included in the Java API.

Chapter 5 deals with the topic of hashing, but it significantly extends the traditional treatment of this topic. It treats the pervasive data structures that use hashing algorithms as a separate data structure category, Hashed Structures. The first part of the chapter illustrates the advantages of hashing via an example, and then it presents the algorithms of a data structure based on a perfect hashing function. The second part of the chapter discusses nonperfect hashing functions, collision algorithms and their performance, and string preprocessing algorithms used by data structures that utilize nonperfect hashing functions. Included is a discussion of optimum hash table size and a $4k + 3$ prime number generator. All these concepts are then applied in the implementation of a data structure based on the division hashing function and high performance collision algorithm. The chapter concludes with a discussion of expandable hashed structure and the use of the HashTable class included in Java's API .

Chapter 6 presents the topic of recursion. The first part of the chapter introduces recursion and provides the student with an understanding of how a recursive method works. The student is taught to think recursively in the second part of the chapter via a methodized approach to recursive algorithm development. Several examples are presented whose recursive solutions can be discovered by directly applying the methodology. Once comfortable with the methodology, the student is presented with other examples that require modification in order to discover their recursive solutions. The chapter concludes with a discussion of the speed and space complexity problems of recursive algorithms and the application of dynamic programming to alleviate these problems. Other applications of recursion appear in the chapters on trees, sorting, and graphs.

Chapter 7 introduces the student to the topic of trees. After a discussion of the terminology of trees in general and binary trees in particular, including the mathematics of binary trees, the algorithms of the binary search tree are introduced. All three cases of the delete algorithm are presented. The structure is implemented using a linked implementation, and a subsequent analysis of its performance leads to a discussion of self-balancing trees, specifically the AVL and re-black trees. The second part of the chapter presents the array-based implementation of a binary tree, which includes the pseudocode of its Insert and Fetch algorithms. The poor performance of the Delete algorithm under this implementation is discussed along with a suggested remedy. The chapter concludes with a discussion of the use of the red-black tree implementation `TreeMap` included in Java's API.

Chapter 8 presents the topic of sorting. It begins with a discussion of the motivation for sorting and demonstrates the need for efficient sorting algorithms. Included is a discussion of the parameters and techniques used to determine the speed of these algorithms. The first algorithm presented is the binary tree sort, which uses the student's knowledge of search trees as a stepping stone to the analysis of sorting algorithms. The remainder of the chapter presents four other classic sorting algorithms, and it implements two of the better performers—the merge and quick sort—recursively. As each algorithm is discussed, its speed and space complexity are determined and summarized in a table for comparative purposes.

Chapter 9 presents the topic of graphs. In the first part of the chapter, they are presented as part of the data structure landscape. After a discussion of the terminology and the mathematics of graphs, the techniques for representing them are introduced and compared, and the algorithms used to operate on them are developed and implemented. These algorithms included both depth-first and breadth-first traversals. The first part of the chapter concludes with an implementation of a graph structure that includes a depth-first traversal. The second part of the chapter discusses the issues of connectivity and paths along with the associated algorithms. These algorithms include the determination of connectivity, spanning trees, and shortest paths based on Warshall's, Dijkstra's, and Floyd's algorithms.

Supplemental Materials

The pedagogical features of the text are significantly enhanced by animation courseware that can be run on any Java-enabled browser. These animations demonstrate the functionality of the algorithms associated with each data structure presented in the text by presenting the changes that take place in main memory as the algorithms execute. Other ancillary materials provided with the text are PowerPoint lecture outlines, the text's source code, spreadsheets that can be used to perform design performance trade-offs between various data structures, and solutions to selected exercises. These supplements can be found at Jones and Bartlett's catalog page, http://www.jbpub .com/catalog/9780763757564.

Acknowledgments

I would like to thank the team at Jones and Bartlett that aided me in the preparation of this book and guided me through the publication process: my acquisitions editor, Tim Anderson; his editorial assistant, Melissa Potter; Melissa Elmore, Associate Production Editor; Kat Macdonald, Production Editor; my copy editor, Diana Coe; and the entire production staff.

I'd also like to thank the reviewers for taking the time to review the manuscript and providing many valuable suggestions, most of which have been incorporated into the textbook: Tom Murphy, Contra Costa College, and Victor Shtern, Boston University.

Most importantly, I'd like to thank my family, friends, and colleagues who not only offered encouragement but also endless patience and understanding during the times when I was too busy to be me. Finally, I'd like to thank St. Joseph's College for the sabbatical that allowed me to get this textbook off the ground.

To the Students

It's my hope that you enjoy reading this book, and that you will experience the joy of accomplishment as you learn material that is fundamental to the remarkable discipline in which we have chosen to immerse ourselves. The pedagogy on which it is based evolved through the classroom experiences I've had with hundreds of students much like you. By the time you finish this book, you will be way ahead of my son-in-law (a lawyer) who says he'd rather wait for *Data Structures: The Movie*. I imagine each of you reading and learning from this book (even before the movie version is released), and I wish you much success in your future careers.

William McAllister

CHAPTER 1

Overview and Java Review

OBJECTIVES

The objectives of this chapter are to familiarize the student with the concepts common to all data structures and to review the Java constructs used to implement them. More specifically, the student will be able to

- Understand the basic terminology of data structures, including data abstraction, encapsulation, linear lists, complexity, homogeneity, and the four basic operations performed on structures in both the key field and the node number mode.

- Explain the difference between programmer-defined and built-in data structures, shallow and deep copies, absolute and relative algorithm speed, and static and nonstatic methods.

- Understand the performance of a data structure, the factors that affect it, and the techniques used to quantify it, including the application of a Big-O analysis.

- Understand the binary search algorithm and be able to explain and verify its $O(\log_2 n)$ performance.

- Understand the significance of a data structure's density and be able to calculate it.

- Understand and be able to declare primitive and reference variables in Java, arrays of primitive and reference variables, and understand their underlying memory models.
- Understand and implement methods, classes, declarations, and operations on objects, and the passing of arguments by value.
- Implement a node definition class and an application class that creates nodes and operates on them.
- Understand and be able to implement inheritance and containership.
- Generalize a method or class using the generic features of Java.

1.1 Data Structures

A thorough knowledge of the topic of *Data Structures* is essential to both software design and implementation. Its subject matter embodies techniques for writing software that performs efficiently, as opposed to software that merely produces correct results. Properly designed data structures can increase the speed of a program and reduce the amount of memory required to store the data that the program processes. In addition, it serves as a bridge between a basic programming course and more advanced topics such as operating systems, networking, and computer organization.

When asked to reflect on their undergraduate careers, most computer scientists consider the core topic of data structures to be the most challenging course in the undergraduate curriculum. Not only is the sheer volume of the material burdensome, but the concepts and algorithms introduced in the course are quite novel. Furthermore, implementation of the concepts into functional software often tax their novice programming abilities. It is not unusual for students to struggle at the beginning of this course until their coding skills improve and they can then focus all of their attention on the underlying concepts and algorithms.

After a brief discussion of data, data structures, and their roles and importance in the field of computer science, this chapter will present topics common to all data structures. It concludes with a review of the Java language, including the topics of objects, inheritance, and generics, which are necessary to implement the concepts presented in subsequent chapters.

1.1.1 What Is Data?

Data is information.

Information such as your name, your address, and your age are all examples of data. The source of the information can be any device attached to a computer system, such as a keyboard, a mouse, a

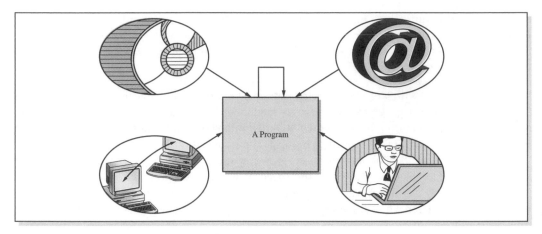

Figure 1.1 Some of the Sources of a Program's Input Data

modem, a network line, a disk drive, or some other mass storage device. Sometimes the program itself can be the source of the data if, during processing, it generates data (Figure 1.1).

All programs, when viewed on a macro level, are the same: when executed they accept input data, process the data, and then output a result (Figure 1.2). In some special cases, the input or output data set is empty, but more often it is not. Occasionally, although the input or output information *appears* to be empty, it is not. For example, consider a program that when executed simply generates a random number. It appears to have no input data; however, random number algorithms require a *seed value*, and although the value is not input by the program user, it still must be supplied for the algorithm to function properly. This seed value is often the current time supplied to the program by the computer's system clock.

Studies show that programs spend 80% of their execution time searching through memory to locate the data they process. When the data set is small, this time is usually insignificant. For example, a program that outputs the largest of 10 numbers stored in memory will identify the largest number after 10 memory accesses. Assuming a memory access takes 100 nanoseconds (10^{-9} seconds), the 10 memory accesses will be complete and the result will be available in 1,000

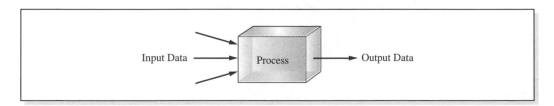

Figure 1.2 Macro View of a Program

nanoseconds. It is difficult to imagine a user growing impatient in one millionth of a second. However, if the information was needed to make a critical mid-course correction to a space probe, or to shut down a runaway nuclear reactor, the time to locate the datum could be significant, even though the data set is small.

When programs deal with large data sets, the time spent searching for a datum is more likely to be significant. Consider a program that searches sequentially through 400 million social security records. If the information requested is the 400 millionth record, and each memory access takes 100 nanoseconds, it will take 40 seconds to locate the information (400×10^6 accesses * 100×10^{-9} accesses per second). Studies show users grow impatient in one to two seconds; they find 40 seconds intolerable (Figure 1.3). Thus, the speed at which a program locates the data to be processed is usually a concern when designing programs that operate on large data sets, and it must also be considered when designing programs that operate on small data sets under stringent time constraints.

Another program design concern is efficient use of main memory. Programs execute most rapidly when both the data that they operate on and their processing instructions reside simultaneously in main memory. However, even on modern computer systems, main memory is a limited resource. Therefore, it is important that the amount of storage required in order for the data to be processed (as well as the program instructions) be kept to a minimum. Techniques for minimizing the data storage requirements of a program and the speed at which the program locates the data it processes are fundamental to the topic of data structures. Data Structures is the area of computer science that addresses these issues in order to ensure that the storage requirements and speed at which the data is accessed is consistent with the requirements of the application.

Figure 1.3 A User's Reaction to a Slow Program

1.1.2 What Is a Data Structure?

The National Institute of Standards and Technology defines a data structure as:

> "A data structure is an organization of information, usually in memory, for better algorithm efficiency."

Therefore, the study of data structures is the study of how to organize the information that a program processes in a way that improves the program's performance. Specifically, the information is organized in a way that facilitates the operations the program's algorithm performs on the data.

For example, suppose salespersons used a program to look up the price of an item in a store's inventory. A good organization of the data would be to place the most popular items at the beginning of the data set, since a sequential search would then rapidly locate them. However, this organization of the data would not as be attractive if the function of the program were to output the store's inventory in alphabetic order.

To improve the program's efficiency, the organization scheme often requires additional storage over and above the size of the program's data set. This extra storage is commonly referred to as *overhead*. Returning to our store example, if we wished to perform rapid price checks *and* rapidly produce inventory printouts, an organization scheme might store the data set twice: ordered by an item's popularity *and* ordered in alphabetic order. Although this would facilitate the operations performed on the data set (price check and inventory output) it would double the data memory required by the application.

Standard for Goodness

A good data structure is one that organizes the data in a way that facilitates the operations performed on the data, while keeping its total storage requirement at, or close to, the size of the data set.

There are two types of data structures: built-in data structures and programmer-defined data structures. Built-in data structures are schemes for storing data that are part of a programming language. Examples of these are memory cell (*variable*) declarations, arrays, and Java's String class.

Programmer-defined data structures are schemes for storing data that are conceived and implemented by the programmer of a particular program. These data structures are constructed from the built-in data structures. Examples of these are parallel arrays, class definitions, hashing schemes, linked lists, trees, stacks, and queues. As programming languages evolve, the built-in data structures have expanded to include some of the programmer defined data structures. For instance, Java's *Application Programmer Interface* includes implementations of hashing schemes, linked lists, trees, stacks, and queues. Many of these data structures are also implemented in the C++ *Standard Template Library*.

1.2 Selecting a Data Structure

The selection of a data structure for a particular application can have a significant effect on the performance of the program. Techniques borrowed from other engineering disciplines are used to ensure that the structure selected satisfies the performance criteria of the application and has a minimal impact on the overall implementation cost of the application.

1.2.1 The Data Structure's Impact on Performance

In an introductory programming course, the programs students write operate on small data sets and execution time constraints are not considered. As such, these programs are evaluated using the following two criteria (standards for goodness):

- The "penmanship" of the program is good.
- For all sets of valid inputs, the program produces the correct outputs.

Here, we will consider penmanship to include such issues as an absence of syntax errors, good variable naming, proper indentation, good organization of the code (including the use of subprograms), and proper use of the language constructs (e.g., appropriate use of `switch` statements vs. `if-else-if` statements).

These criteria are adequate for programs that operate on small data sets. However, as discussed, programs that process large sets of data, or have stringent speed constraints previously imposed on them, must also consider two additional criteria:

- Efficient use of storage—both main memory and external storage.
- Speed of execution.

There is additional criteria that brings us to the study of Data Structures, because the scheme that is selected for storing large data sets can have a significant impact on both speed and memory utilization.

To illustrate this point, consider a program that would service telephone number information requests for a large city. Aside from information requests, listings will be both added to, and deleted, from the data base as residents move into and out of town. In addition, listings will be updated as customers relocate within the town. The conditions and assumptions of the application are given in Table 1.1, as is the operation speed requirement, 0.10 seconds.

Suppose that four software firms have developed a program for this application, each of which uses a different data structure to store the data, as specified in Table 1.2.

Table 1.1

Conditions and Assumptions for a Telephone Information Request Application

Condition	Problem Assumptions
Number of phone listings	100,000,000
Size of each person's name and each listing	16 bytes and 50 bytes
Time to fetch 4 bytes from memory	100 nanoseconds (100×10^{-9} seconds)
Time to execute an instruction	2 nanoseconds (2×10^{-9} seconds)
Maximum time to perform an operation	0.10 seconds

Table 1.2

Data Structures Used by Four Telephone Information Request Programs

Program	Data Structure
1	Unsorted Array
2	Sorted Array
3	Hashing
4	Perfect Hashing

Based on the first set of criteria, all the programs perform equally well: for valid inputs, each program produces valid outputs, and they all are written with good penmanship. However, since they operate on a large data set with a specified time constraint—perform an operation within one-half second—we must also consider the two additional evaluation criteria: efficient use of memory and speed of execution.

To evaluate the speed and memory utilization of the programs, assume each program is put into service for several days. The average time needed to perform four common operations on the data set is monitored, as is the additional storage required by the programs above that used to store the 100,000,000 listings. The results, summarized in Table 1.3, show that the performances of the candidate programs differ greatly. The shaded cells in the table indicate unacceptable performance. Only programs 3 and 4 meet the speed requirement of the problem, and program 4 requires an unacceptable amount of additional memory—memory above that required to store the 100,000,000 listings. (The techniques used to calculate the data in Table 1.3 are discussed in another section of this chapter.) By examining the data in the table, we can clearly see that the choice of a data structure can have a large effect on the execution speed and memory requirements of a program.

Table 1.3

Speed and Overhead of the Candidate Telephone Information Request Program

Program	Seconds to:				Overhead Bytes Required
	Fetch a Listing	Insert a New Listing	Delete a Listing	Update a Listing	
1	5	< 0.10	5	5	0
2	< 0.10	5	5	10	0
3	< 0.10	< 0.10	< 0.10	< 0.10	5.0×10^8
4	< 0.10	< 0.10	< 0.10	< 0.10	1.7×10^{31}

1.2.2 Determining the Performance of a Data Structure

In our hypothetical telephone listing problem, we indicated that the four programs were actually put into service to evaluate their performance. However, this is most often not the way the merits of candidate data structures (i.e., the alternative structures being considered) are evaluated. It would be much too costly to code an entire program just to determine whether the performance of a candidate data structure is acceptable. Rather, this evaluation must take place during the early stages of the design of the program, before any code is written.

To do this, we borrow tools from other engineering disciplines. Consider a group of civil engineers responsible for evaluating several candidate designs for a bridge. Certainly, they would never consider fabricating each design so that they can be tested to determine which design is the best. Cost issues aside, this *build-and-test* approach to design trade-offs would be too time-consuming. Instead, civil engineers perform detailed calculations early in the design process to evaluate candidate designs. Based on the results of these calculations, they select the lowest cost design that satisfies the performance criteria.

Software engineers have adopted this design trade-off technique to evaluate candidate data structures early in the program design process. Consistent with the definition of a data structure, two sets of calculations are performed on each candidate data structure during the trade-off process:

- Calculations to determine the speed of the operations to be performed on the data.
- Calculations to determine the amount of extra storage (overhead) associated with the data structure.

These two calculations are considered to be a measure of the performance of a data structure. A high-performing data structure is one that

- Rapidly operates on the data.
- Minimizes storage requirements.

Unfortunately, due to the architecture of modern computer systems, rapid operation and minimal storage are usually mutually exclusive. Data structures that are very fast normally require high storage overhead; this was the case with our fourth telephone program's data structure. Data structures that minimize memory overhead can be slow; this was the case with our first and second telephone programs' data structure. Thus, the selection of the best structure for a particular application is usually a compromise, or trade-off, between speed and overhead and one other very important factor: cost.

1.2.3 The Trade-Off Process

Once the performance of the candidate data structures has been calculated (i.e., their speed and memory requirements), the trade-off process begins aimed at selecting the best data structure for the application. The selection of the best data structure should always be based on the following guideline:

> Select the least expensive data structure that satisfies the speed requirements and storage constraints of the application.

Thus, there are three factors to consider in the trade-off: cost, speed, and memory overhead. The process is illustrated in Figure 1.4.

Speed requirements can vary widely from one application to another. A program that is monitoring the temperature of a nuclear reactor may have to operate on its data within a few hundred nanoseconds to prevent a meltdown, while a program that updates a bank account balance may have several seconds to perform its operation. When the data processing is performed to update a display viewed by humans, an operation time of 0.1 seconds is more than adequate. Studies show that faster response times are imperceptible to humans. Whatever the speed requirements for a particular problem are, good software engineering practices mandate that they be specified before the program is designed and that they be documented in the project's *Requirements Document*.

The cost of a data structure is primarily the labor cost associated with developing the code to implement the data structure. This includes its design, coding, testing, and documentation. Some

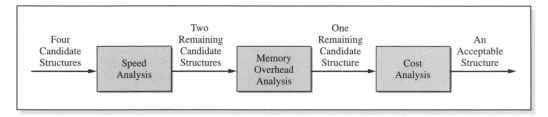

Figure 1.4 Data Structure Selection Process Involving Four Candidate Structures

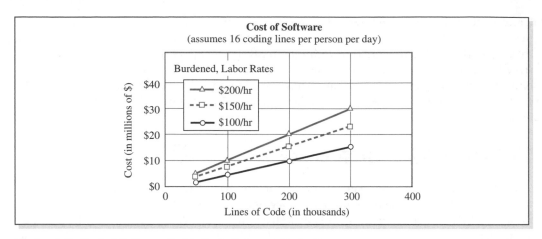

Figure 1.5 Cost of Software that is Part of a Large Project

data structures can be implemented in a few lines of code, while others take thousands of lines. Software engineering studies indicate that the cost of software is directly proportional to the number of lines of code that the software contains. Typical software costs for large software projects are illustrated in Figure 1.5 for various burdened labor rates.[1] The cost shown includes the cost of design, implementation, testing, and documentation. Thus, the most cost-effective data structures are those whose implementations require a minimal amount of code and utilize built-in data structures in their design.

Using data similar to that presented in Figure 1.5, the designer of a data structure can estimate its cost by simply estimating the number of lines of code required to implement the data structure. Once this is done, the most inexpensive structure is selected from those that meet the speed criteria and demonstrate an acceptable level of memory overhead.

To illustrate the trade-off process depicted in Figure 1.4, we will return to our telephone listing application. During the *Requirements Phase* of the project, our system analysis team has met with the customer and has consolidated their findings in the project's *Requirements Document.* Assume that the conditions specified in Table 1.1 have been reproduced from that document. As previously mentioned, four candidate data structures have been proposed for the project (see Table 1.2). These will be passed through the trade-off process illustrated in Figure 1.4.

To begin this process, the speed of the operations are calculated for each of the candidate structures using techniques explained later in this text. The results of these calculations are presented in Table 1.3. Since the required maximum operation time was specified to be less than 0.10 seconds (see Table 1.1), the first and second data structures are eliminated from further consideration. (Their maximum operation times are 6 seconds and 10 seconds respectively.)

---

[1]Burdened labor rates are the cost of one programmer working one hour and include salary, profit, and all associated expenses (e.g., employee benefits, rent, electric, heat, supplies, etc.).

Next, calculations are performed to determine the additional storage required by the two remaining candidate data structures that are necessary to store the 100,000,000 telephone listings. The results of these calculations are presented in the rightmost column of Table 1.3. The overhead associated with the fourth structure (1.7×10^{31} bytes) is unacceptably large, and so it is eliminated, leaving us with the third structure. Its additional memory requirements are only 10% larger than the minimum required to store the phone listings (5,000,000,000 bytes = 100,000,000 listings $\times$ 50 bytes per listing).

Finally, a cost analysis is performed on the third structure. As previously discussed, one simple cost analysis technique is to estimate the number of lines of code required to implement the data structure. Then, a chart similar to Figure 1.5 can be used to estimate the implementation cost. If this cost is acceptable, the structure would be used for the application. If not, other candidate structures would have to be proposed, or the requirements of the project, specified in Table 1.1, would be renegotiated with the customer.

1.3   Fundamental Concepts

All data structures share a common set of concepts that include:

- A common *terminology*.
- The manner in which the information stored in the structures is *accessed*.
- The manner in which the information is *operated on*.
- The manner in which the structures are *implemented*.
- The concepts of *abstraction* and *encapsulation*.

We will begin our study of these topics with a discussion of the common terminology of data structures.

1.3.1   Terminology

Before proceeding further with our study of data structures, it is necessary to gain an understanding of five terms fundamental to the study of data structures: field, node, key field, homogeneous structure, and linear list.

Field:

> A field is an indivisible piece of data.

Our phone listings consist of three fields: a person's name, the person's address, and the person's phone number. By *indivisible*, we mean that if the field were divided further, it would lose all meaning. For example, a seven-digit phone number could be divided into seven separate integers, but in the context of our phone directory, those seven separate integers would have no meaning in that they would no longer represent a phone number.

Node:

> A node is a group of related fields.

In our phone book problem, a single listing is called a node. In some programming languages, node definitions are coded using the structure construct (in C++ the keyword `struct`). Java programmers code node definitions using the class construct, with the node's fields coded as the class' data members. The relationship between the fields of a node must be a belongs-to relationship, so if the name field of a phone book node contains the name "Al Smith," then the address field must contain Al Smith's address, and the phone number field must contain Al Smith's phone number.

Key Field:

> A key field is a designated field in a node whose contents are used
> to identify, or to refer to, the node.

In the case of our phone book information request application, the key field would normally be the name field. The contents of the name field are used to identify which listing is to be fetched from the data set. There can be more than one key field. If the application was also used by the police to trace a call, the phone number field would also be designated as a key field.

The definitions of field, node, and key field are illustrated in Figure 1.6, which refers to the telephone listing application.

Homogeneous data set:

> A set of nodes in which all the nodes have identical fields (number and type)

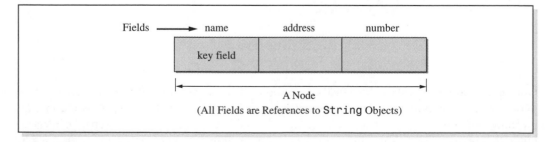

Figure 1.6 A Node and Its Fields

The data set in our telephone listing application is a homogeneous data set because each node in the data set has the same three fields (a person's name, address, and telephone number), and these fields in all the nodes are of the same type (String). Most data sets are homogeneous.

1.3.2 Access Modes

Access is the process by which we locate a node in memory. After the node is accessed or located, then an operation can be performed on it. There are two generic ways or modes used to specify the node to be accessed:

- The node number mode.
- The key field mode.

In the node number mode, the number of the node to be operated on is specified (e.g., fetch back the third node). In the key field mode, the contents of the designated key field are specified (e.g., fetch back the node whose key field contains the value "Al Smith"). Most data structures utilize the key field access mode. However, as we will see, there are some important applications in which the node number mode is used.

1.3.3 Linear Lists

An implicit assumption in the node number mode is that nodes are stored in a linear fashion, called a *linear list*. A collection of n nodes is a linear list if:

- There is a unique first node, N_1.
- There is a unique last node, N_n.
- For any other node, N_i, a unique (one and only one) node, N_{i-1}, comes just before it, and a unique (one and only one) node, N_{i+1}, comes just after it.

Figure 1.7 illustrates a group of nodes organized in two different ways. The organization of the nodes depicted on the left side of the figure satisfies the linear list condition stated above. A is the unique first node, D is the unique last node, and the other nodes have a unique predecessor and ancestor. The organization depicted on the right side of the figure is not a linear list. It does not have a unique first or last node.

1.3.4 Data Structure Operations

The operations performed on data structures can be arranged in a hierarchy. The most fundamental operation is *Insert*, the operation which is used to add a node to the data structure. It is considered to be the most fundamental operation because without it all data sets would be empty. Therefore, this operation must be available for all data sets.

At the next level of the operation hierarchy are the operations *Fetch* and *Delete*. The Fetch operation returns a node from the data set, and the Delete operation eliminates a node from the data set.

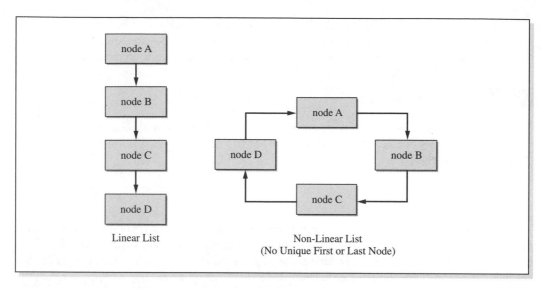

Figure 1.7 Example of a Linear and a Non-Linear List

One level above these two operations is the *Update* operation. It is used to change the contents of *all* the fields of an existing node. It is considered a higher level operation because it can be implemented as a Delete operation (to eliminate the existing node and its contents) followed by an Insert operation (to add a node that contains the new information). Stated from an implementation viewpoint, Update can be implemented with two lines of code: an invocation of the `delete` method, followed by an invocation of the `insert` method. Although simple, this is not as efficient as alternative implementations we will discuss, and all fields of a node must be supplied to the Update operation, *even if only one of them is to be updated.*

At higher levels of the operational hierarchy, operations are added to accommodate the needs of a particular application. One data structure may provide an operation to output the contents of a node, while another may provide an operation to output all nodes in sorted order. Both of these operations would use the Fetch operation. The sorted output operation could be used in our telephone number application to print the telephone directory. The action of the Insert, Delete, Fetch, and Update operations are illustrated in Figure 1.8.

To summarize, the four most fundamental operations performed on data structures are:

- **Insert**, to add a node to the data set.
- **Delete**, to eliminate a node from the data set.
- **Fetch**, to retrieve a node from the data set.
- **Update**, to change the contents of a node in the data set.

These operations can be performed in either the node number or key field access mode. The particular operations provided and the access mode utilized for a given application are specified during the systems analysis phase of the software project.

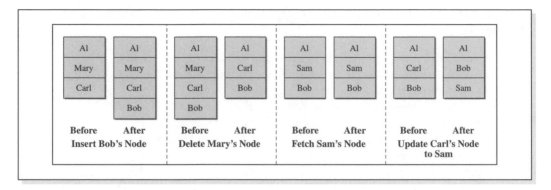

Figure 1.8 Action of the Insert, Delete, Update, and Fetch Operations

Most beginning programmers have used the Fetch and Update operations on a data structure in the node number mode without realizing it and without realizing that these operations are part of the larger Data Structures picture. Consider the built-in structure array that is introduced in all basic programming courses. It is a homogeneous data structure: all of the elements of an array must be the same type (e.g., integers), whose nodes contain one field (e.g., an integer), and the structure is accessed in the node number mode (the index is the node number).

There are two operations allowed on the data structure: Fetch and Update (Insert and Delete are not allowed). One common syntax of the Update operation used in programming languages is to code the node name on the left side of the assignment operator (e.g., Node[3] = 24). This syntax causes the contents of node 3 to be updated to the value 24. A common syntax of the Fetch operation is to code the name of the node on the right side of the assignment operator (e.g., myBalance = Node[3]). This syntax fetches back the contents of a node and then stores the value in the variable myBalance.

1.3.5 Implementing a Programmer-Defined Data Structure

Data structures are implemented in object-oriented programming languages using the class construct. The memory required for the data structure is specified as the class' data members and the operations performed on the information stored in the data structure are coded as the class' methods (subprograms). From a terminology viewpoint, the statement: "George implemented the data structure" simply means that George coded and tested the data structure class.

The best way to implement a data structure is to implement it as a *generic* data structure. Generic data structures are data structures implemented in such a way that they can be used for multiple applications, even though these applications do not have the same node structure (i.e., number of fields and type of information). Generic implementations reduce the cost of software development because once coded for a particular application, they do not need to be recoded for subsequent applications. All of the implementations presented in this book will be based on generic concepts.

To implement a data structure in a generic way, the implementation must follow a few simple guidelines. They are:

- The node definition and the data structure are coded as separate classes.
- The node definition class (sometimes referred to as the *interface* class):
  - Always contains a data member for each field in a node.
  - Usually contains a toString method to facilitate the output of a node's fields.
- The data structure, often referred to as the *implementation* class:
  - Allocates storage to maintain the structure (commonly referred to as *overhead*).
  - Allocates storage for the data set.
  - Provides initialization methods (coded as constructors) to initialize the data structure.
  - Provides methods to perform the required operations on the data set.
  - Usually provides a method to display the contents of all of the nodes.

All data structures coded in this text will use a consistent set of signatures for the basic operations (Insert, Fetch, Delete, and Update). With the exception of the Fetch method, all of the methods return a Boolean value[2] that is set to **false** if they cannot successfully complete their operation. The fetch method returns a reference to the requested node or a **null** reference if the node requested is not in the data set. The signatures for the operations in the key field mode are:

```
public boolean insert(NodeType newNode)
public NodeType fetch(keyType targetKey)
public boolean delete(keyType targetKey)
public boolean update(keyType targetKey, NodeType newContents)
```

where:

NodeType is the name of the class that defines the node,
newNode is (a reference to) the node to be inserted,
targetkey is the contents of the key field of the node to be operated on, and is of type keyType, and,
newContents is (a reference to) a node containing the new node contents.

The signatures for the operations in the node number mode are:

```
public boolean insert (NodeType newNode)
public NodeType fetch (int nodeNumber)
```

---

[2]Returning a Boolean value is simple, but it does not allow the client to determine which of several errors has occurred. Alternatives would either be to return an integer, or for the operation method to throw an exception that contains error information.

```
public boolean delete(int nodeNumber)
public boolean update(int nodeNumber, NodeType newContents)
```

where

nodeNumber is the number of the node to be operated on.

1.3.6 Procedural Abstractions and Abstract Data Types (ADTs)

"Viewing an entity as an abstraction" refers to the idea that we do not need to know the details of how the entity is implemented in order to use it. Very few people know how to implement an internal combustion engine, yet we all use automobiles. Therefore, most drivers have an abstract view of a car. They know what the car does, and how to use it, but they don't know how it works. Abstractions are functional views of an entity.

In computer science, we encounter two abstractions: procedural abstractions and data abstractions. The term *procedural abstraction* means that we do not need to know the implementation details of a method (procedure) in order to use it. We simply need to know what the method does (so we know *when* to use it) and the details of its signature or heading (so we know *how* to use it). Armed with this superficial understanding of methods, we can integrate their functionality into our programs.

Similarly, the term *data abstraction* means that we do not need to know the implementation details of a data structure in order to use it. We simply need to know what the operation methods do (so we know *when* to use them) and their signatures (so we know *how* to use them). We do not need to know the details of how the data is physically stored in memory, nor do we need to know the algorithms of the basic operations methods. A data structure that can be used with this superficial level of understanding is called an *abstract data type*. To most programmers, arrays are abstract data types. We know how to use an array to store data, but we do not know how it does it. For example, to use an array in our programs, we do not need to know that all of its elements are stored in contiguous memory, nor do we need to know how it calculates the memory address of an element given its index.

The term *standard abstract data type* refers to a data structure whose operation method signatures conform to a consistent format. The benefit of this standardization is that an application programmer can easily change the data structure used in an existing application by simply changing one line of the application: the line that declares the data structure object. Since the signatures of the basic operation methods are the same for the original and new data structures, the invocations of the basic operations need not be changed. With the exception of the implementation of the Restricted Data Structures discussed in Chapter 4, the structures implemented in this text will utilize the standard method signatures discussed in the previous section. Standardizing abstract data types reduces the cost of software.

1.3.7 Encapsulation

The principal of encapsulation is a topic of great importance in computer science because it can greatly reduce the cost of software development and maintenance by eliminating many difficult hours of debugging. In addition, encapsulation produces code that is more easily reused, thereby reducing the cost of future software products. Simply stated,

> Encapsulation is the idea that we write code in a way that establishes *compiler enforced protocols* for accessing the data that the program processes.

These protocols usually *restrict* access to the data. The enforcement of the protocols by the compiler is manifested in the compiler's inability to translate a program that violates the protocols.

As an example, suppose that in a particular application, Tom's age is stored in a memory cell named `tomsAge`, and we wish to set his age to sixteen. If the data is *not* encapsulated, we can simply write:

```
tomsAge = 16;
```

This statement could be coded *anywhere* in the application. With no encapsulation, all code in an application has free access to the memory cells that store the program's data.

However, if the data are encapsulated, direct access to these data could be limited to the code of the program's data structure module. In computer science, we would say that encapsulation limits the *scope* of the program statements that can access a data item. Then, if the statement:

```
tomsAge = 16;
```

appeared anywhere else in the program outside this scope, the compiler would issue a syntax error and terminate the translation of the program. To avoid the compile error, the following line of code would be used anywhere outside the data structure module to set Tom's age to sixteen:

```
update(Tom, 16);
```

and the assignment of Tom's age to sixteen would be done inside the `update` method of the data structure class.

The pitfalls of writing code with no encapsulation are not obvious until you have participated in the development of a large program written by a team of programmers. Consider a 1,000,000-line program written with a person's age datum (e.g., `tomsAge`) fully encapsulated inside a data structure. Within this large application, George is assigned to write a small obscure module that rarely executes. To temporarily store the age of an antique piece of **Thom**asson furniture, he writes:

```
tomsAge = 200;
```

and neglects to declare the variable `tomsAge` in his module. Coincidentally, he has chosen the name of the variable inside the data structure that stores Tom's age.

If Tom's age datum is fully encapsulated, a compile error is issued indicating that the variable `toms-Age` is inaccessible. This is sufficient for George to realize he neglected to declare the variable in his module, and he quickly corrects the problem. George then receives his own variable named `tom-sAge`, distinct from the encapsulated variable of the same name used to store Tom's age.

If Tom's age datum were not encapsulated, a compile error would not be issued, and George would deliver his module without a declaration for his local variable: `tomsAge`. Then, after ten years of trouble-free operation, circumstances cause George's module to execute for the first time, and Tom is suddenly 200 years old.

The type of error that George made—forgetting to declare a variable—is unfortunately quite common and, without encapsulation, very time-consuming to find. Yet, it can be nipped in the bud by encapsulation. This is one reason for the rise in popularity of object-oriented programming languages because, through the use of their class construct, we can easily encapsulate data.

The class construct allows us to encapsulate more than data. The code that is allowed to manipulate the data is also encapsulated inside the class construct or module. For example, the code of the `update` method used to change Tom's age to 16 would be part of the class that contained the declaration of the data member used to store Tom's age. The advantage of this *modularization* is that if the data are not being manipulated properly, the focus of the debugging process can be isolated to the code of the methods encapsulated inside the class module or to the arguments sent to these methods. No other portion of the program code needs to be examined. Furthermore, if the classes are designed properly, they can be developed and tested as independent modules and then easily integrated into an application or reused in multiple applications. The reduction in debugging time and the reusability issues associated with encapsulation of data and methods in one entity greatly reduce the time and cost required to develop a software product.

1.4 Calculating Speed (Time Complexity)

To evaluate the merits of candidate data structures during a project's design phase, we must calculate the speed of these data structures, which is related to the speed at which the code of the basic operations (i.e., the `insert`, `fetch`, `delete`, and `update` methods) execute. Paradoxically, during the design phase we have not yet written this code, so the pseudocode versions of the operation algorithms are used in this analysis.

Intuitively, we may consider the speed of an algorithm to be the time it takes to execute (in seconds). However, this measure of speed, which is commonly referred to as *wall* (clock) *time* can vary widely from one execution of the algorithm to another because it is not only dependent on the algorithm but also on many other factors. These factors include the speed of the hardware it is running on, the efficiency of the language translator and operating system, and the number of other processes the platform is executing. To eliminate these platform-dependent factors, a technique called *complexity analysis* is used to analyze algorithms, not only from a speed viewpoint (commonly referred to as *time complexity*), but also from a storage requirement viewpoint (commonly referred to as *space complexity*).

The time complexity of an algorithm is expressed as a mathematical function $T(n)$, where n is usually the number of pieces of data the algorithm processes. As we will see later in this chapter, often there are several terms in this time complexity function, which are determined by analyzing the algorithm. This analysis can be greatly simplified through the use of a mathematical tool called *Big-O Analysis*. Using this tool the algorithm analysis is reduced to determining only one term, the *dominant* term of the function. Before proceeding with our discussion of algorithm speed and the method to determine the time complexity function of an algorithm, we will examine the technique of Big-O analysis.

1.4.1 Big-O Analysis (O Standing for Order of Magnitude)

Big-O analysis is an analysis technique used to set a bound on the upper limit of a mathematical function. The analysis technique is based on the assumption that one of the terms of the function will *dominate*, or contribute, all but a negligible portion of the value of the function, usually as the independent variable(s) gets large. Under this assumption, if we are only interested in the approximate value of the function at a large value of the independent variable, we can simply evaluate the function's dominant term and neglect all of the other terms.

As an example, consider the function $y = 20,000n + 5000 \log_2 n + n^2$. Table 1.4 presents the values of this function and its three terms for increasing values of n. The highlighted values of the terms in the table are those terms that contribute more than one percent of the value of the function.

Table 1.4

Contributions of the Terms of a Function of n, as n Gets Large

n	$20,000n$	$5000 \log_2 n$	n^2	$20,000n + 5000\log_2 n + n^2$
1	2.0×10^4	0.0	1.0	2.0001×10^4
10	2.0×10^5	1.7×10^4	1.0×10^2	2.17×10^5
10^2	2.0×10^6	3.3×10^4	1.0×10^4	2.00×10^5
10^3	2.0×10^7	5.0×10^4	1.0×10^6	2.10×10^7
10^4	2.0×10^8	6.6×10^4	1.0×10^8	3.00×10^8
10^5	2.0×10^9	8.3×10^4	1.0×10^{10}	1.20×10^{10}
10^6	2.0×10^{10}	1.0×10^5	1.0×10^{12}	1.02×10^{12}
10^7	2.0×10^{11}	1.2×10^5	1.0×10^{14}	1.00×10^{14}
10^8	2.0×10^{12}	1.3×10^5	1.0×10^{16}	1.00×10^{16}

For small values of n, $n \leq 10^6$, various combinations of the three terms make significant contributions to the value of the function. Beyond this value of n, the only term contributing more than one percent of the value of the function is the third term. If we were to extend the table beyond $n = 10^8$, this trend would continue. Thus, the term $2n^2$ dominates the function $y = 2000n + 5000\log_2 n + n^2$ as n gets large, so to approximate the value of this function for $n > 10^6$ we simply need to evaluate its third term.

The dominance of one term in a multitermed function is the basis for Big-O analysis. As a result, the following guideline can be used to evaluate the functional relationships associated with an algorithm's time and space complexity.

> To approximate the value of a function of n, as n gets large, it is sufficient to identify its dominant term and evaluate it for adequately large values of n.

In an extension of this concept, constants that multiply the dominant term of a function (e.g., the 2.4 in the term $2.4n^2$) are neglected when we express the proportional relationship between the function and large values of its independent variable. Thus, we would say that the function $y = 5000n + 3000\log_2 n + 2n^2$ is proportional to n^2 as n gets large. In Big-O notation, this is written as: y is $O(n^2)$, for large values of n.

Big-O analysis is used to evaluate functional relationships that arise in all fields of engineering. However, its use in software engineering to evaluate the speed of an algorithm is simpler than its use in other engineering disciplines because there are a limited number of functions that result from the analysis of algorithm complexity. Table 1.5 presents the terms that appear in most algorithm speed functions ordered by their relative magnitude (for large values of n) from smallest to largest.

Table 1.5

Relative Dominance of Common Algorithm Complexity Terms

Dominant Term in an Algorithm's Speed Function	Name of the Dominant Term	Relative Magnitude of the Dominant Term for Large Values of n
c, a constant	Constant	Smallest
$\log_2 n$	Logarithmic	
n	Linear	
$n\log_2 n$	Linear logarithmic	
Powers of n: $n^2 < n^3 < ... < n^i \ (i < n)$	Polynomial	
c^n	Exponential	
$n!$	Factorial	Largest

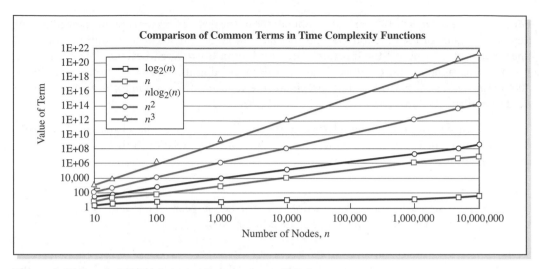

Figure 1.9 Growth Rate of Common Functions as *n* Gets Large

Figure 1.9 presents the magnitude of several of these terms as *n* gets large. It can be seen from this figure that not only is the magnitude of the terms towards the bottom of Table 1.5 larger at a given value of *n*, but also the difference in the magnitude of these terms increases as *n* increases.

It should be noted that there are two other analysis techniques used to determine the *approximate* value of a mathematical function, Big-Omega (Ω) and Big-Theta (Θ). Big-Omega is on the opposite end of the analysis spectrum from Big-O. Whereas Big-O analysis determines the upper bound of a function, Big-Omega determines the lower bound of a function. In terms of algorithms, Big-Omega analysis is used to determine the *minimum* execution speed of an algorithm. For example, the function $y = 20{,}000n + 5000\log_2 n + n^2$ has a Big-O value of $O(n^2)$ while its Big-Omega value is $\Omega(\log_2 n)$. Big-Theta analysis is used to analyze functions whose upper and lower bounds are of the same order of magnitude. For example, the function $y = 10 + n\log_2 n$ has a Big-Theta value of $\Theta(n\log_2 n)$. Not all functions lend themselves to Big-Theta analysis. In the remainder of the textbook we will use Big-O analysis in our discussions of algorithm complexity.

Having gained an understanding of Big-O analysis, we will now return to our discussion of the evaluation of an algorithm's speed.

1.4.2 Algorithm Speed

When discussing algorithm speed, there are two factors to consider:

- The *relative* speed of the algorithm (relative to other algorithms).
- The *absolute* speed of the algorithm.

Relative speed is used to determine whether an algorithm (or code segment) is faster or slower than other algorithms. Absolute speed is used to determine the actual execution time, in seconds, of an algorithm. As we have indicated, absolute speed is a much more difficult calculation, since it is dependent on many platform-specific parameters. The analysis performed to determine both of these speeds can be simplified using Big-O analysis; however, the approximation inherent in this technique may invalidate its use in the calculation of absolute speed for some time-critical applications. We shall first turn our attention to the topic of relative speed.

1.4.3   Relative Speed of Algorithms

To determine the relative speed of several candidate algorithms, we analyze each algorithm's pseudocode, to determine the dominant term in each algorithm's speed function, $T(n)$. The fastest algorithm is the algorithm whose dominant term occupies the highest position in Table 1.5 and the slowest algorithm is the one whose dominant term occupies the lowest position in Table 1.5. Stated another way, the algorithms are ranked in order of speed by their relative positions in Table 1.5; the faster the algorithm, the closer its dominant speed term is to the top of the table.

For example, suppose we are trying to evaluate the relative speed of three candidate algorithms A, B, and C, and that through an analysis of their pseudocode, we determine the dominant terms in their speed function (T_A, T_B, and T_C) to be:[3]

$$T_A \text{ is } O(\log_2 n), \qquad T_B \text{ is } O(n^3), \qquad T_C \text{ is } O(n^2)$$

Examining Table 1.5, we find that $\log_2 n$ occupies the highest position in the table (row 2). Further down the table, we see that n^2 and n^3 occupy a lower position in the table (row 5), but n^3 is to the right of n^2 on that row. Therefore the relative speed order of the algorithms from fastest to slowest is: T_A (the fastest), followed by T_C, followed by T_B (the slowest).

Suppose a more extensive analysis of the algorithms was performed to determine all of terms of their speed functions as:

$$T_A = 300 + 20 \log_2 n$$
$$T_B = 20n + n^3$$
$$T_C = 5n^2 + n \log_2 n.$$

Substituting $n = 10^6$ nodes into these equations we obtain speeds of 6.98×10^2, 1.00×10^{18}, and 5.00×10^{14} for T_A, T_B, and T_C respectively, verifying that our Big-O analysis did indeed identify

---

[3]Most often the independent variable, n, in the speed function is the number of nodes in the data structure, because the number of nodes in the structure usually determines how many instructions the algorithm executes.

the fastest algorithm. It is interesting to note that for small values of n, algorithm C is actually faster than algorithm A, but for values of n larger than 8.1, algorithm A is the fastest.

In our Big-O analysis, we do not need to determine the constant multipliers of the dominant terms in the speed functions (e.g., T_A was $O(\log_2 n)$, not $O(20 \log_2 n)$). This speeds up the analysis of the algorithms because determining the constant multiplier requires a close inspection of the algorithm, which can be a time-consuming process. The multipliers only need be determined when the level of dominance of the terms is the same. For example, if the dominant terms of two speed equations are both $O(n^3)$, then the multipliers will determine which algorithm is the fastest; the higher the multiplier, the slower the algorithm.

In summary, to use Big-O analysis to determine the relative speed of a group of algorithms we must:

- Examine each algorithm's pseudocode to determine the most dominant term in their speed equation, ignoring constant multipliers.
- Rank them from fastest to slowest based on the position their dominant terms occupy in Table 1.5 (faster dominant terms are toward the top of the table).
- If the dominant terms are the same, the constant multipliers must be determined. The higher the constant multiplier, the slower the algorithm.

Relative Speed Case Study: the Binary Search Algorithm

The binary search algorithm is a technique for rapidly finding a data item stored in an array. Given the data item, called a *search value*, the algorithm returns the index of the array element where the search value is stored. In the context of data structures, the search value is usually the contents of the key field of a node, and the array is used to store references to the collection of nodes.

The algorithm *assumes* the data in the array are *sorted*. For this example, we will assume the data are sorted in ascending order. If the array did in fact store nodes, the nodes would be stored in sorted order based on the contents of the key fields of the nodes.

The algorithm defines a *sub-array* as a portion of the given array that includes the search value. The search value can be anywhere in the array, and so initially the sub-array is the entire array. The element accessed is always the middle element of the sub-array. If this is not the desired search value, the algorithm eliminates half of the elements in the sub-array by simply determining if the accessed element is greater than or less than the search value. This process continues until the search value is found.

Assuming that the array is named `data`, it contains n elements, and that the variables `low`, `high`, and `searchValue` are defined as follows:

low stores the index of the lowest element in the sub-array,
high stores the index of the highest element of the sub-array, and
searchValue stores the value being searched for (assumed to be in the array).

Binary Search Algorithm

```
1.    low = 0;
2.    high = (n − 1)
3.    i = (high + low) / 2;
4.    while (searchValue != data[i] && high != low)
5.    { if(searchValue < data[i])
6.        { high = i − 1 } // move high down to eliminate the upper half of the sub-array
7.      else
8.        { low = i + 1 } // move low up to eliminate the lower half of the sub list
9.      i = (high + low) / 2;
10.   }
```

The algorithm assumes that the value being searched for is in the array.

When the algorithm terminates, the variable i contains the index of the array element that stores the value searched for. Having discovered the algorithm, we will now perform a Big-O analysis to determine its *relative* speed so that it can be compared to other candidate search algorithms.

If the search value is stored in the middle of the array, we will find it without executing the loop. This is the best-case scenario. In a worst-case scenario, the search value is the first (or last) element of the array. Assuming the search value is the first element (index 0) and that the array contains 16 elements, then the first value looked at would be the 8th element, then the 4th, then the 2nd, and finally the 1st element. Thus, the loop would execute three times. Extending this reasoning, if there were 32 elements in the array, the elements accessed when looking for an item stored in first element would be the 16th, 8th, 4th, 2nd, and 1st. In this case, the loop would execute 4 times. Extrapolating this reasoning further, Table 1.6 presents the maximum number of times the loop executes T for array sizes between 16 and 1024 elements.

Examining the data in this table, we can deduce the functional relationship between T and n by observing $n = 2^{(T+1)}$. To solve for the time complexity function $T(n)$ we take the $\log_2$ of both sides of the equation, which yields $\log_2(n) = \log_2(2^{(T+1)}) = T + 1$. This means that $T = (\log_2 n) - 1$. Therefore, in the *worst case*, the loop executes $(\log_2 n) - 1$ times, or the algorithm speed is, at worst, $O(\log_2 n)$. Since only one item can be located in one loop iteration, while two items can be found in two loop iterations, four in three iterations, etc., the average number of comparisons is weighted towards the maximum value of $O(\log_2 n)$.

Table 1.6

Maximum Number of Loop Executions in the Binary Search Algorithm when the Search Value is in the First or Last Element of the Array

Number of Loop Executions	Size of the Array
T	n
3	16
4	32
5	64
6	128
7	256
8	512
9	1024

If we were comparing its speed to other algorithms whose speed were also $O(\log_2 n)$, we would need to determine the multipliers of $\log_2 n$. To do this, we need to further analyze the algorithm to determine the number of instructions executed inside the loop.

Inspection of the algorithm reveals that statements 4, 5, and 9 will execute every time through the loop, as will either statements 6 or 8. Therefore the multiplier is four statements, and our refinement to the Big-O analysis of this algorithm would be to say its dominant speed term is $4(\log_2 n - 1)$. Stated another way, this algorithm will locate an item in an n element array after executing, at worst, $4(\log_2 n - 1)$ instructions as n gets large.

This is a fast search algorithm, because for an array of 10^6 elements we can locate a given value after executing, at most, $4(\log_2 10^6 - 1) = 76$ Java instructions. What makes the algorithm fast is that with every *look* into the array, we eliminate the need to examine half of the remaining elements of the array.

1.4.4 Absolute Speed of an Algorithm

Although Big-O analysis identifies the fastest algorithm from several candidates, it could be that the absolute speed of the fastest algorithm is not fast enough for a particular application. In this case, the algorithm discovery process must continue. Conversely, if the fastest algorithm is too costly to implement, or its storage requirements are unacceptably large, perhaps the absolute speed of a slower, but less costly, algorithm would meet the speed and storage requirements of the application.

The most reliable way to determine the absolute speed of an algorithm is to code it, translate it into the machine language of the platform on which it will run, and then measure its wall time as it processes a representative set of input data on that platform. However, this is not often practical during the design process, and so it is useful to perform a more convenient but less accurate analysis technique to approximate absolute speed. Assuming the CPU is dedicated to the execution of the algorithm, we can express execution time, t, of the algorithm as the sum of the execution time of the individual instructions in the machine language translation of the algorithm. Assuming the translation consisted of n instructions, we have:

$$t = t_{m1} + t_{m2} + \ldots + t_{mn}$$

where:

n   is the total number of machine language instructions in the translation of the algorithm, and

t_{mi} is the time required to execute the ith machine language instruction.

In order to obtain a more workable form of the previous equation, we categorize the machine language instructions into groupings based on the number of clock pulses that are required to execute the instruction. Assuming there are g groupings, the above equation becomes:

$$t = t_{m1} + t_{m2} + \ldots + t_{mn} = \sum_{i=1}^{g} (t_i * n_i)$$ **Equation 1.1**

where:

g is the number of instruction groupings,

t_i is the time required to execute an instruction in the ith grouping, and

n_i is the number of instructions in group i.

In the simplest case, instructions are assumed to be in one of two groups ($g = 2$): those that access memory, and those that do not. The reason for distinguishing between instructions that access data in memory from those that do not is that memory access instructions execute much slower than *nonaccess* instructions. Typically, the speed of memory is orders of magnitude slower than the time it takes the CPU to perform math or logic operations, or to transfer data between its registers.

To illustrate this speed difference, consider a system with a 2-gigahertz clock and an average memory access time (the time to read or write a single memory word) of 50 nanoseconds.[4] Assuming

---

[4]For simplicity, it will be assumed that all of the data are resident in the same part of the system's memory hierarchy and, therefore, one memory fetch speed can be used for all memory fetch instructions. In fact, data resident in cache memory can be fetched faster than data stored in RAM memory, which can be fetched faster than data stored in other parts of the memory hierarchy.

that the CPU executes one nonaccess instruction (i.e., math, logic, or register transfer instructions) in one clock pulse, the time to execute a nonaccess instruction, t_{na}, would be

$$t_{na} = (1 \text{ instruction} / \text{clock pulse}) \times (1 \text{ pulse} / 2 \times 10^9 \text{ seconds}) = 0.5 \times 10^{-9} \text{ seconds}$$

$$= 5 \times 10^{-10} \text{ seconds}.$$

The time to execute a memory access instruction t_a would be

$$t_a = 50 \text{ nanoseconds} = 50 \times 10^{-9} \text{ seconds} = 5 \times 10^{-8} \text{ seconds}$$

which is 100 times slower than the 5×10^{-10} seconds to perform a nonaccess instruction.

With g = 2, equation 1.1, which gives the absolute speed of an algorithm in seconds:

$$t = t_1 n_1 + t_2 n_2 = t_{na} \times n_{na} + t_a \times n_a$$

Equation 1.2

where:

t_{na} is the time to execute a memory nonaccess instruction,
n_{na} is the number of memory nonaccess machine language instructions executed,
t_a is the time to execute a memory access instruction, and
n_a is the number of memory access machine language instructions executed.

The execution times (t_{na} and t_a, in equation 1.2) can be determined from the specification of the computer system hardware. To determine the number of instructions in each group (n_{na} and n_a), we examine the algorithm line-by-line to determine which grouping each line falls into. We can then make an assumption regarding the number of machine instructions per pseudocode line. These techniques are illustrated in the following case study.

Absolute Speed Case Study

As an example, consider the following code sequence to sum the elements of the two-dimensional array data consisting of n rows and n columns.

```
1.  row = 0;  t = 0;
2.  while(row < n)
3.  {  column = 0
4.     while(column < n)
5.     {  t = t + data[row, column]
6.        column = column + 1
7.     }
8.     row = row + 1
9.  }
```

To determine n_{na} and n_a, we inspect the algorithm, revealing that Line 1 will execute once; Lines 2, 3, and 8 will execute n times; and Lines 4, 5, and 6 will execute n^2 times. Next we need to identify which of these are not memory access instructions. Modern optimizing compilers will recognize the value of storing variables (such as loop variables or counters) that are accessed repeatedly inside of loops, in CPU registers. Therefore, Lines 1, 2, 3, 4, 6, and 8 are not considered memory access instructions. Line 5, however, refers to a different element of the array every time through the inner loop, and therefore requires a memory access. Line 5 also performs an addition operation. Assuming one CPU operation translates into one machine language instruction, we have:

$$n_{na} = 2 + 3n + 3n^2 \text{ (from Lines 1 + Lines 2, 3, 8 + Lines 4, 5, 6)}$$

$$n_a = n^2 \text{ (from line 5).}$$

Assuming the same hardware as in the previous example ($t_{na} = 5 \times 10^{-10}$ seconds per nonaccess instruction and $t_a = 5 \times 10^{-8}$ seconds per memory access instruction), the execution time, t_a, of the algorithm would be:

$$t = t_{na} \times n_{na} + t_a \times n_a = (5 \times 10^{-10}) \times (2 + 3n + 3n^2) + (5 \times 10^{-8}) \times (n^2).$$

For a 1000×1000 element two dimensional array ($n = 10^3$), this equation evaluates to t = 0.0515 seconds.

It is interesting to note that a Big-O analysis would have resulted in a relative speed of O(n^2), and if the memory access instruction execution time were used for each instruction executed, the algorithm execution time would have been 0.050 seconds (1000^2 instructions * 5×10^{-8} seconds per instruction). This is within 3% of the time determined by the more complex absolute speed analysis.

To summarize, the procedure to calculate absolute speed of an algorithm (to within a good approximation) is:

1. Analyze the algorithm to determine the number of instructions that will be executed. For instructions in loops, this will be a function of n, the number of times the loop executes.
2. Identify the memory access and nonaccess instructions.
3. Add up the number of access and nonaccess instructions to determine n_a and n_{na} respectively.
4. Determine the hardware dependent time to execute the access and nonaccess instructions, t_a and t_{na} respectively.
5. Calculate the speed of the algorithm as: $t = t_{na} \times n_{na} + t_a \times n_a$.

1.4.5 Data Structure Speed

As previously discussed, the speed of a data structure depends upon the speed of its operation algorithms. However, after calculating either the relative or the absolute speed of the algorithms of each candidate data structure, it still may not be obvious which data structure is the fastest.

Consider the following case study. Suppose that two candidate data structures, A and B, are being considered for an application in which only the Insert and Fetch operations will be required. As

Table 1.7		
Insert and Fetch Operation Speed for Two Candidate Data Structures		
Data Structure	**Insert Speed (seconds)**	**Fetch Speed (seconds)**
A	2.0	0.10
B	0.2	0.11

part of the design process, the absolute speed of these algorithms has been calculated for each of the structures as shown in Table 1.7.

By examining the speeds of the operations of the two structures presented in the table, we would probably conclude that B is the best structure. After all, Structure B is 10 times faster in insertion speed, and the two structures are very close in fetch speed.

However, the data presented in the table is insufficient to allow conclusions about which data structure is best for this application. We need another piece of information: the frequency of each operation. Suppose that during a typical day, 1,000,000 fetch operations and no insert operations are performed. In this case, A would be the faster structure. This would be the case for an application in which, after the initial data set is stored, no new nodes are added to the structure. An example of this kind of a data set would be a language dictionary, where the two fields in the nodes are a word and its definition.

As illustrated in this example, to determine the best structure for an application we must consider not only the speed of the operations but also the frequency at which the operations are performed over a given period of time. A good parameter that does this is a frequency-weighted average operation time, t_{avg}, defined as:

$$t_{avg} = (t_1 * f_1 + t_2 * f_2 + t_3 * f_3 + ... + t_n * f_n) / (f_1 + f_2 + f_3 + ... + f_n)$$

where:

t_i, is speed of the ith operation ($i = 1, 2, 3, ..., n$),
n is the number of different operations available on the structure, and
f_i, is frequency of the ith operation ($i = 1, 2, 3, ..., n$).

Applying this to our case study involving the dictionary database involves two operations:

$$n = 2; \text{ and } t_{avg} = (t_1 * f_1 + t_2 * f_2) / (f_1 + f_2).$$

Substituting the data from Table 1.7 for t_1 and t_2; and substituting frequencies of 1,000,000 fetches per day for f_1, and 0 inserts per day for f_2, the average speeds for Structures A and B are:

$$t_{avg} = (2.0 * 0 + 0.10 * 10^6) / (0 + 10^6) = 0.10 \qquad \text{for Structure A}$$

$$t_{avg} = (0.2 * 0 + 0.11 * 10^6) / (0 + 10^6) = 0.11 \qquad \text{for Structure B}$$

The equation for t_{avg} is normally expressed in a simpler form. The denominator is divided into each term of the numerator to give:

$$t_{avg} = (t_1 * p_1 + t_2 * p_2 + t_3 * p_3 + ... + t_n * p_n)$$

where p_i is the probability of the ith operation and is equal to $f_i / (f_1 + f_2 + f_3 + ... + f_n)$

This form of the equation is more convenient, because rather than specifying the number of times each operation is performed over a period of time, we simply specify the probability of the operation occurring (e.g., 10% = 0.1). Keep in mind that the sum of the probabilities for all operations must equal one. Applying this form of the equation to our test case, and realizing the probability of an insert operation is 0% (0.0) and the probability of a fetch operation is 100% (1.0), we obtain:

$$t_{avg} = (t_1 * p_1 + t_2 * p_2) = 2.0 * 0.0 + 0.10 * 1.0 = 0.10 \qquad \text{for Structure A}$$

$$t_{avg} = (t_1 * p_1 + t_2 * p_2) = 0.2 * 0.0 + 0.11 * 1.0 = 0.11 \qquad \text{for Structure B}$$

As a special case, if all operations are equally probable (the p_i's are equal) then the equation for t_{avg} is reduced to an arithmetic average of the operation speeds. To illustrate this, consider four operations, all with equal probabilities (25% = 0.25). Assuming the operation times were 1, 2, 3, and 4 seconds, the arithmetic average would be 10 / 4 = 2.5, and the above formula would yield:

$$t_{avg} = (t_1 * p_1 + t_2 * p_2 + t_3 * p_3 + ... + t_n * p_n)$$
$$= (1 * 0.25 + 2 * 0.25 + 3 * 0.25 + 4 * 0.25) = 0.25 (1 + 2 + 3 + 4)$$
$$= 0.25(10) = 2.5.$$

1.5 Calculating Memory Overhead (Space Complexity)

All encapsulated data structures must allocate sufficient memory to store the information inserted into the data structure. In addition to that storage, they must also allocate storage that is used by the operation algorithms to maintain the structure. This extra memory, in excess of that required to store the nodes' information, is called *overhead*.

Some structures require a minimal amount of overhead storage, while others require a large amount. Since memory is a coveted resource, data structures that minimize overhead are more desirable and are said to be more *memory efficient*.

The parameter (or metric) used to specify how efficiently a data structure uses memory is *density*, D, defined as:

$$D = \text{information bytes / total bytes}$$

$$= \text{information bytes / (information bytes + overhead bytes)}$$

where:

> *information bytes* is the amount of memory required to store the information stored in the structure, in bytes,
> *total bytes* is the total amount of memory allocated to the structure, in bytes, and
> *overhead bytes* is the amount of memory required to maintain the structure, in bytes.

From the previous equation we see that the density, D, equals one when the overhead is zero; otherwise, D is always less than one. In fact, as the overhead memory required by a data structure gets large, D approaches zero, and since all data structures have some overhead, the range of density, D, is:

$$0 < D < 1$$

Stated another way, memory-efficient data structures have a density close to one, while memory-inefficient data structures have densities that approach zero.

Consider our telephone listing nodes, where each node has 50 information bytes and the number of nodes in the structure, n, is 100,000,000. If these nodes are stored in a data structure that utilizes an additional 10 bytes per node to maintain the structure, its density would be 0.83, calculated as:

$$D = \text{information bytes / (information bytes + overhead bytes)}$$

$$= (50 \times n) / ((50 \times n) + (10 \times n))$$

$$= (50 \times 100{,}000{,}000) / ((50 \times 100{,}000{,}000) + (10 \times 100{,}000{,}000))$$

$$= (50) / (50 + 10) = 50 / 60 = 0.83.$$

The overhead memory required by the data structure in the above example is a multiple of the number of nodes in the structure, n. When this is the case, the density of the structure D is not a function of the number of nodes in the structure, since n can be eliminated from both the numerator and the denominator of the density equation. The density of our 100,000,000 node structure would calculate to 0.83 whether there are 100,000,000 nodes or 10 nodes stored in the structure.

Some data structures require a set (or constant) amount of overhead, O, independent of the number of nodes. The density for these types of structures increases as the number of nodes in the data structure increases. To demonstrate this, assume that each node has w information bytes, and thus the density is:

$$D = w * n / (w * n + O) = 1 / (1 + O / (w * n))$$

Since the overhead, O, was assumed constant and the node width, w is constant for a particular data structure, as n gets large, $O / (w * n)$ approaches zero, and therefore D approaches $1 = 1 / (1 + 0)$.

Often data structures are a combination of the two cases discussed previously: they have a set amount of memory overhead, O, as well as an additional amount of overhead per node. The density of these structures also increases, as the number of nodes increases.

1.6 Java Review

There are several Java constructs, operations, and concepts that are used in the implementation of most data structures. These are:

- The declaration of an array of primitive values.
- The definition of a class.
- The declaration of an object.
- Accessing an object.
- Deep and shallow copies.
- The declaration of an array of objects.
- Objects that contain objects as data members.
- Objects that extend objects: inheritance.
- Parent and child references.
- Generic methods and classes.

Familiarity with these topics, which are usually covered in the first course in computer science, is assumed in the subsequent chapters of this book. However, some of these topics are introduced late in the first computer science course, if they are covered at all. As a result, some students have only a superficial knowledge of these topics or no knowledge at all. Therefore, a formal review of these topics is useful before proceeding to subsequent chapters.

1.6.1 Arrays of Primitive Variables

Primitive variables are single instances of integral or real types of information. They are declared using the Java data types `boolean`, `byte`, `short`, `int`, `long`, `char`, `float`, and `double`. Assuming `dataType` represents a primitive type, arrays of these primitive variables are declared using the syntax

```
dataType[] arrayName;
arrayName = new dataType[arraySize];
```

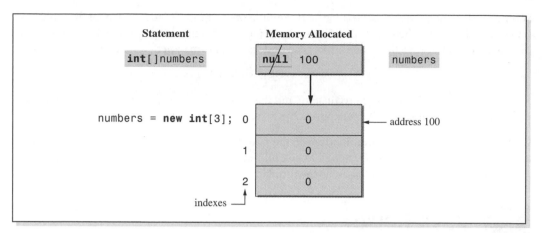

Figure 1.10 Allocation of Storage for an Array of Primitives

where `arraySize` is an integer that specifies the number of elements in the array, and it must be a numeric literal (e.g., 3) or an integer variable (that has been assigned a value).

As an example, to declare an array named *numbers* to store three integers we write:

```
int[] numbers;
numbers = new int[3];
```

It is very useful to understand the memory allocation process resulting from each of the above statements. The first statement (`int[] numbers;`) allocates a reference variable[5] (one that can store a memory location) named `numbers` initialized to the value `null`. The second statement allocates three contiguous memory cells, each of which can store an integer value, and also stores the address of the first integer memory cell into the reference variable `numbers`. Finally, each cell is assigned an index value starting from zero (in ascending order), and each of the integer memory cells is initialized to zero. Figure 1.10 illustrates the two-step memory allocation process resulting from the execution of the two statements. The shaded parts of the figure are a result of the first statement's execution. All other parts of the figure are produced by the second statement.

An alternate syntax can be used to code the two statements as a single statement:

```
int[] numbers = new int[3];
```

The memory allocation of the single-statement syntax is the same as when the two-statement grammar is used.

---

[5]In other programming languages, reference variables are often called pointers.

The array reference variable, like all variables in Java, can only be allocated once in a program, or a *duplicate definition* compile error will result. Therefore, if the size of the array is to change as the program executes, the two-line grammar is required. The code

```
int[] numbers;              // declares the reference variable numbers
numbers = new int[3];       // allocates a three element integer array
       :
       :
numbers = new int[2343];    // resizes and reinitializes the array
```

is syntactically correct, while the code:

```
int[] numbers = new int[3];    // allocates numbers and a three element array
       :
       :
int[] numbers = new int[2343]; // error, re-declaring numbers is not allowed
```

results in a syntax error because the reference variable, numbers, on the above line of code has been declared a second time.

1.6.2 Definition of a Class

A class is a programmer-defined type that consists of data definitions and methods (subprograms) that operate on that data. The name of the class is the name of the newly defined type. The definition of the class (the class statement) does not allocate any memory. As is the case with the built-in primitive types, it simply provides a template for the memory that will be allocated when an instance of this newly defined type (or class) is declared. The simplest grammar for defining a class is:

```
public class ClassName
{   // definition of data members
    // definition of member methods (subprograms)
}
```

where ClassName is the name of the class.

The keyword **public** is called an *access modifier*, and it will be used in all the class definitions in this text,[6] Its use allows a method in any application to declare a reference variable of this class type. In addition, throughout this text the data members of a class will be specified using the **private** access modifier that instructs the translator to enforce the encapsulation of the class' data members.

---

[6]Other Java access modifiers are **private**, **protected**, and **package**.

```
 1. public class Person
 2. { // definition of the data members
 3.     private int age;
 4.     private double weight;

 5.   // definition of member functions
 6.     public Person(int a, double w) // the constructor
 7.     {   age = a;
 8.        weight = w;
 9.     } // end of constructor

10.     public String toString()  // returns annotated value of data members
11.     {  return( "this person's age is: " + age +
12.                 "\nand their weight is: " + weight);
13.     } // end of toString method
14. } // end of Person class
```

Figure 1.11 The Class Person

As an example, consider a class named Person (shown in Figure 1.11) that will contain two data members, age and weight. In addition, the class will contain two methods: a two-parameter constructor that will initialize the data members and a toString method to facilitate the output of the data members' values.

The translator considers the method Person (Lines 6–9 in Figure 1.11) to be a constructor method because it has the same name as the class. A constructor method executes automatically when an instance of the class, an *object*, is declared.[7] Aside from the indentation used in this code, there are two penmanship issues to be followed when coding classes:

- Names of classes should always begin with an uppercase letter (e.g., Person).
- Names of data members and methods (except for the constructors) should always begin with a lowercase letter (e.g., age, weight, toString) and an uppercase letter is used when a new word begins within the name (e.g., toString).

Parameter names used in method headings (e.g., a and w on Line 6) should not be the same as the names of the data members (age and weight on Lines 3 and 4). When they are the same, the compiler creates a new local variable (within the method) with the same name as the data member. All references to the variable within the method are to the local variable and not to the data member. This issue will be discussed further in the next section.

---

[7]Constructor methods are used to construct new objects.

1.6.3 Declaration of an Object

Just as we can declare instances of the built-in type **int** to store an integer, we can declare instances of the programmer-defined type Person to store a person's information. An instance of a built-in type is called a variable, while the instance of a class is called an *object*. Objects can be created in Java using a two-line grammar:

```
ClassName objectName; // declares a reference variable
objectName = new ClassName(argumentList); // declares an object
```

As an example, consider the class Person defined in Figure 1.11. To declare an object in this class named *tom* that is 25 years old and weighs 187.6 pounds, we write:

```
Person tom;                  // allocates a reference variable named tom
tom = new Person(25, 187.6); // creates a person object and places its
                             // address into the reference variable tom
```

Again, it very useful to understand the memory allocation process resulting from each of the previous statements. The first statement (Person tom;) allocates a reference variable named tom that can store the address of a Person object. The value **null** is stored initially in this memory cell.

The second statement allocates an object in the class Person and places the address of the object into the memory cell tom. Inside the newly created object, two memory cells are allocated: an integer called age and a double called weight. Then, since the second statement supplied two arguments (25, 187.6), the two-parameter constructor executes. As coded on Lines 6–9 of Figure 1.11, this constructor places the values 25 and 187.6 into the data members of the newly created object with the statements: age = a; weight = w;. Figure 1.12 illustrates the two-step memory allocation process resulting from the execution of the two statements. The shaded parts of the figure are a result of the first statement's execution. All other parts of the figure are produced by the second statement.

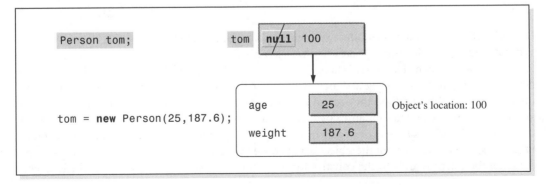

Figure 1.12 Storage Allocation for a Person Object

The name of the reference variable is considered to be the name of the object. It is good penmanship to begin the names of objects with lowercase letters, using an uppercase letter when a new word begins (e.g., `myBalance`).

The two line declaration of the object `tom` discussed previously can be coded as a single statement:

```
Person tom = new Person(25, 187.6);
```

However, as with arrays, the two-line grammar must be used if the object is to be declared more than once in a program. Although the contents of the reference variable, `tom`, can be changed to refer to different objects as the program executes, it (like any other variable), can be declared only once.

The sequence of code that declares the object is referred to as *client code*. This term comes from the idea that just as clients come to a vendor to obtain products, clients come to the class to obtain objects. Therefore, object-oriented programs contain two types of code: client code and class definition code. The authors of the two may be, and often are, different programmers. For example, most beginning programmers are clients of the class `String`, in that they declare `String` objects in their program by writing:

```
String name;
name = new String("bob");
```

or

```
String name = new String("bob");8
```

Each object declared in a program is allocated its own memory locations to store the values of its data members. Consider the client code:

```
Person tom = new Person(25, 187.6);
Person mary = new Person(21, 127.3);
```

Here, two objects (and, of course, two reference variables) are created and initialized as shown in Figure 1.13.

Each object, `tom` and `mary`, contains two memory cells. One named `age` and one named `weight`. What is sometimes confusing is that when we examine the line of code `age = a;` in the constructor of the class `Person` (Figure 1.11, Line 7), we cannot tell which of the memory cells named `age` depicted in Figure 1.13 is being assigned. The constructor, `Person`, simply assigns the first argument to the variable `age` (and the second argument to the variable `weight`) without mentioning an object's name. The determination of which object receives the argument values is decided by the client code. This is typical of object-oriented programming. When the client code creates an object, it specifies the name of the object being created (in this case, `tom` or `mary`) and that object's data members are assigned by the constructor. Therefore, to answer the question of which object's

---

8In the special case of a `String` object we can declare objects using a third grammar: `String name = "bob";`

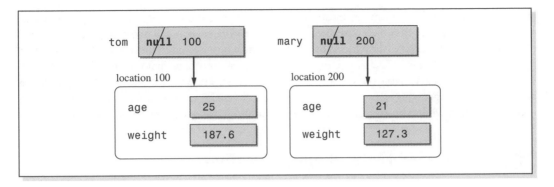

Figure 1.13 Storage Allocation for Two `Person` Objects

age is being assigned a value by the constructor code `age = a;` we must look at the constructor invocation in the client code. For example, if the client code was `Person tom = ` **new** `Person(25, 187.6);` then the variables `age` and `weight` in Tom's object would be assigned by the constructor.

1.6.4 Accessing Objects

After an object is declared, the client code can invoke any publicly accessible method declared in the class. Publicly accessible methods are methods that are declared using the **public** access modifier in their heading. In the class `Person`, the method `toString` is a **public** method since its code begins with the keyword **public** (e.g., **public void** `toString()`). Once again, if we examine the code of the method `toString`, we cannot tell which object's `age` and `weight` the lines:

```
return( "this person's age is: " + age +
        "\nand their weight is: " + weight);
```

are referring to. That reference is specified in the client code. In object-oriented languages, the client specifies the object that the method is to *operate on* (or *access*) by mentioning the object name in the method invocation statement[9] using the following grammar:

```
objectName.methodName();
```

Thus, to output the contents of the `age` and `weight` data members of the object `mary`, the client code would be

```
System.out.println(mary.toString());
```

Accessing information stored in objects is slower than accessing information stored in primitive variables.[10] Suppose that an integer is stored in a primitive variable at location 2000. The integer is fetched

---

[9]An exception is a **static** method, declared using the keywords: **public static,** which is invoked by mentioning the class name followed by the method name (e.g., `Math.sqrt(9)`).

[10]Primitive variables store integers, doubles, etc.

by simply accessing the contents of location 2000. However, if the integer is a data member of an object, it is stored inside the object and accessing the integer then becomes a two-step process. First the reference variable that stores the address of the object must be accessed to locate the object, and then the integer can be accessed. Referring to Figure 1.13, to access Tom's age, first the object's address, 100, stored in the reference variable tom must be accessed, and then, knowing the address of the object, the contents of the integer age can be accessed. Thus, in Java, accessing information in objects requires two memory accesses, while accessing information in primitive variables requires only one memory access.

1.6.5 Standard Method Name Prefixes

One advantage of programming in a high-level language is that the code is much more readable. To further promote readability, Java programmers have adopted a prefix convention for naming methods. The prefix gives insights into the source or destination of the data the method processes. Four of these prefixes are *input*, *show*, *set*, and *get*.

The prefixes input and show are used to indicate that the information is flowing between an *I/O device* and the method. Often this I/O device is a user-interface device (e.g., keyboard or monitor). The other two prefixes, set and get, indicate that the information is flowing between the client code and the method. A set method typically contains a parameter list, and a get method is typically a nonvoid method that contains a **return** statement. Figure 1.14 illustrates the information source and destination implied by these prefixes (as well as toString).

Consistent with these prefixes, a method named getAge added to the class Person would be a method that returned a person's age to the client code, while the method setWeight would be a method the client code could use to store a person's weight in a Person object. Their code would be:

```
public int getAge()              public void setWeight(double w)
{  return age;                    {  weight = w;
}                                }
```

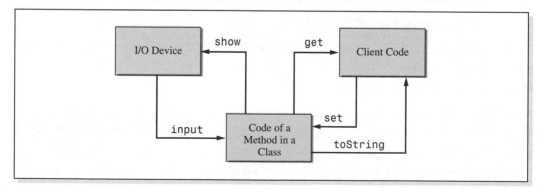

Figure 1.14 Class Method Prefixes

Without `set` and `get` methods, the client code would not be able to access an object's data members, since good programming practice dictates that all class data members are declared with private access to encapsulate the data inside of the class' objects.

Assuming a `Person` object named `tom` stores information about Tom, the following client code fetches Tom's age from his object and then sets his weight to 200 pounds.

```
int tomsAge = tom.getAge();    tom.setWeight(200.0);
```

One more comment on standardized names: The class `Person` contains an example of a method named `toString`, which is a standardized name for a method that returns a string containing the annotated values of a class' data members. As illustrated in Figure 1.14, it is similar to methods that use the `get` prefix in that it returns information to the client code.

1.6.6 Shallow and Deep Copies

Copying information from one primitive variable to another is done with the assignment operator. As an example, assume we have two integer variables i and j that store 10 and 20, respectively. The code `i = j;` copies the value from j into i, leaving j unchanged. After the operation, both i and j store the value 20.

When we are dealing with objects, the copy operation is not as simple, because there are two types of copy operations we can perform on objects: *shallow* and *deep* copies. As we demonstrated, when an object is allocated, the address of the object is stored in a reference variable. To help understand the difference between shallow and deep copies, it is useful to imagine the reference variable floating on the surface of water, with the object (weighed down by its data) sunk to a greater depth. Figure 1.15 depicts two `Person` objects, `tom` and `mary`, using this analogy.

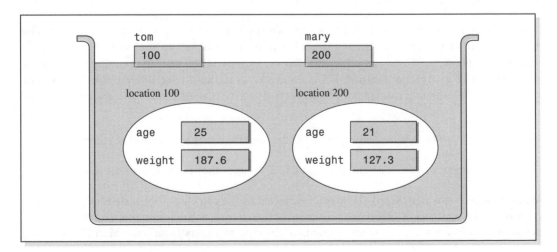

Figure 1.15 Shallow and Deep Copy Water Analogy

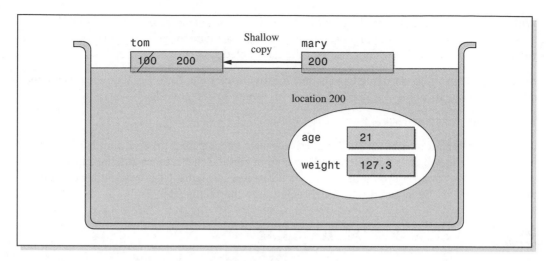

Figure 1.16 A Shallow Copy of the Object `mary` into the Object `tom`

When a shallow copy is performed, the memory affected by the copy is at the shallow depths (the surface of the water). Therefore, shallow copies only affect the contents of the (shallow floating) reference variables. The Java syntax to perform a shallow copy is:

```
referenceVariable1 = referenceVariable2; // shallow object copy
```

Thus, to shallow copy `mary` into `tom`, we write:

```
tom = mary; // shallow copy of mary into tom
```

The action of the statement is the same as when we copy one primitive variable into another. The value 200 stored in the variable `mary` is copied into the variable `tom`, and `mary` would remain unchanged (Figure 1.16). As a result, both reference variables then refer to the same object. Since the address of the object at location 100 is no longer stored in a reference variable, it would be returned to the available storage pool by the Java memory manager. After the shallow copy, the statements

```
System.out.println(tom.toString());  and  System.out.println(mary.toString());
```

would both output an age of 21 and a weight of 127.3, since they both refer to the same object.

When a deep copy is performed, the memory affected by the copy is at deeper depths. Deep copies only affect the contents of objects; the contents of the reference variables remain unchanged. The action of a deep copy is to copy the contents of the data members from one object into the data

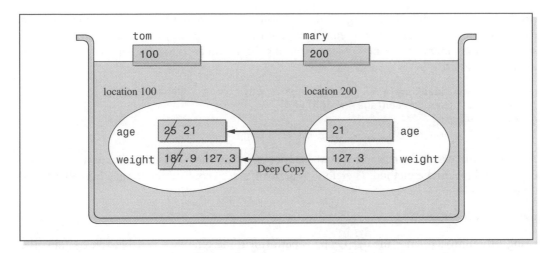

Figure 1.17 A Deep Copy of the Object `mary` into the Object `tom`

members of the other object. The result of a deep copy of Mary's object into Tom's object is shown in Figure 1.17. After the deep copy, the statements

```
System.out.println(tom.toString());   and   System.out.println(mary.toString());
```

would both output an age of 21 and a weight of 127.3 pounds (as they did after the shallow copy was performed). However, in the case of the deep copy, the output is coming from two different objects. Since the reference variables are unaffected by the deep copy, both objects are still referred to (or referenced), and Java's memory manager does not recycle either object. Both objects continue to exist after a deep copy.

Java does not provide an operator to perform a deep copy. Rather, a method must be coded in the class of the objects that copies every data member of one object into the corresponding data member of the other object. For example, one version of a method to deep copy `Person` objects (coded in the class `Person`) would be:

```
public void deepCopy(Person object2)
{  age = object2.age;
   weight = object2.weight;
}
```

Then, to perform a deep copy of object `mary` into object `tom`, we would code:

```
tom.deepCopy(mary);
```

An alternate approach to the coding of a deep copy method is often used in the implementation of data structures. In this approach, the method performs the deep copy into a *newly created* object and returns a reference to the new object. Assuming the method was to deep copy a `Person` object, its code would be:

```
public Person deepCopy() // returns a reference to a Person object
{  Person p = new Person(age, weight);
   return p;
}
```

As we have discussed, the `age` and `weight` mentioned in this method is the age and weight of the object that invokes the method. Therefore, to perform a deep copy of object `mary` into object `tom`, we would code:

```
tom = mary.deepCopy();
```

Using this approach, after the deep copy is performed, the reference variable `tom` contains the address of a newly created object whose data members contain the same values as the object `mary`. Since the variable `tom` references the newly created object, Figure 1.17 does not accurately depict the action of this version of a deep copy method. There are three objects involved here, the object referenced by `mary`, the object referenced by `tom`, and the newly created object returned from the `deepCopy` method whose address will be assigned to the variable `tom`.

1.6.7 Declaration of an Array of Objects

An array of objects is declared using a three-step process. Suppose, for example, we wish to allocate an array of 10 objects. First, as with an array of primitives, we must declare a reference variable in which to store the location of the first element of the array. Second, we must declare the 10-element array. In the case of an array of 10 primitives, this step gives us the 10 primitive storage locations. However, in the case of an array of objects, this step gives us an array of 10 *reference variables* that will store the address of (or *point to*) our 10 objects. It is in the third step that we finally allocate the 10 objects, setting their locations into the array of 10 reference variables.

Specifically, the three steps necessary to allocate an array of *n* objects are:

- Declare a reference variable in which to store the location of the first element of the array.
- Declare an array of *n* reference variables that will store the address of the *n* objects.
- Declare the *n* objects and set their locations into the array of *n* reference variables.

The following code declares an array of three `Person` objects named `employee`, each initialized to 21 years old and 187.6 pounds.

```
Person[] employee;                    // Step 1: allocate the reference variable
employee = new Person[3];             // Step 2: allocate the array of
                                      //         reference variables
for(int i = 0; i < 3, i++)            // Step 3: allocate the objects and set
                                      //         their locations in the array
   employee[i] = new Person(25, 187.6); //        of reference variables
```

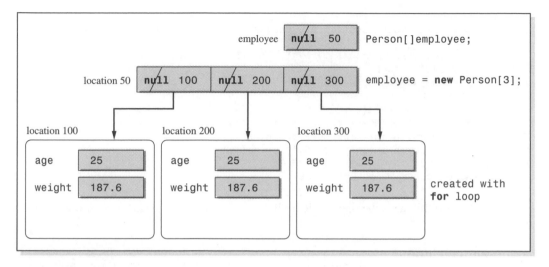

Figure 1.18 Storage Allocation for an Array of Three `Person` Objects

The memory allocation associated with the previous code is illustrated in Figure 1.18.

Alternately, the code could be abbreviated as:

```
Person[] employee = new Person[3];      // Steps 1 and 2: allocate the
                                         //   reference variable and the array
                                         //   of reference variables
for(int i = 0; i < 3, i++)               // Step 3: allocate the objects and set
    employee[i] = new Person(25, 187.6); //   their locations into the array of
                                         //   reference variables
```

1.6.8 Objects that Contain Objects as Data Members

Suppose your friend Bob was asked to conduct several classes at a weight loss clinic, each containing three students, and he has asked you to computerize his record keeping. Obviously, each student in Bob's classes is a person, and each has an age and a weight. In other words, Bob's classes will contain `Person` objects.

Being an object-oriented programmer, you realize that a good model for Bob's venture would be a class named `WeightLossClass` that *contains* `Person` objects. The class would initialize the weight and height of each person and be able to output their data. The code of this class would be:

```
1.  public class WeightLossClass
2.  { // data members
3.      private Person person1, person2, person3; // three Person reference
                                                   // variables
```

```
4.    // methods
5.    public WeightLossClass(int a1, double w1, int a2, double w2, int a2,
                             double w3)
6.    { person1 = new Person(a1, w1);   // allocation of three Person objects
7.      person2 = new Person(a2, w2);
8.      person3 = new Person(a3, w3);
9.    } // end of constructor
10.   public void showAll()
11.   { System.out.println(person1.toString());
12.     System.out.println(person2.toString());
13.     System.out.println(person3.toString());
14.   } // end of showAll method
15. } // end of class WeightLossClass
```

Having established this class, the client code for Bob's application could create two of Bob's classes with the statements:

```
WeightLossClass class1 = new WeightLossClass (21, 300.1, 54, 250.2, 32, 400.3);
WeightLossClass class2 = new WeightLossClass (63, 195.4, 38, 160.5, 73, 195.6);
```

The objects `class1` and `class2` would each contain three `Person` objects. These objects are referenced by the variables declared on Line 3 of the `WeightLossClass` class, and are allocated by the constructor on Lines 6–8. The constructor's parameters are the age and initial weight of the three students. Figure 1.19 shows the memory allocated by the constructor for the `class1` object. Naturally, other methods would have to be added to the class such as a member method to change the weight of the students as they (ideally) lose weight.

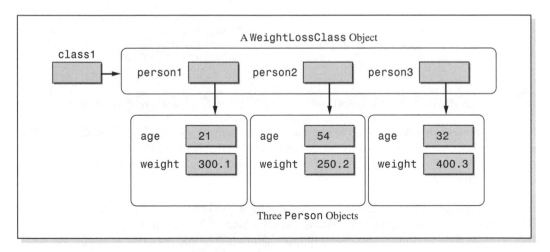

Figure 1.19 A `WeightLossClass` Object Containing Three `Person` Objects

1.6.9 Classes that Extend Classes, Inheritance

Suppose that your friend Bob asked you to improve his WeightLossClass application by adding another piece of information about a student: goal weight. Thus, weight loss clinic attendees may now be considered to be an *extension* of a person in that they have the attributes of a person (age and weight) but also have the additional attribute of goal weight.

Being an object-oriented programmer, you realize you can easily *extend* the class Person to construct a new class, WeightLossClient, using the object-oriented programming concept of *inheritance*. The new class would have all the data members and methods of the Person class as well as the new data member, goal weight. In addition, it would contain a constructor and a toString method to accommodate the additional data member. The code of the new class would be:

```
1.  public class WeightLossClient extends Person
2.  { // member data
3.      private double goalWeight;
4.      // member methods
5.      public WeightLossClient(int a, double w, double g)
6.      { super(a,w); // initializes the age and weight, the inherited
                      // attributes
7.          goalWeight = g;
8.      }
9.      public String toSting()
10.     { String s = super.toString(); // invokes the inherited toString method
                                       // for age and weight
11.         return (s + "\nand the person's goal weight is: " + goalWeight);
12.     }
13. } // end of class WeightLossClient
```

The clause **extends** Person in the heading of the class WeightLossClient indicates that the class inherits all the attributes and methods of the class Person. We say that the class Person is the *parent* (or **super** class) of the *child* class WeightLossClient. Line 3 of the class adds the new (third) data member that will store a person's goal weight. The code **super**(a,w) on Line 6 invokes the parent class' (Person's) constructor to initialize the age and weight data members, and Line 10 invokes the parent class' toString method to fetch the annotated values of the person's age and weight. Line 7 initializes the goal weight, and Line 11 adds the value of the goal weight to the annotated string returned from the Person class' toString method.

To use the new class in Bob's application, the Person objects contained in the class WeightLossClass would be replaced with WeightLossClient objects, and the class' constructor would be expanded to process the goal weight. The revised code follows.

```
1.  public class WeightLossClassRevised
2.  { // data members
3.      private WeightLossClient person1, person2, person3; // 3 Client
                                                           // ref. variables
```

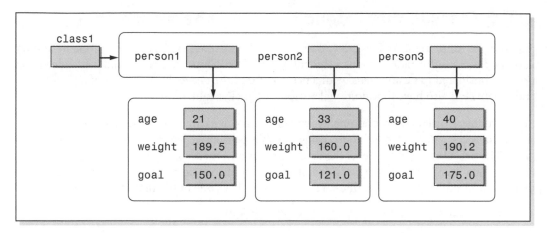

Figure 1.20 A WeightLossClass Revised Object Containing Three Initialized WeightLossClient Objects

```
4.    //  methods
5.    public WeightLossClassRevised(int a1, double w1, double g1,
6.                                  int a2, double w2, double g2,
7.                                  int a3, double w3, double g3)
8.    {  person1 = new WeightLossClient (a1, w1, g1);  // allocation of 3
9.       person2 = new WeightLossClient (a2, w2, g2);  // WeightLossClient
10.      person3 = new WeightLossClient (a3, w3, g3);  // objects
11.   }
12.   public void showAll()
13.   {  System.out.println(person1.toString());
14.      System.out.println(person2.toString());
15.      System.out.println(person3.toString());
16.   } // end of showAll method
17. } // end of class WeightLossClientRevised
```

When a WeightLossClass object is created, the goal weight, along with the age and weight, are specified as arguments to the constructor. Thus, the client code to create Bob's class1 object is now:

```
WeightLossClassRevised class1 = new WeightLossClassRevised(21, 189.5, 150.0,
                                                           33, 160.0, 121.0,
                                                           40, 190.2, 175.0);
```

The resulting object is shown in Figure 1.20.

1.6.10 Parent and Child References

When a new class is created that is an extension of an existing class, we say the new class is a child (or *sub*) class and that the existing class is a parent (or *super*) class. In Java, a parent class reference

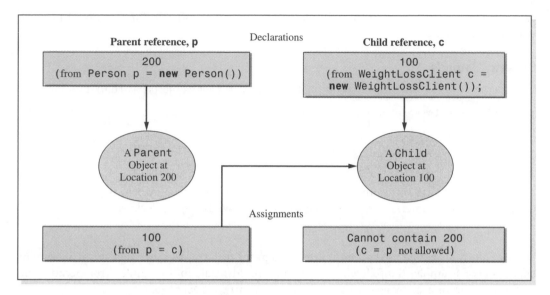

Figure 1.21 Allowable Assignments Between Parent, p, and Child Reference, c, Variables

variable *can* contain the address of a child object; however, a child class reference variable *cannot* contain the address of a parent object. If the reference variables p and c are declared as:

```
Person p = new Person();                    // creates a parent object
WeightLossClient c = new WeightLossClient();  // creates a child object
```

the statement p = c; is valid, and it places the address of the child object into the parent reference variable. The statement c = p; would be invalid because child reference variables cannot refer to parent objects. If, however, a parent reference actually stores the address of a child object, the statement c = (WeightLossClient)p; is valid syntax for placing (or coercing) the address of the child object stored in p, into the child reference variable c. The allowable assignments involving parent and child reference variables are illustrated in Figure 1.21.

To summarize, using an old-fashioned parenting analogy, a parent can point to a child (object), but it is improper for a child to point to a parent (object).

1.6.11 Generic Types

A generic type, or generic typing, is the defining new feature in Java 5.0. It is a language feature that allows the author of a method or class to generalize the type of information with which the method or class will deal. The choice of the type of information is left to the invoker of the method or the declarer of an object. Thus, a generic method can be invoked in one part of a program to process an array of Integer objects, and the same method can be invoked in another part of the program to process an array of Double objects. In the case of a generic class, the type of the class' data members and the parameters of the class' methods can be different for each object instance that the program declares.

Generic Methods

Consider the code shown below that outputs an array of Integer objects passed to it.

```
1.  public static void outputIntegerArray(Integer[] array)    // nongeneric array
                                                              // output method
2.  {  for(int i = 0; i < array.length; i++)
3.         System.out.println(array[i]);
4.  }
```

Assuming this method exists, the invocation statement outputIntegerArray(ages); would be used to output the contents of the array ages that stores five Integers declared as

```
Integer[] ages = {10, 20, 30, 40, 50};
```

However, it could not be used to output the contents of the array weights that stores a group of Doubles. For example, the following statements would result in a compile error because the method is expecting an Integer array and it is sent an array of Doubles.

```
Double[] weights = {10.1, 20.2, 30.3, 40.4, 50.5};
outputIntegerArray(weights);  // compile error
```

Using generics we could generalize the method so that it could be used to output any type of numeric object. The generic version of the output method, renamed outputNumericArray consistent with its generic nature, is shown below.

```
1.  public static <T> void outputNumericArray(T[] array)    // generic version of
                                                            // outputIntegerArray
2.  { for(int i = 0; i < array.length; i++)
3.         System.out.println(array[i]);
4.  }
```

Comparing the generic version of the method to the original version, we see that two simple changes have been made to make the method generic. Both of the changes are made to the method's signature (Line 1). Just before the return type specification, which for this method is void, a *type placeholder* <T> is coded.[11] This indicates to the compiler that this method will use a generic type T in its code, which it does in the parameter list. (The parameter type Integer in the nongeneric version of the method has been change to T in the generic version.) The actual type that T represents will be the type of the argument that appears in an invocation of the generic method. Thus, the following statements would effectively replace T with the type Integer during the first invocation (Line 3), and T would be replaced with the type Double during the second invocation (Line 4).

```
1.  Integer[] ages = {10, 20, 30, 40, 50};.
2.  Double[] weights = {10.1, 20.2, 30.3, 40.4, 50.5};
```

---

[11]The name of the generic placeholder (i.e., T) is arbitrary. Any valid Java identifier can be used.

```
1.   public class PersonGeneric<T, E>
2.   { // definition of the data members
3.       private T age;
4.       private E weight;
5.     // definition of member functions
6.       public PersonGeneric(T a, E w) // the constructor
7.       {  age = a;
8.          weight = w;
9.       }
10.      public String toString()
11.      {  return("this person's age is: " + age +
12.                 "\n and their weight is: " + weight);
13.      } // end of toString method
14.  } // end of PersonGeneric class
```

Figure 1.22 The Person Class Shown in Figure 1.11 Written Generically

```
3.   outputArray(ages);    // Integer substituted for place holder T
4.   outputArray(weights); // Double substituted for placeholder T
```

One restriction placed on the use of generics is that within the code of the method objects cannot be declared in the generic type (e.g., T myObject = **new** T(); is not allowed).

Generic Classes

Type placeholders can be used in the definition of classes to defer the decision as to the type of information that the class deals with until a specific object is declared. Figure 1.22 presents the code of a class named PersonGeneric, which is the code of the class Person (presented in Figure 1.11 modified to make it generic).

As shown on Line 1 of Figure 1.22, to make a class generic we code the generic placeholder(s) at the end of the class' heading. In this case, two placeholders are specified (separated by a comma), which indicates to the compiler that this class' code will use generic types T and E in its code. These will be the types of the class' two data members, and so Line 3 has been modified to use type T, and Line 4 has been modified to use type E. Finally, on Line 6, the types of the constructor's parameters have been changed to the generic types T and E.

With these modifications in place, we can declare an object and specify the types of the age and weight data members for that object when it is declared. For example, the syntax to declare an object tom whose age and weight are both doubles would be:

```
PersonGeneric <Double, Double> tom = new PersonGeneric <Double, Double> (10.23,
                                                                          102.56) ;
```

To declare an object `bill` whose age and weight were they same types as a Person object (integer and double), we would write:

```
PersonGeneric <Integer, Double> bill = new PersonGeneric <Integer, Double>
(1, 15.1)
```

It should be mentioned that the above declarations of the objects `tom` and `bill` take advantage of the *autoboxing* feature added to the Java language in Java 5.0 to simplify the coding examples. The object declaration for Bill's object indicates that placeholders T and E will be references to `Integer` and `Double` objects respectively. Therefore, the constructor on Line 6 of the `PersonGeneric` class (Figure 1.21) must be sent a reference to objects of these types when the object `bill` is created. However, the argument list used to create Bill's object contains primitive constants (i.e., 1 and 15.1), not references to `Integer` and `Double` objects. To prevent a compile error, Java 5.0's autoboxing feature creates these `Integer` and `Double` objects for us. Without the autoboxing feature, the code to declare Bill's object would have to be

```
Integer a = new Integer(1);
Double w = new Double(15.1);
PersonGeneric <Integer, Double> bill = new PersonGeneric <Integer, Double> (a, w);
```

The above three lines cannot be replaced with the line

```
PersonGeneric <int, double> bill = new PersonGeneric <int, double> (1, 15.1);
```

because primitive types (e.g., **int** and **double**) cannot be substituted for type placeholders (e.g., T and E in the class `PersonGeneric`).

Knowledge Exercises

1. What is data?

2. Define the term Data Structure.

3. What is a built-in data structure?

4. What three criteria are used to determine whether a data structure is acceptable for a particular application?

5. What factors determine the cost of software?

6. It has been estimated that a program will consist of 300,000 lines of code. If the burdened cost of a programmer's efforts is $150 per hour, determine the cost of the program.

7. Put the following terms in size order: node, field, data set.

8. An application is to be written that would allow students to find out their GPA (a double) and their total number of credits (an integer), given their student number (an integer).

   (a) Draw a picture of the node used in this application. Include field names and data types.

   (b) Give the node width in bytes.

   (c) Which field would be the key field?

9. You have been asked to write a nonvoid, one-parameter method to access nodes in a data set. What will be the argument passed to your method, and what will be the type of the returned value if the access mode is:

   (a) the key field mode?

   (b) the node number mode?

10. Nodes are stored in a linear list. What node comes just before, and just after, node 6?

11. Give the four basic operations performed on data structures, and tell what each operation does.

12. The nodes in a data set are objects of type: Listing. Give the signatures (the method headings that include types and parameters) for the four basic operations if they are performed in the:

    (a) Node number mode.

    (b) Key field mode (assuming the key field is a String).

13. Define the terms procedural abstraction and data abstraction.

14. Define the term encapsulation.

15. What is the Java keyword that encapsulates data inside an object?

16. Three algorithms A, B, and C, are under consideration for the Insert operation of a particular data set. Through an analysis of these algorithms, their speed functions have been determined to be: Algorithm A: $23n + 36n^2$; Algorithm B: $6 + n\log_2(n) + n$; Algorithm C: $\log_2 n + 36n^2$.

EXERCISES

(a) Calculate the value of these three functions when n, the number of nodes in the data structure, is equal to 1,000,000.

(b) Using Big-O analysis, calculate the value of each function.

(c) Determine the percent difference between the values calculated in parts (a) and (b) for each algorithm.

17. A 1000 element array is used to store integers in ascending order. The array is to be searched using the binary search algorithm for the two integers 5215 and 7282. How many elements of the array would be examined by the algorithm to locate

(a) the integer 5215 stored in element 499?

(b) the integer 7282 stored in element 686?

18. What is the maximum and minimum number of times the search loop will execute when searching through an array of 1,048,576 integers if the search algorithm is

(a) the binary search?

(b) the sequential search?

19. Half of the integers stored in the array data are positive, and half are negative. Determine the absolute speed of the following algorithm, assuming: the time to execute a memory access is 100 nanoseconds and that all other operations (arithmetic, register accesses, etc.) take 10 nanoseconds.

```
for(int i = 0; i<1000000; i++)
{ if(data[i] < 0)
        data[i] = data[i] * 2;
}
```

20. Observations of the "traffic" on a data structure over a certain period of time indicate that 500 Insert operations, 500 Delete operations, 700 Fetch operations, and 200 Update operations were performed on a data set. If Insert operations take 10 nanoseconds, Delete operations take 250 nanoseconds, Fetch operations 200 nanoseconds, and Update operations take 300 nanoseconds, determine:

(a) the probability of performing a Fetch operation over the observation period.

(b) the average speed, in nanoseconds, of the data structure over the observation period.

21. Calculate the density of a data structure whose data set consists of 1,000,000 nodes, assuming the structure requires 1,000,000 bytes of overhead to maintain itself, and:

(a) each node in the data set contains 2000 information bytes.

(b) each node in the data set contains 20 information bytes.

22. Repeat the above exercise assuming the overhead is 10 bytes per node.

23. State the Java code to declare an array of 100 integers named ages.

24. State the Java code to declare an array of three Listing objects named data that are initialized with the no-parameter constructor.

25. Draw a picture of the storage allocated in the previous exercise. Assume the array is stored at location 20, and the three objects are stored at locations 60, 70, and 50.

26. Two objects, `objectA` and `objectB`, are objects in the class `Listing`. The object `objectA` is copied to `objectB`. How many objects exist after the copy, if the copy is performed as:

    (a) a deep copy?

    (b) a shallow copy?

27. Of the two types of copies discussed in the previous exercise, which one produces a clone (an exact duplicate of an existing object)?

28. Give the signature of a method named `deepCopy`, that clones an object in the class `Listing` sent to it as a parameter and returns a reference to the clone.

29. Give the Java invocation to clone the object `objectA` (using the method discussed in the previous exercise) and store a reference to the clone in the variable: `newListing`.

Programming Exercises

30. Write a generic method that could output three numbers of any primitive numeric type sent to it, and include a driver program that demonstrates it functions properly.

31. Write a Java program to accept an item's name and price from the user and output them to the console.

32. Write a Java program to accept the names of *three* items and their prices from the user and outputs them and the *average* price to a message box.

33. Write a Java program to accept three item names and prices, and output them. Also, output the average price if one of the items is named Peas (not case sensitive) *otherwise* output: "no average output".

34. Write a Java program to accept an *unlimited* number of item names and prices, and output them. In addition, output the average price if one of the items is named Peas (not case sensitive) *otherwise* output: "no average output". The inputs will be terminated by a sentinel price of −1. (Do not include the −1 in the average.)

35. Write a Java program to accept a *given* number of item names and prices and then output them in the reverse order in which they were input. In addition, output the average price if one of the items is named Peas (not case sensitive) *otherwise* output: "no average output". (The first user input will be the number of items to process.)

36. Add a static method to the program described in one of the two previous exercises that that outputs "Welcome To St. Joseph's College" before the items and prices are output. The method `main` should invoke this method.

37. Add a method to the program described in the previous exercise that accepts and returns a *single* item name that is input by the user. The prompt presented to the user should be passed to the method as an argument.

38. Modify the program described in one of the four previous exercises so that the average price is calculated by a separate method and returned to the invoker.

39. Modify the program in the previous example so that after it produces its output, it asks the users if they would like to process another group of items. The program should terminate when the user enters "no" (not case sensitive). Otherwise, it continues processing names and ages.

40. Write a class named Listing that contains two data members, name (a String) and number (an integer). The class should have a no-parameter constructor, a two-parameter constructor, and a toString method to facilitate the output of the values of the data members. It should also contain set and get methods for each data member. Write a driver program that is progressively developed (i.e., expands as methods are added to the class Listing) that demonstrates each method in the class functions properly.

41. Write the class whose diagram is shown below *and* write a driver program (progressively developed) to test the class (verify that all the methods function properly). The default (no-parameter constructor) should initialize the String data member name to " " and numeric data member to zero. The input method should allow the user to input the values of an object's data members.

```
┌─────────────────────────────┐
│          Listing            │
├─────────────────────────────┤
│ - String name               │
│ - int age                   │
├─────────────────────────────┤
│ + Listing()                 │
│ + Listing(String, int)      │
│ + String toString()         │
│ + void input()              │
│ + void setName(String)      │
│ + void setAge(String)       │
│ + String getName()          │
│ + int getAge()              │
└─────────────────────────────┘
```

42. Write an application that declares an *array* of three Listings (defined in one of the two previous examples) whose contents are input by the user. After being input, the listings should be output in reverse order.

43. Draw the memory allocated to the Listing objects described in the previous example.

44. Code the definition of the class whose diagram follows. The constructors should allocate the array (data) of Listing object references sized to either 100 elements (the no-parameter constructor) or the number of elements specified by the argument sent to the one-parameter constructor. The method, addListing, will add a new Listing object to the array at index *next*. The showAll method will output the values of the data members of all the Listing

objects. Write a progressively developed driver program to demonstrate that the class functions properly. The class listing is described in Exercise 41.

DataStructure

Listing[] data   // an array of Listing objects
 int size = 100   // the default number of listings in
 // the array
 int next = 0;   // index of next available array element

DataStructure ()   DataStructure (numberOfListings)   **void** addListing (Listing newListing)   **void** showAllListings()

45. Write a program to count the number of times the search loop of the binary search algorithm executes when searching for an integer contained in a one-dimensional array of sorted integers in the range 1 to 65,000. Use the Java method random in the Math class to generate the integer, targetInt, to be located (i.e., targetInt = 1 + (int) Math.random()*65,000). The program should accept an input, n, the number of integers to be located, and then output the average number of times the loop executed after locating the n randomly generated target integers. For comparative purposes, also output the $\log_2 65{,}000$.

46. Write a class named DataStructure that contains a no-parameter constructor and the four basic operation methods inset, fetch, delete and update in the node number mode. The operation methods should use the standard signatures presented in this chapter. Assume that the nodeType is an object in the class Listing. Each method, when invoked, should just output a message to the console that it was invoked. The fetch method should return a **null** reference to Listing object. The class Listing can be the class described in Exercise 41 or coded as an empty class: i.e., **public** class Listing {}. If you use the key field mode signatures, assume a String key type. Write an application that demonstrates that your class is coded properly.

CHAPTER 2

Array-Based Structures

OBJECTIVES

The objectives of this chapter are to familiarize the student with the use of the built-in structure array, the implementation techniques common to all data structures, and the use of these techniques to develop three array-based structures. More specifically, the student will be able to

- Understand the memory-model programming languages used to implement arrays, and the advantages and disadvantages of this representation.

- Explain which of the four basic operations are allowed on the built-in structure array and the Java syntax for using these operations.

- Understand the techniques for designing data structures that make them application independent, and understand the techniques for designing applications that allow them to easily change the data structures they use to store their data.

- Understand the advantages and disadvantages of array-based structures.

- Understand and be able to quantify the performance differences of three array-based structures, and the role of sorting in the performance of these structures.

- Fully implement an array-based structure in the key field mode.

59

- Explain the error conditions associated with the four basic operations, and be able to detect them in a data structure implementation.

- Understand the implementation techniques used to fully encapsulate a data structure and be able to explain the underlying memory model.

- Expand an array-based structure at run-time, and understand the performance penalty associated with that expansion.

- Convert a data structure to a generic implementation using the generic features of Java, and understand how to declare a homogeneous or a heterogeneous object in a generic data structure class.

- Understand Java interfaces and their role in generic data structures, and be able to write and implement an interface.

- Develop an application that declares objects in Java's `ArrayList` class, and understand the advantages and disadvantages of the class.

2.1 The Built-in Structure Array

Early programming languages were, among other things, designed to evaluate mathematical formulas. Since subscripted variables are used extensively in mathematical formulas, these languages provided a built-in data structure for storing them called an array. An array is a data structure rooted in the mathematical concept of subscripted variables, with single subscripted variables, e.g., $x_1, x_2, \ldots, x_i$, modeled by one-dimensional arrays. Virtually all modern programming languages continue to include the structure array as part of their language standard.

It was anticipated that the structure would be widely used, therefore, its designers recognized the need for both high-speed and low-memory overhead in its implementation. From a data structures viewpoint, these two objectives are usually mutually exclusive. They could not have been achieved without some compromises, or restrictions, placed on the structure. A group of compromises was suggested by the characteristics of subscripted variables themselves and the way in which mathematicians use them:

- All of the values stored in the variables are of the same type (e.g., integer, real, etc.).
- Each variable is distinguished by a unique ordinal subscript.
- There is a minimum and maximum value of the subscript.

Since each value stored in the variables is of the same type, the data structure array could be restricted to a *homogeneous* structure. Only *node number access* would be supported, since the unique ordinal subscript could be thought of as a node number. In addition, since the structure would have a specified number of members (within the range of the minimum and maximum value of the subscript) and therefore not grow or shrink, Insert and Delete operations would *not* be allowed.

The designers of the structure imposed two other restrictions on the way arrays would be stored in memory. First, they restricted the storage of the array members (nodes) to contiguous memory.

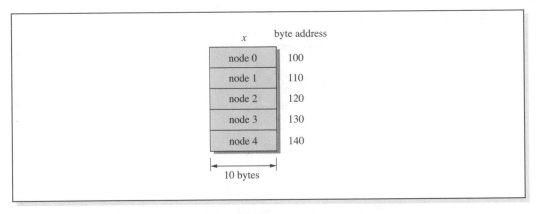

Figure 2.1   The Storage of Five Nodes in the Array x

Furthermore, within this contiguous memory, the nodes would be stored sequentially based on the node number.[1] Figure 2.1 illustrates the storage of a five-element array, x, consistent with these restrictions. Each element of the array x is assumed to contain 10 bytes.

Storing arrays in this way permits rapid access to the nodes since the byte address of a node can be expressed as a simple mathematical function of the node number, N. Specifically, the function is:[2]

$$\text{Address of node } N = A_N = A_o + N \times w$$

where

A_o is the byte address of the first node, called the base address,
w is the node width (number of bytes per node), and
N is the number of the node, starting from $N = 0$.

The function: $A_N = A_o + N * w$, called the *linear list access function,* can be rapidly evaluated by the CPU since it involves only two arithmetic operations.[3] The ability to *calculate* the location of an element of the array from its node number (for a given base address and node width) is what gives the structure array its speed. In addition, since the only overhead associated with structure is the storage for the values of A_o and w, the design goal of low overhead was also achieved.

Returning to the mathematical concept of subscripted variables, the only remaining issue was which subscripted variable would be stored in node 0, node 1, etc. Figure 2.2 shows a typical

---

[1]This sequential ordering is referred to as a linear list, in which there is a unique first node ($node_0$), a unique last node ($node_{max}$), and any other node ($node_i$) is preceded by a unique node ($node_{i-1}$) and followed by a unique node ($node_{i+1}$).

[2]Assumes the nodes are stored in ascending memory locations as shown in Figure 2.1. For descending memory location storage, $A = A_0 - N \times w$.

[3]Actually, many CPUs (e.g., the Intel Processors) can evaluate this function in one machine instruction.

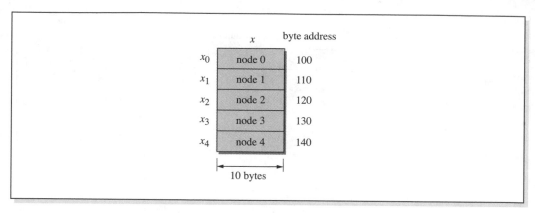

Figure 2.2 The Mapping of Subscripts to Node Numbers for the Array *x*

assignment between the subscript and the node number in which x_0 is stored in node 0, x_1 in node 1, etc.

The relationship between subscript number and node number is called a *mapping function*, and for the assignments depicted in Figure 2.2 it is:[4]

$$N = i$$

where

    N is the node number, and
    i is the variable's subscript.

Combining this mapping function with the linear list access function, we obtain a function to calculate the address of the *i*th subscripted variable as

$$A_N = A_o + N * w = A_o + i * w = Ax_i.$$

As a check of our mapping function, let's calculate the address of the variable x_2. Here $i = 2$, and assuming the base address is $A_o = 100$ and the node width is $w = 10$ (as depicted in Figure 2.2), we calculate the address of the variable to be

$$Ax_i = A_o + i \times w = 100 + (2) \times 10 = 120$$

which is correct, as verified by inspecting the figure.

The inconvenience of typing subscripts demanded a friendlier syntax for arrays. Therefore, subscripts were replaced with indices enclosed in either parentheses or brackets. Java uses brackets.

---

[4]This assumes the subscript begins at zero.

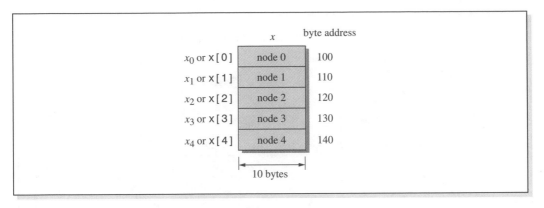

Figure 2.3 The Syntax of Array Indices in Java

Thus, in Java the variable x_i is coded as array element x[i]. The array notation for subscripted variables is shown in Figure 2.3.

Consistent with the restrictions placed on them by their designers, only two of the four basic operations can be performed on the data structure array: Fetch and Update. The syntax of the Fetch operation is simply to code the name of the array element. Thus, to fetch the value of x[2] and output it, we code System.out.println(x[2]). The syntax of the Update operation is to place the name of the element of the array on the left side of an assignment operator. Therefore, to update the value of x[1] to 24, we write x[1] = 24.

All array indices in Java start at zero. Some programming languages allow the minimum index to start at any integer, i_o. When this is the case, the mapping function for a one-dimensional array becomes:

$$Ax[i] = A_o + (i - i_o) \times w$$

2.1.1 Multidimensional Arrays

Most programming languages also include the ability to store multisubscripted variables, (e.g., x_{ijk}). These variables are assigned node numbers in one of two ways: *row major* order or *column major* order. Consider a variable with two subscripts, x_{ij}, with $0 <= i <= 1$, and $0 <= j <= 2$. Figure 2.4 illustrates how each scheme assigns variables to node numbers.

Referring to Figure 2.4, the mapping functions used to calculate the node number, N, given the subscripts i and j are:[5]

$$N = i * (j_{max} + 1) + j \quad \text{for row major order, and}$$

$$N = j * (i_{max} + 1) + i \quad \text{for column major order,}$$

---

[5]Again we assume the subscripts start at zero.

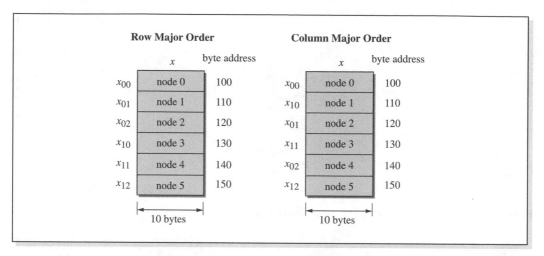

Figure 2.4 Comparison of Row Major and Column Major Orders

where

i and j are the subscripts of the variable,
j_{max} is the maximum value of the index j, and
i_{max} is the maximum value of the index i.

Substituting these expressions for node number into the linear list access function, $A_N = A_o + N * w$, we obtain the address of x_{ij} to be

$$A_N = A_o + N * w = A_o + (i * (j_{max} + 1) + j) * w = A_{ij} \quad \text{for row major order, and}$$

$$A_N = A_o + N * w = A_o + (j * (i_{max} + 1) + i) * w = A_{ij} \quad \text{for column major order.}$$

Once again, these functions can be rapidly evaluated since they involve only basic arithmetic operations.

To verify our mapping functions, let us calculate the row major and column major addresses of x_{02} shown in Figure 2.4. The figure assumes the maximum values of i and j are 1 and 2 respectively, $A_o = 100$, and the node width is w = 10. Under these conditions, we calculate

$$Ax_{02} = A_o + (i * (j_{max} + 1) + j) * w = 100 + (0 * (2 + 1) + 2) * 10 = 120 \quad \text{for row major order, and}$$

$$Ax_{02} = A_o + (j * (i_{max} + 1) + i) * w = 100 + (2 * (1 + 1) + 0) * 10 = 140 \quad \text{for column major order,}$$

which agrees with the addresses shown in Figure 2.4.

The Java syntax for the variable x_{ij} is x[i][j] where the indices i and j always start at zero. Usually programmers visualize two-dimensional arrays arranged in rows and columns, with i representing the row number and j representing the column number. Since the maximum number of rows

(n_r) and columns (n_c) of this visualization is always one more than the maximum subscripts of the variables i_{max} and j_{max}, respectively, the address of the array element x[i][j] can be expressed as

$$Ax[i][j] = A_o + (i \times (j_{max} + 1) + j) \times w = A_o + (i \times n_c + j) \times w \text{ for row major order, and}$$

$$Ax[i][j] = A_o + (j \times (i_{max} + 1) + i) \times w = A_o + (j \times n_r + i) \times w \text{ for column major order,}$$

where

n_r is the number of rows in the array, and
n_c is the number of columns in the array.

Since arrays are built-in structures in modern programming languages, they are treated as an abstract data structure by most programmers. This means that programmers need not know the mapping functions. The only exception to this would be the programmers who write compilers. They need to know all the details of the structure in order to include the mapping function into the compiler's code. These details would include where the base address and number of bytes per node will be stored, whether the nodes will be stored in ascending or descending order, and whether row or column major order will be used for two-dimensional arrays.

2.2 Programmer-Defined Array Structures

By design, the built-in data structure array is fast and its memory overhead is low. However, also by design, its operations are restricted to Fetch and Update. Insert and Delete operations are not allowed and the key field access mode is not supported. These restrictions are acceptable when we are using arrays to emulate subscripted variables, but they are not consistent with requirements of most applications that process data sets.

Most applications access the data they process in the key field mode (e.g., fetch the telephone listing of *Al Jones*), and use the Insert and Delete operations to add nodes to, or eliminate nodes from, the data set (e.g., Mr. Jones has moved into, or out of, town). In addition, nodes in a data set are typically made up of several fields of information rather than a single value.

Despite their limitations, many data structures that support the four basic operations and permit access in the key field mode utilize arrays as their underlying storage scheme. The speed and low overhead of arrays make them an attractive *foundation* for higher level structures to build upon. For example, arrays can be used to store a multifield data set by declaring the array to be an array of node objects,[6] each with multiple data members. In addition, key field mode access can be implemented on array-based structures if the class that defines the node objects has a method to fetch the key from a node object. Although not suited for all applications, data structures that build upon, or enhance, the structure array are in wide use.

---

[6]More accurately, the array is an array of reference variables that stores the address of the objects that contain the nodes' information.

In the remainder of this chapter, we'll examine three of these *array-based* data structures:

- The Unsorted array.
- The Sorted array.
- The Unsorted-Optimized array.

As we will see, all of these data structures

- Can store data sets of multifield nodes.
- Are accessed in the key field mode.
- Permit all four basic operations to be performed on the data set.
- Use an array of objects to store the data set.
- Are fully encapsulated.

What distinguishes one from the other is that each one uses a unique approach to the basic operation algorithms.

The study of these three structures is valuable from several points of view. First, it will demonstrate the use of our calculation and trade-off techniques to uncover the strengths and weaknesses of each structure. Second, the study of these structures will lead us to a discussion of the relative merits of two very basic key field search algorithms: the Sequential and Binary Search algorithms. Finally, the simplicity of these structures will allow us to focus on the implementation techniques common to all the data structures. After we have studied and compared the three, we will fully implement the best performing data structure as the first of the classic data structures presented in the text. The algorithms presented for the three data structures will *not* include error checking (e.g., the node to be operated on is not in the structure or there is insufficient memory to perform an Insert operation) since it does not affect the relative performance of the three structures and its exclusion will simplify the development of their pseudocode. The ability to check for errors will be added to the pseudocode of the best performing structure before it is implemented.

2.2.1 Unsorted Array

This array-based structure, accessed in the key field mode, uses an array of objects to store the data set. The array (named `data`) is sized to the maximum number of nodes that will reside in the structure, *n*. An additional integer type memory cell, `next`, is used to store the index of the array where the next insert will be performed. Initially, all the elements of the array are set to **null**, and `next` is set to zero. Figure 2.5 shows the structure in its initialized state.

To perform an Insert operation, a new node object is allocated with its contents initialized to the contents of the node to be inserted, and then a reference to it is placed into the array at `data[next]`. Then, `next` is incremented by one to prepare for the next insert. Thus, assuming we are to insert the node `newNode` into the structure and that a method to perform a deep copy of a node (named `deepCopy`) exists, the algorithm is:

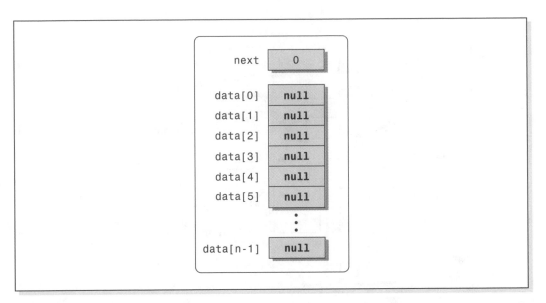

Figure 2.5   The Unsorted Array Structure in Its Initialized State

Unsorted Array Insert Algorithm

1. data[next] = newNode.deepCopy() // stores a deep copy of the node to be inserted, newNode
2. next = next + 1; // prepares for the next insert

Figure 2.6 shows the structure after five nodes have been inserted into the initialized structure. The node with key field Phil was inserted first, then Bill, followed by Carol, then Vick, and finally Mike.

The Delete operation of this structure uses a sequential search to locate the node to be deleted. The search begins at element zero of the array and terminates when the node with the given key is located. Once the node is located, it could be eliminated from the structure in one of two ways:

1. Set the array element that stores the reference to the node to **null**.
2. Move all the node references below the deleted node up one element in the array and then decrement the memory cell next.

The first technique would be the faster approach because it does not spend time moving up the node references; however, our Insert algorithm would never *reuse* the array element associated with the deleted node, since it always performs an insert at data[next], which is already *below*

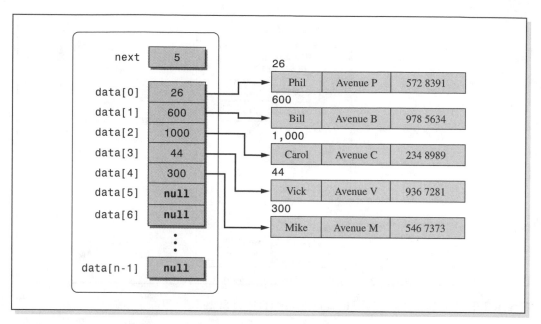

Figure 2.6 The Unsorted Array Structure after Five Nodes Are Inserted

this element. In effect, every time a node was deleted from the structure, the maximum capacity of the structure would be reduced by one node, because the vacated element of the array would never be used again. Therefore, the second technique:

> Move all the node references below it up one element in the array, and then decrement the memory cell next,

which is considerably slower, will be used in our Delete algorithm. The idea of reclaiming the storage associated with a deleted node (in data structures jargon) is called *garbage collection* and all data structures that support the Delete operation must provide some form of garbage collection.

The Delete algorithm (that includes garbage collection) is presented below. It assumes the node with key field contents `targetKey` is to be deleted and that the pseudocode `data[i].key` refers to the contents of the key field of the node referenced by element *i* of the array.

Unsorted Array Delete Algorithm

1. // access the node (assumes the node is in the structure)
2. i = 0;
3. **while**(targetKey != data[i].key)   // targetKey not found

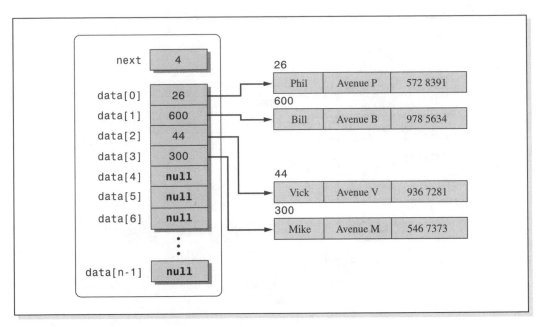

Figure 2.7 Unsorted Array Structure after Carol's Node Is Deleted

```
4. { i++;
5. }
6. // move all the references up to eliminate the node and collect the garbage
7. for(j = i; j < next − 1; j++)
8. { data[j] = data[j + 1];
9. }
10. next = next − 1;
11. data[next] = null;
```

Figure 2.7 shows the data structure after the deletion of the node with key field Carol. Comparing it to Figure 2.6, we see that the references to Vick's and Mike's nodes have each been moved up one element in the array. Carol's reference, which was stored in data[2], has been overwritten with the contents of data[3] (Vick's reference 44). Similarly, data[3] has been overwritten with the contents of data[4].

Now examine the Fetch algorithm. To perform a fetch of the node with the key targetKey, the Fetch algorithm searches sequentially down the array starting at element zero. Once the object

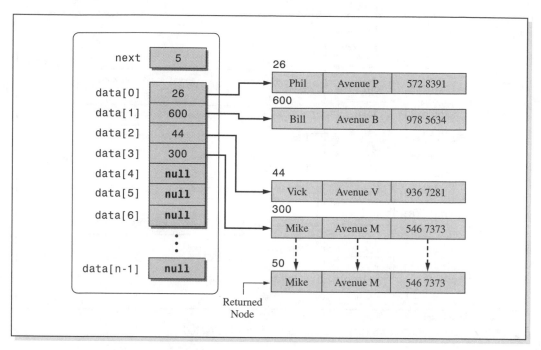

Figure 2.8 Fetching a Deep Copy of Mike's Node from the Unsorted Array Structure

with the given key is found, we simply return a deep copy of it. The pseudocode of the Fetch algorithm is:

Unsorted Array Fetch Algorithm

1. // access the node (assumes the node is in the structure)
2. i = 0;
3. **while** (targetKey != data[i].key())
4. { i++;
5. }
6. // return a copy of the node to the client
7. **return** data[i].deepCopy();

Figure 2.8 illustrates the deep copy operation that takes place after a requested node (in this case Mike's node) has been located using the sequential search coded as the **while** loop in the fetch algorithm.

For the purposes of brevity, we will assume that the algorithm to update the node with the key field `targetKey` to the contents of the node `newNode` uses the Delete and Insert algorithms, previously discussed. Under this assumption, the Update algorithm becomes:

Unsorted Array Update Algorithm

1. Invoke the Delete operation to delete the node with the key field targetKey.
2. Invoke the Insert operation to insert the node newNode.

A more efficient implementation of the Update algorithm would be one in which the actual code to access the node and change its fields would be included in the `update` method because this approach saves the time required to invoke the `delete` and `insert` methods. This implementation is left as an exercise for the student.

Speed of the Structure

To analyze the speed of the structure, we will perform a Big-O analysis to determine the approximate speed as *n* (the number of nodes stored in the structure) gets large. Since the Big-O analysis is an approximate technique and the time to perform a memory access instruction is typically considerably longer than the time to perform a non-access instruction, only memory access instructions will be included in our analysis. Consistent with this approach, instructions inside of loops that repeatedly access the *same* memory cell (e.g., Line 4 of the Delete algorithm) will also not be included in our speed analysis since modern compilers store these variables in CPU registers. Assuming that the CPU has sufficient register space to allow this, the contents of these variables can be used without accessing memory.

Examining the Insert algorithm, its two lines perform three memory accesses: one to fetch the variable `next`, one to write the object's address into `data[next]`, and one to overwrite the variable `next`.[7] Fortunately, these two lines are only executed once per Fetch operation regardless of how many nodes are in the structure. Therefore, three memory accesses are required per Insert operation, and the dominant (and only) term in the Insert operation's speed function is 3, which is O(1).

The Delete algorithm uses a sequential search (Lines 3–5) to locate a node, given its key. Sometimes the node will be at index 0, and line 3 will execute only once. Other times the node will be at index $n - 1$, and line 3 will execute *n* times. Since all locations are equally probable (on the average),

---

[7]For simplicity, the time to execute the method `deepCopy()` is ignored.

the node to be deleted will be in the middle of the array, and the loop will execute an average of approximately $n/2$ times. Once found, the node is deleted by moving up all of the references in the array below the deleted node (Lines 7 and 8). Assuming, on the average, the reference to the deleted node is located in the middle of the array, this loop will also execute an average of approximately $n/2$ times. Within the two loops, Line 3 requires two[8] memory accesses and Line 8 requires two memory accesses. Therefore, the dominant term of the speed equation is $(2 + 2)(n/2) = 2n$, which is $O(n)$.

The Fetch algorithm also uses a sequential search (Lines 3–5) to locate the node to be fetched. Assuming the fetched node is (on the average) referenced from the middle of the array, the search loop executes approximately $n/2$ times. Line 3 requires two memory accesses inside the search loop to access a node and return its key. Line 7 of the algorithm contains a memory access instruction, but it is only executed once, so it does not contribute to the dominant term in the speed equation. Therefore, the two memory accesses inside the loop result in a dominant speed equation term of $2(n/2) = n$, which is $O(n)$.

Table 2.1 summarizes the number of memory accesses (associated with the dominant term in the speed equation) to perform the basic operations on the Unsorted Array structure. The Update operation speed was calculated as the sum of the Delete and Insert speeds.

We will assume the average speed of this structure is too slow for our application and consider another array-based structure: the Sorted Array.

Table 2.1

Dominant Speed Terms of the Unsorted Array Structure

Data Structure	Insert	Delete	Fetch	Update = Delete + Insert	Average[9] Operation Speed	Big-O Average Operation Speed	Average Operation Speed for $n = 10^7$
Unsorted Array	3	$2n$	n	$2n + 3$	$(5n + 6)/4 =$ $1.25n + 1.5$	$O(n)$	1.25×10^7 $+ 1.5$

---

[8]As previously stated, accessing a data member of an object requires two memory accesses: one to fetch the object's address from the array and one to fetch the data member *from* the object.

[9]Assumes all operations are equally probable and is therefore calculated as the arithmetic average of the four operation speeds.

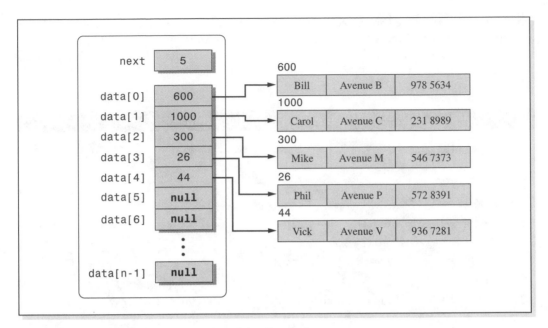

Figure 2.9 Sorted Array Structure Containing Five Nodes

2.2.2 Sorted Array

Examining the results presented in Table 2.1, we see that the Delete, Fetch, and Update algorithms are slow, O(n). To improve the speed of these operations, we can focus our attention on the Delete and Fetch algorithms since an improvement to the Delete algorithm will produce a corresponding improvement in the Update algorithm. Both the Delete and the Fetch operations use a sequential search access algorithm, which is why they are slow. A faster access algorithm will speed up these two operations (as well as the Update operation).

In Chapter 1, we examined the Binary Search algorithm and calculated its speed to be $O(\log_2 n)$ which, as shown in Figure 1.9, is much faster than $O(n)$. However, the algorithm assumes the information in the array being searched is arranged in sorted order. Therefore, as the name of this structure (Sorted Array) implies, in order to take advantage of the speed of the Binary Search algorithm, it will store the nodes in sorted order. Naturally this will require modifications to the Insert algorithm of the previous structure. Before discussing these modifications, let us first turn our attention to the Fetch and Delete algorithms.

Figure 2.9 shows the data structure after the nodes with key fields Phil, Bill, Carol, Vick, and Mike have been inserted into the structure.

Since the nodes are stored in sorted order based on the contents of their key field, the Fetch algorithm can use the Binary Search algorithm to locate a node given its key. Once located, it returns a deep copy of the node, just as the unsorted structure did. The new Fetch algorithm becomes:

Sorted Array Fetch Algorithm

```
1.  // access the node using a binary search (assumes the node is in the structure)
2.  low = 0;
3.  high = next – 1;
4.  i = (low + high) / 2;
5.  while (targetKey != data[i].key)
6.  {  if(targetKey < data[i].key && high != low)
7.     { high = i – 1;      // move high down to eliminate the upper half of the array
8.     else
9.     { low = i + 1; }      // move low up to eliminate the lower half of the array
10.    i = (low + high) / 2;
11. }
12. return data[i].deepCopy();
```

Lines 2–11 are the Binary Search algorithm. They set the variable i to the index of the array element that references the node to be fetched. Line 12 returns a deep copy of this node.

Next, let's consider the Delete algorithm, which also uses the Binary Search algorithm. Once the node to be deleted is found, as in the case of the previous structure, all the nodes below it must be moved up to reclaim the unused storage. Figure 2.10 show the structure after Carol's node has been deleted from the data set depicted in Figure 2.9. The Delete algorithm is:

Sorted Array Delete Algorithm

```
1.  // access the node using a binary search (assumes the node is in the structure)
2.  low = 0;
3.  high = next – 1;
4.  i = (low + high) / 2;
5.  while (targetKey != data[i].key && high != low)
6.  {  if(targetKey < data[i].key)
```

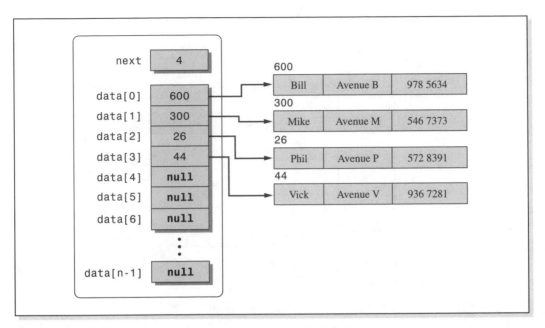

Figure 2.10   Sorted Array Structure after Carol's Node Is Deleted

```
7.    { high = i − 1; }      // move high down to eliminate the upper half of the array
8.    else
9.    { low = i + 1; }      // move low up to eliminate the lower half of the array
10.     i = (low + high) / 2;
11.  }
12. // move all the references up to delete the node and collect the garbage
13. for( j = i; j < next − 1; j++)
14. { data[j] = data[j + 1];
15. }
16. next = next − 1;
17. data[next] = null;
```

Finally, let's consider the revised Insert algorithm. It was not our intent to modify this algorithm, since it was very fast. However, the new Delete and Fetch algorithms use a binary search to locate a node, and so the nodes must be stored in sorted order based on the key field. A newly inserted node can no longer be inserted into the array as the last node (at index next). Rather, it must be placed in its correct sorted position.

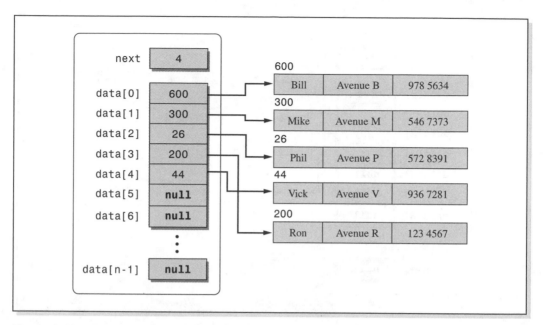

Figure 2.11   Sorted Array Structure after Ron's Node Is Inserted

To find the "correct location" for an inserted node, the Insert algorithm performs a binary search. It continues its search until it finds two adjacent keys that "bracket" the new node's key. Then, it moves all the nodes below these two nodes and the larger of the two nodes down one element to "open up" a spot for the new node. Finally, the contents of the node to be inserted are deep copied into a newly created node, and then a reference to that node is placed in the array element that has been opened up. Figure 2.11 shows the structure after Ron's node is inserted into it. Compare it to Figure 2.10 to visualize action of the algorithm. The pseudocode of the algorithm follows. Since we are interested only in the performance of the algorithm, it ignores the special cases of an Insert operation being performed when the structure contains one or two nodes, which are not significant from a speed complexity viewpoint.

Sorted Array Insert Algorithm

1. // assumes targetKey is the key of the node to be inserted
2. // find the node's place in sorted order using a binary search
3. low = 0;
4. high = next − 1

```
5.  i = (low + high) / 2;
6.  while (!(targetKey < data[i] && targetKey > data[i – 1].key)
7.  {  if(targetKey < data[i].key)
8.     { high = i – 1; }    // move high down to eliminate the lower half of the array
9.     else
10.    { low = i + 1; }    // move low up to eliminate the lower half of the array
11.     i = (high + low) / 2;
12. }
13. // move all the nodes down to "open up" a spot for the new node
14. for( j = next; j >= i; j--)
15. { data[j] = data[j – 1];
16. }
17. next = next + 1;
18. // add a deep copy of the new node to the structure
19. data[i] = newNode.deepCopy();
```

Speed of the Structure

To analyze the speed of this structure, we will perform a Big-O analysis to determine the approximate speed of its operation algorithms as n (the number of nodes stored in the structure) gets large. Again, we will only consider memory access instructions, which typically take considerably longer to execute than non-access instructions, and will ignore instructions in loops that repeatedly access the same memory cell.

Beginning with the Fetch algorithm, Lines 5–11 represents a binary search loop. As discussed in Chapter 1, this executes (in the worst case) approximately $\log_2 n$ times. Lines 5 and 6 require two memory accesses to fetch data[i] and the key field of the node it references. Therefore, the dominant term in this loop's speed equation is $2\log_2 n$, which is $O(\log_2 n)$.

Turning our attention to the Delete algorithm, Lines 5–11 are the same binary search loop as in the Fetch algorithm, so their term in the speed equation is again $2\log_2 n$. The loop on Lines 13–15 reclaims the vacated element of the array by moving the node references up in a sequential manner. As such, it executes an average of approximately $n / 2$ times.[10] Since Line 14 in this loop requires two memory accesses, the dominant term in this loop's speed equation is $2 * n / 2$, which is equal to n. The speed function for this operation is therefore $4\log_2 n + n$, with n being the more dominant term (see Figure 1.9). Therefore, the speed function for the Insert algorithm is $O(n)$.

---

[10]This assumes, on the average, the node referenced from the middle of the array is the node being deleted.

Table 2.2

Dominant Speed Terms of the Sorted Array Structure

Data Structure	Insert	Delete	Fetch	Update = Delete + Insert	Average[11] Operation Speed	Big-O Average Operation Speed	Average Operation Speed for $n = 10^7$
Unsorted Array	3	$2n$	n	$2n + 3$	$(5n + 6)/4 =$ $1.25n + 1.5$	$O(n)$	1.25×10^7 $+ 1.5$
Sorted Array	n	n	$2\log_2 n$	$2n$	$(4n +$ $2\log_2 n)/4 =$ $n + 0.5\log_2 n$	$O(n)$	1×10^7 $+ 12$

Lines 6–12 of the Insert algorithm use the same binary search loop as in the Fetch algorithm except Line 6 performs two additional memory accesses to fetch data[i - 1] and the key of the node it references. Therefore, Lines 6–12's term in the speed equation is $4\log_2 n$. The loop which opens up a "spot" for the new node (Lines 14–16) moves the node references down in a sequential manner. As such, it executes an average of approximately $n / 2$ times. Since Line 15 in this loop requires two memory accesses, the speed equation term for this loop is $2n / 2$, which is equal to n. The speed function for this operation is therefore $4\log_2 n + n$, with n being the more dominant term (see Figure 1.9). Therefore, the speed function for the Insert algorithm is $O(n)$.

Table 2.2 summarizes the number of memory accesses needed to perform the basic operations on the Sorted Array structure and compares it to the previously discussed structure.

Comparing the speed of the operations presented in Tables 2.1 and 2.2, we see that the Binary Search algorithm used in the Sorted Array structure considerably reduced the number of memory access instructions required to perform a Fetch operation. However, the need to maintain the array in sorted order minimized the improvement on the Delete algorithm and made the Insert operation less efficient. Because of this, the average speed of this structure when populated with 10,000,000 nodes (presented in the rightmost column of Table 2.2) is approximately the same. This realization leads us to consider our third array-based structure: the Unsorted-Optimized Array.

---

[11]This assumes all operations are equally probable and is therefore calculated as the arithmetic average of the four operation speeds.

2.2.3 Unsorted-Optimized Array

As the name of this structure implies, it is an *optimized* version of the Unsorted Array structure. Examining the data presented in Table 2.2, the Unsorted structure's Insert operation is the fastest of all the operation algorithms studied so far. Therefore, the new structure will retain this Insert algorithm. The Delete and Fetch algorithms of the new structure will be optimized versions of the Unsorted structure's Delete and Fetch algorithms, optimized to improve their speed.

Both the Delete and Fetch algorithms of the Unsorted Array structure use a sequential search to locate a node, given its key field contents. Since this search starts at the top of the array (element zero) it would execute quickly if the nodes accessed were always referenced by one of the first few elements of the array. This is an unrealistic situation if all nodes in the structure have equal probability of being accessed. However, most often there are some "favorite" nodes that are operated on much more frequently than the others. For example, the phone number of a town's most popular bakery, Maggie's Delights, is accessed much more frequently than the phone number of the Cockroach Cafe.

To take advantage of this characteristic of many data sets, we modify the Unsorted Fetch algorithm to position the references to the most accessed nodes toward the top of the array. This modification is surprisingly simple. After a node is fetched, the position of its reference is swapped with the node reference just above it. Thus, every time a node is accessed, it moves up one position in the array. Eventually, the nodes with the highest probability of being accessed will be positioned at the beginning of the array.

Figure 2.6 shows the data structure after five nodes (Phil, Bill, Carol, Vick, and finally Mike) have been inserted into it using the Unsorted structure's Insert algorithm. Next, let's assume that Carol's node is fetched. Figure 2.12 shows the structure after the Fetch operation is complete. The reference to Carol's node has been moved up one element in the array, switched with the reference to Bill's node. A subsequent (sequential) search for Carol's node will be slightly quicker.

The modified Fetch algorithm is:

Unsorted-Optimized Fetch Algorithm

1. // access the node (assumes the node is in the structure)
2. i = 0;
3. **while** (targetKey != data[i].key)
4. { i++;
5. }
6. node = data[i].deepCopy(); // copy the node before it is relocated

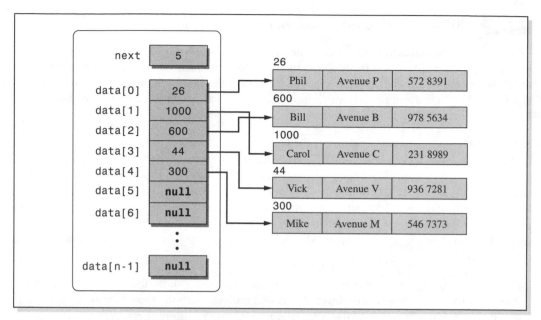

Figure 2.12 Unsorted-Optimized Array after Carol's Node Is Fetched

```
 7. if(i != 0) // move the node reference up one position
 8. { temp = data[i – 1];
 9.    data[i – 1] = data[i];
10.    data[i] = temp;
11. }
12. return node; // return a copy of the node
```

Lines 8–10 of the algorithm is the additional code that moves the node reference up one element in the array unless the node being fetched is referenced by element zero (Line 7).

The Unsorted Delete algorithm will also be modified to improve its speed. It will still perform a sequential search to locate the node to be deleted. However, instead of moving all the node's references up to reclaim the deleted node's array element, we will simply move the last node reference into the deleted node's position. Since the nodes are not stored in sorted order, any node can be moved into this position. The modified Delete algorithm is:

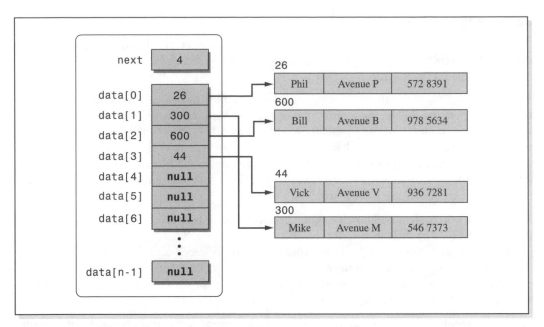

Figure 2.13 Unsorted-Optimized Array after Carol's Node Is Deleted

Unsorted-Optimized Delete Algorithm

1. // access the node (assumes the node is in the structure)
2. i = 0;
3. **while** (targetKey != data[i].key)
4. { i++;
5. }
6. // move the last node into the deleted node's position
7. data[i] = data[next – 1];
8. next = next – 1;

Figures 2.12 and 2.13, respectively, show the data structure before and after Carol's node is deleted. After the deletion, the reference to Mike's node has been written into the element of the array that referenced Carol's node.

Speed of the Structure

We will now examine the speed of the Unsorted-Optimized structure. The Insert algorithm is the same as the Unsorted structure, and therefore the dominant term in its speed equation (as presented in Table 2.1) is 3, which is $O(1)$.

When all the nodes in the structure have an equal probability of being accessed, the speed of the new Fetch operation will be the same as that of the Unsorted structure's Fetch operation, n. But, whenever some nodes are more frequently accessed than others, the number of memory accesses to perform a Fetch operation will be less than n. In the extreme case when the same node is fetched all the time, eventually its reference will find its way to the first element of the array, and only two memory accesses will be required to fetch it. Therefore, the number of memory accesses for our new fetch algorithm is $<= n$, which is $< O(n)$.

In the modified Delete algorithm, we eliminated the need to reposition half of the nodes in the structure in order to reclaim the storage of the deleted node. Therefore, only the search loop (Lines 3–5), which executes $n / 2$ times, contributes to the speed equation. Line 3 of the loop requires two memory accesses, so the speed equation is $2 * n / 2$ (equal to n), which is $O(n)$. However, if the deleted nodes are those most likely to be fetched, the search loop will execute less than $n / 2$ times, and the speed of the algorithm will be $< n$.

Table 2.3 presents the speed of this structure and, for comparative purposes, the speed of the other two array-based structures. As indicated in the rightmost column of the table, even when all operations on the data set are equally probable, the average speed of the Unsorted-Optimized

Table 2.3

Dominant Speed Terms of the Unsorted-Optimized Array Structure

Data Structure	Insert	Delete	Fetch	Update = Delete + Insert	Average[12] Operation Speed	Big-O Average Operation Speed	Average Operation Speed for $n = 10^7$
Unsorted Array	3	$2n$	n	$2n + 3$	$(5n + 6)/4 =$ $1.25n + 1.5$	$O(n)$	1.25×10^7 $+ 1.5$
Sorted Array	n	n	$2\log_2 n$	$2n$	$(4n +$ $2\log_2 n)/4 =$ $n\,(+ 0.5\log_2 n)$	$O(n)$	1×10^7 $(+ 12)$
Unsorted-Optimized Array	3	$\leq n$	$\leq n$	$\leq n + 3$	$(3n + 6)/4 =$ $0.75n\,(+ 1.5)$	$O(n)$	$0.75 \times$ $10^7\,(+ 1.5)$

[12]Assumes all operations are equally probable and is therefore calculated as the arithmetic average of the four operation speeds.

structure is faster than the other two structures, and its speed advantage increases when some nodes have a higher fetch frequency than others. However, from a Big-O analysis viewpoint, all three structures are equivalent (all $O(n)$). The Unsorted-Optimized structure has the best-performing Insert, Delete, and Update algorithms. However, the Sorted Array Structure has the best Fetch algorithm. Therefore, if, after the data set is initially inserted into the data structure, the only operation performed is Fetch, then the preferred structure is the Sorted structure.

Having determined the speed of these three array-based structures, we will now turn our attention to their storage requirements.

Density of the Structure

Density is the measure of how efficiently a data structure utilizes storage. In Chapter 1, it was defined as

$$D = \text{(information bytes) / (total bytes)}.$$

The information bytes for all three array structures is simply the product of the number of nodes, n, and the number of bytes per node, w ($n * w$). The total bytes allocated to the structure is the sum of the information bytes and the structure's overhead. The overhead of these structures is the array of n reference variables that point to the node objects, plus the integer variable next. In Java, reference variables and integers occupy 4 bytes. Therefore, the overhead is $4 * n + 4$. Thus, the density of these structures, D_A, can be expressed as:

$$D_A = \text{(information bytes) / (total bytes)} = (n * w) / ((n * w) + (4n + 4))$$

$$= 1 / (1 + 4/w + 4 / (w * n))$$

where

  w is the information bytes per node (called the node width), and
  n is the number of nodes in the structure.

As n increases, the term $4 / (w * n)$ in the denominator tends toward zero and can be neglected.[13] Therefore, the density of our three array-based structures can be expressed as

$$D_A = 1 / (1 + 4/w)$$

Figure 2.14 presents a graph of $1 / (1 + 4/w)$ vs. node width, w. The figure demonstrates that good densities (0.80 or higher) are achieved for an array-based structure whenever the number of bytes in a node is greater than sixteen.

---

[13]For $n >= 100$, and w $>= 5$, $4 / (wn) <= 0.008$, which is less than 1% of the denominator.

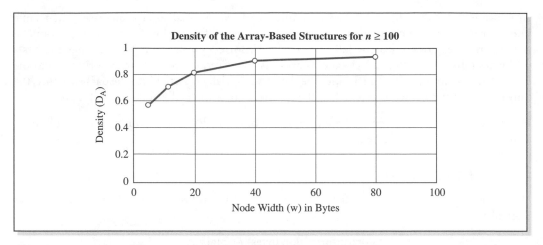

Figure 2.14 Density Variation of Array-Based Structures with Node Width

Table 2.4 summarizes the overall performance (speed and density) of the fastest of our array-based structures: the Unsorted-Optimized array. It is the first of the classic data structures we will implement in this text. Before implementing it, however, we will modify the pseudocode of its basic operations to include error checking. Error checking was not considered when we developed the pseudocode of the three array-based structures because it does not affect the relative performance of these structures, and its exclusion simplified their pseudocode.

2.2.4 Error Checking

Considering the four basic operation algorithms, there are three errors that can occur:

- During an Insert, the structure is full (every element of the array contains a reference to a node object).
- During a Fetch, Delete, or Update operation, the node to be operated on is not in the structure.
- During an Insert operation, there is insufficient memory for the deep copy of the client's node.

The ability to deal with the first two of these errors will be incorporated in the pseudocode of the Unsorted-Optimized Array operation algorithms. The third error will be considered during the implementation of the structure, since the detection of this error is implementation-language specific. In the case of the Fetch, Delete, and Update algorithms, a Boolean value of **true** will be returned if the operation completes without an error. Otherwise, the operations will return a value of **false**. As written, the Fetch algorithm returns a reference to the deep copy of the client's node inserted into the structure. Consistent with this, the modified code will return a **null** reference if there is insufficient array (or system) memory space to complete its operation.

Table 2.4

Performance of the Unsorted-Optimized Array Structure

Data Structure	Insert	Delete	Fetch	Update = Delete + Insert	Average[14]	Big-O Average	Average for $n = 10^7$	Condition for Density > 0.8
				Operation Speed (in memory accesses)				
Unsorted-Optimized Array	3	$\leq n$	$\leq n$	$\leq n + 3$	$(3n + 6)/4$	$O(n)$	$0.75 \times 10^7 + 1.5$	$w > 16$

[14]This assumes all operations are equally probable and is therefore calculated as an arithmetic average of the four operation times.

The pseudocode of the Insert algorithm expanded to include error checking follows. The changes to the original version are shaded and assume that the size of the array is stored in the variable size. As indicated on Line 1 of the algorithm, when the structure is full, next is equal to size. In this case, the algorithm terminates on Line 2 and returns a value of **false**. Otherwise, it performs the insert and returns a value of **true** on Line 5.

Unsorted-Optimized Insert Algorithm with Error Checking

```
1.  if(next == size)  // the structure is full
2.     return false;
3.  data[next]= newNode.deepCopy() // store a deep copy of the node inserted, newNode
4.  next = next + 1;  // prepares for the next insert
5.  return true;  // the node was inserted
```

The following pseudocode is the Fetch algorithm expanded to include error checking. The changes to the original version are shaded. They assume that the size of the array is stored in the variable size. The Sequential Search performed on Lines 3–5 of the algorithm uses the variable i to index through the array. Since the variable next stores the index just beyond the last used index of the array, the condition for a node not present in the structure is when i equals next. Thus, the loop condition on Line 3 has been modified to continue the search only while i is less than next. After the loop terminates, if the node has not been found, i will equal next. Lines 6–7 have been added to detect this, terminate the algorithm, and return a value of **null**.

Unsorted-Optimized Array Fetch Algorithm with Error Checking

```
1.  // access the node
2.  i = 0;
3.  while (i < next && targetKey != data[i].key)
4.  { i++;
5.  }
6.  if(i == next)  // node not found
7.     return null
8.  node = data[i].deepCopy();  // copy the node
9.  if(i != 0)  // move the node reference up one position
10. { temp = data[i – 1];
11.    data[i – 1] = data[i];
12.    data[i] = temp;
13. }
14. return node;  // return a copy of the node
```

The pseudocode of the Delete algorithm expanded to include error checking follows. The modifications to this algorithm are the same as the modifications to the Fetch algorithm except that Line 7 returns **false** instead of **null** when a node is not found. In addition, Line 11 has been added to the algorithm to return a value of **true** after a deletion is performed.

Unsorted-Optimized Delete Algorithm with Error Checking

```
1.   // access the node
2.   i = 0;
3.   while (i < next && targetKey != data[i].key)
4.   { i++;
5.   }
6.   if(i == next) // node not found
7.      return false;
8.   // move the last node into the deleted node's position
9.   data[i] = data[next – 1];
10.  next = next – 1;
11.     return true; // node found and deleted
```

To include error checking in the Update algorithm, the errors returned from the invocations of the Delete and Insert operations are tested (Lines 1 and 3 of the pseudocode below). If either operation returns a value of **false**, the Update algorithm returns **false** (Lines 2 and 4). Otherwise, a value of **true** is returned on Line 6.

Unsorted-Optimized Update Algorithm with Error Checking

```
1.   if (delete(targetKey) == false) // node not in the structure
2.      return false;
3.   else if(insert(newNode) == false) // insufficient memory
4.      return false;
5.   else
6.      return true; // node found and updated
```

2.3   Implementation of the Unsorted-Optimized Array Structure

The Unsorted-Optimized data structure will be implemented in this section.[14] However, since the code of a complete implementation of any data structure can be a bit overwhelming, our first implementation of this structure will be a minimal implementation tied to a particular application (our telephone book listing problem). Once an understanding of this baseline implementation is gained, it will be easier to understand the enhancements that bring it to a full implementation. When fully implemented, the data structure will be coded in a generic way so that it can be used to store nodes particular to any application, and can be easily integrated into these applications. In addition, several *utility* methods will be added to the baseline implementation to make the structure easier for the client to use.

The data in both the baseline and in the full implementation will be encapsulated within the data structure. The only way the client will be able to access the data set will be through the structure's methods. Another feature that the baseline and full implementations will share is that the code that defines the nodes to be stored in the structure will not be part of the class that implements the data structure. Rather, the node definition will be implemented as a separate class. This design feature will be utilized in all implementations presented in this text. Separating the node definition from the data structure class is a first step toward generics, because the data structure is not tied to a particular application's node structure.

2.3.1   Baseline Implementation

We will use a telephone information directory application to demonstrate the functionality and use of our implementations of the Unsorted-Optimized Array structure. In this application, each telephone directory listing will have three fields of String information as shown in Figure 2.15, with the Name field designated as the key field.

Typically, a node definition class contains the data declarations for the node fields and the methods that operate on these fields. Consistent with the idea of a baseline implementation, our node class will initially contain a minimum number of methods. Aside from a constructor, normally a

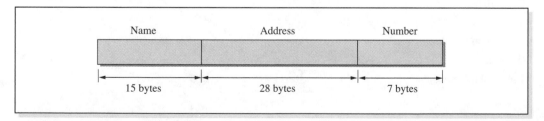

Figure 2.15   Telephone Directory Node

---

[14]This implementation will include error checking.

toString method is provided to facilitate the output of a node. In addition to these, the pseudocode of the four basic operations requires two other methods, one to perform a deep copy and the other to determine if a node's key field is equal to the contents of a given key. Finally, a set method will be provided to demonstrate the encapsulation of the nodes inside the data structure. In summary, the following five methods will be coded in the node definition class:

- A three-parameter constructor to create a node.
- A toString method to return the annotated contents of a node.
- A deepCopy method (used by the data structure to maintain encapsulation).
- A method to compare a given key to the contents of the name field of a node.
- A method to set the value of a node's address field (used as a pedagogical tool to demonstrate data encapsulation).

Node Definition Class

The code of the class that defines our telephone directory node, named Listing, depicted in Figure 2.15 is given in Figure 2.16.

```
1.  public class Listing
2.  {  private String name;   // key field
3.     private String address;
4.     private String number;
5.     public Listing(String n, String a, String num)
6.     {  name = n;
7.        address = a;
8.        number = num;
9.     }
10.    public String toString()
11.    {  return("Name is " + name +
12.              "\nAddress is " + address +
13.              "\nNumber is " + number + "\n");
14.    }
15.    public Listing deepCopy()
16.    {  Listing clone = new Listing(name, address, number);
17.       return clone;
18.    }
19.    public int compareTo(String targetKey)
20.    {  return(name.compareTo(targetKey));
21.    }
22.    public void setAddress(String a) // coded to demonstrate
                                        // encapsulation
23.    {  address = a;
24.    } // end of setAddress method
25. } // end of class Listing
```

Figure 2.16 The Class Listing that Defines a Telephone Listing Node

Lines 2–4 declare the fields of a node. The data access is **private** to encapsulate the data members. By specifying private access, only the code of the methods in this class can directly access the data members. All other attempts to directly access the data, either from the code of the data structure class or the application that uses the data structure, will result in a compile error. Lines 5–9 are the code of a three-parameter constructor. When an object is created in this class, the client code must specify the name, address, and phone number of the listing: e.g., `Listing bill = new Listing("Bill", "1st Avenue", "453 3434";)`. Lines 10–14 are the code of the `toString` method that returns a string containing the annotated contents of a listing.

The deep copy method is coded on Lines 15–18. It copies all the data (from the object that invokes the method) into a newly created object and returns the address of the new object (Line 17). Line 16 does most of the work. First, it creates a new `Listing` reference variable `clone`. Then the Java operator **new** creates a new `Listing` object, and invokes the three-parameter constructor. The values of the data members of the object that invoked the method are sent to the constructor (as arguments), and the constructor sets them into the data members of the newly created object (Lines 6–8). Finally, the address of the new `Listing` object, returned from the operator **new**, is set into the variable `clone`. If there is insufficient storage available to create the new `Listing` object, the **new** operator returns **null**.

Lines 19–21 are a method to determine if the key field (name) of a telephone listing is equal to a given key (`targetKey`). Since the key field of a telephone listing is a `String`, the method can use Java's `compareTo` method to perform its work. This method, invoked on Line 20, returns a value of zero if two strings are equivalent. Finally, Lines 22–24 are a set method to change the contents of the address field of a `Listing` object. Normally it would not be included in a minimal implementation, but is included here for pedagogical reasons (to demonstrate the encapsulation of the Unsorted-Optimized structure's implementation).

Data Structure Class

The class, `UnsortedOptimizedArray`, is the class that implements the Unsorted-Optimized structure's pseudocode (error checking included). It allocates and initializes all the storage for the structure which includes an array named `data`, a memory cell `next` to keep track of where to perform the next insert operation, and a memory cell `size` to store the size of the array. Its methods, which include a no-parameter constructor, perform the four basic operations Insert, Fetch, Delete, and Update in the key field mode.

For purposes of simplicity, the maximum capacity of the data structure in this implementation, which is presented in Figure 2.17, is fixed at 100 nodes. The code of the operation methods is simply the Java version of the Insert, Delete, Fetch, and Update pseudocode previously discussed but with one exception: The `insert` method checks to make sure that there is sufficient system memory to perform the deep copy of the client's node.

Lines 2–4 create three fully encapsulated data members: the integer `next`, which will store the array index of the next Insert operation, the integer `size`, which will store the size of the array, and

```
1.   public class UnsortedOptimizedArray
2.   {  private int next;
3.      private int size;
4.      private Listing[] data;
5.
6.      public UnsortedOptimizedArray()
7.      {  next = 0;
8.         size = 100;
9.         data = new Listing[size];
10.     } // end of constructor
11.
12.     public boolean insert(Listing newNode)
13.     {  if(next >= size)  // the structure is full
14.           return false;
15.        data[next] = newNode.deepCopy(); // store a deep copy of the
                                            // client's node
16.        if(data[next] == null) // insufficient system memory
17.           return false;
18.        next = next + 1; // prepare for the next insert
19.        return true;
20.     } // end of insert method
21.
22.     public Listing fetch(String targetKey)
23.     {  Listing node;
24.        Listing temp;
25.       // access the node using a sequential search
26.        int i = 0;
27.        while(i < next && !(data[i].compareTo(targetKey) == 0))
28.        {  i++;
29.        }
30.        if(i== next) // node not found
31.           return null;
32.       // deep copy the node's information into the client's node
33.        node = data[i].deepCopy();
34.       // move the node up one position in the array, unless it is the
          // first node
35.        if(i != 0) // bubble-up accessed node
36.        {  temp = data[i - 1];
37.           data[i - 1] = data[i];
38.           data[i] = temp;
39.        }
40.        return node;
41.     } // end of fetch method
42.
43.     public boolean delete(String targetKey)
44.     { // access the node using a sequential search
45.        int i = 0;
```

(continues)

Figure 2.17 The Code of the Class SortedOptimizedArray

```
46.         while(i < next && !(data[i].compareTo(targetKey) == 0))
47.         {  i++;
48.         }
49.         if(i == next) // node not found
50.            return false;
51.         // move the last node into the deleted node's position
52.         data[i] = data[next - 1];
53.         data[next - 1] = null;
54.         next = next - 1;
55.         return true; // node found and deleted
56.      } // end of the delete method
57.
58.      public boolean update(String targetKey, Listing newNode)
59.      {  if(delete(targetKey) == false)   // node not in the structure
60.            return false;
51.         else if(insert(newNode) == false)   // insufficient memory
62.            return false;
63.         else
64.            return true;   // node found and updated
65.      } // end of update method
66. } // end of class UnsortedOptimizedArray
```

Figure 2.17 *(continued)*

the array reference data, which will store the address of the array of node references. Both integer variables are initialized by the constructor (Lines 6–10) when a data structure object is created, and the variable data is set pointing to an array of 100 reference variables (Line 9) that can store the addresses of 100 Listing objects.

To utilize this structure, a typical application would code:

```
UnSortedOptimizedArray boston = new UnSortedOptimizedArray();
```

which would create a data structure object named boston. Its data would be initialized as shown in Figure 2.18, which assumes that the array data's base address is 100. For brevity, the variable size is omitted from the figure.

The insert Method

Lines 12–20 implement the Insert operation as the Java equivalent of the pseudocode previously developed, with two additional lines (Lines 16–17) that check for insufficient system memory. If there is not sufficient memory to perform the deep copy of the client's node, the Listing class' deepCopy method returns a **null** reference (Line 15). In this case the insert method returns **false** and terminates (Line 17). The client (application) code to insert a Listing object bill into the data structure object boston could be:

```
boolean success = boston.insert(bill);
```

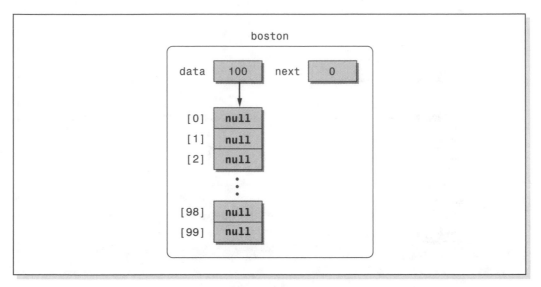

Figure 2.18   An Initialized Unsorted-Optimized Array Structure Named `boston`

Line 15 deep copies the listing into a new `Listing` object and places the address of the new object into the next available element of the encapsulated array `data`. Since the client does not know this address and cannot access the array containing the address, the node is fully encapsulated. The encapsulation is accomplished by "hiding" the address of the newly created listing.

Figure 2.19 shows the process of inserting a copy of the `Listing` object `bill` into the data structure `boston`. It assumes the new `Listing` object, created by the `deepCopy` method, is stored at location 1000.

To illustrate the effectiveness of the encapsulation, suppose that the client code used the class `Listing`'s `setAddress` method to set the address field of the `Listing` object `bill` to "2nd Street," coded as:

```
bill.setAddress("2nd Street")
```

Then, as shown in Figure 2.20, the address contained in the `Listing` object `bill` located at address 5000 would change. However, since the information stored in the data structure is in a different `Listing` object, specifically the `Listing` object located at location 1000 created by the `deepCopy` method, the address of the phone listing stored inside the data structure is unchanged. Consistent with the concept of data encapsulation, the only way the client can change the address field of a listing stored inside the data structure is to invoke the data structure's `update` method.

An alternate, but undesirable, way of coding the `insert` method is to change Line 15 of Figure 2.17 to `data[i] = newListing`. This subtle change would, in effect, unencapsulate the data structure, since Line 15 would then perform a shallow copy. Thus, `data[i]` would store the address of the

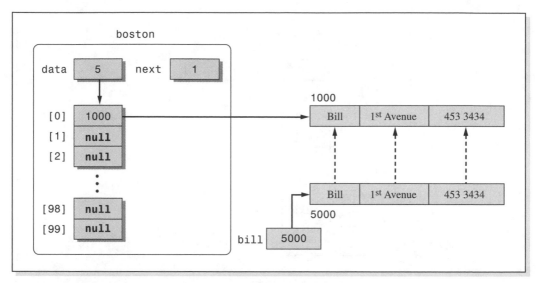

Figure 2.19 The Data Structure boston, After Inserting Bill's Listing

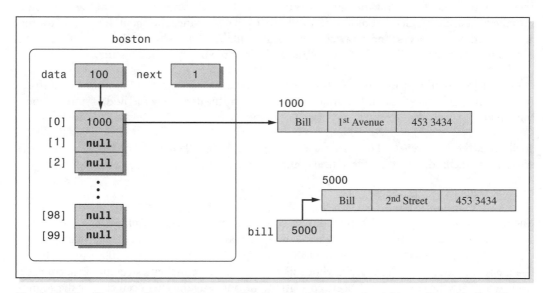

Figure 2.20 The Data Structure boston After the Client Changes the Address Stored in the Client Listing bill

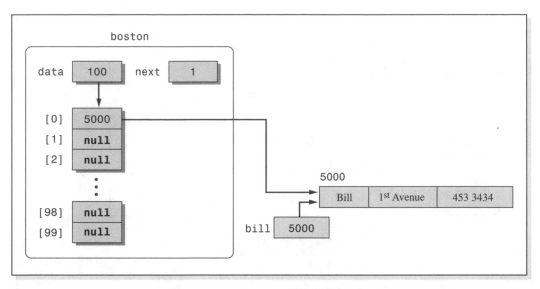

Figure 2.21   The Data Structure `boston`, with a Shallow Copy Coded as Line 15 of the `insert` Method

client's `Listing` object, `bill`, sent over as an argument to the `insert` method (see Figure 2.21). The data structure and the client code now reference the same `Listing` object, and the client statement

```
bill.setAddress("2nd Street");
```

changes the address of the listing stored (actually referenced from) "inside" the data structure. All subsequent fetches of the listing from the data structure would contain the new address. Effectively, the client has changed the data stored in the data structure without invoking the `update` method—a violation of encapsulation.

The `fetch` Method

Lines 22–41 of Figure 2.17 implement the pseudocode of the Fetch operation. The method heading, Line 22, indicates that the method returns a reference to a `Listing` object. This reference will be the address of a deep copy of the node whose key field `targetKey`, is passed to the method as a parameter. It is important that the method return a reference to a deep copy of the requested listing, since, if it returned a shallow copy, the client would then know the address of the object stored inside the data structure. Knowing this object's address, the client would have direct access to it, a violation of encapsulation.

Figure 2.22 shows the data structure with three listings stored in it, before and after the client fetches Tom's listing, using the statement `tom = boston.fetch("Tom")`. Notice the change in the

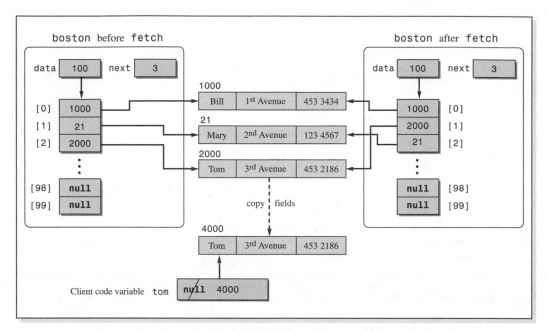

Figure 2.22 The Data Structure, `boston`, Before and After Tom's Listing Is Fetched

contents of the second and third elements of the array after the fetch operation is complete. The reference to the fetched node has begun to *bubble* up to the front of the array.

The `delete` Method

Lines 43–56 of Figure 2.17 implements the pseudocode of the Delete operation. It returns the Boolean value **true** if it successfully deletes a listing. Lines 46–48 perform the sequential search for the requested listing. If found (Line 49), Line 52 eliminates the listing from the data structure by overwriting the reference to it stored in the array data with the address of the last listing in the structure. After this overwriting, the address of the deleted listing is not stored in any reference variable, which causes Java's memory manager to return the storage allocated to the deleted listing's object to the available memory pool.

Figure 2.23 shows the data structure before and after Bill's listing is deleted using the statement: `boolean success = boston.delete("Bill")`. Notice the change in the contents of the first and third elements of the array after the deletion is complete. The reference to the deleted node has been overwritten with the address of Tom's node, and the address of Tom's node is no longer stored in the third element of the array. In addition, the variable `next` has been decremented to "collect the garbage."

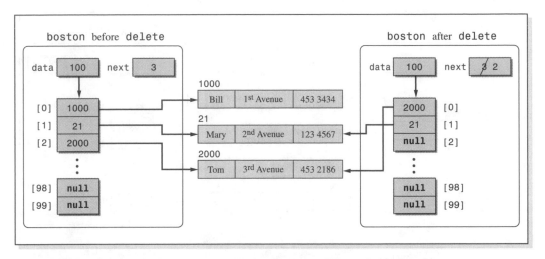

Figure 2.23   The Data Structure, boston, Before and After Bill's Listing Is Deleted

The update Method

Lines 58–65 of Figure 2.17 implement the pseudocode of the Update operation. The value of the key of the node to be deleted (targetKey) and the new contents of the node (contained in the object newNode) are passed into the method (Line 58). It is important to understand that the object containing the old information is not actually updated. Rather, that object is deleted from the data structure (Line 59), and a new Listing object is inserted into the structure (Line 61). Thus, the key field of the node could also be updated during an Update operation.

Figure 2.24 illustrates the data structure before and after Bill's listing is updated by the client statement: boolean success = boston.update("Bill", billsNewListing). The graphics in the figure assume Bill's name has not changed, his new address is "4th Avenue," and his new phone number is "676–7878" (all specified in the object billsNewListing). Notice that the reference to Tom's listing has moved to the front of the array as a result of the deletion of Bill's old listing (the first step in the Update algorithm). Furthermore, the reference to Bill's new listing is at the end of the used portion of the array because it was added with an invocation to the insert method (the second step in the Update algorithm).

Using the Baseline Implementation

Figure 2.25 presents an application program that demonstrates the use of the data structure class UnsortedOptimizedArray. The output it produces is shown in Figure 2.26.

Line 3 of Figure 2.25 creates the data structure boston, an object in the class UnsortedOptimizedArray. Lines 6–8 create three telephone listings (Listing objects) two of which are inserted

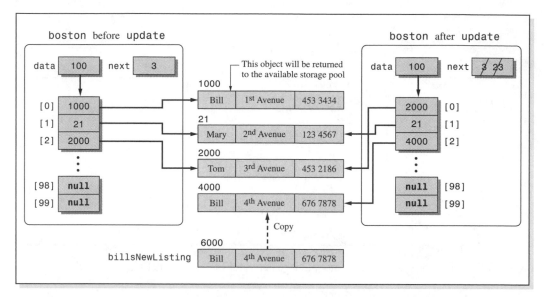

Figure 2.24 The Data Structure, boston, Before and After Bill's Listing Is Updated

into the data structure (Lines 12–13) and then fetched back and output (Lines 15–18), verifying the class's constructor, insert method, and fetch method. Line 14 verifies that the fetch method returns a **null** reference when the requested listing (Tom's) is not in the structure.

Lines 21–25 demonstrate the data structure's encapsulation. Line 22 changes the contents of the address field of the *client's* object mary to 9th Avenue. Line 23 outputs the modified client object to verify that the contents of the address field have been changed. This should not affect Mary's listing in the data structure because it is encapsulated inside the structure. Line 24 fetches back the listing with key field contents "Mary" from the structure, which is then output on Line 25. Since the output is the original listing with the address field unchanged, the data structure's encapsulation is verified.

Lines 28–31 demonstrate the use of the delete method. First, an attempt is made to delete a listing not in the structure (Tom's listing, Line 29), which produces an output of **false**. Then Bill's listing is deleted (Line 30), which produces an output of **true** because Bill's listing was in the structure. The subsequent attempt to fetch Bill's listing (Line 31) results in an output of **null** because Bill's listing has been deleted from the structure.

Lines 34–40 demonstrate the use of the update method. First, an attempt is made to update a listing not in the structure (Tom's listing, Line 35), which produces the correct output, **false**. Then, Bill's listing is reinserted into the structure (Line 36) and successfully updated to the contents of Tom's listing (Line 37 produces an output of true). After the Update operation is performed, the subsequent attempt to fetch a listing whose key field is Bill (Line 38) is unsuccessful (**null** output), while the fetch of the listing whose key field is Tom (Line 39) is successful and the listing is output.

```
1.   public class MainUnsortedOptimizedArray
2.   {  public static void main(String[] args)
3.   {  UnsortedOptimizedArray boston = new UnsortedOptimizedArray();
4.      Listing temp;
5.      // Test of the constructor
6.      Listing bill = new Listing("Bill", "First Avenue", "345 7474");
7.      Listing mary = new Listing("Mary", "Second Avenue", "123 4567");
8.      Listing tom = new Listing("Tom", "Third Avenue", "999 9999");
9.
10.     // Test of the insert and fetch methods. Outputs true, true, null,
        // Bill and Mary
11.     System.out.println("*** Test of the insert and fetch methods ***");
12.     System.out.println(boston.insert(bill));
13.     System.out.println(boston.insert(mary));
14.     System.out.println(boston.fetch("Tom"));
15.     temp = boston.fetch("Bill");
16.     System.out.println(temp.toString());
17.     temp = boston.fetch("Mary");
18.     System.out.println(temp.toString());
19.
20.     // Test of encapsulation. Output Mary's new listing, then the
        // encapsulated listing (which should be unchanged)
21.     System.out.println("*** Test of the data encapsulation ***");
22.     mary.setAddress("Ninth Avenue");  // will not change the
                                          // encapsulated listing
23.     System.out.println(mary.toString());
24.     temp = boston.fetch("Mary");
25.     System.out.println(temp.toString());
26.
27.     // Test of the Delete method. Next three outputs should be false,
        // true, and null
28.     System.out.println("*** Test of the delete method ***");
29.     System.out.println(boston.delete("Tom"));
30.     System.out.println(boston.delete("Bill"));
31.     System.out.println(boston.fetch("Bill"));
32.
33.     // Test of the Update method. Output should be false, true, and
        // null, followed by Bill's updated listing (Tom's listing)
34.     System.out.println("\n*** Test of the update method ***");
35.     System.out.println(boston.update("tom", mary));
36.     boston.insert(bill);
37.     System.out.println(boston.update("Bill", tom));
38.     System.out.println(boston.fetch("Bill"));
39.     temp = boston.fetch("Tom");
40.     System.out.println(temp.toString());
41.     System.exit(0);
42.   } // end of main method
43. } // end of class MainUnsortedOptimizedArray
```

Figure 2.25 An Application that Demonstrates the Use of the Class UnsortedOptimizedArray

```
*** Test of the insert and fetch methods ***
true
true
null
Name is Bill
Address is First Avenue
Number is 345 7474

Name is Mary
Address is Second Avenue
Number is 123 4567

*** Test of the data encapsulation ***
Name is Mary
Address is Ninth Avenue
Number is 123 4567

Name is Mary
Address is Second Avenue
Number is 123 4567

*** Test of the delete method ***
false
true
null

*** Test of the update method ***
false
true
null
Name is Tom
Address is Third Avenue
Number is 999 9999
```

Figure 2.26   The Output from the Application Program Shown in Figure 2.25

2.3.2 Utility Methods

The motivation for beginning with a baseline implementations of the UnsortedOptimizedArray structure and a class that described a node in a telephone listing data base was purely pedagogical. It allowed us to gain an understanding of the basic implementation techniques within a minimal amount of code. Having gained that understanding, in this section we will expand the code of the class Listing, shown in Figure 2.16, and the class UnsortedOptimizedArray, shown in Figure 2.17, adding some common *utility* methods that make them easier for clients to use.

An input method will be added to the class Listing that, when invoked by the application program, will allow the user to input the contents of a telephone listing. The code shown below is an example of how the method could be used by a client application to add 50 telephone listings, input by the user, to the data structure boston.

```
Node newListing = new Node();
for(int i = 0; i < 50; i++)
{  newListing.input();
   boston.insert(newListing);
}
```

Two methods will be added to the DataStructure class:

- A constructor to permit the client to specify the maximum number of nodes that can be stored in the structure when it is created.
- A showAll method that outputs the contents of the entire data structure.

The relationship between the three new methods and the application's user is depicted in Figure 2.27.

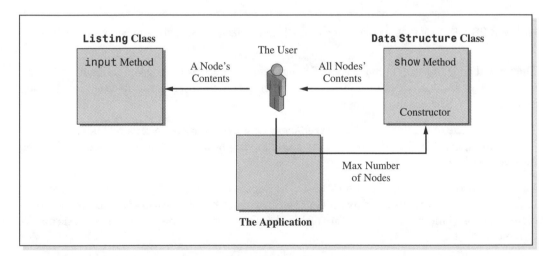

Figure 2.27   The Three-Method Expansion of the Baseline Implementation of the Unsorted-Optimized Array Structure

```
1.  public class Node
2.  {  private String name;  // key field
3.     private String address;
4.     private String number;
5.     public Node(String n, String a, String num)
6.     {  name = n;
7.        address = a;
8.        number = num;
9.     }
10.    public String toString()
11.    {  return("Name is " + name +
12.              "\nAddress is " + address +
13.              "\nNumber is " + number + "\n");
14.    }
15.    public Node deepCopy()
16.    {  Node clone = new Node(name, address, number);
17.       return clone;
18.    }
19.    public int compareTo(String targetKey)
20.    {  return(name.compareTo(targetKey));
21.    }
22.    public void setAddress(String a) // coded to demonstrate
                                        // encapsulation
23.    {  address = a;
24.    }
25.    public void input()
26.    {  name = JOptionPane.showInputDialog("Enter a name");
27.       address = JOptionPane.showInputDialog("Enter an address");
28.       number = JOptionPane.showInputDialog("Enter a number");
29.    } // end of inputNode method
30. } // end of class Node
```

Figure 2.28   Recoding of the Class Node to Include a Default Constructor and an input Method

The revised code of the Listing class, which has been renamed Node, is given in Figure 2.28. The new input method is coded on Lines 25–29, which places the user input directly into the data members name, address, and number.

The revised code of the UnsortedOptimizedArray class, which has been renamed UOAUtilities, is given in Figure 2.29 All references to the class Listing now refer to its expanded version, the class Node (e.g., Lines 4 and 18).

The new constructor is coded as Lines 12–16. It uses an integer passed into it (the parameter on Line 12) to size the structure's array on Line 14. Since the value of s is also saved in the class' data member size (Line 15), no changes are required to the error checking performed in basic operation methods (e.g., Line 19).

```
1.  public class UOAUtilities
2.  { private int next;
3.    private int size;
4.    private Node[] data;
5.
6.    public UOAUtilities()
7.    { next = 0;
8.      size = 100;
9.      data = new Node[size];
10.   } // end of constructor
11.
12.   public UOAUtilities(int s)
13.   { next = 0;
14.     data = new Node[s];
15.     size = s;
16.   } // end of constructor
17.
18.   public boolean insert(Node newNode)
19.   { if(next >= size)  // the structure is full
20.       return false;
21.     data[next] = newNode.deepCopy(); // store a deep copy of the
                                         // client's node

22.     if(data[next] == null)
23.       return false;
24.     next = next + 1; // prepare for the next insert
25.     return true;
26.   } // end of insert method
27.
28.   public Node fetch(String targetKey)
29.   { Node node;
30.     Node temp;
31.     // access the node using a sequential search
32.     int i = 0;
33.     while(i < next && !(data[i].compareTo(targetKey) == 0))
34.     { i++;
35.     }
36.     if(i == next) // node not found
37.       return null;
38.     // deep copy the node's information into the client's node
39.     node = data[i].deepCopy();
40.     // move the node up one position in the array, unless it is the
          // first node
41.     if(i != 0) // bubble-up accessed node
42.     { temp = data[i - 1];
43.       data[i - l] = data[i];
44.       data[i] = temp;
45.     }
```

(continues)

Figure 2.29 The Unsorted-Optimized Array Implementation with an Additional Constructor and a showAll Method

```
46.        return node;
47.     } // end of fetch method
48.
49.     public boolean delete(String targetKey)
50.     { // access the node using a sequential search
51.        int i = 0;
52.        while(i < next && !(data[i].compareTo(targetKey) == 0))
53.        {  i++;
54.        }
55.        if(i == next) // node not found
56.          return false;
57.        // move the last node into the deleted node's position
58.        data[i] = data[next - 1];
59.        data[next - 1] = null;
60.        next = next - 1;
61.        return true; // node found and deleted
62.     } // end of the delete method
63.
64.     public boolean update(String targetKey, Node newNode)
65.     {  if(delete(targetKey) == false)  // node not in the structure
66.          return false;
67.        else if(insert(newNode) == false)   // insufficient memory
68.          return false;
69.        else
70.          return true;   // node found and updated
71.     } // end of update method
72.     public void showAll()
73.     {  for(int i = 0; i < next; i++)
74.          System.out.println(data[i].toString());
75.     } // end of showAll method
76. } // end of class UOAUtilities
```

Figure 2.29   *(continued)*

The showAll method is coded as Lines 72–75. It outputs the nodes by invoking the Node class' toString method Line (74) inside a **for** loop. The loop uses the variable next (Line 73) to decide when the output is complete.

The following code is an example of how the new constructor and the showAll method could be used by the client application to declare and output all the nodes in a 100,000 listing structure named boston.

```
UOAUtilities boston = new UOAUtilities (1000000);
boston.showAll();
```

Having completed the expansions to the baseline implementation of our Unsorted-Optimized, array-based structure, we will now discuss an additional feature that will make the structure easier for the client to use.

2.4 Expandable Array-Based Structures

When any array is created, its size must be specified. Thus, the array-based implementations developed in this chapter either required the client to specify the maximum number of nodes that would be stored in the structure, or the maximum was set by the structure's constructor to a default value. In either case, the maximum value was used to size the structure's array, and it was checked by the Insert operation before it attempted to add a node to the structure.

There are many applications in which the maximum number of nodes in the structure cannot be anticipated (with any certainty) at the time the data structure is created. And so, there is an alternate implementation of the insert method aimed at these applications. When the structure's array is full, the insert method copies the entire contents of the structure's array into a larger array and then inserts the node into the expanded structure. Under this scheme, the only time the Insert operation would return false is when the system memory is exhausted.

In some programming languages, copying an array of objects from one array to another is a time consuming process. This is not the case in Java, because Java implements an array of objects as an array of reference variables that point to the objects (see Figure 2.24). Therefore, only the reference variables need to be copied into the expanded array, making the process as efficient as copying an array of primitive values.

The pseudocode of the algorithm written to expand a Java array follows. It assumes data is the array to be expanded, larger is the expanded array, and temp is an array reference variable.

A Java Array Copy Algorithm

1. temp = data; // set temp to reference the array to be expanded, data
2. data = larger; // both data and larger now reference the expanded array
3. // the code to copy the contents of temp into data is coded here
4. temp = **null**; // send the original array to the systems memory manager
5. larger = **null**; // only data should reference the expanded array

The comment on Line 3 of the algorithm must be replaced with the code that copies the object references from temp into data. This can be done using a loop or by invoking the Java method arraycopy, which is contained in the System class. When a loop is used, the following code would replace Line 3.

```
for(int i = 0; i < temp.length-1; i++)
   data[i] = temp[i];
```

where temp.length returns the number of elements in the array to be expanded, temp.

Java's arraycopy method copies a specified number of items from a source array to a destination array. The source and destination starting indices are supplied to the method, as is the number of elements to be copied. Since we want to copy the entire contents of the array `temp` starting at index zero into the array `data` starting at index zero, the invocation would be:

```
System.arraycopy(temp, 0, data, 0, temp.length);
```

The use of the method `arraycopy` is preferred because it is about 50% faster than the loop technique. On an absolute speed basis, tests performed on a PC using an AMD Athlon XP 3000+ processor with a 2.17-gigahertz clock showed that the `arraycopy` method was able to copy a 500,000 element array of object references in 0.06 seconds. What this means is that an Insert operation performed at a time when an array-based structure is full would require an extra 0.06 seconds to expand the structure's 500,000 element array. This level of performance would be adequate for most applications. Still, there are many real-time applications that could not tolerate a 0.06-second delay. One other potential downside is that expanding an array can result in a somewhat unpredictable `"java.lang.OutOfMemoryError: Java heap space"` run-time error.

All things considered, for small- to moderately-sized array-based structures, an `insert` method that can expand the size of the structure's array greatly enhances the usefulness of these structures. A good middle ground implementation would add a Boolean parameter to the structure's constructor to allow the client to specify whether or not the expandable feature of the `insert` method should be employed for a particular application. This implementation is left as an exercise for the student.

2.5   Generic Data Structures

The development of software is an expensive and time-consuming process. Therefore, whenever possible, we should write *reuseable* software. In the context of data structures, reusability is achieved by writing data structures that are application independent, or *generic*. Generic data structures, by definition, can store any kind of node and, therefore, can be used in any application. (Naturally, the performance of the structure would have to be consistent with the requirements of the application.) Stated another way, if the final implementation of our Unsorted-Optimized array structure (the class `UOAUtilities`) was generic, it could not only be used to store the data for a telephone listing application, but also an employee record application, a store inventory application, or any other type of data intense application *without modifying its code*.

Generic implementations of data structures fall into two groupings: *homogeneous* and *heterogeneous* (nonhomogeneous) generic data structures. Both groups can store data sets comprised of any type of node (e.g., telephone listings or employee records). However, in a homogeneous generic data structure, *all nodes* stored in a particular data structure object must be of the same type (e.g., all nodes in the data set are telephone listings *or* they are all employee records). In a heterogeneous structure, the nodes in a single data structure object need *not* be all of the same type (e.g., employee records and telephone listings can be stored in the same object). The difference between homogeneous and heterogeneous structures is illustrated in Figure 2.30.

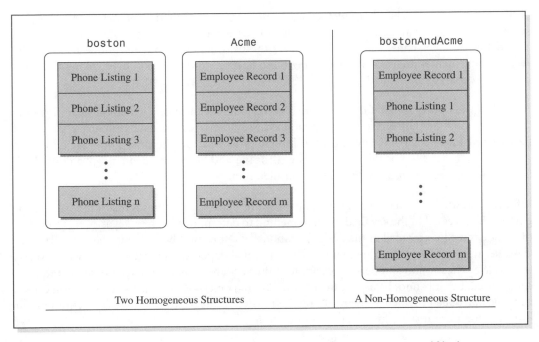

Figure 2.30 Phone Listings and Employee Records Stored in Homogeneous and Nonhomogeneous Data Structures

In the remainder of this section, we will examine the features of a data structure's design that makes it generic and show how to implement these features in Java.

2.5.1 Design Considerations

The first consideration in designing and implementing generic data structures is to separate the node definition and the data structure's definition into two separate classes since different applications deal with different types of nodes. Typically, the nodes in different applications have a different number of fields, along with different field names, widths, and data types. By defining the node in a separate class we need not rewrite the data structure class when the node composition changes. In addition, the task of coding the node class is appropriately passed on to the application programmers who know the composition of the nodes. In the baseline and expanded implementations of the array-based structures presented in this chapter, the node definition was coded in a separate class. Therefore, both of these implementations conformed to this generic design feature.

A second consideration is that the data structure's code must not mention the names of the data fields that make up a node. If it did, it would again be tied to a particular node composition of a particular application. The two implementations of the Unsorted-Optimized Array structure presented in Figures 2.17 and 2.29, both conformed to this generic design feature. Neither class mentioned the variables `name`, `address`, or `number`; the field names of our telephone listings. The second implementation avoided mentioning these in its `showAll` method by invoking the node definition class' `toString` method.

A third consideration is that if the structure is going to be encapsulated, a method to perform the deep copy must be part of the node definition class. Otherwise, the data structure class would have to have knowledge of the node composition in order to create the clone node (see Line 16 of Figure 2.28). Since the node definition classes `Listing` and `Node` provided a `deepCopy` method, both of our implementations satisfied this consideration.

A fourth consideration in designing and implementing generic structures is that if the structure is going to be accessed in the key field mode, a method to determine if a given key is equal to the key of a node must be provided in the node definition class. It cannot be coded in the data structure class, because how we determine that two keys are equal depends on the key's type, which varies from one application to another. For example, if the keys are numeric, the relational operator == can be used, but it cannot be used if the keys are `String` objects. Since the node definition classes `Listing` and `Node` provided a `compareTo` method to determine if two keys were equal, both of our implementations satisfied this generic consideration.

The final two design considerations address the fact that nodes can be instances of any class (e.g., `Listing` objects, or `Node` objects, or `Employee` objects, or `CarType` objects, etc.), and their key fields can be any type (not just a `String` object). Neither of our two implementations addressed these issues. In the first implementation, the name of the node definition class had to be `Listing` because many lines of the data structure's code specifically mention that type (e.g., Lines 4, 9, 12, 22, etc. of Figure 2.17). Similarly, the second implementation shown in Figure 2.29 can only store nodes that are instances of the class `Node` (see Lines 4, 9, 14, 18, 28, etc.). Both implementations assume the key field sent to the `fetch`, `delete`, and `update` methods is an object in the class `String` (e.g., Lines 28, 49, and 64 of Figure 2.29). Our final implementation of the Unsorted-Optimized, array-based structure will address these last two issues, making it a generic implementation. Before proceeding to that implementation, it is useful to summarize the design and implementation features that make a data structure class generic:

1. The node definition and the data structure are coded as two separate classes.
2. The data structure cannot mention the names of the data fields that make up a node.
3. If the structure is going to be encapsulated, a method to perform a deep copy of a node must be coded in the node definition class.
4. If the structure is going to be accessed in the key field mode, a method to determine if a given key is equal to the key of a node must be coded in the node definition class.
5. The data structure code cannot mention the name of the node class.
6. The data structure code cannot mention the type of the key.

2.5.2 Generic Implementation of the Unsorted-Optimized Array

As previously mentioned, in our two implementations of the Unsorted-Optimized structure, we have incorporated the first four design features of a generic implementation. In this section, we will develop a completely generic implementation of this structure by incorporating the fifth and sixth design features into the code of the class UOAUtilities (presented in Figure 2.29). The revised structure will be able to store nodes of any type, whose key field is of any type. Prior to the release of Java 5.0, this was accomplished by changing the types of the node *and* key field references in the data structure class to Object references. However, for reasons we will discuss later, the generic typing features in Java 5.0 offer a better alternative.

As mentioned in Chapter 1, generic typing is a language feature that allows the author of a class to generalize the type of information with which a class (or a method) will deal. Then, the specific type of information is specified by the client when an object in that class is declared. For example, if the name of a generic data structure class were UOA, then the following two declarations of the data structure objects boston and newYork would be used to store Listing objects in the data structure boston, and Node objects in the data structure newYork.

```
UOA boston <Listing> = new UOA();
newYork <Node> = new UOA();
```

Although generic typing is the best alternative for coding generic data structures, its use is not as simple as substituting generic type placeholders for the data member types as presented in the Java review example in Chapter 1. The class in that example did *not* allocate new objects of the generic type, and it did not invoke any methods to operate on objects of the generic type. Both of these complications must be dealt with to complete the conversion of our data structure class into a generic class.

In the interest of simplicity, we will discuss the conversion of one section of the class UOAUtilities' code at a time, so that that we can focus on one conversion issue at a time. However, the line numbers in each section of converted code (presented in Figures 2.31–2.35) will be sequential and will roughly parallel the line numbers of the class UOAUtilities presented in Figure 2.29. To begin with, we will consider modifications to the data declarations and the class' constructors (Lines 1–16 of Figure 2.29), which are highlighted in the revised code presented in Figure 2.31. The name of the new (and eventually generic) class is assumed to be UOA.

As was discussed in Chapter 1, to make data members generic, a generic placeholder is added to the end of the class heading. In this case, the placeholder <T> has been added to the end of Line 1, and the type Node on Line 4 has been replaced with the generic type, T. However, we cannot simply replace the type Node on Lines 9 and 14 with the generic type T because the translator will not allow us to declare an array of references to a generic type. To do so would imply that there is a constructor in the class T, which at this point is an undefined class. Therefore, the arrays on these lines are declared to be arrays of Object references. The class Object is predefined in Java, and since the class Object is the parent class of all Java classes, references will be able to store the address of any type of node. Finally, on Lines 9 and 14 the location of the array of Object references must be coerced into the location of an array of type T since the variable data on Line 4 is now declared to store the location of an array of type T.

```
1.    public class UOA<T>
2.    {  private int next;
3.       private T[] data;
4.       private int size;
5.
6.       public UOA()
7.       {  next = 0;
8.          size = 100;
9.          data = (T[]) new Object[100];
10.      } // end of constructor
11.
12.      public UOA(int s)
13.      {  next = 0;
14.         data = (T[]) new Object[s];
15.         size = s;
16.      } // end of constructor
```

Figure 2.31   The Changes Made to the Data Members and Constructors of the Class UOAUtilities (Figure 2.29) to Make Them Generic

```
17.
18.      public boolean insert(T newListing)
19.      {  KeyMode node = (KeyMode) newListing;
20.         if(next >= size)
21.            return false;   // check for too many listings
22.         data[next] = (T) node.deepCopy();
23.         if(data[next] == null) // check for insufficient memory
24.            return false;
25.         next = next + 1;
26.         return true;   // insert performed
27.      } // end of insert method
```

Figure 2.32   The Changes Made to the insert Method of the Class UOAUtilities (Figure 2.29) to Make It Generic

Next we will consider modifications to the insert method, Lines 18–26 of Figure 2.29. These changes are highlighted in the revised code presented in Figure 2.32. Referring to that figure, one line has been added (Line 19), and two lines have been changed (Lines 18 and 22). The change to Line 18 is simply to change the parameter type Node to the generic type placeholder T. The change to Line 22 necessitates the addition of Line 19, so we will discuss Line 22 first.

The invocation to the method deepCopy (Line 22) can no longer operate on the object referenced by newNode, as it did on Line 21 of Figure 2.29, because newNode is now of type T (Line 18) and the translator cannot look into the class T to verify the method's signature.[15] The remedy is to reference the object to be operated on with the variable node, which is defined on the left side of Line 19 to be a KeyMode reference, and then place the address of the node to be inserted into the

---

[15]The generic type T is not associated with a class until an application declares an object in the class UOA.

variable node (right side of Line 19). However, the translator still wants to verify the signature of the method deepCopy, and at this point KeyMode is an undefined symbol. Therefore, the programmer of the data structure must code a Java interface named KeyMode and define the signature of the method deepCopy in it. The actual implementation of the method will be coded where we have always coded it, in the application's node definition class. One restriction is that the node definition classes must add the phrase "implements KeyMode" to its heading. The coercions (KeyMode) and (T) on Lines 19 and 22 respectively are necessary to match the types on the left side of the assignment operators.

The interface KeyMode would be written (by the coder of the data structure class) as:

```
public interface KeyMode
{  public abstract KeyMode deepCopy();   // performs a deepCopy of the
                                          // invoking object
}
```

As we discuss the changes to the other methods in the class UOAUtilities, we will add two more method signatures to this interface.

Next we will consider modifications to the fetch method, Lines 28–47 of Figure 2.29. These changes are highlighted in the revised code presented in Figure 2.33. Referring to that figure, one line has been added (Line 36), and five lines have been changed (Lines 29, 30, 31, 34, and 41).

```
28.
29.      public KeyMode fetch(Object targetKey)
30.      {  KeyMode node = (KeyMode) data[0];
31.        // access the node using a sequential search
32.         T temp;
33.         int i = 0;
34.         while(i < next && node.compareTo(targetKey) != 0)
35.         {  i++;
36.            node = (KeyMode) data[i];
37.         }
38.         if(i == next)   // the node with the given key was not found
39.            return null;
40.         // deep copy the nodes information into returned node
41.         node = node.deepCopy();
42.         // move the node up one position in the array, unless it is the
                // first node
43.         if(i != 0)   // bubble-up accessed node
44.         {  temp =  data[i - 1];
45.            data[i - 1] = data[i];
46.            data[i] = temp;
47.         }
48.         return node;
49.      } // end of the fetch method
```

Figure 2.33   The Changes Made to the fetch Method of the Class UOAUtilities (Figure 2.29) to Make It Generic

Most of the changes here are made for the same reasons as the changes we made to Line 22 of the insert method: A method cannot operate on objects referenced by variables of type T. In the case of the fetch method, there are two invocations. The method compareTo is invoked on Line 33 of Figure 2.29, and the method deepCopy is invoked on Line 39. Both of these methods operate on the entity referenced by data[i]. Since the variable data now stores a T reference (Line 4 of Figure 2.31), the translator cannot verify the method signatures. The remedy is the same as that discussed for the insert method. Both invocations are changed to operate the KeyMode reference variable node (Lines 34 and 41 of Figure 2.33), whose declaration is on Line 30, and the signature of the method compareTo is added to the interface KeyMode. Line 36 was added so that the reference stored in the variable node is changed each time through the loop. Since the fetch method returns the reference stored in the variable node, and node's type has been changed to be of type KeyMode (Line 30), the fetch method's returned type (on Line 29) has been changed from Node to KeyMode. Finally, the type of the insert method's parameter on Line 29 has been changed to an Object reference so that the key is not restricted to String objects.

The expanded KeyMode interface is now:

```
public interface KeyMode
{  public abstract KeyMode deepCopy();   // performs a deepCopy of the
                                         // invoking object
    public abstract int compareTo(Object other);  // returns 0 for equality
}
```

Next we will consider modifications to the delete method (Lines 49–62 of Figure 2.29). These changes are highlighted in the revised code presented in Figure 2.34. Referring to that figure, one line has been added (Line 57), and three lines have been changed (Lines 51, 52,

```
50.
51.    public boolean delete(Object targetKey)
52.    {  KeyMode node = (KeyMode) data[0];
53.    // access the node using a sequential search
54.       int i = 0;
55.       while (i < next && node.compareTo(targetKey) != 0)
56.       {  i++;
57.          node = (KeyMode) data[i];
58.       }
59.       if(i == next) // the node was not found
60.          return false;
61.      // move the last node into the deleted node's position
62.       data[i] = data[next - 1];
63.       data[next - 1] = null;
64.       next = next - 1;
65.       return true;
66.    } // end of delete method
```

Figure 2.34 Changes Made to the delete Method of the Class UOAUtilities (Figure 2.29) to Make It Generic

```
67.
68.     public boolean update(Object targetKey, T newNode)
69.     {   if(delete(targetKey) == false)
70.             return false;
71.         else if(insert(newNode) == false)
72.             return false;
73.         else
74.             return true;
75.     } // end of update method
```

Figure 2.35 Changes Made to the update Method of the Class UOAUtilities (Figure 2.29) to Make It Generic

and 55). The rationale for these changes is the same as that discussed for the analogous changes made to the insert method: to direct the translator to the interface KeyMode to verify the signature of the compareTo method and to allow any type key to be passed into the method.

The modifications to the update method (Lines 64–71 of Figure 2.29) are highlighted in the code presented in Figure 2.35. Only the types of the method's parameters were changed so that the key field need not be a reference to a String object, and to make the invocation on Line 71 compatible with the insert method's new signature. The modified insert method is expecting an argument of type T (Line 18 of Figure 2.32). Therefore, the type of the argument (newNode) passed it has been changed on Line 68 of Figure 2.35.

Finally, although the toString method in the class UOAUtilities need not be changed, its signature is added to the interface KeyMode to remind the application programmer to include it in the node definition class. For convenience, all of the code in the generic implementation of the Unsorted-Optimized array is presented in Figure 2.36, and the code of the expanded interface KeyMode is presented in Figure 2.37.

```
1.  public class UOA<T>
2.  {   private int next;
3.      private T[] data;
4.      private int size;
5.
6.      public UOA()
7.      {   next = 0;
8.          size = 100;
9.          data = (T[]) new Object[100];
```

(continues)

Figure 2.36 Fully Implemented Generic Version of the Unsorted-Optimized Array-Based Structure

```
10.    } // end of constructor
11.
12.    public UOA(int s)
13.    {  next = 0;
14.       data = (T[]) new Object[s];
15.       size = s;
16.    } // end of constructor
17.
18.    public boolean insert(T newListing)
19.    {  KeyMode node = (KeyMode) newListing;
20.       if(next >= size)
21.         return false;  // check for too many listings
22.       data[next] = (T) node.deepCopy();
23.       if(data[next] == null) // check for insufficient memory
24.         return false;
25.       next = next + 1;
26.       return true;  // insert performed
27.    } // end of insert method
28.
29.    public KeyMode fetch(Object targetKey)
30.    { // access the node using a sequential search, returns null for
         // not found
31.       KeyMode node = (KeyMode) data[0];
32.       T temp;
33.       int i = 0;
34.       while(i < next && node.compareTo(targetKey) != 0)
35.       {  i++;
36.          node = (KeyMode) data[i];
37.       }
38.       if(i == next)  // the node with the given key was not found
39.         return null;
40.     // deep copy the nodes information into returned node
41.       node = node.deepCopy();
42.     // move the node up one position in the array, unless it is the
         // first node
43.       if(i != 0)  // bubble-up accessed node
44.       {  temp =  data[i - 1];
45.          data[i - 1] = data[i];
46.          data[i] = temp;
47.       }
48.       return node;
49.    } // end of the fetch method
50.
51.    public boolean delete(Object targetKey)
52.    {  KeyMode node = (KeyMode) data[0];
53.     // access the node using a sequential search
54.       int i = 0;
```

(continues)

Figure 2.36 (continued)

```
55.         while (i < next && node.compareTo(targetKey) != 0)
56.         {  i++;
57.            node = (KeyMode) data[i];
58.         }
59.         if(i == next) // the node was not found
60.            return false;
61.         // move the last node into the deleted node's position
62.         data[i] = data[next - 1];
63.         data[next - 1] = null;
64.         next = next - 1;
65.         return true;
66.      } // end of delete method
67.
68.      public boolean update(Object targetKey, T newNode)
69.      {  if(delete(targetKey) == false)
70.            return false;
71.         else if(insert(newNode) ==  false)
72.            return false;
73.         else
74.            return true;
75.      } // end of update method
76.
77.      public void showAll()
78.      {  for(int i = 0; i < next; i++)
79.            System.out.println(data[i].toString());
80.      } // end of toString method
81. } // end of class UOA
```

Figure 2.36   *(continued)*

```
public interface KeyMode
{  public abstract KeyMode deepCopy(); // performs a deepCopy of the
                                       // invoking object
   public abstract int compareTo(Object targetKey); // returns 0 for
                                                     // equality
   public abstract String toString(); // added to prevent Objects toString
                                       // method from executing,
                                       // technically not necessary
}
```

Figure 2.37   The Interface KeyMode

2.5.3 Client-Side Use of Generic Structures

To use our generic data structure class UOA, the application programmer simply declares an object (or objects) in the class UOA, specifying the type of the nodes it will store, and implements the interface Key-Mode in the node definition class. This means that the node definition class must include a coding of a deepCopy method, a compareTo method, and a toString method whose signatures are those specified in the interface (Figure 2.37). Naturally, the node definition class should also include the declaration of the fields of a node, constructors as required by the application, and any utility methods that the application uses to operate on the nodes (e.g., an input method for the application's user to input the values of a node). The translator will check that the phrase "implements KeyMode" appears in the class' heading and that the class includes the code of all the methods mentioned in the interface. As previously mentioned, the coding of the deepCopy and compareTo methods is properly left to the application programmer who knows the character of the nodes and what it means to say that two key objects are equal.

To declare two Unsorted-Optimized, array-based structures named carDealer1 and carDealer2, each able to store a maximum of 700 objects of the class Car, the client code would be:

```
UOA <Car> carDealer1 = new UOA <Car> (700);
UOA <Car> carDealer2 = new UOA <Car> (700);
```

As part of Java's generic feature, these declarations are compiler enforced homogeneous structures. Any attempt to store anything other than a Car object in these structures, for example,

```
Truck myTruck = new Truck;
carDealer1.insert(myTruck);
```

results in a compile error.

As an example, Figures 2.38 and 2.39 present the code of a telephone directory application. Figure 2.38 presents the class PhoneListing that defines the nodes used the application. Since the

```
1.   public class PhoneListing implements KeyMode //'s three methods
2.   {  private String name;  // key field
3.      private String address;
4.      private String number;
5.      public PhoneListing(String n, String a, String num)
6.      {  name = n;
7.         address = a;
8.         number = num;
9.      }
10.     public String toString()
11.     {  return("Name is " + name +
12.             "\nAddress is " + address +
13.             "\nNumber is " + number + "\n");
14.     }
15.     public KeyMode deepCopy()
16.     {  PhoneListing clone = new PhoneListing (name, address, number);
17.        return clone;
18.     }
19.     public int compareTo(Object targetKey)
20.     {  String tKey = (String) targetKey; // targetKey is a String
21.        return(name.compareTo(tKey));
22.     } // end of compareTo method
23. } // end of class PhoneListing
```

Figure 2.38 The Node Definition Class PhoneListing

```
1.  public class MainUOA
2.  { public static void main(String[] args)
3.    { UOA <PhoneListing> NYC = new UOA<PhoneListing>(500);
4.      PhoneListing bob = new PhoneListing("Bob", "23 1st Avenue",
                                            "133-4573");
5.      PhoneListing roy = new PhoneListing("Roy", "421 east 24th Street",
                                            "897-2232");
6.
7.      NYC.insert(bob);
8.      NYC.insert(roy);
9.      System.out.println(NYC.fetch("Roy").toString());
10.     System.out.println(NYC.fetch("Bob").toString());
11.   } // end of main method
12. } // end of class MainUOA

    Output:
    Name is: Roy
    Address is: 421 East 24th Street
    Number is: 897-2232

    Name is: Bob
    Address is: 23 1st Avenue
    Number is: 133-4573
```

Figure 2.39   A Phone Book Application That Uses the Generic Class UOA and Its Output

application will use our unsorted-optimized generic structure UOA, it implements the interface KeyMode. Figure 2.39 presents the code of the application and the output it produces.

2.5.4 Heterogeneous Generic Data Structures

A generic data structure can be used as a heterogeneous structure if the type parameter is left out of the object declaration. For example, if the declaration for the data structure given in the previous section were changed to:

```
UOA carDealer1 = new UOA(700);
```

then any type of objects whose definition class implements the interface KeyMode (Car objects, Truck objects, etc.) could be stored in it. In this case, the statements

```
UOA carDealer1 = new UOA(700);
Car myCar = new Car();
carDealer1.insert(myCar);
Truck myTruck = new Truck();
carDealer1.insert(myTruck);
```

would *not* result in a compile error. It should be noted that for most applications it is better programming practice to declare two homogeneous data structures that each store one type of node, rather than one heterogeneous structure that stores two different types of nodes.

2.6 Java's `ArrayList` Class

The Java Application Programmer Interface provides a class named `ArrayList` that is similar to the language's array construct but in fact has much more in common with the array-based structures developed in this chapter. Like arrays, access into the structure is in the *node number mode*[16] via an integer index whose minimum value is zero, and the structure is *unencapsulated*. Unlike arrays, the structure `ArrayList` supports all four basic operations (Insert, Fetch, Delete, and Update), is implemented using generics, cannot store primitive types,[17] and can be used either as compiler-enforced homogeneous or heterogeneous structure. Considering these characteristics, an `ArrayList` is actually an unencapsulated node number mode access version of our generic array-based structure.

The `ArrayList` structure does have one additional feature that neither arrays nor our array-based structures possess. Although we can specify an initial number of nodes to be stored in the structure,

```
ArrayList <Node> NYC = new ArrayList<Node>(200);   // initially 200 node
                                                   // capacity
```

an `ArrayList` object can expand at run-time beyond its initial size to accommodate unanticipated Insert operations. As discussed, Insert operation implementations that support run-time expansion run more slowly than those that do not.

Table 2.5 presents the names of the basic operation methods in the class `ArrayList` and some examples of their use. It assumes that the `ArrayList` structure boston was declared as a heterogeneous structure with the statement:

```
ArrayList boston = new ArrayList();  // initial size defaults to 10 nodes
```

that the variables `tom` and `mary` store references to `Node` objects and `temp` can store a Node reference.

---

[16]The one exception is that the Insert operation assigns the next node number to the inserted node, which makes the structure a little awkward to use.

[17]Java 5.0 gives the appearance of allowing primitives to be inserted into an `ArrayList` object but it actually wraps the primitive in a `Wrapper` object before inserting it.

Table 2.5

Some of the Methods Available in the API class ArrayList

Basic Operation	ArrayList Method Name	Coding Example[18]	Comments

Insert	add	`boston.add(tom); // uses index 0`
		`boston.add(mary); // uses index 1`
		`boston.add(21); // uses index 2`
			the 21 gets wrapped

Fetch	get	`temp = (Node) boston.get(1) // fetch mary`
		`temp = (Node) boston.get(0) // fetch tom`
		`int i = (Integer) boston.get(2) // fetch 21`
			coercion not necessary for homogeneous uses

Delete	remove	`boston.remove(1); // mary is deleted`	21 moves up to index 1

Update	set	`boston.set(0, mary); // tom now mary`
		`boston.set(1, 999.89); // 21 now 999.89`
			the 999.89 gets wrapped

[18]Assumes the code is executed in the order shown.

Knowledge Exercises

1. Which of the four basic operations does the built-in structure array support?

2. Draw a picture of the memory allocated to a five-element, one-dimensional array of integers called numbers. Assume the first element of the array is stored at location 500, the array is stored in ascending memory locations, and that the integers occupy 4 bytes each. On the left side of the array, indicate the number of each element, and on the right side of the array indicate the memory location number (beginning at 500).

3. Give the mapping function used to calculate the address of the kth element of a one-dimensional array of integers, assuming element zero is stored at location 500, the array is stored in ascending memory locations, and that an integer occupies 4 bytes of memory.

4. 20 integers are stored in a two-dimensional array of four rows and five columns. The name of the array is ages.

   a) Draw a picture of the rows and columns of the array, indicating the column numbers across the top of the array and the row numbers along the left side.

   b) Place an x in the cell of your picture whose contents is modified by the statement: ages[2][3] = 20;

   c) Give the memory location of the cell ages[2][3] assuming the array is stored in row major order in ascending memory locations beginning at location 500. Assume each cell is 4 bytes.

5. Give the change to Line 7 of an Unsorted Array structure's Fetch algorithm to unencapsulate the structure after the Fetch operation is completed.

6. A data structure is to be chosen that will allow the customers to look up the price of an item, given its item number. The data set will only be loaded once and never modified. Of the three array-based structures discussed in this chapter, which would be best suited for this application?

7. The Sorted Array structure accesses nodes using the Binary Search algorithm, and the Unsorted-Optimized Array structure uses a Sequential Search to access nodes. Knowing that a binary search is significantly faster than a sequential search, explain why it is that the *average* speed of the Unsorted-Optimized array structure is faster than that of the Sorted Array structure. (Assume all four basic operations are equally probable.)

8. Referring to the data structure depicted in Figure 2.8, what memory location would be returned by the Fetch algorithm if Mike's node was requested and the structure was not encapsulated?

9. Give the differences in the basic operation algorithms of the Unsorted and Unsorted-Optimized Array structures that made the latter structure faster. Under what conditions would both structures' Fetch algorithms be equivalent from a speed viewpoint?

10. The Unsorted-Optimized array structure is used to store a data set. Calculate its density if:

    a) Each of the client's nodes contains 8 bytes of information and there are 50 nodes in the data set.

    b) Each of the client's nodes contains 200 bytes of information and there are 1,000,000 nodes in the data set.

11. Give the average number of memory accesses of the Unsorted-Optimized array structure whose data set is described in part (b) of the previous exercise:

    a) Assuming all operations on the data set are equally probable.

    b) Assuming only Insert operations will be performed on the data set.

12. Plot the variation in density with the number of nodes, n, in an array-based structure. Assume each node contains 10 information bytes and that the range of n is $2 <= n <= 100$.

13. Define the data structures term *garbage collection*.

14. Describe the garbage collection method for the Unsorted-Optimized array structure.

15. You have coded an application for your friend's business that uses an Unsorted-Optimized array to store the venture's data. One day your friend informs you that the speed of the operations performed on the data set seems to be getting faster and faster. Explain how this could happen.

16. An application's data set will consist of five different types of nodes. Is the data set homogeneous or heterogeneous?

17. Give the six design features that should be followed when designing generic data structures.

18. Give the pseudocode of an `update` method for the Unsorted structure that does not invoke the `delete` and `insert` methods and does check for errors.

Programming Exercises

19. A database is to be developed to keep track of student information at your college. It will include names, identification numbers, and grade point averages. The data set will be accessed in the key field mode, with the student's name being the key field. Code a class named `StudentListings` that defines the nodes. Your class should include all the methods in the class shown in Figure 2.28 except for the `setAddress()` method. It should also include a no-parameter constructor. Test it with a progressively developed driver program that verifies the functionality of all of its methods.

20. Code a class that implements the Sorted Array structure, and write a progressively developed driver program that verifies the functionality of all of its methods. Assume that it is to store a data set whose nodes are described in Exercise 19. Include error checking in the code of the

basic operation methods, a constructor to permit the client to specify the maximum size of the data set, and a method to display the contents of entire data set in sorted order.

21. Code an application program that keeps track of student information at your college: names, identification numbers, and grade point averages in a *fully encapsulated* (homogeneous) Sorted array-based data structure. When launched, the user will be asked to input the maximum size of the data set, the initial number of students, and the initial data set. Once this is complete, the user will be presented with the following menu:

    Enter: 1 to *insert* a new student's information,

           2 to *fetch* and output a student's information,

           3 to *delete* a student's information,

           4 to *update* a student's information,

           5 to *output* all the student information in sorted order, and

           6 to *exit* the program.

    The program should perform an unlimited number of operations until the user enters a 6 to exit the program.

22. A database is to be developed to keep track of faculty information at your college. Faculty member's names, departments, areas of expertise, and e-mail addresses will all be included. The data set will be accessed in the key field mode, with the area of expertise being the key field. Code a class named `ProfessorListing` that defines the nodes. Your class should include all the methods in the class shown in Figure 2.28 except for the `setAddress()` method. It should also include a no-parameter constructor. Include a progressively developed driver program that verifies the functionality of all of the class's methods.

23. Code an application program to store a data set consisting of `StudentListing` and `ProfessorListing` objects (see Exercises 19 and 22) in two Sorted Array structures. When launched, the user will be asked to input the maximum size of both data sets, the initial number of students, the initial number of professors, and the initial data set. Once this is complete, the user will be presented with the following menu:

    Enter: 0 to *exit* the program.

           1 to *insert* a new *student's* information,

           2 to *fetch* and output a *student's* information,

           3 to *delete* a *student's* information,

           4 to *update* a *student's* information,

           5 to *insert* a new *professor's* information,

           6 to *fetch* and output a *professor's* information,

           7 to *delete* a *professor's* information,

           8 to *update* a *professor's* information, and

           9 to *output* the entire data set in sorted order.

The program should perform an unlimited number of operations until the user enters a 0 to exit the program.

24. Modify the class presented in Figure 2.29 so that the Insert operation doubles the size of the array when it senses the structure is full. The feature should be activated by a Boolean parameter set by the client code when the structure is declared. Write a driver program to demonstrate that the class functions properly.

25. Code a GIU program that visually demonstrates the changes to the contents of the array, and the other data members that make up an Unsorted-Optimized array object, when each of the four basic operations is performed. When the program is launched, the structure should be shown in its initialized state. Six buttons should be available to the user: one button for each of the four basic operations, a *reinitialize* button, and a *quit* button. Text boxes should be available to allow the user to input a node's information and key field contents.

26. Code the application described in Exercise 21, using a generic implementation of the data structure described in Exercise 20.

27. Code the application described in Exercise 23, but use the Java API class ArrayList as the application's data structure. (Will there be a need to ask the user for the maximum size of both data sets?)

CHAPTER 3

Restricted Structures

OBJECTIVES

The objectives of this chapter are to familiarize the student with the features, implementation, and uses of the restricted structures, Stack and Queue, and to master a methodized approach to converting a data structure to a generic implementation. More specifically, the student will be able to

- Understand the operation and access mode limitations implicit in restricted structures and the motivation for accepting those restrictions.

- Explain the operations and access modes of the Stack and Queue data structures, and be able to implement an array-based version of them that includes error checking.

- Write an application program that uses a stack or a queue to store the data it processes.

- Understand and be able to quantify the performance of restricted structures.

- Understand the advantages of postfixed arithmetic expression notation and be able to write an application that evaluates these arithmetic expressions.

Expand a Stack or Queue implementation to include a reinitialization operation, a peek operation, tests for full and empty, and the ability to expand these structures dynamically at run-time.

■ Recognize several common applications of restricted structures.

■ Understand a methodology used to convert a data structure to a generic implementation using the generic features of Java, and be able implement a generic data structure using the methodology.

■ More fully understand the implications of a Java interface and its role in coding generic data structures.

■ Understand the operations of a priority queue.

■ Develop an application that declares objects in Java's Stack class, and understand the advantages and disadvantages of this API class.

3.1 Restricted Structures

All of the array-based structures presented in Chapter 2 have high density and support all four of the basic operations: Insert, Delete, Fetch, and Update. As such, they can be used to store a data set for any application as long as their speed is within the performance parameters of the application.

Restricted structures are not as ubiquitous in that they are not appropriate for all applications. By design, they target a small subset of applications (see Figure 3.1) that share a common "pattern" of operations and are so ideally suited for this subset of applications that no other data structure would even be considered during the design process. A good analogy would be a very talented rock band whose music appeals to a very small percentage of the population. Although their

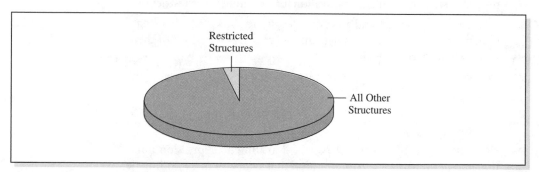

Figure 3.1 Limited Use of Restricted Structures

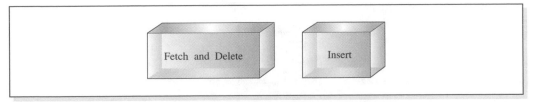

Figure 3.2 The Two Basic Operations Allowed on Restricted Structures

music does not appeal to everyone, the band has a small cult-like following who would not even consider listening to anyone else's music.

Restricted structures receive their name because they place severe restrictions on the way the application program accesses its data set. Both the operations performed (Insert, Delete, Fetch, and Update) and the mode in which these operations are performed (node number or key field mode) are restricted.

The restrictions placed on the operations performed on the data set, as illustrated in Figure 3.2 are:

- The Update operation is not supported.
- The Fetch and Delete operations are combined into one operation.
- The Insert operation is supported.

Combining the Fetch and Delete operations implies that whenever a node is fetched from the data set, it is automatically removed from the structure. Thus, restricted structures are aimed at applications that recall a node once, and only once. In addition, since the Update operation is not supported, applications targeted by restricted structures are those that never change the contents of the nodes stored in the data set.

The restrictions placed on the *access modes* are even more severe than those placed on the operations in that:

- The key field access is not supported.
- The node number access is supported, but is severely restricted.

Under the restricted form of node number mode access associated with these structures, node number has no meaning. The client code does not specify the node number of the node inserted into the data set, nor does it specify the node number of the node to be fetched (and deleted). Rather, the client code simply specifies that the Insert operation, or combined Fetch-and-Delete operation, be "performed." The Insert operation "arranges" the nodes in a chronological insertion order. Then, depending on the restricted structure we are dealing with, the combined Fetch-and-Delete operation operates on the node that has been in the structure either the shortest or the longest amount of time.

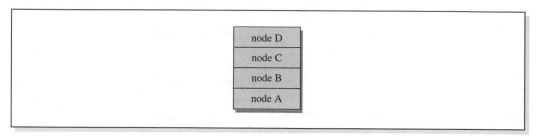

Figure 3.3   A Restricted Structure after Nodes A, then B, then C, and Finally D Have Been Inserted

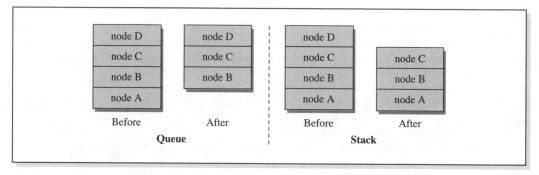

Figure 3.4   A Queue and a Stack Before and After a Fetch-and-Delete Operation Is Performed

For example, consider the nodes with key fields A, B, C, and D inserted into a restricted structure—first A, then B, then C, and finally D (see Figure 3.3). Because the structure is a restricted structure, we can't say "fetch-and-delete B," nor can we say "fetch-and-delete the second node." All we can say is "fetch-and-delete" and depending on the restricted structure, either A will be returned and then deleted from the structure, or D will be returned and then deleted from the structure.

The two most widely used restricted structures are Queue and Stack. In the case of a Queue, when a Fetch-and-Delete operation is performed, the node that has been in the structure the *longest* amount of time is fetched and then deleted. In the case of a Stack, the node that has been in the structure the *shortest* amount of time is fetched and then deleted (see Figure 3.4). A third restricted structure, Deque (not as widely used as Queues and Stacks), combines the functionality of a Stack and a Queue into one structure.

Although extremely restrictive, the operational behavior of these restricted structures mimics the manner in which some important and common application programs access their data set. As a result, restricted structures are an important topic in computer science. We will begin our study by examining the structure Stack.

3.2 Stack

The structure Stack obtains its name from the analogy that the nodes are stacked one on top of the other in the structure just as coins would be stacked (see Figure 3.5). A new coin, or node, is always placed on the *top* of the stack. Since the coins are stacked, the only way to remove a coin (or node) without toppling them is to remove the one that is on the top of the stack, which is the one that has been on the stack the *least* amount of time. Removal of any other coin (or node) from the stack is not allowed since it would cause the stack to fall. Thus, the last node inserted into the structure is always the node returned on the next combined Fetch-and-Delete operation. Because of this, the structure is referred to as a Last-In-First-Out structure, and the acronym LIFO is often used to describe the structure Stack.

3.2.1 Stack Operations, Terminology, and Error Conditions

The Insert operation on a Stack structure is called a *Push* operation, and the combined Fetch-and-Delete operation is called a *Pop* operation. Nodes are said to be stored *on* a stack and removed *from* a stack. Thus, we say that nodes are "pushed onto" a stack and "popped from" a stack. The *last* node pushed onto a stack is said to be at the *top* of the stack and the *first* node pushed onto the stack is said to be at the *bottom* of the stack.

When there are no nodes on a Stack, the stack is said to be *empty*. If the stack has reached its maximum node capacity, it is said to be *full*. A Pop operation cannot be performed on an empty stack, and a Push operation cannot be performed on a full stack; both situations result in an error. The error associated with a Pop operation on an empty stack is called an *underflow* error, and the error associated with a Push operation on a full stack is called an *overflow* error. Figure 3.6 illustrates the results of a series of Push and Pop operations on a Stack structure that has a maximum capacity of three nodes.

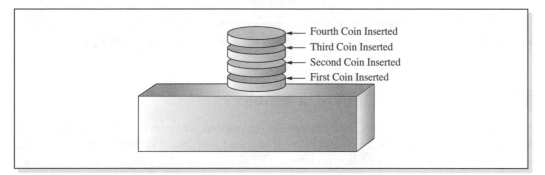

Figure 3.5 A Stack of Four Coins

Operation	Result	The Stack After the Operation
push(nodeA)	nodeA is stored	nodeA
pop()	nodeA is returned	empty
pop()	**Underflow Error**	empty
push(nodeB)	nodeB is stored	nodeB
push(nodeC)	nodeC is stored	nodeC / nodeB
push(nodeD)	nodeD is stored	nodeD / nodeC / nodeB
push(nodeE)	**Overflow Error**	nodeD / nodeC / nodeB
pop()	nodeD is returned	nodeC / nodeB
pop()	nodeC is returned	nodeB
pop()	nodeB is returned	empty
pop()	**Underflow Error**	empty

Figure 3.6 Several Operations on a Stack that Has a Maximum Capacity of Three Nodes, and the Results They Produce

3.2.2 Classical Model of a Stack

In the classical model of a Stack, the Push and Pop operations are the only operations allowed on the structure. In addition, the maximum number of nodes to be stored in the structure (size of the stack) is specified when the structure is created. This classical model is often expanded to include other operations and features such as:

- The ability to reinitialize the stack to empty.
- The ability to test for an empty stack (underflow condition).

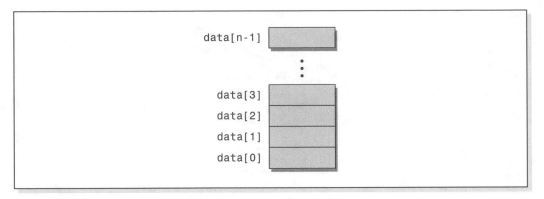

Figure 3.7 Typical Depiction of the *n* Element Array `data` Used to Store References to Nodes Pushed onto a Stack

- The ability to test for a full stack (overflow condition).
- The ability to pop a node from the stack without deleting it from the structure.[1]
- The ability to store an "unlimited" number of nodes on the stack.[2]

In the interest of simplicity, we will ignore these expanded features for now and limit our discussion of the structure Stack to the classical model and its implementation. Once an understanding of the classical model is obtained, we will discuss the changes necessary to incorporate the expanded features. The last feature, the ability to store an unlimited number of nodes on the stack, will be discussed again when we study linked lists in Chapter 4. For now, an attempt to push more than a specified maximum number of nodes onto the stack will result in an overflow error.

Throughout this chapter, an *n* element array of object references named `data` will be part of our Stack object, and it will be used to store the locations of the nodes pushed onto the stack. Typically, this array will be shown with its first element (index 0) at the bottom of the graphic, and its last element (index $n - 1$) at the top of the graphic (see Figure 3.7) In Chapter 4 we will discuss a second implementation of a stack that does not utilize an array.

Operation Algorithms

As we have stated, the classical model of a Stack is a fully encapsulated structure that supports two operations: Push and Pop. In addition to the array `data` used to store the locations of nodes pushed onto the stack, the algorithms for these two operations require that each Stack object contains two other integer data members:

- `size`, used to store the maximum number of nodes the stack can hold.
- `top`, used to store the index into the array, `data`, where the last Push operation was performed.

---

[1]This operation is commonly referred to as a Peek operation.

[2]That is, within the limits of the system's available storage.

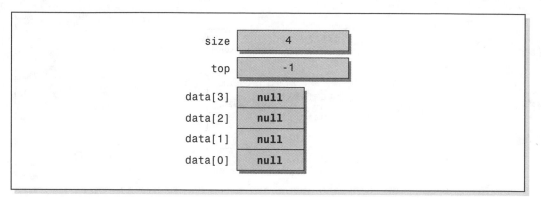

Figure 3.8 Data Members of a `stack` Object Capable of Storing Four Nodes in Its Initialized State

Stated another way, when a Push operation is performed, `data[top]` will store the address of the node pushed onto the stack. The memory cell `top`, as its name implies, will be used to "keep track" of the top of the stack.

To determine the initial state of the Stack structure, we will assume that nodes pushed onto the stack will be stored in the array `data` sequentially, in the order in which they are pushed, beginning at element zero. Thus, the location of the first node pushed onto the `Stack` object is stored in `data[0]`, the location of the second node pushed is stored in `data[1]`, the location of the third node pushed is stored in `data[2]`, etc. Initializing the memory cell `top` to −1 and incrementing it *before* the location is set into `data[top]`, guarantees that the first node will be stored at location zero and that all subsequent nodes pushed will be store sequentially. Thus, the initial condition for the variable `top` (which will also indicate that the stack is empty) is:

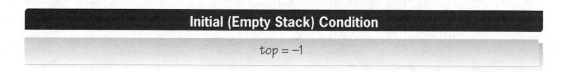

Initial (Empty Stack) Condition

$$top = -1$$

Figure 3.8 shows all of the data members of a `Stack` object capable of storing four nodes in their initialized state.

Turning our attention to the operation algorithms, our Push operation will not only insert a node into the structure but it will also check for an overflow error. Since `top` stores the index of the last node pushed, the test for overflow is when `top` is equal to the maximum index of the array, `size-1`. Thus, the Push algorithm that adds the node whose location is stored in the memory cell `newNode` into the `Stack` object depicted in Figure 3.8 is:

Push Algorithm

```
1.  if(top == size − 1)
2.     return false;  // ** overflow error **
3.  else
4.  { top = top + 1;
5.     data[top] = newNode.deepCopy();
6.     return true;  // push operation successful
7.  }
```

Line 5 of the algorithm accomplishes the encapsulation of the data structure by performing a deep copy of the node added to the structure and storing the location of the *copy* of the client's node in the structure.

Figure 3.9 shows the data members of a four element Stack object in its initial state, after three Push operations have been performed (Mike's node, Vick's node, and finally, Carol's node), and in its full state (after Bill's node is placed on the stack). In its full state, the variable top is equal to 3, or size - 1, so the next Push operation will not be performed. Rather, the Push operation will end after returning **false** on Line 2.

Let us now turn our attention to the Pop operation. The Pop operation fetches and deletes a node from the structure. The node operated upon is the node that has been in the structure the least amount of time. The variable top stores the index of the element in the array (data) that contains a reference to this node. A successful Pop operation returns this reference to the client.

To complete the Pop operation, top must be set to the index of the next node to be popped from the stack and the fetched node must be deleted from the structure. Since the nodes are stored in chronological order, decrementing top sets it to the index of the next node to be popped. That is, if data[2] was at the top of the stack, after a pop operation data[1] would be the new top of the stack. Decrementing top also, effectively, deletes the fetched node from the structure. Since the deleted node's reference is now stored "above" the top of the stack it cannot be accessed by subsequent Pop operations as they always decrement top. The only way the variable top can ever store the index of a popped node's location is after a Push operation which increments top (Line 4 of the Push algorithm). However, before the Push operation ends, the reference to the previously popped node is overwritten with the location of the newly pushed node (Line 5 of the Push algorithm).

When the last node is popped from the structure, the decrementing of the variable top returns it to its initial (empty) condition, -1. Thus, the test for underflow (an empty stack) is when top contains -1. When an underflow error occurs, the Pop operation returns a **null** reference to the client, as shown in the following pseudocode version of the algorithm.

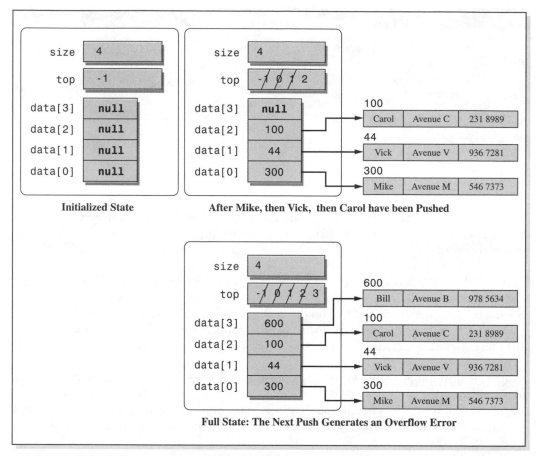

Figure 3.9 A Stack Object in its Initial, Intermediate, and Full States

Pop Algorithm

1. **if**(top == −1)
2.   **return null;** // ** underflow error **
3. **else**
4. { topLocation = top;
5.   top = top − 1;
6.   **return** data[topLocation]; // return a shallow copy
7. }

Figure 3.10 shows the changes in the data members of a four element Stack object after performing two Pop operations on a stack that contains two objects: Mike's node and Vick's node. The first Pop operation returns the location of Vick's node to the client, and the second Pop operation

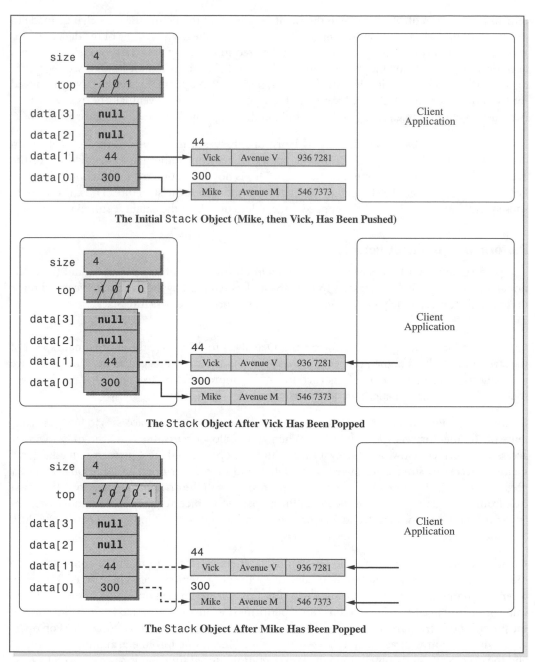

Figure 3.10 Pop Operations Performed on a Four Element stack Object Containing Two Nodes

returns the location of Mike's node to the client. As shown in the figure, the only change made to the Stack object's data members during the Pop operation is the decrementing of the data member top. The locations of the popped nodes are still stored in the array data. However, since top has been decremented during the Pop operations, these node locations cannot be accessed by subsequent Pop operations. Their inaccessibility to subsequent Pop operations has effectively removed the two nodes from the stack. The location of these popped nodes will eventually be overwritten by two Push operations (e.g., after Carol's and Bill's nodes are pushed as shown in Figure 3.11).

It should be noted that, unlike the Fetch algorithms discussed in Chapter 2, the Pop algorithm does *not* return a deep copy of the node popped (fetched) but rather passes the address of the actual node stored in the structure to the client. This is not a violation of encapsulation since the Pop operation, unlike a Fetch operation, deletes the node from the structure. Thus, if the client subsequently makes changes to the popped node it does not affect the database stored in the stack.

Performance of the Structure

The performance of a Data Structure is dependent on the speed of its operations and the additional memory (above that necessary to store the nodes) required by the structure. We will discuss these two factors separately as we examine the performance of the structure Stack.

Speed of the Structure   We will perform a Big-O analysis to determine the approximate speed of the structure Stack, as *n*, the number of nodes stored in the structure, gets large. Once again we will only consider memory access instructions in this approximation technique because they are much slower than arithmetic, logic, and register transfer instructions.

Examining the Push operation algorithm, Line 1 performs two memory accesses to fetch the contents of the memory cells top and size. When an overflow occurs, these are the only memory accesses performed. However, during a successful Push operation, Line 4 performs an additional memory access to store top's incremented value, and Line 5 performs an additional memory access to store the location of the copy of the pushed node in the array data. Therefore, the worst case from a speed viewpoint is a successful Push operation which requires four memory accesses (two for Line 1, one for Line 4, and one for Line 5) and the dominant (and only) term in the Push operation's speed function is 4, which is O(1).

Examining the Pop algorithm, Line 1 requires one memory access to fetch the contents of the memory cell top. When an underflow occurs, this is the only memory access performed. However, when a Pop operation is successful, one memory access is performed on Line 5 to overwrite the value of memory cell top. In addition, Line 6 performs one memory access to fetch the location of the popped node from the array data.[3] Therefore, the worst case scenario is a successful Pop operation which requires three memory accesses (one for Line 1, one for Line 5, and one for Line 6) and the dominant (and only) term in the Pop operation's speed function is 3, which is O(1).

---

[3]An optimizing compiler would store the variable topLocation used on Lines 4 and 6 of the algorithm in a CPU register. Thus, no memory accesses would be required to assign, or use, the value stored in it.

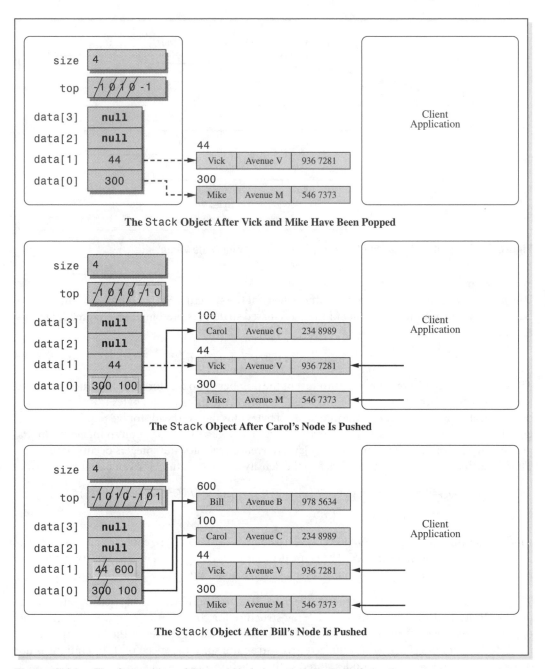

Figure 3.11 The Overwriting of Popped Node Locations by Push Operations

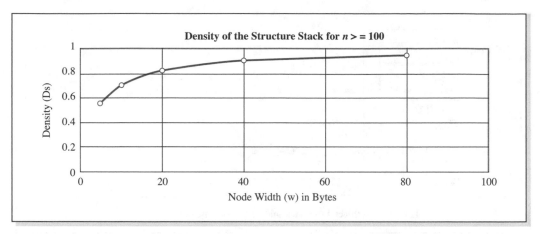

Figure 3.12   Density Variation of an Array-Based Stack with Node Width

Density of the Structure   The analysis of the density of the structure Stack is similar to the analysis performed to determine the density of the array-based structures presented in Chapter 2. Density is defined as

$$D = \text{(information bytes)} / \text{(total bytes)}.$$

The information bytes are simply the product of the number of nodes stored in the structure, n, and the number of information bytes per node, w. Therefore, the information bytes is $n * w$. The total bytes allocated to the structure is the information bytes plus the overhead storage required to maintain the structure. The overhead is the array of n reference variables that point to the node objects, plus the integer variables top and size. In Java, reference variables and integers occupy four bytes. Therefore, the overhead is $4 * n + 4 + 4$, and the density of the structure, D_S, can be expressed as

$$D_S = \text{(information bytes)} / \text{(total bytes)} = (n * w) / ((n * w) + (4n + 8))$$
$$= 1 / (1 + 4/w + 8 / (n * w))$$

which is approximately equal to $1 / (1 + 4/w)$ as n gets large. Figure 3.12 presents a graph of an approximation of D_S for n greater than 100. The figure demonstrates that good densities (0.80 or higher) are achieved whenever the number of information bytes in a node, w, is greater than 16 bytes.

Table 3.1 summarizes the performance of the Stack structure and includes the performance of the previously studied Unsorted-Optimized Array structure for comparative purposes. From a density viewpoint, the performance of the two structures is the same. However, the Stack structure is much faster than the Unsorted-Optimized Array structure since the speed of its operations is not proportional to the number of nodes stored in the structure, n.

Implementation

The implementation of the classical Stack structure is presented in Figure 3.13 as the Java class Stack. It is implemented as a homogeneous, fully encapsulated structure that stores Listing

Table 3.1

Performance of the Stack Structure

| Data Structure | Operation Speed (in memory accesses) | | | | | | Condition for Density > 0.8 |
	Insert	Delete	Fetch	Update = Delete + Insert	Average[4]	Big-O Average	Average for $n = 10^7$	
Unsorted-Optimized Array	3	$\leq n$	$\leq n$	$\leq n + 3$	$(3n + 6)/4$	O(n)	$0.75 \times 10^7 + 1.5$	w > 16
Stack	4 (Push)	combined with Fetch	3 (Pop)	not supported	$7/2 = 3.5$	O(1)	3.5	w > 16

[4]Assumes all operations are equally probable and is therefore calculated as an arithmetic average of the four operation times.

objects. Its code, and the code of the class Listing (see Figure 3.14), are consistent with all of the generic design features discussed in Chapter 2 except that the stack can *only* store Listing class objects. A fully generic implementation of the structure, using the generic features of Java 5.0, will be presented later in the chapter.

Line 2 of the class Stack shown in Figure 3.13, declares the array data to be an array of references to Listing objects. As was the case for the structure implementations presented in Chapter 2, the code of the class Stack does not mention any of the data members of a Listing object, which is a first step toward a generic implementation of this data structure.

```
1.   public class Stack
2.   {  private Listing[] data;
3.      private int top;
4.      private int size;
5.      public Stack()
6.      {  top = -1;
7.         size = 100;
8.         data = new Listing[100];
9.      }
10.     public Stack(int n)
11.     {  top = -1;
12.        size = n;
13.        data = new Listing[n];
14.     }
15.     public boolean push(Listing newNode)
16.     {  if(top == size - 1)
17.           return false;  // ** overflow error **
18.        else
19.        {  top = top + 1;
20.           data[top] = newNode.deepCopy();
21.           return true;  // push operation successful
22.        }
23.     }
24.     public Listing pop()
25.     {  int topLocation;
26.        if(top == -1)
27.           return null;  // ** underflow error **
28.        else
29.        {  topLocation = top;
30.           top = top - 1;
31.           return data[topLocation];
32.        }
33.     }
34.     public void showAll()
35.     {  for(int i = top; i >= 0; i--)
36.           System.out.println(data[i].toString());
37.     } // end of showAll method
38. } // end of class Stack
```

Figure 3.13   Implementation of a Classical Stack Structure

The class has two constructors that begin on Lines 5 and 10 that initialize the structure's data members and allocate the array data. The first constructor is a default constructor that allows for a maximum of 100 nodes to be stored on the stack before an overflow error occurs. The array of 100 reference variables is declared on Line 8. The second constructor includes an integer parameter (n on Line 10) which allows the client to specify the maximum number of nodes to be stored on the stack. Line 13 of this constructor allocates the array of n reference variables.

The push and pop methods, which begin on Lines 15 and 24, are simply the Java equivalent of the Push and Pop algorithms' pseudocode previously presented in this chapter. The push method's heading (Line 15) includes a Listing parameter which the client uses to specify the location of the node to be pushed onto the stack. The method returns a Boolean value set to **false** to indicate an unsuccessful operation (stack overflow). The heading of the Pop operation (Line 24) indicates that the method returns a reference to the Listing object, the object popped from the stack (**null** if the stack is empty). As mentioned in the discussion of the Pop algorithm, since the popped node is also deleted from the structure, returning a shallow copy of the node (Line 31) does not compromise the structure's encapsulation.

The showAll method (Lines 34–37) outputs the nodes from the top of the stack to the bottom. This is done by initializing the output loop's variable (Line 35) to top and decrementing it every time through the loop.

Figure 3.14 presents the class Listing that defines the nodes to be stored on the stack. It provides a method to deep copy a node and a toString method; implicit assumptions in the code of the

```
1.   public class Listing
2.   {   private String name;
3.       private String address;
4.       private String number;
5.       public Listing()
6.       {   name = "";
7.           address = "";
8.           number = "";
9.       }
10.      public Listing(String n, String a, String num)
11.      {   name = n;
12.          address = a;
13.          number = num;
14.      }
15.      public String toString()
16.      {   return ("Name is " + name + "\n" +
17.                  "Address is" + address + "\n" +
18.                  "Number is" + number + "\n");
19.      }
20.      public Listing deepCopy()
21.      {   Listing clone = new Listing(name, address, number);
22.          return clone;
23.      } // end of deepCopy method
24. } // end of class Listing
```

Figure 3.14 The Class Listing Consistent with the Three Assumptions Implicit in the Class Stack

```
1.  public class MainStack
2.  {  public static void main(String[] args)
3.     {  Stack s = new Stack(3);
4.        Listing l;
5.        Listing l1 = new Listing("Bill",  "1st Avenue", "123 4567");
6.        Listing l2 = new Listing("Al",    "2nd Avenue", "456 3232");
7.        Listing l3 = new Listing("Mike",  "3rd Avenue", "333 3333");
8.        Listing l4 = new Listing("Carol", "4th Avenue", "444 4444");
9.      // an attempt to pop an (empty) stack will return null
10.       System.out.println(s.pop());
11.     // perform three pushes to fill the stack and then output it
12.       System.out.println(s.push(l1));
13.       System.out.println(s.push(l2));
14.       System.out.println(s.push(l3));
15.       s.showAll();
16.     // perform three pop operations to empty the stack
17.       l = s.pop();
18.       System.out.println(l.toString());
19.       l = s.pop();
20.       System.out.println(l.toString());
21.       l = s.pop();
22.       System.out.println(l.toString());
23.     // an attempt to perform a pop on an empty stack will return null
24.       l = s.pop();
25.       System.out.println(l);
26.       System.exit(0);
27.    } // end of main method
28. } // end of class MainStack
```

Figure 3.15 An Application Program that Utilizes the Class Stack

class Stack. It is a shorter version of the class Listing presented in Chapter 2 (see Figure 2.16). Since restricted structures do not support the key field mode of access, a compareTo method need not be included in the class and (for brevity) it does not include a setAddress method for demonstrating encapsulation. Figure 3.15 presents a Stack application to demonstrate the use of the class Stack. The output it produces is presented in Figure 3.16.

```
null
true
true
true
Name is Mike
Address is 3rd Avenue
Number is 333 3333

Name is Al
Address is 2nd Avenue
Number is 456 3232

Name is Bill
Address is 1st Avenue
Number is 123 4567

Name is Mike
Address is 3rd Avenue
Number is 333 3333

Name is Al
Address is 2nd Avenue
Number is 456 3232

Name is Bill
Address is 1st Avenue
Number is 123 4567

null
```

Figure 3.16   The Output Generated by the Application Program Presented in Figure 3.15

3.2.3 A Stack Application: Evaluation of Arithmetic Expressions

The structure Stack is used extensively in computer science because the LIFO processing of information appears in the algorithms of many important applications. These applications include artificial intelligence, tree traversals, graph traversals (demonstrated in Chapter 7 and 9), and compilers. Specifically, compilers use stacks to pass information to and from subprograms, to "remember" the return addresses of nested subprogram invocations, and to evaluate arithmetic expressions.

In most programming languages, arithmetic expressions are written in *infixed* form because this is the way we are taught to write arithmetic strings in grammar school. When an arithmetic expression is written in infixed form, the operator is always written in between the operands. Thus, the infixed notation to add 2 and 4 is: 2 + 4.

Arithmetic expressions involving more than one term written in infixed notation can be ambiguous. For example, consider the infixed expression: 2 + 3 * 4. This could evaluate to 20 = (2 + 3) * 4, or 14 = 2 + (3 * 4). When parentheses are not used, ambiguities are resolved by a set of rules called *precedence* rules. These *rules of precedence* state (among other things) that multiplication is always performed before addition. Thus, when we consider the rules of precedence, the multiplication contained in the infixed expression 2 + 3 * 4 is performed first, and the expression evaluates to 14. If we want the addition to be performed first, we enclose the term 2 + 3 in parentheses. Parentheses override the rules of precedence. Thus, the infixed expression: (2 + 3) * 4 evaluates to 20.

Dealing with the rules of precedence and groupings of parentheses at run-time would be a very time consuming process which would slow down the execution of programs involving multiple arithmetic expressions. As a result, modern language compilers translate arithmetic expressions into alternate notations at compile time. These alternate notations eliminate the ambiguities implicit in infixed notations, and thus eliminate the need to consider precedence rules and parentheses at run-time. The result is executable modules that run faster. Stated another way, programmers write arithmetic expressions in infixed notation using parentheses to override the rules of precedence. Compilers produce executable modules in which arithmetic expressions have been translated into a nonambiguous alternate notation that does not require precedence rules and/or parentheses to resolve ambiguities.

The two alternate notations used by compilers are *postfixed* or *prefixed* notations. A post-fixed notation places the operator after the two operands, and a prefixed notation places the operator before the two operands. Thus, the postfixed notation for adding two and four is 2 4 +, while the same arithmetic expression is written in prefixed notation as + 2 4. The nice thing about these two notations is that they do not suffer from ambiguities. As a result they do not have precedence rules and parentheses need not be used to override these rules.

Of these two notations, most compilers use postfixed notation in their executable modules. The infixed arithmetic expression: 2 + 3 * 4 is written in postfixed notation as 2 3 4 * +, which evaluates to 14, while the infixed notation expression (2 + 3) * 4 is written in postfixed notation as: 2 3 + 4 * which evaluates to 20. After checking the syntax of an infixed notation arithmetic expression, a two-step process is used to generate the code used to evaluate it at run-time. The compiler:

1. Converts the infixed notation expression to the equivalent postfixed notation expression.
2. Applies the postfixed notation evaluation algorithm to the resulting expression.

The data structure Stack is used in both of these steps. In this section, we will demonstrate the use of a stack in the second step of this process, the postfixed notation evaluation algorithm.

The postfixed notation evaluation algorithm begins on the left side of the postfixed expression and searches through the expression until an operator is encountered, or the end of the expression is reached. When an operator is encountered, the operator is applied to the previous two operands in the expression, and the arithmetic result replaces the two operands *and* the operator in the postfixed expression. This process is continued from that point rightward replacing each operator encountered, and the two operands that precede it, with the result of applying the operator to the two operands. When the end of the expression is reached, the value of the entire expression is the numeric value just preceding the end of the expression.

As an example, consider the postfixed expression 2 3 + 4 *, which should evaluate to 20. We begin on the left looking for operators. As such, we skip the 2 and the 3, and arrive at the operator +. This is applied to the two previous operands, 2 and 3, to obtain 5. The value 5 replaces the + operator and the 2 and 3 (its two previous operands) in the postfixed string, reducing it to the postfixed string: 5 4 *. Proceeding to the right looking for operators, the operand 4 is skipped and then the operator * is encountered. It is applied to the two previous operands, 5 and 4, which yields 20. This value replaces the two operands, 4 and 5, and the operator * to yield the new postfixed string, 20. Proceeding again to the right we encounter the end of the string, and so the value of the string is the previous (and only remaining) numeric value in the string, 20. The steps involved in the evaluation of the post-fixed string discussed in this paragraph (2 3 + 4 *) are shown in Table 3.2 along with the evaluation of the postfixed arithmetic expression 2 3 4 * +.

Because an operator always operates on the two operands last encountered, and then these operands are never used again (can be deleted), the data structure, Stack, is ideally suited for storing postfixed expression operands. As we proceed from left to right through the postfixed string, we push the operands onto a stack until we encounter an operator. Then the stack is popped twice to obtain the two previous operands, and the result of applying the operator to these two operands is pushed onto the stack. If the postfixed expression is syntactically correct, when we encounter the end of the expression string, there will be only one operand on the stack which is the value of the arithmetic expression. Figure 3.17 presents the postfixed arithmetic expression evaluation algorithm using a stack, s, to store the operands. In it, a single operand, or operator, is referred to as a *token*.

Table 3.2

Evaluation of Two Postfixed Arithmetic Expressions 2 3 + 4 * and 2 3 4 * +

Step	Postfixed String	Operator Encountered	Two Previous Operands	Value	New Postfixed String (value replaces operator and operands)
1	2 3 + 4 *	+	2, 3	5	5 4 *
2	5 4 *	*	5, 4	20	20
3	20	none, so 2 3 + 4 * evaluates to 20			
1	2 3 4 * +	*	3, 4	12	2 12 +
2	2 12 +	+	2, 12	14	14
3	14	none, so 2 3 4 * + evaluates to 14			

Figure 3.18 shows the progression of the contents of the stack, s, as the postfixed string: 2 3 4 * + is evaluated using the algorithm depicted in Figure 3.17.

3.2.4 Expanded Model of a Stack

As previously mentioned, in the classical model of a Stack the Push and Pop operations are the only operations allowed on the structure. This model is often expanded to include methods to perform some, or all of the following operations:

- To reinitialize the stack to empty.
- To test for an empty stack (underflow condition).
- To test for a full stack (overflow condition).
- To pop a node from the stack *without* deleting it from the structure.
- To expand the stack at run-time within the limits of system memory.

The method to reinitialize a stack to empty simply sets the data member *top* to its initial condition: top = -1. With top set to −1, a Pop operation will return an underflow error (which it should, since the stack has been reinitialized). The elements of the array data need not be set back to

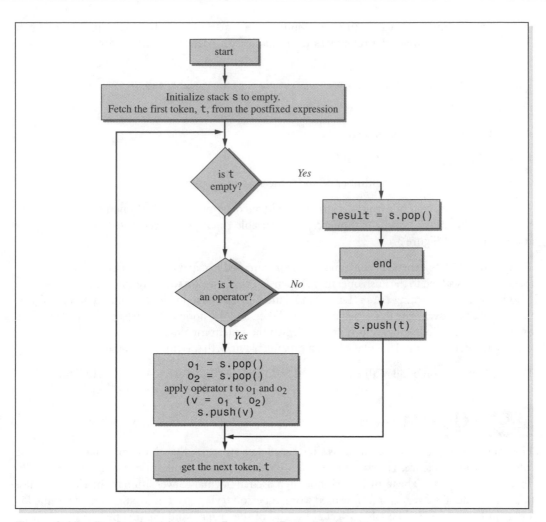

Figure 3.17 The Postfixed Arithmetic Expression Evaluation Algorithm

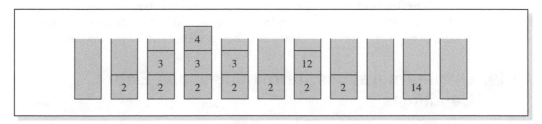

Figure 3.18 The Progression of the Contents of a Stack used to Evaluate the Postfixed Arithmetic Expression: 2 3 4 * +

their initial condition (`null`). To do so would be a waste of time because subsequent Push operations will overwrite the references to the nodes stored in the array before the stack was reinitialized.[5]

The method to determine if a stack is empty simply tests the variable `top`:

```
if(top == -1)   // stack empty,
```

as does the method to determine if a stack is full:

```
if(top == size - 1)   // stack full,
```

where `size` is the maximum number of nodes the structure can store.

The method to fetch a node from the structure *without* deleting it is typically named: *Peek*. It is the same algorithm as the Pop algorithm except the variable `top` is not decremented during the operation (Line 30 of Figure 3.13).

To allow the stack to expand at run-time, the algorithm used to expand arrays discussed in Chapter 2 (Section 2.4) is added to the Push operation. When a Push operation would result in an overflow condition, instead of returning **false** (Line 17 of Figure 3.13) the `push` method would expand the size of the stack's array, overwrite the variable `size`, and then add the node to the expanded structure. The only time the method would return **false** is when the system memory is exhausted. Chapter 4 will present an alternative implementation of an expandable stack that is not array-based.

The implementation of all of these expanded features is left as an exercise for the student.

3.3 Queue

The data structure Queue, like Stack, is a restricted data structure that shares an equally important role in computer science. The structure obtains its name from the concept of a waiting line that, by definition, is a queue. The term *queue* is not often used in normal conversation in the United States, but in England it is a very commonly used word. A person trying to cut into a ticket holder's line for a play in London would be told to "get at the end of the *queue*," and the first person to be seated would be the person at the front of the queue. Similarly, the first node inserted into a Queue structure is always the first node returned from the structure by the combined Fetch-and-Delete operation, and nodes are inserted at the end of a queue. Because of this, the structure is referred to as a First-In-First-Out structure (FIFO). A proper understanding of the difference between a queue and a stack is that a queue is a "fair" waiting line, whereas a stack is a very "unfair" waiting line.

3.3.1 Queue Operations, Terminology, and Error Conditions

We say that nodes are inserted *into* a queue and removed *from* a queue. As with all restricted structures, nodes are stored in chronological order in a queue. The node that has been in the structure

---

[5]The only advantage to setting all elements of the array `data` to **null** is that it more rapidly returns the copies of the client's nodes to the Java memory manager.

the longest amount of time is said to be at the *front* of the queue, and the node that has been in the structure the least amount of time is said to be at the *rear* of the queue. The Insert operation on a Queue structure is called an *Enqueue* operation and the combined Fetch-and-Delete operation is called a *Dequeue* operation. Figure 3.4 illustrates the operational difference between the Queue and Stack data structures. It assumes that prior to performing the combined Fetch-and-Delete operation, the insertion order of the nodes into the structures were first A, then B, then C, and finally D.

When there are no nodes in a queue, it is said to be *empty*. If the queue has a maximum node capacity, when this capacity is reached the queue is said to be *full*. A Dequeue operation cannot be performed on an empty queue, and an Enqueue operation cannot be performed on a full queue; both situations result in an error. The error associated with a Dequeue operation on an empty queue is called an *underflow* error, and the error associated with an Enqueue operation on a full queue is called an *overflow* error.

A superficial difference between the Stack and Queue structures is the way they are abstractly depicted. As the name Stack would imply, nodes on a stack are always shown in a vertical arrangement (see Figure 3.5), while nodes in a queue are represented in a horizontal arrangement, as shown in Figure 3.19.

There is also a difference in the terminology used to refer to the first and last node inserted into these two structures. As we have learned, consistent with the vertical image of a stack, the last node inserted into a stack is said to be at the *top* of the stack, and the first node inserted into a stack is said to be at the *bottom* of the stack. Consistent with the idea of a waiting line and the horizontal depiction of a queue, the first node inserted into the structure (e.g., Node A in Figure 3.20) is said to be at the *front* of the queue and the last node inserted into a queue (e.g., Node D in Figure 3.20) is said to be at the *rear* (or *back*) of the queue.

Enqueue (Insert) operations are always performed at the rear of a queue, and Dequeue (combined Fetch-and-Delete) operations are always performed at the front of a queue. Figure 3.21 shows the

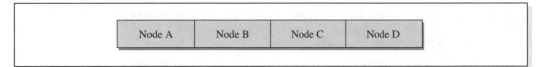

Figure 3.19   Abstract Depiction of a Queue

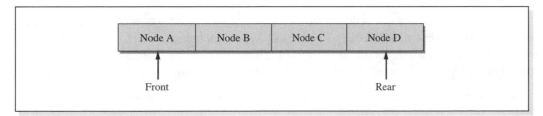

Figure 3.20   The Nodes at the Front and Rear of a Queue

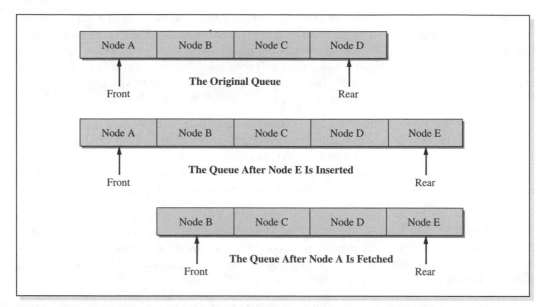

Figure 3.21   A Queue After an Enqueue and Dequeue Operation

queue depicted in Figure 3.20 after node E is inserted and then after a Dequeue operation is performed.

3.3.2 Classical Model of a Queue

In the classical model of a Queue, the Enqueue and Dequeue operations are the only operations allowed on the structure, and the maximum number of nodes to be stored in the structure (size of the queue) is set when the structure is created. As is the case with the structure Stack, this classical model of a Queue is often expanded to include other operations and features such as:

- The ability to reinitialize the queue to empty.
- The ability to test for an empty queue (underflow condition).
- The ability to test for a full queue (overflow condition).
- The ability to fetch a node from the queue *without* deleting it from the structure.[6]
- Expand the queue at run-time within the limits of system memory.

In the interest of simplicity, we will ignore these expanded features for now and limit our discussion of the structure Queue to the classical model and its implementation. Once an understanding of the classical model is obtained, we will discuss the changes necessary to incorporate the expanded features. The last feature, the ability to store an unlimited number of nodes, will be

---

[6]This operation is commonly named a *Peek* operation.

discussed again when we study linked lists in Chapter 4. For now, an attempt to add more than a specified maximum number of nodes to the queue will result in an overflow error.

Operation Algorithms

Our classical model of a Queue will be a fully encapsulated structure that supports two operations: Enqueue is used to insert nodes into the structure, and Dequeue is used to fetch (and delete) nodes from the structure. An *n* element array of object references named `data` will be used to store the locations of the nodes inserted into the queue. In addition to this array, the two operation algorithms require that each `Queue` object contains four other integer data members:

- `size`, used to store the maximum number of nodes the queue can hold.
- `numOfNodes`, used to store the number of nodes currently stored in the structure.
- `front`, used to store the index into the array `data` where the next Dequeue operation will be performed.
- `rear`, used to store the index into the array `data` where the next Enqueue operation will be performed.

Thus, when an Enqueue operation is performed, a reference to the newly inserted node is stored in data[rear], and data[front] stores the address of the next node to be fetched (and deleted) from the queue. Figure 3.22 shows all of the data members of a `Queue` object capable of storing four nodes[7] shown in their initialized state.

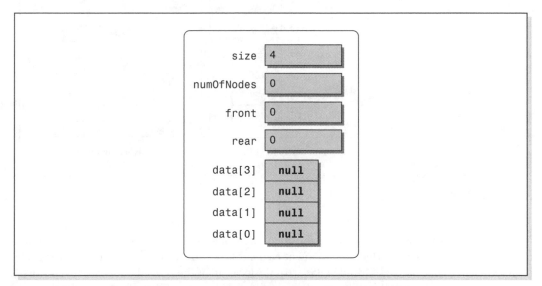

Figure 3.22 The Data Members of a Four-Node Queue in their Initialized State

[7]Although the standard graphic of a queue exhibits the nodes in a horizontal arrangement, the array data used to store references to the nodes will be shown arranged vertically inside a queue object.

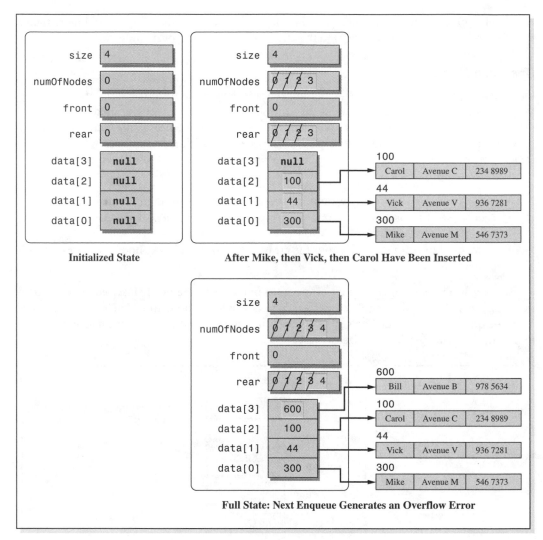

Figure 3.23 A Queue Object in its Initial, Intermediate, and Full States

The locations of the nodes inserted onto the queue are stored in the array data sequentially in the order in which they are inserted, beginning at element zero. Thus, the location of the first node inserted into a queue object is stored in data[0], the location of the second node inserted is stored in data[1], etc. Initializing the memory cell rear to 0, and incrementing it *after* the inserted node's location is set into data[rear] guarantees that the location of the first node inserted will be stored at location zero, and that all subsequent nodes inserted into the queue will be stored sequentially.

Figure 3.23 shows the data members of a four-element Queue object in its initial state, after three Enqueue operations have been performed (first Mike's node was added, then Vick's node, and finally Carol's node), and in its full state (after Bill's node is inserted into the queue). The test for a full queue is when the memory cells `size` and `numOfNodes` are equal.

When we implement a queue, a problem develops that does not surface during the implementation of a stack. Consider the full queue depicted at the bottom of Figure 3.23. Since `front` contains the element number of the array `data` that stores the location of the node to be fetched next, when a Dequeue (Fetch-and-Delete) operation is performed, the node referenced by `data[0]` is returned and `front` is incremented to prepare for the next Dequeue operation. After this operation the queue is no longer full, and element zero of the array `data` is now available to store the location of the next node inserted into the queue. However (as depicted in Figure 3.23) every time a node is inserted into the queue the variable `rear` is simply incremented, and therefore it will never return to its initial value, 0. Thus, the next insert will not utilize element zero of the array `data`. Worse yet, simply incrementing the value of `rear` has set it to 4 (as shown in the lower portion of Figure 3.23), which is an illegal (out of bounds) index into the array `data`.

The solution to this dilemma is the concept of a circular queue. All queues implemented using arrays utilize this concept. When the memory cell `rear` of a four-element circular queue reaches the value 3, it is not incremented during the Enqueue operation. Rather, it is reset to zero to "reclaim" the unused portion of the array `data`. Therefore, the memory cell `rear`, associated with a four-element queue, takes on the values 0, 1, 2, 3, 0, 1, 2, 3, 0, etc. There are two ways of implementing this. One is:

```
if(rear === size - 1)
  rear = 0;
else
  rear = rear + 1;
```

The alternate method, which is the method more commonly used is:

```
rear = (rear + 1) % size;
```

where % is the modulus (remainder) operator.

Thus, the Enqueue algorithm to add the node whose location is stored in the memory cell `newNode` is:

Enqueue Algorithm

1. **if**(numOfNodes == size)
2.   **return false**; // ** overflow error **
3. **else**
4. { numOfNodes = numOfNodes + 1;
5.   data[rear] = newNode.deepCopy();
6.   rear = (rear + 1) % size;
7.   **return true**; // Enqueue operation successful
8. }

Line 5 of the algorithm enforces the encapsulation of the data structure by performing a deep copy of the node to be added to the structure and then storing the location of the cloned node in the structure.

Let us now turn our attention to the Dequeue (combined Fetch-and-Delete) operation algorithm. Since nodes are stored in chronological order in the array `data`, after a node is fetched from the queue, the element of the array just "after" the node fetched from the queue contains the location of the next node to be fetched. For example, if the node whose location is stored in `data[1]` was just fetched from the queue, the location of the next node fetched would be stored in `data[2]`. Thus, the memory cell `front` must be incremented during a Dequeue operation to keep track of the next node to be fetched from the queue.

Eventually, `front` will store a value that, if incremented, will exceed the bounds of the array. To prevent this from happening, just as in the Enqueue algorithm, the modulus operator is used during the incrementing of the variable `front`:

```
front = (front + 1) % size;
```

Its use causes the variable `front` to remain in the range 0 to size − 1, and prevents an "array-out-of-bounds" error from occurring during a Dequeue operation. A successful Dequeue operation returns the location of the node at the front of the queue; otherwise, a **null** value is returned. The test for an empty queue is when the variable `numOfNodes` contains a zero. Thus, the Dequeue algorithm is:

Dequeue Algorithm

```
1.  if(numOfNodes == 0)
2.     return null; // ** underflow error **
3.  else
4.  { frontLocation = front;
5.     front = (front + 1) % size;
6.     numOfNodes = numOfNodes − 1;
7.     return data[frontLocation];
8.  }
```

Figure 3.24 shows the changes in the data members of a four-element queue after performing two Dequeue operations on a queue that contains three objects: Mike's node, Vick's node, and Carol's node. The first Dequeue operation returns the location of Mike's node to the client, and the second Dequeue operation returns the location of Vick's node. As shown in the figure, the only changes made to the Queue object's data members during these Dequeue operations are the incrementing of the data member `front` and the decrementing of the memory cell `numOfNodes`. The locations of the fetched nodes are still stored in the array `data`; however, the changes made to

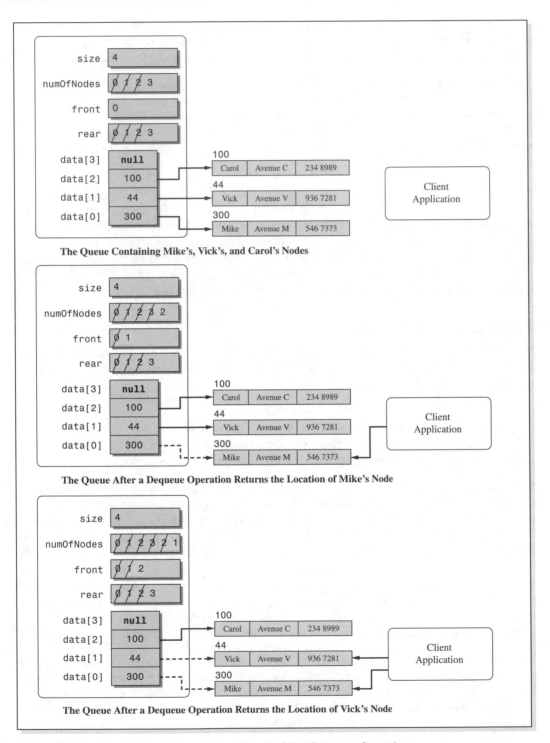

The Queue Containing Mike's, Vick's, and Carol's Nodes

The Queue After a Dequeue Operation Returns the Location of Mike's Node

The Queue After a Dequeue Operation Returns the Location of Vick's Node

Figure 3.24 Data Member Changes as a Result of Two Dequeue Operations

front and numOfNodes during the Dequeue operations prevent these elements from being accessed until they are overwritten by subsequent Enqueue operations. The fact that they are inaccessible until they are overwritten has effectively removed the two nodes from the queue.

The overwriting process is shown at the bottom of Figure 3.25, which depicts the changes to the data members as a result of the insertion of Ryan's node into the queue. After Bill's node was inserted into the structure (middle section of the figure), rear has recycled to zero (as a result of the modulo size arithmetic on Line 6 of the Enqueue algorithm). This reclaims the element zero of the array data, previously used to store a reference to Mike's node, which is then overwritten with the location of Ryan's node.

Before ending our discussion of the Dequeue algorithm, it should be noted that unlike the Fetch algorithms associated with the array-based structures discussed in Chapter 2, and like the Pop operation discussed previously in this chapter, the Dequeue algorithm does not return a deep copy of the node fetched. Rather it passes the address of the actual node stored in the structure to the client. This is not a violation of encapsulation since the Dequeue and Pop operations, unlike a Fetch operation, deletes the returned node from the structure. Thus, if the client subsequently makes changes to the node it does not affect the database stored in the queue.

Performance of the Structure

We will now turn our attention to the performance of the structure Queue considering first the speed of the structure, and then the additional memory (above that necessary to store the nodes' information), required to maintain the structure.

Speed of the Structure   In the interest of consistency, we will again include only memory access instructions in our Big-O analysis since it is an approximation technique and the time to perform nonmemory access instruction is negligible within this approximation.

Examining the Enqueue operation algorithm, Line 1 performs two memory accesses (one to fetch the contents of the memory cell numOfNodes, and the other to fetch the contents of the memory cell size). When an overflow occurs, these are the only memory accesses performed. However, when an Enqueue operation is successful, Line 4 performs one additional memory access (to rewrite the incremented value of numOfNodes). Line 5 requires two memory accesses (one to fetch the value of the memory cell rear, and the other to store the location of the copy of the inserted node in the array data). Finally, Line 6 requires one additional memory access to store the incremented value or rear. Therefore, the worst case scenario from a speed viewpoint is a successful Enqueue operation which performs six memory accesses (two for Line 1, one for Line 4, two for Line 5, and one for Line 6) and the dominant (and only) term in the Enqueue operation's speed function is 6, which is $O(1)$.

The dominant term in the Dequeue operation's speed function is also $O(1)$. When an underflow error occurs, only one memory access is performed (Line 1). However, when the structure is not empty, Line 4 requires one additional memory access to fetch the value of the memory cell front, and Line 5 requires two memory accesses (one to access the memory cell size, and one to overwrite the value of

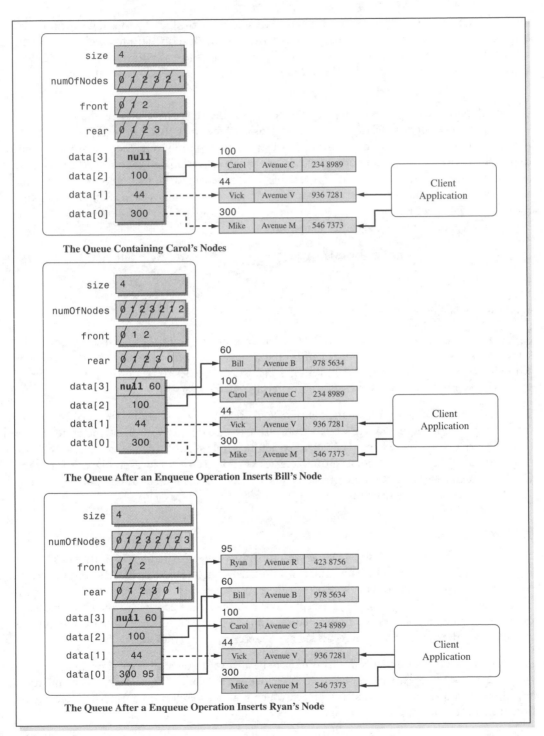

Figure 3.25 Data Member Changes as a Result of Two Enqueue Operations

memory cell `front`). Line 6 requires one memory access to overwrite the contents of the memory cell `numOfNodes`, and Line 7 requires one memory access to fetch the location of the fetched node from the array `data`. In all, six memory accesses (one for Line 1, one for Line 4, two for Line 5, one for Line 6, and one for Line 7) are performed, $O(1)$, to complete a successful Dequeue operation.

Density of the Structure   The analysis of the density of the structure Queue is the same as the analysis previously performed to determine the density of the Stack structure, except that a Queue uses an additional eight bytes of overhead. Both structures require n reference variables to point to the client's node objects, and both structures use an integer variable `size` to store the size of the array `data`. A stack requires one addition variable, `top`, to keep track of the top of the stack, while three variables `numOfNodes`, `front`, and `rear` are required to maintain a queue. Remembering that reference variables and integers occupy four bytes, the overhead is $4 * n + 4 * 4$ bytes, and the density of the structure Queue, D_Q, can be expressed as:

$$D_Q = \text{(information bytes) / (total bytes)} = (n * w) / ((n * w) + (4n + 16))$$

$$= 1 / (1 + 4 / w + 16 / (n * w))$$

where w is the width of the client's nodes.

As the number of nodes, n, gets large $16 / (n * w)$ approaches zero and $D_Q \approx (1 + 4/w)$. This is the same expression we obtained for the density of the structure Stack as n gets large (> 100), which is plotted in Figure 3.12. The figure demonstrates that good densities (0.80 or higher) are achieved whenever the number of bytes in a node is greater than sixteen.

Table 3.3 summarizes the performance of the Queue structure and includes the performance of the two previous structures for comparative purposes. From a density viewpoint, the performance of all three structures is the same. The Queue structure is only slightly slower than the Stack structure (with a calculated average speed of 6 accesses vs. 3.5 accesses); however, like the Stack, the Queue is much faster than the array structure since its speed is also not a function of n, the number of nodes stored in the structure.

Implementation

The implementation of the classical Queue structure is presented in Figure 3.26 as the class `Queue`. It is implemented as a homogeneous, fully encapsulated structure that stores `Listing` nodes. Its code, and the code of the class `Listing` (see Figure 3.14), are consistent with all of the generic design features discussed in Chapter 2 except that the stack can *only* store `Listing` class objects. A fully generic implementation of the structure, using the generic features of Java 5.0 and the methodology presented in Section 3.4, is left as an exercise for the student.

Line 2 of the class `Queue` declares the array `data` to be an array of references to `Listing` objects. As was the case for the previous structures we implemented, the code of the class does not mention any of the data members of a `Listing` object, which is a first step toward a generic implementation of this data structure.

Table 3.3

Performance of the Queue Structure

Data Structure	Operation Speed (in memory accesses)							Condition for Density > 0.8
	Insert	Delete	Fetch	Update = Delete + Insert	Average[8]	Big-O Average	Average for $n = 10^7$	
Unsorted-Optimized Array	3	$\leq n$	$\leq n$	$\leq n + 3$	$\leq (3n + 6)/4$	$O(n)$	$\leq 0.75 \times 10^7 + 1.5$	$w > 16$
Stack	4 (Push)	combined with Fetch	3 (Pop)	not supported	$7/2 = 3.5$	$O(1)$	3.5	$w > 16$
Queue	6 Enqueue	combined with Fetch	6 Dequeue	not supported	$12/2 = 6$	$O(1)$	6	$w > 16$

[8]Assumes all operations are equally probable and is therefore calculated as an arithmetic average of the four operation times.

```
1.   public class Queue
2.   {  private Listing[] data;
3.      private int size;
4.      private int numOfNodes;
5.      private int front;
6.      private int rear;
7.      public Queue()
8.      {  size = 100;
9.         numOfNodes = 0;
10.        front = 0;
11.        rear = 0;
12.        data = new Listing[100];
13.     }
14.     public Queue(int n)
15.     {  size = n;
16.        numOfNodes = 0;
17.        front = 0;
18.        rear = 0;
19.        data = new Listing[n];
20.     }
21.     public boolean enque(Listing newNode)
22.     {  if(numOfNodes == size)
23.           return false;  // ** overflow error **
24.        else
25.        {  numOfNodes = numOfNodes + 1;
26.           data[rear] = newNode.deepCopy();
27.           rear = (rear + 1) % size;
28.           return true;  // push operation successful
29.        }
30.     }
31.     public Listing deque()
32.     {  int frontLocation;
33.        if(numOfNodes == 0)
34.           return null;  // ** underflow error **
35.        else
36.        {  frontLocation = front;
37.           front = (front + 1) % size;
38.           numOfNodes = numOfNodes - 1;
39.           return data[frontLocation];
40.        }
41.     }
42.     public void showAll()
43.     {  int i = front;
44.        for(int c = 1; c <= numOfNodes; c++)
45.        {  System.out.println(data[i].toString());
46.           i = (i + 1) % size;
47.        }
48.     } // end of showAll method
49. } // end of class Queue
```

Figure 3.26 Implementation of a Classical Queue

The class has two constructors that begin on Lines 7 and 14. The first of these constructors is a default constructor that allows for a maximum of 100 nodes to be stored in the Queue before an overflow error occurs. The array of 100 reference variables is declared on Line 12. The second constructor includes an integer parameter (n on Line 14) that allows the client to specify the maximum number of nodes to be stored in the Queue. Line 19 of this constructor allocates the array of n reference variables.

The enque and deque methods, which begin on Lines 21 and 31 respectively, are simply the Java equivalent of the pseudocode versions of the Enqueue and Dequeue algorithms presented earlier in this chapter. The method enque's heading (Line 21) includes a Listing parameter that the client uses to pass the location of the node to be inserted into the method. A Boolean value is returned to indicate overflow (false if an overflow occurs). The heading of the deque method (Line 31) indicates that it returns a reference to the Listing object fetched from the queue (**null** if the queue is empty). As mentioned in the discussion of the Stack structure, since the fetched node is also deleted from the structure, returning a shallow copy of the node (Line 39) does not compromise the structure's encapsulation.

The showAll method (Lines 42–48) outputs the nodes from the front of the Queue to the rear. This is done by counting the number of nodes output until the total is equal to the number of nodes in the structure (Line 44). Each time through the loop, the index i, which was initialized to the front of the queue on Line 43, is incremented using modulo size arithmetic (Line 46).

As mentioned previously, Figure 3.14 presents the class Listing that describes the nodes stored by our Queue implementation. It provides a method to deep copy a node and a toString method, an assumption implicit in the code of the class Queue. Figure 3.27 presents an application program to demonstrate the use of the class Queue. The output it produces is presented in Figure 3.28.

3.3.3 Queue Applications

Queue's FIFO characteristic models a waiting line (which is how the structure received its name). As such, it is used extensively in computer applications where information is to be processed in the order it is received. One such application is a print spooler for a multitasking operating system. When several applications that produce output are running at the same time[9] and share a single printer, the output they produce is buffered to disk files. When an application completes its output, the disk file is added to a queue of files that are being written to the printer. As a result, the output from these applications appears on the printer in the order in which these applications complete their execution.

Queues are also used extensively in the field of operations research, in some sorting algorithms, in the graph traversal algorithms discussed in Chapter 9, and in the algorithm used to convert infixed strings to postfixed strings.

---

[9]Actually applications only appear to be running at the same time on a multitasking operating system. In fact they share the CPU in sequential time slices, but the time slices are so small that the applications appear to be running simultaneously.

```
1.  public class MainQueue
2.  { public static void main(String[] args)
3.    { Queue q = new Queue(3);
4.      Listing l;
5.      Listing l1 = new Listing("Bill",  "1st Avenue", "123 4567");
6.      Listing l2 = new Listing("Al",    "2nd Avenue", "456 3232");
7.      Listing l3 = new Listing("Mike",  "3rd Avenue", "333 3333");
8.      Listing l4 = new Listing("Carol", "4th Avenue", "444 4444");
9.      // an attempt to perform a dequeue on an initialized (empty) queue
        // will return null
10.     System.out.println(q.deque());
11.     // perform three enqueues to fill the queue and then output the
        // queue
12.     System.out.println(q.enque(l1));
13.     System.out.println(q.enque(l2));
14.     System.out.println(q.enque(l3));
15.     System.out.println(q.enque(l4));
16.     q.showAll();
17.     // perform three dequeue operations to empty the queue
18.     l = q.deque();
19.     System.out.println(l.toString());
20.     l = q.deque();
21.     System.out.println(l.toString());
22.     l = q.deque();
23.     System.out.println(l.toString());
24.     // an attempt to perform a dequeue on an empty queue will return
        // null
25.     l = q.deque();
26.     System.out.println(l);
27.     System.exit(0);
28.   } // end of main method
29. } // end of class Queue
```

Figure 3.27 An Application Program that Utilizes the Class `Queue`

3.3.4 Expanded Model of a Queue

In the classical model of a Queue, the Enqueue and Dequeue operations are the only operations permitted on the structure. Often, as previously discussed, restricted structures are expanded to include additional features (repeated here for convenience).

- To reinitialize the queue to empty.
- To test for an empty queue (underflow condition).
- To test for a full queue (overflow condition).
- To fetch a node from the queue *without* deleting it from the structure.
- To expand the queue at run-time.

The method to reinitialize a queue simply sets the variables `front`, `rear`, and `numOfNodes` back to their initial values. The elements of the array `data` need not be set back to their initial condition

```
null
true
true
true
false
Name is Bill
Address is 1st Avenue
Number is 123 4567

Name is Al
Address is 2nd Avenue
Number is 456 3232

Name is Mike
Address is 3rd Avenue
Number is 333 3333

Name is Bill
Address is 1st Avenue
Number is 123 4567

Name is Al
Address is 2nd Avenue
Number is 456 3232

Name is Mike
Address is 3rd Avenue
Number is 333 3333

null
```

Figure 3.28   The Output Generated by the Application Presented in Figure 3.27

(`null`). To do so would be a waste of time because subsequent Enqueue operations will overwrite the references to the nodes stored in the array before the queue was reinitialized.

The method to determine if a queue is empty simply tests the variable `numOfNodes` to determine if it is zero. If the variables `size` and `numOfNodes` are equal, the queue is full. The method to fetch a node from the structure *without* deleting it, typically named `peek`, is the same algorithm as the `deque` method except the variable `front` is not incremented and `numOfNodes` is not decremented.

To allow the queue to expand at run-time, the algorithm used to expand arrays discussed in Chapter 2 (Section 2.4) is added to the enque method. When an Enqueue operation would result in an overflow condition, instead of the method returning **false** (Line 23 of Figure 3.26) it would expand the size of the queue's array, adjust the variables front, rear, and size and then add the node to the expanded structure. The only time the method would return **false** is when the system memory is exhausted. Chapter 4 will present an alternative implementation of an expandable restricted structure that is not array-based.

The implementation of all of these expanded features is left as an exercise for the student.

3.4 Generic Implementation of the Classic Stack, a Methodized Approach

Earlier in this chapter we implemented a classic Stack structure (Figure 3.13) in a way that could be easily modified into a generic implementation. It separated the node definition and the data structure into two separate classes, and the data structure class did not mention the field names of the nodes. In addition, the node definition class contained a toString method and a deepCopy method. As coded, however, it can only store objects that are instances of a class named Listing. In this section we will modify the class to make it fully generic; that is, it will be able to store objects of any class. The generic typing features of Java 5.0 discussed in Chapters 1 and 2 will be used to generalize the class. In describing this generalization, we will take a different pedagogical approach than we did in Chapter 2 (Section 2.4). Here, we will *methodize* the process of converting the code (presented in Figure 3.13) into a four-step process.

3.4.1 Generic Conversion Methodology

Step One   Since we are trying to eliminate the dependence of the class' code on the type Listing, the first step in this process is to add a generic placeholder (in this case <T>) at the end of the method's heading (Line 1 in Figure 3.29). This will be the generic name of the node type stored in the structure.

Step Two   The next step is to replace all references to the type Listing with our generic type. This gives us the highlighted replacements on the left side of Lines 2, 8, 13, 15, and 24 of Figure 3.29. (For now, ignore the fact that the code on Lines 8 and 13 have been commented out and recoded on the right side of these lines.) It would be nice if this were all we had to do, but Java is a heavily typed language and so the process continues.

```
1.  public class GenericStack<T>
2.  { private T[] data;
3.      private int top;
4.      private int size;
5.      public GenericStack()
6.      {  top = -1;
7.         size = 100;
8.      // data = new T[100];    data = (T[]) new Object[100];
9.      }
10.     public GenericStack(int n)
11.     {  top = -1;
12.        size = n;
13.     // data = new T[n];    data = (T[]) new Object[n];
14.     }
15.     public boolean push(T newNode)
16.     {  if(top == size - 1)
17.           return false;  // ** overflow error **
18.        else
19.        {  top = top + 1;
20.        // data[top] = newNode.deepCopy(); data[top] = (T) node.deepCopy();
21.           return true;   // push operation successful
22.        }
23.     }
24.     public T pop()
25.     {  int topLocation;
26.        if(top == -1)
27.           return null;   // ** underflow error **
28.        else
29.        {  topLocation = top;
30.           top = top - 1;
31.           return data[topLocation];
32.        }
33.     }
34.     public void showAll()
35.     {  for(int i = top; i >= 0; i--)
36.           System.out.println(data[i].toString());
37.     } // end of showAll method
38. } // end of class GenericStack
```

Figure 3.29   Some of the Generic Revisions of the Class Stack Presented in Figure 3.13

Step Three   Wherever the keyword **new** operates on the placeholder T, we must substitute the class Object for the placeholder T. The translator will not let us generate a reference to the type T; it is an undefined type. This is the case on Lines 8 and 13. The fully corrected versions of lines 8 and 13 appear on the right side of the lines, which also includes coercion, because the variable data is now declared on Line 2 to be a T reference.

```
public interface GenericNode
{  public abstract GenericNode deepCopy(); // clones the invoking object
   public abstract String toString(); // added to prevent Object's
                                      // toString method from executing
}
```

Figure 3.30   The Interface `GenericNode`

Once we substitute `Object` for `T` on these lines, the translator gives us some additional help via an incompatible type error: `"found: java.lang.Object[], required: T[]"`; type `T[]` is required to match the new type of the variable `data`.

Step Four   Wherever a method is invoked that operates on an object of type `T`, we can expect a `"cannot find symbol"` compile error. This is because the translator cannot look into the class `T` to verify the existence, or at least the signature, of the method. The invocation of the method `deepCopy` on Line 20 in Figure 2.39 is an example of this problem, because the type of `newNode` was changed to `T` on Line 15 in Step 2. The remedy here is to collect all the method signatures into an interface, and implement the interface[10] in the node definition class. The corrected version of Line 20 is coded on the right side of the line, which requires that the symbol `node` be defined as a local variable in the `push` method (and that the reference returned from the method `deepCopy` be coerced into the array `data`, `T`). Assuming the name of the interface is `GenericNode`, the declaration of the variable node would be:

```
GenericNode node = (GenericNode) newNode;
```

which must be added to the `push` method. It not only defines the symbol `node`, but also directs the translator to look into the interface `GenericNode` for `deepCopy`'s signature (which was our Step Four problem). The only remaining issue is to code the interface `GenericNode` and add the phrase `"implements GenericNode"` to the end of heading of the node definition class (problem solved).

The code of the interface is given in Figure 3.30, and the final version of the generic code, the class `GenericStack`, is given in Figure 3.31. All the additions and revisions to the code of the class presented in Figure 3.13 to make it fully generic are highlighted.

Consistent with the idea of divide and conquer, it is often easier to code a fully generic data structure, as we did, in two steps. First, the data structure class and a node class used to debug it are coded using the design features incorporated into the classes depicted in Figures 3.13 and 3.14. Once the data structure class is debugged, then the four-step methodology developed in this section is used to convert it to a fully generic data structure class.

---

[10]A class that implements an interface codes all of the methods whose signatures are defined in the interface. In addition, the phrase `"implements interfaceName"` must appear at the end of the class' heading.

```
1.   public class GenericStack<T>
2.   {  private T[] data;
3.      private int top;
4.      private int size;
5.      public GenericStack()
6.      {  top = -1;
7.         size = 100;
8.         data = (T[]) new Object[100];
9.      }
10.     public GenericStack(int n)
11.     {  top = -1;
12.        size = n;
13.        data = (T[]) new Object[n];
14.     }
15.     public boolean push(T newNode)
16.     {  GenericNode node = (GenericNode) newNode;
17.        if(top == size - 1)
18.          return false;   // ** overflow error **
19.        else
20.        {  top = top + 1;
21.           data[top] = (T) node.deepCopy();
22.           return true;   // push operation successful
23.        }
24.     }
25.     public T pop()
26.     {  int topLocation;
27.        if(top == - 1)
28.          return null;   // ** underflow error **
29.        else
30.        {  topLocation = top;
31.           top = top - 1;
32.           return data[topLocation];
33.        }
34.     }
35.     public void showAll()
36.     {  for(int i = top; i >= 0; i--)
37.           System.out.println(data[i].toString());
38.     } // end of showAll method
39.  } // end of class GenericStack
```

Figure 3.31   Generic Version of the Class Stack Presented in Figure 3.13

3.5 Priority Queues

Priority queues can be thought of as a restricted data structure in that they normally support just an Insert operation (often named Add) and a combined Fetch-and-Delete operation (often named Poll). In addition, the access to the nodes in the structure is restricted in that they are fetched and deleted in an order based on a priority assigned to each node. Normally, the node with the lowest priority is returned from a Poll operation, although some priority queues return the node with the highest priority. Various strategies are used to decide which node should be returned in the event of a priority "tie". In many cases priority ties are resolved by returning the node that has been in the structure the longest, thus the name *Priority Queue*.

Priority Queues can be implemented in a variety of ways, but one of the most efficient ways is to use a scheme called a heap, which will be examined in Chapter 8. The implementation of a Priority Queue is left as an exercise for the student in that chapter.

3.6 Java's Stack Class

The Java Application Programmer Interface provides a class named Stack that is implemented as a *generic*, *expandable*, but *unencapsulated* data structure. The structure stores *objects,* not primitive types,[11] and can be used either as a compiler enforced *homogeneous* or a *heterogeneous* structure. An EmptyStackException is thrown when a Pop operation is performed on an empty Stack object. The structure is dynamic and expands at run-time to accommodate an unlimited number of Push operations. A no-parameter constructor is provided to create Stack objects. For example, the declaration

```
Stack<Node> NYC = new Stack<Node>();
```

creates a compiler enforced empty stack named NYC that can only store Node objects.

Table 3.4 presents the names of the basic operation methods in the class Stack and some examples of their use. It assumes that the Stack structure boston was declared as a heterogeneous structure

```
Stack boston = new Stack();
```

that the variable tom, mary, and temp can store references to Node objects, and that the coding examples are performed in the order shown (from the top row to the bottom row).

---

[11]Java 5.0 gives the appearance of allowing primitives to be inserted into a Stack object, but it actually wraps the primitive in a Wrapper object before inserting it.

Table 3.4

Methods Available in the API class `Stack`

Basic Operation	Stack Method Name	Coding Example[12]	Comments
Test for Empty	empty	`if(boston.empty())` `System.out.println("boston is empty");`	Returns **true** if empty, otherwise **false**.

Push	push	`boston.push(tom); // adds tom to boston`
		`boston.push(mary); // adds mary to boston`
		`boston.push(21); // adds 21 to boston`
			boston expands dynamically.
			The 21 gets wrapped.

Find a Node's Position on the Stack	search	`if(boston.search(tom) != 1)`
		`System.out.println(Tom's node is not " +`
		`at the top of the stack");`
			Returns a node's position on the stack.

Pop	pop	`int i = (Integer) boston.pop() // fetch 21`
		`temp = (Node) boston.pop() // fetch mary`
		`temp = (Node) boston.pop() // fetch tom`
			Coercion not necessary for homogeneous uses.
			Next pop throws an exception.

Peek	peek	`boston.push(tom);` `boston.peek(1); // tom fetched`	tom is not deleted.

[12]Assumes the below code is executed in the order shown.

Knowledge Exercises

1. Which of the two access modes cannot be used to access restricted structures?

2. Which of the four basic operations do restricted structures support (indicate if any are combined)?

3. Name two restricted structures.

4. Tell what the following acronyms stand for and which restricted structures they are associated with:

   a) LIFO

   b) FIFO

5. Give the names of the operations that can be performed on the following structures, and tell what the operations do.

   a) A Stack

   b) A Queue

6. Nodes A, B, and C are placed on a stack in the order first A, then B, and finally C.

   a) Draw a picture of the stack using the standard abstract graphic.

   b) What would be stored in the variable top?

   c) A Pop operation is performed. What node is returned?

7. What error occurs if

   a) A Pop operation is performed on an empty stack?

   b) A Push operation is performed on a full stack?

8. Describe the action of the stack Peek operation.

9. In the implementations of the Stack operation presented in this chapter, what does the memory cell top store, the index of the array where the nextPush or the nextPop will be performed?

10. Rewrite the stack Push algorithm presented in this chapter assuming that top was initialized to 0 instead of -1.

11. Rewrite the stack Pop algorithm presented in this chapter assuming that top was initialized to 0 instead of -1.

12. Give the line numbers of the code presented in Figure 3.13 that perform the garbage collection for the structure Stack.

13. Evaluate the following arithmetic expressions written in postfixed notation:

   a) 45 3 21 + $-$ 10 *

   b) 3 6 * 45 2 + *

   c) 12 3 * 2 /

14. Write the following arithmetic expressions in postfixed notation:

    a) $45 + 6/2$

    b) $(3 + 4 + 7)/2$

    c) $(b^2 - 4 * a\,c)/(2\,a)$

15. Nodes A, B, and C are placed on an initialized queue in the order first A, then B, and finally C.

    a) Draw a picture of the queue using the standard abstract graphic.

    b) Indicate the position of the rear of the queue.

    c) Indicate the position of the front of the queue

    d) A Dequeue operation is performed. What node is returned?

16. In the implementations of the structure Queue presented in this chapter, what is stored in the memory cells front and rear?

17. Give the integer range of the values that rear can assume after the statement: rear = x % 54; executes (assume x is an integer).

18. Give the line numbers of the code presented in Figure 3.26 that perform the garbage collection for the structure Queue.

Programming Exercises

19. Expand the implementation of the class Stack presented in Figure 3.13 to include methods to: reinitialize the stack to empty, test for an empty stack (underflow condition), test for a full stack (overflow condition), and to perform a Peek operation. Include a progressively developed driver program to demonstrate the functionality of each new method.

20. Expand the implementation of the class Stack presented in Figure 3.13 so that it expands every time a Push operation is performed that would cause an overflow. Initially, it should accommodate a maximum of three nodes. Include a progressively developed driver program to demonstrate the functionality of each new class.

21. Write a program to evaluate an arithmetic expression written in postfixed notation. The arithmetic expression will be input as a String (by the user) and will contain only integer operands. Use the following code sequence to parse (i.e., remove) the integers and the operators from the input string, mathExpression:

```
import java.util;
String thisToken;
StringTokenizer tokens = new StringTokenizer(mathExpression);
while(tokens.hasMoreTokens())
{   thisToken = tokens.nextToken();
// processing for thisToken goes here
}
```

EXERCISES

22. Expand the implementation of the class Queue presented in Figure 3.26 to include methods to reinitialize the queue to empty, test for an empty queue (underflow condition), test for a full queue (overflow condition), and to perform a Peek operation. Include a progressively developed driver program to demonstrate the functionality of each new method.

23. Using the generic capabilities of Java 5.0, modify the implementation of the structure Queue presented in Figure 3.26 to make it generic. Include a driver program that demonstrates the functionality of the class with two homogeneous Queue objects that store two different kinds of nodes.

24. Write a program to convert an infixed arithmetic expression that includes nested parentheses to the equivalent postfixed string. The infixed expression will be input from the keyboard, and the postfixed expression should be output to the console.

25. Code a GUI program that visually demonstrates the changes to contents of the array, and the other data members that make up a Queue object (see Figure 3.23) when an Enqueue or a Dequeue operation is performed. When the program is launched, the structure should be shown in its initialized state. Four buttons should be available to the user: an "Enqueue" button, a "Dequeue" button, a "reinitialize" button, and a "quit" button. Provide text boxes for the input of the nodes' fields and for the output of a fetched node.

26. Code a GUI program that visually demonstrates the changes to contents of the array, and the other data members that make up a Stack object (see Figure 3.9) when a Push or a Pop operation is performed. When the program is launched, the structure should be shown in its initialized state. Four buttons should be available to the user: a "Push" button, a "Pop" button, a "reinitialize" button, and a "quit" button. Provide text boxes for the input of the nodes' fields and for the output of a fetched node.

27. Marty the mouse is to navigate his way through a ten-foot by twenty-foot rectangular room whose floor is made of red and white one-foot square tiles. Marty hates red tiles and will only walk on white tiles. There is a piece of cheese at the exit. Write a program that outputs the row and column numbers of the white tiles Marty walks on as he finds his way to the cheese. Model the floor of the room using a two-dimensional array of integers, one element per tile. A value of 0 indicates a white tile, a value of 1 indicates a red tile. Assume the maze is navigable, and that the maze entrance location and exit location will be input by the user. (*Hint:* you will need two stacks for this application. One will store the path Marty has followed so he can backtrack if he encounters a dead end. A special location is pushed on this stack whenever Marty is at a tile from which he can proceed in more than one direction. As Marty steps onto a tile, if there are alternate tiles he could have stepped onto they are pushed onto the second stack.)

CHAPTER 4

Linked Lists and Iterators

The objectives of this chapter are to familiarize the student with the features, implementation, and uses of linked structures and list iterators. More specifically, the student will be able to

- Explain the advantages of linked structures and be able to quantify their performance.

- Understand the memory model programmers use to represent linked structures and the resulting advantages and disadvantages of this representation.

- Understand the classic linked structures Singly Linked list (and its circular, sorted, and double-ended variations), Doubly Linked list, and Multilinked lists.

- Implement a fully encapsulated version of any of the classic linked structures.

- Understand the ways in which a linked structure can be used to implement a dynamically expandable Stack or Queue and the advantages of that implementation.

■ Understand list iterators; be familiar with their access advantages and the classic operations used to position iterators, be able to identify applications that benefit from their use, and be able to quantify their performance advantages.

■ Write an application that attaches an iterator to a data structure and use the iterator to access the structure.

■ Implement several types of iterator classes including one that allows the application programmer to declare multiple iterator objects, attach them to the application's structure, and access the structure using them.

■ Develop an application that declares objects in Java's API LinkedList class, understand the advantages and disadvantages of the class, and operate on the structure using the class' operation methods.

■ Develop an application that attaches a Java API ListIterator object to a Java LinkedList object and access the linked list structure using the iterator.

4.1 Noncontiguous Structures

All of the data structures we have discussed in the previous chapters use an array to store references to the data set. When an array is created the system's memory manager must locate a contiguous portion of memory large enough to accommodate the array, since arrays are always stored in contiguous memory. In order to do this, the size of the array must be known. That is why the array-based implementations developed in the previous chapters either required the client to specify the maximum number of nodes that would be stored in the structure, or the maximum was set to a default value by the structure's constructor. In either case, the maximum value was used by the memory manager to locate and allocate the contiguous portion of memory for the array's elements.

A data structure that does not require contiguous memory can, at times, be very advantageous. Consider three application programs: A, B, and C, all running on a system at the same time with the system's RAM memory shared as shown in Figure 4.1. Although there are still 60 kilobytes (KB) of unused memory, it is fragmented into three 20KB sections. Thus, the largest RAM resident array-based structure that could be declared by any of the three applications is one that could store 5000 nodes, because the structure's 5000 element array of reference variables requires 20KB of storage (4 bytes per reference variable). An attempt to declare a larger array would either produce an "insufficient system memory" error or cause the operating system to allocate the storage further up the memory hierarchy, thus slowing down the application. However, any of the applications using a *noncontiguous* structure could expand by 60KB within RAM memory since it could use all three of the unused portions of RAM.

In this chapter, we will study the most fundamental category of noncontiguous data structures: linked lists. These structures, like all linked structures, can rapidly expand to accommodate a

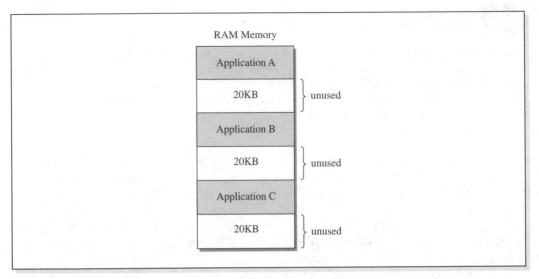

Figure 4.1   Three Applications Sharing Main Memory

virtually unlimited number of nodes, one node at a time. Aside from its compatibility with fragmented memory, a subtle but important advantage this structure has over an array-based structure is that it always uses all the memory assigned to it. Consider an array-based structure that can accommodate one million nodes with only half of the nodes currently inserted into it. At this point in the structure's life, it has been allocated 2MB (= 4 bytes $\times$ 500,000 elements) of storage it really does not need since half of the elements of the array are not being used. Linked lists, like noncontiguous structures, are more frugal. They are only assigned as much storage as they currently need.

There are many applications in which the maximum number of nodes in the structure cannot be anticipated with any certainty at the time the data structure is created. Consider an application that stores information transmitted from a deep space probe whose mission is to discover new stars and planets. The very nature of the mission precludes our ability to predict the maximum number of heavenly bodies that will make up the data set. These types of applications require *dynamic* data structures; structures that can be expanded at run-time. If the implementation language does not provide the ability to rapidly expand an array (as Java does), then noncontiguous structures are the only viable alternative. Linked lists, implemented in *all* programming languages, are so easily expanded that at run-time their insert algorithm expands the structure every time a node is added to it.

Because of their ability to utilize fragmented memory, utilize all the memory assigned to them, and expand rapidly regardless of the implementation language, noncontiguous structures such as linked lists are widely used.

4.2 Linked Lists

There are several types of linked lists, but all of them share two common characteristics:

- Every node in the structure has at least one field, called a *link* field, that stores the location of another node (with the exception of the unique last node, if there is one).
- Each node's location is stored in at least one other node (with the exception of the unique first node, if there is one).

Figure 4.2**a** illustrates these two characteristics using a data set that contains four nodes: X, B, T, and G. Rather than storing the nodes addressed in a fixed size array, each node has two *link fields* that contain the addresses of other nodes. Considering Node T to be the unique first node (see Figure 4.2**b**), we can follow either the first (left) or the second (right) link field contents (beginning at Node T) to locate all the other nodes. For example, starting at Node T and "following" the second link fields, Node G, stored at location 973, is encountered next. This is followed by Node X stored at location 20, and finally Node B, stored at location 332. Since the node locations can be determined in this way (by traveling "through" the other nodes), we no longer need to store the node references in contiguous memory, an assumption implicit in the access function used to locate array elements. Link fields free us from the constraint of contiguous memory; however, the sequential nature of accessing linked lists through the link fields tends to reduce the speed of these

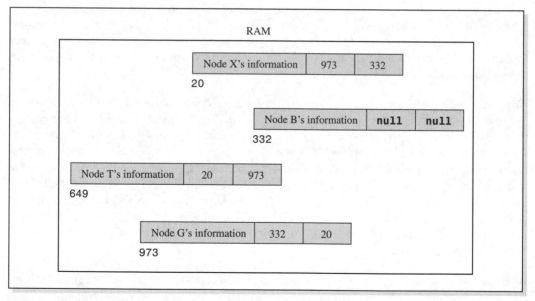

Figure 4.2a   A Linked List with Two Link Fields

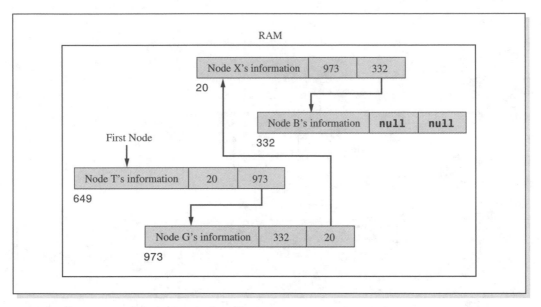

Figure 4.2b One Sequential Access Path Through the Nodes of a Linked List

structures. The process of moving from the first node to the second node to the third node, etc., by using the contents of the link fields to locate the next node, is called *traversing* the list.

4.3 Singly Linked Lists

The simplest form of a linked list is the singly linked list. A singly linked list is one in which:

- Each node has one link field.
- The nodes form a linear list:
  - there is a unique first node, n_1,
  - there is a unique last node n_j, and
  - any other node n_k is proceeded by node n_{k-1} and followed by node n_{k+1}.

As an example, Figure 4.3 shows the nodes X, B, T, and G arranged in a singly linked list. Each node has one link field, and Node T is the unique first node. Its address is stored in a single reference variable called the *list header*. Node B is the unique last node. Each of the other two nodes, X and G, have a unique node just before it (T is before X, and X is before G) and a unique node just after it (G is after X, and B is after G).

Although Figure 4.3 accurately depicts the arrangement of the nodes in memory, most often singly linked lists are not illustrated this way. Rather, the "standard" graphical depiction of a singly

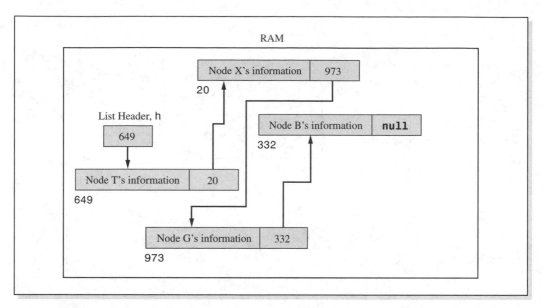

Figure 4.3 Four Nodes: X, B, G, and T Stored in a Singly Linked List

linked list, shown in Figure 4.4, is used to depict the nodes. In the standard depiction, the nodes are shown horizontally, in traversal order, with the unique first node on the left and the unique last node on the right. The list header is drawn above the unique first node. Arrows emanating from the link fields are used to point to the next node in the sequence. A series of dots indicates that one or more nodes in the list have not been drawn.

Representing a linked list in this way often makes it easier to develop and understand the basic operation algorithms for singly linked lists. What is sometimes forgotten when using this standard graphical depiction is that, although the nodes are shown "next" to each other, they are indeed scattered around in memory. This fact is more easily remembered when we add memory addresses to the standard depiction of a singly linked list, as shown in Figure 4.5. (For brevity, the list header reference variable is simply denoted as h in this figure.)

4.3.1 Basic Operation Algorithms

The basic operation algorithms for a singly linked list can be a bit confusing because they all involve manipulating the link fields of the nodes in the structure. The best way to approach the discovery of these algorithms, or any other algorithm associated with linked lists, is to first draw a picture of the structure and then modify the picture to incorporate the changes required to perform the operation. After the operation algorithm has been developed graphically, it is then verified and transformed into pseudocode.

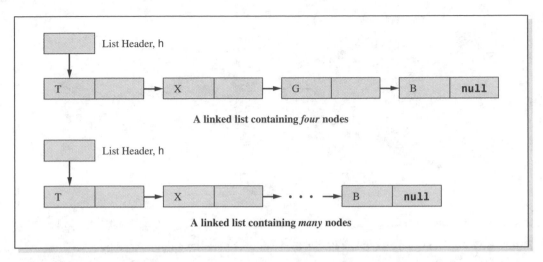

Figure 4.4 Standard Depictions of Singly Linked Lists

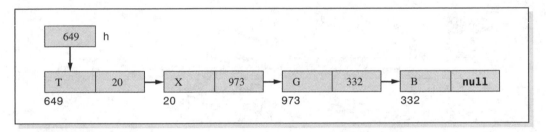

Figure 4.5 A Standard Depiction of a Singly Linked List with Node Addresses and Link Field Contents Shown

As an example, consider an algorithm to position a new node, referenced by the variable r, into our four-node singly linked list between Nodes X and G (referenced by q and p). The first step in developing the algorithm is to draw a picture of the structure before the operation is performed (see Figure 4.6). The modifications necessary to perform the insert are then added to the picture. Since the new node is to be inserted between Nodes X and G, two modifications are necessary:

1. The arrow coming from the link field of Node X must be changed to point to the new node.
2. The link field of the new node must be made to point to the Node G.

These modifications are shown as the dotted arrows in Figure 4.7, numbered 1 and 2.

Before coding the algorithm, we verify it graphically by moving down (or traversing) the linked list to make sure that the adjusted link fields have the effect of inserting the new node in between Nodes X and G. Starting the list header, we first encounter (or visit) Node T. T's link field brings us to Node X, X's link field now brings us to the new node, the new node's link field brings us to

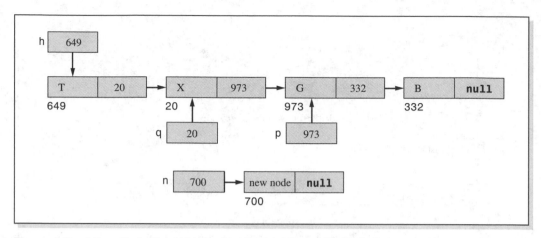

Figure 4.6   A Four-Node Linked List before the Insertion of the Node Referenced by r

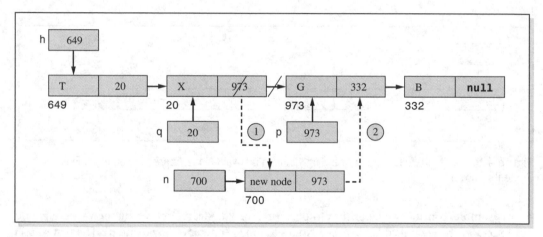

Figure 4.7   The Graphical Representation of the Two-Step Algorithm to Insert the Node Referenced by r Between Nodes X and G

Node G, and G's link field brings us to Node B. Thus, the order of the nodes is T, X, the new node, G, and B, which verifies the algorithm.

We are now ready to code the two steps of our algorithm shown graphically in Figure 4.7. Assuming the name of the link field is: next, and that it can be accessed with the notation: reference-Variable.next, the code of the algorithm is:

```
q.next = n // reset X's link field to point to the new node
n.next = p // set the new node's link field to point to node G
```

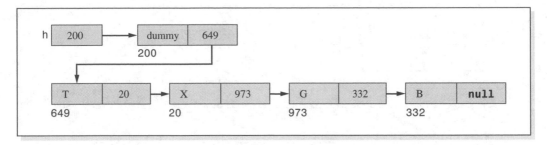

Figure 4.8 Inclusion of a Dummy Node into the Standard Depiction of a Singly Linked List

These two lines of pseudocode place the address 700 (stored in the variable n) in Node X's link field, and stores the address 973 (stored in the variable p) in the newly inserted node's link field.

Before using this graphical technique to discover and verify the basic operation algorithms, two changes to the standard graphical depiction of a singly linked list will be discussed. The first change is to insert a *dummy node* between the list header and the real first node. The dummy node will not store client information (thus the term dummy). It is added to the structure to simplify the code of the Insert and the Delete algorithms because without it, performing these operations on an empty structure becomes a special case. The grayed area of Figure 4.8 reflects the changes to the linked list depiction presented in Figure 4.5 necessary to incorporate the dummy node.

The second change is to introduce a lower level of detail into Figure 4.8 consistent with the manner in which the operation algorithms will be implemented. In the implementation, the left field of each node that makes up the singly linked list will *not* contain the client's information. Rather, it will contain a reference to a deep copy of the information. Thus, both fields of the "nodes" in our singly linked list will be reference variables. The left field will be named l, and the right field will be named next. l will point to a deep copy of the client's information (a Listing object), and next will point to the subsequent node (a linked list Node object) in the singly linked list. This implementation level view of the structure is shown in Figure 4.9.

At the implementation level, the nodes in the linked list are analogous to the array of reference variables that was part of the structures presented in previous chapters in that they store the addresses of the deep copies of the client's objects. However, since it is a linked list, each node also stores the address of the next node in the linked list. A thorough understanding of the material presented in Figure 4.9 is necessary to understand the structure implementations presented in this chapter.

Initialization

One of the ironies of linked lists is that, although they can contain a virtually unlimited number of nodes (within the limits of system storage), the class that defines them usually contains only one data member: the list head h. In addition, after the structure is initialized, it only contains one

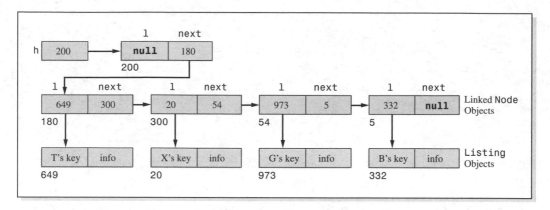

Figure 4.9   Implementation-Level View of a Singly Linked List

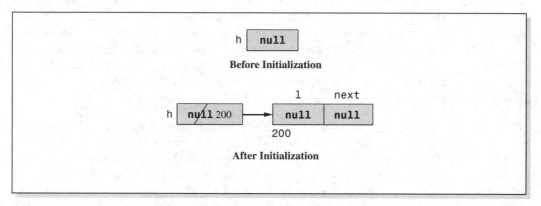

Figure 4.10   Singly Linked List Before and After Initialization

linked node, the dummy node. Consistent with our graphical technique for developing the operation algorithms, Figure 4.10 shows a linked list object before and after its initialization algorithm is executed.

To verify the initialization algorithm, we traverse the list shown in Figure 4.10 starting at the list head. The list head points us to the dummy node, and then the dummy node's link field, being **null**, ends the traverse. As long as we accept the condition of an empty list as a **null** value stored in the link field of the dummy node, the algorithm is verified. Assuming the left and right fields of the dummy node are named l and next, respectively, and that the dummy node is an object in the class Node, the pseudocode of the verified initialization algorithm can be written as:

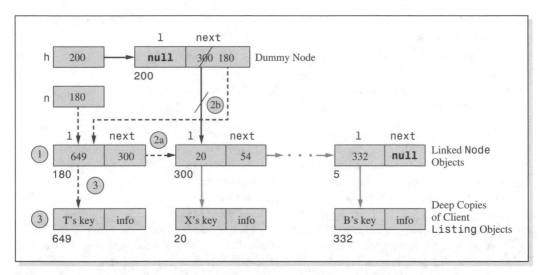

Figure 4.11　The Steps to Insert T's Node into the Singly Linked List Depicted in Figure 4.9

The Singly Linked List Initialization Algorithm

h = new Node(); // create the dummy node with h referencing it
h.l = **null**;　// set the fields of the dummy node to **null**
h.next = **null**;　// condition for an empty list

Insert Algorithm

In order to encapsulate the structure, the Insert algorithm will add a *deep copy* of the client's information to the data set. Since the access to the nodes is sequential, the fastest and simplest way to add the deep copy to the structure is to insert the new node at the beginning of the linked list, just after the dummy node. This approach to the insertion algorithm will cause the structure to resemble a stack in that the most recently inserted node will be the most readily accessible node, an issue we will return to later in this chapter.

Figure 4.11 shows the changes required to insert a deep copy of client's Listing, T, at the beginning of a linked list. The circled numbers in the figure indicate the order in which the changes are made, as described below.

1. Create a new linked list Node object.
2. Add the new linked list Node object to the beginning of the linked list.

    a) Set the `next` field of the linked list `Node` object to the contents of the `next` field of the dummy node.

    b) Place the address of the new linked list `Node` object into the `next` field of the dummy node.

3. Create a deep copy of the client's information, and reference it from the `l` field of the new linked list `Node` object.

To verify the graphical version of the Insert algorithm depicted in Figure 4.11, we traverse the list starting at the list head. This brings us to the dummy node, and the dummy node's link field (`next`) now brings us to the new linked list node (by following the dotted arrow from the `next` field of the dummy node). Then, the `next` field of the new linked list node brings us to the remainder of the linked list (by following the dotted arrow from the `next` field of the new linked list node). Also, the `l` field of the new linked list node references the deep copy of the client's information. Since the newly inserted node is accessible via the dummy node, the other nodes in the structure are still accessible, and the deep copy of the client's inserted information is also accessible, we have verified the graphical representation of the algorithm. It is important to note that if Step 2b is performed before 2a, the entire linked list, except for the newly inserted node, is effectively deleted from the structure.

The next step in the development of the algorithm is to translate the graphical representation into pseudocode. Following the order of the numbered changes to the linked list depicted in Figure 4.11, the four-step pseudocode version of the verified Insert algorithm is written as:

The Singly Linked List Insert Algorithm

```
1.   Node n = new Node(); // create a new linked list Node object
2a. n.next = h.next; // add the linked Node object to the front of the linked list
2b. h.next = n;
3.   n.l = newListing.deepCopy(); // deep copy the client's information, reference the copy
```

where `newListing` is an object that contains the information to be inserted into the linked list. It should be noted that, because of the presence of the dummy node in the list, the Insert algorithm functions properly on an empty (initialized) list as well. The verification of this is left as an exercise for the student.

The Fetch Algorithm

Because the only access to the information stored in the structure (the deep copies of the client's listings) is through the nodes in the singly linked list, in order to locate a listing we must traverse the linked list. Traversing is performed using a linked node reference (e.g., `p`), which is initialized to reference the first node in the linked list. Then `p` is moved down the linked list by repeatedly assigning it the contents of the `next` field of the node it references, until the listing is found. Once

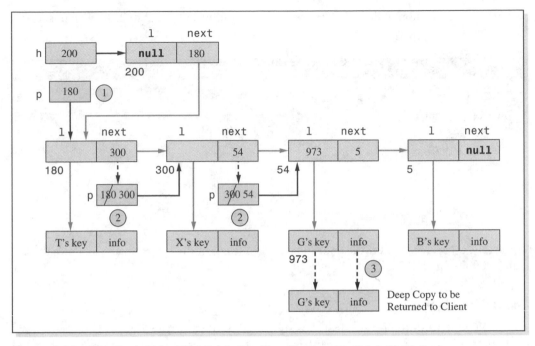

Figure 4.12 The Singly Linked List Fetch Algorithm (Illustrated to Fetch G's Listing)

found, a deep copy of the listing is returned. If the requested listing is not in the list, then p will eventually assume a **null** value when it reaches the last node in the linked list, which terminates an unsuccessful search.

Figure 4.12 shows the singly linked list depicted in Figure 4.9, modified (gray boxes) to include the graphical representation of the Fetch algorithm. In this case, the listing to be fetched is G. The four dashed arrows in the figure indicate that the algorithm is copying information from one area of memory to another. The circled numbers indicate the order of the operations required to accomplish a Fetch operation, which are:

1. Initialize the Node reference, p, to reference the first node in the list.
2. Traverse p down the list until it locates the information to be fetched.
3. Return a deep copy of the information to be fetched.

To verify the graphical representation of the algorithm depicted in Figure 4.12 we first observe that by copying the contents of the next field of the dummy node (180) into p, it is set to point to the first node in the linked list. Then, by repeatedly copying the contents of the next field of the node that p references into p (first 300, and then 54), p traverses the list and locates the listing to be fetched (G). At this point, we observe that the location of the listing to be fetched is contained in the l field of the node p references, and a deep copy of it is returned to the client. This verifies the graphical version of the algorithm.

The pseudocode version of the three-step graphical algorithm, expanded to include an unsuccessful search, is:

The Singly Linked List Fetch Algorithm

1. Node p = h.next; // set p to refer to the first node in the list
2. **while** (p != **null** && targetKey != p.l.key) // traverse the list
   { p = p.next; }
3. **if** (p != **null**) // return a deep copy of the listing to be fetched
       return p.l.deepCopy();
   else
       return null; // the request node is not in the list

The algorithm returns **null** if the node to be fetched is not in the structure and assumes the key searched for is targetKey.

The Delete Algorithm

The first two steps of the Delete algorithm are identical to the first two steps of the Fetch algorithm in that it begins by initializing a reference variable, p, to the first node in the linked list and then traverses p down the list in order to locate the listing to be deleted. To delete the listing from the structure, the linked list node that references it is deleted from the linked list. To accomplish this, the next field of the node preceding it is modified to "jump over" it. As illustrated in Figure 4.13 (where it is assumed that G is the listing to be deleted), the jump is performed by resetting the preceding linked node's next field to the location of the node after the deleted node.

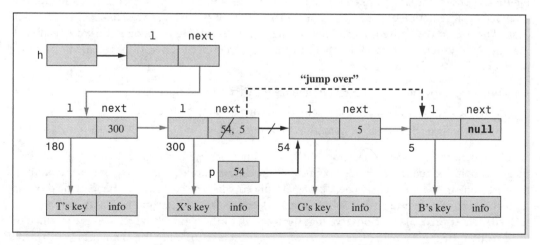

Figure 4.13 Deleting the Listing G by "Jumping" Around Its Linked List Node

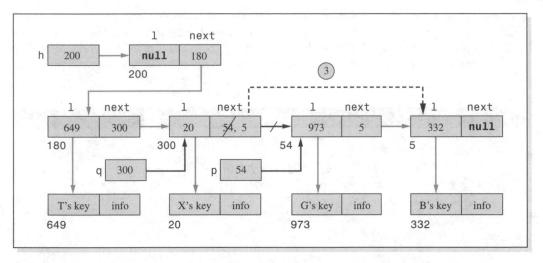

Figure 4.14 The Delete Algorithm After p and q Have Been Positioned At, and Before, the Node to Be Deleted, G

One problem arises: when the traverse is complete and p is referencing the node to be deleted, there is no way of determining the location of the preceding node. The next field references point forward, not backward, in the linked list. The remedy is to use another node reference, q, to store the location of the proceeding node. The reference variable q follows p down the list. Initially, q is set pointing to the dummy node, which is another reason the dummy node was included in the structure. Figure 4.14 shows the positioning of the reference variables, p and q, after a successful traversal to locate the node G.

Figure 4.14 also shows the graphical representation of the portion of the Delete algorithm that is different from the three-step Fetch algorithm; the jump over the linked node to be deleted. As indicated by the circled 3 in the figure, this jump replaces Step 3 of the Fetch algorithm. The only other changes to the Fetch algorithm are to expand Steps 1 and 2 to initially store the location of the dummy node in the variable q (in Step 1) and then to set q to p (in Step 2).

To verify the graphical version of the algorithm depicted in Figure 4.14, we traverse the list beginning at the dummy node referenced by h. The next field of the dummy node brings us to the linked node that references Node T. Then, the next field of the node that references Node T brings us to the linked node that references Node X. Finally, the next field of the linked node that references Node X brings us to the linked node that references Node B, which completes the traverse. Since Node G was not encountered in the traverse, and all the other nodes were, the algorithm is verified.

One final point should be made regarding the garbage collection process used in this algorithm. Because of the "jump over" step of this algorithm, the deleted linked node is no longer referenced (by a linked node). Therefore it, and the deleted Listing object, are returned to the available memory pool by the Java memory manager.

Having verified the graphical representation of the Delete algorithm, we will now present the pseudocode version. As discussed above, the first two steps of the algorithm are the first two steps of the Fetch algorithm expanded to include the use of the trailing reference variable, q. The pseudocode returns **false** if the node to be deleted is not in the structure and assumes the key of the listing to be deleted is targetKey.

The Linked List Delete Algorithm

1. Node q = h; // set the trailing reference, q, to refer to the dummy node
   Node p = h.next; // set p pointing to the first linked node (after the dummy node)
2. **while** (p != **null** && targetKey != p.l.key) // traverse the list
   { q = p;   // make q trail p throughout the traverse
     p = p.next; }
3. **if** (p != **null**)
   { q.next = p.next; } // "jump over" the deleted node
      return true;
   else
      return false;

The Update Algorithm

Once again, the Update algorithm will be an invocation of the Delete algorithm to eliminate the listing to be updated from the structure, followed by an invocation of the Insert algorithm to place a clone of the new information into the structure. Therefore, the Update algorithm to change the listing whose key is targetKey to the contents of the listing newNode is:

The Singly Linked List Update Algorithm

1. Invoke the Delete operation to delete the node with the key field, targetKey
2. Invoke the Insert operation to insert the node: newNode

4.3.2 Implementation

The implementation of the singly linked list structure is presented in Figure 4.15 as the Java class, SinglyLinkedList. It is implemented as a homogeneous, fully encapsulated structure. The code presented in Figure 4.15 is consistent with many of the concepts of generics presented in Chapter 2. For example, it does not mention the names of any of the fields of the client's nodes, and the definition of these nodes is coded as a separate class (see Figure 2.16). The class provides a deepCopy method in order to encapsulate the structure, a compareTo method to determine if a given key is equal to the key of a client node stored in the structure, and a toString method to return the contents of a node. The implementation is not fully generic in that the client's node class must be

```
1.  public class SinglyLinkedList
2.  {  private Node h; // list header
3.     public SinglyLinkedList()
4.     {  h = new Node(); // dummy node
5.        h.l = null;
6.        h.next = null;
7.     }
8.     public boolean insert(Listing newListing)
9.     {  Node n = new Node();
10.       if(n == null) // out of memory
11.         return false;
12.       else
13.       {  n.next = h.next;
14.          h.next = n;
15.          n.l = newListing.deepCopy();
16.          return true;
17.       }
18.    }
19.    public Listing fetch(String targetKey)
20.    {  Node p = h.next;
21.       while(p != null  && !(p.l.compareTo(targetKey) == 0))
22.       {  p = p.next;
23.       }
24.       if(p != null)
25.         return p.l.deepCopy();
26.       else
27.         return null;
28.    }
29.    public boolean delete(String targetKey)
30.    {  Node q = h;
31.       Node p = h.next;
32.       while(p != null && !(p.l.compareTo(targetKey) == 0))
33.       {  q = p;
34.          p = p.next;
35.       }
36.       if(p != null)
37.       {   q.next = p.next;
38.          return true;
39.       }
40.       else
41.          return false;
42.    }
43.    public boolean update(String targetKey, Listing newListing)
44.    {  if(delete(targetKey) == false)
45.         return false;
46.       else if(insert(newListing) == false)
47.         return false;
48.       return true;
49.    }
```

Figure 4.15 The Implementation of the Singly Linked List Structure

```
50.    public void showAll()
51.    {  Node p = h.next;
52.       while(p != null) // continue to traverse the list
53.          {  System.out.println(p.l.toString());
54.             p = p.next;
55.          }
56.    }
57.    public class Node
58.    {  private Listing l;
59.       private Node next;
60.       public Node()
61.       {
62.       }
63.    } // end of inner class Node
64. } // end SinglyLinkedList outer class
```

Figure 4.15 (continued)

named Listing, and the key field must be a String. A fully generic implementation of the structure, using the generic features of Java 5.0 and the techniques described in Chapters 2 and 3, Section 2.5 and 3.4, is left as an exercise for the student.

Line 2 declares the list header, h, that will store the address of the dummy node, an object in the class Node. This class defines the objects that will make up the linked list, and its code appears as Lines 57–63. Node objects have two data members: l, a reference to a Listing object, and next, a reference to a Node object (Lines 58–59). The class Node is defined as an inner class[1] of the class SinglyLinkedList because:

- The code of the class SinglyLinkedList can then directly access the two data members, l and next, of the class Node (e.g., Lines 5–6).
- Only the code of the class SinglyLinkedList will declare objects in the class Node.

The singly linked list initialization algorithm is coded on Lines 3–7, the outer class' constructor. Line 4 creates the dummy node referenced by the list header. The insert, delete, and fetch operation methods (Lines 8–42) are the Java equivalent of the pseudocode algorithms presented in the previous section with error checking added to the insert method (Lines 10 and 11). The only nuance is on Lines 21 and 32, in that they use the Listing class' compareTo method to compare the String keys. Lines 43–49 are the update method (which is the same coding of the update methods presented in Chapter 2). It invokes the delete and insert methods (Lines 44 and 46) to perform its operation. Finally, the showAll method (Lines 50–56) traverses the list outputting each listing until p reaches the end of the linked list (p == null; on Line 52).

---

[1]An inner class is a class defined within a class.

```
1.   public class MainSinglyLinkedList
2.   {  public static void main(String[] args)
3.      {  SinglyLinkedList boston = new SinglyLinkedList();
4.         Listing l1 = new Listing("Bill", "1st Avenue", "123 4567");
5.         Listing l2 = new Listing("Al", "2nd Avenue", "456 3232");
6.         Listing l3 = new Listing("Mike", "3rd Avenue", "333 3333");
7.         boston.insert(l1); // test insert
8.         boston.insert(l2);
9.         boston.insert(l3);
10.        boston.showAll();
11.        l3 = boston.fetch("Mike"); // test fetch of Mike
12.        System.out.println(l3.toString());
13.        boston.delete("Al"); // test delete of Al
14.        boston.showAll();
15.        boston.update("Mike", l2); // test update of Mike to Al
16.        boston.showAll();
17.        System.exit(0);
18.     } // end main method
19. } // end class MainSinglyLinkedList
```

Figure 4.16 A `SinglyLinkedList` Telephone Listing Application

To demonstrate the use of the class `SinglyLinkedList`, an application program that processes a telephone listing data set is presented in Figure 4.16. The output it generates is presented in Figure 4.17. Notice that the listings output by invoking the `showAll` method on Line 10 are in the reverse order (compared to the order in which they were inserted into the structure on Lines 7–9) because, as we have mentioned, new listings are inserted at the beginning of the linked list. The class that defines the telephone listings, presented in Figure 4.16, complies with the assumptions implicit in the coding of the class `SinglyLinkedList`.

4.3.3 Performance of the Singly Linked List

As we have discussed, the major advantage of a singly linked list is its ability to rapidly expand to accept a virtually unlimited number of nodes in a fragmented memory environment, regardless of the implementation language. We would suspect the major disadvantage of the structure would be its speed, since it uses a sequential search to locate a node. To evaluate the overall performance of the structure `SinglyLinkedList`, we will first examine the speed of its operation algorithms, and then the amount of overhead memory required to implement the structure.

Speed

To analyze the speed of the structure, we will perform a Big-O analysis to determine the approximate speed as n, the number of listings stored in the structure, gets large. Because the time to perform a memory access instruction is typically considerably longer than the time to perform a

```
Name is Mike
Address is 3rd Avenue
Number is 333 3333

Name is Al
Address is 2nd Avenue
Number is 456 3232

Name is Bill
Address is 1st Avenue
Number is 123 4567

Name is Mike
Address is 3rd Avenue
Number is 333 3333

Name is Mike
Address is 3rd Avenue
Number is 333 3333

Name is Bill
Address is 1st Avenue
Number is 123 4567

Name is Al
Address is 2nd Avenue
Number is 456 3232

Name is Bill
Address is 1st Avenue
Number is 123 4567
```

Figure 4.17   The Output Generated by the `SinglyLinkedList` Telephone Listing Application shown in Figure 4.16

nonaccess instruction, only memory access instructions will be included in our analysis. In addition, instructions inside of loops that repeatedly access the *same* memory cell will not be included in our speed analysis either, since modern compilers store these variables in CPU registers.

Examining the Insert algorithm, all four lines of pseudocode access memory. However, they are only executed once per Insert operation, independent of the number of nodes in the structure. Therefore, six memory accesses are required per Insert operation (one on Line 1, three on Line

2a,[2] one on Line 2b, and one on Line 3). Thus the dominant (and only) term in the Insert operation's speed function is 6, which is $O(1)$.

The Fetch algorithm uses a sequential search (beginning on Line 2) to locate a listing given its key, targetKey. Sometimes it will be at the beginning of the linked list and the loop will not execute, and other times the listing will be at the end of the list and the loop will execute $n - 1$ times. Since all locations are equally probable, the loop will execute an average of approximately $n / 2$ ($\approx (n - 1) / 2$) times.

Line 1 and the lines after (and including) Line 3 are not in the search loop so they will be ignored. Inside the loop, a total of three memory accesses are performed: one to fetch p.l, one to fetch the key, and one to fetch p.next (assuming p would be stored in a CPU register). Since these accesses are performed approximately $n / 2$ times, the dominant term in the speed equation is $3(n / 2) = 1.5n$, which is $O(n)$.

The Delete algorithm also uses a sequential search (beginning on Line 2) to locate the node to be deleted. Assuming the variables p and q are stored in CPU registers, there are three memory accesses performed inside the search loop: one to fetch p.l, one to fetch the key, and one to fetch p.next. The lines outside of the search loop contain memory access instructions, but they are only executed once so they do not contribute to the dominant term in the speed equation. As in the case of the Insert algorithm, the sequential search loop will be executed an average of approximately $n / 2$ times. Therefore, the three memory accesses performed inside the loop result in a dominant term of $3(n / 2) = 1.5n$, which is $O(n)$.

Overhead

Let us now turn our attention to the overhead of the structure. Referring to Figure 4.9, the overhead of the structure is the storage associated with the list header and the nodes that form the linked list, including the dummy node. The list header, the fields of the dummy node, and the fields of the n nodes on the linked list are all reference variables. Therefore, the overhead is one header reference variable, plus two dummy node reference variables, plus $2n$ linked node reference variables, for a total of $3 + 2n$ reference variables. Since reference variables occupy four bytes, the total overhead storage required by this structure is $4(3 + 2n)$ bytes.

Density is defined as

$$D = (\text{information bytes}) / (\text{total bytes}),$$

where the information bytes is simply the product of the number of Listing objects, n, and the number of information bytes per Listing object, w. The total bytes allocated the structure is the

---

[2]Once n and h are accessed on lines 1 and 2a, modern compilers would store them in CPU registers for the remainder of the algorithm.

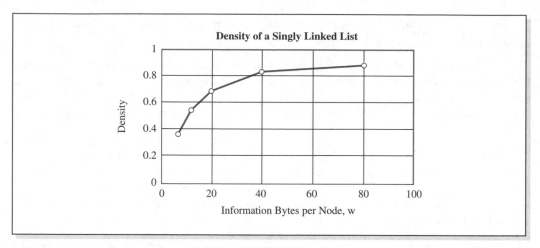

Figure 4.18   Density of the `SinglyLinkedList` Structure Containing More than 100 Nodes

sum of the information bytes, $n * w$, and the overhead bytes, $4(3 + 2n)$. Therefore the density can be expressed as

$$D_A = \text{(information bytes)} / \text{(total bytes)} = (n * w) / ((n * w) + 4(3 + 2n))$$
$$= 1 / (1 + 12 / (n * w) + 8 / w)$$

(which is approximately equal to $1 / (1 + 8 / w)$ as n gets large).

Figure 4.18 presents a graph of this function for $n > 100$ (which makes the term $12 / (n * w)$ negligible). The figure demonstrates that good densities (0.80 or higher) are achieved whenever the number of bytes in a node is greater than 33. Table 4.1 summarizes the performance of the singly linked list structure and includes the performance of the previously studied structures for comparative purposes. While not quite as fast as the Unsorted-Optimized array structure, its noncontiguous feature makes it an attractive alternative to the array-based structure for node widths greater than 33 bytes.

4.3.4 A Stack Implemented as a Singly Linked List

Often, a singly linked list is used to implement the data structure Stack as an alternative to the array-based implementation presented in Chapter 3. The advantage of this alternate implementation is that it can be rapidly expanded in all programming languages to accommodate a virtually unlimited number of Push operations, and it is compatible with a fragmented memory environment.

Table 4.1

Performance of a Singly Linked List

Data Structure	Operation Speed (in memory accesses)						Condition for Density > 0.8
	Insert	Delete	Fetch	Update = Delete + Insert	Average[3]	Big-O Average	Average for $n = 10^7$
Unsorted-Optimized Array	3	$\leq n$	$\leq n$	$\leq n + 3$	$\leq (3n + 6)/4$	$O(n)$	$\leq 0.75 \times 10^7 + 1.5$	$w > 16$
Stack and Queue	5	combined with fetch	4.5	not supported	$9.5/2 = 5$	$O(1)$	5	$w > 16$
Singly Linked List	6	$1.5n$	$1.5n$	$1.5n + 6$	$(4.5n + 12)/4$ $= 1.13n + 3$	$O(n)$	$1.13 \times 10^7 + 3$	$w > 33$

[3]Assumes all operations are equally probable and is therefore calculated as an arithmetic average of the four operation times.

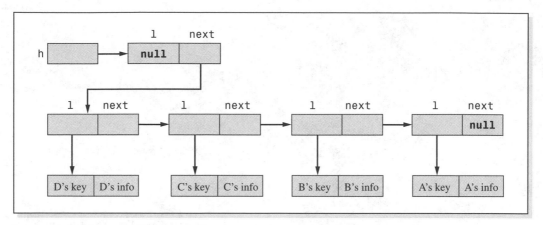

Figure 4.19 A Singly Linked List After A, B, C, and D Are Inserted (or Pushed)

The singly linked list Insert operation can be thought of as a stack Push operation, if we consider the front of the singly linked list to be the top of the stack. Since the inserted node is always placed in the front of the linked list, the nodes are stored in a "stack-like" reverse order. This is illustrated in Figure 4.19 which shows a linked list after the nodes A, B, C, and finally D are inserted.

The singly linked list Fetch operation however, appears to be far from a stack Pop operation. It is performed in the key field mode and does not delete the fetched node from the structure. Aside from these problems, neither the `fetch` nor the `insert` methods are named properly. Stack operation methods should be named `pop` and `push`.

The best remedy is to define a new stack structure class, copy the `SinglyLinkedList` data members, constructors, inner class `Node`, and the `insert` method code into it and then rename the `insert` method `pop`. The `pop` method in this class would be a new method that has the standard (no parameter) `push` signature, and always returns and deletes the first node in the list. Figure 4.20 presents the graphical representation of this Pop algorithm which places the address of the popped listing into the variable `p`. The circled numbers in the figure indicate the sequence of the two steps of the algorithm, and the dash-dot arrow indicates the writing of address 649 into `P`. Figure 4.21 presents the equivalent pseudocode with the test for underflow added to it.

The implementation of this linked list-based stack is left as an exercise for the student.

An Alternative Linked Stack

As an alternative to coding a new class to implement a dynamic stack, there is a "trick" we can use to force the linked list Fetch operation to always fetch the first node from the structure and to also

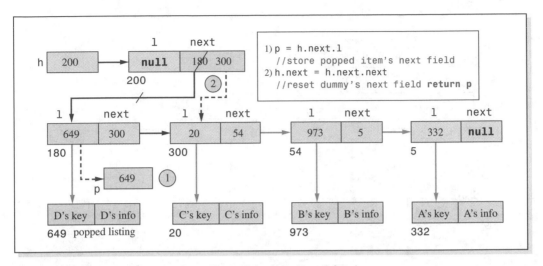

Figure 4.20 A Pop Operation for a Singly Linked List-Based Stack

The Pop Algorithm for a Singly Linked List-Based Stack

1. **if**(h.next == **null**) // list empty
2. **return null**
3. **else**
4. { p = h.next.l // step 1 of Figure 4.20
5. h.next = h.next.next; // step 2 of Figure 4.20
6. **return** p;
7. {

Figure 4.21 The Pop Operation for the Dynamic Implementation of a Stack

force the Delete operation to remove it from the structure. Thus, utilizing this trick, a Pop operation can be accomplished by performing a Fetch operation followed by a Delete operation.

The trick is to set the key field of each of the client's nodes inserted into the structure to the same value (e.g., "X") before they are inserted. Naturally, if the definition of the nodes is not changed, the contents of the key fields will be lost. This problem will be dealt with later in this section. Figure 4.22 shows a linked list after nodes A, B, C, and finally D are inserted into the structure. Then, to perform a Pop operation, we invoke the fetch method followed by the delete method and specify this common value of the key field as the argument sent to the fetch and delete methods (e.g., fetch(X), delete(X)). Since both methods start their sequential search at the first node in

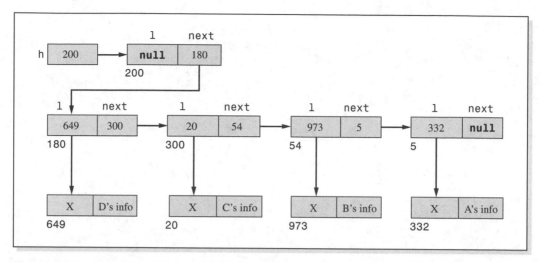

Figure 4.22 Singly Linked List after A, B, C, and D Are Inserted (Pushed) with their Key Fields Set to X

the linked list, and this node (and all nodes in the structure) contain the key value X, the first node in the linked list is returned and then deleted.

Considering the data stored in the stack depicted in Figure 4.22, the fetch method invocation: fetch("X") will return D. The delete method invocation: delete("X") will remove D from the structure. Since D was the last node inserted into the structure, these two invocations have performed a stack Pop operation. If the two invocations are repeated three more times, C will be fetched and deleted, followed by B, and then A. Thus, the structure is behaving like the restricted LIFO Stack structure.

Figure 4.23 shows an application program that uses our trick to make the object boston, an object in the class SinglyLinkedList, behave like a stack. The code is followed by the output it produces. Consistent with the trick, the key fields of the nodes declared on Lines 4–6 have all been set to "X". The nodes are pushed onto the structure using the insert method (Lines 8–10). Then they are popped from the structure and output using the fetch, delete, and toString methods (Lines 12–20). The key "X" is used in each Fetch-and-Delete operation. The LIFO sequence of the output verifies that our trick has indeed caused the SinglyLinkedList object, boston, to behave like a stack.

Although this trick can be used in application programs to simulate a stack that accommodates a virtually unlimited number of Push operations, its use is undesirable for four reasons:

- To retain the contents of the key field, an additional field must be added to the node.
- It requires the application programmer to have knowledge of the "trick."
- The push and pop operation methods are not named push and pop.

```
1.   public class MainSinglyLinkedListStack
2.   {  public static void main(String[] args)
3.      {  SinglyLinkedList boston = new SinglyLinkedList();
4.         Listing l1 = new Listing("X", "1st Avenue", "123 4567");
5.         Listing l2 = new Listing("X", "2nd Avenue", "456 3232");
6.         Listing l3 = new Listing("X", "3rd Avenue", "333 3333");
7.         // three "push" operations
8.         boston.insert(l1);
9.         boston.insert(l2);
10.        boston.insert(l3);
11.        // three "pop" operations
12.        l3 = boston.fetch("X"); // first "pop"
13.        boston.delete("X");
14.        System.out.println(l3); // automatically invokes the toString
                                   // method
15.        l3 = boston.fetch("X"); // second "pop"
16.        boston.delete("X");
17.        System.out.println(l3); // automatically invokes the toString
                                   // method
18.        l3 = boston.fetch("X"); // third "pop"
19.        boston.delete("X");
20.        System.out.println(l3);
21.        System.exit(0);
22.     } // end of main method
23.  } // end of class MainSinglyLinkedListStack
```

Program output:

Name is X
Address is 3rd Avenue
Number is 333 3333

Name is X
Address is 2nd Avenue
Number is 456 3232

Name is X
Address is 1st Avenue
Number is 123 4567

Figure 4.23   A Program That Uses a Singly Linked List Structure As a Stack and Its Output

- If the client neglects to invoke the delete method after each fetch invocation, the stack "simulation" breaks down (the Pop operation becomes a Peek operation).

A more desirable approach to utilizing the trick is to write a new class, StackSLL, that includes a SinglyLinkedList object as a data member. Knowledge of the trick is then imbedded into the push and pop methods of the StackSLL class, which unburdens the application programmer. As shown in the top part of Figure 4.24, the client will pass StackListing objects to, and from, the

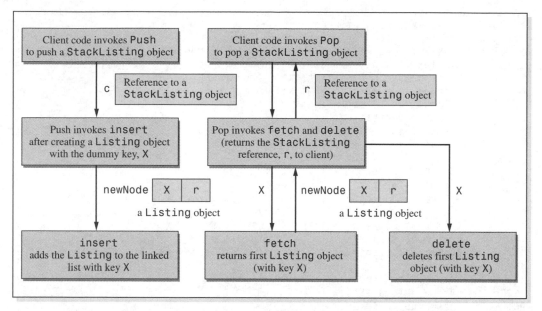

Figure 4.24 Invocation Sequence and Argument Flow for a Stack Implemented Using the Class
`SinglyLinkedList`

push and pop methods respectively. These objects will contain the client's information to be stored
in the structure. The push method will invoke the singly linked list insert method, and the pop
method will invoke the singly linked list's fetch and delete methods. Since the linked list methods
pass Listing objects, the dummy key and a reference, r, to a deep copy of the client's StackListing
object will be combined by the push method to form a redefined two-field Listing object before it
invokes insert. The pop method will invoke the fetch method to fetch a Listing object from the
front of the singly linked list. The location of the StackListing object, r, contained in the Listing
object will be returned to the client by the pop method after it invokes delete.

The top portion of Figure 4.25 shows the redefined fields of the singly linked list Listing object
consistent with this approach. The rightmost field of the object, r, is a reference to a StackListing object. It also shows the fields of a StackListing object for a client application that stores
telephone listings on our stack. Figure 4.26 shows a StackSLL structure after the four nodes A, B,
C, and finally D have been pushed onto the structure. The implementation of the class StackSLL
is left as an exercise for the student.

4.4 Other Types of Linked Lists

A singly linked list is the simplest form of a linked list. Other types of linked lists include circular
singly linked lists, double-ended singly linked lists, sorted singly linked lists, doubly linked lists,
circular doubly linked lists, and multilinked lists. We will now briefly discuss these structures.

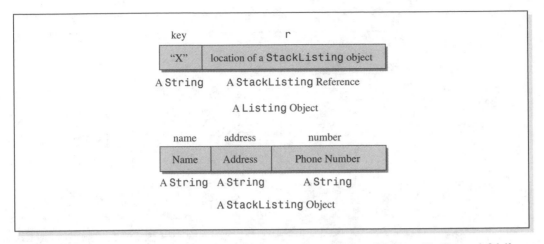

Figure 4.25 The Fields of the `Listing` and `StackListing` Objects Mentioned in Figure 4.24 (for a Phone Listing Application)

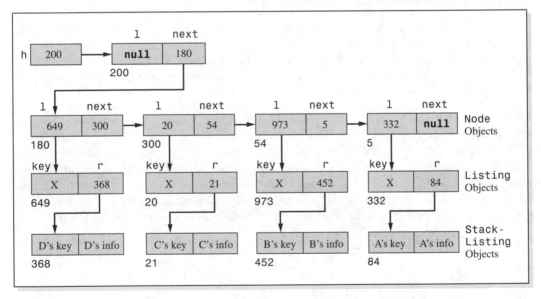

Figure 4.26 The Memory Model for the Stack Implemented as Shown in Figure 4.24

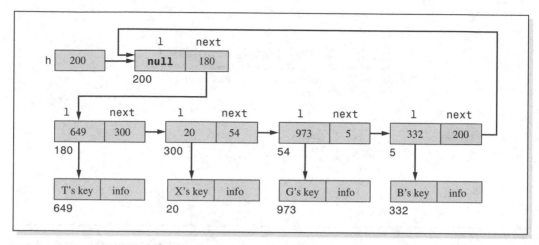

Figure 4.27 A Circular Singly Linked List

4.4.1 Circular Singly Linked List

A circular singly linked list is a singly linked list in which the next field of the *last* node in the list references the *first* node in the list. When a dummy node is used in the implementation, the last node in the list references the dummy node. Otherwise, it references the actual first node. Figure 4.27 shows a circular singly linked list (whose implementation uses a dummy node) with four client nodes, T, X, G, and B stored in it.

The implementation of a circular singly linked list is basically the same as a singly linked list with a few minor additions to account for the last node's circular reference to the dummy node. When the list is created, the next field of the dummy node is set to reference itself (h.next = h). The only other change is to the sequential search performed in the Fetch and Delete algorithms. Rather than an unsuccessful search ending at a **null** reference, it ends when a reference to the dummy node is encountered. Therefore, the comparison of p with **null** on Lines 2 and 3 of both the Fetch and Delete pseudocode algorithms are changed to comparisons of p with h (the list header) as

    while (p != h && targetKey != p.l.key) // continue to traverse the list

and

    if(p != h) // perform the operation

4.4.2 Double-Ended Singly Linked List

A double-ended singly linked list is a singly linked list in which insertions are permitted at the front (as usual) *and* rear (a new feature) of the list. A newly inserted linked node can become either the new first node *or* the new last node in the list.

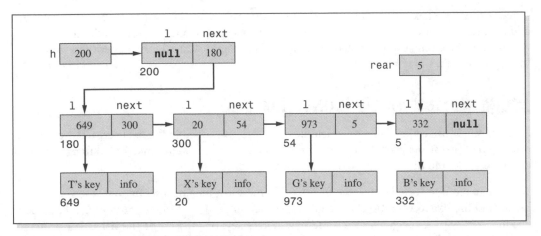

Figure 4.28   A Double-Ended Singly Linked List

To implement this structure a reference variable, rear, is added as a data member to the
SinglyLinkedList class along with an additional insert method. The variable rear references
the last node in the structure (Figure 4.28), and the additional insert method is used to insert
nodes at the end of the linked list.[4] When the list is empty (all the nodes have been deleted) rear
is **null**. When a node is inserted at the end of the list, the last node's next field and the variable
rear are changed to reference the new (last) node. An empty list is treated as a special case in the
new Insert algorithm. Assuming the new linked node is referenced by the variable newLink, the
pseudocode to add a new linked node at the end of the list is:

if(rear == **null**) // special case, empty list
  { rear = newLink;
    h.next = newLink; }
else
{ rear.next = newLink;
   rear = newLink;
}

To complete the Insert algorithm, the l field of the newly added linked node is set to reference a
clone of the client's listing.

Deleting the last node in the list is also treated as a special case. Referring to Step 3 of the singly
linked list Delete algorithm, prior to returning **true**, the following is added:

if(p == rear)
   rear = **null**;

---

[4]Alternately, a parameter can be added to the singly linked list insert method to indicate which end of the list is to receive
the new node.

Often a double-ended singly linked list is used to implement the structure Queue. Nodes are added at the rear of the queue using the new `insert` method. Nodes are removed (fetched) from the front of the queue using the algorithm depicted in Figure 4.21 (the Pop operation for a stack implemented as a singly linked list).

4.4.3 Sorted Singly Linked List

A sorted singly linked list is one in which the nodes are positioned in the list in sorted order based on the contents of their key field. Figure 4.29 shows a sorted singly linked list after four client nodes (B, G, X, and finally T) have been inserted.

To arrange them in sorted order, the Insert algorithm must include a sequential search down the list to find the "correct location" for a newly inserted node. The search continues until a node is encountered with a key *greater than* the new node's key, or the end of the list is encountered. Assuming the reference variable used to traverse the list is p, newNode references the item to be inserted into the structure, and the client's node definition class included a getKey method, the traversal would continue as follows:

while (p != **null** && newNode.compareTo(p.l.getKey()) > 0) // continue traversal

The compareTo method would have to return a positive integer whenever the key of the object that invoked it (newNode) is greater than the argument passed to it (p.l.getKey()).[5] The new linked node is inserted between the node referenced by p and its predecessor, or as the new last node. The technique for inserting a node in between two nodes is illustrated in Figure 4.7, and the sequential search to find the new item's correct position is similar to the sequential search in the Delete algorithm in that a reference variable q trails the variable p during the traversal.

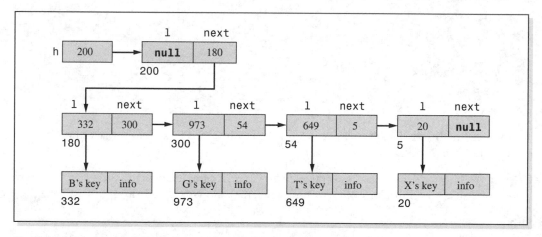

Figure 4.29 A Sorted Singly linked List

---

[5]The compareTo method in the Strmq class, which is invoked by the compareTo method in the Listing class (Figure 2.16), does this.

The major advantage of a sorted singly linked list structure is that its showAll method outputs the nodes in sorted order based on their key field contents. In addition, when the delete or fetch method is invoked to operate on a listing that is *not* in the structure, their average speed is doubled. Since the listings are stored in sorted order, the search portion of these algorithms can be modified to end when it encounters a key greater than the key of the listing to be operated on. This, on the average, will occur after traversing halfway down the linked list.

On the negative side, the sequential search added to the Insert algorithm decreases the speed of both the Insert and Update operations. Therefore, for some applications that require sorted output and perform many Insert operations, it is more efficient to store the nodes in an unsorted singly linked list and then simply sort the nodes inside the showAll method before they are output. Sorting methods used in this approach are discussed in Chapter 8.

4.4.4 Doubly Linked List

A doubly linked list is a singly linked list in which each node in the list has an additional linked reference field that refers to the node just before it in the list. Figure 4.30 shows a doubly linked list with three nodes T, X, and G stored in it. The additional reference variable is named back. As shown in the figure, the dummy node also contains the additional reference field, back.

The Fetch algorithm of this structure is the same as the singly linked list's Fetch algorithm. Since inserts are still performed at the front of the list, the Insert algorithm is modified to set the back reference of the first node in the list to the location of the inserted (new) node, and to set the back

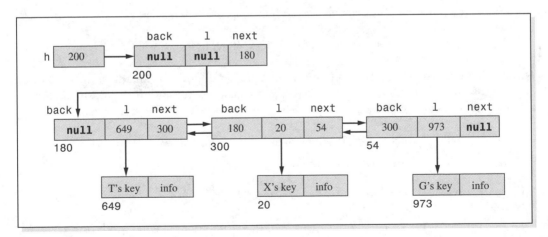

Figure 4.30   A Doubly Linked List

reference of the inserted node to **null**. Assuming the new doubly linked list node is referenced by the variable newLink, the additional code in the Fetch algorithm is:

```
h.next.back = newLink;
newLink.back = null;
```

The singly linked list Delete algorithm must also be modified to implement this structure. When a node is deleted from a singly linked list, the next field of the node that precedes it is reset to effectively jump around the deleted node (see Figure 4.13). An analogous section of code must be added to the Delete algorithm to adjust the back reference of the node following the deleted node; it too must also be made to jump around the deleted node. To accomplish this, the Delete algorithm places the address of the node preceding the deleted node into the back field of the node that follows the deleted node. Deletion of the last node in the list is treated as a special case in which the addition code is not executed. Thus, the code added to the Delete algorithm is:

```
if(p.next != null) // not deleting the last node in the structure
p.next.back = p.back;
```

Doubly linked list structures are used for applications that require a backward traversal through the list. The density of the structure is slightly lower than that of the singly linked list due to the additional four bytes of overhead associated with the back field of each node. Specifically, the overhead is one header reference variable, plus three dummy node reference variables plus $3n$ doubly linked node reference variables, for a total of $4 + 3n$ reference variables. Since reference variables occupy four bytes, the total overhead is $4(4 + 3n)$ bytes.

To compute the density of this structure we recall that density is defined as

$$D = \text{(information bytes) / (total bytes)}.$$

The information bytes is simply the product of the number of nodes, n, and the number of bytes per client listing, w. The total bytes allocated to the structure, the sum of the information bytes and the overhead bytes, is $n * w + 4(4 + 3n)$. Therefore the density can be expressed as

$$D = \text{(information bytes) / (total bytes)} = (n * w) / ((n * w) + 4(4 + 3n))$$
$$= 1 / (1 + 16 / (n * w) + 12/w),$$

which is approximately equal to $1 / (1 + 12/w)$ as n gets large.

Figure 4.31 presents the variation of the density of this structure with node width (for $n \geq 100$), and includes the density of the singly linked list for comparative purposes. The figure shows that the doubly linked list structure achieves a density greater than 0.80 for node widths greater than 60 bytes.

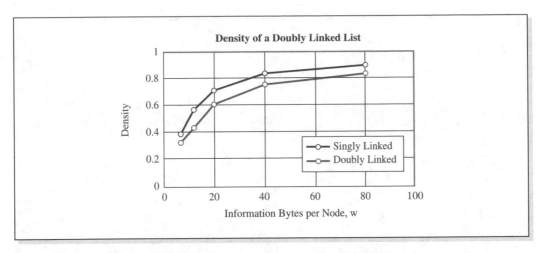

Figure 4.31 Density of a Doubly Linked List that Stores 100 Nodes

4.4.5 Multilinked List

Multilinked lists are linked lists in which the nodes are stored in a way that allows more than one traversal path through the nodes (e.g., Figure 4.2b). Consider our phone book listings. Suppose an application required the listings to be output in both name and phone number order. A multi-linked list that allowed a traversal in alphabetic name order *and* in phone number order would be ideally suited for this application.

Figure 4.32 presents a multilinked data structure implemented as two *sorted* singly linked lists. The first singly linked list, which is shown at the top of the figure and whose header is h1, orders the listings in name order. Assuming the lowest phone number is T's followed by B's, G's, and finally X's, the second singly linked list (shown at the bottom of the figure and whose header is h2) orders the listings in phone number order.

In the implementation of this structure, two sorted singly linked objects (e.g., list1 and list2) are declared as data members of the new multilinked structure class. Although a listing inserted into the multilinked data structure would be fully encapsulated, the implementation of the insert method of the sorted singly linked lists would be modified to unencapsulated the listings. This would permit (as shown in Figure 4.32) the two singly linked list objects to share access to the same clone of the client's information. The insert method of the multilinked structure would clone the client's listing, and send a reference to it to the sorted singly linked list's insert method which would *shallow copy* the cloned listing into the list.

A second modification to the singly linked list's insert method would be necessary. An integer parameter would be added to its parameter list to indicate which field in the cloned listing is to be used as the sort field. Its expanded signature would be:

```
public boolean insert(int sortField, Listing newNode)
```

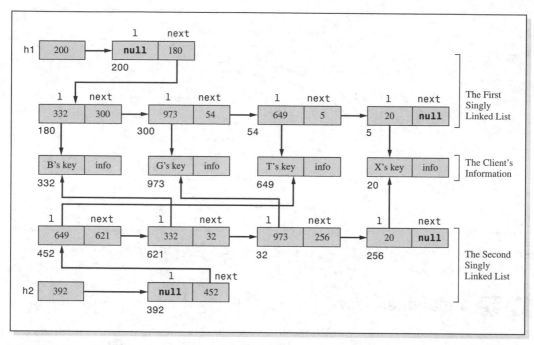

Figure 4.32   A Multilinked List with Two Orderings

The class that defines the client's listings would have to include two getKey methods (e.g., getKey1 and getKey2) used by the linked list's insert method to fetch the contents of one sort field, or the other. The decision as to which one to invoke would be based in the value of the new sortField parameter sent to it. Assuming that the listing to be inserted is an object in the class Listing, and that it is referenced by the variable newNode, the multilinked structure's insert method would be:

```
Listing clone = deepCopy(newNode);
list1.insert(1, clone);
list2.insert(2, clone);
```

where list1 and list2 are the two sorted singly linked list objects declared as data members of the new multilinked structure class. The sorted singly linked list insert method would be modified to contain the additional code:

```
if(sortField == 1)
   String key = getKey1();
else
   String key = getKey2();
```

and to use the contents of the variable key to position the node in the sorted singly linked list objects.

The showAll method of the multilinked list class would also contain an additional integer parameter that the client could set to indicate which of the two sorted orders would be used in the output. Its signature would be: **void** showAll(**int** listNumber). The client would invoke the method in one of two ways: myList.showAll(1) or myList.showAll(2). The multilinked structure's showAll method would then invoke the Listing class' showAll method using the code sequence:

```
if(listNumber == 1)
   list1.showAll()
else
   list2.showAll();
```

If the application required that a Delete operation be performed on the data set, the simplest implementation would be to require the client to specify two key values, key1 and key2, when the delete method is invoked. Then, the delete method would eliminate the node from the data structure by invoking the sorted singly linked class' delete method twice:

```
link1.delete(key1);
link2.delete(key2);
```

A more involved (but more client-friendly) implementation would only require the client to pass one key to the multilinked class' delete method and the method would fetch the other key from the node before it was deleted from one of the lists. Then the delete method would be invoked again with that key to delete the node from the other list.

The density of this structure is lower than the other linked structures presented in this chapter because of the overhead associated with the second sorted singly linked list. As we have previously shown, the overhead associated with a singly linked list, containing n listings, is $4(3 + 2n)$ bytes. To generalize our calculation of density for this structure, we will assume that the nodes are sorted on L different fields, requiring our structure to contain L singly linked lists.[6] Thus the total overhead for the structure is $4L(3 + 2n)$ bytes. Remembering that the information bytes in the structure is simply the product of the number of nodes, n, and the number of information bytes per client node, w, its density is:

$$D = (\text{information bytes}) / (\text{total bytes}) = (n * w) / ((n * w) + 4L(3 + 2n))$$

$$= 1 / (1 + 12L / (n * w) + 8L / w)$$

which is approximately equal to $1 / (1 + 8L / w)$ as n gets large.

Figure 4.33, which assumes a node width $n \geq 100$, presents the density of this structure for values of L equal to 2 and 4. For comparative purposes it includes the density variation of the singly and doubly linked structures. A density of 0.80 is achieved for node widths greater than 65 bytes for two orderings, and a node width greater than 130 bytes for four orderings.

---

[6]L is equal to 2 in the structure depicted in Figure 4.32.

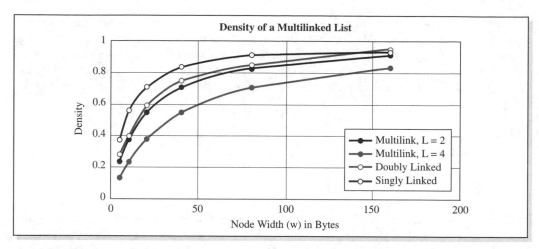

Figure 4.33   Densities of Multilinked Lists that Store more than 100 Nodes in Two or Four Orderings

4.5   Iterators

An iterator is an object that the *client* can use to sequentially access the nodes in a linear list. Singly linked lists and arrays are examples of linear lists. Typically, the iterator's class provides methods for positioning the iterator object at the first item in the list, advancing the iterator to the next item, and determining if the iterator is at the end of the list. In addition, the iterator's class provides methods to operate on the item at the iterator's current position.

Iterators can be a very convenient means of access for certain applications. For example, suppose we wanted to add an area code to every listing in a telephone directory stored in a singly linked list (see Figure 4.9). In this case, an Update operation performed in the key field mode is not particularly useful because we would have to generate the names of all of the telephone customers in order to operate on each node. In addition, even if the Update method was coded in the node number mode, using it to change the area code of every item in the database would be a time consuming process since each invocation begins its traversal at the front of the list. When updating the first listing, one node would be traversed. Two nodes would be traversed to update the second listing, three nodes for the third listing, etc. Thus, the total number of nodes traversed to update each of n nodes is: $1 + 2 + 3 + \ldots + n = n(n + 1) / 2$, which is $O(n^2)$.

An iterator object, on the other hand, retains its position in the list after an operation is performed. Therefore, if the iterator's class contained an update method, after updating one listing, it would simply traverse one more node in order to update the next listing. The total number of nodes traversed to update each of n nodes would be: $1 + 1 + 1 + \ldots + 1 = n$, which is $O(n)$. In summary, the use of the iterator would speed up the update of the listings by n times.

Table 4.2

Several Iterator Methods of an Iterator Class to be Added to the Class `SinglyLinkedList`

Iterator **Method**	**Description**
public void reset()	positions the iterator at the dummy node
public boolean hasNext()	returns **true** if there is a node after the iterator's current position
public Listing next()	moves the iterator to the next node *and* then returns a reference to a clone of its listing
public void set(Listing newListing)	replaces the listing, stored at the iterator's current position, with a clone of `newListing`. The iterator's position is not changed.

Most iterator classes provide methods, whose signatures are somewhat standardized, to operate on the information stored in a linear list. These methods typically included the method add (to perform an Insert operation), the method next (to perform a Fetch operation), the method remove (to perform a Delete operation), and the method set (to perform an Update operation). Other common iterator methods are reset, used to position the iterator at the beginning of the list, and hasNext to determine if the iterator is at the end of the list. Iterator classes that operate on doubly linked lists include a method previous, for traversing the iterator backward through the list, and a method hasPrevious, to determine if the iterator is at the beginning of the list.

To illustrate the use of some of these methods, let us again consider the problem of adding an area code to a telephone listing data set. We will assume that the iterator class containing the methods described in Table 4.2 has been added to the class `SinglyLinkedList` (see Figure 4.15), and that an iterator object, i, has also been added to the class as a **public** data member.

We will also assume that the methods getNumber and setNumber have been added to the class Listing (see Figure 2.16) to fetch (getNumber) and change (setNumber) the contents of a Listing object's phone number field. Under these assumptions, the iterator object, i, is used in the following code sequence to efficiently add the area code "631" to every listing in the telephone directory boston, a `SinglyLinkedList` object:

```
Listing listing;
String number;
boston.i.reset();                  // position the iterator, i, at the dummy node
// add an area code to all the listings
while(boston.i.hasNext())          // there are more listings
{  listing = boston.i.next();      // fetch the next listing from the structure
```

```
    number = listing.getNumber();      // add the area code to the existing listing's
                                        //   phone number
    number = "631 " + number;
    listing.setNumber(number);
    boston.i.set(listing);             // update the listing in the list
}
```

As previously discussed, the efficiency of this code resides in the first line of the **while** loop (`listing = boston.i.next()`) because the iterator, `i`, retains its position in the list after the line executes. This eliminates the need to begin a new traversal through the list during each loop iteration.

4.5.1 Implementation of an Iterator

There are two common techniques used to implement an iterator class. One technique defines the class inside the data structure class (i.e., as an inner class), and the iterator object (as previously suggested) is a public data member of the data structure class. This technique is used when the data structure is encapsulated, since it maintains the encapsulation of the structure. In this implementation, the `Iterator` class' methods insert and return *clones* (deep copies) of the client's listings.

In the second technique, the iterator class is defined outside of the data structure class, and the iterator object is declared in the client code. This technique is used when the data structure is not encapsulated, since it gives the client direct access to the information contained in the structure. In this implementation, the iterator class' methods insert and return *shallow* copies of the client's listings.

Figure 4.34 presents the code of a class named `SinglyLinkedListIterator`, which is an expanded version of the class `SinglyLinkedList` presented in Figure 4.15.[7] The expansion includes the definition of an iterator class, named `Iterator`, that implements the four methods presented in Table 4.2 and the declaration of an `Iterator` object as a data member in the class. The inner class implementation of the iterator was used since the class `SinglyLinkedList` is a fully encapsulated structure.

Line 3 declares the `Iterator` reference variable, `i`, as a **public** data member. Its access is public so that the client can use it to access the `Iterator` class' methods. The actual `Iterator` object is created on Line 6 of the class' constructor. Lines 7–9, the code of the four basic operation methods (Lines 10–51), the showAll method (Lines 52–58), and the definition of the class Node (Lines 59–65) are the same as the code of the class `SinglyLinkedList` presented in Figure 4.15.

Lines 66–87 is the code of the inner class `Iterator`. It contains one data member `ip`, a singly linked Node reference variable declared on Line 67. This variable will be used to store the position of the iterator. Initially it refers to the dummy node (Line 69).

The reset method (Lines 71–73) re-initializes the variable `ip` (Line 72) to again position the iterator at the dummy node. The hasNext method (Lines 74–79) determines if the iterator is not at

---

[7]Better programming practice would be to implement the class `SinglyLinkedListIterator` as an *extension* of the class `SinglyLinkedList`, but that would require the reader to refer to the code of both classes during subsequent discussions in this chapter.

```
1.  public class SinglyLinkedListIterator // expands SinglyLinkedList
                                           // (see Fig. 4.15)
2.  {  private Node h; // list header
3.     public Iterator i;
4.     public SinglyLinkedListIterator()
5.     {  h = new Node(); // allocates the dummy node
6.        i = new Iterator();
7.        h.l = null;
8.        h.next = null;
9.     }
10.    public boolean insert(Listing2 newListing)
11.    {  Node n = new Node();
12.       if(n == null) // out of memory
13.         return false;
14.       else
15.       { n.next = h.next;
16.         h.next = n;
17.         n.l = newListing.deepCopy();
18.         return true;
19.       }
20.    }
21.    public Listing2 fetch(String targetKey)
22.    {  Node p = h.next;
23.       while(p != null  &&  !(p.l.compareTo(targetKey) == 0))
24.       {  p = p.next;
25.       }
26.       if(p != null)
27.          return p.l.deepCopy();
28.       else
29.          return null;
30.    }
31.    public boolean delete(String targetKey)
32.    {  Node q = h;
33.       Node p = h.next;
34.       while(p != null && !(p.l.compareTo(targetKey) == 0))
35.       {  q = p;
36.          p = p.next;
37.       }
38.       if(p != null)
39.       {  q.next = p.next;
40.          return true;
41.       }
42.       else
43.          return false;
44.    }
45.    public boolean update(String targetKey, Listing2 newListing)
46.    {  if(delete(targetKey) == false)
47.          return false;
```

Figure 4.34   The Class SinglyLinkedList (Figure 4.15) Expanded to Include an Iterator Object

```
48.        else if(insert(newListing) == false)
49.           return false;
50.        return true;
51.     }
52.     public void showAll()
53.     {  Node p = h.next;
54.        while(p != null) // continue to traverse the list
55.        {  System.out.println(p.l.toString());
56.           p = p.next;
57.        }
58.     }
59.     public class Node
60.     {  private Listing2 l;
61.        private Node next;
62.        public Node()
63.        {
64.        }
65.     } // end of inner class Node
66.     public class Iterator
67.     {  private Node ip;
68.        public Iterator()
69.        {  ip = h;
70.        }
71.        public void reset()
72.        {  ip = h;
73.        }
74.        public boolean hasNext()
75.        {  if(ip.next != null)
76.           return true;
77.           else
78.           return false;
79.        }
80.        public Listing2 next()
81.        {  ip = ip.next;
82.           return ip.l.deepCopy();
83.        }
84.        public void set(Listing2 newListing)
85.        {  ip.l = newListing.deepCopy();
86.        }
87.     } // end of inner class Iterator
88. } // end class SinglyLinkedListIterator
```

Figure 4.34 (continued)

```
1.  public class Listing2
2.  {   private String name; // key field
3.        private String address;
4.        private String number;
5.        public Listing2(String n, String a, String num)
6.        {   name = n;
7.            address = a;
8.            number = num;
9.        }
10.       public String toString()
11.       {   return("Name is " + name +
12.                   "\nAddress is " + address +
13.                   "\nNumber is " + number + "\n");
14.       }
15.       public Listing2 deepCopy()
16.       {   Listing2 clone = new Listing2(name, address, number);
17.           return clone;
18.       }
19.       public int compareTo(String targetKey)
20.       {   return(name.compareTo(targetKey));
21.       }
22.       public String getNumber() // fetch the phone number
23.       {   return number;
24.       } // end of getNumber method
25.       public void setNumber(String n) // change the phone number
26.       {   number = n;
27.       } // end of setNumber method
28. } // end of Listing2 Class
```

Figure 4.35 The Class `Listing2` with Methods to "Get" and "Set" a Listing's Phone Number

the end of the list by testing the next field of the node at the iterator's location for a non-**null** value (Line 75). If it is **null**, the method returns **false** indicating there is no next node.

Lines 80–83 are the code of the method next, which fetches a Listing object from the structure *after* moving the iterator. Line 81 moves the iterator to the next node in the linked list, and then Line 82 returns a deep copy of the listing referenced by that node. Similarly, the set method (Lines 84–86) stores a reference to a deep copy of a Listing object at the current iterator position (Line 85). The invocation of the Listing class' method deepCopy, on Lines 82 and 85, maintains the encapsulation of the structure.

Figure 4.35 presents the code of the Listing class presented in Figure 2.16 (less the setAddress, renamed Listing2, method) expanded to include the setNumber and getNumber methods (Lines 22–27). These two methods permit the client to access the phone number fields of a listing. Figure

```
1.   public class MainSinglyLinkedListIterator
2.   {  public static void main(String[] args)
3.      {  SinglyLinkedListIterator boston = new SinglyLinkedListIterator();
4.         String number;
5.         Listing2 l1 = new Listing2("Bill", "1st Avenue", "123 4567");
6.         Listing2 l2 = new Listing2("Al", "2nd Avenue", "456 3232");
7.         Listing2 l3 = new Listing2("Mike", "3rd Avenue", "333 3333");
8.         boston.insert(l1);  // test insert
9.         boston.insert(l2);
10.        boston.insert(l3);
11.     // output all the listings using the iterator, i
12.        while(boston.i.hasNext())
13.        {  System.out.println(boston.i.next());  // automatically invokes
                                                     // toString
14.        }
15.     // add an area code to all the listings using the iterator, i
16.        boston.i.reset();
17.        while(boston.i.hasNext())
18.        {  l1 = boston.i.next();
19.           number = l1.getNumber();
20.           number = "631 " + number;
21.           l1.setNumber(number);
22.           boston.i.set(l1);
23.        }
24.     // output the updated listings using the iterator, i
25.        boston.i.reset();
26.        while(boston.i.hasNext())
27.        {  System.out.println(boston.i.next()); // automatically invokes
28.                                                 // toString
29.        }
30.        System.exit(0);
31.     } // end of method main
32. } // end of iterator application
```

Figure 4.36   An Application that Uses an iterator, i, to Efficiently Add a 631 Area Code to Phone Directory Listings

4.36 is an application program that creates a phone listing data set stored in the SinglyLinkedList-Iterator object boston (Lines 3–10). Then the object's iterator is used to output the data set[8] (Lines 12–14), add an area code to each listing's phone number (Lines 16–23), and output the revised data set (Lines 25–29). The two sets of output it generates is presented in Figure 4.37.

---

[8]The iterator, i, and the toString methods are used in place of the showAll method in order to illustrate the iterator's use.

```
Name is Mike
Address is 3rd Avenue
Number is 333 3333

Name is Al
Address is 2nd Avenue
Number is 456 3232

Name is Bill
Address is 1st Avenue
Number is 123 4567

Name is Mike
Address is 3rd Avenue
Number is 631 333 3333

Name is Al
Address is 2nd Avenue
Number is 631 456 3232

Name is Bill
Address is 1st Avenue
Number is 631 123 4567
```

Figure 4.37   The Output Generated by the Application Shown in Figure 4.36, Demonstrating the Addition of a 631 Area Code

4.5.2 Multiple Iterators

Some applications require two or more iterators to be operating on a list simultaneously. Programs with multiple threads often have this requirement. For example, an iterator in one thread could be used to transfer a data set over a modem, while an iterator in a second thread could be used to output the data set to a printer. One alternative is to add more iterator references to the data structure class as data members, and then to create the corresponding iterator objects in the data structure's constructor.

For example, to increase the number of iterators in the class `SinglyLinkedListIterator` (Figure 4.34) from one to three, the code:

```
public Iterator j;  // second iterator
public Iterator k; // third iterator
```

would be added to the class after Line 3, and the code:

```
j = new Iterator();
k = new Iterator();
```

would be added to the class' constructor after Line 6. Then, the client code could position the three iterators i, j, and k at different locations in the list.

A more flexible alternative is to add a parameter to the SinglyLinkedListIterator class' constructor to allow the client to specify the number of iterators required for a particular application. In this approach, the iterators are implemented as an array of iterator references. Line 3 of the class would become:

```
public Iterator[] i;
```

The constructor's heading, Line 4 would become:

```
public SinglyLinkedListIterator(int numberOfIterators)
```

and Line 6 of the constructor would be replaced with:

```
i = new Iterator[numberOfIterators];
for(int count = 0; count < numberOfIterators; count++)
    i[count] = new Iterator();
```

where numberOfIterators is the name of the parameter the client would use to specify the number of iterators used in the application. Then the client code to allocate a singly linked list structure with 10 iterators and to output the list using the third iterator would be:

```
SinglyLinkedListIterator boston = new SinglyLinkedListIterator(10);
                    :
                    :
// output all the listings using iterator, 3
boston.i[3].reset();
while(boston.i[3].hasNext())
    System.out.println(boston.i[3].next());
```

External Iterators

Another approach to implementing multiple iterators is to implement them in a way that allows the *client code* to declare the iterator object references (e.g., Iterator iterator1, iterator2;). The advantage to this approach is that the client can choose the names of the iterators (as well as the number of iterators). In this implementation, the Iterator class can no longer be an inner class (i.e., coded inside the class SinglyLinkedListIterator). Once the iterator class is removed from this class, the class Node (Lines 59–65 of Figure 4.34) must also be removed from the class SinglyLinkedListIterator because otherwise the iterator class could not declare a Node reference to store the iterator's current position (Line 67 of Figure 4.34).

Figures 4.38, 4.39, and 4.40 present the Node, Iterator, and SinglyLinkedListIterator classes as three separate classes renamed NewNode, SLLIterator, and SllExternalIterator respectively.

```
1.  public class NewNode
2.  {   Listing2 l;  // package access data members
3.      NewNode next;
4.      public NewNode()
5.      {
6.      }
7.  }
```

Figure 4.38   The class NewNode with Package Access Data Members

```
1.  public class SllIterator  // implements a list iterator
2.  {   private NewNode ip;
3.      private NewNode h;
4.      public SllIterator(NewNode h)
5.      {   ip = h;
6.          this.h = h;
7.      }
8.      public void reset()
9.      {   ip = h;
10.     }
11.     public boolean hasNext()
12.     {   if(ip.next == null)
13.             return false;
14.         else
15.             return true;
16.     }
17.     public Listing2 next()
18.     {   ip = ip.next;
19.         return ip.l.deepCopy();
20.     }
21.     public void set(Listing2 newListing)
22.     {   ip.l = newListing.deepCopy();
23.     } // end of method set
24. } // end of the class SllIterator;
```

Figure 4.39   The External Iterator Class, SllIterator

Some subtle, but important changes have been made to the code of all three classes to make them syntactically correct.

To begin with, Lines 12 and 19 of Figure 4.39 and Lines 5 and 6 of Figure 4.40 (among several others), will not compile since the variables next and l are declared in the class NewNode, which has been separated from the other two classes. The solution to this problem is to change the access modifier of the variables next and l from **private** (see Lines 60 and 61 of Figure 4.34) to *package*

```
1.   public class SllExternalIterator
2.   {  private NewNode h;
3.      public SllExternalIterator()
4.      {  h = new NewNode();
5.         h.next = null;
6.         h.l = null;
7.      }
8.      public boolean insert(Listing2 newListing)
9.      {  NewNode n = new NewNode();
10.        if(n == null) // out of memory
11.           return true;
12.        else
13.        {  n.l = newListing.deepCopy();
14.           n.next = h.next;
15.           h.next = n;
16.           return false;
17.        }
18.     } // end insert method
19.     public Listing2 fetch(String targetKey)
20.     {  NewNode p = h.next;
21.        while(p != null && p.l.compareTo(targetKey) != 0)
22.        {  p = p.next;
23.        }
24.        if(p == null)
25.           return null;
26.        else
27.        {  return p.l.deepCopy();
28.        }
29.     } // end of fetch
30.     public boolean delete(String targetKey)
31.     {  NewNode q = h;
32.        NewNode p = q.next;
33.        while(p != null && !targetKey.equals(p.l.getKey()))
34.        {  q = q.next;
35.           p = p.next;
36.        }
37.        if(p == null)
38.           return true;
39.        else
40.        {  q.next = p.next;
41.           return false;
42.        }
43.     } // end of delete method
44.     public boolean update(String targetKey, Listing2 newListing)
45.     {  if(delete(targetKey) == true)
46.           return true;
47.        else if(insert(newListing) == true)
48.           return true;
```

Figure 4.40 The Singly Linked List Class, SllExternalIterator, that Supports an External Iterator Class, SllIterator

```
49.         return false;
50.      } // end of update
51.      public void showAll()
52.      {  NewNode p = h.next;
53.         while(p != null)
54.         {  System.out.println(p.l); // automatically invokes the
                                        // toString method
55.            p = p.next;
56.         }
57.      } // end of showAll method
58.      public SllIterator iterator()
59.      {  return (new SllIterator(h));
60.      } // end of iterator method
61. } // end of class SllExternalIterator
```

Figure 4.40   (continued)

access. This is done by removing the keyword **private** from the declaration of these variables as shown on Lines 2 and 3 of the class NewNode (Figure 4.38), and placing all three classes in the same Java package (directory). A data member of a class with package access can be accessed from any other class defined in the package.

Separating the class definitions causes a second syntax problem. The list header, h, defined on Line 2 of Figure 4.40 is no longer accessible from the Iterator class (e.g., Line 5 of Figure 4.39). The solution to this problem is to add a method (typically) named iterator to the class SllExternalIterator (Lines 58–60 of Figure 4.40). This is the method the client will use to create the external iterator objects. For example, assuming the name of the client's singly linked list object is boston, in order to create two iterator objects (iterator1 and iterator2) the client would invoke the method iterator as shown below:

```
SllIterator iterator1, iterator2;
iterator1 = boston.iterator();
iterator2 = boston.iterator();
```

The method iterator then invokes the SllIterator class' constructor (Line 59 of Figure 4.40), passes it the contents of the singly linked list header, h, and returns the location of the newly created SllIterator object to the client. When the code of the SllInterator class constructor executes (Lines 4–7 of Figure 4.39), it stores the location of the singly linked list passed to it as the parameter h (Line 4 of Figure 4.39) not only in the variable, ip, but also in its own NewNode reference variable h (Line 6 of Figure 4.39), declared on Line 3 of Figure 4.39. This is the variable used by the reset method to reinitialize the iterator to the beginning of the list (Line 9 of Figure 4.39).

Figure 4.41 presents an application program that declares three (external) SllIterator references i1, i2, and i3 (Line 12), to operate on the data structure boston, an object in the class SllExternalIterator (Line 3). The iterators are "attached" to the structure boston on Lines 13–15. Iterator

```
1.  public class MainSllExternalIterator
2.  {  public static void main(String[] args)
3.      {  SllExternalIterator boston = new SllExternalIterator();
4.         String number;
5.         Listing2 l1 = new Listing2("Bill", "1st Avenue", "123 4567");
6.         Listing2 l2 = new Listing2("Al", "2nd Avenue", "456 3232");
7.         Listing2 l3 = new Listing2("Mike", "3rd Avenue", "333 3333");
8.         Listing2 aListing;
9.         boston.insert(l1);   // test insert
10.        boston.insert(l2);
11.        boston.insert(l3);
12.        SllIterator i1,i2,i3;
13.        i1 = boston.iterator();
14.        i2 = boston.iterator();
15.        i3 = boston.iterator();
16.      // output all the listings using iterator 1
17.        while(i1.hasNext())
18.        {  aListing = i1.next();
19.           System.out.println(aListing); // Java automatically invokes
                                          // the toString method;
20.        }
21.      // add an area code to all the listings using iterator 2
22.
23.        while(i2.hasNext())
24.        {  l1 = i2.next();
25.           number = l1.getNumber();
26.           number = "631" + number;
27.           l1.setNumber(number);
28.           i2.set(l1);
29.        }
30.      // output all the updated listings using iterator 3
31.
32.        while(i3.hasNext())
33.        {  System.out.println(i3.next());
34.        }
35.        System.exit(0);
36.    } // end of main method
37. } // end of class
```

Figure 4.41   An Application That Declares Its Own Iterators to Operate on a Singly Linked List

i1 is used on Lines 17–20 to traverse the linked list structure and output original data set. Iterator i2 is used on Lines 22–29 to traverse the structure and add the area code "631" to all the phone numbers, and finally iterator i3 is used on Lines 31–34 to traverse the structure and output the modified data set.

4.6 Java's `LinkedList` Class and `ListIterator` Interface

The Java class `LinkedList`, contained in the package `java.util`, is an unencapsulated generic implementation of a double-ended, doubly linked list structure. The structure does not support key field mode access, but rather is accessed in the node number mode or through the use of a client declared external iterator. The class contains methods to insert and fetch objects (`add` and `get`), to easily allow a `LinkedList` object to be used as a Stack or a Queue (`addFirst`, `getFirst`, `removeFirst`, `addLast`), and to attached a client defined iterator object to a `LinkedList` object. The class implements `ListIterator`, using techniques similar to those presented in Figures 4.39 and 4.40, providing methods for performing forward and backward traversals through a `LinkedList` object.

Table 4.3 presents a description of some of the methods in the class `LinkedList`, and Table 4.4 presents some of the methods specified in the `ListIterator` interface. Figure 4.42 presents a brief application program (and the output it produces) that demonstrates the use of the iterator methods `add`, `hasPrevious`, `previous`, and `next` to access and operate on a data structure named `dataBase`, a `LinkedList` object. The items inserted into the structure are objects in the class `Listing2` (Figure 4.35). The application also demonstrates the structure's lack of encapsulation.

Table 4.3

Some of the Methods in the Java API Class `LinkedList`

Basic Operation	Method Names	Example	Comments

Insert	add
	addLast
	addFirst
		myList.add(5, bill);
		myList.addFirst(bill);
		myList.addLast(bill);
			Inserts the object bill as the fifth, first, and last items, respectively, into the structure myList.

Fetch	get
	getFirst
	getLast
		myList.get(5);
		myList.getFirst();
		myList.addLast();
			Returns a shallow copy of the fifth, first, and last items, respectively, from the structure myList.

Delete	remove,
	removeFirst,
	removeLast
		myList.remove(5);
		mylist.removeFirst();
		mylist.removeLast();
			Deletes the fifth, first, and last items, respectively, from the structure myList.

Update	set	myList.set(5, tom)	Updates the fifth item in the structure myList to the object tom.
Attach a ListIterator object	listIterator	ListIterator i = myList.listIterator()	Iterator i is positioned at the first item in the structure myList.

Table 4.4

Some of the Methods in the Java API Interface `ListIterator`

Basic Operation	Method Names	Example	Comments
Insert	`add`	`i.add(bill);`	Inserts the object `bill` into the structure at the current iterator position and moves the iterator forward.
Fetch	`next,` `previous`	`i.next();` `i.previous();`	Moves the iterator one position forward or backward (respectively) in the structure, and returns a shallow copy of the object at that position.
Delete	`remove`	`i.remove();`	Deletes the object at the current iterator position from the structure.
Update	`set`	`i.set(5, tom);`	Updates the item at the current iterator in the structure to the object `tom`.
Testing	`hasNext,` `hasPrevious`	`i.hasNext();` `i.hasPrevious();`	Returns **true** if the iterator is not at the last or first objects (respectively) in the structure.

```
1.   import java.util.*;
2.   public class MainAPILinkedListAndIteratorClasses
3.   {  public static void main(String args[])
4.      {  LinkedList dataBase = new LinkedList();
5.         Listing2 b;
6.         Listing2 a;
7.         Listing2 bill = new Listing2("Bill", "1st Avenue", "123 4567");
8.         Listing2 al = new Listing2("Al", "2nd Avenue", "456 3232");
9.         // declare a ListIterator attached to the structure database
10.        ListIterator i = dataBase.listIterator();
11.
```

Figure 4.42 An Application that Demonstrates the use of the Java API class `LinkedList` and the `ListIterator` Interface Methods

```
12.        // add two phone listings to the data set
13.        i.add(bill);
14.        i.add(al);
15.
16.        // return the iterator to the front of the list
17.        while(i.hasPrevious())
18.            i.previous();
19.
20.        // fetch back the two listings and output them
21.        a = (Listing2) i.next();
22.        b = (Listing2) i.next();
23.        System.out.println(a);
24.        System.out.println(b);
25.
26.        // demonstrate the structure is un-encapsulated
27.        // change Bill's phone number to 999 9999
28.        bill.setNumber("999 9999");
29.        // return the iterator to the front of the list
30.        while(i.hasPrevious())
31.            i.previous();
32.        // fetch and output Bill's listing from the structure
33.        a = (Listing2) i.next();
34.        System.out.println(a);
35.    } // end of main method
36. } // end of class MainAPILinkedListAndIteratorClasses
```

Program output:

Name is Bill
Address is 1st Avenue
Number is 123 4567

Name is Al
Address is 2nd Avenue
Number is 456 3232

Name is Bill
Address is 1st Avenue
Number is 999 9999

Figure 4.42   (continued)

Knowledge Exercises

1. What is one advantage of a linked list structure over array-based structures?

2. What is one advantage of array-based structures over a linked list structure?

3. Explain the term "fragmented memory."

4. What is "dynamic" about dynamic data structures?

5. What is the only condition that would cause the Insert operation of a dynamic data structure to return a "data structure full" error?

6. There are many types of linked lists; however, the nodes in all of them have one thing in common. What is it?

7. The last node in a singly linked list, by definition, does not store the *address* of another node. Instead, what does it store?

8. All singly linked lists contain a reference variable called a "list header". What is sorted in it?

9. What is the advantage of implementing a stack using a singly linked list?

10. A data set consisting of four information nodes A, X, P, and C, is stored in a singly linked list. A field in each node named next is used to "link" them together. The memory locations of the nodes are: 200, 30, 500, and 60, respectively. The memory cell h is the list header. The nodes are to be stored in alphabetic order in the linked list.

    a) Draw a picture, similar to Figure 4.2a, showing the relative position of the nodes in main memory.

    b) Add arrows to the picture drawn in part (a) to show the ordering of the nodes starting at the list header (see Figure 4.3).

    c) Give the contents of the list header.

    d) Give the contents of the next field of each node.

    e) Draw the standard depiction (see Figure 4.4) of the four nodes in the linked list.

    f) Add the node locations to your answer to part (e), as shown in Figure 4.5.

    g) Assuming a field named back, was added to each node to order them in reverse alphabetic order, give the contents of this field for each node.

11. Draw the implementation level depiction (see Figure 4.9) of the nodes described in the previous example. (Make up the memory location of the dummy node and the locations of the other linked nodes that are used to implement the structure.)

12. Figure 4.10 depicts an initialized singly linked list. Verify that the singly linked list Insert algorithm is correct when it is used to add a new Listing to an *empty* singly linked list.

13. Suppose that when a node is added to a singly linked list, it becomes the new *last* node. Assuming the list header is named h, and the link field is named next, give the pseudocode algorithm for this approach to the Insert algorithm.

14. Give the dominant term in the speed function of the Insert algorithm described in the previous exercise.

15. The reference variable p references a node in the middle of a long singly linked list, and q points to the node just before the node that p references.

   a) Give the standard graphical representation of the list including the reference variables p and q.

   b) Modify the graphic to show the deletion of both the node p points to and the node that follows it.

   c) Give the pseudocode to accomplish the deletion of the two nodes.

16. Two linked lists, L1 and L2, are pointed to by the lists headers h1 and h2 respectively. A reference variable, p, stores the address of a node in list L1. The entire list L2, is to be inserted into list L1 just after the node referenced by p.

   a) Give the standard graphical representation (Figure 4.4) of the two lists. Include the reference variable, p.

   b) Modify the graphic to show the steps necessary to accomplish the insertion of the list L2 into the list L1.

   c) Give the pseudocode to accomplish the insertion of the list L2.

17. For the two linked lists described in the previous example, give an algorithm to "shuffle" the two linked lists into one linked list. After the shuffle operation the odd nodes (i.e., the first, third, fifth, etc.) will be the nodes from L1, and the even nodes (i.e., the second, fourth, sixth, etc.) will be the nodes from L2. (Hint: develop the algorithm graphically and then translate it to pseudocode.)

18. Give the pseudocode of the four basic operation algorithms of a *sorted* singly linked list. (Hint: develop the algorithm graphically and then translate it to pseudocode.)

19. Give the speed functions of the four basic operations for a *sorted* singly linked list and the average operation speed (assume all operations are equally probable).

20. Give the ratio of the average speed of an Unsorted-Optimized array structure to the average speed of a SinglyLinkedList structure, assuming each structure contains one million information nodes and all operations are equally probable.

21. Describe the garbage collection method for the SinglyLinkedList structure, and give the line number of the code presented in Figure 4.15 that accomplishes (i.e., actually initiates) the "garbage collection."

22. A SinglyLinkedList structure is used to store a data set. Calculate its density if:

   a) Each of the client's information nodes contains 8 bytes of information, and there are 50 nodes in the data set.

   b) Each of the client's information nodes contain 200 bytes of information, and there are one million nodes in the data set.

EXERCISES

23. Give a plot showing the variation in density with the number of nodes, n, stored in a Singly-LinkedList structure. Assume each node contains 10 information bytes and that the range of n is $2 \leq n \leq 100$.

24. Give an example of when it would be more efficient to use an iterator to access the nodes in a singly linked list.

Programming Exercises

25. A database is to be developed to keep track of student information at your college. It will include their names, identification numbers, and grade point averages. The data set will be accessed in the key field mode, with the student's name being the key field. Code a class named Listing that defines the nodes. Your class should include all the methods in the class shown in Figure 2.28. Test it with a progressively developed driver program that demonstrates the functionality of all of its methods.

26. Using the generic capabilities of Java 5.0, modify the implementation of the structure SinglyLinkedList presented in Figure 4.15 to make it fully generic. Include a driver program that demonstrates the functionality of the class with two homogeneous SinglyLinkedList objects that store two different kinds of nodes.

27. Code an application program that keeps track of student information at your college (see Exercise 25). Include their names, identification numbers, and grade point averages in a fully encapsulated, homogeneous singly linked list. When launched, the user will be asked to input the initial number of students and the initial data set. Once this is complete, the user will be presented with the following menu:

Enter: 1 to *insert* a new student's information,

2 to *fetch* and output a student's information,

3 to *delete* a student's information,

4 to *update* a student's information,

5 to *output* all the student information, and

6 to *exit* the program.

The program should perform an unlimited number of operations until the user enters a 6 to exit the program. If the user requests an operation on a node not in the structure, the program output should be "node not in structure." Otherwise, the message "operation complete" should be output.

28. Code a class that implements a homogeneous stack structure using a singly linked list. The Push operation will insert a node at the front of the linked list, and the Pop operation will fetch and delete the node at the front of the linked list. Include a progressively developed driver program to demonstrate the functionality of the Push and Pop operations.

29. Code an application program that keeps track of student information at your college. Include their names, identification numbers, and grade point averages in a fully encapsulated, homogeneous *sorted* singly linked list structure. When launched, the user will be asked to input the initial number of students and the initial data set. Once this is complete, the user will be presented with the following menu:

Enter: 1 to *insert* a new student's information,

2 to *fetch* and output a student's information,

3 to *delete* a student's information,

4 to *update* a student's information,

5 to *output* all the student information in sorted order, and

6 to *exit* the program.

The program should perform an unlimited number of operations until the user enters a 6 to exit the program. If the user requests an operation on a node not in the structure, the program output should be "node not in structure." Otherwise, the message "operation complete" should be output.

30. Redo the application described in the previous exercise using a doubly linked list to store the nodes. Add a seventh user option to output all the nodes in descending order.

31. Implement the dynamic version of a stack illustrated in Figures 4.24–4.26 using the class `SinglyLinkedList` presented in Figure 4.15. Provide a driver program that demonstrates that the Push and Pop operations function properly.

32. Code a class named `SLLQueue` that uses a double-ended singly linked list to implement a Queue as described in this chapter. Provide a driver program that demonstrates the constructor, `enqueue`, and `dequeue` methods function properly.

33. Redo Exercise 27, but this time use the Java API class `LinkedList` to store the nodes. The list should be accessed in the node number mode. Add a seventh option to the class to increase all the student GPA's by a given amount using an iterator object.

34. Code a GIU program that visually demonstrates the changes that take place to the linked nodes, and the other data members, that make up a `SinglyLinkedList` object when each of the four basic operations are performed. When the program is launched, the linked list should be shown in its initialized state. Six buttons should be available to the user: one for each of the four basic operations, a "reinitialize" button, and a "quit" button. Text boxes should be provided to permit the user to enter a node's information prior to an Insert or Update operation, and to display the results of a Fetch operation.

CHAPTER 5

Hashed Data Structures

OBJECTIVES

The objectives of this chapter are to familiarize the student with the features, uses, and implementation of hashing and hashed data structures, and to understand how to convert these data structures to generic implementations. More specifically, the student will be able to

- Explain the advantages and disadvantages of hashed structures and be able to quantify their performance.

- Understand the various memory models programmers use to represent static and dynamic hashed structures, and understand the advantages and disadvantages of these representations.

- Understand the role of key preprocessing algorithms, hashing functions, and collision algorithms in hashed data structures and be familiar with the features of these that lead to good performance.

- Understand basic numeric and alphanumeric key preprocessing algorithms, hashing functions, and collision algorithms and be able to implement them.

- Implement a fully encapsulated perfect hashed structure accessed in the key field mode, and be able to understand and quantify its performance.

- Implement a fully encapsulated nonperfect hashed structure accessed in the key field mode, and be able to understand and quantify its performance.

- Convert a hashed data structure to a generic implementation, and understand the role of the Java `hashCode` method in this conversion.

- Develop an application whose data structure is an object in Java's API `HashTable` class, understand the advantages and disadvantages of the class, and operate on the structure using the class's operation methods.

- Understand the techniques used to dynamically expand a hashed structure at run-time, and the performance of dynamic hashed structures.

5.1   Hashed Data Structures

Each of the data structures we have studied so far—array-based structures, restricted structures (Stacks and Queues), and linked lists—have strengths and weaknesses. All of these structures have high densities. Restricted structures are fast, but they do not support access in the key field mode. The array-based and linked list structures do offer access in the key field mode, but are slow because they use a sequential search to locate a node.

Hashing is an alternate search technique (more accurately a set of techniques) for locating a node in the key field mode. Unlike the Sequential Search algorithm, hashing algorithms are fast. When you want speed, think hashing. Because of their ability to rapidly locate a node, data structures that use hashing access algorithms are in wide use.

In this chapter we will study several hashing algorithms and the data structures that use them. These data structures, called hashed data structures, vary in speed. However, when properly implemented, all of them are faster than the structures we have studied thus far.

There is a down side to hashed structures. For some applications, their overhead can be very high. However, there are many applications where the overhead of even the fastest hashed structure approaches zero. With their guarantee of speed and the possibility of low overhead, hashed data structures should always be considered in our designs.

5.2   Hashing Access Algorithms

Hashing access algorithms are a collection of algorithms that share a common characteristic: the given key is used to *compute* an index or a location into a *primary* storage area. Since the primary storage area is a group of sequentially numbered storage cells, it is normally implemented as an array. Sometimes the nodes themselves are stored in the primary storage area at the computed location (see Figure 5.1a), and sometimes *paths* to the nodes are stored there. The paths, stored in

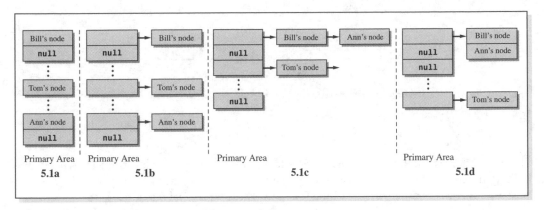

Figure 5.1 Four Uses of the Primary Storage Area

the primary storage area array, can be a reference variable that stores a node's location (see Figure 5.1**b**), the beginning of a linked list that contains nodes (see Figure 5.1**c**), or the location of a secondary array that stores a group of nodes (see Figure 5.1**d**).[1]

This ability to compute an index into the primary storage area from the given key is what gives hashing access algorithms their speed because computations are performed rapidly by modern CPU's. In contrast, sequential access algorithms perform time-consuming memory accesses to fetch keys from the data structure in order to compare them to a given key. Memory accesses are slow, computations are fast; thus, sequential algorithms are slow, hashing algorithms are fast.

The computation of the index into the primary storage area is performed using a mathematical function, h, that uses the given key as the independent variable. This function, called the *hashing access function*, is expressed as:

$$i_p = h(k)$$

where: i_p is the index (in Java, an integer greater than or equal to zero) into the primary storage area,

  h is the hashing (or mapping) function of a particular hashing access algorithm, and
  k is the contents of the key field of the node being accessed.

Figure 5.2 illustrates the *hashing process* used to determine a primary storage index.

---

[1]Of the four schemes depicted in Figure 5.1 only the middle two can be implemented in Java.

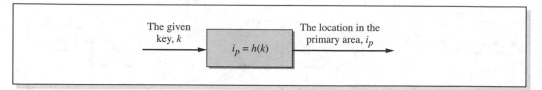

Figure 5.2 The Hashing Process

The function, h, is said to *hash* or *map* a key into a primary storage area location. There are many hashing functions. Two of the most simplistic functions used for numeric keys are the *Division* Hashing function and the *Direct* Hashing function. These functional relationships are:

$$i_p = h(k) = k \bmod N = k \% N \qquad \text{Division Hashing function}$$
$$i_p = h(k) = k \qquad\qquad\qquad\quad \text{Direct Hashing function}$$

where: N is the number of storage locations allocated to the primary storage area

      k is the given key.

Comparing the two hashing functions, the Division function uses the division *remainder* as the primary index, while the Direct Hashing function uses the key as the primary index. The number of storage locations allocated to the primary storage area, N, should not be confused with the maximum number of nodes that will be stored in the structure, n_{max}. There are times when they are equal, but most often they are not. In hashing jargon, the ratio n_{max}/N is referred to as the maximum *loading factor*.

If the key is negative or non-numeric (e.g., -36 or "Jones") then some form of *preprocessing* is performed on the key to convert it to a numeric, non-negative value called a *pseudo* key and then the pseudo key, pk, is used as the independent variable in the hashing function. Figure 5.3 illustrates the expanded process of converting a key to a primary storage area location when preprocessing is required.

Preprocessing algorithms, and other motivations for using them, will be discussed in subsequent sections of this chapter.

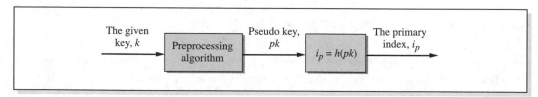

Figure 5.3 The Hashing Process with Preprocessing

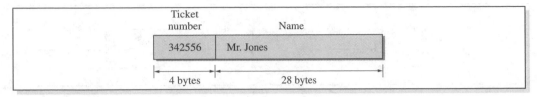

Figure 5.4 A Stadium Ticket Database Node

Table 5.1

Comparison of the Division and Direct Hashing Algorithms

Ticket Number (Key Value)	Calculated Location Using the Two Access Algorithms	
	Division Algorithm ($N = 10{,}054$)	Direct Algorithm
342556	720	342,556
000000	0	0
999999	4463	999,999
211854	720	211,854

5.2.1 A Hashing Example

To illustrate the use of the Division and Direct Hashing algorithms, we will consider a stadium ticket database that will store the ticket number (key field) and the purchaser's name for an event to be held in a 10,054 seat stadium. The ticket number is a six digit encoding of the seat number, the event number, and the event date in the range 000000 to 999999. Figure 5.4 depicts a typical node and the information for ticket number 342556.

For this example, we will assume that all 10,054 tickets will be stored in the data structure, and that there will be 10,054 storage locations (one per ticket) allocated to the primary storage area for the division algorithm ($N = 10{,}054$). Under these assumptions, the index computed for ticket number 342556 by our two hashing functions is:

$i_p = h(k) = k \% N = 342{,}556 \% 10{,}054 = 720$ Division Hashing function

$i_p = h(k) = k = 342{,}556$ Direct Hashing function

These indices and the indices computed for several other ticket numbers are tabulated in Table 5.1. The ticket numbers presented in this table were selected to illustrate two issues that arise when using these two access algorithms. The first issue is the Division algorithm's inability to map keys into unique indices, and the second issue is the potential of high overhead associated with the

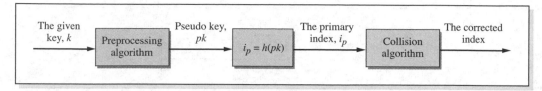

Figure 5.5   The Hashing Process with Preprocessing and Collision Resolution

Direct Hashing algorithm. We will first turn our attention to the problem of nonunique indices associated with the Division algorithm.

As shown on rows 1 and 4 of Table 5.1, the Division algorithm maps the keys 342556 and 211854 into the same index, 720 (342,556 % 10,054 = 720 and 211,854 % 10,054 = 720). The mapping of two keys into the same index is called a *collision*, and the resolution of a collision is left to another collection of algorithms called (you guessed it) *collision algorithms*. Unfortunately, collision algorithms reduce the speed of access since they require another processing step usually involving multiple memory accesses. Figure 5.5 illustrates the inclusion of a collision algorithm into the process of converting a key to a primary storage area location.

There is a class of hashing algorithms, called *perfect hashing* algorithms that map every key into a unique primary storage area index. This unique mapping means that collisions cannot occur, and therefore structures that use perfect hashing algorithms do not include collision algorithms. As a result, they perform better from a speed viewpoint. Our Direct Hashing function is an example of a perfect hashing algorithm since a unique ticket number becomes the unique index.

However, all that glitters is not gold. As shown in the third column of Table 5.1, the information for the lowest and highest ticket numbers, 000000 and 999999, are stored in primary storage locations 0 and 999,999 respectively. Therefore, we would have to allocate 1,000,000 locations to the primary storage area even though only 10,054 of them (one for each seat in the stadium) would be used. The maximum loading factor would be low (0.01 = 10,054 / 1,000,000), which is indicative of a low density structure. In contrast, the Division algorithm can only generate indices in the range 0 to $N - 1$ (the range of the remainder when dividing by N), and since N was chosen to be the number of tickets, its memory requirements are much more modest.

If properly designed, however, the maximum loading factors of perfect hashing functions for *some* applications can approach a value of one. A perfect hashing function that minimizes the unused portions of the primary storage area is called a *minimum* perfect hashing function. Unfortunately, designing a hashing function that even approaches a minimal function is not a simple process. Aside from the complexity of their design, a minimal hashing function is usually tied to a particular application, requires that the designer know the particular subset of the application's keys that will be stored in the data structure, and is valid only for that subset of keys. For example, to design a minimal perfect hashing function for our stadium application we would have to know the subset of ticket numbers that correspond to the 10,054 tickets for a particular event number and date. Once designed, the hashing function would only be valid for that (*static*) set of ticket numbers and, therefore, it could not be used for other events.

These restrictions limit the use of perfect hashing functions and a further discussion of their design process is, with one exception, beyond the scope of this book. The exception is a set of applications where perfect hashing can be easily applied because the Direct Hashing function can be used *without* producing low densities; these applications share common characteristics which make the Direct Hashing algorithm approach a minimal perfect hashing algorithm. In the next section, we examine the features of the applications that make this possible and develop a *perfect hashed* data structure based on the Direct Hashing algorithm. The data structures discussed in the remainder of this chapter will utilize *nonperfect* hashing algorithms.

5.3　Perfect Hashed Data Structures

Before we examine the features of an application that make the Direct Hashing algorithm approach a minimal hashing algorithm, we will formally state the definition of a perfect hashing function. Consistent with our previous discussions, we can define a perfect hashing function as:

Perfect Hashing Function

A perfect hashing function is a function that maps each key, in a *static* set of keys, into a *unique* index in the primary storage area.

A *static set of keys* is the subset of all possible values of the key for which the function is valid. For example, if the keys were comprised of letters, a static set of keys would be the keys "Bob," "Mary," "Alice," and "Tim" and the hashing function would be designed to process only these four keys. As a result, there would be no guarantee that the function would produce a valid index when processing a key outside of the predefined subset (e.g., "Harry").

By *unique index* we mean that each location in the primary storage area is dedicated to a particular value of the key. No other key is mapped into that location by the hashing function. When preprocessing is used, the combination of the preprocessing algorithm and hashing function must produce a unique index for each key. The unique mapping eliminates the occurrence of collisions, which degrade the speed performance of hashed data structures. As a result, hashed data structures based on perfect hashing algorithms, which we will refer to as *perfect hashed structures*, are the fastest of all the data structures we will study.

To identify the feature of an application that permits the Direct Hashing function to approach a minimal perfect hashing function we will revisit the use of this algorithm in our stadium ticket database example. The reason the loading factor was low for that application was that there were 1,000,000 possible ticket numbers (key values) and a place in the primary storage area had to be provided for each of them, even though only 10,054 of these keys would actually by stored. Now consider the case where the 10,054 ticket numbers no longer include an encoding of the event number and date. In this case, the ticket numbers can be the seat numbers and there are only 10,054 possible key values; meaning, we only need to allocate 10,054 locations in the primary storage area, all of which will be used. Thus, an application's feature that permits the Direct Hashing function to approach a minimal perfect hashing function is:

> **Condition Under Which the Direct Hashing Function Approaches a Minimal Perfect Hashing Function**
>
> Of the set of all possible key values, most (or all) of them will be stored in the structure.

Even when conditions are such that a moderate percentage of all possible keys will be represented in the data structure, a Direct Hashing algorithm-based structure can produce acceptable densities. For example, when only half the keys are represented, a density greater than 0.8 is achieved as long as the node width is greater than 32 bytes. One caveat is in order: when the keys are non-numeric, the percentage of the possible key values represented in the structure is usually too low to produce acceptable densities.

We will now develop a data structure based on the Direct Hashing function.

5.3.1 Direct Hashed Structure

Before developing the operation algorithms for this structure, we will discuss a numeric key preprocessing algorithm commonly used with this structure to process numeric keys. We will not discuss a string key preprocessing algorithm because string preprocessing for perfect hashing schemes that produce acceptable densities is highly application specific and beyond the scope of this book.

The Subtraction Preprocessing Algorithm

In a numeric key application when the minimum key value (k_{min}) is nonzero, a subtraction preprocessing algorithm is used to compute a pseudo key. As shown in Figure 5.3, the calculated pseudo key is then used in the Direct Hashing algorithm. This prevents the Direct Hashing algorithm from generating negative indices when the minimum key is negative, and improves the density when the minimum key is positive. In the latter case, without preprocessing, the minimum index generated by the direct hashing algorithm would be k_{min}, and the low area of primary storage (indices 0 to $k_{min} - 1$) would be unused. The Subtraction Preprocessing algorithm is:

Table 5.2

Pseudo Keys Calculated using the Subtraction Algorithm

	Minimum Key = −3		Minimum Key = 112	
	The Given Key, k, (The Index Without Preprocessing)	The Index With Preprocessing $pk = k - k_{min} = k - (-3)$	The Given Key, k, (The Index Without Preprocessing)	The Index With Preprocessing $pk = k - k_{min} = k - 112$
	−3	0	112	0
	−2	1	113	1
	−1	2	114	2
	0	3	115	3
	1	4	116	4
	2	5	117	5

Subtraction Preprocessing Algorithm

$$pk = k - k_{min}$$

where:

   pk is the calculated pseudo key,

   k is the given key that can assume negative values, and

   k_{min} is the minimum value the key can assume.

Table 5.2 illustrates the use of the algorithm for minimum key values of −3 and 112, which prevents a negative index from being produced by the Direct Hashing function.

Primary Storage Area

As mentioned in Section 5.2, the primary storage area is normally implemented as an array, but, we must decide what will be stored in the array. We have two choices in Java: Each element of the primary storage array can store a reference to a single node (just as they did in the Unsorted-Optimized array structure discussed in Chapter 2), or each element can store a *path* to a group of nodes (see Figures 5.1c and d). We will use the first option: each element of the array will store a reference to a single node, because it is simpler. The second option will be discussed later in the chapter.

When an array of references is created in Java, each element is initialized to **null**. Realizing this, we will use a **null** element to indicate that the node whose key maps into the element is not in the structure. Figure 5.6 shows the primary storage area in its initialized state.

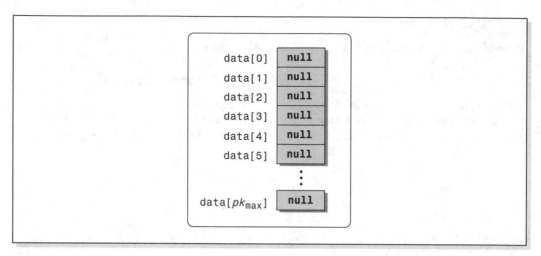

Figure 5.6 Primary Storage Area in its Initialized State

Operation Algorithms

Having decided on what will be stored in the array and the condition for a nonexistent node, we can now examine the basic operation algorithms. The four basic operation algorithms for our perfect hashed structure all begin the same way. We use the Direct Hashing function, preceded by a preprocessing algorithm when necessary, to determine the index into the primary storage area, i_p. Then, using this element of the array as the reference to the node, we perform the operation on the node.

To insert a node into the structure, we deep copy the node into a newly created node, and store a reference to the new node in element i_p of the primary storage array. Assuming the name of the primary storage array is data, that the node to be inserted is referenced by newNode, and its key is targetKey, the pseudocode of the Inset algorithm is:

Direct Hashed Insert Algorithm

```
1. // access the primary storage area
2. pseudoKey = preProcessing(targetKey);
3. ip = pseudoKey;    // direct hashing function
4. // insert the new node
5. data[ip] = newNode.deepCopy();
```

This is an encapsulated Insert operation because the address of the newly created node is stored inside the data structure, not the address of the client's node. Figure 5.7 shows the structure after

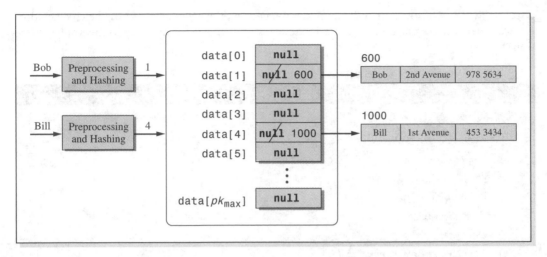

Figure 5.7 A Direct Hashed Structure after Bill's and Bob's Listings have Been Inserted

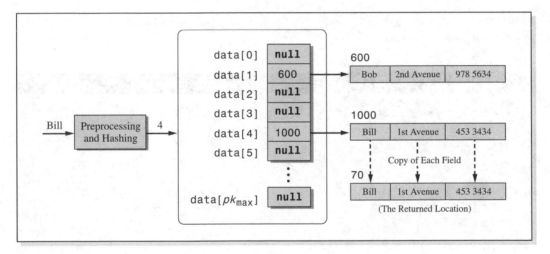

Figure 5.8 The Process of Fetching Bill's Listing

two telephone listing nodes have been added to the structure. It assumes that the preprocessing and hashing algorithms map the keys "Bill" and "Bob" into indices 4 and 1 respectively.

The Fetch operation returns a deep copy of the requested node or a **null** value if the requested node is not in the structure. Returning a deep copy hides the address of the listing stored inside the data structure from the client and thus maintains the structure's encapsulation. Figure 5.8 illustrates the process of fetching Bill's listing. Assuming the name of the primary storage array is data, that the key of the node to be deleted is targetKey, the pseudocode of the Fetch algorithm (which defers the language-specific checking for insufficient system memory to the implementation) is:

The Direct Hashed Fetch Algorithm

1. // access the primary area
2. pseudoKey = preProcessing(targetKey);
3. i_p = pseudoKey; // direct hashing function
4. //return a copy of the node or a **null** reference
5. **if**(data[i_p] == **null**)
6. { return **null**; }
7. **else**
8. { **return** data[i_p].deepCopy(); }

To perform a Delete operation, we simply set element: data[ip] to **null**. The pseudocode of the Delete algorithm is:

The Direct Hashed Delete Algorithm

1. // access the primary area
2. pseudoKey = preProcessing(targetKey);
3. i_p = pseudoKey; // direct hashing function
4. // delete the node
5. **if**(data[i_p] == **null**)
6. { **return false**; }
7. **else**
8. { data[i_p]= **null**;
9.   return **true**; }

Figure 5.9 shows the data structure after Bob's listing is deleted, but before the deleted node's storage is collected by Java's run-time memory manager.

As we have done with previously studied data structures, for the purposes of brevity, we will use the Delete and Insert operations in the Update algorithm. Assuming that the node with the key field targetKey is to be updated to the contents of the node newNode, the pseudocode of the Update algorithm (which defers the language-specific checking for insufficient system memory to the implementation) is:

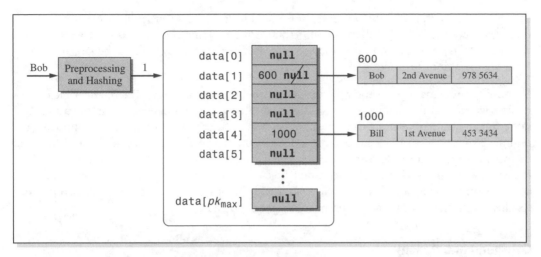

Figure 5.9   Data Structure after Bob's Listing is Deleted

The Direct Hashed Update Algorithm

1. **if** (delete(targetKey) == **false**) // node not in the structure
2.   **return false**;
3. **else**
4. { insert(newNode);
5.   **return true**; }

Performance

We will now examine the performance of the Direct Hashed data structure, by examining the speed of the basic operation pseudocode, and the amount of overhead memory required to implement this code.

Speed of the Structure

To analyze the speed of the structure, we will perform a Big-O analysis to bound the number of memory access instructions executed as n, the number of nodes stored in the structure, gets large. We will assume that an optimizing compiler will use a CPU register to store a memory cell's value after the first time it is accessed.

Looking at the Insert, Fetch, and Delete algorithms, Line 2 of each algorithm invokes the preprocessing algorithm. The number of instructions executed in this algorithm is not a function of the number of nodes in the structure, and an optimizing compiler would store most of the code's variables in CPU registers. The one exception would be if the keys were non-numeric, which is a case we are not considering. When our Subtraction Preprocessing algorithm is used, a total of two memory accesses is required to preprocess a key; one memory access to fetch the key, and one to fetch the maximum key value.

Examining the remainder of the pseudocode instructions in the Insert, Fetch, and Delete algorithms, we see that the number of instructions executed is also not dependent on the number of nodes in the structure. Rather, the algorithms perform one access into the primary storage array on Line 5 of each algorithm to access data[i], and the Delete algorithm performs an additional memory access on Line 8 to overwrite data[i]. Therefore, a total of one memory access is performed during an Insert or Fetch operation (three with preprocessing), and two memory accesses are performed during a Delete operation (four with preprocessing). Thus the speed complexity for these operations, including the preprocessing term, is $O(1)$.

Overhead and Density

Certainly, the speed of this structure is very good news. Let us now turn our attention to the overhead and density of the structure. As we have previously discussed, this could be very high or very low depending on the application. The source of the overhead for this structure is the same as that of the array-based structures. It is the array of reference variables, the primary storage area array. Unlike the array-based structures however, where the array was sized to the maximum number of nodes that would be stored in the structure at one time, the Direct Hashed structure's array is sized to the maximum value of the key (or pseudo key when preprocessing is performed). Thus, the overhead can become significant if the number of nodes that will be stored in the structure is small compared to the size of the set of all possible keys.

The density of any data structure, D, is defined as:

$$D = \text{information bytes} / \text{total bytes},$$

with:

$$\text{total bytes} = \text{information bytes} + \text{overhead}.$$

Using the notation:

n is the number of nodes stored in the structure,
w is the width of a node, in bytes,
N is the number of elements in the primary storage array, and
w_a is the width of each element of the array, in bytes,

the information bytes and total bytes of the data structure becomes:

$$\text{information bytes} = n * \text{w, and}$$
$$\text{total bytes} = \text{information bytes} + \text{overhead} = n * \text{w} + N * w_a.$$

Thus, the density of our Direct Hashed structure, D_{dh}, becomes:

$$D_{dh} = \text{information bytes} / (\text{information bytes} + \text{overhead}) = (n * w) / (n * w + N * w_a)$$

Dividing the numerator and denominator of the right side of this equation by $n * w$ we obtain:

$$D_{dh} = [(n * w) / (n * w)] / [(n * w + N * w_a) / (n * w)] = 1 / (1 + N/n * w_a/w)$$

Examining the previous equation, we see that the density is dependent on two ratios:

- N / n, the ratio of the size of the array to the number of nodes stored in the structure, (the inverse of the loading factor).
- w_a / w, the ratio of the size of the array elements to the node width.

The term N / n (the inverse of the loading factor) in the denominator of this equation was not present in the density equation of the array-based structures, and the density of this structure is highly dependent on it (and thus the loading factor). When the loading factor is one, the density of this structure is the same as the density of the array-based structures and we have the best of both worlds: speed and high density.[2]

In Java, reference variables occupy 4 bytes, and so $w_a = 4$. Substituting this value for w_a in the above density equation and replacing N / n with the the reciprocal of the loading factor l, we obtain:

Density of a Direct Hashed Data Structure

$$D_{dh} = 1 / (1 + 4 / (l * w))$$

Where:

w is the width of a node, in bytes, and

l is the loading factor (n / N).

Figure 5.10 presents the variation in density with a loading factor for the Direct Hashed structure for various client node widths, w. Substituting a density of 0.8 into the density equation and solving for $w * l$, we see that a density of 0.8 or better is achieved when $w * l \geq 16$, or $w \geq 16/l$. Figure 5.11 presents the client node widths that result in a density of 0.8 or greater at various loading factors. This figure demonstrates that there is a there is a wide range of loading factors that produce good density as long as the client's nodes are wide enough.

Table 5.3 summarizes the performance of the Direct Hashed structure, and includes the performance of the previously studied structures for comparative purposes. Its speed is the fastest of all the data structures we have studied, or will study, and its density for some applications can be high. The implementation of this perfect hashed structure is left as an exercise for the student.

---

[2]Assuming the node width, w (as shown in Chapter 2), is greater than 16.

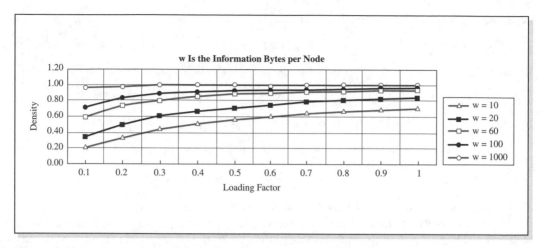

Figure 5.10   Density of the Direct Hashed Structure

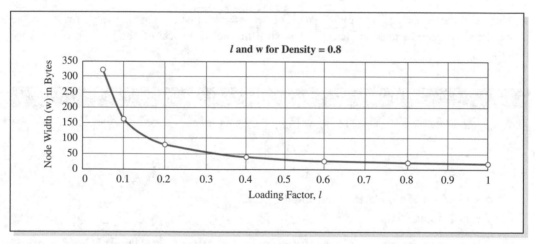

Figure 5.11   Node Widths and Loading Factors that Result in a Density of 0.8

5.4   Nonperfect Hashed Structures

When the conditions of an application require high speed but are such that perfect hashing cannot be used (e.g., the key set is not static, the density would be too low, or an efficient perfect hashing function cannot be discovered), a hashed structure based on a nonperfect hashing algorithm provides the next fastest alternative. These structures, which we will refer to simply as *hashed structures*, do *not* provide a unique location in the primary storage area for every allowable value of the key. As a result, two or more keys can map into the same primary storage index. When this

Table 5.3

Performance of the Direct Hashed Data Structure (w is the node width, l is the loading factor)

| Data Structure | Operation Speed (in memory accesses) | | | | | | Condition for Density > 0.8 |
	Insert	Delete	Fetch	Update = Delete + Insert	Average[3]	Big-O Average	Average for $n = 10^7$	
Unsorted-Optimized Array	3	$\leq n$	$\leq n$	$\leq n + 3$	$\leq (3n + 6)/4$	$O(n)$	$\leq 0.75 \times 10^7 + 1.5$	$w > 16$
Stack and Queue	5	combined with Fetch	4.5	not supported	$9.5/2 = 5$	$O(1)$	5	$w > 16$
Singly Linked List	6	$1.5n$	$1.5n$	$1.5n + 6$	$(4.5n + 12)/4 = 1.13n + 3$	$O(n)$	$1.13 \times 10^7 + 3$	$w > 33$
Direct Hashed (with Subtraction Pre-processing)	1 or (3)	2 or (4)	1 or (3)	3 or (7)	$7/4 = 1.75$ or $(17/4 = 4.25)$	$O(1)$	1.75 or (4.25)	$w * l > 16$

[3]Assumes all operations are equally probable and is therefore calculated as an arithmetic average of the four operation times.

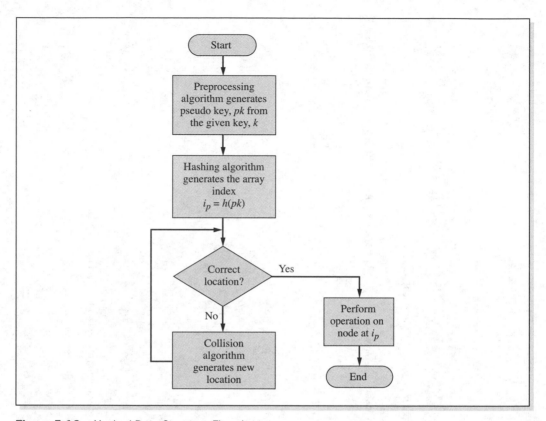

Figure 5.12 Hashed Data Structure Flowchart

happens, we say that a collision has occurred and so the mapping process must be expanded (as depicted in Figure 5.5) to include a collision resolution algorithm.

There are many collision algorithms, preprocessing algorithms, and hashing functions used by hashed data structures to determine the primary storage area location for a given key. Regardless of the particular algorithms used, they are generally executed as shown in Figure 5.12. If the array index generated by the preprocessing and hashing algorithms result in a collision, a collision algorithm is repeatedly executed (see bottom of Figure 5.12) until a correct location (which, in the case of the Insert operation, is an unused location) is found.

For example, suppose that Bill's listing was to be inserted into a hashed data structure that already contained Bob's listing referenced by element 1 of the primary storage array. Let us assume, as shown on the left side of Figure 5.13a, that the key "Bill" is preprocessed and hashed into index 4, and that element 4 of the primary storage array was unused. Bill's listing would then be stored in the structure referenced by element 4 (see Figure 5.13a).

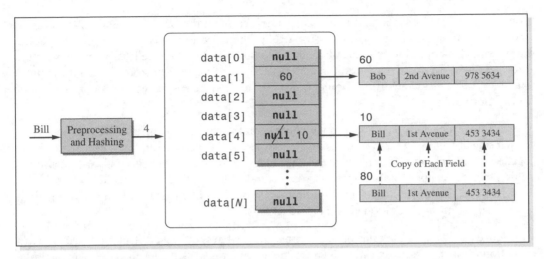

Figure 5.13a   Inserting Bill's Information

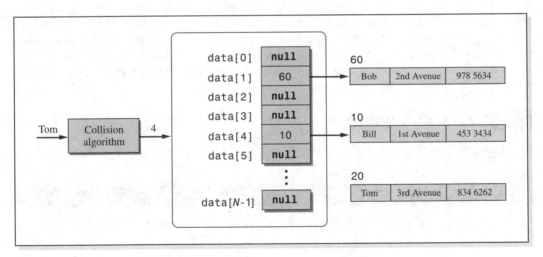

Figure 5.13b   The First Unsuccessful Attempt to Insert Tom's Information

Now suppose that Tom's listing is to be inserted next and that the key "Tom" is also preprocessed and hashed into index 4 (see Figure 5.13**b**). A collision has occurred. We cannot reference Tom's listing with element 4 since it is already pointing to Bill's listing. Technically speaking, when Bill's information is inserted first, index 4 is no longer the correct place to store Tom's information. Therefore, the collision algorithm would be executed to determine a correct (unused) location for Tom's information.

Where Tom's information will be inserted depends on the collision algorithm used. As shown on the left side of Figure 5.13**c**, some collision algorithms use the incorrect index to generate the next location to be considered. It is possible that the index produced by the collision algorithm also has some other node stored in that element (see Figure 5.13**c**). In this case, this new index is also incorrect, and the collision algorithm continues to execute until a correct, or unused, element of the primary storage area is located (see Figure 5.13**d**).

Continued execution of the collision algorithm is the weakness of hashed structures, because each execution of the collision algorithm involves memory accesses. Consider the case where half the nodes are accessed before a correct location is found. Then the speed of the algorithm, in Big-O notation, is O(n / 2). This is approximately the speed of the array-based and linked list structures we previously studied, and the speed advantage of hashed structures is lost.

Thus, it is important that the preprocessing, hashing, and collision algorithms of a hashed data structure be carefully chosen in order to minimize the number of collisions. Before studying three specific algorithms and the features that minimize collisions, we will examine the strategy used to size the primary storage area array for a hashed structure because the size of this array can also have an effect on the number of times the collision algorithm executes. This discussion will begin with a definition of the term *search length*.

5.4.1 Search Length

Search length, L, a parameter used to describe the speed of all data structures is defined as:

Search Length
The number of memory accesses required to locate the node.

As we have seen, perfect hashed data structures dedicate a unique location in the primary storage area for each allowable value of the key. There are no collisions, and thus the search length for perfect hashed structures is always one (one access into the primary storage area to fetch the location of the node).

For a hashed structure, when an operation is performed without a collision, the search length is also one. Most often, however, there are multiple collisions. Since the number of collisions varies from one operation to another, an average search length, L_{avg}, is used as a measure of the speed of

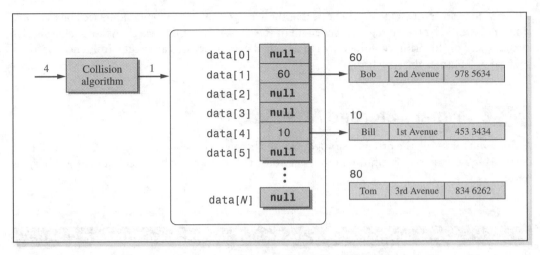

Figure 5.13c   The Second Unsuccessful Attempt to Insert Tom's Information

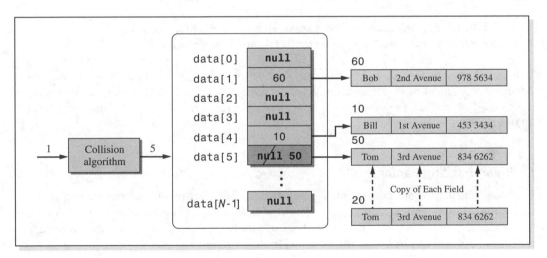

Figure 5.13d   The Successful Attempt to Insert Tom's Information

a hashed data structure. One would hope that the average search length would be well below $n/2$, since $n/2$ would be the average search length of the (slow) sequential search. As we shall now discuss, the size of the primary storage area of a hashed data structure can greatly influence the average search length of the structure.

5.4.2 Primary Storage Area Size

A guideline for sizing the primary storage area of a hashed data structure is that it be a small percentage higher than the maximum number of nodes that the structure will contain, n_{max}. Thus, we have:

Size of the Primary Storage Area, N, for a Hashed Structure
size of the primary storage area $= N = n_{max} + p * n_{max}$

where:

n_{max} is the maximum number of nodes to be stored in the structure, and
p is a percentage expressed in decimal form (i.e., for 10%, $p = 0.10$).

Usually, for reasons we will discuss shortly, a value of $p = 33\%$ results in optimum performance. Applying this guideline to our stadium ticket database problem in which 10,054 nodes are to be stored ($n_{max} = 10{,}054$), the size of the primary storage array would be 13,371 elements (10,054 + 10,054 * 0.33).

Optimum Loading Factor

For hashed structures we normally talk about two loading factors, the current loading factor, l, and the maximum loading factor l_{max}. The current loading factor is computed using the number of nodes currently in the structure, n, and the maximum loading factor is computed using the maximum number of nodes that will be stored in the structure, n_{max}.

Loading Factors
$l = n / N$ (current loading factor)
$l_{max} = n_{max} / N$ (maximum loading factor)

where:

> n is the number of nodes the structure *currently* contains,
> N is the number of elements in the primary storage array, and
> n_{max} is the the maximum number of nodes that will be stored in the structure.

As nodes are added to a hashed structure, the current loading factor increases until finally, when every node in the database is stored in the data structure, the two loading factors are equal.

When we size the primary storage area of a hashed data structure using the optimum value of p (33%), the maximum loading factor is fixed at 0.75:

$$l_{max} = n_{max} / N = n_{max} / (n_{max} + p * n_{max}) = 1 / (1 + p) = 1 / (1 + 0.33) = 0.75$$

From a density viewpoint, a higher loading factor would be better. However, from a speed viewpoint the number of collisions that occur are lower when the loading factor is low because more of the primary storage area is unused. The optimum value ($l_{max} = 0.75$ with $p = 33\%$), was chosen as a *middle ground* where the number of collisions (search length) is acceptably low and the density is still relatively high. This middle ground is possible because, while the density decreases in a *linear* fashion with loading factor, the average search length decreases in a more rapid *nonlinear* fashion[4] (see Figure 5.14). As a result, at a loading factor near 1.0 (where the density is high) a

---

[4]The actual functional relationship is: average search length $= L_{avg} \leq 1/(1 - l)$. See Appendix B for its derivation, which assumes that all N primary storage area locations are equally probable to be generated each pass through the collision algorithm.

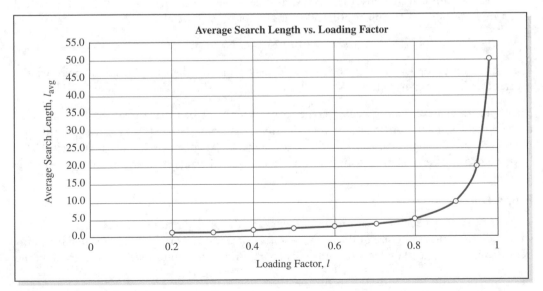

Figure 5.14 Variation of Average Search Length with Loading Factor for Hashed Structures

decrease in loading factor produces a much larger decrease in search length than it does a decrease in density. This trend continues until we reach a maximum loading factor of 0.75 (called the *optimum loading factor*) at which we reach a point of diminishing returns. At this point, as shown in Figure 5.14, the average search length is between three and four memory accesses. Further reductions in the loading factor produce relatively insignificant decreases in the average search length while producing significant decreases in density.

To demonstrate that the density is relatively high at the optimum loading factor, we will derive an expression for the density of a hashed data structure, D_h, in terms of the loading factor and evaluate it for a loading factor of 0.75. The density can be expressed as

$$D_h = \text{information bytes} / (\text{information bytes} + \text{overhead bytes})$$
$$= (n * w) / (n * w + N * w_a)$$

where:

> n is the number of nodes stored in the structure,
> w is the number of information bytes per node,
> N is the size of the primary storage area array, and
> w_a is the number of bytes per primary storage area array element.

Dividing numerator and denominator by n, and realizing that w_a is 4 (i.e., reference variables in Java occupy 4 bytes), D_h becomes

$$D_h = w / (w + 4 * N/n) = w / (w + 4/l)$$

where l is the loading factor, n/N. (This is the same density equation derived for the Direct Hashed structure in section 5.3.1.) Substituting a loading factor of 0.75, we obtain

$$D_h = w / (w + 4/0.75) = w / (w + 5.33).$$

This function, plotted in Figure 5.15, yields densities greater than 0.8 for client node widths greater then 22 bytes per node.

Therefore, to achieve good speed (average search lengths of between three and four memory accesses) while maintaining relatively high densities, hashed data structures are designed so that the maximum loading factor is 0.75. At this loading factor the primary storage area array is 33% larger than n_{max} (the maximum number of nodes stored in the data structure at any given time).

Prime Numbers

There is one other issue to be considered when sizing the primary storage area. For reasons that we will discuss later, if the size of the primary storage area (N) is a prime number,[5] then the number of collisions for certain hashing and collision algorithms is minimized. Euclid proved, in the

---

[5]A prime number is a positive integer that can only be divided evenly by itself and one.

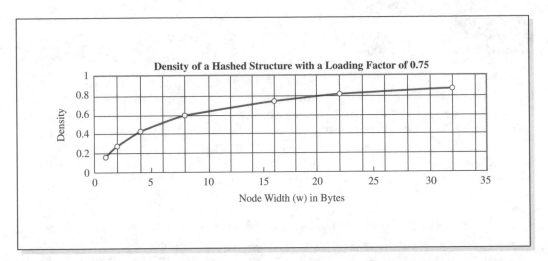

Figure 5.15 Density of Hashed Structures at the Optimum Loading Factor (0.75)

third century BC, that there are an infinite number of prime numbers. Table 5.4 presents the prime numbers less than 7000.

The performance of some hashing and collision algorithms improves even further if we choose only primes of the type "$4k + 3$". Only a subset of the prime numbers are $4k + 3$ primes. A prime, P, is a $4k + 3$ prime if there is an integer k such that $P = 4 * k + 3$. Therefore, to determine if a prime is a $4k + 3$ prime we set the prime equal to $4 * k + 3$, solve for k, and see if k is an integer. If it is, the prime is a $4k + 3$ prime. Otherwise, it is not.

To illustrate this test, we will arbitrarily choose P to be the prime 61. Then, setting $61 = 4 * k + 3$ and solving for k we have

$$61 = 4 * k + 3 \quad \text{or} \quad 61 - 3 = 4 * k \quad \text{or} \quad (61 - 3) / 4 = k \quad \text{or} \quad 15.5 = k.$$

Since k is not an integer, 61 is not a $4k + 3$ prime.

Alternately, if we choose the prime 67, we find that

$$67 = 4 * k + 3 \quad \text{or} \quad 67 - 3 = 4 * k \quad \text{or} \quad (67 - 3) / 4 = k \quad \text{or} \quad 16 = k.$$

Therefore, since k is an integer, 67 is a $4k + 3$ prime.

To take advantage of the speed increase associated with prime numbers, we will increase the size of the primary storage area array to be the $4k + 3$ prime just above that calculated with our general

Table 5.4

Prime Numbers Below 7000

2, 3, 5, 7, 11, 13, 17, 19, 23, 29, 31, 37, 41, 43, 47, 53, 59, 61, 67, 71, 73, 79, 83, 89, 97, 101, 103, 107, 109, 113, 127, 131, 137, 139, 149, 151, 157, 163, 167, 173, 179, 181, 191, 193, 197, 199, 211, 223, 227, 229, 233, 239, 241, 251, 257, 263, 269, 271, 277, 281, 283, 293, 307, 311, 313, 317, 331, 337, 347, 349, 353, 359, 367, 373, 379, 383, 389, 397, 401, 409, 419, 421, 431, 433, 439, 443, 449, 457, 461, 463, 467, 479, 487, 491, 499, 503, 509, 521, 523, 541, 547, 557, 563, 569, 571, 577, 587, 593, 599, 601, 607, 613, 617, 619, 631, 641, 643, 647, 653, 659, 661, 673, 677, 683, 691, 701, 709, 719, 727, 733, 739, 743, 751, 757, 761, 769, 773, 787, 797, 809, 811, 821, 823, 827, 829, 839, 853, 857, 859, 863, 877, 881, 883, 887, 907, 911, 919, 929, 937, 941, 947, 953, 967, 971, 977, 983, 991, 997, 1009, 1013, 1019, 1021, 1031, 1033, 1039, 1049, 1051, 1061, 1063, 1069, 1087, 1091, 1093, 1097, 1103, 1109, 1117, 1123, 1129, 1151, 1153, 1163, 1171, 1181, 1187, 1193, 1201, 1213, 1217, 1223, 1229, 1231, 1237, 1249, 1259, 1277, 1279, 1283, 1289, 1291, 1297, 1301, 1303, 1307, 1319, 1321, 1327, 1361, 1367, 1373, 1381, 1399, 1409, 1423, 1427, 1429, 1433, 1439, 1447, 1451, 1453, 1459, 1471, 1481, 1483, 1487, 1489, 1493, 1499, 1511, 1523, 1531, 1543, 1549, 1553, 1559, 1567, 1571, 1579, 1583, 1597, 1601, 1607, 1609, 1613, 1619, 1621, 1627, 1637, 1657, 1663, 1667, 1669, 1693, 1697, 1699, 1709, 1721, 1723, 1733, 1741, 1747, 1753, 1759, 1777, 1783, 1787, 1789, 1801, 1811, 1823, 1831, 1847, 1861, 1867, 1871, 1873, 1877, 1879, 1889, 1901, 1907, 1913, 1931, 1933, 1949, 1951, 1973, 1979, 1987, 1993, 1997, 1999, 2003, 2011, 2017, 2027, 2029, 2039, 2053, 2063, 2069, 2081, 2083, 2087, 2089, 2099, 2111, 2113, 2129, 2131, 2137, 2141, 2143, 2153, 2161, 2179, 2203, 2207, 2213, 2221, 2237, 2239, 2243, 2251, 2267, 2269, 2273, 2281, 2287, 2293, 2297, 2309, 2311, 2333, 2339, 2341, 2347, 2351, 2357, 2371, 2377, 2381, 2383, 2389, 2393, 2399, 2411, 2417, 2423, 2437, 2441, 2447, 2459, 2467, 2473, 2477, 2503, 2521, 2531, 2539, 2543, 2549, 2551, 2557, 2579, 2591, 2593, 2609, 2617, 2621, 2633, 2647, 2657, 2659, 2663, 2671, 2677, 2683, 2687, 2689, 2693, 2699, 2707, 2711, 2713, 2719, 2729, 2731, 2741, 2749, 2753, 2767, 2777, 2789, 2791, 2797, 2801, 2803, 2819, 2833, 2837, 2843, 2851, 2857, 2861, 2879, 2887, 2897, 2903, 2909, 2917, 2927, 2939, 2953, 2957, 2963, 2969, 2971, 2999, 3001, 3011, 3019, 3023, 3037, 3041, 3049, 3061, 3067, 3079, 3083, 3089, 3109, 3119, 3121, 3137, 3163, 3167, 3169, 3181, 3187, 3191, 3203, 3209, 3217, 3221, 3229, 3251, 3253, 3257, 3259, 3271, 3299, 3301, 3307, 3313, 3319, 3323, 3329, 3331, 3343, 3347, 3359, 3361, 3371, 3373, 3389, 3391, 3407, 3413, 3433, 3449, 3457, 3461, 3463, 3467, 3469, 3491, 3499, 3511, 3517, 3527, 3529, 3533, 3539, 3541, 3547, 3557, 3559, 3571, 3581, 3583, 3593, 3607, 3613, 3617, 3623, 3631, 3637, 3643, 3659, 3671, 3673, 3677, 3691, 3697, 3701, 3709, 3719, 3727, 3733, 3739, 3761, 3767, 3769, 3779, 3793, 3797, 3803, 3821, 3823, 3833, 3847, 3851, 3853, 3863, 3877, 3881, 3889, 3907, 3911, 3917, 3919, 3923, 3929, 3931, 3943, 3947, 3967, 3989, 4001, 4003, 4007, 4013, 4019, 4021, 4027, 4049, 4051, 4057, 4073, 4079, 4091, 4093, 4099, 4111, 4127, 4129, 4133, 4139, 4153, 4157, 4159, 4177, 4201, 4211, 4217, 4219, 4229, 4231, 4241, 4243, 4253, 4259, 4261, 4271, 4273, 4283, 4289, 4297, 4327, 4337, 4339, 4349, 4357, 4363, 4373, 4391, 4397, 4409, 4421, 4423, 4441, 4447, 4451, 4457, 4463, 4481, 4483, 4493, 4507, 4513, 4517, 4519, 4523, 4547, 4549, 4561, 4567, 4583, 4591, 4597, 4603, 4621, 4637, 4639, 4643, 4649, 4651, 4657, 4663, 4673, 4679, 4691, 4703, 4721, 4723, 4729, 4733, 4751, 4759, 4783, 4787, 4789, 4793, 4799, 4801, 4813, 4817, 4831, 4861, 4871, 4877, 4889, 4903, 4909, 4919, 4931, 4933, 4937, 4943, 4951, 4957, 4967, 4969, 4973, 4987, 4993, 4999, 5003, 5009, 5011, 5021, 5023, 5039, 5051, 5059, 5077, 5081, 5087, 5099, 5101, 5107, 5113, 5119, 5147, 5153, 5167, 5171, 5179, 5189, 5197, 5209, 5227, 5231, 5233, 5237, 5261, 5273, 5279, 5281, 5297, 5303, 5309, 5323, 5333, 5347, 5351, 5381, 5387, 5393, 5399, 5407, 5413, 5417, 5419, 5431, 5437, 5441, 5443, 5449, 5471, 5477, 5479, 5483, 5501, 5503, 5507, 5519, 5521, 5527, 5531, 5557, 5563, 5569, 5573, 5581, 5591, 5623, 5639, 5641, 5647, 5651, 5653, 5657, 5659, 5669, 5683, 5689, 5693, 5701, 5711, 5717, 5737, 5741, 5743, 5749, 5779, 5783, 5791, 5801, 5807, 5813, 5821, 5827, 5839, 5843, 5849, 5851, 5857, 5861, 5867, 5869, 5879, 5881, 5897, 5903, 5923, 5927, 5939, 5953, 5981, 5987, 6007, 6011, 6029, 6037, 6043, 6047, 6053, 6067, 6073, 6079, 6089, 6091, 6101, 6113, 6121, 6131, 6133, 6143, 6151, 6163, 6173, 6197, 6199, 6203, 6211, 6217, 6221, 6229, 6247, 6257, 6263, 6269, 6271, 6277, 6287, 6299, 6301, 6311, 6317, 6323, 6329, 6337, 6343, 6353, 6359, 6361, 6367, 6373, 6379, 6389, 6397, 6421, 6427, 6449, 6451, 6469, 6473, 6481, 6491, 6521, 6529, 6547, 6551, 6553, 6563, 6569, 6571, 6577, 6581, 6599, 6607, 6619, 6637, 6653, 6659, 6661, 6673, 6679, 6689, 6691, 6701, 6703, 6709, 6719, 6733, 6737, 6761, 6763, 6779, 6781, 6791, 6793, 6803, 6823, 6827, 6829, 6833, 6841, 6857, 6863, 6869, 6871, 6883, 6899, 6907, 6911, 6917, 6947, 6949, 6959, 6961, 6967, 6971, 6977, 6983, 6991, 6997

sizing guideline ($N = 1.33n_{max}$). This minor increase in N does not produce a significant decrease in density. Thus, the optimum size of a hashed data structure's primary storage area array is:

Optimized Size of the Primary Storage Area, N, for a Hashed Structure

N = next highest $4k + 3$ prime 33% above the maximum number of nodes that will exist in the structure at any given time, n_{max}.

As an example, suppose that we were going to store 5000 nodes in a hashed data structure. To calculate the size of the primary storage area, first we multiply 5000 by 1.33 (to add 33%) and obtain 6650. Referencing the table of primes, the first prime greater than 6650 is 6653. Testing 6653 to determine if it is a $4k + 3$ prime, we find it is not ($k = (6653 - 3) / 4 = 1662.5$). The next highest prime is 6659, which is a $4k + 3$ prime ($k = (6659 - 3) / 4 = 1664$). Thus, the size of the primary storage area array would be 6659 elements.

The code presented in Figure 5.16 calculates, and returns, the next highest $4k + 3$ prime a given percent (pct) above a given integer (n).

The method determines the requested $4k + 3$ prime by testing successively higher odd *candidate* integers the given percentage above n to determine if they are prime numbers. When a prime number is found, the prime is then tested to determine if it is a $4k + 3$ prime. The process continues, until a $4k + 3$ prime is found.

Lines 6–8 make an initial guess of the $4k + 3$ prime to be the next odd integer (2 is the only even prime) the given percent above n. Lines 9–27 is an outer loop that continues until the prime, found in the inner loop (Lines 10–20) is a $4k + 3$ prime. The test for a $4k + 3$ prime is performed on Line 21.

The test to determine if the candidate is, in fact, a prime is performed by the **for** loop of Lines 12–15. The candidate prime is divided by every integer between the square root of the candidate prime and 2. If the remainder of the division is zero (Line 13) then the candidate is not a prime. In this case, the candidate prime is increased to the next highest odd integer (Line 17) and this new candidate prime is tested.

Starting the divisor, d, in the **for** loop at the square root of the candidate prime, saves many iterations through the loop. A more brute force approach would start the divisor at one less than the candidate prime. For instance, for a candidate prime of 10,000,001, d would be initialized to 10,000,000, and the loop would execute 9,999,998 times. However, if we initialize d to 3263 (the square root of 10,000,001) the loop executes only 3262 times.

To determine the validity of this technique, we must verify that if an integer, p, is not evenly divisible by an integer less than the square root of p, it is not evenly divisible by an integer greater than the square root of p. The proof of this statement is in Appendix C, but we can gain an intuitive understanding of its validity by considering the following example:

```
1.   public static int fourKPlus3(int n, int pct)
2.   {  boolean fkp3 = false;
3.      boolean aPrime = false;
4.      int prime, highDivisor, d;
5.      double pctd = pct;
6.      prime = (int)(n * (1.0 + (pctd / 100.0))); // guess the prime pct
                                                    // percent larger than n
7.      if(prime % 2 == 0) // if even make the prime guess odd
8.          prime = prime + 1;
9.      while(fkp3 == false) // not a 4k + 3 prime
10.     {  while(aPrime == false) // not a prime
11.        {  highDivisor = (int)(Math.sqrt(prime) + 0.5);
12.           for(d = highDivisor; d > 1; d--)
13.           {  if(prime % d == 0)
14.                  break; // not a prime
15.           }
16.           if(d != 1) // prime not found
17.               prime = prime + 2;
18.           else
19.               aPrime = true;
20.        } // end of the prime search loop
21.        if((prime - 3) % 4 == 0)
22.            fkp3 = true;
23.        else
24.        {  prime = prime + 2;
25.           aPrime = false;
26.        }
27.     } // end of 4k + 3 prime search loop
28.     return prime;
29. }
```

Figure 5.16   Method to Calculate a 4k + 3 Prime Number

Suppose the candidate prime was 100. Its square root is 10. If the **for** loop were allowed to proceed through all the integers at and below 10, it would consider divisors of 10 through 2 and would determine that 10, 5, 4, and 2 are all evenly divisible into 100. If it were to examine the integers above the square root of 100, it would find that 50, 25, and 20 are all evenly divisible into 100. But 50 * 2 = 100, which means that since 50 is an even divisor, 2 would also have to be (100 / 2 = an integer, 50). Thus, by testing 2 we eliminate the need to test 50. Similarly by testing 4 we are, in effect, also testing 25, 5 also tests 20, with 10 (the square root of the candidate prime) being a symmetry (pivot) point.

Having gained an understanding of how to size the primary storage area array in a way that minimizes collisions while producing acceptable densities, we will now turn our attention to a discussion of the preprocessing, hashing, and collision algorithms used in hashed data structures.

5.4.3 Preprocessing Algorithms

As shown in Figure 5.5, a preprocessing algorithm maps keys into pseudo keys. Most hashing functions require that some form of preprocessing be performed when the key field is alphanumeric or it can assume negative values, because their independent variable must be a positive integer.

When the keys can assume negative values, the Subtraction algorithm discussed in section 5.3.1 can be used, although hashed structures employ a wide variety of algorithms to preprocess both numeric and alphanumeric keys. Generally speaking, most string preprocessing algorithms combine the bits that make up the characters of the key into four bytes, and the resulting bit pattern is then evaluated as a positive integer. One of these preprocessing algorithms is coded into the method hashCode(), discussed in section 5.4.6, which is a member of the Java String class.

Naturally, a good preprocessing algorithm will produce pseudo keys that infrequently collide. Three widely used preprocessing algorithms used in hashed structures are: folding, Pseudorandom Averaging, and Digit Extraction. They are often used to preprocess both numeric and nonnumeric keys. We will begin our discussion of these algorithms with a folding algorithm.

Fold-Shifting Preprocessing Algorithm

Generally speaking, folding algorithms divide the key field into groups of bits, with the size (number of bits) of each group being the desired size of the pseudo key. Then the groupings are treated as numeric values, and arithmetically added to produce the pseudo key. Typically, one grouping near the middle of the key, called the *pivot*, is selected as the first operand in the addition. To maintain the size of the pseudo key, arithmetic overflow from the higher order bit is ignored. Thus, folding can be used to convert keys of any size into integer pseudo keys.

A popular version of a folding algorithm, called *Fold-shifting*, is illustrated in Figure 5.17. The top half of the figure is presented purely for pedagogical purposes in that the algorithm's operands and additions are shown in the decimal (base 10) system. The 9 digit numeric key 987845369 is transformed into the 3 digit pseudo key 201, using 845 as the pivot. A more realistic but slightly more complicated application of the algorithm is shown at the bottom of the figure. The nonnumeric key "Al McAllister" (with the blank removed), is converted into a 32 bit integer pseudo key. The middle four characters, "Alli", are used as the pivot point and the Unicode bit patterns[6] of the four characters to the left and right of it are added to it. The resulting integer, 4,132,249,406, is used as the 32 bit integer pseudo key.

A variation on this basic technique reverses the characters in the groupings before the addition is performed.

---

[6]Java uses 32 bit Unicodes to represent characters. The first 256 characters in the Unicode table (hexadecimal 0000 to 00FF) are the ISO 8859-1 extension of the ASCII code set. Figure 5.17 assumes that the eight leading zeros of each Unicode character in the key have already been stripped away.

For the numeric key: 987845369, the key is folded about 845.
The addition is performed as:

$$
\begin{array}{r}
845 \\
987 \\
\underline{369} \\
2201
\end{array}
$$

Thus, the pseudo key would be 201

For the non-numeric key: "AlMcAllister", the key is folded about the second grouping, `Alli`.
The addition is performed as:

```
                A         l         l         i
  Alli     0100 0001 0110 1100 0110 1100 0110 1001

                A         l         M         c
+ AlMc     0100 0001 0110 1100 0100 1101 0110 0011

                s         t         e         r
+ ster   + 0111 0011 0111 0100 0110 0101 0111 0010

           1111 0110 0100 1101 0001 1111 0011 1110
```

Treating this result as a positive 32 bit integer, the pseudo key would be 4, 132, 249, 406.

Figure 5.17   Fold-Shifting Key Conversion

The Java coding of the fold-shifting algorithm for non-numeric keys is presented in Figure 5.18. It preprocesses `String` keys of any length into a 32 bit integer pseudo key. It does *not* ignore white space and is case sensitive (e.g., "Bob Smith", "BobSmith", and "bob smith" map to the pseudo keys 1,780,691,972, 706,950,148 and 1,344,743,749, respectively). It should be kept in mind, however, that there are many keys that, when processed by this algorithm, yield the same pseudo key (e.g., "MaryLynnTodd" and "MaryToddLynn" both produce the pseudo key 297,122,485) so the algorithm is not suited for use in perfect hashed structures.

The loop on Lines 7–17 process all the characters of the key. Starting on the left side of the key, Lines 8–10 build four character groupings and place them into the variable grouping. Line 11 checks to see if the grouping is complete; that is if grouping contains four characters or contains the (possibly incomplete) last grouping. Line 12 builds the pseudo key by adding the grouping to it. When the last grouping is processed, the absolute value of the pseudo key is returned on Line 18.[7]

---

[7]Returning the absolute value of the pseudo key effectively ignores overflow into the sign (leftmost) bit of the pseudo key.

```
1.  public static int stringToInt(String aKey)
2.  {  int pseudoKey = 0;
3.     int n = 1;
4.     int cn = 0;
5.     char c[] = aKey.toCharArray();
6.     int grouping = 0;
7.     while (cn < aKey.length()) // still more characters in the key
8.     {  grouping = grouping << 8; // pack next 4 characters
9.        grouping = grouping + c[cn];
10.       cn = cn + 1;
11.       if(n == 4 || cn == aKey.length())    // 4 characters are processed,
                                               // or no more characters
12.       {  pseudoKey = pseudoKey + grouping; // add grouping to pseudokey
13.          n = 0;
14.          grouping = 0;
15.       }
16.       n = n + 1;
17.    } // end while
18.    return Math.abs(pseudoKey);
19. }
```

Figure 5.18 A Fold-Shifting Non-Numeric Key Conversion Method

Pseudorandom Average Preprocessing

Pseudorandom preprocessing is a technique used to distribute keys somewhat *randomly* about the primary storage area array. Generally speaking, introducing randomness into the preprocessing algorithm tends to reduce collision frequencies. The algorithm is:

Pseudorandom Preprocessing

$$pk = p_1 * k + p_2$$

where:

> pk is the pseudo key,
>
> k is the key, and
>
> p_1 and p_2 are prime numbers.

The prime numbers are usually small and, once chosen, retain their values over the life of the data structure. As an example, consider the numeric key: 89,351. Assuming the primes p_1 and p_2 were chosen to be 13 and 53, respectively, then the pseudo key would be

$$pk = 13 * 89351 + 53 = 1,161,616.$$

Usually arithmetic overflow occurring in this calculation is ignored. Pseudorandom preprocessing can also be applied to non-numeric key applications after the key is converted to a numeric equivalent, perhaps using the folding technique previously discussed.

Digit Extraction Preprocessing

Digit extraction, like folding, is a technique used to reduce the length of multiposition (or multidigit) keys, and also to introduce randomness into the pseudo keys it generates. Several key positions (e.g., m of them) are retained to form the pseudo key; all other key positions are ignored. Thus, the multiposition key is mapped into an m position pseudo key formed by concatenating the retained m key position values.

Key positions that add uniqueness to the keys are usually passed onto the pseudo key. For example, consider keys with fifteen positions and every other position's value common to all keys. Two typical keys would be: **123456789012345** and **928436281042542**. These common value positions would be ignored and only the first, third, etc. key positions would be retained. In this example, m would be 8, and the key 123456789012345 would map into the pseudo key, 13579135. This technique can be used to preprocess non-numeric as well as numeric keys. Naturally, non-numeric keys would require further preprocessing (e.g., Fold-shifting).

In the case of non-numeric keys the bit patterns of the characters that make up the keys are examined to determine which bits are not contributing any uniqueness. These bit locations are then ignored. For example, Java's Unicode representation of lowercase letters all begin with 0000 0000 011 (e.g., "a" is 0000 0000 0110 0001 and "b" is 0000 0000 0110 0010). Therefore, if the keys were comprised of just lowercase letters, only the rightmost five bits of the key's characters would be retained and processed through the Fold-shifting algorithm.

5.4.4 Hashing Functions

There are many hashing functions used in hashed structures to compute the index into the primary storage area, i_p. These include both the Direct Hashing function and the Division Hashing function previously discussed. Assuming preprocess is performed, they are:

$i_p = h(pk) = pk$ Direct Hashing function

$i_p = h(pk) = pk \bmod N = pk \% N$ Division Hashing function

where:

N = the number of storage locations allocated to the primary storage area, and

pk is the given key.

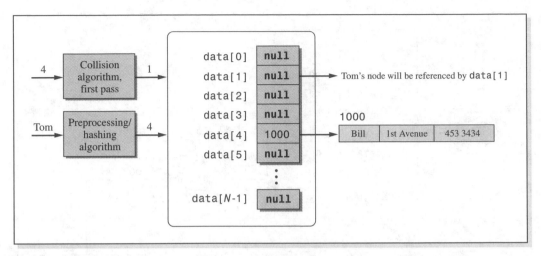

Figure 5.19 Open Addressing Collision Resolution of "Tom" Colliding with "Bill" During an Insert Operation

When preprocessing is not performed,[8] the pseudo key, *pk*, in the previous equations is replaced with the value of the key. Most hashed data structures, however, do perform some form of preprocessing. Of the two algorithms, the Division algorithm is more commonly used in hashed structures.

5.4.5 Collision Algorithms

Collision algorithms can be divided into two categories: those algorithms that compute an index into the primary storage area and those that do not. The former group is called *open addressing* collision algorithms and the latter group is called *non-open addressing* collision algorithms.

When open addressing is used, each element of the primary storage area stores a reference to a *single node*, and the collision algorithm *always* generates indexes into the primary storage area array. During an Insert operation, if the location generated by the preprocessing/hashing algorithms is occupied, an open addressing collision algorithm looks for the unused or *open address* in the primary storage area array. Thus the name: *open addressing*. Figure 5.19 illustrates the resolution of the collision of the key "Tom" with "Bill" by an open addressing collision algorithm.

---

[8]When the Direct Hashing function is used and preprocessing is either not performed or the preprocessing algorithm produces unique pseudo keys, a hashed data structure is a perfect hashed data structure.

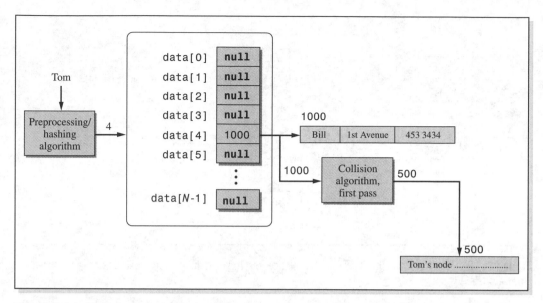

Figure 5.20 Non-Open Addressing Collision Resolution of "Tom" Colliding with "Bill" During an Insert Operation

When non-open addressing is used, each element of the primary storage area can store a reference to *multiple nodes* (see Figures 5.1c and 5.1d). This reference locates *all* the nodes that the preprocessing /hashing algorithms map into the element (*synonyms*). Thus, during an Insert operation, if the location generated by the preprocessing/hashing algorithms is already occupied, a non-open addressing collision algorithm stores the reference to the inserted node *outside* the primary storage area array. Figure 5.20 illustrates the resolution of the collision of the key "Tom" with "Bill" by a non-open addressing collision algorithm.

We will begin our study of collision algorithms with a study of open addressing collision algorithms.

Linear and Quadratic Probing Collision Algorithms

Linear Probing and Quadratic Probing are two similar open addressing collision algorithms, expressed as:

$i_p = i_p + 1$ Linear Probing collision algorithm

$i_p = i_p + p^2$ Quadratic Probing collision algorithm

where:

> i_p is the index into the primary storage area array, and
> p is the pass number (1, 2, 3, ...) through the collision algorithm loop depicted in the lower portion of Figure 5.12.

Table 5.5

Indices Generated by the Linear and Quadratic Collision Algorithms, for an Initial (Home) Address of 4

Collision Algorithm Pass Number, p	Index Generated by the Collision Algorithm	
	Linear	Quadratic
1	5	5
2	6	9
3	7	18
4	8	34
5	9	59
6	10	95
7	11	144
8	12	208
9	13	289
10	14	389
11	15	510
12	16	654
13	17	823
14	18	1019
15	19	1244
16	20	1500
17	21	1789
18	22	2113

Both algorithms calculate the index of the next candidate location in the primary storage area by adding an increment to the current, unsuccessful location. In the case of the Linear algorithm the increment is 1, which amounts to a sequential search upward through the primary storage area. The increment added to the current location in the Quadratic algorithm is the square of the pass number through the collision algorithm's loop. Assuming the preprocessing/hashing algorithm produced an initial, or *home*, index of 4, Table 5.5 gives the subsequent indices generated by both algorithms, for the first 18 passes through each algorithm.

Since both algorithms continue to add a positive increment to the unsuccessful index it will continue to grow as the pass number increases, and eventually it will exceed the maximum allowable index of the primary storage area array, $N - 1$. For example, if N is 19 and the home address is 4, then the Linear algorithm generates indices that are out of bounds after pass 14 and the Quadratic algorithm produces invalid indices after pass 3 (see the shaded cells in Table 5.5). To prevent this from happening, the algorithms are modified to perform modulo N arithmetic which guarantees that the calculated index remains in the allowable range of the primary storage array, $0 \leq i_p \leq N - 1$. The modified algorithms are:

$i_p = (i_p + 1) \% N$ Linear Probing collision algorithm
$i_p = (i_p + p^2) \% N$ Quadratic Probing collision algorithm

where:

i_p is the index into the primary storage area array, and
p is the pass number $(1, 2, 3, \dots)$ through the collision algorithm loop depicted in the lower portion of Figure 5.12.

For $N = 19$, both modified algorithms produce indices in the range 0 to 18, and the indexing into the primary storage area array is never out of bounds. Table 5.6 presents the indices for the first 18 passes through the revised algorithms.

Although modulo N arithmetic has solved the index-out-of-bounds problem, these two collision algorithms are rarely used. The data in Table 5.6 reveals three undesirable characteristics intrinsic to these two algorithms that renders them two of the poorer performers in the world of open addressing collision algorithms. These undesirable characteristics are:

- Multiple accesses of an element of the primary storage array (Quadratic algorithm)
- Primary clustering (Linear algorithm)
- Secondary clustering (Quadratic algorithm)

The rightmost column of Table 5.6 illustrates the problem of multiple accesses. Beginning with a home address of 4, and after 18 passes through the Quadratic collision algorithm, the algorithm has generated the index 4 twice (pass numbers 9 and 18) and the indices 9 and 18 three times each (pass numbers 2, 10, 15, and 3, 8, and 16, respectively). This is a waste of eight passes through the algorithm, because if the locations 4, 9, and 18 were unacceptable the first time they were generated, there is no need to consider them again. Furthermore, indices 1, 7, 10, 13, 14, and 17 have not been generated.

The Linear Collision algorithm inevitably leads to the problem of primary clustering. Primary clustering occurs when the nodes mapped into the same home address by the preprocessing/ hashing algorithms, are located in a tight *cluster* near the home address. Consider the insertion of six nodes, A, B, C, D, E, and F whose collisions will be resolved using the Linear collision algorithm. Let us assume that A, B, C, D, and E's home address is 4, and that F's home address is 6.

Table 5.6

Indices Generated by the Modified Linear and Quadratic Collision Algorithms, for an Initial (Home) Address of 4

Pass Number, p	Collision Algorithm	
	Linear	Quadratic
1	5	5
2	6	9
3	7	18
4	8	15
5	9	2
6	10	0
7	11	11
8	12	18
9	13	4
10	14	9
11	15	16
12	16	8
13	17	6
14	18	12
15	0	9
16	1	18
17	2	3
18	3	4

Furthermore we will assume that the nodes are inserted in the order A, B, C, D, E, and finally F. If the structure was empty to begin with, A would be inserted without a collision at location 4. Referring to the middle column of Table 5.6, B would be inserted (after one pass through the collision algorithm) at location 5; C (after two passes) would be inserted at location 6, etc. Figure 5.21 depicts the structure after nodes A through E have been inserted.

The grouping of nodes A through E near their home location (4) is a primary cluster. There are two problems with primary clustering. Not only do they slow down operations on the nodes

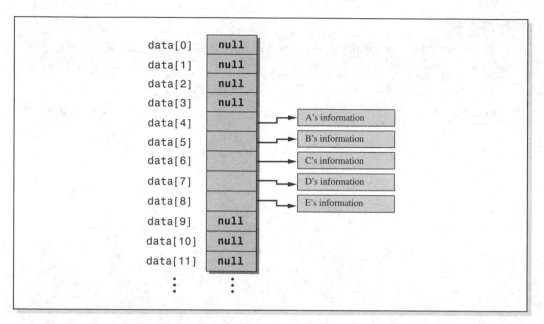

Figure 5.21   A Primary Cluster Produced by the Linear Collision Algorithm after Inserting Five Nodes with the Same Home Address (4)

whose home address is the home address of the cluster (e.g., nodes B, C, D, and E), but they also slow down operations on nodes whose home address is anywhere within the cluster. For example, in the absence of the primary cluster, F (whose home address is 6) would be inserted without a collision. However, because of the primary cluster, three passes through the collision algorithm are required to insert F; location 7 is tried first, then location 8, and finally location 9. If nodes B, C, D, and E were scattered about primary storage, F would probably be inserted at location 61 without a collision.

Secondary clustering occurs when nodes with the same home address, although scattered throughout the primary storage area, generate the same sequence of collision addresses. The Quadratic collision algorithm generates secondary clusters. Consider the insertion of five nodes, A, B, C, D, and E. We will assume that the nodes are inserted in the order A, B, C, D, and E; that the Quadratic collision algorithm is used to resolve collisions; and that the home address of all five nodes is 4. If the structure was empty to begin with, A would be inserted without a collision at location 4. As shown in the rightmost column of Table 5.6, B would insert (after pass 1 through the collision algorithm) at location 5, C (after pass 2) would insert at location 9, etc., resulting in the situation depicted in Figure 5.22. Because all of these nodes follow the same collision path, clustering has occurred. But since they are scattered about the primary storage area array, the cluster is referred to as a secondary cluster (rather than a primary cluster). Secondary clusters only suffer from one of the primary cluster problems: they slow down the operations on nodes whose home address is the home address of the cluster (e.g., 4 in our example).

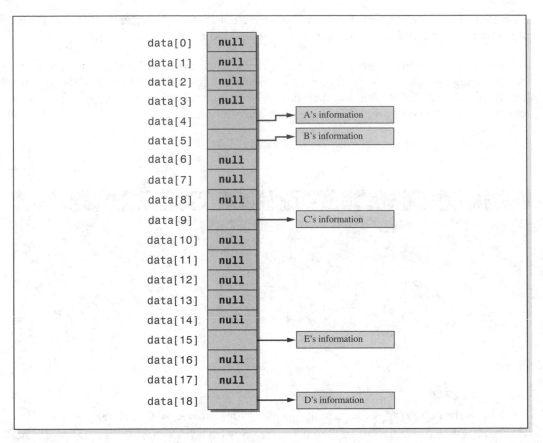

Figure 5.22 A Secondary Cluster Produced by the Quadratic Collision Algorithm after Inserting Five Nodes with the Same Home Address (4)

The way to reduce clustering is to make the collision algorithm dependent on the key (or pseudo key). Then, nodes with different keys that hash into the same home address will follow different collision paths. Using this technique, many open addressing collision algorithms greatly reduce the probability of the occurrence of primary and secondary clustering. One of these is the Linear Quotient collision algorithm, which also eliminates the problem of multiple accesses into the primary storage area.

The Linear Quotient Collision Algorithm

The Linear Quotient (or LQ) collision algorithm, like the Linear and Quadratic collision algorithms, uses modulo N arithmetic to keep the calculated indices within the bounds of the primary storage area array. In addition, like these algorithms, it computes the next location by adding an offset to the previously computed location. Unlike these algorithms, however, the offset is a function of the key (or pseudo key) which tends to minimize secondary clustering.

As the name of the algorithm suggests, the offset is a division *quotient* and the functional relationship involving this quotient is a *linear* one. Specifically, the quotient is the result of dividing the key (or pseudo key) by N, with one exception. When the quotient is evenly divisible by N, it is replaced with a somewhat arbitrarily chosen $4k + 3$ prime.

Referring to the quotient as q, the algorithm is stated as

Linear Quotient Collision Algorithm

if $(q \% N) \mathrel{!=} 0$ // q is not evenly divisible by N

$\quad i_p = (i_p + \text{offset}) \% N = (i_p + q) \% N$

else

$\quad i_p = (i_p + \text{offset}) \% N = (i_p + p_{4k+3}) \% N$

---

where:

> $q = pk / N$,
> N is the number of elements in the primary storage area (a $4k + 3$ prime),
> pk is the value of the integer pseudo key (or key when no preprocessing is performed), and
> p_{4k+3} is any $4k + 3$ prime other than N.

The unusual part of this algorithm involves the quotient, q. Its initial computation is straightforward (pk / N). However, if the remainder of the division of q by N is zero, then a *default* $4k + 3$ prime (other than N) is used in the collision algorithm. Once picked, the default value remains constant for the entire life of the data structure. To see why the default prime is a necessary part of the algorithm, we rewrite the first part of the algorithm as

$$i_p = (i_p + q) \% N = (i_p \% N + q \% N).$$

Since i_p is always calculated using modulo N arithmetic, i_p is always in the range 0 to $N - 1$ and therefore $i_p \% N = i_p$. Therefore, the previous equation becomes

$$i_p = (i_p + q \% N).$$

This means that when $q \% N = 0$ the above equation degenerates to $i_p = i_p$ and all passes through the collision algorithm produce the same index (the home address).

For example, let us assume N is 19, and a quotient of 57 which *is* evenly divisible by 19. Furthermore, we will assume a home index of 6, which resulted in a collision. Then, if q were used in the collision algorithm, the next address calculated would also be 6:

$$i_p = (6 + 57) \% 19 = (63 \% 19) = 6.$$

However, using a default prime, p_{4k+3}, in the collision algorithm, rather than the quotient 57, guarantees a nonzero offset since prime numbers are not evenly divisible by any number other than themselves. For example, if the default prime chosen for our data structure was 23, the next index calculated by the collision algorithm would 10:

$$i_p = (6 + 23) \% 19 = (29 \% 19) = 10.$$

Table 5.7 further illustrates the use of the LQ collision algorithm. It is a tabulation of the collision algorithm pass number vs. the indices calculated during the first 18 passes through the algorithm for 3 pseudo keys. N was assumed to be 19 and the default prime, p_{4k+3}, was assumed to be 23. The values of the 3 pseudo keys are 593, 5058, and 251 for the indices tabulated in columns 2 (Case 1), 3 (Case 2), and 4 (Case 3) respectively. All 3 keys map into the same home address, 4, as calculated by the Division Hashing algorithm (593 % 19 = 5058 % 19 = 251 % 19 = 4).

To begin the collision algorithm we calculate the quotient, q. As shown in the headings of the table, the quotients are 31 (= 593 / 19), 266 (= 5058 / 19), and 13 (= 251 / 19). Next we calculate q % N for each of the keys to determine the offset to be used in the collision algorithm. If it evaluates to zero, q is evenly divisible by N and the default prime will be used as the offset. Otherwise, q will be used as the offset. The values of q % 19 and the resulting offset are shown in the column headings of the table. The key value 5058 uses the default prime as an offset (266 % 19 = 0). The resulting three equations for the primary storage index i_p is also present in the column headings of the table. These equations were used to generate the indices presented in the table.

It is a useful exercise for the student to calculate the home address (4), the offsets (31, 23, and 31), and the first two or three indices presented in the table for each of the three pseudokeys. (Note: the Division Hashing algorithm is used to calculate the home address.)

Having gained an understanding of the calculation processes of the Linear Quotient collision algorithm, we will now examine it from the viewpoint of multiple accesses and clustering, beginning with the problem of multiple accesses.

Multiple accesses occur when the collision algorithm produces an index already visited on a previous pass (probe). Inspecting the indices presented in the Table 5.7, we see that for all three cases the indices between 0 and 18 (with the exception of index 4 which is the previously visited home address) are generated once, and only once. The data presented in the table is typical of the performance of this algorithm; it has remarkable (and very desirable) feature of never recalculating a location in the primary storage area, for all possible values of the offset. Therefore, the algorithm does not produce multiple accesses.

Table 5.7

Indices Generated by the Linear Quotient Collision Algorithm for Three Keys that Map into the Same Home Address (4)

Pass Number p	Primary Storage Area Size, $N = 19$ Home Address, $i_p = 4$ Default Prime, $P_{4k+3} = 23$		
	Case 1, $pk = 593$ $q = 593/19 = 31$ $q \% 19 = 31 \% 19 = 12$ $i_p = (i_p + 31) \% 19$	Case 2, $pk = 5058$ $q = 5058/19 = 266$ $q \% 19 = 266 \% 19 = 0$ $i_p = (i_p + 23) \% 19$	Case 3 $pk = 251$ $q = 251/19 = 13$ $q \% 19 = 13 \% 19 = 13$ $i_p = (i_p + 13) \% 19$
1	$i_p = 16$	$i_p = 8$	$i_p = 17$
2	9	12	11
3	2	16	5
4	14	1	18
5	7	5	12
6	0	9	6
7	12	13	0
8	5	17	13
9	17	2	7
10	10	6	1
11	3	10	14
12	15	14	8
13	8	18	2
14	1	3	15
15	13	7	9
16	6	11	3
17	18	15	16
18	11	0	9

Now let us turn our attention to the problem of primary clustering. Primary clustering occurs whenever the collision path generates a set of sequential indices. For the LQ collision algorithm, this will occur when the term q % N, or p_{4k+3} % N, equals 1. Since there are $N - 1$ possible values for these terms (the range of the remainders when dividing by N), the probability of them evaluating to 1 is $1 / (N - 1)$. As N gets large, $1 / (N - 1)$ approaches zero and, therefore, the LQ hashing has a low probability of primary clustering.

Finally, let us consider the problem of secondary clustering. Secondary clustering occurs when two keys with the same home address follow the same nonsequential collision path. The home address for all three pseudo keys presented in Table 5.7 is the same, 4. Yet, when we examine the indices presented in the table, we see that all three pseudo keys follow a different collision path. If this is true for all keys that map into the same home address, then this algorithm does not exhibit secondary clustering.

Consider the key 954. For $N = 19$, its quotient is 50 and its home address (4) is the same as the keys presented in Table 5.7.[9] Since 50 % 19 is not 0, the index equation in the collision algorithm is

$$i_p = (i_p + 50) \text{ % } 19.$$

During the first pass through the collision algorithm this equation yields an index of 16 (i.e., (4 + 50) % 19 = 16). The second pass produces an index of 9 (i.e., (16 + 50) % 19). Unfortunately, these and all subsequent passes yield the same collision path as pseudo key 593 (see Table 5.7) and the algorithm, under these conditions, exhibits secondary clustering. Clustering occurs because the offset 50 (for key 954) when divided by 19 yields the same remainder, 12, as when the offset 31 (for key 593) is divided by 19. Since both calculations start from the same home address, 4, all calculated indices will be the same.

Therefore, whenever two pseudo keys map into the same home address, *and* their offsets divided by N yield the same remainder, the algorithm exhibits secondary clustering. There are $N - 1$ choices for this remainder (1 to $N - 1$), and when we use the optimum loading factor to size the array, three-fourths of the home addresses will be occupied. Thus, the probability of secondary clustering occurring for any two keys is $\leq [¾ * 1 / (N - 1)]$. As N gets large, $1 / (N - 1)$ approaches zero and, therefore, the LQ collision algorithm has a low probability of secondary clustering.

The low probability of clustering, the ability to generate unique indices each pass through the algorithm, and its simplicity make the Linear Quotient algorithm an excellent candidate for resolving collisions in hashed data structures. Before demonstrating its use in an implementation of a hashed data structure, we will examine a problem that all open addressing collision algorithms demonstrate: the *Delete problem*.

---

[9]Its home address is 4 because we have assumed the Division algorithm is used for the hashing algorithm, 4 = 954 % 19.

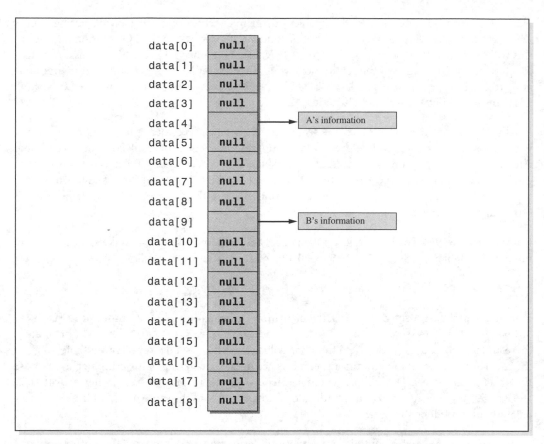

data[0]   null
data[1]   null
data[2]   null
data[3]   null
data[4]   → A's information
data[5]   null
data[6]   null
data[7]   null
data[8]   null
data[9]   → B's information
data[10] null
data[11] null
data[12] null
data[13] null
data[14] null
data[15] null
data[16] null
data[17] null
data[18] null

Figure 5.23   A Hashed Structure After Nodes A and B are Inserted, B Colliding with A

The Delete Problem

To illustrate this problem, let us assume that we try to fetch node B from an empty data structure, and its home index, as determined by the preprocessing and hashing algorithms, is 4. Finding a **null** reference stored in that element of the array, we would correctly conclude that B is not in the structure. Now suppose that nodes A and B are inserted into the empty structure in the order, first A, and then B. Let us also assume that they both have the same home address, 4, and that the collision algorithm placed B at location 9 (see Figure 5.23).

Now consider what happens when we try to fetch node B from the structure. The first place we look is its home address, 4. Finding node A there, we *cannot* conclude that node B is not in the data structure since, when it was inserted, it could have (and in fact did) collide with node A. Therefore, we use the collision algorithm to probe further into the primary storage area. On the first pass through the collision algorithm we find it, or if it is not in the structure, we encounter a **null** reference.

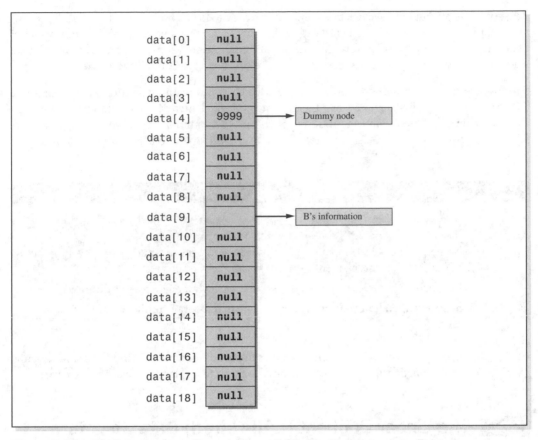

Figure 5.24 The Data Structure Shown in Figure 5.38 after Node A has been Deleted

Now suppose that node A is deleted and that the reference to it, at index 4, is set to **null**. A subsequent searched for node B uncovers a **null** reference at its home address, index 4, and we would conclude (erroneously) that node B is not in the data structure. This example illustrates the Delete problem which occurs when a node on a collision path is deleted (i.e., A) and then an operation is attempted on a node further down the collision path (i.e., B). By setting the deleted node's reference in the primary storage area to **null**, we have effectively lost the *record* that the other nodes have collided with it.

The usual solution to this problem is to set the deleted node's reference in the primary storage area array to a value other than its initial **null** value. Referring to the initial value (**null**) as v_1 and the *other value* as v_2, v_1 indicates there was never a node reference at that location, while v_2 indicates that there was once a node there, but it has been deleted. Both v_1 and v_2 must be chosen to be nonlegitimate node references. Usually v_1 is chosen to be **null**, and v_2 is chosen to be a pointer to a dummy node. Assuming values of **null** and 9999 for v_1 and v_2 respectively, Figure 5.24 shows the data structure after A has been deleted. Now, when we try to locate node B, the home address contains a pointer to the dummy node indicating that there once was a node at this location which B could have collided with. Therefore, we must continue the search for B by invoking the collision algorithm. In this case, on the first pass through the collision algorithm, B is located.

Suppose we tried to locate some other node, C, which is not in the structure but whose home address is also 4. Finding a reference to the dummy node in element 4, we would invoke the collision algorithm repeatedly until a **null** reference was encountered which would terminate the search. The solution to the Delete problem for all four basic operations is summarized in Figure 5.25.

The Delete Problem Solution

- Initialize the primary storage area to a value, v_1 (usually **null**).
- The Fetch and Delete operations continue searching primary storage until the node is found, or the element of primary storage contains v_1.
- When deleting a node, its reference is set to v_2 (usually a reference to a dummy node).
- The Insert operation continues searching primary storage until a value of v_1 or v_2 is found.

Having discussed all aspects of the hashing process depicted in Figure 5.5, and the preprocessing, hashing, and collision algorithms, we are now in a position to implement a hashed structure.

5.4.6 The Linear Quotient (LQHashed) Data Structure Implementation

In this section we will implement a hashed data structure LQHashed. The keys will be assumed to be strings of any length, therefore preprocessing will be necessary to map then into numeric pseudo keys. The Fold-shifting algorithm, coded as the method stringToInt (see Figure 5.18), will be the preprocessing algorithm.

The client will specify the maximum number of nodes to be stored in the structure. This value, adjusted by the optimum loading factor (0.75), will be used by the method fourKPlus3 (see Figure 5.16) to determine the size the primary storage area array, N. Since the preprocessing algorithm returns the absolute value of a 32 bit signed integer, the range of the pseudo keys will be 0 to 2,147,483,648. To avoid indexing beyond the bounds of the primary storage area array, the Division Hashing algorithm will be used to map the pseudo keys into indices. The value of v_1 will be **null**, and v_2 will be the address of a dummy node. As previously stated, collisions will be resolved with the Linear Quotient collision algorithm. The default quotient will be the (arbitrarily chosen) $k4 + 3$ prime, 9967.

As usual, the update algorithm will be implemented as an invocation to the delete method, followed by an invocation to the insert method. The flowcharts for the other three operation algorithms,

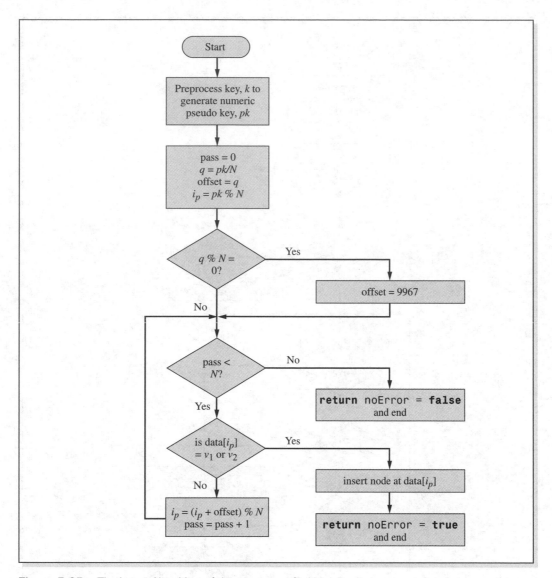

Figure 5.25 The Insert Algorithm of the LQHashed Structure

Insert, Fetch, and Delete (which are adaptations of the algorithm depicted in Figure 5.12) are given in Figures 5.25, 5.26, and 5.27 respectively. The following notation is used in these figures:

k is the given key; pk is the numeric pseudo key;
data is the name of the primary storage area array;
ip is used as an index into the primary storage area;
pass is a count of the number of times the collision algorithm (loop) executes;
v_1 is the value initially stored in the primary storage array elements (**null**); and
v_2 is the reference to a dummy node.

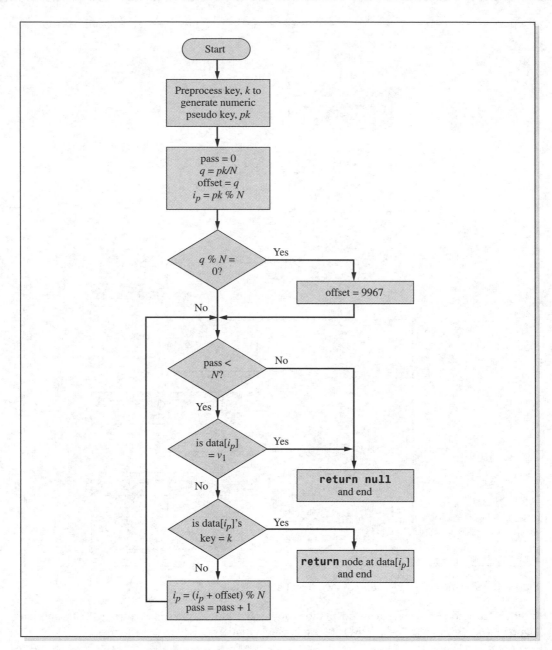

Figure 5.26   The Fetch Algorithm of the `LQHashed` Structure

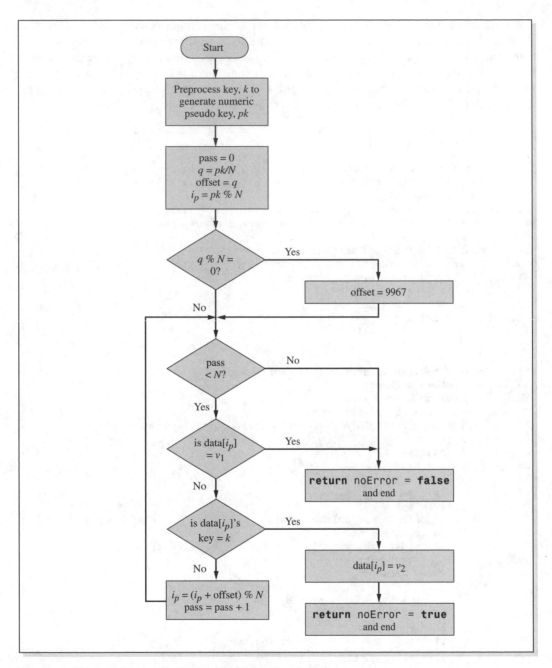

Figure 5.27 The Delete Algorithm of the LQHashed Structure

Our implementation will be a fully encapsulated homogeneous implementation of a hashed data structure that stores nodes in the class Listing. The code, which is presented in Figure 5.28, is consistent with the many of the concepts of generics presented in Chapter 2. It does not mention the names of any of the fields of the nodes, and the definition of the nodes to be stored in structure is coded as a separate class (see Figure 2.16). This class provides a deepCopy method in order to encapsulate the structure, a method compareTo to determine if a given key is equal to the key of

```
1.   public class LqHashed
2.   {  int N;
3.      int n = 0; // the number of nodes in the structure
4.      int defaultQuotient = 9967; // the default 4k + 3 prime
5.      double loadingFactor = 0.75;
6.      Listing deleted; // the dummy node, v2 (v1 = null)
7.      private Listing[] data; // the primary storage array
8.
9.      public LqHashed(int length)
10.     {  int pct = (int)((1.0 / loadingFactor - 1) *100.0);
11.        N = fourKPlus3(length, pct);
12.        data = new Listing[N];
13.        deleted = new Listing("","","");
14.        for(int i = 0; i < N; i++)
15.           data[i] = null;
16.     } // end of constructor
17.
18.     public boolean insert(Listing newListing)
19.     {  boolean noError;
20.        boolean hit = false;
21.        int pass, q, offset, ip;
22.        int pk = stringToInt(newListing.getKey()); // preprocess the key
23.        if(((((double) n) / N) < loadingFactor) // insert the node
24.        {  pass = 0;
25.           q = pk / N;
26.           offset = q;
27.           ip = pk % N;
28.           if(q % N == 0)
29.              offset = defaultQuotient;
30.           while(pass < N)
31.           {  if(data[ip] == null || data[ip] == deleted)
32.              {  hit = true;
33.                 break;
34.              }
35.              ip = (ip + offset) % N;
36.              pass = pass + 1;
37.           } // end while
38.           if(hit == true)  // insert the node
39.           {  data[ip]=newListing.deepCopy();
```

(continues)

Figure 5.28 Implementation of the Hashed Data Structure LQHashed

```
40.              n++;
41.                  return noError = true;
42.             }
43.           else
44.               return noError = false;
45.          }
46.        else // structure full to loading factor, insert not performed
47.            return noError = false;
48.    } // end of the insert method
49.
50.    public Listing fetch(String targetKey)
51.    {  boolean noError;
52.       boolean hit = false;
53.       int pass, q, offset, ip;
54.       int pk = stringToInt(targetKey);   // preprocess the key
55.       pass = 0;
56.       q = pk / N;
57.       offset = q;
58.       ip = pk % N;
59.       if(q % N == 0)
60.           offset = defaultQuotient;
61.       while(pass < N)
62.       {  if(data[ip] == null) // node not in structure
63.             break;
64.          if(data[ip].compareTo(targetKey) == 0) // node found
65.          {  hit = true;
66.             break;
67.          }
68.          ip = (ip + offset) % N;  // collision occurred
69.          pass = pass + 1;
70.       } // end while
71.       if(hit == true) // return a deep copy of the node
72.           return data[ip].deepCopy();
73.       else
74.           return null;
75.    } // end of the fetch method
76.
77.    public boolean delete(String targetKey)
78.    {  boolean noError;
79.       boolean hit = false;
80.       int pass, q, offset, ip;
81.       int pk = stringToInt(targetKey);   // preprocess the key
82.       pass = 0;
83.       q = pk / N;
84.       offset = q;
85.       ip = pk % N;
86.       if(q % N == 0)
87.           offset = defaultQuotient;
88.       while(pass < N)
```

Figure 5.28   (continued)

```
89.      {  if(data[ip] == null) // node not in structure
90.           break;
91.         if(data[ip].compareTo(targetKey) == 0) // node found
92.         { hit = true;
93.            break;
94.         }
95.         ip = (ip + offset) % N;   // collision occurred
96.         pass = pass + 1;
97.      }
98.      if(hit == true)  // delete the node
99.      { data[ip] = deleted;
100.        n--;
101.        return noError = true;
102.     }
103.     else
104.        return noError = false;
105.  } // end of the delete method
106.
107.  public boolean update(String targetKey, Listing newListing)
108.  {  if(delete(targetKey) == false)
109.        return false;
110.     else if(insert(newListing) == false)
111.        return false;
112.     return true;
113.  } // end of the update method
114.
115.  public void showAll()
116.  {  for(int i = 0; i < N; i++)
117.        if(data[i] != null && data[i] != deleted)
118.           System.out.printIn(data[i].toString());
119.  } // end showAll method
120.
121.  public static int fourKPlus3(int n, int pct) // from Figure 5.16
122.  {  boolean fkp3 = false;
123.     boolean aPrime = false;
124.     int prime, highDivisor, d;
125.     double pctd = pct;
126.     prime = (int)(n * (1.0 + (pctd / 100.0))); // guess the prime pct
                                                   // percent larger than n
127.     if(prime % 2 == 0) // if even make the prime guess odd
128.        prime = prime + 1;
129.     while(fkp3 == false) // not a 4k + 3 prime
130.     {  while(aPrime == false)  // not a prime
131.        {  highDivisor = (int)(Math.sqrt(prime) + 0.5);
132.           for(d = highDivisor; d > 1; d--)
133.           {  if(prime % d == 0)
134.                 break;
135.           }
136.           if(d != 1) // prime not found
```

Figure 5.28   (continued)

```
137.                    prime = prime + 2;
138.                else
139.                    aPrime = true;
140.            } // end of the prime search loop
141.            if((prime - 3) % 4 == 0)
142.                fkp3 = true;
143.            else
144.            { prime = prime + 2;
145.                aPrime = false;
146.            }
147.        } // end of 4k + 3 prime search loop
148.        return prime;
149.    } // end fourKPlus3 method
150.    public static int stringToInt(String aKey) // from Figure 5.18
151.    {   int pseudoKey = 0;
152.        int n = 1;
153.        int cn = 0;
154.        char c[] = aKey.toCharArray();
155.        int grouping = 0;
156.        while (cn < aKey.length()) // still more characters in the key
157.        {   grouping = grouping << 8; // pack next 4 characters
158.            grouping = grouping + c[cn];
159.            cn = cn + 1;
160.            if(n==4 || cn == aKey.length()) // 4 characters are processed
                                                // or no more characters
161.            {   pseudoKey = pseudoKey + grouping; // add grouping to
                                                      // pseudo key
162.                n = 0;
163.                grouping = 0;
164.            }
165.            n = n + 1;
166.        } // end while
167.        return Math.abs(pseudoKey);
168.    } // end stringToInt method
169. } // end class LqHashed
```

Figure 5.28 (continued)

a node in the structure, and a method toString to return the contents of a node. Since this is the first structure we have studied whose Insert algorithm needs access to the key field of the node being inserted (in order to preprocess and hash the key), a getKey method will be added to the class Listing. The code of the method follows:

```
public String getKey()
{   return name;
}
```

The implementation is not fully generic in that the node class must be named Listing and the key field must be a String. A fully generic implementation of the structure, using the generic features of Java 5.0 and the techniques described in Chapters 2 and 3 (Section 2.5 and 3.4) will be left as an exercise for the student.

Lines 121–149 is the method that generates the $4k + 3$ prime (previously presented in Figure 5.16) used to size the primary storage area. Lines 150–169 is the preprocessing method to convert string keys, of *any* length, into numeric pseudo keys (previously presented in Figure 5.18).

The default prime is set to the $4k + 3$ prime 9967 on Line 4, and the loading factor is set to the optimum value of 0.75 on Line 5. This will minimize collisions while maintaining an acceptable density. Lines 9–16, the class' one parameter constructor, allocates the primary storage area array (Line 12), and allocates a dummy node (Line 13) that will be used for the value of v_2 (i.e., to indicate that a node has been deleted). The client will use the method's parameter (length) to specify the maximum number of nodes to be stored in the structure. The size of the primary storage area (a $4k + 3$ prime) is calculated on Line 11. Finally, on Lines 14 and 15, the constructor initializes all elements of primary storage to v_1 (chosen to be **null**).[10]

The insert method on Lines 18–48, the fetch method on Lines 50–75, and the delete method on Lines 77–105 are the Java equivalent of the algorithms presented in Figures 5.25, 5.26, and 5.27, respectively, except for the code added to the insert and delete methods to keep track of the current loading factor and to not allow it to exceed the optimum value (0.75). Each of these methods uses the method stringToInt to preprocess String keys into numeric pseudo keys (Lines 22, 54, and 81). As previously mentioned, they presuppose that the class Listing, presented in Figure 2.16, has been expanded to include a method getKey that returns the key field of a Listing object.

Line 23 of the insert method will only allow an Insert operation to be performed if the current loading factor (n / N) is below the optimum loading factor. The **while** loop (Lines 30–37) performs a search for an unused location in the primary storage area: a **null** reference or a reference to the dummy node (Line 31). When found, the variable hit is set to **true** (Line 32), and a deep-Copy of the node is inserted into the structure (Line 39). Then, Line 40 increases the number of nodes in the structure by 1, to keep track of the current loading factor.

Line 72 of the fetch method returns a deepCopy of the requested node, thus maintaining the structure's encapsulation. When a node is deleted, Line 99 of the delete method resets the reference to it in the primary storage area to the dummy node. References to this node are considered unused by the insert method (Line 31) but do not cause the search loops of the fetch and delete methods to terminate (Lines 62 and 89). When a node is deleted, the number of nodes in the structure, n, is decremented by the delete method (Line 100) to keep track of the current loading factor. Finally, the Boolean expression on the right side of Line 117 prevents the showAll method from outputting the dummy node.

---

[10]Actually, in the language Java, all reference variables are initialized to **null** when created (Line 12). Lines 14–15 therefore, are redundant, but are included to make the initialization more obvious to the reader.

Performance of the LQHashed Structure

The speed and density of the LQHashed data structure will now be examined to determine its performance.

Speed

To analyze the speed of the structure, we will again perform a Big-O analysis to determine the approximate number of memory access instructions executed as n, the number of nodes stored in the structure, gets large. We will ignore instructions in loops that repeatedly access the same memory cell because optimizing compilers store these values in CPU registers. Each of the algorithms presented in Figures 5.25–5.27 performs preprocessing on non-numeric keys. During the preprocessing each character of the key has to be fetched from memory to be fold-shifted into the pseudo key. Assuming there are m characters in the key, m memory accesses would be performed during the preprocessing. In addition, the calculation of the quotient requires one memory access to fetch the value of N and an optimizing compiler would fetch the reference to the dummy node, v_2 prior to entering the loop. This would require one memory access. Thus, prior to entering the collision loop, $m + 2$ memory accesses are performed.

The remaining term in the speed equations is contributed by the collision loop in the Insert, Fetch, and Delete algorithms (bottom of Figures 5.25–5.27). Since the structure's maximum loading factor is the optimum loading factor (0.75), Figure 5.14 indicates we can expect average search lengths (resulting from repeated collisions) to be approximately 4.

In fact, the search length of this structure is even better than that illustrated in Figure 5.14 since the formula the figure is based upon, as stated in Appendix B, assumes that "All N primary storage area locations are *equally* probable to be generated each pass through the collision algorithm." This is not the case for the Linear Quotient collision algorithm. As we have seen, once a location is generated by the algorithm it is not generated again (see Table 5.7). When all locations have an equal probability of being generated (as Appendix B assumes), the probability of a collision on the ith pass through the collision algorithm is n / N. However, if we do not *revisit* locations as we proceed down a collision path, the probability of a collision on the ith pass through the collision algorithm is $(n - i) / (N - i)$, since i locations have been eliminated from consideration. Since $(n - i) / (N - i)$ is less than n / N for all positive values of i[11] the collision probability of the LQ algorithm decreases with each probe, resulting in slightly shorter search lengths.

Returning to our speed calculation, the Insert algorithm performs one memory access every pass through the loop to fetch the reference stored at data[ip]. Thus, the loop's speed term (in the speed equation) is four,[12] which, when combined with the memory access performed prior to entering the loop, ($m + 2$) gives a speed equation of $m + 6$.

---

[11]$(n - i) / (N - i)$ decreases as i increases since n is always less than N and, thus, n will reach zero before N.

[12]One access times four passes.

Both the Fetch and the Delete algorithms perform two memory accesses every pass through the loop. One to fetch `data[ip]`, and one to fetch the key of the node referenced by `data[ip]`. Thus, the loop's speed term (in these operations' speed equation) is eight,[13] which, when combined with the memory access performed prior to entering the loop, $(m + 2)$ gives a speed equation of $m + 10$.

Before ending our discussion of the speed of this structure, it should be mentioned that there is one situation that causes the speed of the Fetch and Delete operations to fall off sharply: when a significant portion of *unused* primary storage contains the value v_2 *and* the node to be fetched or deleted is not in the structure. To see why this happens, we must remember that the Fetch and Delete algorithms can only end on one of three conditions (see Figures 5.26 and 5.27):

1. The node to be operated on is located.
2. A value of v_1 (**null**) is encountered.
3. The collision loop executes $N - 1$ times.

Since the node to be operated on is not in the structure, condition 1 cannot end the algorithms. In addition, when the traffic on the structure is such that nodes are often deleted and others inserted, there may be no **null** values in the primary storage array. The deletions have overwritten them with the reference to the dummy node, v_2. Therefore, condition 2 cannot end the algorithms and the only way they can terminate is on condition 3. In this case, the collision loop executes $N - 1$ times performing $(N - 1) * 2$ time-consuming memory accesses. This is as slow as a sequential search.

One remedy for this situation is for the Fetch and Delete algorithms to temporarily suspend operations on the data structure when the number of v_2 primary storage references becomes excessive. Then, all the nodes are inserted into a newly declared array, except for the references to the dummy node. The array reference `data` is set to reference the new array. Finally, the count of the v_2 references can be set to zero because the **null** references in the newly created array were not overwritten with the references to the dummy node. The code to accomplish this, which assumes the new array is named `temp`, is given below.

```
temp = data; // set temp referencing primary storage
data = new Listing[N]; // allocate a new array data
for (int i = 0; i < N; i++)
{  if(temp[i] != null && temp[i] != v2)
        insert(temp[i]); // insert nodes into array data
}
V2count = 0; temp = null; // no v2 references; recycle the array
```

To keep track of the number of the number of v_2 references in the data structure, a counter is incremented whenever a node is deleted from the structure, and the counter is decremented whenever a node is inserted into an element previously written to v_2. Then, when the sum of this counter and n (the number of nodes in the structure) produce a loading factor above 0.75, operations on the structure are temporarily suspended and the previously discussed remedy is performed.

---

[13]Two accesses times four passes.

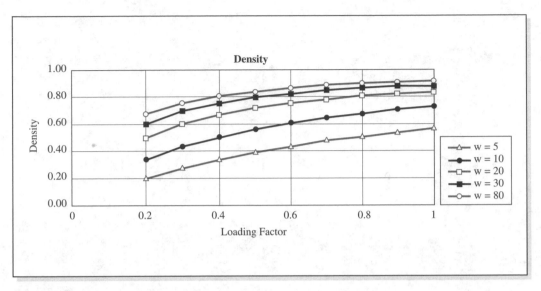

Figure 5.29   Density of the LQHashed Structure for Various Node Widths

Density

Our LQHashed structure uses the optimum loading factor (0.75) to size the primary storage area array which, as we have discussed, strikes a balance between good speed and space complexity. To demonstrate this, in Section 5.4 of this chapter, we derived a formula for the density of a hashed data structure in terms of loading factor:

$$D = w / (w + 4 * N / n) = w / (w + 4 / l)$$

where:

  w is the node width, in bytes,
  N is the size of the primary storage area array, and
  l is the loading factor.

Substituting our structure's loading factor (0.75) into this equation, its density D_{LQ} becomes

$$D_{LQ} = w / (w + 4 / 0.75) = w / (w + 5.33).$$

Figure 5.15, which is a plot of this function, demonstrates that the density of the LQHashed structure, like all hashed data structures with loading factors of 0.75, is good (> 0.80) for node widths of 23 bytes or more. Figure 5.29, which presents the density of a hashed structure for various loading factors and node widths, shows that only minimal improvements in density can be made by increasing the loading factor above 0.75.

Table 5.8 presents the overall performance of this structure, along with the performance of the structures we have previously studied for comparative purposes. Its speed is not quite as good as

Table 5.8

Performance of the LQHashed **Data Structure (**m **is the number of positions in the key,** l **is the loading factor, and** w **is the node width)**

Data Structure	Insert	Delete	Fetch	Update = Delete + Insert	Average[14]	Big-O Average	Average for $n = 10^7$	Condition for Density > 0.8
Unsorted-Optimized Array	3	$\leq n$	$\leq n$	$\leq n + 3$	$\leq (3n + 6)/4$	$O(n)$	$\leq 0.75 \times 10^7 + 1.5$	$w > 16$
Stack and Queue	5	combined with Fetch	4.5	not supported	$9.5/2 = 5$	$O(1)$	5	$w > 16$
Singly Linked List	6	$1.5n$	$1.5n$	$1.5n + 6$	$(4.5n + 12)/4$ $= 1.13n + 3$	$O(n)$	$1.13 \times 10^7 + 3$	$w > 33$
Direct Hashed (with Sub-traction Pre-processing)	1 or (3)	2 or (4)	1 or (3)	3 or (7)	$7/4 = 1.75$ or $(17/4 = 4.25)$	$O(1)$	1.75 or (4.25)	$w * l > 16$
LQHashed	$m + 6$	$m + 10$	$m + 10$	$2m + 16$	$(5m + 42)/4$	$O(1)$	$1.25m + 11$	$w > 23$

[14]Assumes all operations are equally probable and is therefore calculated as an arithmetic average of the four operation times.

that of the Direct Hashed data structure whose search length is always 1. However, its ability to deliver densities of 80% for all applications (whose node widths are above 23 bytes), and its ability to process String keys of any length make it a more than acceptable alternative when the density of the Direct Hashed structure is unacceptable, or when the key field is a long string.

For example, in our stadium ticket case study in which the seat number, date, and event number is encoded into a six digit ticket number, the loading factor of the DirectHashed structure was shown to be 0.01 (Section 5.2.1) and, therefore, the above equation for density yields D = 0.074 (the node with for this application was 32 bytes). In most cases, this would be a prohibitively low density. In contrast, since the node width is greater than 23 bytes, the LQHashed structure has a density greater than 0.80. From a speed complexity viewpoint, both structures are O(1).

Generic Implementation Considerations

Although the implementation of the LQHashed structure presented in Figure 5.28 is not fully generic (it can only store objects in the class Listing), it is consistent with many of the concepts of generics presented in Chapters 2 and 3. It does not mention the names of any of the fields of the nodes, and the definition of the nodes to be stored in the structure is defined in a separate class (Figure 2.16 was expanded to include a getKey method). To convert it to a full generic class, the techniques discussed in Chapters 2 and 3 (Sections 2.5 and 3.4) that make use of the generic features of Java 5.0 can be used. However, these techniques will have to be expanded slightly if the generic implementation of this structure is to allow keys that are not String objects because the preprocessing method stringToInt (in the data structure class) assumes that the key field is a String object. If the key is other than a String object, the method would have to be rewritten to produce integer pseudo keys for that type of object.

There are two approaches that could be taken to accomplish this rewrite. One approach would be to define a new data structure class that extends the class LQHashed (using OOP inheritance techniques, see Section 1.6) and overwrite the stringToInt method (which would now be improperly named, but we'll deal with that in a moment). Another approach would be to remove the string-ToInt method from the class LQHashed and require that it be defined as a method in the class of the key. In this case, its signature is usually changed so that it no longer operates on an argument sent to it, but on the object that invoked it. For example, if the key were an object in the class Car-Type, and the name of the method was a generic name like hashCode, then the signature of the method would be

```
public int hashCode()
```

and the method would be coded in the class CarType. The invocation in the data structure class to determine the pseudo key, pk, (e.g., Line 22 of Figure 5.28) for the CarType key convertible would be changed to:

```
int pk = convertible.hashCode();
```

As we will see later in this chapter, this is the approach taken in the implementations of the generic hashed data structures included in the Java Application Programmer Interface. In fact, many of the classes included in the Java API (e.g., `Integer`, `Double`, and `String`) include an implementation of a method named `hashCode`, whose signature is **public int** `hashCode()`. Therefore, if the invocations of the method `stringToInt` in Figure 5.28 are changed to invocations of the method `hashCode`, the structure `LQHashed` could store nodes whose keys were objects in the class `Double`, `Integer`, or `String`. For example, Line 22 of Figure 5.28 would be changed to

```
int pk = newListing.getKey().hashCode();
```

5.4.7 Dynamic Hashed Structures

The hashed structures studied so far require the client to specify the maximum number of nodes to be stored in the structure when it is created. The primary storage area array is sized using this value and an attempt to insert more than the specified number of nodes into the structure results in an insert error. A more flexible alternative is to allow the data structures to dynamically expand, while the data structure is in service. The number of nodes specified by the client is typically used to establish the *initial* size of the structure, but the structure will be allowed to grow beyond its initial size to accommodate additional nodes. This approach can make the speed of hashed data structures available to applications where the maximum number of nodes cannot be accurately predicted.

Dynamic expansion of the data structure can be accomplished in a variety of ways. The size of the primary storage area array can be increased to accommodate additional node references, or the additional storage can be provided outside of the primary storage area. Hybrid structures combine both approaches. These various schemes are illustrated in Figure 5.30. Two popular approaches to providing additional storage outside of the primary storage area is to provide either a linked list or an array to store the additional node references. Whichever approach is taken, the

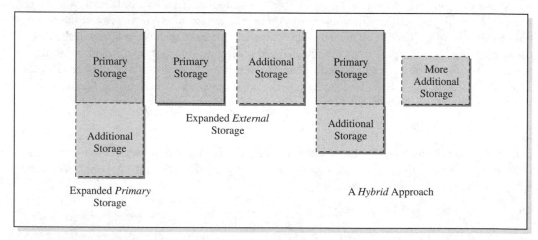

Figure 5.30 Three Approaches to Dynamic Hashed Structures

ability of these structures to accommodate virtually an unlimited number of nodes and still provide the speed of a hashed data structure, makes them very attractive for many applications.

We will conclude our study of hashed data structures by briefly examining two dynamic hashed data structures. The first one, which is implemented in a Java Application Programmer Interface package, will be examined from the client's viewpoint. The other structure will be examined at a lower level, to gain insights into the implementation of dynamic structures.

Java's Dynamic `Hashtable` Data Structure

The Java class `Hashtable`, contained in the package `java.util`, is an implementation of a *dynamic* hashed data structure. As such, it expands beyond its initial size to accommodate virtually an unlimited number of nodes. As implemented, it is a nonhomogeneous, unencapsulated generic data structure accessed in the key field mode. The key can be any type of object.

The structure is a dynamic hybrid; it expands its primary storage area *and* resolves collisions by providing additional storage for node references outside of the primary storage area. When the number of references stored in the primary storage area array is such that the loading factor exceeds a specified maximum, the size of the primary storage area is increased. Although keys can be any type of object, as previously discussed, the key's class should overwrite the method `hash-Code`. This method is invoked by the operation methods in the `Hashtable` class to preprocess a key into an integer. The key's class should also overwrite the method `equals`. The signature of both of these methods is given in the description of the class `Object` to be:

```
public boolean equals()
public int hashCode()
```

The classes `String`, and the wrapper classes for the numeric types (i.e., `Byte`, `Double`, `Float`, `Integer`, `Long`, and `Short`) all overwrite these methods. Therefore, keys that are instances of these classes can be properly processed into pseudo keys.[15]

The class `Hashtable` has four constructors. The default constructor sets the maximum loading factor to 0.75 and the initial size of the primary storage area to 101 elements. The one parameter constructor also defaults the maximum loading factor to 0.75, but allows the client to specify the initial size of the primary storage area. The client can specify both the maximum loading factor and the initial size of the primary storage area using the class' two parameter constructor. A fourth constructor initializes the structure to a copy of an existing `Hashtable` structure by copying the references in the primary storage area array of the existing structure into the newly created structure.

The Insert, Fetch, and Delete operation methods are named `put`, `get`, and `remove`, respectively. The methods `get` and `remove` return **null** if the specified key is not in the structure. The structure

---

[15]If a key's class does not overwrite these two methods the implementation in the class `Object` is used and the pseudo key returned from the method `hashCode` is based on the node's location rather than the node's key.

recalculates the loading factor every time an `insert` is performed. When the loading factor exceeds the specified maximum, an internal reorganization takes place. A **protected** method named `rehash` is invoked to expand the primary storage area, and all the nodes are reinserted into the expanded structure. This process reduces the speed of the structure and so it is advisable to specify the initial size of the structure in a way that minimizes the number of times the structure is reorganized. Descriptions of the other methods in the class are given in the Java online documentation (http://java.sun.com/j2se/1.3/docs/api/java/util/Hashtable.html).

An application that uses the `Hashtable` data structure, and the output it produces, is given in Figure 5.31. On Line 3, the application uses the Java 5.0 generic type parameters (i.e., `<String, Listing>`) to declare the structure to be a homogeneous structure that can store only `Listing` objects whose key field is a `String` object. The code of the class `Listing` is presented in Figure 2.16.

The lack of the structure's encapsulation is demonstrated on Lines 21–24. If the structure were encapsulated, Line 23 would have output Bill's address that was updated to "99th Street" on Line 18. Instead it outputs the address "18 Park Avenue" that the client set using the `setAddress` method.

If the generic type parameters were not used in the declaration of the object `dataBase` on Line 4, then the structure would be heterogeneous and any type node with any type key could be stored in the data structure. In this case, the reference returned from a `get` operation would have to be coerced before they were assigned to reference variables; e.g., `b = (Listing) dataBase.get("Bill");`.

Linked Hashed Data Structures

A common design of a dynamic hashed structure is the Linked Hashed structure.[16] It does not expand primary storage to accommodate additional nodes, but rather provides additional storage outside of the primary storage area in the form of multiple linked lists.

Each of the N locations of the primary storage area array (commonly called a *bucket*) is a header of a singly linked list. All of the nodes that hash into a given location of primary storage are stored in the linked list associated with that (home) location. For example, if nodes A, B, and C all mapped into location 4, and node D mapped into location 10, the nodes would be stored as shown in Figure 5.32.[17] Thus, not only are the linked lists used to dynamically grow the structure, but they are also used to resolve collisions. Collision resolution is performed through a sequential search down the linked lists, rather than a search through the primary storage area.

When a collision occurs during an Insert operation, the length of the linked list (headed by the key's home address) is increased by one node. Normally, for speed considerations the new node is inserted at the beginning of the linked list, and so the elements of primary storage refer to the most recently inserted node that hashed into that element.

---

[16]Also called a Chained Hashed structure.

[17]We have assumed a linked list implementation *without* a "dummy" node between the list header and the list.

```
1.    import java.util.Hashtable;
2.    public class MainAPIHashtable
3.    {  public static void main(String[] args)
4.       {  Hashtable <String, Listing> dataBase = new Hashtable<String, Listing>();
5.          Listing b, t;
6.          Listing bill = new Listing("Bill", "1st Avenue", "999 9999");
7.          Listing tom = new Listing("Tom", "2nd Avenue", "456 8978");
8.          Listing newBill = new Listing("William", "99th Street", "123 4567");
9.          // inserts
10.         dataBase.put("Bill", bill);
11.         dataBase.put("Tom", tom);
12.         // fetches
13.         b = dataBase.get("Bill");
14.         t = dataBase.get("Tom");
15.         System.out.println(b);
16.         System.out.println(t);
17.         // effectively an update of Bill's address
18.         dataBase.put("Bill", newBill);
19.         b = dataBase.get("Bill"); // fetches Bill's updated node
20.         System.out.println(b);
21.         // demonstration of the lack of encapsulation
            // Client can change the contents of the node with a set method
22.          newBill.setAddress("18 Park Avenue");
23.          b = dataBase.get("Bill");
24.          System.out.println(b);
25.         // delete operation
26.          dataBase.remove("Bill");
27.          b = dataBase.get("Bill");
28.          System.out.println(b);
29.       } // end of main method
30.    } // end class MainAPIHashtable
```

Program Output

Name is Bill
Address is 1st Avenue
Number is 999 9999

Name is Tom
Address is 2nd Avenue
Number is 456 8978

Name is William
Address is 99th Street
Number is 123 4567

Name is William
Address is 18 Park Avenue
Number is 123 4567

null

Figure 5.31 An Application Program that Uses the Java `Hashtable` Data Structure

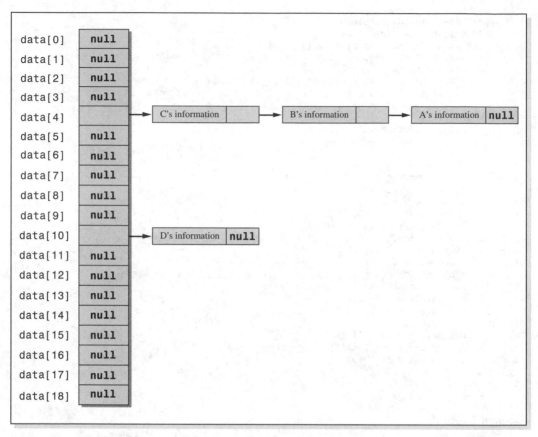

Figure 5.32 A Dynamic Linked Hashed Structure (with Nodes A, B, and C Hashing into the Same Location of Primary Storage)

Most implementations of this structure permit the client to specify a *best guess* at the maximum number of nodes to be stored in the structure, n. Then the primary storage area is sized to a percentage of n. The size of primary storage area, N, does not necessarily have to be greater than n for this structure since the nodes are stored in the linked lists. In the extreme case, when N is 1, the structure degenerates into a singly linked list.

The overhead of this structure is the storage associated with the primary storage area array ($N * 4$) and the storage associated with the implementation of the linked list. The storage associated with the linked list implementation includes two reference variables for each node in the structure; one variable to store the node's address and one to store the address of the next item in the linked list (see Figure 4.9 with the dummy node eliminated). Assuming reference variables occupy 4 bytes, the density of this structure, D_{LH}, can be expressed as

$$D_{LH} = \text{information bytes} / (\text{information bytes} + \text{overhead bytes}) =$$
$$= (n * w) / (n * w + [N * 4 + n * 2 * 4])$$
$$= (n * w) / (n * [w + 8] + N * 4),$$

where:

>n is the number of nodes in the structure,
>
>w is the information bytes per node,
>
>N is the size of the primary storage area (= number of linked lists), and each reference variable occupies 4 bytes.

Dividing the numerator and denominator of the right side of this equation by $n * w$ we obtain

$$\frac{1}{(1 + 8/w) + (N * 4)/(n * w)} = \frac{1}{(1 + 8/w) + (N/n)/(4/w)}$$

Substituting $1 / l_p$, for N / n the density of the Linked Hashed structure becomes

$$D_{LH} = \frac{1}{(1 + 8/w) + (1/l_p) * (4/w)}$$

where:

>l_p is a *pseudo* loading factor n / N.

Examining the fraction on the right side of the equation, we see that as the node width or the pseudo loading factor increases, the denominator decreases, and the density improves. This is typical of the hashed structures studied thus far. What is atypical of this structure, and the reason we use the term *pseudo* loading factor, is that the ratio n / N can be allowed to exceed 1, since we no longer have to provide a location in the primary storage area array for each node. We only need to provide a location for each linked list.

The variation in the density with the pseudo loading factor for various node widths, w, is shown in Figure 5.32. For a given node width, the increase in density with loading factor appears to be insignificant beyond a loading factor of three. Now, assuming the preprocessing and hashing function distributes the keys' home addresses evenly over the primary storage area, the average number of nodes in each of the N linked lists is n / N. For example, 30 nodes ($n = 30$) distributed over 10 lists ($N = 10$) results in 3 nodes per list (30 / 10). Since the average number of nodes in the linked lists adversely affects the speed of the structure, and further increases in the loading factor do little to improve the density, a loading factor of 3 is a good balance between speed and density for this structure. At a loading factor of 3, the density is 0.8 for node widths (w) greater than or equal to 37 bytes.

Now let us examine the speed of the structure in more detail beginning with the Insert algorithm. In Chapter 4 we determined that an average of six memory accesses are required to insert a node at the beginning of a linked list. However, this structure requires one less memory access because the preprocessing and hashing algorithms calculate the location of the memory cell that references the new node rather than using the list header to locate a dummy node. Thus, an Insert operation is performed with an average of five memory accesses.

The average search length for a Fetch or Delete operation is related to the average number of nodes in the linked lists. A goal of the preprocessing and hashing algorithms used in this structure is to keep the length of the linked lists equal or *balanced* by randomly mapping the keys over the primary storage area. In this case, as previously stated, each linked list will contain n / N nodes since the number of linked lists is the size of the primary storage area, N.

Assuming an average node would be halfway down one of the linked lists, $(n / N) / 2$ nodes would be traversed to locate it. As discussed in Chapter 4, traversing a linked list requires two memory accesses per node traversed, therefore the average number of memory accesses required to locate a node would be

$(n / N) / 2$ nodes traversed * 2 memory accesses per node traversed $= n / N$ memory accesses.

Since n/N is, by definition, the loading factor, the average number of memory accesses during a Fetch or Delete operation is equal to the loading factor. Therefore, if the linked lists can be kept balanced, the x-axis in Figure 5.33 is also the average number of memory accesses (speed) of the Fetch-and-Delete operations, not considering the memory accesses required to preprocess non-numeric keys. When we consider the number of preprocessing memory accesses, m, and the fact that little gain in density is realized if we increase the loading factor beyond a value of 3, the number of memory access for a Fetch or Delete operation becomes $m + n/N = m + 3$.

Table 5.9 presents the overall performance of this structure, compared to structures previously studied. Not only is its speed and performance excellent (assuming the linked lists remain balanced), but its dynamic characteristic make it an excellent choice for many applications.

An interesting variation of the Linked Hashed structure is a hybrid structure, expandable in two directions. In addition to the size of a linked list increasing every time a collision occurs, the primary storage area is also expandable. When the average length of the linked lists grows to a point where the speed of the structure is unacceptable, the primary storage area is expanded and the nodes are reinserted into the structure.

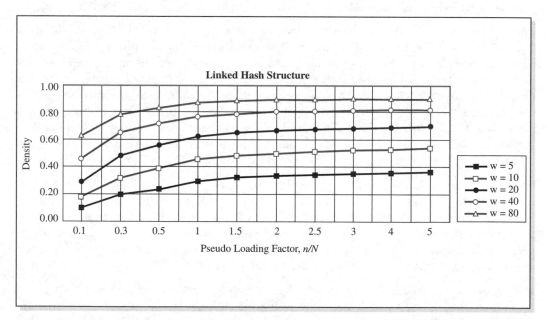

Figure 5.33   Variation of Density with Loading Factor for a Linked Hashed Structure

Table 5.9

Performance of the Linked Hashed Data Structure (m is the number of position in the key, l is the loading factor, w is the node width

Data Structure	Operation Speed (in memory accesses)				Big-O Average	Average[18]	Average for $n = 10^7$	Condition for Density > 0.8
	Insert	Delete	Fetch	Update = Delete + Insert				
Unsorted-Optimized Array	3	$\leq n$	$\leq n$	$\leq n+3$	$\leq (3n+6)/4$	$O(n)$	$\leq 0.75 \times 10^7 + 1.5$	$w > 16$
Restricted Structures, Stack and Queue	4	combined with Fetch	3	not supported	$7/2 = 3.5$	$O(1)$	3.5	$w > 16$
Singly Linked List	6	$1.5n$	$1.5n$	$1.5n + 6$	$(4.5n + 12)/4 = 1.13n + 3$	$O(n)$	$1.13 \times 10^7 + 3$	$w > 33$
Direct Hashed (with Subtraction Pre-processing)	1 or (3)	2 or (4)	1 or (3)	3 or (7)	$7/4 = 1.75$ or $(17/4 = 4.25)$	$O(1)$	1.75 or (4.25)	$w \star l > 16$
LQHashed	$m + 6$	$m + 10$	$m + 10$	$2m + 16$	$(5m + 42)/4$	$O(1)$	$1.25m + 11$	$w > 23$
Linked Hashed, $l = 3$	$m + 5$	$m + 3$	$m + 3$	$2m + 8$	$(5m + 19)/4$	$O(1)$	$1.25m + 4.8$	$w > 37$

[18]Assumes all operations are equally probable and is therefore calculated as an arithmetic average of the four operation times.

EXERCISES

Knowledge Exercises

1. Give the major advantage of any hashed data structure over array-based and linked list structures?

2. What is the potential downside to hashed data structures compared to array-based and linked list structures?

3. What characteristic common to all hashing access algorithms makes them fast in the key field mode?

4. For a hashed data structure implemented in Java, give the two alternatives for what is is stored in the primary storage area array?

5. Define loading factor.

6. Define the term collision in the context of data structures.

7. True or false, collisions improve the performance of a hashed data structure?

8. Keys are numeric values between 0 and 10,000. Assuming 200 nodes are to be stored in a hashed data structure that uses the direct hashing function, how many elements will be in the primary storage area array?

9. Assuming the Direct Hashing function and the Subtraction preprocessing algorithm is used to map keys into indices, give the index it maps the key 2000 into, assuming:

   a) The range of the keys is 0 to 999,999.

   b) The range of the keys is 100 to 999,999.

10. Give the Division Hashing function and the index it maps the key 2000 into, assuming a primary storage area array size of 61 elements and:

    a) The range of the keys is 0 to 999,999.

    b) The range of the keys is 100 to 999,999.

11. Nodes are to be stored in a hashed data structure that utilizes the direct hashing function. Assuming the key field was an integer ranging from 2000 to 100,000 and the structure will store a maximum of 60,000 nodes:

    a) Compute the loading factor of the structure.

    b) Compute the density of the structure assuming a node width of 100 bytes.

    c) Give the node width that results in a density of 0.7.

12. A key maps into index 200 of a Direct Hashed data structure's primary storage array. A Fetch operation is to be performed. How will we tell if the node is not in the structure?

13. What would be the density *and* maximum loading factor of the structure described in Exercise 11 if 9000 nodes were to be stored in the structure?

14. Which data structure is faster: a perfect or a nonperfect hashed structure?

15. Define search length.

16. What is the average search length of a perfect hashed data structure?

17. Considering density and speed, what is the optimum loading factor for a hashed data structure that uses a nonperfect hashing function, *and* what is the average search length at that loading factor?

18. Which of the following integers are $4k + 3$ primes?

    a) 4726

    b) 2003

    c) 9109

19. Pseudo keys are in the range 0 to 200,000 and a maximum of 9000 nodes will be stored in a nonperfect hashed data structure. Give the size of the primary storage area array (number of elements) that will produce the optimum loading factor.

20. Give the density of the structure described in Exercise 19 assuming the node width is:

    a) 10 bytes

    b) 200 bytes

21. Assuming keys are comprised of upper- and lowercase letters, give the bit pattern *and* base 10 numeric value of the pseudo key that would result from processing the key "Mary" using the algorithm illustrated in Figure 5.17.

22. What would be the base 10 value of the pseudo key produced by fold-shifting the key "Bob-Jones" to produce a 16-bit numeric pseudo key. Use the characters "bJ" as a pivot.

23. A pseudorandom preprocessing scheme is being used in a hashed data structure with the primes $p_1 = 11$ and $p_2 = 5$. Give the pseudo keys for the following keys:

    a) 198

    b) 24

24. State the difference between an open addressing and a non-open addressing collision algorithm.

25. The primary storage area in a nonperfect hashed data structure is a 103 element array. A key has been mapped into index 102, and a collision has occurred. Give the indices calculated by the next three passes through the collision algorithm if the collision algorithm is the modified version of the:

    a) Linear Probing

    b) Quadratic Probing

26. Define the terms:

    a) Primary clustering

    b) Secondary clustering

EXERCISES

27. Why is the array used for a restricted hashing scheme always sized to a $4k + 3$ prime?

28. Give the Linear Quotient collision algorithm and describe how it gets its name?

29. Describe the "delete problem" associated with nonperfect hashed data structures and state the standard remedy.

30. Give the density of a hashed structure with a loading factor of 0.6 assuming each node contains 30 information bytes.

31. Objects to be stored in a data structure each have 1000 bytes of information, which includes the key field comprised of 5 digits. A maximum of 1500 nodes will be in the structure at one time. How many elements will be in the primary storage area array, if the nodes are stored using a:

    a) Direct hashing function?

    b) Division hashing function?

32. Give the density of the two structures described in Exercise 31.

33. A maximum of 300 nodes are to be stored in a hashed data structure. Give the size of the primary storage area that would maximize the performance of the structure.

34. A 23 element array has been allocated to store nodes using the LQHashed data structure discussed in this chapter. Give the array index used to store the nodes with the following keys, assuming they are inserted in the order given:

    a) 4618

    b) 391

    c) 6941

    d) 547

    Note: Use the $4k + 3$ prime 19 to resolve any problems with the quotients.

35. Give the advantage of dynamic hashed structures over nondynamic hashed structures.

36. Give an advantage and a disadvantage of the array-based approach to a dynamic hashed structure over the linked approach.

37. In the context of dynamic hashed structures, what is a bucket?

38. Assuming 30,000 nodes are equally distributed over a dynamic linked hashed structure, give the size of the primary storage array for optimum performance.

39. Java contains a class that implements a dynamic hashed data structure.

    a) Give the name of the class.

    b) Give the import statement necessary to use the class.

    c) How does it resolve collisions?

    d) Is the structure a fully encapsulated structure?

EXERCISES

Programming Exercises

40. Implement the perfect hashed data structure discussed in this chapter and provide an application that demonstrates that its four basic operation methods function properly. Your application should store nodes for a stadium ticket application where the ticket numbers range from 2000 to 100,000 for a 60,000 seat stadium. The ticket number will be the key field and the nodes will also store the purchaser's name. See Figure 5.4 for a description of the field widths.

41. Code a method that outputs the prime numbers between any two given integers. Supply a driver program that allows the user to input the range of the prime numbers.

42. Code a method that outputs the density of a Direct Hashed data structure given the number of nodes in the structure, the node width in bytes, and the number of elements in the primary storage area.

43. Code a method that maps an automobile license plate number into a unique integer. License plates can consist of any permutation of up to four capital letters and the digits 0 through 9. Supply a driver program that demonstrates that the method functions properly.

44. Write a program that demonstrates that the Linear Quotient collision algorithm generates every primary storage array index before repeating one. The size of the primary storage area and the initial home address will be input by the user. Supply a driver program that demonstrates that the method functions properly.

45. A database is to be developed to keep track of student information at your college: their names, identification numbers, and grade point averages. The data set will be accessed in the key field mode, with the student's identification number being the key field. Code a class named `Listing` that defines the nodes. The class must comply with the five conditions (assumptions) of a generic, homogeneous, fully encapsulated data structure. As such, your class should include all the methods in the class shown in Figure 2.28. Test it with a progressively developed driver program that demonstrates the functionality of all of its methods.

46. Code an application program that keeps track of student information at your college: their names, identification numbers (the key field), and grade point averages in a fully encapsulated, Direct Hashed data structure. When launched, the user will be asked to input the maximum size of the data set, the initial number of students, and the initial data set. Once this is complete, the user will be presented with the following menu:

    Enter: 1 to *insert* a new student's information,

    2 to *fetch* and output a student's information,

    3 to *delete* a student's information,

    4 to *update* a student's information,

    5 to *output* all the student information, and

    6 to *exit* the program.

EXERCISES

The program should perform an unlimited number of operations until the user enters a 6 to exit the program. Assume the identification numbers will be in the range 1000 to 50,000.

47. Code the application described in Exercise 46 using a hashed structure based on the Quadratic collision algorithm, but now the student's name will be the key field.

48. Code the application described in Exercise 46 using a Java's `Hashtable` data structure.

49. Code the application described in Exercise 46 using a Linked Hashed data structure.

50. The code presented in Figure 5.28 processes nodes whose keys are `Strings`. Modify its code so that it processes keys that are objects in any class. Provide a driver program to demonstrate the modifications function properly.

51. Modify the code presented in Figure 5.28 so that it is a fully generic class using the generic features of Java 5.0. Is should be able to processes nodes and keys that are objects in any class. Provide a driver program to demonstrate the modifications function properly.

CHAPTER 6

Recursion

OBJECTIVES

The objectives of this chapter are to introduce the student to the topic of recursion, to teach the student how to think recursively, and how to formulate and implement recursive solutions. More specifically, students will be able to

- Understand the concept of recursion and recursive definitions.

- Understand how recursive algorithms produce their result, and understand the execution path of methods that implement them.

- Implement a recursive algorithm, and understand its iterative counterpart.

- *Think recursively.* Understand a methodized approach to formulating many recursive algorithms that includes the discovery of a *base case*, *reduced problem*, and *general solution*, and understand the flowchart that integrates these into a recursive solution.

- Extend their ability to think recursively by generalizing the methodized approach to include problems that require multiple base cases, reduced problems, and general solutions.

- Understand, and be able to explain, the advantages of recursive solutions as well as the limitations and problems associated with recursion.

- Understand a technique called *dynamic programming*, and its role in improving the speed complexity of recursive algorithms.

- Understand a general problem solving technique called *backtracking* that utilizes recursion, understand its use in the solution of the Knights Tour problem, and be able to apply the technique to the solution of other problems such as the Queens Eight problem.

6.1 What Is Recursion?

Most of us at some point in our lives have been told not to define something in terms of itself. We were told that the word we are defining should be not be used in its definition. Usually, this is good advice. When asked to define a dog, the statement "a dog is a dog" gives no insight into what a dog really is. Yet there are times when it is not only allowable to use the word we are defining in its definition, but actually advisable; when the word is used to only *partially* define itself.

For example, to define the word ancestor it is not permissible to say "an ancestor is an ancestor," but the statement

"An ancestor is a parent *or* an ancestor of a parent"

is a permissible definition even though the word ancestor is used in the definition. The phrase "ancestor of a parent" is only part of the definition; the other part is the phrase "a parent."

This type of definition is called a recursive definition. Typically, recursive definitions consist of something we are familiar with (e.g., a parent), and some sort of *recurrence relation* involving the word we are trying to define and the familiar entity (e.g., *ancestor* of a *parent*). The strength of a recursive definition is that the recurrence relation, or *repetitive part* of the definition, is used to succinctly expand the scope of the definition.

For example, suppose we wish to determine the meaning of the statement

"Mary is an ancestor of George."

Using the nonrepetitive portion of the definition of ancestor (an ancestor is a parent) the statement becomes "Mary is a *parent* of George," and its meaning is clear. However, the word ancestor in the original statement could also mean "an ancestor of a parent." In this case the statement becomes

"Mary is *an ancestor of a parent* of George."

To find the meaning of this statement we could use the nonrepetitive portion of the definition of ancestor (an ancestor is a parent). Then the statement becomes "Mary is a *parent* of a parent of

George," and the original statement means Mary is George's grandparent. Alternately, we could again use the repetitive portion of the definition of ancestor (an ancestor is an ancestor of a parent). In this case, the statement becomes

"Mary is *an ancestor of a parent* of a parent of George."

This could mean that Mary is George's great grandparent or a more distant relative;

"Mary is *an ancestor of a parent* of a parent of a parent of George."

Thus, we see that our original recursive definition of ancestor "an ancestor is a parent *or* an ancestor of a parent" is a succinct way of saying an ancestor is a parent, or a grandparent, or a great grandparent, or a great great grandparent, etc.

Recursive definitions are also used in computer science in the statement of algorithms. A recursive algorithm is an algorithm defined at least *partially* in terms of itself. Not all problems have recursive solutions. However, for those that do, the recursive algorithm often offers an elegant and succinct alternative to iterative algorithms.[1]

When most people are introduced to the concept of a recursive algorithms, they usually find them difficult to understand and even somewhat magical. After an initial examination of a recursive algorithm, we are often convinced it will not work, that it is incomplete, or that it only addresses a subset of the problem. This is because only a small percentage of the population has the innate ability to think recursively. The majority of us have to acquire this cognitive ability. We have to be trained to think recursively.

There are two levels of recursive thinking we should aspire to. They are, the ability to *understand* a recursive algorithm and, at a deeper level, the ability to *formulate* a recursive algorithm; the former skill being a necessary foundation for the latter.

6.2 Understanding Recursive Algorithms

One way of learning how to understand recursive algorithms is to compare a nonrecursive definition of an algorithm to its recursive definition. Another way is to code the recursive version of the algorithm and trace its execution path. Let us begin with the former technique and consider the problem of calculating *n* factorial.

---

[1]Iterative algorithms are algorithms that involve loops.

6.2.1 *n* Factorial

The function *n* factorial, written as *n*!, is defined for non-negative values of *n* as:

for $n = 0$, $n! = 1$

for all positive values of *n*, $n! = n * (n - 1) * (n - 2) * (n - 3) * \ldots * 1$.

This definition is a *nonrecursive* definition of *n* factorial because the factorial operator (!) is not used in its own definition. Using this nonrecursive definition, we calculate $0! = 1$ and $4! = 4 * 3 * 2 * 1 = 24$.

The second portion of this definition, $n! = n * (n - 1) * (n - 2) * (n - 3) * \ldots * 1$, can be written recursively by realizing that

$$n! = n * (n - 1) * (n - 2) * (n - 3) * \ldots * 1 = n * [(n - 1) * (n - 2) * (n - 3) * \ldots * 1]$$
$$= n * (n - 1)!$$

Using this equality in the second part of the nonrecursive definition it becomes

for $n = 0$, $n! = 1$

for all positive values of *n*, $n! = n * (n - 1)!$

which is the recursive definition of *n*!. It is a recursive definition because unless $n = 0$, *n* factorial is defined in terms of another factorial, $(n - 1)!$. The nonrecursive definition explicitly tells you how to calculate *n*! as: $n * (n - 1) * (n - 2) * (n - 3) * \ldots * 1$. The recursive definition does not explicitly tell you how to calculate n!, but rather seems to assume that you already know something about the factorial function. That is, that you already know how to calculate $(n - 1)!$.

Like most recursive definitions, this definition of *n*! seems to beg the question "how do I calculate *n*!?" It can be likened to you asking your friend John the value of *n* factorial. John, being blessed with the ability to think recursively, begs the question by responding "I'll call Mary and ask her the value of $n - 1$ factorial, and then I'll have the answer for you." What John plans to do is multiply Mary's answer (the value of $n - 1$ factorial) by *n* to determine the answer to your question. Thus, for $n = 4$, once John calls Mary and she tells him that the value of 3 factorial is 6, he can then calculate 4 factorial as: $4! = 4 * 3! = 4 * 6 = 24$.

The only remaining question is how will Mary know the value of 3 factorial? Strangely enough, the answer is that she doesn't need to know it because Mary, like John, is blessed with the ability to think recursively. Therefore, Mary also has an uncontrollable urge to beg questions. Using the same thought process John used, Mary calls her friend Sue and asks her the value of 2 factorial, who asks Bob the value of 1 factorial, who (at long last) asks Al the value of 0 factorial. Finally, Al no longer needs to beg the question because Al, like everyone else in the world, knows that 0 factorial is 1 (by definition).

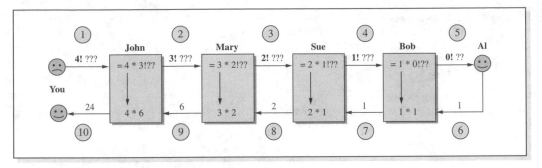

Figure 6.1   The Ten-Step Recursive Process to Evaluate 4!

Al responds immediately with his answer 1, which Bob uses to calculate 1! as 1! = 1 * 0! = 1 * 1 = 1, which is used by Sue to calculate 2! = 2 * 1! = 2 * 1 = 2, which is used by Mary to calculate 3! = 3 * 2! = 3 * 2 = 6, which is finally used by John to calculate 4! = 4 * 3! = 4 * 6 = 24.

This ten-step recursive process performed by John, Mary, Sue, Bob, and Al to determine the value of 4 factorial is illustrated in Figure 6.1.

Each person that took part in our recursive algorithm, except for John, is called a *level* in the recursive solution. In our example, there were four levels of recursion: Mary, Sue, Bob, and Al, with Al said to be at the *deepest* level of recursion. Typically, in a recursive process we enter deeper and deeper recursive levels with problems that get progressively closer and closer to the nonrepetitive part of the recursive algorithm; the portion of the definition whose solution is "known to everyone." In the jargon of recursion, this part of the algorithm is called the *base case*. In our example, Bob's problem (1!), was closer to the nonrepetitive part of the definition, 0!, than Sue's problem (2!), which was closer to 0! than Mary's problem (3!), etc. Once we reach the base case, the recursive process works its way back up the recursive levels, most often using solutions supplied by the level just below, to determine the solution to the original problem.

6.2.2   The Code of a Recursive Algorithm

Let us now turn our attention to the alternate way of learning how to understand recursive algorithms, coding the algorithm, and tracing its execution path. To begin with, we will express the recursive algorithm for $n!$ in pseudocode.

1. **if** ($n == 0$)
2.   **return** (1);
3. **else**
4. { nMinus1Factorial = $(n-1)!$
5.   **return** (n * nMinus1Factorial)
6. }

```
1.  public class Factorial
2.  {  public static long nFactorial(long n)
3.     long nMinus1Factorial;
4.     if(n == 0)
5.        return (1);
6.     else
7.     {  nMinus1Factorial = nFactorial(n - 1);
8.        return (n * nMinus1Factorial);
9.     }
10. }
```

Figure 6.2   The Coding of the Recursive Algorithm for *n* Factorial

Lines 1 and 2 are the portion of the algorithm that is known to everyone (the base case), and Lines 3–6 are the recurring portion of the algorithm.

In most programming languages, recursive algorithms are coded as subprograms (methods). Some languages use a special syntax to indicate that the subprogram is implementing a recursive algorithm. This is not the case in Java. Any Java method can implement a recursive algorithm. Figure 6.2 presents the class Factorial with one method, nFactorial, that implements our pseudocode algorithm for *n*!. The value of *n* is sent to it as an argument and the method returns the value of *n*!.

Line 2 of Figure 6.2 declares the method, nFactorial, to be a static method. When a static method is invoked, it is not preceded by an object name. This is appropriate for this method since it does not operate on, or use, an object's member data.[2] The method invokes itself on Line 7 to determine the values of $(n - 1)!$. This is one of the indications that a method implements a recursive algorithm; it invokes itself. When this is the case, the method is said to be *directly recursive*. Alternately, a method could be *indirectly recursive*. An indirectly recursive method invokes some other method that invokes it, or the other method invokes another method that invokes it, etc.

Figure 6.3 is an application program that uses the method nFactorial to calculate 4!. The output it produces appears at the bottom of the figure.

Line 4 invokes the method nFactorial to determine the value of 4 factorial. Since the method is a static method (Line 2 of Figure 6.2), Java requires the name of the class be coded before the name of the method when it is invoked (Line 4).

6.2.3   Tracing a Recursive Method's Execution Path

In order to more easily trace the execution path of the recursive method shown in Figure 6.2, we will add statements to it that generate a significant amount of additional output. These statements will produce an output whenever:

- the method is invoked (Line 2 of Figure 6.2 executes),

---

[2]Recursive methods can operate on an object's member data, in which case the method is coded as a nonstatic method.

```
1.   public class MainFactorial
2.   {  public static void main(String[] args)
3.      {  long n = 4;
4.         System.out.println(n + " factorial is " + Factorial.nFactorial(n));
5.      }
6.   }
```

Output

4 factorial is 24

Figure 6.3   An Application Program to Calculate 4! and its Output

- the method returns a value (Lines 5 or 8 of Figure 6.2 executes), and
- the method invokes itself (Line 7 of Figure 6.2 executes).

Although we are more interested in the output than the details of the code that produces it, in the interest of completeness the revised code is shown in Figure 6.4. The expanded method is named nFactorialTrace, and the expanded class is named FactorialTrace.

The data members count and time (Lines 2 and 3) have been added to the class to count the number of times the method nFactorialTrace is invoked and to simulate the passage of time. These variables are incremented on Lines 6 and 7 every time the method is invoked. In addition, the variable time is also incremented whenever a value is returned (Lines 12 and 21). Lines 8 and 9 have been added to produce an output every time the method is invoked. Lines 13, 14, 22, and 23 have been added to produce an output every time the method returns a value. Line 19 produces an output every time the method invokes itself.

Let us now turn our attention to the output produced by the application program shown in Figure 6.3, assuming the invocation on Line 4 has been changed to invoke our revised method.[3] The output it produces, when calculating 4!, is shown in Figure 6.5. Assuming that one increment of the variable time is a second, we see that the application takes 10 seconds to execute (at time 1, at time 2, etc.). As indicated by the second line of the figure, at time 1a, nFactorial is invoked for the first time by the application program to calculate 4 factorial ($n = 4$). This invocation does not complete (return the value 24) until 10 seconds have past (see the bottom of Figure 6.5), because the algorithm is recursive and it has invoked itself at time 1b to determine 3!. With each tick of the clock the program enters a deeper level of recursion.

At time 6 the base case (0!) is encountered and the recursion begins to *unwind*, returning the value of 0! from the fifth invocation to the fourth invocation. At time 7, 1! is returned from the fourth invocation to the third invocation; at time 8, 2! is returned from the third invocation to the second invocation; and at time 9, 3! is returned from the second invocation to the first invocation.

---

[3]Line 4 of Figure 6.3 would become: FactorialTrace.nFactorialTrace(n);

```
1.   public class FactorialTrace
2.   {  public static int count = 0;
3.      public static int time = 0;
4.      public static long nFactorialTrace(long n)
5.      {  long value;
6.         count++;
7.         time++;
8.         System.out.println("at time " + time);
9.         System.out.println("\tnFactorial has been INVOKED for the " + count +
10.                            "th time," + " with n = to " + n);
11.        if(n == 0)
12.        {  time++;
13.           System.out.println("\nat time " + time);
14.           System.out.println("\tRETURNING 0! = 1" + " from the " +
15.                              count-- + "th invocation of nFactorial");
16.           return 1;
17.        }
18.        else
19.        {  System.out.println("\tnFactorial is INVOKING ITSELF with n = to " +
                                 (n - 1));
20.           value = n * nFactorialTrace(n - 1);
21.           time++;
22.           System.out.println("at time " + time);
23.           System.out.println("\tRETURNING " + n + "! = " + value + " from the "
24.                              + count-- + "th invocation of nFactorial");
25.           return value;
26.        }
27.     } // end of nFactorialTrace method
28.  } // end of the class FactorialTrace
```

Figure 6.4   The Class `FactorialTrace`

Finally, at time 10, the value of 4! is returned to the application program from the first invocation of nFactorialTrace and the application program outputs this value. Thus, 10 seconds has passed from the time of the first invocation to nFactorialTrace is initiated (to determine the value of 4!) to the time that the invocation terminates (returning 24). During this time, four other invocations of nFactorialTrace are initiated, executed, and terminated.

Figure 6.6 illustrates the five invocations of the method nFactorialTrace (or nFactorial) for $n = 4$. The circles numbered 1 through 5 indicate the five invocations of the method (i.e., the *winding up* of the recursion), and the circles 6 through 10 indicate the returns from the five invocations (the *unwinding* of the recursion).

1. At time 1
   a. nFactorial has been INVOKED for the 1th time, with n = to 4
   b. nFactorial is INVOKING ITSELF with n = to 3
2. At time 2
   a. nFactorial has been INVOKED for the 2th time, with n = to 3
   b. nFactorial is INVOKING ITSELF with n = to 2
3. At time 3
   a. nFactorial has been INVOKED for the 3th time, with n = to 2
   b. nFactorial is INVOKING ITSELF with n = to 1
4. At time 4
   a. nFactorial has been INVOKED for the 4th time, with n = to 1
   b. nFactorial is INVOKING ITSELF with n = to 0
5. At time 5
   nFactorial has been INVOKED for the 5th time, with n = to 0
6. At time 6
   RETURNING 0! = 1 from the 5th invocation of nFactorial
7. At time 7
   RETURNING 1! = 1 from the 4th invocation of nFactorial
8. At time 8
   RETURNING 2! = 2 from the 3th invocation of nFactorial
9. At time 9
   RETURNING 3! = 6 from the 2th invocation of nFactorial
10. At time 10
    RETURNING 4! = 24 from the 1th invocation of nFactorial

4 factorial is 24

Figure 6.5 Trace of the Recursive Invocations when nFactorialTrace Calculates 4!

One final analogy to aid our understanding of how recursion works is shown in Figure 6.7. The invocations and the returns from the invocations can be likened to a cascading row of dominos that fall from left to right during the recursive invocations, and then are reset upright from right to left during the returns from the invocation. The left hand domino (analogous to the first invocation of the method) stays down the longest waiting to be set upright (analogous to the first method receiving its returned value).

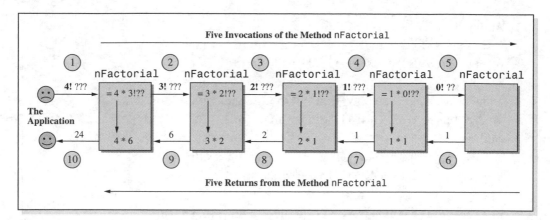

Figure 6.6 The Execution Sequence of the Method nFactorial for *n* = 4

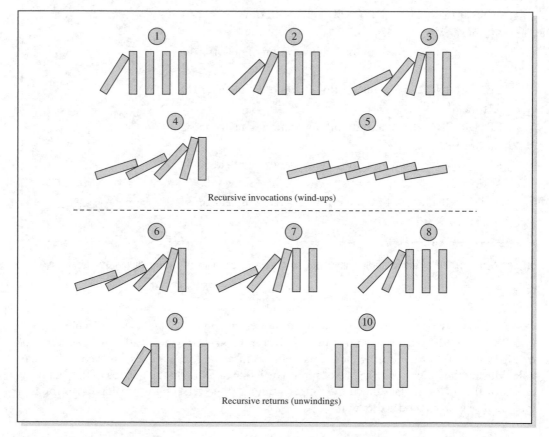

Figure 6.7 Recursive Invocation and the Return Falling Domino Analogy

6.3 Formulating a Recursive Algorithm

Having gained an understanding of recursive algorithms and how they execute, we now turn our attention to the techniques for formulating recursive algorithms. These techniques can be methodized, and the methodology can be directly applied to the formulation of recursive algorithms for some problems. However, there is still a certain amount of "art" remaining in the development of recursive algorithms because our methodology requires a bit of creativity to adapt it to certain problems, and a good deal of creativity to adapt it to many other problems. That being said, an understanding of the methodized approach is still a valuable skill to acquire because it not only furthers our understanding of recursion but can also take us far into the development of most recursive algorithms. More importantly, it reveals insights into the thought processes of those blessed with the innate ability to think recursively.

6.3.1 Definitions

Before examining the methodology of developing recursive algorithms, we will define the terms *base case*, *reduced problem*, and *general solution* used in this methodology. (Don't worry; we won't define them recursively.) The problem of computing $n!$ will be used to illustrate the definitions.

Base Case

The base case is the *known portion of the problem solution*. It is the portion of the solution that "everyone knows," the nonrecursive portion of the solution. In the n factorial problem, the base case is $0! = 1$. Often the base case is referred to as the *escape clause* because it allows the algorithm to escape from the recursive invocations.

Reduced Problem

The reduced problem is *a problem very "close" to the original problem, but a slight bit closer to the base case*. In the n factorial problem, the reduced problem is $(n - 1)!$, which is as close to the original problem $(n!)$ as we can get, and it is closer to the base case $(0!)$. One important quality of the reduced problem is that when it is repeatedly reduced, it degenerates into the base case. By repeatedly reduced, we mean that the relationship between the original problem and the reduced problem is repeatedly applied to the reduced problem. In our case, $(n - 1)!$ becomes $(n - 2)!$, which becomes $(n - 3)! \ldots$, which becomes $(0)!$ the base case. If it does not eventually degenerate into the base case, the algorithm will enter an infinite loop. This is one of the dangers of an incorrectly chosen reduced problem (often referred to as a *false base case* because the statement "the reduced problem degenerates into the base case" is false).

General Solution

The general solution is the *solution to the original problem expressed in terms of the reduced problem*. In other words, the general solution uses the solution to the reduced problem to solve the

Table 6.1			
The Base Case, Reduced Problem, and General Solution for $n!$			
Original Problem	**Base Case**	**Reduced Problem**	**General Solution**
$n!$	$0! = 1$	$(n - 1)!$	$n! = n * (n - 1)!$

original problem. In the n factorial algorithm, the general solution *uses* the reduced problem as a multiplier of n, in that the general solution in the $n!$ recursive algorithm is $n * (n - 1)!$.

The base case, reduced problem, and general solution for the $n!$ recursive algorithm are summarized in Table 6.1. Having gained an understanding of these terms, we will now be able to explore the methodology of recursive thinking.

6.3.2 Methodology

To begin with, it is worth repeating that not all recursive algorithms can be formulated using this methodology. Although it can be followed verbatim to produce a recursive algorithm for *some* problems with recursive solutions, it must be modified to solve most problems. However, it does serve as starting point for all problems with recursive solutions, and can usually be "tweaked," morphed, or modified to accommodate most problems.

The methodology consists of four steps:

1. Determine the base case.
2. Determine the reduced problem.
3. Determine the general solution.
4. Combine the base case, reduced problem, and general solution to form the recursive algorithm.

General Flowchart

Before we examine the techniques involved to complete the first three steps, we will turn our attention to Step 4 of the methodology. The completion of Step 4 can be a trivial effort because many times the base case, reduced problem, and general solution are combined as shown in the flowchart presented in Figure 6.8. Although the shadowed box in the flowchart looks as innocent as the others, it isn't. What you see is just the "tip of the iceberg" because it is the recursive portion of the algorithm. If we enter this box of the flowchart, the algorithm begins again, initiating another level (a lower level) of recursion.

The first three boxes of the flowchart will be repeatedly executed until the second box determines that the current level of recursion is the base case. At this point we "escape" from the repeated

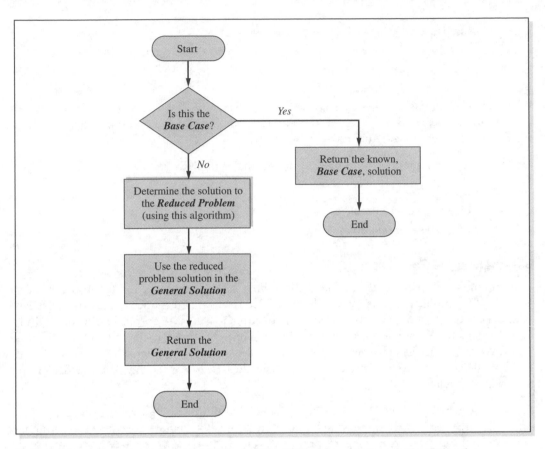

Figure 6.8 A Common Approach to Step 4 of the Methodology for Formulating Recursive Algorithms

execution of boxes 1–3, return the base case solution, and the recursion begins to unwind. If the reduced problem does not eventually reach the base case, then the algorithm will never end. This is why, in the definition of the reduced problem we stated that "one important quality of the reduced problem, is that when it is repeatedly reduced, *it degenerates into the base case.*"

To demonstrate how the flowchart is used, let us assume we have already completed Steps 1, 2, and 3 (using techniques not yet discussed) to determine the base case, reduced problem, and general solution for *n*! shown in Table 6.1. Then, mechanically following the flowchart to combine these three parts of our problem solution, the pseudocode algorithm for *n*! would be:

1. **if** (n == 0) // this is the base case
2.   **return** 1; // return the known (base Case) solution
3. **else**

```
4.  { nMinus1Factorial = (n − 1)!;  // determine the solution of the reduced problem
5.      gs = n * nMinus1Factorial;  // use the reduced problem in the general solution
6.      return gs; // return the general solution
7.  }
```

When this algorithm is coded into a Java method (e.g., Figure 6.2), the term $(n − 1)!$ on Line 4 of the algorithm is replaced with an invocation to the method, and Lines 5 and 6 of the algorithm can be combined into one (return) statement.

Let us now turn our attention to Steps 1, 2, and 3 of the methodology:

1. Determine the base case.
2. Determine the reduced problem.
3. Determine the general solution.

Determining the Base Case

Determining the base case is the easiest of these three steps. Here, we try to identify a particular instance of the problem, a special case, whose solution is known. Often the base case is trivial. For example, the base case for a recursive algorithm to output a string is to output a string of length 1, a single character. Sometime it is a defined solution. This is the case for $n!$ because $0!$ is defined as $0! = 1$. When the problem involves an integer variable n, the base case often occurs when n is 0 or 1. If both 0 and 1 are acceptable values for n, usually the base case is the one that is farthest from the original problem, $n = 0$.

Many list search algorithms (e.g., the Binary Search algorithm) can be written recursively. Two common base cases for a recursive search algorithm is when the item we are currently examining in the list is the item we are looking for, or the list is empty.

Determining the Reduced Problem

Once we determine the base case, the reduced problem is usually determined next. Of the four steps in our methodology, this is usually the most difficult and requires the most imagination and creativity. The best technique for this is to consider the original problem and the base case in the definition of a reduced problem. The reduced problem should

- be a problem "similar" to the original problem,
- be a small "step" away from the original problem in the "direction" of the base case, and
- degenerate into the base case when repeatedly reduced.

In other words, the reduced problem should be "in between" the original problem and the base case, but much closer to the original problem than to the base case, and eventually become the base case.

For example, problems similar to $n!$ that are in the direction of the base case, $0!$ are $(n − 1)!$, $(n − 2)!$, $(n − 3)!$ etc. Which one should we pick for the reduced problem? The first of these is certainly the closest to the original problem, but if $n = 1,000,000$ then all three of them, when compared to the base case, are very close to the original problem. To select the correct reduced problem from these we turn to the last part of the definition of a reduced problem which states it should "degenerate into the base case when repeatedly reduced."

Suppose we were to choose $(n - 2)!$ and n were odd, say $n = 5$. Then the reduced problem would be $(5 - 2)! = 3!$. Considering $3!$ to be an original problem and reducing it again, we obtain $(3 - 2)! = 1!$ One more reduction gives $(1 - 2)! = -1!$. Since these repeated reductions of the reduced problem do not become the base case $(0!)$, $(n - 2)!$ is not a valid reduced problem. The only reduced problem that, when repeatedly reduced, degenerates into the base case for all values of n, is $(n - 1)!$. Therefore, it is selected as the reduced problem.

Determining the General Solution

To determine the general solution, we ask ourselves the question, "how can I use the reduced problem to generate, or solve, the original problem?" In the case of $n!$, where the reduced problem is $(n - 1)!$, the answer is to multiply the reduced problem by n. Therefore, the general solution to $n!$ is $n * (n - 1)!$.

Summary of the Methodology

Table 6.2 summarizes the techniques used in our four step methodology to formulate recursive algorithms. Although this methodology does not produce a recursive algorithm for many problems, it does train us to think recursively. It also serves as a starting point for all problems and can be modified to accommodate most problems.

6.3.3 Practice Problems

As we have discussed, most recursive algorithms do not fall into our "cookie cutter" methodology. They often have multiple base cases, they use the reduced problem several times in the general solution, the reduced problem is *not* a "small step" from the original problem, or they have alternate general solutions. The discovery of these recursive algorithms require some creativity and, as a result, can be quite challenging. However, the old axiom "practice makes perfect" certainly applies to the learning process of how to think recursively; practice can help move us toward that set of people who naturally think recursively.

To minimize the frustration associated with this practice, it is advisable to start with problems that follow our methodology, then progress to those that "almost" follow it, and finally, venture into what some students refer to as "wide open territory." Table 6.3 presents practice problems that require different levels of innovation and creativity. The problems in the leftmost column of the table require the least amount of creativity, while the problems in the rightmost column require the most creativity. Before concluding this section, we will formulate and implement recursive algorithms for four of these problems (two from the first column of the table, one from the

Table 6.2

The Four-Step Methodology for Developing Recursive Algorithms

Step	Techniques
1. Determine the base case.	Look for a known solution, a trivial case, a special case, a defined value, or when $n = 0$ or 1
	(e.g., 0! is defined as 1; an empty list; or a search item is found).
2. Determine the reduced problem.	Look for a problem
	• similar to the original problem,
	• in between the original problem and the base case,
	• much closer to the original problem than to the base case, and
	• that, when repeatedly reduced,[4] degenerates into the base case
	(e.g., $(n - 1)!$; search a sub list).
3. Determine the general solution.	Think of how the reduced problem can be used to solve original problem
	(e.g., $n! = n * (n - 1)!$).
4. Combine the base case, reduced problem, and general solution to form the recursive algorithm.	Use Figure 6.8 or morph it to accommodate the problem
	(e.g., for $n!$ use it verbatim).

[4]By "repeatedly reduced," we mean that the relationship between the original problem and the reduced problem is repeatedly applied to the reduced problem.

second column, and one from the third column). The remaining problems are left as an exercise for the student. The base case(s), reduced problem(s), and general solution(s) for the all the problems are given in Table 6.8, which is presented at the end of Section 6.4.

x^n

Let's consider the problem of determining x^n for all non-negative integer values of n. To discover a recursive algorithm for this problem, our methodology can be followed verbatim. It involves a positive integer variable n, and so the base case often occurs when n is 0 or 1. x^0 and x^1 are both

Table 6.3

Practice Problems to Improve our Ability to Think Recursively

Increasing Order of Difficulty ———————————————————————➔

Generally Follows the Methodology	Multiple Base Cases and Reduced Problems	Uses the Reduced Problem Twice	Multiple Base Cases
$n!$	Generating the nth term in the Fibonacci sequence	Towers of Hanoi	Finding the greatest common denominator of two positive integers
A number raised to a positive integer power, x^n	Binary search of an array	Traversing a binary tree (see Chapter 7)	
Sum of the integers from n to 1		Quick Sort (see Chapter 8)	
Product of two integers, $m * n$		Merge Sort (see Chapter 8)	
Generate the nth term in the triangular series			
Output the characters of a string in reverse order			

legitimate candidates for the base case because their values, 1 and x respectively, are known by definition. However, as we have stated, usually the base case is the one that is farthest from the original problem which is x^n. Since, for positive values of n, 0 is further from n than 1 is, the base case for this problem is usually chosen to be $x^0 = 1$.

Our reduced problem should be similar to the original problem, x^n, between it and the base case, x^0, and much closer to x^n than to x^0. Candidate reduced problems are x^{n-1}, x^{n-2}, etc. Of these, x^{n-1} is the only one that will degenerate into x^0 for all n when repeatedly reduced. Therefore, the reduced problem is chosen to be x^{n-1}.

To determine the general solution, we ask ourselves the question, "how can I use the reduced problem to generate, or solve, the original problem?" In this case the question becomes "what can I do to x^{n-1} to make it x^n?" The answer is to multiply it by x. Therefore the general solution is $x^n = x * x^{n-1}$.

Table 6.4			
The Base Case, Reduced Problem, and General Solution for x^n			
Original Problem	**Base Case(s)**	**Reduced Problem(s)**	**General Solution(s)**
$n!$	$0! = 1$	$(n-1)!$	$n! = n * (n-1)!$
x^n	$x^0 = 1$	x^{n-1}	$x^n = x * x^{n-1}$

```
1.   public static double xTON(double x, int n)
2.   {  if(n == 0)   // base case
3.         return  1;
4.      else
5.      {  double rp = xTON(x, n - 1); // calculate the reduced problem
6.         double gs = x* rp; // calculate the general solution
7.         return gs; // return the general solution
8.      }
9.   }
```

Figure 6.9   A Recursive Method to Compute x^n

Table 6.4 summarizes the base case, reduced problem, and general solution for x^n and includes the problem of $n!$ for comparative purposes.

Finally, the base case, reduced problem, and general solution are combined as shown in Figure 6.8 to produce the recursive algorithm for x^n. Figure 6.9 presents the code of a method xTON that implements the algorithm.

*n*th Term of the Fibonacci Sequence

Calculating the nth term of the Fibonacci sequence is a good problem to study next because although the discovery of its recursive algorithm generally follows our methodology, there are two nuances. It is an example of a problem with multiple base cases and two reduced problems; however, both are easily detected because the series is usually defined recursively. The Fibonacci sequence, f_n is defined as

the first term, $f_1 = 1$,
the second term, $f_2 = 1$, and
all other terms, $f_n = f_{n-1} + f_{n-2}$.

Thus, the terms of the sequence are: 1, 1, 2, 3, 5, 8, 13, 21, 34....

From its definition we see the nuance it presents to our methodology. There are *two* trivial solutions, when $n = 1$ and when $n = 2$. These become our base cases.

The next steps in our methodology are to determine the reduced problem and the general solution. Since the definition is recursive, they are easy to discover. Two reduced problems are used to calculate f_n, f_{n-1}, and f_{n-2}, and our general solution is $f_n = f_{n-1} + f_{n-2}$.

Table 6.5

The Base Case, Reduced Problem, and General Solution for the nth term in the Fibonacci Sequence

Original Problem	Base Case (s)	Reduced Problem (s)	General Solution
$n!$	$0! = 1$	$(n-1)!$	$n! = n * (n-1)!$
x^n	$x^0 = 1$	x^{n-1}	$x^n = x * x^{n-1}$
nth term in the Fibonacci sequence, f_n	$f_1 = 1, f_2 = 1$	f_{n-1} and f_{n-2}	$f_n = f_{n-1} + f_{n-2}$

```
1.   public static long fibonacci(int n)
2.   {   if(n == 1 || n == 2) // one of 2  base cases
3.           return 1;
4.       else
5.       {  long rp1 = fibonacci(n - 1); // first reduced problem
6.          long rp2 = fibonacci(n - 2); // second reduced problem
7.          long gs = rp1 + rp2; // general solution
8.          return gs;
9.       }
10.  }
```

Figure 6.10   A Recursive Method to Determine the nth Term of the Fibonacci Sequence

Table 6.5 summarizes the base case, reduced problem, and general solution for this problem and includes the problems of $n!$ and x^n for comparative purposes.

Finally, the base cases, reduced problems, and general solution are combined as shown in Figure 6.8, to produce the recursive algorithm for the nth term of the Fibonacci sequence. Figure 6.10 presents the code of the method `fibonacci` that implements the algorithm.

Reverse a String, s, of Length n

To discover a recursive algorithm for this problem, our methodology can be followed verbatim. However, this problem is more challenging because the general solution is a little more difficult to determine.

We will assume that the problem will be to *output* a given string s of length n in reverse order. Thus, the string "Bill" should be output as "lliB". Once again the problem involves a positive integer variable n, and so the base case often occurs when n is 0 or 1. Both $n = 0$ and $n = 1$ are legitimate base cases; for $n = 0$, output nothing and for $n = 1$, output the string s. However, we will again choose the base case to be the one that is furthest from the original problem, $n = 0$. In this case, we would not produce an output.

Our reduced problem should be similar to the original problem (reverse a string, s, of length n), between it and the base case (reverse a string, s, of length 0), and much closer to the original problem than it is to the base case. Candidate reduced problems are a reversed string of $n - 1$ characters, $n - 2$ characters, etc., but of these, the first is the only one that will degenerate into the base case for all n when repeatedly reduced. For example, if the reduced problem reverses a string of $n - 2$ characters and n is 3, two reductions ($3 - 2 = 1$, and $1 - 2 = -1$) would skip the base case. Therefore, the reduced problem is chosen to output a string of $n - 1$ characters in reverse order.

To determine the general solution, we ask ourselves the question, "how can I use the reduced problem to generate, or solve, the original problem?" The reduced problem can be used to output $n - 1$ characters of the string backward. The remaining character must be output by the general solution. But which character would that be? The answer lies in which group of characters the general solution uses the reduced problem to output. If it's the first $n - 1$ characters, then the general solution must output the last character, and vice versa. Either approach will work. We will take the former approach. Since the last character must be output first, the general solution is to output the last character and then use the reduced problem to output the first $n - 1$ characters in reverse order.

Table 6.6 summarizes the base case, reduced problem, and general solution for this problem, and includes the problems of $n!$ and x^n for comparative purposes.

Finally, the base case, reduced problem, and general solution are combined as shown in Figure 6.8 to produce the recursive algorithm outputting a string backward. Figure 6.11 presents the code of a method stringReverse that implements the algorithm. The method charAt on Line 5 is a method in the Java String class that returns a character in a string, with the first character being at position 0. Thus, the last character in an n character string is at position $n - 1$.

Table 6.6

The Base Case, Reduced Problem, and General Solution for Reversing a String of Length n!

Original Problem	Base Case(s)	Reduced Problem(s)	General Solution
$n!$	$0! = 1$	$(n - 1)!$	$n! = n * (n - 1)!$
x^n	$x^0 = 1$	x^{n-1}	$x^n = x * x^{n-1}$
nth term in the Fibonacci sequence, f_n	$f_1 = 1, f_2 = 1$	f_{n-1} and f_{n-2}	$f_n = f_{n-1} + f_{n-2}$
Reverse a string, s, of length n	$n = 0$: do nothing	output $n - 1$ characters reversed	Output the nth character; Output the first $n - 1$ characters reversed

```
1.  public static void stringReverse(String s, int n)
2.  {   if(n == 0) // base case
3.         return;
4.      else // general solution
5.      { System.out.print(s.charAt(n - 1)); // output the last character
6.         stringReverse(s, n - 1); // reduced problem (recursion)
7.      }
8.  }
```

Figure 6.11 A Recursive Method to Reverse the Characters of a String

Towers of Hanoi

This problem is a more challenging one because both the reduced problem and general solution are a little more difficult to determine. However, our general methodology is still applicable. There is another important reason for discussing this problem. The previous problems discussed are more easily solved using loops rather than recursion. Their recursive solutions were developed for pedagogical reasons. However, the Towers of Hanoi problem is typical of problems in which the recursive solution is much simpler than the iterative solution. This class of problems is the reason we study recursion.

The Towers of Hanoi is a puzzle conceived by the French mathematician Eduardo Lucas in 1883. The objective is to move n rings from one tower (designated "S" for source tower) to another tower (designated "D" for destination tower). A third tower (designated "E" for extra tower) is available for the temporary storage of rings. The rings are each of a different radius and are initially stacked on tower S in sized order, with the largest radius ring on the bottom. When moving the rings three rules apply.

1. The rings must be moved one at a time.
2. A small ring can never be placed on top of a larger ring.
3. When a ring is removed from a tower it must be placed on a tower before another ring is removed.

Our problem will be to discover a recursive algorithm that outputs the moves to relocate n rings from tower S to tower D without violating the rules.

Applying our methodology, we first look for a base case. As with the previous problems, we are again dealing with an integer variable, n, the number of rings to be relocated. Thus, we would suspect that the base case is when there are no rings, $n = 0$, or there is one ring, $n = 1$, to move. Considering the rules of the puzzle, $n = 1$ is a trivial case whose solution everyone knows. Simply move one ring from tower S to tower D; end of puzzle.

The next step is to find the reduced problem. Since the base case is for one ring and the original problem involves n rings, we would suspect (as in the previous problems) that the reduced problem would involve $n - 1$ rings. So far, so good. But there is a problem. In the previous problems the reduced problem was identical to the original problem except that $n - 1$ was substituted for n. In this problem, however, if we move $n - 1$ rings from tower S to tower D then the largest ring is left on tower S and it can't be moved to tower D without violating Rule 2. The solution here is to generalize the reduced problem so that it could be used to move $n - 1$ rings from any tower to any other tower.

Table 6.7

The Base Case, Reduced Problem and General Solution for the Towers of Hanoi

Original Problem	Base Case(s)	Reduced Problem(s)	General Solution
$n!$	$0! = 1$	$(n-1)!$	$n! = n * (n-1)!$
x^n	$x^0 = 1$	x^{n-1}	$x^n = x * x^{n-1}$
nth term in the Fibonacci sequence, f_n	$f_1 = 1, f_2 = 1$	f_{n-1} and f_{n-2}	$f_n = f_{n-1} + f_{n-2}$
Reverse a string, s, of length n	$n = 0$: do nothing	output $n-1$ characters reversed	Output the nth character; Output the first $n-1$ characters reversed.
Towers of Hanoi for n rings	$n = 1$, move 1 ring from tower S to D	Move $n-1$ rings from any tower to any other tower	Move $n-1$ rings from tower S to E; Move 1 ring from tower S to D; Move $n-1$ rings from tower E to D.

Now we will examine the general solution. According to our methodology, the general solution should use the reduced problem to solve the original problem. And so the question is, if we have n rings on tower S and the ability to move $n-1$ rings from any tower to any other tower, which towers would we select? For our answer we look back to our initial discussion of $n!$ where we said that if we could find someone who knew $(n-1)!$ we would know $n!$ ($= n * (n-1)!$). An analogous argument is applied twice in this problem. If we could find someone who could move $n-1$ rings from tower S to E and then someone who could move the $n-1$ rings from E to D, and in between move the nth (largest) ring from tower S to D, we would have our general solution. The unique thing here is that it was not obvious that the reduced problem had to be generalized and used twice in the general solution. Once to move $n-1$ rings from tower S to E, and a second time to move them from tower E to D.

Table 6.7 summarizes the base case, reduced problem and general solution for this problem and includes the previously discussed problems for comparative purposes.

Finally, the base case, reduced problem, and general solution are combined as shown in Figure 6.8 to produce the recursive algorithm for the Towers of Hanoi puzzle. Figure 6.12 presents the code of a method `hanoi` that implements the algorithm. The method's first parameter, n, is the number

```
1.  public static void hanoi(int n, int S, int D, int E)
2.  {  if(n == 1) // base case
3.         System.out.println("move 1 ring from tower " + S +
                              " to tower " + D);
4.      else // general solution
5.      {  hanoi(n - 1, S, E, D); // reduced problem (recursion)
6.         System.out.println("move 1 ring from tower " + S +
                              " to tower " + D);
7.         hanoi(n - 1, E, D, S); // reduced problem (recursion)
8.      }
9.  }
```

Output for the following invocation: `hanoi(3, 1, 2, 3);`

move 1 ring from tower 1 to tower 2
move 1 ring from tower 1 to tower 3
move 1 ring from tower 2 to tower 3
move 1 ring from tower 1 to tower 2
move 1 ring from tower 3 to tower 1
move 1 ring from tower 3 to tower 2
move 1 ring from tower 1 to tower 2

Figure 6.12 A Recursive Method to Solve the Towers of Hanoi Puzzle and its Output for Three Rings

of rings to be moved. Its last three parameters accept the integer tower numbers of the source (S), destination (D), and extra (E) towers. Also included in the figure is the output of the method for three rings ($n = 3$) being moved from tower number 1 to 2, with tower 3 being the extra tower.

6.4 Problems with Recursion

The elegance of the Towers of Hanoi recursive algorithm often attracts us to recursive solutions. But all that glitters is not gold. Aside from the fact that the ability to think recursively does not come naturally to most people, there are two major problems associated with the use of recursive algorithms in our programs:

- They tend to run slowly.
- At run-time, they can consume an unacceptably large amount of main memory.

Both of these problems are amplified by the manner in which modern compilers transfer the execution path, and the shared information, to and from methods. When a method is invoked, the values of the shared information[5] (arguments and returned value) must be passed between the

---

[5]Or the locations of the shared information if the parameters are nonprimitive types (i.e., objects).

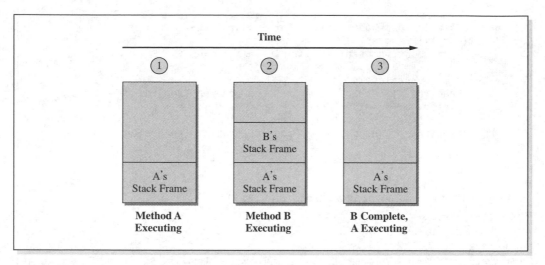

Figure 6.13 Changes to the Run-time Stack as Method A Invokes Method B, and then Method B Completes Execution

invoker and the method. In addition, in order to continue the program after the method completes execution, the address of the line of code after the method invocation (often referred to as the *return address*) and the contents of the CPU's registers at the time of the invocation (often referred to as the *state of the machine*) must be "remembered." Finally, storage must be allocated for the method's local variables.

The memory allocated to this information is part of a stack called the *run-time stack*, and the collection of information is referred to as a *stack frame*. Every time a method is invoked a new stack frame is pushed onto the stack, and when an invocation is complete the information is popped off the stack. Figure 6.13 shows the progression of the run-time stack after method A begins execution (stack status 1), after it invokes method B (stack status 2), and after method B completes execution (stack status 3).

The pushing and popping of the run-time stack takes time, and the stack occupies main memory. For a program that invokes nonrecursive methods, this time and memory use is most often negligible[6] because the nesting of non-recursive method calls usually does not exceed a depth of 10 methods. However, recursive methods often call themselves hundreds or thousands of times as would be the case to calculate 2000!. Every time we enter a lower level of recursion, a new stack frame is built. The time to create and push each frame, and the memory associated with all the frames can become excessive. At best, a recursive method runs slowly and consumes memory. At worst, programs that invoke recursive methods run unacceptably slowly and, since most operating

---

[6]When it is not, many compilers give the programmer the option of replacing the invocation with the actual code of the method. The C++ keyword to accomplish this is "inline."

systems dedicate a limited amount of memory to the run-time stack, can terminate in a run-time "Stack Overflow" error.

The safe alternative is to abandon the elegance of a recursive algorithm in favor of an iterative algorithm. Iterative algorithms are algorithms involving loops, and any recursive algorithm has an iterative counterpart. For example, the iterative version of $n!$ is

```
1.  public static int fact(int n)
2.  {  value = 1;
3.     for(int i = 1; i <= n; i++)
4.         value = value * i;
5.     return value;
6.  }
```

Tests run on a AMD XP 3000 Windows-based platform running at 2.17 GHz with 448 MB of RAM, show that the iterative solution for $n!$ runs three times faster than the recursive solution, and since the iterative solution eliminates recursive invocations it cannot end in a run-time stack overflow error.

6.4.1 Dynamic Programming Applied to Recursion

Incorporating dynamic programming into recursive algorithms allows us to retain the elegance of recursive solutions while approaching the speed and run-time stack requirements of iterative solutions. It is a technique for efficiently computing solutions to problems that involve recurrences by storing partial results. To apply dynamic programming to recursive algorithms we look for parts of the algorithm that repeatedly calculate the same values. Then, the first time these values are calculated, they are stored in a memory resident table. From that point on, rather than recalculate these values they are simply fetched from the table.

For example, consider a program that calculates the value of 4! and then 5! with two invocations to a method that implements a recursive algorithm of the factorial function. As illustrated in Figure 6.6, in the process of calculating the value of 4! the recursive algorithm also calculates the value of 3!, 2!, and 1!. A dynamic version of this algorithm would store these calculated values (as well as the value of 4!) in a table during the first invocation of the method. Then, when 5! is calculated, 4! would not be recalculated but simply read from the table. This saves not only computational time, but also reduces stack overflow errors by reducing the number of levels of recursion for all but the first invocation of the recursive method.

In the case of $n!$, a one-dimensional array could be used to store the calculated values with the value of n used as an index into the array. Thus, 1! would be stored at index 1, 2! stored at index 2, etc. The first column in Figure 6.14 shows the array in its initialized state, and the second shows the array contents after the recursive algorithm calculates the value of 4!. Then, when 5! is calculated, the value 4! is simply read from the table and multiplied by 5, eliminating the need for recursion. Before ending, the method would write the value of 5! (120) to the table, as shown in the third column of Figure 6.14.

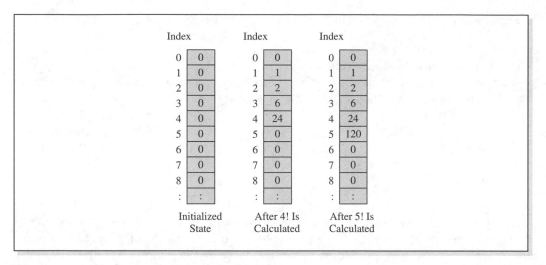

Figure 6.14 The Changes to the Contents of an Array used in the Dynamic Recursive Algorithm for *n*!

In summary, although recursive algorithms are not all glitter they do have an important place in algorithm design. For applications whose levels of recursion do not overflow the run-time stack and are not time critical, recursive algorithms offer concise and elegant solutions to some rather difficult problems (e.g., the Towers of Hanoi, tree traversal discussed in Chapter 7, and sorting algorithms discussed in Chapter 8). In addition, the inclusion of dynamic programming into many recursive algorithms can eliminate the speed and stack overflow problems inherent in recursive solutions.

As an example of the use of dynamic programming in recursive methods, consider the code shown in Figure 6.15 that calculates and outputs the first 45 terms of the Fibonacci sequence. Each term of the series is calculated on Line 5 using an invocation to the method `fibonacci` defined on Lines 9–17. The program takes 45 seconds to execute when run on an AMD Athlon XP 3000+ processor with a 2.17 GHz clock. When recoded using the techniques of dynamic programming (see Exercise 21), it executes in less than one second on the same processor.

6.5 Backtracking, an Application of Recursion

Backtracking is a problem solving technique that can be used to resolve a class of problems in which the objective is to proceed to a goal from a starting point by successively making *n* correct choices from a finite selection of choices. The backtracking algorithm either determines a set of *n* correct choices that achieves the goal, or it determines that the goal is unattainable. Typical goals are to reach the exit of a maze from a given starting point, Sudoku puzzle solutions, to place eight queens on a checkerboard such that no queen can capture another queen (the Queens Eight

```
1.  public class MainFibonacciTerms
2.  {  public static void main(String[] args)
3.     {  int lastTerm = 45;
4.        for(int i = 1; i <= lastTerm; i++)
5.        {  System.out.println("fibonacci" + i + " " + fibonacci(i));
6.        }
7.     } // end main
8.
9.     public static long fibonacci(int n)
10.    {  if(n == 1 || n == 2) // one of 2  base cases
11.          return 1;
12.       else
13.       {  long rp1 = fibonacci(n - 1); // first reduced problem
14.          long rp2 = fibonacci(n - 2); // second reduced problem
15.          long gs = rp1 + rp2;  // general solution
16.          return gs;
17.       }
18.    } // end fibonacci method
19. } // end class MainFibonacciTerms
```

Figure 6.15 A Program to Output the First 45 Terms of the Fibonacci Sequence using a Recursive Method to Calculate the Terms

problem), or to move a knight from a given starting point around a checkerboard such that it moves to every square on the board once, and only once (the Knights Tour problem).

The algorithm uses a trial-and-error technique to decide the *n* correct choices that attain the goal. At each of the *n* decision points, it selects or *tries* a choice from among the choices it has not yet tried at that decision point, and then it proceeds to the next decision point and repeats the process. If the choice at a decision point does not lead to the goal, another choice is tried at that decision point. When the choices at a decision point are exhausted, the algorithm backs up (thus the name *backtracking*) through the previous decision points until it finds a decision point with an untried choice. That choice is substituted for the backtracked decision point's previous choice, and the algorithm again proceeds to the next decision point. If the algorithm backs up to the first decision point and there are no untried choices, it concludes that the goal is unattainable.

The decision choices can be depicted as shown in Figure 6.16, which is referred to as a *decision tree*. The problem's starting point, S, is represented by the top circle (called the *root* of this inverted tree) with each level of circles in the tree representing a decision point. Referring to Figure 6.16, A and B (called the root's *children*) represent the set of choices for the first decision point, the choices available at the starting point. A's children, C, D, and E, represent the choices available if A is chosen at the first decision point (the starting point), and B's children, F and G, represent the choices available if B is chosen at the first decision point. Generally speaking, the children of a node represent the choices for the next decision point assuming their *parent* (e.g., A or B) was chosen at a previous decision point. As decisions are made by the backtracking algorithm, it proceeds down the levels of the decision tree. If none of the children of a parent chosen at a given

Table 6.8

Base Cases, Reduced Problems, and General Solutions for the Problems Presented in Table 6.3

Problem	Base Case	Reduced Problem	General Solution
Calculate $n!$	$0! = 1$	$(n-1)!$	$n! = n * (n-1)!$
Calculate x^n	$x^0 = 1$	x^{n-1}	$x^n = n * x^{n-1}$
Calculate the sum of the integers from n to 1, S_n	$n = 1, S_n = 1$	S_{n-1}, the sum of the integers from $(n-1)$ to 1	$S_n = n + S_{n-1}$
Calculate the product of two integers, $p = m * n$	$n = 0, p = 0$ $n = 1, p = m$	$m * (n-1)$	$p = m + m * (n-1)$
Calculate the nth term in the triangular series, T_n	$n = 1, T_n = 1$	T_{n-1}	$T_n = n + T_{n-1}$
Output an n character string backwards	$n = 0$, do nothing	output $(n-1)$ characters backward	Output last character; Output $(n-1)$ characters backward.
Calculate the nth term of the Fibonacci sequence, f_n	$f_1 = 1, f_2 = 1$	f_{n-1}, f_{n-2}	$f_n = f_{n-1} + f_{n-2}$
Binary search of an array to find X	**if** array size $= 0$, X not present. **if** middle array element $= X$, return middle element's index	Binary search subarray.	**if** middle element $> X$, make the subarray the upper half of the array, **else** make it the lower half of the array. Binary search subarray.
Towers of Hanoi to move n rings from tower S to D using tower E	**if** $n = 1$, move one ring from S to D	move $n - 1$ rings from any tower to any tower	Move $n - 1$ rings from S to E; Move one ring from S to D; Move $n - 1$ rings from E to D.
Traversing a Binary Tree (in LNR order)	**if** no subtree, don't traverse it	traverse a sub tree	Traverse the root's left subtree; Visit the root node; Traverse the root's right subtree.
Calculate the greatest common denominator of two integers m and n $(m > n)$, $GCD(n,m)$	$n = 1, GCD(m,n) = 1$ $n = 0, GCD(m,n)$ is m	$GCD(n, m \% n)$	$GCD(n,m) = GCD(n, m \% n)$
Merge Sort (described in Chapter 8)	If one item to be sorted, do nothing	Merge Sort the upper or lower half of the list	Merge Sort upper half of list; Merge sort lower half of list; Combine the sorted lower and upper halves of the lists.

(continues)

Table 6.8

Base Cases, Reduced Problems, and General Solutions for the Problems Presented in Table 6.3 *(continued)*

Problem	Base Case	Reduced Problem	General Solution
Quick Sort (described in Chapter 8)	If one item to be sorted, do nothing	Quick Sort any area of a list	Partition the list; Move items into their correct partition; Quick Sort the left partition; Quick Sort the right partition.

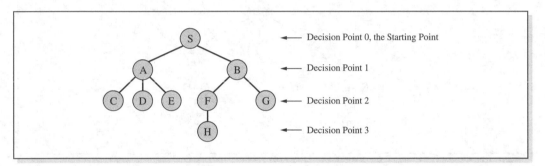

Figure 6.16   Depiction of a Decision Tree

level lead to the goal, the algorithm backtracks up to the previous level and makes an alternate decision at that level (here comes the "r" word), recursively. Assuming that the choices depicted at each level of the tree shown in Figure 6.16 were selected in a left to right order, the choices made by the backtracking algorithm to arrive at H would be A, C, backtrack, D, backtrack, E, backtrack, backtrack, B, F, H.

For example, consider the problem of traveling along the squares of a maze from a given starting square to a goal square. The set of choices for each move are to proceed straight, turn left, or turn right. However, for the maze depicted in Figure 6.17 not all of these moves are valid for every square. Although all three choices are valid for the square in row 0, column 1 (denoted 0,1), only two of them are valid for the square 1,1 (i.e., to proceed straight or to turn left). Turning right when at square 1,1 is not a valid choice. After entering any of the squares in column 0, there are no valid choices. The only option after entering any of these squares would be to backtrack.

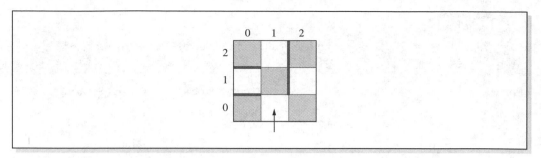

Figure 6.17 A Nine Cell Maze

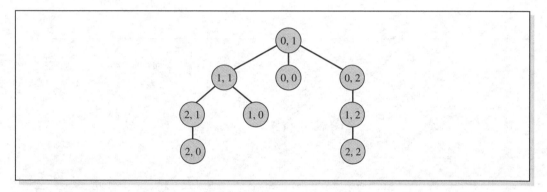

Figure 6.18 The Decision Tree for the Valid Next Move Choices of the Maze Shown in Figure 6.17

The decision tree shown in Figure 6.18 represents all the valid choices for the squares of the maze depicted in Figure 6.17 when it is entered at square 0,1. The placement of the nodes in the tree assumes the choices are selected in a left to right order, and that proceeding forward is always considered first, then a left turn, and then a right turn. If the goal was to arrive at square 1,2, the backtracking algorithm would traverse the maze as follows: 0,1; 1,1; 2,1; 2,0; backtrack to 2,1; backtrack to 1,1; 1,0; backtrack to 1,1; backtrack to 0,1; 0,0; backtrack to 0,1; 0,2; 1,2.

At each point in the decision tree we encounter a new problem similar to the original problem—the problem of making correct choices in order to reach a goal. However, the new problem is one choice closer to the goal because we have just made a choice at the previous decision point. Considering this, and also considering the goal to be our end point or base case, most often a backtracking algorithm is coded recursively. The reduced problem is considered to be the problem of making the remaining correct choices.

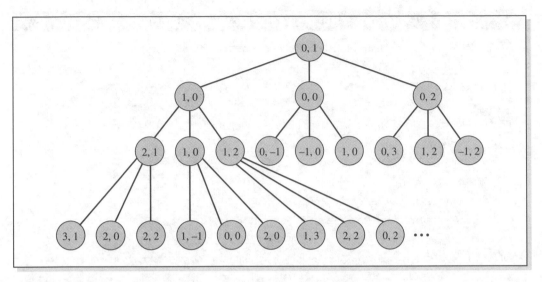

Figure 6.19 The First Four Levels of the Decision Tree for the Valid and Invalid Next Move Choices of the Maze Shown in Figure 6

Before presenting a generalized version of the backtracking algorithm that can be adapted to a variety of problems, we should discuss one more point about decision trees. The two decision trees presented previously in this chapter contained only valid choices. For example, after moving onto square 1,1 from square 0,1 (in the maze depicted in Figure 6.17), moving right is not an option, so square 1,2 was not included as a child of square 1,1 in the decision tree. Generally speaking, it is usually better to include all choices in the decision tree, and allow the backtracking algorithm to determine the validity of each choice because it tends to generalize our algorithm. This approach will allow us to rearrange the walls of the maze and still use the same decision tree. The first four levels of the expanded version of the maze's decision tree are presented in Figure 6.19.

6.5.1 A Generalized Backtracking Algorithm

A generalized recursive version of the backtracking algorithm, named makeNextDecision, is given below. It is generalized in that several of its lines simply indicate *what* is to be done because the decision as to *how* it is to be done is particular to a specific problem. The algorithm is passed the choice made at the last decision point so that only that choice's children (in the decision tree) will be considered during the next decision. The selection from among these choices is performed on Line 4 by a method named nextChoice that returns the next choice at a decision point from among the decision point's untried choices.

Generalized Recursive Backtracking Algorithm

boolean makeNextDecision(lastDecisionChoice)

```
1.  atGoal = false;
2.  choiceNumber = 0;  // initialize the choice number for this decision point
3.  while(atGoal == false && choiceNumber < numberOfChoices)  // more choices
4.  { thisDecisionChoice = nextChoice(choiceNumber, lastDecisionChoice);
5.    if(thisDecisionChoice is valid)
6.    { record thisDecisionChoice
7.      if(goal has been reached)  // base case
8.        return true; // reached the goal
9.      else
10.     { atGoal = makeNextDecision(thisDecisionChoice); // reduce problem
11.       if(atGoal == false)  // backtrack has occurred
12.       { un-record this DecisionChoice
13.       } // end if
14.     } end else
15.   } end if
16.   choiceNumber = choiceNumber + 1;
17. } end while
18.   return atGoal;
```

The algorithm begins by initializing the Boolean variable atGoal to **false** and the variable choiceNumber to zero. Line 3 begins a loop that works its way sequentially through the choices at a decision point looking for one that eventually leads to the goal. Each pass through the loop the variable choiceNumber is incremented (Line 16), and the loop continues while the goal has not been reached (atGoal == **false**) and then there are more choices to consider at this decision point (choiceNumber < numberOfChoices).

The variable choiceNumber is passed to the method nextChoice on Line 4 to request that the next choice (initially the 0th choice) be determined and returned. The method nextChoice is assumed to exist and is particular to the problem being solved. (Lines 5, 6, 7, and 12 are also particular to the problem being solved.) Normally the choice is not only a function of the choice number, but also a function of the previous decision, which is also passed to the method as the second argument. At the beginning of the maze problem depicted in Figures 6.17 and 6.19, the previous decision would be to start at square 0,1, and 1,1 would be returned as the next choice (since, as specified in the decision tree, the move order is forward, left, and then right).

The code of the Boolean condition on Line 5 would be particular to an application, and in most cases coded as a separate function. When Line 5 determines that a choice is not valid, the body of the `if` statement (Lines 6–15) does not execute and the choice is ignored. Then, Line 16 increments the `choiceNumber`, and the next choice is considered.

Line 6 and Line 12 are also particular to a specific problem. When a choice is valid, Line 6 makes a record of the choice. For the maze problem, the choice could be recorded by storing the chosen square's row and column number in an array, and unrecorded by eliminating them from the array. The choice is recorded so that if the goal is reached, the sequence of correct choices can be displayed. Another reason for recording the choice is that, for some problems, the determination of a valid choice performed on Line 5 depends on the choices made at previous decision points. For example, if a square on the Knight's Tour checkerboard was visited by the knight as a result of a choice made at a previous decision point, that square is no longer a valid choice for subsequent decision points. Line 12 eliminates the choice from the record of choices if the next decision point results in a backtrack.

Line 7 is the base case, i.e., the current choice has achieved the goal. Its Boolean condition is also particular to an application. In the case of the maze problem, the goal is reached when the choice is the goal square. In the Queens Eight problem the goal has been reached when eight queens have been placed on the board. If the goal has not been reached, the algorithm is invoked recursively on Line 10 (the reduced problem) to continue the decision process. If the method returns **false**, indicating that the goal could not be reached using the current choice, the choice is unrecorded (Line 12), and the choice number is incremented (Line 16) so that the next choice at this decision point can be considered.

Adapting the generalized backtracking algorithm to a particular application requires a bit of creativity. However, the amount of creativity can be reduced by methodizing the adaptation process.

6.5.2 Algorithm Adaptation Methodology

As previously mentioned, Lines 4, 5, 6, 7, and 12 are particular to a given problem. The scheme used to represent the choices is also particular to a given problem. Therefore, when applying the backtracking algorithm to a problem we have to decide how to represent the choices, how to determine if the goal has been reached (for Line 7 of the algorithm), how to record and unrecorded a choice (for Lines 6 and 12 of the algorithm), how to determine the next choice (for Line 4 of the algorithm), and how to determine if a choice is valid (for Line 5 of the algorithm). In the spirit of divide and conquer, once we have made decisions on these issues we code a data structure to represent the choices, and code five methods that can be invoked on Lines 4, 5, 6, 7, and 12 of the algorithm. Next, the algorithm itself is coded and, finally, an application program is written to perform initialization, record the starting point, and invoke the backtracking algorithm to determine the choices that lead to the goal. These steps are summarized in the following methodology.

Methodology for Applying the Generalized Backtracking Algorithm

1. Decide how to represent the n choices, and declare a data structure that will store the n choices.
2. Decide how to determine if the goal has been reached, and write a method that can be invoked on Line 7 of the algorithm.
3. Decide how to record and unrecord a choice, and write a method that can be invoked on Lines 6 and 12 of the algorithm.
4. Decide how to determine the next choice, and write methods that can be invoked on Line 4 of the algorithm.
5. Decide how to determine if a choice is valid, and write a method that can be invoked on Line 5 of the algorithm.
6. Write the generalized backtracking algorithm, and include invocations to the methods developed in the previous steps on Lines 4, 5, 6, 7, and 12.
7. Write an application that performs initialization, records the starting point, invokes the generalized backtracking method, and then outputs the choices that lead to the goal.

We will now illustrate the application of the methodology by using it to code a solution to the Knights Tour problem.

The Knights Tour, an Adaptation Example

The Knights Tour problem begins by placing a knight on a square of a checkerboard. Then, using only valid knight moves, we are to determine a sequence of moves during which the knight arrives at each square of the checkerboard once, and only once. The shaded boxes in Figure 6.20 show the eight valid moves for a knight, as per the rules of chess, assuming that the knight is initially

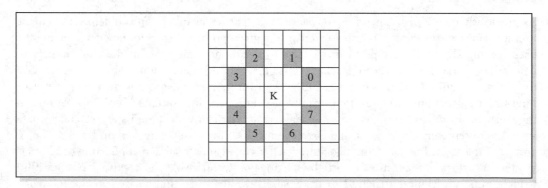

Figure 6.20 The Eight Valid Moves for the Knight Positioned at Square K

positioned in the box K. (The rules of chess also demand, of course, that after the move, the knight is on the checkerboard.)

The eight moves have been arbitrarily assigned a sequential choice number (0 through 7) as indicated by the digit in the shaded boxes of Figure 6.20. When the moves are chosen in this order (i.e., move to the right two boxes and up one box as a first choice, move to the right one box and up two boxes as a second choice, etc.), the sequence of valid moves for a tour beginning in row 4 and column 0 of a 5 × 5 checkerboard is depicted in the top part of Figure 6.21. The numbers in the squares of the checkerboard represent the move number during which the knight landed on the squares (1 being the starting point, 25 being the end point). The bottom part of the figure presents the number of times the algorithm backtracked to each of the 25 decision points. For example, the 4 in square 4,3 of the lower part of the figure indicates that the decision point that determined the eighth move (see square 4,3 of the upper part of the figure) was backtracked to

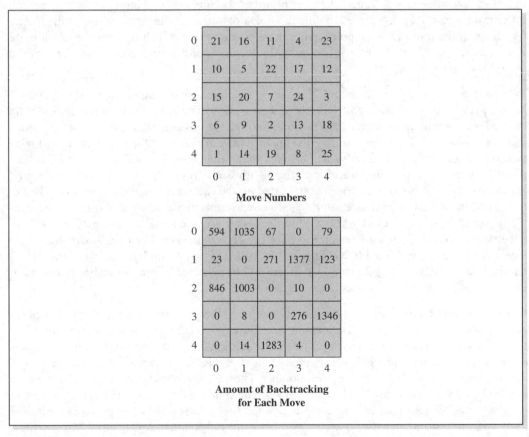

Figure 6.21   A Valid Knights Tour Beginning at Row 4, Column 0 and the Amount of Backtracking Performed

four times during the solution. Similarly, square 3,1 in the figure indicates that the decision point that determined the ninth move was backtracked to eight times.

The five recorded choices for the eighth move (four of which are unrecorded as a result of the four backtracks to the eighth decision point), and the nine recorded choices for the ninth move (eight of which are unrecorded), are depicted in Figure 6.22. Each of the five checkerboards in the figure depict one of the five recorded choices for the eighth move, denoted as 8/1 (the first recorded choice) on the top checkerboard, 8/2 (the second recorded choice) on the second from the top checkerboard, and 8/3, 8/4, and 8/5 on subsequent checkerboards. Also shown in each checkerboard are the positions chosen for the first seven moves, denoted in the squares as 1 to 7.

The seventh move positions the knight on square 2,2. The first choice for move 8 is to move the knight from that square to square 1,4, as shown in the top of the figure. From that square, the first valid choice for move 9 is square 0,2. However, all subsequent combinations of choices for the tenth, eleventh, twelfth, ... twenty-fifth moves do not produce a solution, which results in the first backtrack and the move to square 0,2 is unrecorded. The only other valid choice for the ninth move from square 1,4 is to square 3,3. This also does not lead to a solution, resulting in the second backtrack to the ninth decision point. Since there are no other valid choices for the ninth move from square 1,4 the first backtrack to the eighth decision point is performed, and the move to square 1,4 is unrecorded.

Referring to the second checkerboard, the next valid choice for the eighth move (to square 0,1 from square 2,2) is recorded, and then the knight is moved from that square to the first valid choice for the ninth move, square 2,0. (It should be noted at this point that the square 0,3 is not a valid choice for the eighth move because the square had been visited on the fourth move.) Moving to square 2,0 or square 1,3 from square 0,1 (the only valid choices for the ninth move) do not result in a solution. After backtracking to the eighth decision point, the remaining three valid choices for the eighth move are tried. As indicated on the checkerboard at the bottom of the figure, the fifth, and last, valid choice for the eighth move results in a solution. If it had not, the algorithm would have backtracked to the seventh decision point, the move to square 2,2 would have been unrecorded, and the only remaining valid choice for the seventh move, square 4,2, would have been tried to see if it led to a solution. It is suggested that an understanding of the move's choices and the backtracking illustrated in Figure 6.22 be mastered before proceeding to the application of the methodology to this problem.

In Step 1 of our methodology we determine how we will represent the eight move choices. To accomplish a move we simply add an increment to the knight's current row and column numbers. For example, if the knight is currently at row 4 and column 0 (and the row and column numbers are assigned as depicted in Figure 6.21), move choice 0 would be accomplished by adding a -1 to the row number and a $+2$ to the column number. Thus, to store the choices we simply store the row and column increments for the eight moves. The simplest data structure to store the increments is a two-dimensional array of integers (named rowColIncrement) composed of eight rows and two columns, and then use the choice number as the index into the array's row. The scheme is depicted in Figure 6.23 where the column increment is stored in column 0 of the array, and the row increment is stored in column 1 of the array. The row assignment of the increments in the array reflects the move order depicted in Figure 6.20.

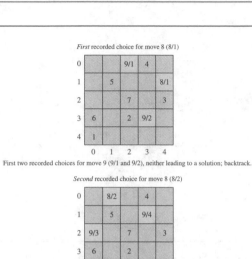

First recorded choice for move 8 (8/1)

First two recorded choices for move 9 (9/1 and 9/2), neither leading to a solution; backtrack.

Second recorded choice for move 8 (8/2)

Third and fourth recorded choices for move 9 (9/3 and 9/4), neither leading to a solution; backtrack.

Third recorded choice for move 8 (8/3)

Fifth and sixth recorded choices for move 9 (9/5 and 9/6), neither leading to a solution; backtrack.

Fourth recorded choice for move 8 (8/4)

Seventh and eighth recorded choices for move 9 (9/7 and 9/8), neither leading to a solution; backtrack.

Fifth recorded choice for move 8 (8/5), and the choice that leads to a solution

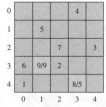

The ninth recorded choice for move 9, which leads to the solution.

Figure 6.22 The Choices Recorded for Moves Eight and Nine during the Four Backtracks to Decision Eight

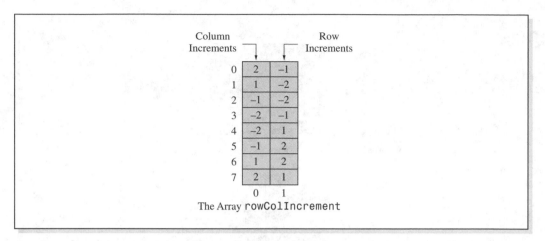

Figure 6.23   The Representation of the Eight Valid Knight Move Increments Depicted in Figure 6.20

The Java code to declare and initialize the array is:

```
static int [][] rowColIncrement = new int[8][2];
rowColIncrement[0][0] =  2;      rowColIncrement[0][1] = -1;
rowColIncrement[1][0] =  1;      rowColIncrement[1][1] = -2;
rowColIncrement[2][0] = -1;      rowColIncrement[2][1] = -2;
rowColIncrement[3][0] = -2;      rowColIncrement[3][1] = -1;
rowColIncrement[4][0] = -2;      rowColIncrement[4][1] =  1;
rowColIncrement[5][0] = -1;      rowColIncrement[5][1] =  2;
rowColIncrement[6][0] =  1;      rowColIncrement[6][1] =  2;
rowColIncrement[7][0] =  2;      rowColIncrement[7][1] =  1;
```

The next step (Step 2) of the methodology is to decide how to determine if the goal has been reached. For a checkerboard with n rows and n columns, the goal has been reached when we make n^2 successful moves (which include the starting square). Assuming the number of rows and columns are stored in the variables nRows and nCols, and that the number of moves made is stored in the variable thisMoveNumber, the goal is reached when thisMoveNumber = nRows * nCols. This step is concluded with the coding of the method goalHasBeenReached given below. It will be invoked by Line 7 of the generalized backtracking algorithm.

```
public static boolean goalHasBeenReached(int thisMoveNumber)
{  if( thisMoveNumber == nRows*nCols)
      return true;
   else
      return false;
}
```

In Step 3 of our methodology, we decide how to record and unrecord a choice. To record the move we will "mark" the square of the checkerboard the knight lands on. In order to display the sequence of the moves, we will mark the square with the move number as depicted in the upper part of Figure 6.21. We will represent the checkerboard as a two-dimensional array of integers named board, consisting of nRows and nCols defined as

```
static int[][] board = new int[nRows][nCols];
```

Assuming that an unvisited square is marked with a zero, this step concludes with the coding of the two methods recordThisDecisionChoice and unrecordThisDecisionChoice given below. These methods will be invoked from Lines 6 and 12 of the generalized backtracking algorithm, respectively.

```
public static void recordThisDecisionChoice(int row, int column,
                                            int thisMoveNumber)
{   board[row][column] = thisMoveNumber;
}

public static void unrecordThisDecisionChoice(int row, int column)
{   board[row][column] = 0;
}
```

In Step 4 of our methodology, we decide how to determine the next choice for a move when the current move does not lead to the goal. The simplest thing to do is to select the moves sequentially in the order given in Figure 6.20, which is consistent with the fact that every time through the **while** loop of the generalized backtracking algorithm, the variable choiceNumber is incremented by one. The row and column of the next move will simply be determined by adding the row and column increments stored in the array rowColIncrement (depicted in Figure 6.23) at row index choiceNumber, to the row and column numbers that represent the knight's current location (the location we are moving from). The two methods nextChoiceRow and nextChoiceColumn, which would be invoked by Line 4 of the generalized backtracking algorithm, accomplish this.

```
public static int nextChoiceRow(int choiceNumber, int fromRow)
{   int nextRow;
    nextRow = fromRow + rowColIncrement[choiceNumber][1];
    return nextRow;
}
public static int nextChoiceColumn(int choiceNumber, int fromCol)
{   int nextColumn;
    nextColumn = fromCol + rowColIncrement[choiceNumber][0];
    return nextColumn;
}
```

In Step 5 of our methodology, we decide how to determine if a choice is valid. Since our moves will be fetched from the array depicted in Figure 6.23 that represents valid knight moves (see Figure 6.20), the only way they could be invalid is if the move places the knight off the board or on a square already visited. A square whose row and column numbers are stored in row and col is on the board if

```
0<= row  nRows    and  0<= col  nCols,
```

and it has not been visited if

```
board[row][col] == 0.
```

The method `thisDecisionChoiceIsValid`, which follows, and would be invoked from Line 5 of the generalized backtracking algorithm, tests these conditions.

```
public static boolean thisDecisionChoiceIsValid(int row, int column)
{   if(row >= 0 && row < nRows &&
        column >= 0 && column < nCols &&
        board[row][column] == 0)
        return true;
    else
        return false;
}
```

In Step 6 of our methodology, we code the generalized backtracking algorithm, the method `makeNextDecision`, incorporating into it the methods developed in the first five steps of our methodology. Before coding it, we have to decide on the parameter(s) of the method that will represent the previous (last) decision choice. In the Knights Tour problem that would be the row and column number of the knight's current position. We will also include the last move number as a third parameter because it is incremented and then used in the method `recordThisDecisionChoice` (to keep track of where the knight has been). It is also used in the `goalHasBeenReached` method (to determine if the solution is complete). Thus, the signature of the method becomes

```
public static boolean makeNextDecision(int lastMoveNumber,
                                       int fromRow, int fromCol)
```

Having defined the method's parameters, we complete Step 6 of the methodology by coding the method. Lines 31–55 of Figure 6.24 presents the Java implementation. The invocations to the methods developed in the previous steps of our methodology are highlighted on Lines 39–43 and 48. In addition, Lines 33 and 34 have been added to perform initialization particular to this problem.

Finally, in Step 7 we complete our solution by writing an application that performs some initialization, records the starting point, invokes the generalized backtracking method, and then outputs the choices that lead to the goal. The application is presented in Figure 6.24 as Lines 1–29, which includes the declaration of the data structures previously discussed (Lines 4–5) and the initialization of the valid knight moves (Lines 9–16). The methods developed in Steps 2–5 of the methodology are included in Figure 6.24 as Lines 57–92.

The Queens Eight Problem

Table 6.9 summarizes the decisions made during Steps 2–5 of the methodology to adapt the generalized backtracking algorithm to the Knights Tour problem. In addition, it presents the analogous decisions that adapt the algorithm to the Queens Eight problem, assuming that each queen will be placed in a different column and therefore the backtracking algorithm is only used to determine queens' row numbers. The coding of the solution to this problem is left as an exercise for the student. (The entire solution of the maze problem, the decisions made during Steps 2–5 of

```
1.   public class MainKnightsTour
2.   {  static int firstRow = 4; static int firstCol = 0; // starting position
                                                           // of the knight
3.      static int nRows = 5;    static int nCols = 5;     // number of columns
                                                           // and rows
4.      static int[][] board = new int[nRows][nCols];  // stores the move number
                                                        // of the Knight
5.      static int[][] rowColIncrement = new int[8][2];   // stores valid
                                                           // Knight move choices
6.
7.      public static void main(String[] args)
8.      {  boolean success;
9.         rowColIncrement[0][0] =  2;        rowColIncrement[0][1] = -1;
10.        rowColIncrement[1][0] =  1;        rowColIncrement[1][1] = -2;
11.        rowColIncrement[2][0] = -1;        rowColIncrement[2][1] = -2;
12.        rowColIncrement[3][0] = -2;        rowColIncrement[3][1] = -1;
13.        rowColIncrement[4][0] = -2;        rowColIncrement[4][1] =  1;
14.        rowColIncrement[5][0] = -1;        rowColIncrement[5][1] =  2;
15.        rowColIncrement[6][0] =  1;        rowColIncrement[6][1] =  2;
16.        rowColIncrement[7][0] =  2;        rowColIncrement[7][1] =  1;
17.
18.        board[firstRow][firstCol] = 1;
19.        success = makeNextDecision(1, firstRow, firstCol);
20.        if(success == true)
21.        {  for(int i = 0; i < nRows; i++)
22.           {  System.out.println();
23.              for(int j = 0; j < nCols; j++)
24.              { System.out.print(board[i][j] + "\t");
25.              }
26.           }
27.        }
28.        else System.out.println("no solution");
29.     } // end of main method
30.
31.     public static boolean makeNextDecision(int lastMoveNumber
32.                                    int fromRow, int fromCol)
33.     {  int thisMoveNumber = lastMoveNumber + 1;
34.        int numberOfChoices = 8;
35.        int choiceNumber = 0;
36.        boolean atGoal = false;
37.
38.        while(atGoal == false && choiceNumber < numberOfChoices)
39.        {  int row = nextChoiceRow(choiceNumber, fromRow);
40.           int col = nextChoiceColumn(choiceNumber, fromCol);
41.           if(thisDecisionChoiceIsValid(row, col))
42.           {  recordThisDecisionChoice(row, col, thisMoveNumber);
43.              if(goalHasBeenReached(thisMoveNumber))
```

(continues)

Figure 6.24 The Solution to the Knights Tour Problem

```
44.                return true;
45.            else // make next decision
46.            {  atGoal = makeNextDecision(thisMoveNumber, row, col);
47.                if (atGoal == false) // had to backtrack
48.                {  unrecordThisDecisionChoice(row, col);
49.                } // end if
50.            } // end else
51.        } // end if
52.        choiceNumber = choiceNumber + 1;
53.    } // end while
54.    return atGoal;
55.  }
56.
57.  public static int nextChoiceColumn(int choiceNumber, int fromCol)
58.  {  int nextColumn;
59.    nextColumn = fromCol + rowColIncrement[choiceNumber][0];
60.    return nextColumn;
61.  }
62.
63.  public static int nextChoiceRow(int choiceNumber, int fromRow)
64.  {  int nextRow;
65.    nextRow = fromRow + rowColIncrement[choiceNumber][1];
66.    return nextRow;
67.  }
68.
69.  public static boolean thisDecisionChoiceIsValid(int row, int column)
70.  {  if(row >= 0 && row < nRows   &&
71.      column >= 0 && column < nCols  &&
72.      board[row][column] == 0)
73.      return true;
74.    else
75.      return false;
76.  }
77.
78.  public static void recordThisDecisionChoice(int row, int column,
79.                                              int thisMoveNumber)
80.  {  board[row][column] = thisMoveNumber;
81.  }
82.
83.  public static void unrecordThisDecisionChoice(int row, int column)
84.  {  board[row][column] = 0;
85.  }
86.
87.  public static boolean goalHasBeenReached(int thisMoveNumber)
88.  {  if(thisMoveNumber == nRows*nCols)
89.      return true;
90.    else
91.      return false;
92.  }
93. }
```

Figure 6.24   The Solution to the Knights Tour Problem *(continued)*

Table 6.9

Decisions Necessary to Adapt the Generalized Backtracking Algorithm to the Knights Tour and Queens Eight Problems

Problem	How to Represent the Valid Choices	How to Decide if Goal is Reached	How to Record and Unrecord a Choice	How to Determine the Next Choice	How to Discern a Valid Choice
Knights Tour	Array of 8 row and column increments.	$nRows * nCols$ valid moves have been made.	Record: place the move number in the square. Unrecord: place a zero in the square.	Add the next choice's row and column increment to the row and column number of the last choice.	$0 <= row < nRows$ $0 <= col <= nCols$ (square row, col is on the board) and the square contains a zero.
Queens Eight	Not necessary.	Eight queens have been placed.	Record: place a 1 in the square. Unrecord: place a zero in the square.	Column number is one more than the previous *decision* point's column. Row number of the last choice is incremented by one mod nRows.	No other queen is on this row or the square's two diagonals.

the algorithm adaptation methodology, and the coding of the solution, is left as an exercise for the student.)

When coding the method `thisDecisionChoiceIsValid` for the Queens Eight problem (see the last column of the Table 6.9) we make use of two facts regarding the diagonals of a checkerboard:

1. For each square on an upper left to lower right running diagonal, the *difference* of the square's row and column numbers is a constant (different for each diagonal). For example, on the diagonal from 1,0 to 4,3 the difference is 1.

2. For each square on a lower left to upper right running diagonal, the *sum* of the square's row and column numbers is a constant (different for each diagonal). For example, on the diagonal from 3,0 to 0,3 the sum is 3.

These sums and differences can be used to index into two one-dimensional arrays used to record which diagonals have queens on them. For example, if a queen had been placed on square 2,1 then element 1 of one of the arrays would be marked occupied, as would element 3 of the other array. A third one-dimensional array can be used to keep track of the rows that have queens on them using the queen's row number as an index into this array.

Knowledge Exercises

1. State the definition of recursion.

2. True or false:

   a. *All* algorithms can be stated recursively.

   b. Some algorithms can *only* be stated recursively.

   c. For most people, recursive algorithms are more difficult to discover and understand than nonrecursive algorithms.

   d. All recursive algorithms must have an escape clause.

   e. Recursive algorithms, if not properly coded, can terminate with a stack overflow error; if true, why?

3. The menu of Juan's Taco Tower states "when ordering a Sombrero Meal you get a taco, and a soda, and your choice of an ice cream sundae *or* a Sombrero Meal."

   a. What part of the Sombrero Meal's description is recursive?

   b. What is the base case (escape clause) in the description of a Sombrero Meal?

   c. Can I order a Sombrero Meal consisting of:

      1. 1 taco, 1 soda, and 1 ice cream sundae?

      2. 2 tacos, 1 soda, and 1 ice cream sundae?

3. 2 tacos, 3 sodas, and 1 ice cream sundae?

4. 1 taco and 1 soda?

5. 1 taco, 1 soda, and 2 ice cream sundaes?

4. Define:

   a. Base case

   b. Reduced problem

   c. General solution

5. Give the generic flowchart for a recursive method that has one base case.

6. Give the four steps in the methodized approach to formulating a recursive algorithm.

7. Give an advantage of a recursive algorithm over an iterative algorithm.

8. Give two advantages of an iterative algorithm over a recursive algorithm.

9. A recursive method is used to calculate 6^4. The base case is 6^0.

   a. What is the first value returned from the recursive invocations?

   b. What is the second value returned from the recursive invocations?

10. Draw a figure similar to Figure 6.6 that shows the values calculated by a recursive method invoked to determine the value of 5^3.

11. Give the base case, reduced problem, and general solution of the recursive algorithm for:

   a. $n!$

   b. x^y

   c. The product of two integers a and b.

   d. The sum of the integers from a to b, $a > b$.

   e. Outputting an array of characters, c, given the starting and ending indices.

   f. Binary search of an array to locate the value aKey.

12. Give the signatures of the methods that implement the recursive algorithms of Exercises 11(a)–(f).

13. Give the pseudocode of the methods that implement the recursive algorithms of Exercises 11(a) through 11(f).

Programming Exercises

14. Code a recursive solution for Exercise 11(d), *and* provide a driver program to test your solution.

15. Code a recursive solution for Exercise 11(e), *and* provide a driver program to test your solution.

16. Code a recursive solution for Exercise 11(f), *and* provide a driver program to test your solution.

17. Code a recursive solution for Exercise 11(c), *and* provide a driver program to test your solution.

18. Code a recursive method that calculates the greatest common denominator of two integers *and* provide a driver program that demonstrates that it functions properly.

19. Apply the techniques of dynamic programming to improve the performance of the method coded in Exercise 14, and provide a driver program that demonstrates that it is faster than the nondynamic version of the code in Exercise 14.

20. Code a program that outputs the first 45 terms in the Fibonacci sequence by invoking a non-dynamic recursive method that calculates the nth term of the series.

21. Apply the techniques of dynamic programming to improve the performance of the method `fibonacci` that is presented in Figure 6.15 and provide a driver program that demonstrates that it functions properly.

22. Determine the value of n such that the dynamic version of the recursive algorithm for x^y is 20 seconds faster than the nondynamic version. Include a description of the platform (CPU make and model, clock speed, amount of RAM memory, and the operating system).

23. Your pet mouse Marty can find his way out of a maze, unassisted, much to the delight of his fans. The maze is divided into a two-dimensional grid of six rows and six columns of black and white tiles. Tiles are identified by their row number, followed by their column number. Rows and columns are numbered sequentially from 0 to 5 with box 0,0 in the upper left corner. Black tiles cannot be stepped on so Marty must proceed along the white tiles of the maze to reach the exit. Marty always enters the maze from below, stepping onto tile 5,1 which is always a white tile. From there he can advance to any adjacent white tile, but cannot travel diagonally from tile to tile. If possible, Marty will always continue straight ahead. Being left handed his second choice is always to turn left, then right, and finally (if he has reached a dead end), his last and only remaining choice is to retreat backward. The maze is modeled by a 6 × 6 array of integers with a black tile represented as a 1, and a white tile represented as a 0. Write a program that invokes a recursive backtracking method and outputs the row and column numbers of the tiles Marty steps on as he finds his way through the maze. Include all the boxes backtracked onto because Marty chose a path that ended in a dead end.

24. Each square of the following 10 × 10 checkerboard has a toll associated with it that must be paid when you enter the square. You wish to travel from the bottom-most row to the top-most row and minimize the total of the tolls along the way. Write a program to output the row and column numbers of a route that minimizes the tolls. When making a move, the row number *must* increase by 1 and the column number can change by −1, 0, or +1. Tolls range from 0 to 9, and row 1 and column 1 is the lower leftmost square of the checkerboard. The

program should invoke a dynamic recursive method, minToll, to determine the minimum toll to get to each of the top row cells, $i = 10$, of the checkerboard calculated as

$\text{minToll}[i][j] = \text{toll}[i][j] + \text{minimum of } (\text{minToll}[i-1][j-1], \text{minToll}[i-1][j], \text{minToll}[i-1][j+1])$

	Column									
	1	2	3	4	5	6	7	8	9	10
10	6	4	7	4	8	3	6	7	2	4
9	9	1	4	7	3	6	8	6	1	4
8	4	8	1	9	7	9	2	3	5	4
7	1	8	6	6	8	4	8	3	8	2
6	7	3	7	4	4	1	5	9	9	4
5	1	6	3	2	1	4	3	3	7	9
4	5	3	8	4	2	6	7	9	3	5
3	6	4	3	8	7	1	2	4	7	4
2	8	8	3	6	5	8	3	9	1	5
Row 1	0	3	5	6	1	2	7	1	9	4

25. There is a kind of puzzle formatted as a 9 by 9 grid of cells grouped into nine 3 by 3 boxes. To solve this puzzle the numbers 1 through 9 must appear once, and only once, in each row, column, and 3 by 3 box. The puzzle begins with several cells filled in. Use the generalized backtracking algorithm to solve this kind of puzzle.

CHAPTER 7

Trees

The objectives of this chapter are to familiarize the student with the features, implementation, and uses of tree structures. More specifically, the student will be able to

■ Understand the standard *graphics* used to depict trees, the *terminology* of trees, and the *mathematics* of binary trees.

■ Understand the linked and array-based memory models programmers use to represent binary tree structures, and the advantages and disadvantages of these representations.

■ Understand the classic *binary search tree* structure and its operation algorithms, including their use of a method that locates a node in the tree.

■ Explain the advantages and disadvantages of binary search tree structures, and be able to quantify their performance.

■ Implement a fully encapsulated version of a binary search tree.

■ Understand the standard tree traversal techniques (including inorder, preorder, and postorder), the use of these techniques, and be able to implement them recursively.

- Understand the extension of the binary search tree structure to an *AVL* tree and a *Red-Black* tree, and understand the techniques these structures use to keep the tree balanced.

- Understand the topic of recursion more fully by examining several recursive tree algorithms.

- Develop an application that declares a structure in Java's API `TreeMap` class, understand the advantages and disadvantages of the class, and operate on the structure using the class' operation methods.

7.1 Trees

In the previous chapters we have studied three types of data structures that allow access in the key field mode: array-based structures, linked lists, and hashed structures. Each of these structures has unique attributes that make them attractive in certain applications. The hashed structures are, by far, the fastest structures when we consider all four basic operations. The array-based structures are the simplest to implement and the speed of two of their operations (Insert for the unsorted version and Fetch for the sorted version) match the hashed structures. The linked list structures do not require contiguous memory and, therefore, are the most efficient structures to expand. In addition, the speed of the Insert operation for unsorted linked list structures approaches the speed of the hashed structures.

Tree structures, like linked lists, do not require contiguous memory, making them just as efficient to expand. In addition, when properly implemented, the speed of these structures greatly exceeds that of the array-based and linked structures and approaches the overall speed of the hashed structures. From a density viewpoint, they require higher node widths than the other structures to reach acceptable densities. However, they are the only structure we will study that can easily model data in a hierarchical (as opposed to a linear) form and can process nodes in sorted order without sacrificing operation speed. These attributes make them attractive for many applications.

7.1.1 Graphics and Terminology of Trees

Before proceeding to a discussion of the algorithms used to operate on trees, it is necessary to gain an understanding of the depictions and terminology of trees. The standard depiction of a tree is shown in Figure 7.1, which presents a tree containing eight nodes. Each node in the tree is represented by a circle with lines emanating from it. These lines connect a node to other nodes in the structure that come after it, and are analogous to the arrows in the standard depiction of a linked list. The annotation inside the circle normally refers to the contents of the key field of the node. As was the case with linked lists, these graphical depictions will be used extensively in this chapter to develop the algorithms used to operate on trees and to facilitate our understanding of them.

We will now turn our attention to the terminology of trees, beginning our discussion with the term *directed tree*. We will see that most tree terminology employs two analogies; the terms root,

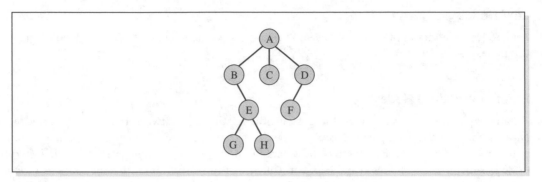

Figure 7.1   Standard Depiction of a Tree

leaf, forest, and, of course, tree are terms borrowed from nature, and the terms parent, child, and grandparent are terms borrowed from the traditional family unit.

Directed (or General) Tree

A directed (or *general* tree), is a structure in which

- There is a designated unique first node,
- Each node in the structure, except for the unique first node, has one and only one node before it, and
- Each node in the structure has 0, 1, 2, 3,… nodes after it.

Consider the tree depicted in Figure 7.1. If we designate node A to be the unique first node, then it is a directed tree because

- There is a unique first node, A, which has no node before it,
- Nodes B, C, and D are preceded *only* by node A; node E is preceded *only* by node B; node F is preceded *only* by node D; and nodes G and H are preceded *only* by node E, and
- Nodes C, F, G, and H have 0 nodes after them; nodes B and D have one node after them; node E has two nodes after it; and node A has three nodes after it.

Root Node

A *root* node is the unique first node in the structure. The root node does not have a node before it. Each tree has one, and only one, root node that is always drawn at the top of the standard depiction of a tree. Node A is the root node of the tree presented in Figure 7.1.

Leaf Nodes

Leaf nodes are nodes in the tree that have no (0) nodes after them. Nodes C, F, G, and H in Figure 7.1 are leaf nodes.

Parent (or Father) Nodes

An analogy to a family is often used to describe the relationship between the nodes of a tree. A *parent* node is a node's unique predecessor. Referring to the tree shown in Figure 7.1, node A is the parent of nodes B, C, and D; node B is the parent of node E; node D is the parent of node F; and node E is the parent of nodes G and H. A consequence of this definition is that all nodes in a tree are parent nodes except for the leaf nodes. Sometimes in the literature, a patriarchal analogy is used in which case the term *father* is substituted for the term parent.

Child (or Son) Nodes

A *child* node is a node that comes directly after a node in a tree. Referring to the tree presented in Figure 7.1, nodes B, C, and D are the children of node A; node E is the child of node B; node F is the child of node D; and nodes G and H are the children of node E. A consequence of this definition is that all nodes in a tree are child nodes except for the root node, and when we also consider the definition of a parent node we can conclude that all nodes in a tree are both child *and* parent nodes except for the leaf nodes and the root node. When the patriarchal analogy is used, a child is referred to as a *son*.

Grandchild Nodes, Great Grandchild Nodes, etc.

A *grandchild* of a node is a child of a child of a node. Referring to the tree presented in Figure 7.1, nodes E and F are the grandchildren of node A, and nodes G and H are the grandchildren of node B. Extending this genealogy, nodes G and H are also the *great* grandchildren of node A.

Grandparent Nodes, Great Grandparent Nodes, etc.

A *grandparent* of a node is the parent of the parent of a node. Referring to the tree presented in Figure 7.1, node A is the grandparent of nodes E and F, and node B is the grandparent of nodes G and H. Extending this genealogy, node A is the *great* grandparent of nodes G and H.

Outdegree of a Node

The *outdegree* of a node is the number of children it has. Referring to the tree presented in Figure 7.1, node A has outdegree three, node E has outdegree two, node D has outdegree one, and nodes C, F, G, and H have outdegree zero. Leaf nodes always have outdegree zero.

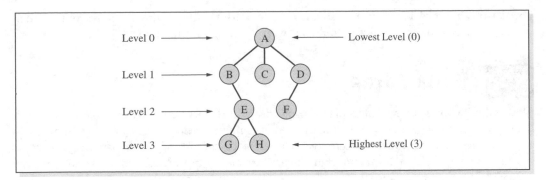

Figure 7.2 The Level Numbers of a Tree With Four Levels

Outdegree of a Tree

The outdegree of a tree is equal to the *largest* outdegree of *any* of the nodes in the tree. The tree presented in Figure 7.1 has outdegree three.

Levels of a Tree

The *levels* of a tree are a sequential numbering assigned to the descendents of the root node, with the root node at level 0. The root node's children are at level 1, the root node's grandchildren are at level 2, etc. Since the level numbers begin at 0, the number of levels of a tree is always one more than the highest *level number* in the tree. Figure 7.2 presents the levels of the tree depicted in Figure 7.1, which has a total of four levels.

When we begin our study of trees, this level numbering system can be a bit confusing since the lowest level number is at the top of the standard tree depiction, and vice versa.

Visiting a Node

We *visit* a node in a tree by first locating the node, and then performing some operation on it. Typical operations performed on a node are to fetch the contents of the node, output the node, determine if it has a child, etc.

Traversing a Tree

Traversing a tree is the process of visiting each node in the tree once, and only once. For example, if the operation to be performed on the nodes of the tree presented in Figure 7.1 was to output the key values of each node, then a valid traversal would output the keys in the order: A, B, C, D, E, F, G, and finally, H. An equally valid output traversal would be to output the nodes in the order: A, B, E, G, H, C, D, and finally, F. Although it is true that many traversal orders are possible, three of these possibilities (named *preorder*, *inorder*, and *postorder* traversals) are most often used. These popular traversal orders will be discussed later in this chapter. Outputting the nodes in the order A, B, E, G, H, A, C, D, and finally, F would be an invalid traversal since node A is visited twice.

7.2 Binary Trees

Most of the material in the remainder of this chapter deals with binary trees. They are a subset of directed trees that occupy a very important place in the field of computer science. A *binary tree*, by definition, is a directed tree with maximum outdegree two. This implies that each node in a binary tree can have a maximum of two children. That is, nodes in a binary tree can only be leaf nodes, have one child, or have two children. The tree presented in Figure 7.1 is not a binary tree because the root node has three children. Figure 7.3 presents six valid binary trees. Before beginning our study of the algorithms associated with binary trees, we will discuss some the terminology and mathematics particular to binary trees.

7.2.1 Terminology

Left Child (Left Son) of a Node

When the standard tree graphic is used to depict a binary tree, a node's *left child* is the child of the node to the *viewer's* left. For example, in tree **f** presented in Figure 7.3, node B is A's left child,

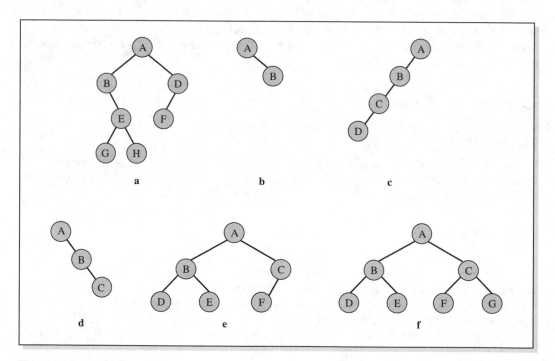

Figure 7.3 Valid Binary Trees

and node G is C's left child. When the patriarchal analogy is used, a left child is referred to as a *left son*.

Right Child (Right Son) of a Node

When the standard tree graphic is used to depict a binary tree, a node's *right child* is the child of the node to the *viewer's* right. For example, in tree **f** presented in Figure 7.3, node C is A's right child, and node G is C's right child. Again, when the patriarchal analogy is used, a right child is referred to as a *right son*.

Left Subtree of a Node

The *left subtree* of a node is the tree whose root is the left child of the node. Referring to tree **a** in Figure 7.3, the left subtree of node B is the empty tree (containing no nodes), while the left subtree of node A contains the nodes B, E, G, and H, with node B being the root of the subtree.

Right Subtree of a Node

The *right subtree* of a node is the tree whose root is the right child of the node. Referring to tree **a** in Figure 7.3, the right subtree of node B is the tree containing the nodes E, G, and H, with E being the root of the subtree.

Complete

A binary tree is *complete* if all the levels of the tree are fully populated. Thus, except for the leaf nodes, all the nodes in a complete tree have two children. Tree **f** in Figure 7.3 is the only tree in the figure that is complete because at least one nonleaf node in all of the other trees has less than two children.

Balanced

A tree is *balanced* if all the levels of the tree below the highest level are fully populated. This implies that all complete trees are balanced. Trees **b**, **e**, and **f** in Figure 7.3 are examples of balanced trees.

Complete Left (or Right)

A tree is *complete left* if it is balanced *and* all the nodes at the highest level are on the left side of the level. Tree **e** presented in Figure 7.3 is complete left. A tree is *complete right* if it is balanced *and* all the nodes at the highest level are on the right side of the level. Tree **b** presented in Figure 7.3 is complete right.

This concludes our discussion of the terminology of binary trees. We will now turn our attention to the mathematics of binary trees, which is used later in this chapter when we evaluate the performance of these structures.

7.2.2 Mathematics

Maximum Number of Nodes at Level *l* of a Binary Tree

Consider tree **f** in Figure 7.3. All of its levels are fully populated; that is, they contain the maximum number of nodes that could exist at these levels. Counting the number of nodes at each level, we find that for any binary tree there is a maximum of

> 1 node at level $l = 0$,
> 2 nodes at level $l = 1$, and
> 4 nodes at level $l = 2$.

Extrapolating these observations (or alternately fully populating higher levels of the tree and counting the nodes) we find that there would be a maximum of

> 8 nodes at level $l = 3$,
> 16 nodes at level $l = 4$, and
> 32 nodes at level $l = 5$.

It is now easy to deduce the functional relationship between the maximum number of nodes at a level, nl_{max}, and the level number, l, to be:

Maximum Number of Nodes, nl_{max}, at Level *l* of a Binary Tree

$$nl_{max} = 2^l$$

Equation 7.1

Thus, the maximum number of nodes at level 15 of a binary tree is 2^{15}, or 32,768 nodes.

Maximum Number of Nodes in a Tree with *L* Levels

A tree with L levels will contain a maximum number of nodes when all of its levels are fully populated; that is, the tree is complete. Figure 7.4 presents three complete trees comprised of 1, 2, and 3 levels.

Table 7.1 tabulates the number of levels in each of these trees (L) vs. the total number of nodes they contain (nL_{max}) extrapolated to include complete trees with 4 and 5 levels. (This extrapolation

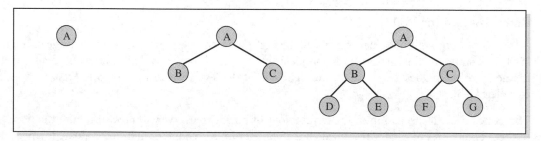

Figure 7.4 Complete Binary Trees with 1, 2, and 3 Levels

Table 7.1

Maximum Number of Nodes, nL_{max}, in a Binary Tree With L Levels

L	nL_{max}
1	1
2	3
3	7
4	15
5	31

can be verified by drawing complete 4 and 5 level trees and counting the total number of nodes.)

From the data presented in Table 7.1, we can deduce the functional relationship between nL_{max} and L to be

Maximum Number of Nodes, nL_{max}, in a Binary Tree with L Levels

$$nL_{max} = 2^L - 1$$

Equation 7.2

which is also the number of nodes in a complete binary tree with L levels. Thus, a complete binary tree with 16 levels would have a total of $2^{16} - 1 = 65,535$ nodes with slightly over half these nodes ($32,768 = 2^{15}$) at the highest level (level $l = 15$).

Minimum Number of Levels in a Tree with N Nodes

The number of levels in a tree with N nodes will be a minimum when the tree is balanced because all levels except the lowest level are fully populated (e.g., compare trees **e** and **c** in Figure 7.3). Assuming N is such that the tree is not only balanced but also complete (e.g., tree **f** in Figure 7.3), then $N = nL_{max}$ and using Equation 7.2 we obtain

$$N = nL_{max} = 2^L - 1$$

or

$$2^L = N + 1.$$

Remembering, from the definition of a logarithm, $x^y = z$ implies $y = \log_x z$ we can solve the above equation for L to obtain

$$L = \log_2(N + 1).$$

This is the number of levels in a complete binary tree containing N nodes.

Number of Levels in a Complete Binary Tree Containing N Nodes

$$L = \log_2(N + 1)$$

Equation 7.3

If N is such that the tree is balanced but not complete ($N < nL_{max}$), then the highest level of the tree would not be fully populated and Equation 7.3 will not yield an integer value. In this case, in order to include the highest level of the tree in the computed value of L, we use the ceiling of the previous function to determine the minimum number of levels in the tree. Thus, we have

Minimum Number of Levels in a Tree Containing N Nodes
(which is also the number of levels in a balanced binary tree)

$$L = \text{ceiling}(\log_2(N + 1))$$

Equation 7.4

For example, a binary tree containing 600 nodes must have at least 10 levels (= ciel($\log_2$(600 + 1)) = ciel(9.23) = 10), and the highest level of the tree would not be fully populated because $\log_2$(600 + 1) is not an integer.

Armed with knowledge of tree graphics, tree terminology, and the mathematics of binary trees, we are now prepared to explore the algorithms used to operate on trees. We will begin with a discussion of a special kind of binary tree, a *binary search tree*.

7.3 Binary Search Trees

Consider the tree shown in Figure 7.5 consisting of six nodes, each containing a one letter key. Let us assume we are to fetch the node with key field P. We begin our search, as we begin all searches for nodes stored in trees, at the root node. The key field of this node is fetched and examined, and our search ends successfully after one memory access.

Now suppose we are searching for the node with key field K. Starting at the root node, the first memory access returns the key P, and the search must continue. Now we need to make a decision whether to visit the left child (node N), or right child (node V), of node P. Let us assume we make the correct choice and visit node N next, and then make another correct choice visiting node N's

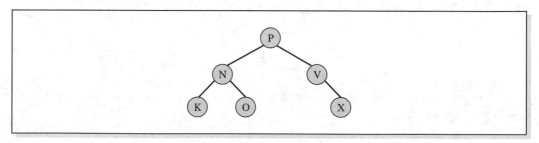

Figure 7.5   Six Nodes with One Letter Key Each Stored in a Binary Tree

left child next. Under these assumptions we will locate node K after three memory accesses, searching through the nodes in the order P, N, K.

But suppose we make incorrect choices at every decision point. In this case a typical search order could be: P, V, X, N, O, K. Under this "worst case" scenario, six memory accesses are required to locate the node K. Obviously deciding to visit N after P, and then K after N would be a better choice, but we can only be certain of making a correct decision at each decision point if we have some way of knowing that K is in the left subtrees of P and N. Enter the *binary search tree*.

A binary search tree is a binary tree that allows us to always identify the "correct" child (subtree) to visit after an unsuccessful memory access. This is made possible by the manner in which the nodes are arranged in a binary tree as stated in its definition.

> ### Binary Search Tree
>
> A binary search tree is a binary tree in which the key field value of the *root node* is *greater than* the key field values of *all* of the nodes in the root's *left subtree*, and *less than* the key field values of *all* of the nodes in the root's *right subtree*. In addition, each subtree in the tree is also a binary search tree.

Consider the tree presented in Figure 7.6 whose nodes have integer key values. Under our definition, this tree is a binary search tree. The value of the key field of the tree's root node, 50, is *greater than* all the keys in its *left subtree* (40, 35, 47, and 43), and it is also *less than* all the keys in its *right subtree* (63, 55, 70, 68, and 80). In addition, all subtrees in the tree are also binary trees, which can be verified by inspecting them. For example, consider the subtree whose root node is 63. This subtree is also a binary search tree because all keys in 63's left subtree (55) are less than 63, and all of the keys in the root's right subtree (70, 68, and 80) are greater than 63.

Other examples of binary search trees are trees **b** and **d** in Figure 7.3, the leftmost tree in Figure 7.4, and the tree shown in Figure 7.5. Conversely, because of the arrangement of the nodes in the

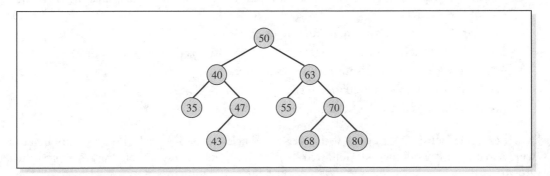

Figure 7.6   A Binary Search Tree

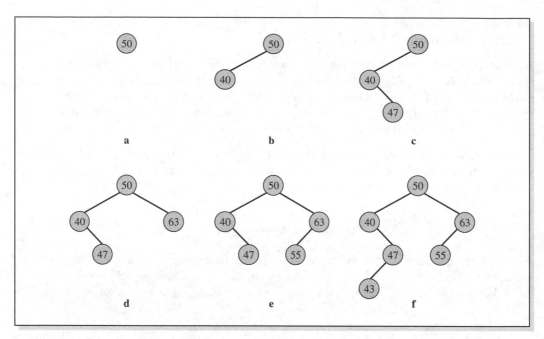

Figure 7.7   The Progressive Build-up of a Six Node Binary Search Tree

trees depicted in Figure 7.3, trees **a**, **c**, **e**, and **f** are not binary search trees, nor are the trees depicted in the middle and right side of Figure 7.4.

The positioning of the nodes in a binary search tree consistent with its definition is performed by the Insert operation. The following five step process accomplishes this.

1. The first node inserted becomes the root node.
2. For any subsequent node, consider the root node to be a root of a subtree, and start at the root of this subtree.
3. Compare the new node's key to the root node of the subtree.
    3.1. If the new node's key is *smaller*, then the new subtree is the root's *left* subtree.
    3.2. Else, the new subtree is the root's *right* subtree.
4. Repeat Step 3 until the new subtree is empty.
5. Insert the node as the root of this empty subtree.

As an example, consider six nodes with integer key fields to be inserted into an empty binary search tree: first key 50, then 40, followed by 47, 63, 55, and finally 43. Figure 7.7 depicts the growth of the tree as the nodes are inserted. Since the tree is initially empty, as per Step 1 of the process, 50 becomes the root node (see Figure 7.7**a**).

The node with key 40 is to be inserted next. Step 2 of the process tells us to consider the tree whose root is 50 as a subtree. Comparing the root of this subtree to the key value 40 (Step 3 of the process) we find it is less than the root, and the new subtree is therefore the left subtree of 50 (Step 3.1). Since this subtree is empty, Step 5 tells us to make the new node the root of the empty left subtree of 50 (see Figure 7.7**b**).

The node with key 47 is to be inserted next. Step 2 of the process tells us to consider the tree whose root is 50 as a subtree. Comparing the root of this subtree to the key value 47 (Step 3 of the process) we find it is less than the root, and the new subtree is therefore the left subtree of 50 (Step 3.1). This subtree's root is 40, and since it is not empty, Step 4 tells us to repeat Step 3. Comparing the root of this subtree to the key value 47 (Step 3 of the process) we find it is greater than the root, and the new subtree is therefore the right subtree of 40 (Step 3.2). Since this subtree is empty, Step 5 tells us to make the new node the root of the empty right subtree of 40 (see Figure 7.7**c**).

The node with key 63 is to be inserted next. Step 2 of the process tells us to consider the tree whose root is 50 as a subtree. Comparing the root of this subtree to the key value 63 (Step 3 of the process) we find it is greater than the root, and the new subtree is therefore the right subtree of 50 (Step 3.2). Since this subtree is empty, Step 5 tells us to make the new node the root of the empty right subtree of 50 (see Figure 7.7**d**).

The remaining nodes are inserted into the tree structure in a similar fashion, following the steps of the insertion process, and the tree grows as shown in Figure 7.7**e–f**. The subsequent addition of four more nodes to this tree: key 70 first, then keys 80 and 35, and finally, key 68, produces the tree shown in Figure 7.6.

Armed with an understanding of how nodes are arranged in binary search trees inherent in their definition, the process of deciding which subtree to visit after an unsuccessful access is simple. If the key value of the node just accessed is less than the key of the node being searched for, we visit the right subtree; otherwise we visit the left subtree.

Knowing which subtree to visit significantly improves the time required to locate a node in a *balanced* binary tree. Consider a balanced tree with 65,535 nodes and assume we are trying to fetch a node stored in the *highest* level of the tree. Equation 7.4 tells us that the tree has 16 levels. By making a correct subtree decision at each level, the node would be located after only 16 memory accesses.

However, there are times when even knowing what subtree to visit does not significantly reduce the number of memory accesses performed when searching for a node. Consider a tree that is not complete or one that is not balanced. Rather, it is highly skewed, like tree **c** in Figure 7.3, with one node at each level of the tree. In this case, there would be 65,535 levels in the tree, and even though we make the correct subtree decision (proceed to the left subtree) after each unsuccessful access, it will take 65,535 memory accesses to locate a node at the highest level of the tree. Thus, although binary search trees do allow us to make a correct subtree decision when searching for a node, the speed advantages associated with this decision-making process can only be realized if the tree is balanced, or close to balanced.

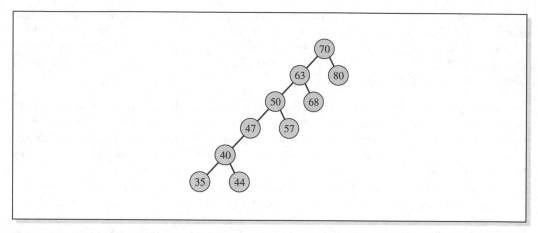

Figure 7.8   An Imbalanced Binary Search Tree

The most basic binary search tree operation algorithms make no attempt to keep the tree balanced, and they can produce skewed trees like the tree depicted in Figure 7.8. (This tree would be generated if the keys depicted in Figure 7.7 were inserted into the tree in the order: 70, 63, 68, 80, 50, 57, 47, 40, 44, and finally 35.) However, a characteristic common to most data sets (that will be identified when we study the performance of binary search trees) often produces trees that are close to (or actually) balanced. As a result, even the most basic search tree structure is a practical structure and, in the interest of simplicity, we will begin our study of search trees by examining its operation algorithms. Once we have gained an understanding of this structure, we will discuss more complicated binary tree structures, such as AVL trees and Red-Black trees, whose operation algorithms keep the tree balanced for all data sets.

7.3.1   Basic Operation Algorithms

Before discussing the pseudocode of the basic operations on binary search trees, we need to expand our understanding of the circle symbol used in the tree graphics presented thus far in this chapter. A deeper level of understanding of what this symbol represents is essential to the development of the pseudocode and its implementation.

The Graphical Circle Symbol Meaning

We have previously interpreted the circles in the graphical representations of a tree as the symbol that represents a node, and the annotation inside of it as the contents of the node's key field. At the implementation level, the circle symbol has two other interpretations, each tied to one of the two standard implementations of a binary tree; the *linked* implementation and the *array* implementation. The meaning of the circle symbol under the linked implementation of a binary tree will be discussed first, since this implementation is in much wider use. The array implementation will

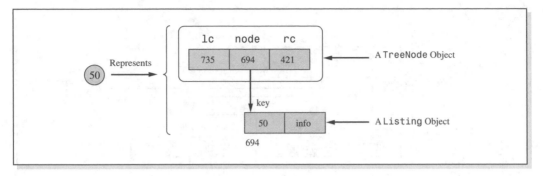

Figure 7.9   The Linked Implementation Level Meaning of the Circle Symbol

be discussed in a subsequent section of this chapter in which we will also compare the advantages of the two implementations.

In the linked implementation, the circle represents two objects: a `TreeNode` object and a `Listing` object (see Figure 7.9). The `TreeNode` object has three data members, all of which are reference variables. Referring to Figure 7.9, the left- and rightmost data members, named `lc` and `rc` respectively, store the location of the nodes' left and right children. The other data member, `node`, contains the location of the information stored in the structure, a `Listing` object.

Figure 7.10 shows the standard graphic of a three node tree (the left side of the figure) and the actual storage it represents (the center and right portions of the figure) under the linked implementation. The information that has been inserted into the tree structure (three `Listing` objects) are shown at the right of the figure. The contents of the key fields are 50, 63, and 40 which correspond to the key field values shown in the standard tree graphic at the left side of the figure. As shown in the figure, the items inserted into the tree are not actually arranged in a tree structure. Rather, the `TreeNode` objects (shown in the center of the figure) form the tree structure.[1] The **null** values in the `lc` and `rc` data members of the lower two `TreeNode` objects indicate that they do not have any children.

It is important that we become familiar with this lower level representation of the circle symbols (presented in Figures 7.9 and 7.10) before moving on to the development of the operation algorithms. The best way to approach the coding of these algorithms (or any other operation to be performed on a tree structure) is to first draw these lower-level graphics and then modify them to incorporate the changes necessary to perform the operation. Once the operation algorithm has been graphically developed and verified, it is much more easily coded.

---

[1]This is analogous to the implementation of a singly linked list (see Figure 4.9) in which the `Node` objects were arranged in the linked list, not the `Listing` objects.

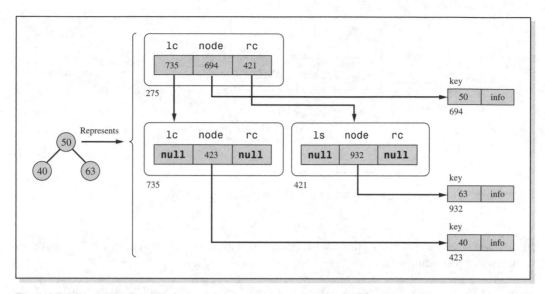

Figure 7.10   Actual Storage Represented by the Standard Depiction of a Three-Node Tree

Having gained an understanding of the circle symbol under the linked implementation of a binary tree, we are now ready to develop the operation algorithms for a binary search tree under the linked implement.

Initialization Algorithm

One of the ironies of a binary tree structure (as was the case with linked lists) is that, although a binary tree can store virtually an unlimited number of nodes, initially it contains only one data member, root, a reference variable. This variable will store the location of the tree's root node as depicted in Figure 7.11.

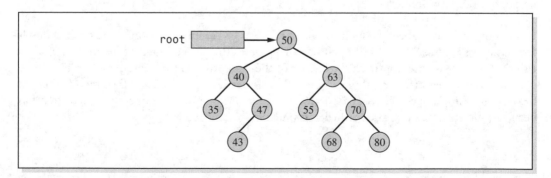

Figure 7.11   A Ten-Node Binary Tree

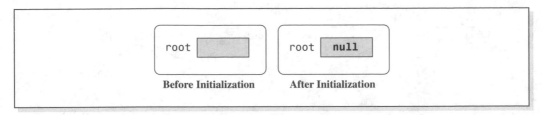

Figure 7.12   A Binary Search Tree Object Before and After Initialization

Consistent with the graphical technique for developing the operation algorithms employed in Chapter 4, Figure 7.12 shows a binary search tree object, before and after its initialization algorithm is executed. The initialization sets the variable root to **null**. Thus, the initialization algorithm is:

Binary Search Tree Initialization Algorithm

1.   root = **null**;

Whenever the tree is empty, the value of root will be **null**. We will now turn our attention to the Insert, Fetch, Delete, and Update algorithms.

Insert Algorithm and the `findNode` Method

As depicted in Figure 7.7, the process of inserting nodes into a binary search tree places all newly inserted nodes into the tree as leaf nodes. Therefore, the Insert algorithm must first decide which of the nodes in the tree will be the new leaf's parent. This decision process is depicted in Figure 7.13 in which the node with a key value of 52 is being inserted into the tree. The process involves repositioning two reference variables: P (for parent) and C (for child) until C contains a **null** value.

The reference variables P and C are first set pointing to the root node (see Figure 7.13**a**). The key of the node to be inserted, 52, is compared to the node referenced by C. Since 52 is *greater* than the key of the node referenced by C, we know the new node belongs in the right subtree of C, and its parent, therefore, must be in the *right* subtree of the node referenced by C. Therefore, C is set to reference the right child of C (see Figure 7.13**b**).

Again, 52 is compared to the node referenced by C. Since 52 is now *less than* the key of the node referenced by C, we know the new node belongs in the left subtree of C. P is set to C, but now C is set to reference the *left* child of C (see Figure 7.13**c**). This process continues moving through the levels of the tree until C contains a **null** reference (see Figure 7.13**d**). At this point the search for the new node's parent ends with P containing a reference to what will become the new node's parent.

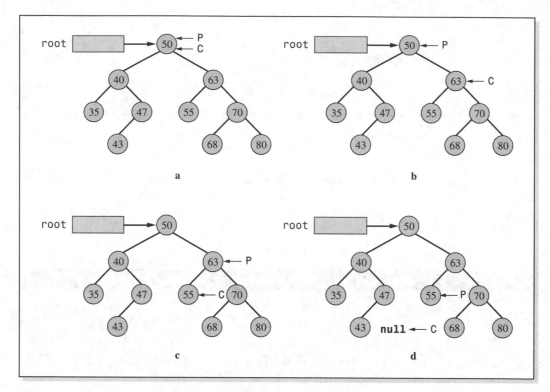

Figure 7.13   Finding the Parent of a Newly Inserted Node with Key Value 52

The only remaining question is whether the new node will be the parent's left or right child. This is easily determined by comparing the new node's key to the key of the parent node. If the new node's key is less than its parent's key, the new node becomes the parent's left child, otherwise it becomes the parent's right child.

To express the steps of the Insert algorithm depicted in Figure 7.13 in pseudocode, it is useful to assume that a method, findNode, exists that locates a node in a binary search tree given its key value, targetKey. Let us also assume the method has two parameters: C and P, and that it sets C to the location of the node with the given key and sets P to the location of C's parent. Thus, if the method were searching the tree depicted in Figure 7.13 for the node with key field 55, then its search process would be as depicted in parts **a, b,** and **c.**

Now for some implementation trickery. Let us further assume that when the method was given a key that was not in the tree, it halted its search when the parameter C assumed a **null** value. Under this assumption, if it were searching for the node with key value 52, its search process would be as depicted in Figures 7.13**a, b, c,** and **d.** Thus (and here is the implementation trickery), the *unsuccessful* search mode of this method could be used to locate the parent of a node to be inserted into a binary search tree[2] if the key sent to it was the new node's key. Although C would return set to **null**, P would contain the location of the parent of the new node (see Figure 7.13**d**).

Remembering the steps discussed above and depicted in Figure 7.13, the pseudocode of the method findNode that returns a Boolean value of **true** after a successful search for the key targetKey is:

Pseudocode of the findNode Algorithm (Iterative Version)

```
1.  P = root;
2.  C = root;
3.  while(C != null)
4.  { if(targetKey == C.node.key) // node found
5.      return true;
6.   else  // continue searching
7.   { P = C;
8.      if(targetKey < C.node.key) // move into left subtree
9.        C = C.lc;
10.     else  // move into the right subtree
11.       C = C.rc;
12.  } // end else clause
13. } // end while
14. return false;
```

Alternately, the findNode can be coded recursively. Following our recursive methodology we need to identify the original problem, bases cases, reduced problem, and general solution. The original problem is to locate the node whose key is targetKey in a tree whose root is given, and set C pointing to the node and P pointing to its parent. Stated more succinctly, findNode(root, targetKey, P, C). The base cases would be when the tree is empty or when the key is found (C is referencing the targetKey). The reduced problem would be just one step closer to the base cases: to look for the key in either the right or left subtree of C. The pseudocode of findNode's recursive algorithm follows, assuming the location of the tree is initially stored in root.

---

[2]This use of the findNode method assumes that we will never insert two Listings with the same key value into the structure (an assumption used in the development of all data structures presented in this text).

Pseudocode of the `findNode` Algorithm (Recursive Version)

1. **if**(root == **null**) // first base case
2.   **return false;**
3. C = root;
4. **if**(targetKey == C.node.key) // second base case
5.   **return true;**
6. P = C;
7. **if**(targetKey < C.node.key) // look in the left subtree
8.   root = C.ls;
9. **else** // look in the right subtree
10.   root = C.rs
11. **return** findNode(root, targetKey, P, C); // reduced problem and general solution

The recursion is on Line 11 where the algorithm invokes itself and passes to it the root of either the left subtree (Line 8) or the right subtree (Line 10).

Returning to the Insert algorithm, after using the method `findNode` to locate the parent of the new node to be inserted into the search tree, we must place a reference to a deep copy of the inserted information (a `Listing` object) into a `TreeNode` object and add the `TreeNode` object into the tree structure. Assuming the key 52 is to be inserted into the tree depicted in Figure 7.13**d**, Figure 7.14 shows the process to complete its insertion.

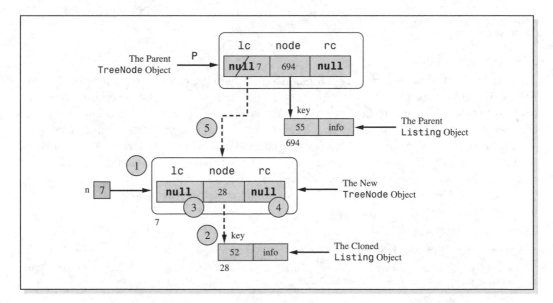

Figure 7.14 Inserting a Node whose Key Value is 52 into a Binary Tree as P's Left Child

Finally, the pseudocode version of this graphical representation of the algorithm is given below. It inserts a deep copy of the Listing object referenced by newListing into the tree structure whose root is referenced by root. The line numbers correspond to the circled step numbers in Figure 7.14.

Binary Tree Insert Algorithm

```
1.   TreeNode n = new TreeNode();
2.   n.node = newListing.deepCopy(); // copy the node and make it a leaf node
3.   n.lc = null;
4.   n.rc = null;
5a.  if (root == null) // the tree is empty
5b.     root = n;
5c.  else // the tree is not empty
5d.  { findNode(root, newListing.key, P, C); // find the new node's parent
5e.     if (newListing.key < P.node.key) // new node is parent's left child
5f.        P.lc = n;
5g.     else // new node is parent's right child
5h.        P.rc = n;
5i.  }
```

Fetch Algorithm

The graphical representation of the Fetch algorithm is essentially depicted in Figure 7.13**a**, **b**, and **c**, which actually illustrates the process performed by the findNode method to position the reference variable C on the item to be fetched (in this case, key 55). Once located, the Fetch algorithm returns a deep copy of the Listing. In the following pseudocode version of the algorithm, the key value of the item to be fetched is targetKey and the root of the tree is referenced by root.

Binary Search Tree Fetch Algorithm

```
1.   found = findNode(root, targetKey, P, C); // place the location of the node in C
2.   if(found == true)
3.      return C.node.deepCopy();
4.   else
5.      return null;
```

As developed earlier in the chapter, the method findNode returns **true** if it locates a Listing whose key value is targetKey (Line 1), and sets the argument C to the location of the TreeNode

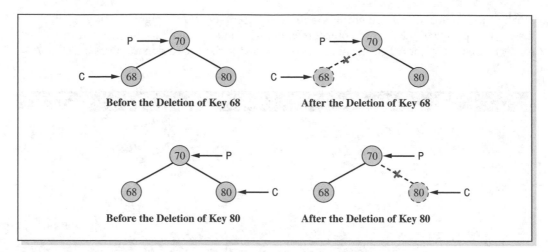

Figure 7.15 Case 1 of the Binary Search Tree Delete Algorithm

object that references the Listing. In this case, Line 3 returns a reference to a deep copy of the node. If the node is not found, a **null** value is returned (Line 5).

Delete Algorithm

This algorithm is the most complicated algorithm studied thus far in this text. In the spirit of "divide and conquer," it is traditionally broken down into three cases:

- Case 1: the node to be deleted has *no children*, is a *leaf*.
- Case 2: the node to be deleted has *one child*, or subtree.
- Case 3: the node to be deleted has *two children*, or subtrees.

The portion of the algorithm associated with each case becomes more complex as we move from Case 1 to Case 3. Therefore, the algorithm will be developed in that order.

Case 1: The Node to be Deleted has *No* Children (is a *Leaf*)

This portion of the Delete algorithm, depicted in Figure 7.15, simply breaks the connection between the deleted node, C, and the parent node, P, by setting P's reference to the node to **null**. Since the deleted node is a leaf node, and therefore has no children, we do not have to concern ourselves with retaining the location of the nodes in the deleted node's subtree; it has no subtree. The top half of Figure 7.15 illustrates the process of deleting a leaf node that is a left child, and the bottom half of the figure assumes the node to be deleted is a right child.

Assuming the key value of the item to be deleted is targetKey and the tree is referenced by root, the pseudocode version of Case 1 of the algorithm (depicted in Figure 7.15) is:

Binary Search Tree Delete Algorithm, Case 1

```
1.   found = findNode(root, targetKey, P, C);
2.   if(found == false) // node not found
3.      return false;
4.   if (C.lc == null  &&  C.rc == null) // Case 1
5.   { if (P.lc == C) // the deleted node is a left child
6.        P.lc = null;
7.   else              // the deleted node is a right child
8.        P.rc = null
9.   return true;
10.  } // end of Case 1
```

The algorithm begins by using the findNode algorithm (Line 1) to set C and P pointing to the node to be deleted *and* to its parent, respectively. Line 4 verifies that the node to be deleted has no children (Case 1). Then the algorithm decides if the node is a left or right child (Line 5) by comparing the left reference of the parent node to the location of the node, C. Finally, it sets the appropriate reference to the node to **null** (Lines 6 and 8).

Case 2: The Node to be Deleted has *One* Child or Subtree

This portion of the Delete algorithm separately considers the following four possibilities (depicted in Figure 7.16) involving the node to be deleted (C) and its parent (P).

2a. C is a *left* child of P, and C has a *left* child or subtree (see Figure 7.16**a**).
2b. C is a *left* child of P, and C has a *right* child or subtree (see Figure 7.16**b**).
2c. C is a *right* child of P, and C has a *left* child or subtree (see Figure 7.16**c**).
2d. C is a *right* child of P, and C has a *right* child or subtree (see Figure 7.16**d**).

Simply stated, the node to be deleted could *be either* a left or right child, and it could *have either* a left or right child (or subtree).

The Delete algorithm associated with the four possibilities depicted in Figure 7.16, is shown in Figure 7.17. In each of the four possibilities, the node is deleted by resetting the parent's reference to it, to reference the deleted node's child (the root of its subtree).

Before writing the pseudocode version of this algorithm, we will discuss one subtle, but important, point. In the upper right portion of Figure 7.17, the deletion causes the deleted node's subtree to change from a *right* subtree (of C) to a *left* subtree (of P). This is precisely what should happen since, although all the keys in the subtree were greater than C's key (the subtree was to the right of C), they must be less than P's key or the subtree would not have been to the left of P. More specifically, all the keys in the subtree depicted in the upper right portion of Figure 7.17, must be between 33 and 69. Therefore, they should become a left subtree of P. An analogous situation

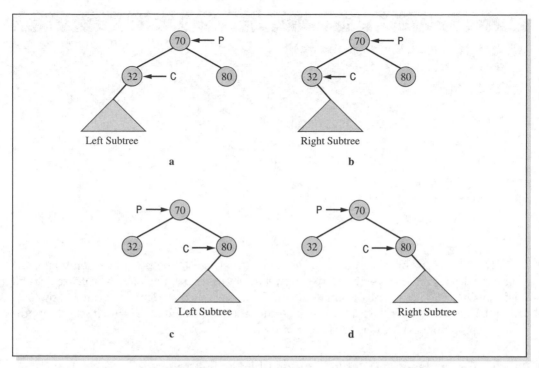

Figure 7.16   The Four Possibilities of Case 2 of the Binary Search Tree Delete Algorithm

occurs in the possibility depicted in the lower left portion of Figure 7.17. In this case, all of the keys in 80's subtree must be between 71 and 79.

Assuming the key value of the item to be deleted is targetKey and the root of the tree is referenced by root, the pseudocode version of Case 2 of the algorithm (depicted in Figure 7.17) is:

Binary Search Tree Delete Algorithm, Case 2

```
1.   found = findNode(root, targetKey, P, C);
2.   if(found == false) return false; // node not found
3.   if(C.lc != null && C.rc == null || C.rc != null && C.lc == null) // Case2
4.   { if(P.lc == C) // deleted node is a left child, Case 2a or 2b
5.      { if(C.lc != null) // deleted node has a left child, Case 2a
6.          P.lc = C.lc;
7.        else
8.          P.lc = C.rc;
9.      } // end of deletion of a left child
```

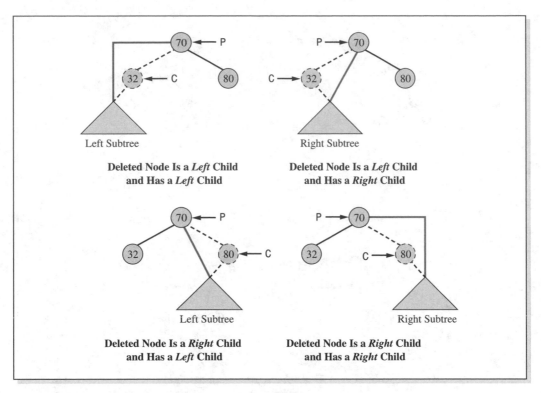

Figure 7.17   Case 2 of the Binary Search Tree Delete Algorithm

```
10.   else // deleted node is a right child, Case 2c or Case 2d
11.   { if(C.lc != null) // deleted node has a left child, Case 2c
12.       P.rc = C.lc;
13.   else
14.       P.rc = C.rc;
15.   } // end of deletion of a right child
16. return true;
17. } // end of Case 2
```

The algorithm begins by using the findNode algorithm (Line 1) to set C and P pointing to the node to be deleted *and* to its parent, respectively. Line 3 verifies that the node to be deleted has one, and only one, child (Case 2). Then it determines if the node to be deleted is a left or right child (Line 4) by comparing the left reference of the parent node to the location of the node. Finally, it eliminates the node to be deleted (as shown in Figure 7.17) by setting the parent's

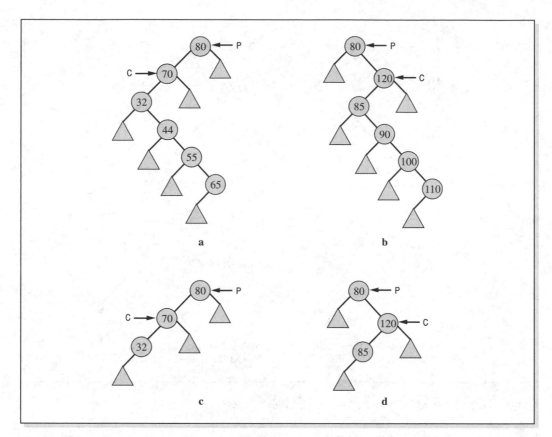

Figure 7.18   The Four Possibilities of Case 3 of the Binary Search Tree Delete Algorithm

appropriate reference (left child or right child) to the left or right child of the node to be deleted (Lines 6, 8, 12, or 14).

Case 3: The Node to be Deleted has *Two* Children or Subtrees

The final portion of the Delete algorithm separately considers the four possibilities (depicted in Figure 7.18) involving the node to be deleted (C) and its parent (P). The triangle symbol in the figure represents a subtree.

3a.   C is a *left* child of P, and C's left child *has* a right subtree (see Figure 7.18**a**).
3b.   C is a *right* child of P, and C's left child *has* a right subtree (see Figure 7.18**b**).
3c.   C is a *left* child of P, and C's left child *has no* right subtree (see Figure 7.18**c**).
3d.   C is a *right* child of P, and C's left child *has no* right subtree (see Figure 7.18**d**).

Simply stated, the node to be deleted could *be either* a left or right child, and its left child could *have either* a right subtree or not.

In the first two of these four possibilities (depicted in Figures 7.18**a** and 7.18**b**) the node referenced by C is deleted from the tree using the same process. For the tree depicted in Figure 7.18**a**, the process is illustrated in Figure 7.19.[3] The node to be deleted (in this case the node with key value 70) is simply replaced with a node relocated from its left child's right subtree (in this case the node with key value 65). This node is chosen as the replacement node because its position in the tree guarantees that it is the largest key in 70's left subtree, and it is less than all of the keys in 70's right subtree. Thus, it can be relocated to the deleted node's position without violating the definition of a binary search tree. In general, the replacement node is always chosen to be the node positioned at the far right side of the deleted node's left subtree, which is the largest node in the deleted node's left subtree.

To locate this node, two reference variables l and nl (standing for "largest" and "next largest"), are initially positioned as shown in Figure 7.19**a**. They then traverse through their right children (shown in Figures 7.19**b** and 7.19**c**) until l is referencing a node with no right child. Once this node is located, it is copied into the node to be deleted referenced by C (see Figure 7.19**d**). (More accurately, a reference to it is copied into the node field of the TreeNode referenced by C.) Finally, to prevent two copies of the node referenced by l from being in the structure, nl's right child reference is set pointing to the left subtree of the relocated node (see Figure 7.19**e**). Because of its position in the tree, the keys of all of the nodes in this subtree are greater than the key of the node referenced by nl, making it a legitimate right subtree of this node.

The remainder of the Case 3 portion of the Delete algorithm (Subcases 3c and 3d) addresses the other two possibilities for a node with two children; the left child of the node to be deleted does not have a right subtree (see the bottom half of Figure 7.18). The graphical depiction of this portion of Case 3 is shown in Figure 7.20. The left side of the figure assumes the node to be deleted is a left child, and the right side of the figure assumes the node to be deleted is a right child. In both cases, the node to be deleted and its parent is referenced by the variables C and P, respectively.

Once again, a reference variable nl is set to reference the left child of the node to be deleted (see Figures 7.20**a** and 7.20**b**). To keep from losing the right subtree of the node to be deleted, it becomes nl's right subtree, which was previously empty (see Figures 7.20**c** and 7.20**d**). Finally, the deleted node is removed from the tree by making P's left child (see Figure 7.20**e**), or P's right child (see Figure 7.20**f**), the left child of the deleted node.

Assuming the key value of the item to be deleted is targetKey and the tree is referenced by root, the pseudocode version of Case 3 of the Delete algorithm follows. It combines the processes presented in Figures 7.19 and 7.20. For clarity, the names of the reference variables nl and l have been changed to nextLargest and largest respectively.

---

[3]It is left as an exercise for the student to verify that the process is identical for the tree depicted in Figure 7.18**b**.

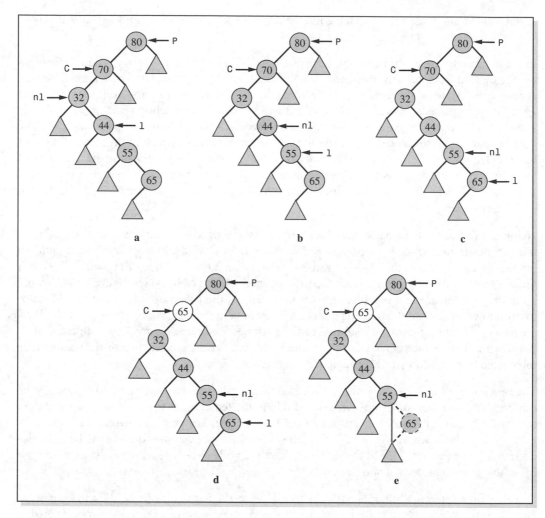

Figure 7.19 Part "a" of Case 3 of the Binary Search Tree Delete Algorithm (the node to be deleted has a key of 70)

Binary Search Tree Delete Algorithm, Case 3

1. found = findNode(root, targetKey, P, C);
2. **if**(found == **false**) **return false**; // node not found
3. **if**(C.lc != **null** && C.rc != **null**) // Case 3
4. { nextLargest = C.lc;
5.   largest = nextLargest.rc;
6.   **if**(largest != **null**) // left child of deleted node has a right subtree, Cases 3a–b

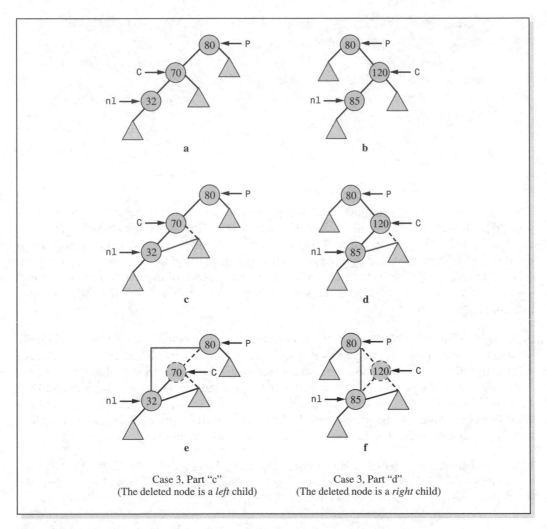

Figure 7.20 Parts "c" and "d" of Case 3 of the Binary Search Tree Delete Algorithm

```
7.    { while(largest.rc != null) // move down the right edge of right subtree
8.        { nextLargest = largest;
9.          largest = largest.rc;
10.       } // end of while loop, replacement node has been located
11.       C.node = largest.node; // "relocate" the replacement node
12.       nextLargest.rc = largest.lc; // save left subtree of the relocated node
13.    } // end of right subtree exists case
14.    else // left child of deleted node does not have a right subtree, Cases 3c–d
```

```
15.    { nextLargest.rc = C.rc; // save the right subtree of the deleted node
16.      if(P.lc == C)   // deleted node is a left child
17.        P.lc = nextLargest;  // deleted node's parent jumps around deleted node
18.      else              // deleted node is a right child
19.        P.rc = nextLargest;  // deleted node's parent jumps around deleted node
20.    } // end of no right subtree case
21.    return true;
22. } // end of Case 3
```

The algorithm begins by using the findNode algorithm (Line 1) to set C and P pointing to the node to be deleted *and* its parent, respectively. Line 3 verifies that the node to be deleted has two children (Case 3). Then, the locations of the node's left child, and the child's right child are set into the variables nextLargest and largest, respectively (Lines 4 and 5). If the left child has a right subtree (Line 6), then Lines 7–13 execute, which is the pseudocode of the algorithm shown in Figure 7.19. Otherwise, Lines 14–21 execute, which is the pseudocode version of the algorithm shown in Figure 7.20.

Referring to Figures 7.19a–c, the while loop (Lines 7–10) locates the node that will replace the node to be deleted. Once this node is located, Lines 11–12 perform the deletion (see Figure 7.19d) and reclaim the repositioned node's left subtree (see Figure 7.19e). Figure 7.21 shows the changes to the relevant TreeNode objects (see the unshaded fields in the figure) made by Lines 11 and 12 of Case 3 of the Delete algorithm at the implementation level. Since the deleted node, and the TreeNode object that was associated with the largest key in the subtree (65), is no longer referenced by a variable in the structure, they will be recycled by Java's memory manager.

When the deleted node's left child does not have a right subtree (see Figure 7.20), Line 15 of the algorithm performs the action depicted in Figures 7.20c and 7.20d, and Lines 17 and 19 actually delete the node from the structure (see Figures 7.20e and 7.20f).

7.3.2 Performance

The performance of a data structure is dependent upon the speed of its operations and the additional memory (above that necessary to store the clones of the client's information) required by the structure. In this section, we will discuss the speed of the structure's operations first, and then discuss the structure's overhead. Throughout our speed discussions, we will *assume* that the binary search tree is balanced, which, as we have seen, has a significant impact on the speed of the structure. For data sets that do not produce balanced binary search trees, the speed of the operations would be slower than that presented in this section. At the end of this chapter, we will consider alternate binary tree structures that always result in balanced (or close to balanced) trees.

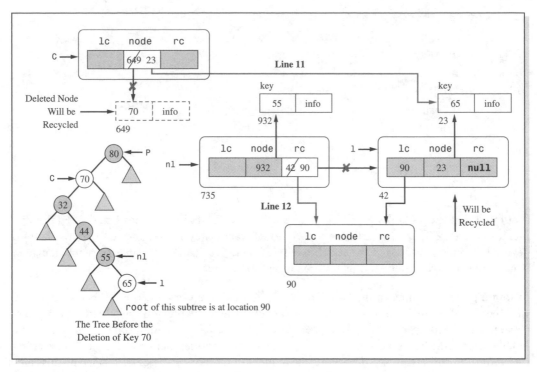

Figure 7.21   Memory Changes Resulting from Lines 11 and 12 of Case 3 of the Delete Algorithm

Speed of the Structure

As we have done in the previous chapters, we will perform a Big-O analysis to determine the approximate speed of the binary search tree structure as *n*, the number of nodes stored in the structure, gets large. Since a Big-O analysis is a bounding technique, and the time to perform a memory access instruction is typically considerably longer than the time to perform a nonaccess instruction, only memory access instructions will be included in our analysis.

Since all of the basic operation algorithms use the findNode algorithm, we will analyze it first.

Pseudocode of the findNode Algorithm (Iterative Version)

1. P = root;
2.   C = root;
3.   **while**(C != **null**)
4.   { **if**(targetKey == C.node.key) // node found
5.   **return true**;

```
6.    else // continue searching
7.    { P = C;
8.        if(targetKey < C.node.key) // move into the left subtree
9.            C = C.lc;
10.       else // move into the right subtree
11.           C = C.rc;
12.   } // end else clause
13. } // end while
14. return false;
```

Assuming that the variables P and C will be stored in CPU registers, Lines 1 and 2 require one memory access to fetch the variable root. Although targetKey is used inside the **while** loop to descend through the levels of the search tree (see Figure 7.13), since its value does not change, it would only be fetched once and then stored in a CPU register.

Examining the remainder of the loop, Line 4 requires two memory accesses to fetch C's key. The variables involved in Lines 7 and 8 have already been used in previous statements so they are already in the registers of the CPU and, therefore, do not require any additional memory accesses. Finally, *either* Line 9 *or* Line 11 executes requiring one additional memory access to access either C's left or right child reference. Therefore, the number of memory accesses performed by this algorithm is: $2 + 3T$, where T is the number of times the loop executes.

To determine the value of T, we recall that every time the loop executes we move one level higher into the tree. This means that T will be in the range 1 (when locating the root node) to $\log_2(n + 1)$ (when locating a node at the highest level of our, assumed to be, balanced tree: see equation 7.4). At most, half the nodes in a balanced tree are at the highest level of the tree.[4] This occurs when the tree is not only balanced, but also complete (the highest level is fully populated). Therefore, at most, half the nodes will require $\log_2(n + 1)$ passes through the loop, and the other half of the nodes will require less passes (1, or 2 ..., or $\log_2(n + 1) - 1$). This makes $T <= \log_2(n + 1)$, and the number of accesses to locate a node in balanced binary tree using the findNode algorithm is:

The Number of Memory Accesses Performed by the findNode Algorithm

$$<= 2 + 3\log_2(n + 1)$$ **(assumes a balanced tree)**

Having developed an expression for the speed of the findNode algorithm, we will now determine the speed of the basic operation algorithms beginning with the Insert Algorithm. For convenience, it is presented again as follows:

---

[4]This is proven in the appendix using Equations 7.1 and 7.3.

Binary Tree Insert Algorithm

```
1.   TreeNode n = new TreeNode();
2.   n.node = newListing.deepCopy(); // copy the node and make it a leaf node
3.   n.lc = null;
4.   n.rc = null;
5a.  if (root == null) // the tree is empty
5b.     root = n;
5c.  else // the tree is not empty
5d.  { findNode(root, newListing.key, P, C); // find the new node's parent
5e.     if (newListing.key < P.node.key) // new node is parent's left child
5f.        P.lc = n;
5g.     else // new node is parent's right child
5h.        P.rc = n;
5i.  }
```

Lines 1, 2, 3, and 4 require a total of four additional accesses: one access per line to store values in the variables n, n.node, n.lc, and n.rc. Next, Lines 5a–b or c–h execute. Lines 5a–b require less memory accesses (i.e., two: one to fetch the variable root and one to store n in root) than 5c–h so we will ignore them. We have previously determined that Line 5d requires less than $2 + 3\log_2(n + 1)$ memory accesses. Line 5e requires four memory accesses (one to access P, one to access P.node, one to fetch P.node's key, and one to fetch newListing's key). Finally, one access is required to store n in either P.lc or P.rc (Lines 5f and 5h). Therefore, *assuming the tree is balanced*, the Insert algorithm requires $<= 11 + 3\log_2(n + 1)$ accesses: four for Lines 1–4, $(2 + 3\log_2(n + 1)$, for Line 5d, four for Line 5e, and one for either Lines 5f or 5h) which is $O(\log_2 n)$.

We will now analyze the speed of the Fetch algorithm, which is repeated for convenience.

Binary Search Tree Fetch Algorithm

```
1.   found = findNode(root, targetKey, P, C); // insert the new leaf node
2.   if(found == true)
3.     return C.node.deepCopy();
4.   else
5.   return null;
```

As we have shown, Line 1 requires less than $2 + 3\log_2(n + 1)$ memory accesses. Examining Line 3, we see that it requires two memory accesses: one to access C and 1 to access C.node.

Table 7.2

Number of Nodes in the Levels of a Six-Level Complete Binary Tree

Level Number, *l*	Nodes at Level *l*	Total Number of Nodes Below this Level
0	1	0
1	2	1
2	4	3
3	8	7
4	16	15
5	32	31

Thus, the Fetch algorithm requires less than $4 + 3\log_2(n + 1)$ memory accesses which is $O(\log_2 n)$.

Since there are three parts to the Delete algorithm, in order to analyze its performance we will need to determine what percentage of the nodes in a balanced binary tree fall into Cases 1, 2, and 3 of the algorithm; that is, how many nodes have 0, 1, or 2 children. Then, these percentages will be used to calculate a *weighted average* speed of the algorithm.

Consider the *complete* binary tree with three levels shown in Figure 7.3f. Counting the nodes in this tree, we find that Level 0 contains 1 node; Level 1 contains 2 nodes; and Level 3 contains 4 nodes. Table 7.2 tabulates this data and extrapolates it to a six-level complete binary tree. In addition, its rightmost column presents the total number of nodes *below* each level, *l*, of the six-level tree. Comparing the data in the rightmost column to that in its middle column, we can observe that each level of the tree contains one more node than the total number of nodes in all the levels below it. This is typical of all complete binary trees. Thus, if there are *n* nodes in a complete binary tree, and *x* represents the number of nodes in the highest level of the tree, then the total number of nodes in all the other (lower) levels of the tree is $x - 1$ and the total number of nodes in the tree, *n*, is $n = x + x - 1$.

Now let us add one more level to our complete tree, which we will assume, on the average, will be half populated. The tree is no longer complete, but it is balanced. Being half populated, instead of containing twice as many nodes as the level below it, $2x$, the newly added level only contains $2x / 2 = x$ nodes. Thus, the total number of nodes, *n* becomes:

$$n = x + x - 1 + x = 3x - 1.$$

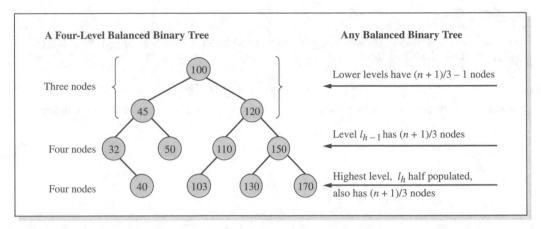

Figure 7.22 Distribution of the Number of Nodes in a Balanced Binary Tree Whose Highest Level is Half Populated (*n* is the number of nodes in the tree)

where x is the number of nodes at the next to highest level of the new tree, l_{h-1}. Solving this equation for x we obtain $x = (n + 1)/3$, and therefore:

For Any Balanced Binary Tree Containing *n* Nodes Whose Highest Level is Half Populated

The number of nodes in *each* of two highest levels of the tree is $x = (n + 1) / 3$ **Equation 7.5**

The *total* number of nodes in all other levels of the tree is $x - 1 = (n + 1) / 3 - 1$ **Equation 7.5**

For example, consider the balanced binary tree shown in Figure 7.22 whose highest level is half populated. The total number of nodes in the tree is 11. Counting the number of nodes at each level of the tree we can verify that there are $(11 + 1) / 3 = 4$ nodes at each of the two highest levels, and a total of $(n + 1) / 3 - 1 = 3$ nodes in the levels below the two highest levels.

We are now in a position to determine how many of the nodes in a balanced binary tree, whose highest level is half populated, have (most probably) zero, one, or two children. Equation 7.5 indicates that (approximately) one-third of the nodes reside in the highest level of the tree. Since all of the nodes at this level are leafs, these one-third n nodes have no children. Equation 7.6 indicates that (approximately) one-third of the nodes reside in the levels below the next to the highest level, l_{h-1}. Since all of these level *and* level l_{h-1} are fully populated, these (one-third n nodes) all have two children each. The remaining one-third of the nodes reside at level l_{h-1}. It can be demonstrated that, since the level below it is half populated, most probably, half of these nodes will have one child. With half of the nodes at level l_{h-1} having one child, the only way to half populate the highest level is if half of the remaining nodes at level l_{h-1} have two children, and the rest of the nodes at l_{h-1} must have zero children.

Table 7.3

The Number of Nodes in a Balanced Binary Tree (Whose Lower Level is Half Populated) with Zero, One, and Two Children

Level(s)	Population	Percent of Nodes		
		With No Children	With One Child	With Two Children
below l_{h-1}	~ $1/3n$	0%	0%	100%
l_{h-1}	~ $1/3n$	25%	50%[5]	25%
highest	~ $1/3n$	100%		
all	n	~ 1/3 * 25% + 1/3 * 100% = ~ 42%	~ 1/3 * 50% = ~ 16%	~ 1/3 * 100% + 1/3 * 25% = ~ 42%

[5]A reasonable assumption.

Consistent with the previous analysis, Table 7.3 summarizes the most probable distribution of the nodes with zero, one, or two children in a balanced binary tree whose lowest level is half populated. The bottom row of the table is a weighted sum of the three rows above it. As indicated in this row, when deleting nodes from a balanced binary tree (whose highest level is half populated), 42% of the time we will be deleting a node with zero children (Case 1 of the Delete algorithm), 16% of the time we will be deleting a node with one child (Case 2 of the Delete algorithm), and 42% of the deleted nodes will have two children (Case 3 of the Delete algorithm). Having determined the weighting factors to be applied to the speeds of Cases 1, 2, and 3 of the Delete algorithm (42%, 16%, and 42%, respectively), we will now analyze each case individually to determine their speed.

The analysis will begin with an observation: each of the three cases of the Delete algorithm begins with an invocation of the findNode method which, when the three cases are combined into one Delete method, will only be invoked once. Therefore, we will ignore this line during our analysis of the three cases and include its $2 + 3\log2(n + 1)$ memory access after we have determined the weighted average speed of the three cases.

In order to more easily analyze Case 1 of the Delete algorithm, its pseudocode, developed earlier, follows:

Binary Search Tree Delete Algorithm, Case 1

```
1.   found = findNode(root, targetKey, P, C);
2.   if(found == false) // node not found
3.     return false;
4.   if (C.lc == null && C.rc == null) // Case 1
5.   { if (P.lc == C) // the deleted node is a left child
6.       P.lc = null;
7.     else              // the deleted node is a right child
8.       P.rc = null
9.   return true;
10.  } // end of Case 1
```

Ignoring findNode's accesses, Line 4 requires three memory accesses to access C, C.lc, and C.rc. Line 5 requires two additional memory accesses to access P, and then P.lc. Lines 6 or 8 require one memory access to store a **null** value in either P.lc or P.rc. Thus, Case 1 of the delete algorithm requires a total of six memory accesses (which is O(1)).

The pseudocode of Case 2 of the Delete algorithm, previously developed, is:

Binary Search Tree Delete Algorithm, Case 2

```
1.   found = findNode(root, targetKey, P, C);
2.   if(found == false) return false; // node not found
3.   if(C.lc != null && C.rc == null || C.rc != null && C.lc == null) // Case2
4.   { if(P.lc == C) // deleted node is a left child, Case 2a or 2b
5.     { if(C.lc != null) // deleted node has a left child, Case 2a
6.         P.lc = C.lc;
7.       else
8.         P.lc = C.rc;
9.     } // end of deletion of a left child
10.    else // deleted node is a right child, Case 2c or Case 2d
11.    { if(C.lc != null) // deleted node has a left child, Case 2c
12.        P.rc = C.lc;
13.      else
14.        P.rc = C.rc;
15.    } // end of deletion of a right child
16.  return true;
17.  } // end of Case 2
```

Line 3 requires three memory accesses to access C, C.lc, and then C.rc. Line 4 requires two additional memory accesses to access P, and then P.lc. Either Lines 5–9 or Lines 11–15 execute next. Each group of code requires the same number of memory accesses. We will analyze Lines 5–8. The only additional memory access performed in this section of pseudocode is the writing into the memory cell P.lc on either Line 6 or 8. Therefore, ignoring findNode's accesses, Case 2 of the Delete algorithm requires six memory access (which is O(1)).

The pseudocode of Case 3 of the Delete algorithm, previously developed, is:

Binary Search Tree Delete Algorithm, Case 3

```
1.   found = findNode(root, targetKey, P, C);
2.   if(found == false) return false // node not found
3.   if(C.lc != null && C.rc != null) // Case 3
4.   { nextLargest = C.lc;
5.       largest = nextLargest.rc;
6.       if(largest != null) // left child of deleted node has a right subtree, Cases 3a-b
7.       { while(largest.rc != null) // move down the right edge of the right subtree
8.           { nextLargest = largest;
9.               largest = largest.rc;
10.         } // end of while loop, replacement node has been located
11.         C.node = largest.node; // "relocate" the replacement node
12.         nextLargest.rc = largest.lc; // save left subtree of the relocated node
13.     } // end of right subtree exists case
14.     else  // left child of deleted node does not have a right subtree, Cases 3c-d
15.     { nextLargest.rc = C.rc; // save the right subtree of the deleted node
16.         if(P.lc == C)  // deleted node is a left child
17.             P.lc = nextLargest;  // deleted node's parent jumps around deleted node
18.         else                     // deleted node is a right child
19.             P.rc = nextLargest;  // deleted node's parent jumps around deleted node
20.     } // end of no right subtree case
21.     return true;
22. } // end of Case 3
```

We will again ignore Line 1 of the algorithm, the invocation of the findNode method, because it will only be invoked once for all three cases of the Delete algorithm. The remainder of the algorithm can be divided into three portions. The upper portion (Lines 3–6), the middle portion

(Lines 7–13) which executes if the left child of the deleted node has a right subtree, and the lower portion (Lines 14–20) which executes if the left child of the deleted node does not have a right subtree. Examining the upper portion, Line 3 requires three memory accesses to access C, C.lc, and then C.rc. The variables nextLargest (first used on Line 4 and largest (first used on Line 5 and again on Line 6) are variables local to this algorithm. An optimizing compiler would store them in CPU registers, and therefore accessing them does not require memory access. However, Line 5 does require one additional memory access to fetch nextLargest.rc. Therefore, the upper portion of the algorithm requires a total of four memory accesses.

Examining the middle portion of the algorithm (Lines 7–13), the loop on Lines 7–10 require one memory access to fetch the memory cell largest.rc every time the loop executes. Lines 11 and 12 require a total of four memory accesses to access C.node, largest.node, nextLargest.rc, and largest.lc. This give a total of $1T + 4$ memory accesses, where T is the number of times the loop that begins on Line 7 executes.

To find T, we must find the average number of nodes traversed as we move down the right subtree of the left child of the deleted node (see Figure 7.19). Since we are in Case 3 of the algorithm, the deleted node cannot be at the highest level of the tree because Case 3 nodes have two children, and the nodes on the highest level have no children. Furthermore, since we are in the middle portion of the Case 3 algorithm, the deleted node's left child must have a right subtree. Therefore, the deleted node cannot be on the next to the highest level either, since the left children of nodes at this level are leafs (they are on the highest level). Thus, this portion of the Case 3 algorithm deals only with nodes below the next to the highest level of the tree.

Figure 7.23 shows a tree with 10 levels. Suppose we were deleting the root node of the tree. Then the variables nextLargest and largest (*nl* and *l* of Figure 7.19) would be positioned at nodes 40 and 45 respectively. Therefore, to move *l* to the highest level of the tree, the loop would execute 7 times. This can be verified by counting the number of nodes from node 45 to the lowest level of the tree shown in Figure 7.23. Similarly, if the node to be deleted was on level 1 of the tree, the variables nextLargest and largest would be positioned at levels 2 and 3, respectively, and the loop would execute six times. Extending this logic, Column (b) of Table 7.4 presents the number of times the loop executes to delete a node at each level of a 10-level tree operated on by the middle portion of Case 3 of the algorithm. Column (c) of the table presents the number of nodes at each level of the tree, and column (d) presents the number of times through the loop to delete all the nodes at a level of the tree. Assuming all the nodes in the tree are equally likely to be deleted; we can compute a weighted average number of times through the loop by dividing the sum of Column (c) by the sum of Column (d). Thus, for our 10-level tree, the most probable number of times the loop in the middle portion of the algorithm executes is: 247 / 255 = 0.97 times, or T is approximately 1.

This result may seem surprising, but it is typical of balanced binary search trees of any size. Since most of the nodes in a balanced binary tree reside in the higher levels of the tree, their deletion requires very few passes through the loop. In fact, as illustrated in the dark shaded row of Table 7.4,

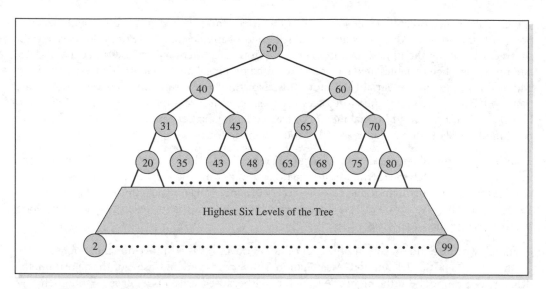

Figure 7.23 A 10-Level Binary Tree

Table 7.4

Number of Times the Loop in the Middle Portion of the Delete Algorithm is Executed for Each Node in a 10-Level Balanced Tree

(a) Level Number of the Deleted Node	(b) Number of Times Through the Loop, T	(c) Nodes at This Level	(d) Total Times Through Loop for All Nodes at This Level = (b) * (c)
0	7	1	7
1	6	2	12
2	5	4	20
3	4	8	32
4	3	16	48
5	2	32	64
6	1	64	64
7	0	128	0
Totals		255	247

the majority of the nodes deleted by this portion of the Case 3 algorithm (128 of the 255 nodes) require zero passes through the loop. Substituting an average value of $T = 1$ into the expression for the number of memory accesses performed by the middle portion of the algorithm ($1T + 4$, as derived previously), we find that an average of five memory accesses are performed to delete a node processed by the middle portion of the Case 3 algorithm.

The lower portion of the algorithm (Lines 14–20) requires one memory access to write into `next-Largest.rc` (Line 15), one access to write into `P.lc` (Line 16), and one access to write into `P.lc` or `P.rc` (Lines 17 or 19). Thus, the lower portion of the Case 3 algorithm requires three memory accesses.

To summarize our findings, the upper, middle, and lower portion of Case 3 of the delete algorithm requires four, five, and three memory accesses, respectively. We will use the worst case performance scenario for the Case 3 algorithm, which is when the upper portion and the middle (rather than the lower) portion of the algorithm execute. This execution path requires a total of nine memory accesses to delete a node: four memory accesses performed for the upper portion and five performed by the middle portion of the algorithm, which is O(1).

To combine all three cases of the Delete algorithm, we add the number of memory accesses required by Line 1 of the algorithm $2 + 3\log2(n + 1)$ (the invocation of `findNode`), to the number of memory accesses required by Cases 1, 2, and 3 of the Delete algorithm (six, six, and nine, respectively) with the weighting factors of Table 7.3 (0.42, 0.16, 0.42) applied to them. The result is that the most probable number of memory accesses for the Delete algorithm is:

$$2 + 3\log_2(n + 1) \text{ accesses for } \texttt{findNode} + 6 * 0.42 * \text{ accesses for Case 1 } +$$
$$6 * 0.16 * \text{ accesses for Case 2 } + 9 * 0.42 * \text{ accesses for Case 3 } = 3\log_2(n + 1) + 9.3$$

which is $O(\log_2 n)$ memory accesses per deletion.

Density

Let us now turn our attention to the overhead of a binary search tree structure. The overhead is the storage associated with the `TreeNodes` (see Figure 7.9) that actually make up the binary tree and the reference variable, `root`, that stores the address of the root of the tree. Therefore, the total overhead is 1 reference variable associated with the variable `root` plus $3n$ reference variables associated with the client's n information `Listings` in the structure. This gives a total of $1 + 3n$ reference variables of overhead. Since reference variables occupy 4 bytes, the total overhead is therefore $4(1 + 3n)$ bytes.

Density is defined as:

$$D = (\text{information bytes}) / (\text{total bytes}) = (\text{information bytes}) / (\text{information bytes} + \text{overhead})$$

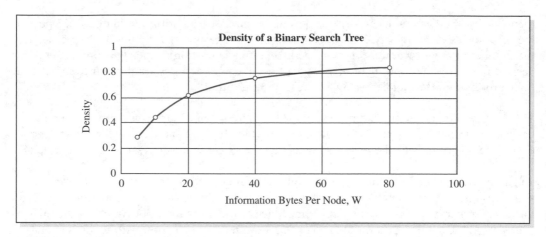

Figure 7.24 Density of the Binary Search Tree Structure for $n > 100$

The information bytes is simply the product of the number of client `Listings` n and the number of bytes per `Listing`, w. Therefore, the density can be expressed as:

$$D_A = \text{(information bytes)} / \text{(information bytes + overhead)} = (n * w) / ((n * w) + 4(1 + 3n))$$

$$= 1 / (1 + 4 / (n * w) + 12/w)$$

which is approximately equal to $1/(1 + 12/w)$ as n gets large. Figure 7.24 presents a graph of the approximation of this function for $n > 100$.

The figure demonstrates that good densities (0.80 or higher) are achieved whenever the number of information bytes per node is greater than 48.

Table 7.5 summarizes the performance of the *balanced* Binary Search Tree structure, and includes the performance of the previously studied structures for comparative purposes. When storing large data sets, the speed of the binary tree structure (presented in the next to the last column of the table) approaches the speed of the hashed data structures. The speed advantages of this structure, its ability to expand to accommodate an unlimited number of nodes, and (as we will see) its ability to process nodes in sorted order make it a popular data structure for many applications.

7.3.3 Implementation

This implementation, named `BinaryTree`, will be a fully encapsulated homogeneous implementation of a binary search tree structure. The code, presented in Figure 7.25, is consistent with the many of the concepts of generics presented in Chapter 2 in that it does not mention the names of any of the fields of the nodes and the definition of the nodes to be stored in the structure is defined in a separate class (see Figure 2.16). The node definition class provides a `deepCopy` method in order to encapsulate the structure, a `compareTo` method to determine if a given key is

Table 7.5

Performance of the Balanced Binary Search Tree Structure (m is the number of positions in the key, l is the loading factor, and w is the node width)

Data Structure	Insert	Delete	Fetch	Update = Delete + Insert	Average[6]	Big-O Average	Average for $n = 10^7$	Condition for Density > 0.8
Unsorted-Optimized Array	3	$<= n$	$<= n$	$<= n + 3$	$<= (3n+6)/4 = 0.75n + 1.5$	$O(n)$	$<= 0.75 \times 10^7 + 1.5$	$w > 16$
Stack and Queue	5	combined with Fetch	4.5	not supported	$9.5/2 = 5$	$O(1)$	5	$w > 16$
Singly Linked List	6	$1.5n$	$1.5n$	$1.5n + 6$	$(4.5n + 12)/4 = 1.13n + 3$	$O(n)$	$1.13 \times 10^7 + 3$	$w > 33$
Direct Hashed (with subtraction preprocessing)	1 or (3)	2 or (4)	1 or (3)	3 or (7)	$7/4 = 1.75$ or $(17/4 = 4.25)$	$O(1)$	1.75 or (4.25)	$w * l > 16$
LQHashed	$m + 6$	$m + 10$	$m + 10$	$2m + 16$	$(5m + 42)/4 = 1.25m + 11$	$O(1)$	$1.25m + 11$	$w > 23$
Balanced Binary Search Tree	$11 + 3 * \log_2(n+1)$	$9.3 + 3 * \log_2(n+1)$	$4 + 3 * \log_2(n+1)$	$20.3 + 6 * \log_2(n+1)$	$11.2 + 4 * \log_2(n+1)$	$O(\log_2 n)$	105	$w > 48$

[6]Assumes all operations are equally probable and is therefore calculated as an arithmetic average of the four operation times.

```
1.    public class BinaryTree
2.    {  TreeNode root;
3.       public BinaryTree()
4.       {  root = null;
5.       }
6.       public boolean insert(Listing newListing)
7.       {  TreeNodeWrapper p = new TreeNodeWrapper();
8.          TreeNodeWrapper c = new TreeNodeWrapper();
9.          TreeNode n = new TreeNode();
10.         if(n == null) // out of memory
11.            return false;
12.         else // insert the node
13.         {  n.node = newListing.deepCopy(); // fill in the TreeNode's fields
14.            n.lc = null;
15.            n.rc = null;
16.            if(root == null) // tree is empty
17.            {  root = n;  }
18.            else
19.            {  findNode(newListing.getKey(), p, c); // find the node's parent
20.               if(newListing.getKey().compareTo(p.get().node.getKey()) < 0)
21.                    p.get().lc = n; // insert new node as a left child
22.               else
23.                    p.get().rc = n; // insert new node as a right child
24.            }
25.            return true;
26.         }
27.      } // end insert method
28.      public Listing fetch(String targetKey)
29.      {  boolean found;
30.         TreeNodeWrapper p = new TreeNodeWrapper();
31.         TreeNodeWrapper c = new TreeNodeWrapper();
32.         found = findNode(targetKey, p, c); // locate the node
33.         if(found == true)
34.            return c.get().node.deepCopy();
35.         else
36.            return null;
37.      } // end of fetch method
38.      public boolean delete(String targetKey)
39.      {  boolean found;
40.         TreeNodeWrapper p = new TreeNodeWrapper();
41.         TreeNodeWrapper c = new TreeNodeWrapper();
42.         TreeNode largest;
43.         TreeNode nextLargest;
44.         found = findNode(targetKey, p, c);
45.         if(found == false) // node not found
46.            return false;
47.         else // identify the case number
```

(continues)

Figure 7.25 Listing of the Implementation of a Binary Search Tree Structure

```
48.           {  if(c.get().lc == null && c.get().rc == null) // case 1: deleted
                                                             // node has no
                                                             // children
49.           {  if(p.get().lc == c.get()) // deleted node is a left child
50.               p.get().lc = null;
51.             else                        // deleted node is a right child
52.               p.get().rc = null;
53.           } // end case 1
54.           else if(c.get().lc == null || c.get().rc == null) // case 2:
                                                              // 1 child
55.           {  if(p.get().lc == c.get()) // deleted node is a left child
56.             {  if(c.get().lc != null) // deleted node has a left child
57.                   p.get().lc = c.get().lc;
58.                 else
59.                   p.get().lc = c.get().rc;
60.             }
61.             else                        // deleted node is a right child
62.             {  if(c.get().lc != null) // deleted node has a left child
63.                   p.get().rc = c.get().lc;
64.                 else
65.                   p.get().rc = c.get().rc;
66.             }
67.           } // end case 2
68.           else // case 3: deleted node has two children
69.           {  nextLargest = c.get().lc;
70.              largest = nextLargest.rc;
71.              if(largest != null) // left child has a right subtree
72.              {  while(largest.rc != null) // move down right subtree
73.                 {  nextLargest = largest;
74.                    largest = largest.rc;
75.                 }
76.                 c.get().node = largest.node; // overwrite deleted node
77.                 nextLargest.rc = largest.lc; // save the left subtree
78.              }
79.              else  // left child does not have a right subtree
80.              {  nextLargest.rc = c.get().rc; // save the right subtree
81.                 if(p.get().lc == c.get()) // deleted node is a left child
82.                    p.get().lc = nextLargest;   // jump around deleted node
83.                 else                        // deleted node is a right child
84.                    p.get().rc = nextLargest;   // jump around deleted node
85.              }
86.           } // end of case 3
87.         return true;
88.         }
89.     } // end of delete method
90.     public boolean update(String targetKey, Listing newListing)
91.     {  if(delete(targetKey) == false)
92.            return false;
```

(continues)

Figure 7.25 Listing of the Implementation of a Binary Search Tree Structure *(continued)*

```
93.          else if(insert(newListing) == false)
94.              return false;
95.          return true;
96.      } // end of update
97.      public class TreeNode
98.      {  private Listing node;
99.         private TreeNode lc;
100.        private TreeNode rc;
101.        public TreeNode()
102.        {
103.        }
104.     } // end of class TreeNode
105.     private boolean findNode(String targetKey, TreeNodeWrapper parent,
106.                              TreeNodeWrapper child)
107.     {  parent.set(root);
108.        child.set(root);
109.        if(root == null) // tree is empty
110.            return true;
111.        while(child.get() != null)
112.        {  if(child.get().node.compareTo(targetKey) == 0) // node found
113.            return true;
114.          else
115.          {  parent.set(child.get());
116.             if(targetKey.compareTo(child.get().node.getKey()) < 0)
117.                 child.set(child.get().lc);
118.             else
119.                 child.set(child.get().rc);
120.          }
121.        } // end while
122.        return false;
123.     } // end of findNode
124.     public class TreeNodeWrapper
125.     {  TreeNode treeRef = null;
126.        public TreeNodeWrapper()
127.        {
128.        }
129.        public TreeNode get()
130.        {  return treeRef;
131.        }
132.        public void set(TreeNode t)
133.        {  treeRef = t;
134.        }
135.     } // end of class TreeNodeWrapper
136. } // end class BinaryTree
```

Figure 7.25   Listing of the Implementation of a Binary Search Tree Structure *(continued)*

equal to the key of a node in the structure, and a `toString` method to return the contents of a node. Like the hashed data structures studied in Chapter 5, this structure's Insert algorithm needs access to the key field of the node being inserted. Therefore, a `getKey` method will have to be added to the class `Listing`. The code of the method is given as follows:

```java
public String getKey()
{   return name; }
```

A fully generic implementation of the structure, using the generic features of Java 5.0 and the techniques described in Chapters 2 and 3 (Sections 2.5 and 3.4) will be left as an exercise for the student.

Lines 97–104 are a definition of the class `TreeNode`. This class defines the objects that will make up the binary search tree. A `TreeNode` object contains three reference variables (Lines 98–100): `node` (a reference to a `Listing` object), `lc`, and `rc` (both references to `TreeNode` objects). The variable `node` will reference the deep copy of the client's information inserted into the structure, while `lc` and `rc` are the references to the tree node's left and right children, respectively. The class is defined as an inner class (of the class `BinaryTree`) for two reasons. Most importantly, this allows the code of the class `BinaryTree` to directly access a `TreeNode` object's data members (e.g., Lines 13–15). In addition, only the code of this class will need to declare `TreeNode` objects.

Line 2 declares the reference variable, `root`, that will store the address of the root `TreeNode`. It is initialized to the empty tree condition on Line 4 by the class' constructor.

The `findNode` method is coded on Lines 105–123. It is the Java coding of the iterative pseudocode version of the algorithm developed earlier in this chapter, with two exceptions. First, lines 109 and 110 have been added to check for an empty tree. Second, aside from a Boolean value, this method must also return two node locations: the location of the node whose key is `targetKey`, and the location of its parent. The only way for a Java method to return more than one item, is by way of its parameter list. However, since parameters in Java are always value parameters, the arguments passed into the method by the client are unchanged when the method returns back to the invoker. The solution to this dilemma is to make the items to be changed by the method *data members* of an object. References to these objects are passed to the method which then changes the data members in the objects. Thus, the parameters are not the items to be modified, but references to the objects containing the items to be modified. A Java class created for this purpose, to allow a method to return a changed value via a parameter, is called a *wrapper* class.

This explains why the second and third parameters of method `findNode` (Line 105–106) are of type `TreeNodeWrapper` rather than type `TreeNode`. The class `TreeNodeWrapper` is defined as a second inner class on Lines 124–135. `TreeNodeWrapper` objects contain one data member, a reference to a `TreeNode` (Line 125). This variable can be set, or fetched, using the methods of the class coded on Lines 129–134. The method `findNode` uses these methods to begin its search for the node with the given key at the root of the tree (Lines 107 and 108), and to move the `TreeNodeWrapper` objects' parent and child references through the levels of the tree (Lines 115, 117, and 119). The `Listing` class' method `compareTo` is used to decide if the node has been found and, if not, to decide if the search should proceed into the left, or right, subtree of the node just examined (Line 16).

The Insert, Fetch, and Delete operation methods on Lines 6–89, are the Java coding of the pseudocode algorithms previously developed in this chapter. However, they pass TreeNodeWrapper objects to the method findNode (e.g., Lines 7, 8, and 19), and use the get method (e.g., Lines 21 and 34) of the class TreeNodeWrapper to access the returned information (the location of the parent of the node to be operated on, or the location of node itself). Lines 90–96 is the update method, which is the same coding of the update methods presented in previous chapters. It invokes the delete and insert methods (Lines 91 and 93) to perform its operation.

Finally, the class does not contain a showAll method. Outputting all the nodes in a binary tree structure is not as simple as when the nodes are stored in the structures previously discussed. The showAll method will be presented in the next section after a detailed discussion of the techniques used to *traverse* binary trees.

To demonstrate the use of the class BinaryTree, an application program that processes a telephone listing data set is presented in Figure 7.26, and the output it generates is presented in Figure 7.27. The Listing class that defines the telephone listings, would be similar to the class Listing presented in Figure 2.16 of Chapter 2, modified to include a getKey method that returns the key field of a Listing object.

7.3.4 Standard Tree Traversals

Traversing a data structure is the process of performing a processing operation on each node in the structure, once and only once. When we perform the processing instruction on a node, we are said to have "visited" the node. Typical processing operations are to modify the contents of a particular field of the nodes, output the contents of the nodes, or to count the nodes to determine how many are in the structure.

We have already studied traversal methods. The showAll method coded in the data structure implementations presented in the previous chapters, is an example of an output traversal. The linear nature of these data structures allowed us to traverse them using a loop construct. For example, in the case of the array-based structures, the hashed structures, and the restricted structures the loop variable simply indexed sequentially through the array associated with these structures from the first to the last element. The linked list traversal used a **while** loop to sequentially travel through the nodes stored in the structure via the next (or link) field, until the last node in the structure (the node with a **null** next field) was output.

The algorithm for traversing a tree structure is not as simplistic because a tree is not a linear structure. After visiting the unique first node (the root node) it is not clear which node to visit next. For example, the left child of the root node could be visited second, and the root's right child third, or vice versa. Actually, any of the nodes in the tree could be considered the second node in the traversal, and in fact, the root node does not necessarily have to be the first node operated on.

Furthermore, once we proceed into one of the two subtrees of a node another problem develops; the location of the subtree *not* visited is no longer available. Thus, the traversal algorithm must maintain a history of the subtree locations *not* visited (as it proceeds down the levels of the tree)

```
1.   public class MainBinaryTree
2.   {public static void main(String[] args)
3.    {BinaryTree t = new BinaryTree();
4.     Listing l;
5.     Listing l1  = new Listing("Ann",    "1st Avenue",  "111 1111");
6.     Listing l2  = new Listing("Bill",   "2nd Avenue",  "222 2222");
7.     Listing l3  = new Listing("Carol",  "3rd Avenue",  "333 3333");
8.     Listing l4  = new Listing("Mike",   "4th Avenue",  "444 4444");
9.     Listing l5  = new Listing("Pat",    "5th Avenue",  "555 5555");
10.    Listing l6  = new Listing("Sally",  "6th Avenue",  "666 6666");
11.    Listing l7  = new Listing("Ted",    "7th Avenue",  "777 7777");
12.    Listing l8  = new Listing("Vick",   "8th Avenue",  "888 8888");
13.    Listing l9  = new Listing("Will",   "9th Avenue",  "999 9999");
14.    Listing l10 = new Listing("Zack",   "11th Avenue", "101 0101");
15.    Listing l11 = new Listing("Zeek",   "12th Avenue", "121 2121");
16.   // insert and fetch nodes
17.    t.insert(l9);
18.    t.insert(l7);
19.    t.insert(l10);
20.    t.insert(l2);
21.    t.insert(l8);
22.    t.insert(l1);
23.    t.insert(l4);
24.    t.insert(l3);
25.    t.insert(l6);
26.    t.insert(l5);
27.    System.out.println(t.fetch("Carol"));
28.    System.out.println(t.fetch("Sally"));
29.    System.out.println(t.fetch("Ted"));
30.   // delete nodes
31.    t.delete("Carol"); // a node with NO children
32.    System.out.println(t.fetch("Carol"));
33.    t.delete("Sally"); // a node with ONE child
34.    System.out.println(t.fetch("Sally"));
35.    t.delete("Ted"); // a node with TWO children
36.    System.out.println(t.fetch("Ted"));
37.   // update nodes
38.    t.update("Bill", l3);
39.    System.out.println(t.fetch("Carol"));
40.    System.out.println(t.fetch("Bill"));
41.    System.exit(0);
42.   } // end of main method
43. } // end class MainBinaryTree
```

Figure 7.26 An Application that Uses a Binary Search Tree Structure

Name is Carol
Address is 3rd Avenue
Number is 333 3333

Name is Sally
Address is 6th Avenue
Number is 666 6666

Name is Ted
Address is 7th Avenue
Number is 777 7777

null
null
null
Name is Carol
Address is 3rd Avenue
Number is 333 3333

null

Figure 7.27   The Output Generated by the Application Program Presented in Figure 7.26

in order to insure that all nodes of the tree are visited. For example, if the traversal always chose the left subtree first, the locations of all the right subtrees would have to be stored.

Although it is true that many traverse orders are possible,[7] most of them are rarely, if ever, used. The most often used traverses fall into two groups:

- Those that visit *all the nodes at a given level* (siblings) before proceeding to the next level, called *breadth-first* traverses.
- Those that visit *all children* of a node, before visiting the nodes siblings, called *depth-first* traverses.

The most often used traverses in the depth-first group have been given names indicative of the order in which they visit the nodes. Consider the binary tree shown in Figure 7.28.

Designating the left subtree as **L**, the root node as **N**, and the right subtree as **R**, a traversal that first visited all the nodes in the left subtree, then visited the root node, and then visited all the nodes in the right subtree is named an LNR traversal, or LNR *scan*. This scan, and the other possible scans designated by the five other permutations of these three letters, are defined below.

LNR   traverse the **l**eft subtree, then visit the root **n**ode, then traverse the **r**ight subtree.
LRN   traverse the **l**eft subtree, then traverse the **r**ight subtree, then visit the root **n**ode.

---

[7]For any tree containing *n* nodes, *n*! different traverses are possible.

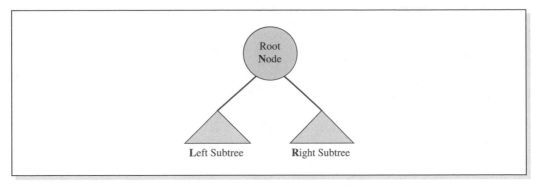

Figure 7.28 A Binary Tree

NLR visit the root **n**ode, then traverse the **l**eft subtree, then traverse the **r**ight subtree.
NRL visit the root **n**ode, then traverse the **r**ight subtree, then traverse the **l**eft subtree.
RLN traverse the **r**ight subtree, then traverse the **l**eft subtree, then visit the root **n**ode.
RNL traverse the **r**ight subtree, then visit the root **n**ode, then traverse the **l**eft subtree.

The three traversals that visit the subtrees in a left-to-right order: LNR, LRN, and NLR have alternate names. (By "left-to-right" order we mean that during these traversals the left subtree is always traversed before the right subtree.) The prefixes *pre*, *in*, and *post* are used in the alternate names to indicate when the *root node* is visited during the traversal. Thus:

- NLR is called a ***pre***order scan (because the root node is visited *before* visiting the left and right subtrees).
- LNR is called an ***in***order scan (because the root node is visited *in between* visiting the left and right subtrees).
- LRN is called a ***post***order scan (because the root node is visited *after* visiting the left and right subtrees).

Returning to the discussion of the six scans, a question arises; how do we traverse the subtrees during these scans? That is, what is the order in which the nodes in the left or right subtrees are visited? The answer is simple. The subtrees are traversed in the same order as the original tree. Therefore, if an LNR traversal is being performed on the tree, then the subtrees are traversed using an LNR traversal. The LNR definition (and that of the other five traversals) is recursive in that an LNR traversal uses an LNR traversal to traverse the subtrees. The LNR traversal is more accurately stated as:

LNR Traversal

- Traverse the entire left subtree *using an LNR traversal recursively.*
- Visit (operate on) the root node.
- Traverse the entire right subtree *using an LNR traversal recursively.*

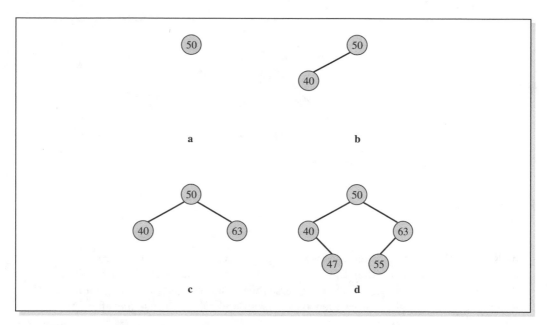

Figure 7.29 Four Binary Search Trees

The base case of this recursive definition is when the subtree is empty. In this case we do nothing (which most everyone is good at). Thus, the recursive LNR algorithm to traverse the tree whose root node is referenced by the variable root, whose left child is referenced by lc, and whose right child is referenced by rc, is:

LNR Recursive Traversal Algorithm Named LNRtraversal (assumes LNRtraversal is passed the root of the tree to be traversed)

1. **if**(root.lc != **null**) // traverse the left subtree
2.   LNRtraversal(root.lc);
3. visit(root); // operate on the root node
4. **if**(root.rc != **null**) // traverse the right subtree
5.   LNRtraversal(root.rc);

To gain an understanding of the recursion in the algorithm, we will examine the algorithm's execution for the trees shown in Figure 7.29. For simplicity, we will assume that the operation performed on a node by Line 3 of the algorithm (when a node is visited) is to output the node's key field.

First let us consider the simple case of performing an LNR traversal on a tree with just one node, a root node (see Figure 7.29a). The **if** statement on Line 1 evaluates to **false** (the root node does not have a left subtree) and Line 2 does not execute. Line 3 operates on the root node, and the root node's key (50) is output. Finally, the **if** statement on Line 4 evaluates to **false** (the root node's right subtree is empty) and the algorithm ends. This traversal does not execute the recursive part of the LNR algorithm (Lines 2 and 5). The confusing part of a traversal is the use of recursion to output the nodes in the subtrees.

Consider the LNR traversal of the tree with two nodes shown in Figure 7.29**b**. This time the **if** statement on Line 1 evaluates to **true** (the root has a left subtree) and Line 2 executes. Line 2 is recursive. It invokes LNRtraversal recursively to perform an LNR traversal on the tree whose root is the node with key field 40, and the algorithm begins again. In this invocation, the variable root refers to the node whose key is 40.

The **if** statement on Line 1 evaluates to **false** (the tree whose root is 40 does not have a left subtree), and Line 2 does not execute. Line 3 operates on the root node, and the key 40 is output at this point. Finally, the **if** statement on Line 4 evaluates to **false** (40's right subtree is empty), and the recursive invocation of the algorithm ends.

Having completed Line 2 of the original execution of the algorithm, Line 3 operates on the root node of the tree, and the key 50 is output at this point. Finally, the **if** statement on Line 4 evaluates to **false** (50's right subtree is empty), and the algorithm ends.

If the right subtree were not empty (as in Figure 7.29**c**) the **if** statement on Line 4 would perform an LNR traversal on the tree whose root is the node with key field 63. In this invocation, the variable root refers to the node whose key is 63. The **if** statement on Line 1 evaluates to **false** (the root node, 63, does not have a left subtree), and Line 2 does not execute. Line 3 operates on the root node, and the key 63 is output. Finally, the **if** statement on Line 4 evaluates to **false** (63's right subtree is empty) and the recursive invocation of the algorithm ends. This completes Line 5 of the original execution of the algorithm, and it ends.

Finally, consider the tree presented in Figure 7.29**d** with nodes whose key fields are 50, 40, 63, 47, and 55. The LNR algorithm's traversal process would be (reading from left to right):

Line 2	Line 3	Line 5
Traverse all the nodes in the *left* subtree of 50, in LNR order recursively	then output 50 (the root node)	then traverse all the nodes in the *right* subtree of 50, in LNR order recursively

Thus, to output the entire tree using an LNR traversal, we must first traverse the left subtree of 50 in LNR order. To accomplish this, we treat this subtree as an independent tree whose root has a key value of 40 to be traversed also (recursively) in LNR order. Thus, the traversal process to traverse the left subtree of 50 (*first* level of recursion) is (reading from left to right):

Line 1	Line 3	Line 5
The left subtree of 40 is empty, skip Line 2	output 40 (the root node)	then traverse all the nodes in the *right* subtree of 40, in LNR order recursively

Line 1 of the algorithm determines that the left subtree of 40 is empty, and Line 2 does not execute. Line 3 outputs the root node of the subtree, 40, producing the first output. To complete the traversal of the left subtree of 50, Line 5 traverses the right subtree of 40 using an LNR traversal. To accomplish this, we treat the subtree as an independent tree whose root has a key value 47 (see Figure 7.29**d**) to be traversed also (recursively) in LNR order. Thus, the traversal process to traverse the right subtree of 40 (*second* level of recursion) would be (reading from left to right):

Line 1	Line 3	Line 4
The left subtree of 47 is empty, skip Line 2	then output 47 (the root node)	The right subtree of 47 is empty, skip Line 5

Line 1 of the algorithm determines that the left subtree of 47 is empty, and Line 2 does not execute. Line 3 outputs the root node of the subtree, 47, producing the second output. To complete the traverse of the right subtree of 40, Line 4 of the algorithm determines that 47's right subtree is empty, and Line 5 does not execute. This completes the second level of recursion (used to output the right subtree of 40), as well as the first level of recursion (to output the left subtree of 50), and so the root of the original tree, 50, is output (the third output).

To complete the LNR scan of the tree in Figure 7.29**d**, we must traverse the right subtree of 50 in LNR order. To accomplish this, we treat this subtree as an independent tree whose root has a key value 63 to be traversed also (recursively) in LNR order. Thus, the traversal process to traverse the right subtree of 50 (first level of recursion) is (reading from left to right):

Line 2	Line 3	Line 4
Traverse all the nodes in the *left* subtree of 63, in LNR order recursively	then output 63 (the root node)	The right subtree of 63 is empty, skip Line 5

Line 2 traverses the left subtree of 63 using an LNR traversal. To accomplish this, we treat this subtree as an independent tree whose root has a key value 55 (see Figure 7.29**d**) to be traversed also (recursively) in LNR order. Thus, the traversal process to traverse the left subtree of 63 (second level of recursion) is (reading from left to right):

Line 1	Line 3	Line 4
The left subtree of 55 is empty, skip Line 2	then output 55 (the root node)	The right subtree of 55 is empty, skip Line 5

Line 1 of the algorithm determines that the left subtree is empty, and Line 2 does not execute. Line 3 outputs the root node of the subtree, 55, producing the fourth output. To complete the traverse of the left subtree of 63, Line 4 of the algorithm determines that the right subtree of 55 is empty, and Line 5 does not execute. This completes the second level of recursion (to traverse the left subtree of 63).

Returning to the first level of recursion used to traverse the right subtree of 50, Line 3 executes and outputs the root node of 50's right subtree, 63 (producing the fifth output). Next, Line 4 executes and, since the right subtree of 63 is empty, the first level of recursion ends. This completes the execution of Line 5 of the initial invocation of the algorithm (to traverse the tree whose root is 50) and the LNR traversal of the tree depicted in Figure 7.29**d** is complete. The output produced is 40, 47, 50, 55, 63.

To summarize the execution of the tree traversal algorithms, the subtrees are traversed using a recursive tree traversal whose escape clause is an empty subtree. Figure 7.30 shows the results of LNR, NLR, and RNL output traversals of an expanded version of the tree presented in Figure 7.29**d**. This figure can be studied to gain an understanding of these recursive traversal algorithms.

As shown in Figure 7.30, the LNR and RNL traversals output the nodes in ascending and descending key order respectively. This is not the case for LNR or RNL output traversals performed on *all* binary trees, but only those binary trees that are *also* binary search trees. Examining the tree presented in Figure 7.30, we can verify that it is, in fact, a binary search tree. Therefore, aside from good performance, binary search trees have the additional feature that LNR and RNL scans process the nodes in key field sorted order.

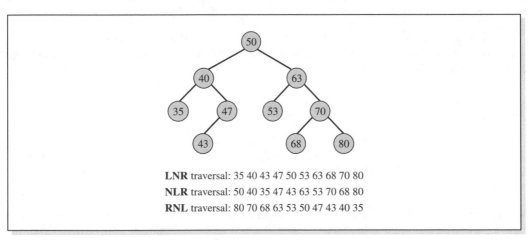

LNR traversal: 35 40 43 47 50 53 63 68 70 80
NLR traversal: 50 40 35 47 43 63 53 70 68 80
RNL traversal: 80 70 68 63 53 50 47 43 40 35

Figure 7.30   Three Output Traversals of a Binary Tree

```
1.    public void LNRoutputTraversal(TreeNode root)
2.    {  if(root.lc != null)
3.          LNRoutputTraversal(root.lc);   // traverse the entire left subtree
4.       System.out.println(root.node);   // output the root node
5.       if(root.rc != null)
6.          LNRoutputTraversal(root.rc);   // traverse the entire right subtree
7.    }
```

Figure 7.31   The LNR Output Traversal

```
1.    public void showAll()
2.    {  if(root == null)  // check for an empty tree
3.          System.out.println("the structure is empty");
4.       else
5.          LNRoutputTraversal(root);
6.    } // end of showAll method
```

Figure 7.32   The ShowAll method for a Binary Search Tree

The showAll Method

Now that we have gained an understanding of tree traversal techniques, we can complete the coding of the class BinaryTree by coding its showAll method used by the client to output the contents of all of the nodes stored in the structure. We will arbitrarily select an LNR traversal to visit all the nodes in the tree, and so the nodes will be output in ascending order based on the values of the key fields of the nodes. Both the traversal method and the showAll method are normally included as member functions of the data structure class (see Figure 7.25).

The implementation of the LNR output traversal shown in Figure 7.31 is simply the Java version of this algorithm with console output substituted for Line 3 of the algorithm (Line 4 of the method).

The code of the showAll method is presented in Figure 7.32. If the tree to be output is not empty (checked on Line 2), the method simply invokes the LNRoutputTraversal method, passing it the location of the root of the tree (Line 5).

7.3.5 Balanced Search Trees

As previously discussed, the speed of a balanced binary search tree is $O(\log_2 n)$. With the exception of hashed structures, they are faster than all the other data structures presented thus far. Balancing a tree minimizes the number of levels in the tree, and since one comparison is made per level to locate a node in a search tree, balancing a tree also maximizes the speed of the structure's operations.

The binary search tree Insert algorithm presented in this chapter made no attempt to keep the tree balanced, and so for some data sets the $O(\log_2 n)$ speed of the structure is not realized. Consider the four node data set with one letter keys: A, B, C, and D. Let us assume that the node whose key is A is inserted first, then B, then C, and finally the node with key D is inserted. Because each newly inserted node's key is greater than all the nodes currently in the tree, each node is inserted as the rightmost descendent and the tree develops (as shown in Figure 7.33) highly skewed to the right.

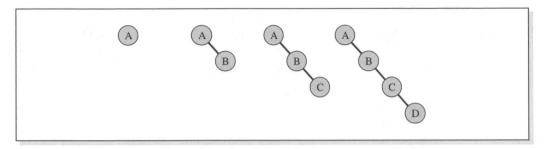

Figure 7.33   A Binary Search Tree after Inserting Keys A, then B, then C, and then D

Whenever nodes are inserted into a binary search tree in sorted key order, each node inserted creates a new level of the tree, making the number of levels in the tree equal to the number of nodes in the tree. Under these conditions, the speed of the structure degenerates to that of a singly linked list, O(n). To prevent this from happening, the data set can be randomized before it is initially inserted into the data structure.

Although randomizing the nodes before the tree is built usually results in an initial search tree that is balanced (or close to balanced), once the data structure is "in service" subsequent insertions and deletions can cause it to become highly imbalanced. One way to prevent this from happening is to keep track of the number of nodes, n, and the number of levels, l, in the tree. Whenever an Insert (or Delete) operation is performed, the number of levels in the tree, l, is compared to the number of levels in a balanced binary tree with n nodes: $ciel(\log_2(n + 1))$. If the difference between the actual number of levels in the tree is larger than that of a balanced tree by some specified tolerance, dL_{max}, all the nodes are removed from the tree, randomized, and reinserted into the tree. This usually brings the tree back into balance within the desired tolerance.

When this technique is used to keep a binary search tree balanced, the Insert and Delete operation uses the parameter $dL = l - ciel(\log_2(n + 1))$ to monitor how far the tree is out of balance. The tree is rebuilt when this parameter is greater then the chosen value of dL_{max}. The choice of the value of dL_{max} is not self evident. Although the speed of the operation algorithms is optimized when the tree is balanced, $dL = 0$, rebuilding the tree takes time. If dL_{max} is chosen too small, the tree is frequently rebuilt, and the processing time associated with the rebuilding degrades the overall performance of the structure. Conversely, if dL_{max} is chosen too large, the speed of the basic operations degrades as dL increases. Ultimately, the optimum value of dL_{max} for a particular application is dependent on the character of the data set and the distribution of the operations performed on the structure. The modification of the Binary Search Tree implementation developed in this chapter (see Figure 7.25) to keep the tree balanced within a client specified tolerance is left as an exercise for the student.

AVL Trees

A more efficient technique for keeping a binary search tree balanced was developed by two mathematicians, G. M. Adelson-Velskii and E. M. Landis, in the 1960s. This specialized binary search tree, named an *AVL Tree* in honor of its inventors (*Adelson-Velskii and Landis*) is always kept close to balanced in that the height of the left and right subtrees of the root do not differ by more

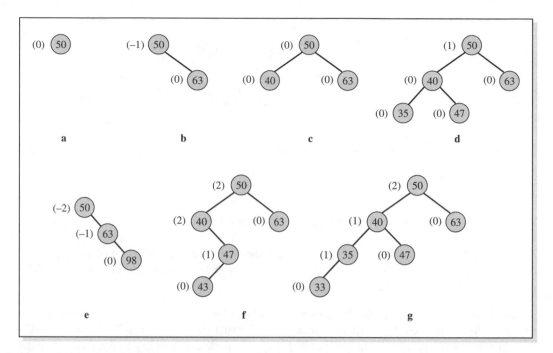

Figure 7.34   The AVL Balance Factors for Nodes in Balanced and Imbalanced Binary Search Trees

than one. The balancing is accomplished by expanding the Insert and Delete algorithms to rebalance the tree without having to randomize the nodes and reinsert them back into the tree. The Fetch and Update algorithms are the same as the binary search tree algorithms previously presented in this chapter.

A parameter called a *balance factor* is used to decide when to rebalance the tree. Each node in the tree has a balance factor associated with it, which is calculated and stored as an additional piece of information for each node. The value of a node's balance factor is, by definition, the difference in the number of levels in the node's left and right subtrees. Figure 7.34 presents several trees with the value of each node's balance factor shown to its left (in parentheses). The trees are arranged in the figure such that all the trees in the upper portion of the figure are balanced, and the trees in the lower portion of the figure are imbalanced.

Examining the trees in the figure, we see that the balance factors of all of the nodes in the balanced trees are 1, 0, or −1, whereas this is not the case for the imbalanced trees. This characteristic, which is a consequence of the definition of a balanced tree and the definition of a balance factor, is typical of all balanced and imbalanced AVL trees.

To see why, consider the complete trees shown in Figures 7.3f and 7.34c. Because each level of a complete tree is fully populated, the left and right subtrees of every node in the tree contain the same number of levels. As a result, all nodes in a complete tree (which is one type of balanced tree) have balance codes of 0. The other type of balanced tree is one in which a nonfully populated level is added to a complete binary tree (see Figure 7.34**d**). All of the nodes at the added level are leafs and so their balance factors are zero. The addition of the new level can only cause the balance factors of the nodes at the other levels of the tree to increase or decrease by at most one, since only one level was added to the tree. The balance factor of all of these nodes was zero before the new level was added, and therefore their new balance factors must be in the range ± 1.

In AVL jargon, a node with a +1 balance factor is said to be *left high*, a node with a 0 balance factor is said to be *even high*, and a node with a -1 balance factor is said to be *right high*. Left high, even high, and right high are denoted LH, EH, and RH, respectively. The AVL tree algorithms check to make sure that an insertion (or a deletion) has not caused the balance factors of the nodes in the tree to exceed ± 1; that is, all the nodes are either LH, EH, or RH. If this is the case, the tree is still balanced, and the operation is complete.

When a node is inserted or deleted, we start at the node's parent and work our way up the tree looking for a node with an unacceptable balance factor (other than LH, EH, or RH). This node and its descendants are subjected to a *rotation* to rebalance the tree. After the rotation, we continue to work our way up the tree, performing other rotations wherever necessary.

For example, consider the insertion of a node whose key value is 33 into the tree shown in Figure 7.34**d**. Before the insertion, all the nodes are EH (even high) with the exception of the tree's root node, 50, which is LH (left high). When the root node of a tree is left high, we say the tree is left high. Figure 7.34**g** shows our left high tree after key value 33 is inserted (using the binary search tree insertion algorithm) along with the new values of the balance factors. Working our way up the tree beginning at the parent of the inserted node we move from key 35, to 40, and finally find a node with a balance factor out of the range ± 1 (the node 50). This indicates that the tree, rooted by 50, is out of balance. In addition, the insertion of node 33 has also made the left subtree of 50 left high (i.e., node 40's balance factor has changed to +1). When this is the case we say that the tree has become *left-of-left*; the operation created a *left* high subtree in a *left* high tree.

To restore balance to a left-of-left tree, a *right* rotation is performed on node 50. The rotation is a right rotation because there are too many levels in 50's left subtree as indicated by its +2 balance factor. Beginning with the tree shown in Figure 7.35**a**, the right rotation positions the nodes as shown in Figure 7.35**b**. (This leaves 40's original right child 47 without a parent, which is a problem we will resolve momentarily.) The root node 50 is moved (rotated) rightward and downward making 40 the new root of the tree, and 50 is now its right child. Since the rotation moves the left subtree of 50 up one level, the resulting tree has one less level. The balance factors of the right rotated tree, as shown in Figure 7.35**b**, are now in the range ± 1. This means this tree is in balance.

For some trees, this rotation completes the rebalancing operation. But since node 40 had a right child (47, or possibly a larger right subtree) in the original tree, the right rotation algorithm continues. The right rotation of any node (in our case 50) always causes it to have no left child. In addition, since it was originally to the right of the *orphaned* node (47) or subtree, it must be larger than the orphaned node (or all of the nodes in the orphaned subtree). Therefore, node 47 (or the

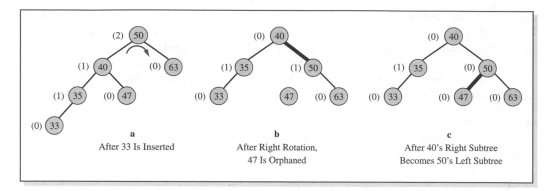

Figure 7.35 The AVL Single Right Rotation to Rebalance a Left High Tree with a Left High Subtree (the Tree of Figure 7.34d After the Node with Key Field 33 Is Inserted)

subtree whose root 47) can become the left subtree of 50 (Figure 7.35**c**) and the resulting tree is still a binary search tree. This repositioning of the subtree whose root is 47 completes the rebalancing of our tree. The balance factors of the resulting tree shown in Figure 7.35**c**, verifies that the right rotation of node 50 has produced a search tree that is once again balanced.

The AVL tree insertion algorithm includes three other rotation algorithms to deal with imbalanced trees whose balance factor distributions are different than that depicted in Figure 7.35**a**. The rebalancing procedure described is used when an operation on a node creates a left high subtree (the subtree rooted by node 40 in Figure 7.34**g**) of a previously left high tree (the tree rooted by node 50 in Figure 7.34**d**). The other three cases are when the operation creates a

- *right* high subtree in a *right* high tree,
- *right* high subtree in a *left* high tree, or
- *left* high subtree in a *right* high tree.

When the operation creates a *right* high subtree in a *right* high tree (as depicted in the left and center portions of Figure 7.36, a rebalancing process similar to the one described above is performed except that the right rotation is replaced with a left rotation (see the center and left portions of Figure 7.36).

When the tree's imbalance results from an operation that produces a *right* high subtree of a *left* high tree, or a *left* high subtree of a *right* high tree, then two rotations are necessary to restore an AVL tree to a balanced condition. Consider the left high search tree depicted in the upper left portion of Figure 7.37. After key 44 is inserted (see the upper right portion of Figure 7.37), node 50's balance factor become +2 requiring a rotation. Unlike the situation depicted in the left portion of Figure 7.35, this time, the left subtree of 50 has gone *right* high. A *right* high subtree of a *left* high tree has been created requiring two rotations. First, a left rotation is performed on node 40 resulting in the tree depicted in Figure 7.37**c**. Then a right rotation is performed on node 50 resulting in the tree depicted in Figure 7.37**d**.

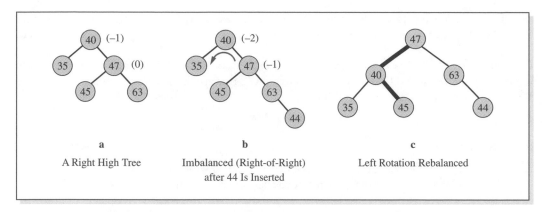

Figure 7.36   The Rebalancing of a Right High Tree with a Right High Subtree

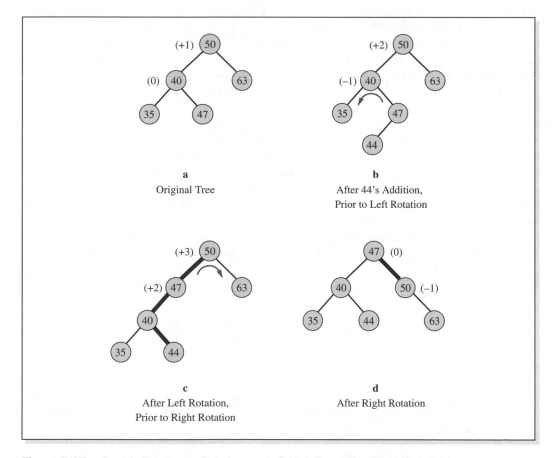

Figure 7.37   Double Rotation to Rebalance a Left High Tree with a Right High Subtree

When the operation creates a *left* high subtree in a *right* high tree, first a right rotation is performed on the root of the subtree, and then a left rotation is performed on the root of the tree.

Both the Insert and Delete algorithms are usually expressed, and coded, recursively. As previously mentioned, the Fetch and Update algorithms of an AVL tree are the same as the binary search tree algorithms previously developed in this chapter.

Red-Black Trees

Another form a self balancing binary tree is a *Red-Black* tree, which was invented by Rudolf Bayer in 1972. Originally named a Binary B-tree, it has become one of the more popular self balancing tree algorithms.

Red-Black trees and AVL trees share many characteristics. Their Fetch and Update algorithms are the same (the binary search tree algorithms previously presented in this chapter), and both trees incorporate rotations into the binary search tree's Insert and Delete algorithms to resolve imbalance. Neither an AVL tree nor a Red-Black tree is perfectly balanced, although an AVL tree typically comes closer to a balanced tree than a Red-Black tree. In fact, a Red-Black tree can contain twice as many levels ($2 * \log_2(n + 1)$ levels) as a balanced tree. That being said, the Red-Black tree does outperform the AVL tree because its rebalancing process is more efficient. The Java API structure `TreeMap` is a Red-Black tree.

The tree gets its name from the fact that the algorithm assigns each node in the tree one of two colors, red or black. With the exception of the root node which is always black, during the insertion or deletion of a node the color of the other nodes in the tree can—and often do—change during the rotations these operations perform. Aside from the normal ordering that all binary search trees comply to (small keys in the left subtree, large keys in the right subtree) Red-Black trees must comply to additional ordering conditions. If a node is red, its children must be black, and every path from a node to a `null` link (a leaf's left or right `null` reference) must contain the same number of black nodes. All of the conditions of a Red-Black tree are summarized as follows:

Ordering Conditions of a Red-Black Tree

1. Every node in the tree must be red or black.
2. The root of the tree is always black.
3. If a node is red, its children must be black.
4. Every path from a node to a `null` link (a leaf's left or right `null` reference) must contain the same number of black nodes.
5. The tree must be a binary search tree. (Every node in a node's left and right subtree is less than and greater than it, respectively.)

In an AVL tree when the balance factors exceed ± 1, balancing rotations are performed. In a Red-Black tree, lack of compliance with Conditions 3 and 4 initiates rotations that keep the tree near balanced. For example, an implication of Condition 4 is that a newly inserted node must be red or it will initiate a balancing rotation. If it were black, then the black path to it would be increased by 1, making the path longer than the other black paths in the tree. This would violate Condition 4. If the new node were inserted as a red node (and thus not initiate a rotation), when a subsequent node was inserted as its child, a rotation would be initiated. This rotation would be necessary because the newly inserted node would have to be red to comply with Condition 4, but its parent is also red which violates Condition 3.

The rotations performed by Red-Black trees are somewhat similar to the rotations performed by AVL trees, but are more complicated because they also involve color changes. The important feature of Red-Black trees is that the coloring of the nodes adds sufficient information to the tree to initiate color adjustments and rotations *as we move down through the tree* looking for the insertion point (or the node to be deleted). These rotations keep the tree near balanced making the additional upward traversal required to balance an AVL tree unnecessary. The fact that Red-Black trees perform only one traversal during their Insert and Delete operations is what gives Red-Black trees their performance advantage.

A further discussion of the rotational procedures and color changes performed during the insertion and deletion downward traversals is beyond the scope of this text. However, our discussion of the details of the AVL rotations provide a good foundation for future study.

7.3.6 Array Implementation of a Binary Search Tree

For some applications, an array-based implementation of a binary tree offers a more efficient means of representing a binary tree than the linked approach utilized up to this point in this chapter. Rather than storing the address of the client's information `Listing` object in a `TreeNode` object, which also stores the address of the left and right children (see Figure 7.10), in this alternate implementation the `Listing`'s address is stored in an element of an *array* of references variables (see Figure 7.38).

The location of the information at the root of the tree is always stored at index 0 of the array. Therefore, for the array depicted in Figure 7.36 the root `Listing` object has a key value of 50. Since each element of the array of reference variables can only store one address, that of a single `Listing` object, the implementation makes an assumption about where in the array the addresses of the children are stored. The assumption, called the "$2i + 1, 2i + 2$ rule," is stated as:

> ### Children Locations in the Array Implementation of a Binary Tree
>
> For a Listing whose address is stored at index *i* of the array,
> its *left child*'s address will be stored at index $2i + 1$, and
> its *right child*'s address will be stored at index $2i + 2$.

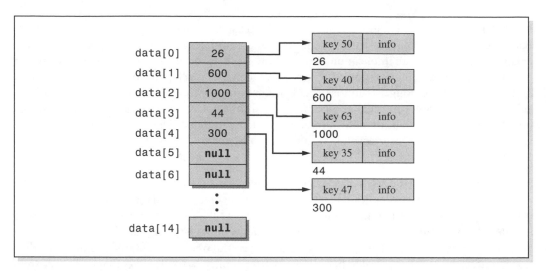

Figure 7.38 Array Implementation of a Binary Tree

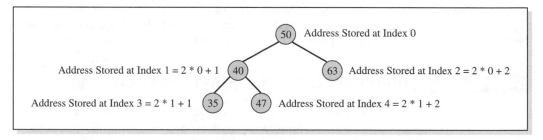

Figure 7.39 The Binary Tree "View" of the Array Presented in Figure 7.38

For example, in Figure 7.38 we can locate the addresses of the two children of the root (stored at index $i = 0$) by examining the contents of elements $1 = 2 * 0 + 1$, and element $2 = 2 * 0 + 2$. Thus, the root's children are the Listings with key values 40 and 63. Since the address of the node with key value 40 is stored at element 1 of the array, its two children's addresses are stored in elements $3 = 2 * 1 + 1$, and $4 = 2 * 1 + 2$. Using this rule, any array can be viewed as a tree. The tree represented by the array shown in Figure 7.38 is depicted in Figure 7.39.

When the tree is completely empty, all elements of the array are set to **null**. In addition, if a Listing does not have a left or right child, then the reference variable used to store the address of the nonexistent child is **null**. Again referring to the array implementation of a binary tree depicted in Figure 7.38, we know that the Listings with keys 63, 35, and 47 do not have any children since the array elements that the $2i + 1$, $2i + 2$ rule associates with their children, elements 5, 6, 7, 8, 9, and 10, all contain **null** values.

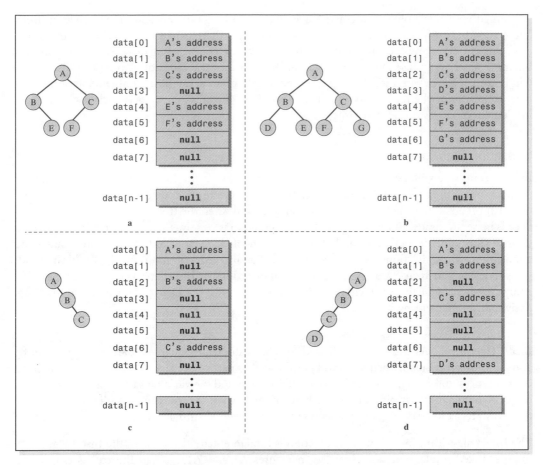

Figure 7.40 Four Binary Trees and Their Array Representations

Not only can an array be viewed as a binary tree using the $2i + 1$, $2i + 2$ rule, but the rule is often used to store a binary tree in an array. For example, consider the four binary trees shown in Figure 7.40. The array representations of the four trees are given just to their right. In each of the arrays, all of the elements after element 7 contain a **null** value. To build the arrays, we begin by placing the address of the root into element 0 of the array. Then to place the address of the other List-ings into the array, we use the $2i + 1$, $2i + 2$ rule to calculate their indices. Referring to Figure 7.40**c**, since B is the right child of A, its address is stored in element $2 = 2 * 0 + 2$, and since C is the right child of B, its address is stored in element $6 = 2 * 2 + 2$. An equivalent—and often easier—method for placing the addresses into the array is to go across the levels of the tree from left to right, starting at level 0, and then working our way down the levels of the tree placing the Listing objects' addresses into sequential elements of the array. Referring to Figure 7.40**b**, A's address would be stored in element 0, B's in element 1, C's in element 2, D's in element 3, etc. If a child were missing, the element would receive a **null** value (see element 3 of Figure 7.40**a**).

Mapping the `Listing` objects into array elements by working our way across the tree levels from left to right beginning at level 0, is much more convenient then using the $2i + 1, 2i + 2$ rule. However, this is only a graphical technique. Whenever we are coding an array implementation of a binary tree, we always use the $2i + 1, 2i + 2$ rule to determine the index of a node. This distinction will become clearer when we develop the pseudocode of an array-based implementation in the next section and when we study the Heap Sort algorithm in Chapter 8 (which uses the array implementation to store a binary tree).

Operation Algorithms

In this section we will develop the pseudocode algorithms for the Insert and Fetch operations of an array-based binary search tree structure. As we will see, one advantage this scheme has over the linked approach is that these algorithms are simpler, and when the tree is balanced their performance is better. A disadvantage is that the Delete operation is very inefficient from either a speed or density viewpoint, depending upon how it is implemented. As a result, this structure is suited for applications where deletions are not necessary, or they are held to a minimum. With this in mind, we will develop an array-based tree structure that just supports Insert and Fetch operations. After analyzing these algorithms we will discuss the problems with the Delete algorithm and the alternatives for implementing it.

Insert Operation   As with the array-based structures studied in Chapter 2, an array named `data` and an integer variable named `size` will be allocated as part of the structure. The array will store the references to the client's nodes inserted into the tree, and the variable `size` will store the number of elements in the array. As previously mentioned, when the tree is empty all the elements of the array are set to **null**. Figure 7.41 shows the structure in its initialized state.

The Insert algorithm for this implementation is fundamentally the same as the Insert algorithm for the linked implementation depicted in Figures 7.7 and 7.13. When the tree is empty, the inserted node becomes the root node. Otherwise, we repeatedly move into the left or right subtree depending on the relationship between the root node's key and the key of the node to be inserted. The $2i + 1, 2i + 2$ rule is used to determine the location of the root of the subtree. The search for an insertion point continues until a **null** reference is located in the array *or* the calculated index is out of bounds. In the former case, the node is inserted and the algorithm returns **true**, otherwise it returns **false**. Assuming the listing to be inserted is referenced by the variable `newListing`, the pseudocode of this process is given as follows:

Array-Based Binary Search Tree Insert Algorithm

```
1.  i = 0;
2.  while(i < size && data[i] != null) // continue search for an insertion point
3.  { if(data[i].key > newListing.key) // go into left subtree
4.      i = 2 * i + 1;
```

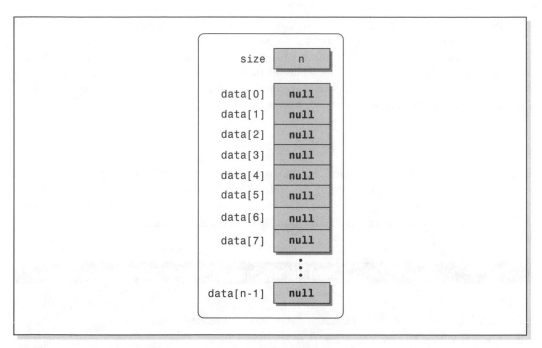

Figure 7.41   The Array-Based Binary Tree in its Initialized State

```
5.    else // go into the right subtree
6.        i = 2 * i + 2;
7.  } // end search
8.  if (i >= size) // node position exceed the bounds of the array
9.      return false;
10. else // insert the node
11. { data[i] = newListing.deepCopy();
12.     return true;
13. }
```

Lines 2–7 perform the search for the insertion point assigning the variable i to either $2i + 1$ or $2i + 2$. When the tree is empty, data[0] is **null**, the loop does not execute, i remains 0, and the first node inserted into the tree is stored in data[0]. Line 8 checks to make sure the loop did not end on an out-of-bounds condition and if not, Lines 10–12 perform the encapsulated Insert operation.

It should be noted that there are two ways for this structure to return **false**, indicating that the node could not be added to the structure. Both are detected by the Boolean expression i < size on Line 2. The first way, is that every element in the array is used. The second way, is that the node insertion order is such that the tree is imbalanced or highly skewed as is the tree depicted in Figure 7.34e. When this happens, the array is far from full when the index calculated by the $2i + 1$, $2i + 2$ rule is out of bounds. For example, the Insert operation will return **false** when an attempt is made to insert the eleventh (and largest) node into a highly right skewed structure whose array size is 1023 elements. This unfortunate characteristic will be discussed in more detail when we consider the density of this structure.

Fetch Operation

The Fetch operation uses the same search technique as the Insert algorithm except that the search can now end on an additional condition, the node is found. A **null** reference encountered during the search indicates that the given key is not in the structure. The pseudocode for the Fetch operation follows, which assumes the key of the node to be fetched is targetKey.

Array-Based Binary Search Tree Fetch Algorithm

```
1.  i = 0;
2.  while(i < size && data[i] != null && data[i].key != targetKey) // search
3.  { if(data[i].key > newListing.key) // go into left subtree
4.        i = 2 * i + 1;
5.    else  // go into the right subtree
6.        i = 2 * i + 2;
7.  } // end search
8.  if (i >= size || data[i] == null) // node not found
9.      return null;
10. else // return the node
11.     return data[i].deepCopy();
```

The Boolean condition on Line 2 has been expanded so that the search ends if the given key is found. The test for an unsuccessful search on Line 8 has also been expanded to include the case when the index is not out of bounds but the node is not in the structure, data[i] == **null**. A successful search ends on Line 11, where a deep copy of the located node is returned to the client.

Implementation

The implementation of this structure will be left as an exercise for the student. With the exception of the class' constructor, the implementation is a line-for-line translation of the pseudocode algorithms previously presented. The constructor requires some further discussion.

As we mentioned when we discussed the pseudocode of the Insert operation, the density of this structure can degrade rapidly if the tree is imbalanced. However, there is a range of imbalance within which the density is good and, if the speed of the structure is acceptable to the client, the structure can be quite serviceable. Therefore, the constructor's parameter list will include all the information necessary to size the array in a way that the density of the structure meets the client's minimum needs. The size of the array, N, will be calculated by the constructor as

$$N = n \left(1 / D_{BSA} - 1 \right) w / 4,$$

where:

N is the size of the array $(N >= n)$,
D_{BSA} is the desired density $(D_{BSA} <= (1 / (1 + 4 / w)))$,
n is the maximum number of nodes to be stored in the structure, and
w is the node width in bytes.

The derivation of the equation will be presented when we discuss the performance of this structure. Since there are three independent variables in this equation, the class' constructor will contain three parameters. Assuming the name of the array is `data` and the name of the class is `BinaryTreeArray`, the code of the constructor is given below.

```
public BinaryTreeArray (int n, int w, int d)
{   if(d > 1 / (1 + 4/w))
        size = n;
    else
        size = n * (1/d - 1)*(w / 4);
    data = new Listing[size];  .
}
```

7.3.7 Performance

As we have indicated, the performance of this structure can be very good or very bad depending on how well the tree is balanced. Generally speaking, as the tree becomes more imbalanced its speed degrades to that of a singly linked list, as was the case for our linked implementation. Unlike the linked implementation, however, the density of this structure also degrades rapidly as the tree becomes more and more imbalanced.

Speed

We will first examine the speed of the Insert algorithm. Again, assume that an optimizing compiler will make use of the CPU's registers to minimize the number of memory accesses required to fetch (or assign) local, and other, variables used several times in the algorithm. Lines 2 and 3 require two memory accesses: one to fetch the variable `data[;]` and one to fetch its key. (The variables `size` and `newListing.key` would be stored in CPU registers during the loop's execution.) Lines 4 and 6 do not require any memory accesses because the variable `i` would also be stored in a CPU register. Therefore, a total of two memory accesses are performed during each iteration of the loop, which executes once per level of the tree. If the tree is highly skewed, there will be n levels in the tree and the loop will execute an average of $n / 2$ times. If the tree is balanced, the loop will execute, on the average,

$\le \log_2(n + 1)$ times (as shown is Section 7.3.2). Therefore, the number of memory accesses performed by Lines 2–7 will be between $2\log_2(n - 1)$ and $2n$ depending on how well the tree is balanced.

The remainder of the algorithm (Lines 8–12) accesses memory one additional time to write the reference to the cloned node into data[i] (Line 11). This brings the total number of memory accesses for the Insert algorithm to between $1 + 2\log_2(n - 1)$ and $1 + 2n/2$ depending on how well the tree is balanced (between $O(\log_2(n))$ and $O(n)$).

The search process for the Fetch algorithm (Lines 2–7) is identical to that of the Insert algorithm except that the memory access required to fetch the key of the node referenced by data[i] is performed on Line 2 instead of Line 3. Thus, the search portion of both algorithms requires the same number of memory accesses. The remainder of the Fetch algorithm does not require any additional memory accesses. Therefore, the total number of memory accesses for the Fetch algorithm is between $2\log_2(n - 1)$ and n depending on how well the tree is balanced (between $O(\log_2(n))$ and $O(n)$).

Density

To calculate the density, D, we recall that:

$$D = \text{(information bytes)} / \text{(total bytes)}.$$

The information bytes are simply the product of the number of nodes, n, and the number of bytes per node, w. The total bytes allocated the structure is the sum of the information bytes and the overhead bytes. Assuming there are N elements in the array, and that reference variables occupy 4 bytes, the overhead is $4N$. Thus, the density of the array-based structure, D_{BSA} is

$$D_{BSA} = \text{(information bytes)}/\text{(total bytes)} = (n * w) / ((n * w) + 4 (N)))$$
$$= 1 / (1 + 4N / (nw))$$

where:

> N is the size of the array,
> n is the maximum number of nodes to be stored in the structure, and
> w is the node width in bytes.

The value of N in the above formula for density depends on how well balanced the tree is. Its minimum value, which produces the maximum density for this structure, is n because we must provide an element in the array to store the address of each of the n nodes in the tree. However, N can be considerably larger than n.

Consider the trees shown in Figure 7.40a, c, and d. The parent–child relationships in these trees are such that there are elements of the array that are not used, and so $N > n$. The worst case is when the tree is highly skewed to the right. In this case, assuming the tree contains n nodes (and therefore n levels), the array must be sized to $N = 2^n - 1$ elements. For example, the tree shown in Figure 7.38c has only 3 ($= n$) nodes but the array must be sized to 7 ($= N$) elements.

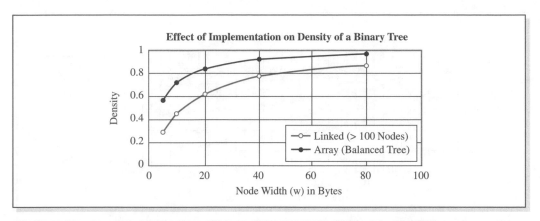

Figure 7.42 Density of the Linked and Array-Based Implementations of a Binary Tree

The best case scenario occurs when the tree is left balanced or complete (see Figure 7.40**b**). This is the case when $N = n$. Thus the range of N for an array-based tree containing n nodes is $n \leq N \leq 2^n - 1$. Substituting these limiting values for N into this equation, this density of a left balanced tree, D_{LB}, and that of a right skewed tree, D_{RS} becomes

$$D_{LB} = 1 / (1 + 4N / (nw)) = 1 / (1 + 4n / (nw)) = 1 / (1 + 4/w) \text{ for the } \textit{left balanced} \text{ tree}$$

and

$$D_{RS} = 1 / (1 + 4N / (nw)) = 1 / (1 + 4(2^n - 1) / (nw)) \text{ for the } \textit{right skewed} \text{ tree.}$$

Because the term 2^n dominates the terms in the denominator of the equation for D_{RS}, it approaches zero even for moderate values of n. Therefore, from a memory overhead viewpoint, the array-based implementation is not practical for trees that are far out of balance. However, when the tree is left balanced (or complete), the density of the array-based structure is better than the linked implementation. Figure 7.42 compares the density of the linked implementation (from Figure 7.24) and the array-based implementation for left balanced (or complete) trees.

Before we end our discussion of density, it is useful to gain some insights into the range of imbalance for which the array-based structure still offers good density. As derived previously, the density of this structure is

$$D_{BSA} = 1 / (1 + 4N / (nw)) = 1 / (1 + (N / n)(4 / w))$$

Figure 7.43 shows the variation in density with the parameter N / n, the ratio of the size of the array to the number of nodes in the structure, for various values of node widths. As shown in this figure, densities above 0.80 can still be obtained in array-based binary trees when $N / n = 32$ as long as the node widths are greater than 640 bytes.

The ratio of N / n is related to the degree of imbalance in the tree, in that, when N / n is 2, we have provided twice as many "spots" in the tree as will be occupied. This means that the tree is one level larger than it would have to be if the tree were balanced. When $N / n = 4$, we have provided four

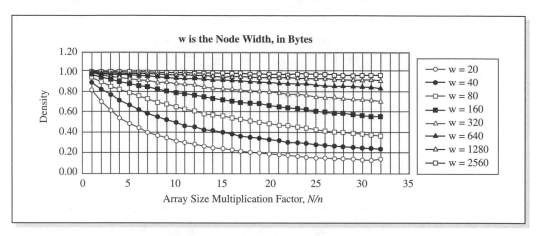

Figure 7.43 Variation in Density of the Array-Based Binary Tree with N/n and Node Width

times as many spots in the tree as will be occupied. This means that the tree is two levels larger than it would have to be if the tree were balanced. Following this logic, the number of extra levels in a tree containing n nodes is $\log_2 N / n$. Therefore, for a given node width and required minimum density, the $\log_2$ of N / n (as determined from Figure 7.43) can be used as the upper bound of range of imbalance for which the density meets the required minimum. For example, for a node width of 640 bytes and a minimum required density of 0.84, Figure 7.43 indicates that N / n must be 32. Thus, the tree can be imbalanced by as many as 5 (= $\log_2 32$) levels and the density of the structure will still be within the desired range (≥ 0.84).

Another handy formula is one that can be used to determine the degree of imbalance to achieve a density of 0.8 for a given node width. Substituting a density of 0.8 into the density equation and solving for N / n we obtain

$$N / n = (1/0.8 - 1) \text{ w} / 4 = (1.25 - 1) \text{ w} / 4 = 0.0625\text{w}.$$

This function is plotted in Figure 7.44. Finally, from the density equation we can determine the size of the array for a desired density, given the node width, and number of nodes as

$$N = n (1/D_{BSA} - 1) \text{ w} / 4.$$

It should be noted that there is an upper limit to the desired density of any array-based structure because even if all elements of the array are used, $N / n = 1$, the overhead is nonzero (4 * N). Substituting $N = n$ in the previous equation and solving for the density we obtain

$$D_{max} = (1 / (1 + 4 / \text{w}))$$

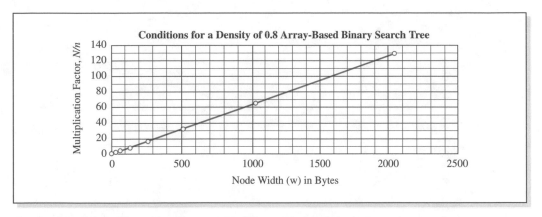

Figure 7.44   Conditions for a Density of 0.8 for an Array-Based Binary Tree

Table 7.6 presents the performance of the array-based binary search tree and includes the performance of the previously studied structures for comparative purposes. When balanced, its speed is only exceeded by the hashed structures, and it is the best performing structure from a density viewpoint. However, the structure does not support the Delete and Update operations.

Delete Operation Alternative

If we were to use the linked implementation's Delete algorithm for the array-based implementation, its speed would be very slow for all but the first case of the algorithm: deleting a leaf node. To see why, consider the case where we want to delete the root node from the tree shown in Figure 7.40**d**. The node B would become the root node so its reference would have to move from data[1] to data[0]. Then, to maintain the parent–child relationship, C's reference would have to be moved to data[1], and D's to data[3]. For all but very small trees, the number of memory accesses required to maintain the parent–child relationships make the linked implementation's Delete algorithm prohibitively slow for an array-based tree.

An alternative algorithm adds a Boolean field to each node to indicate that a node has been deleted from the structure. The Insert algorithm sets this field to **false**. To delete a node, this field is simply set to **true**. The search portions of Delete and Fetch are modified to ignore any node whose deleted field is **true**. The downside of this scheme is that the storage occupied by a deleted node is never reclaimed. However, it does offer a viable scheme for applications where only a few nodes will be deleted. The implementation is left as an exercise for the student.

7.3.8 Java's `TreeMap` Data Structure

The Java class `TreeMap`, contained in the package `java.util`, is an implementation of a Red-Black tree. As implemented, it is an unencapsulated generic data structure accessed in the key field

Table 7.6

Performance of the Balanced Binary Search Tree Structure (m is the number of positions in the key, l is the loading factor, and w is the node width)

Data Structure	Operation Speed (in memory accesses)							Condition for Density > 0.8
	Insert	Delete	Fetch	Update = Delete + Insert	Average[8]	Big-O Average	Average for $n = 10^7$	
Unsorted-Optimized Array	3	$<= n$	$<= n$	$<= n + 3$	$<= (3n + 6)/4$ $= 0.75n + 1.5$	$O(n)$	$<= 0.75 \times 10^7 + 1.5$	$w > 16$
Stack and Queue	5	combined with Fetch	4.5	not supported	$9.5/2 = 5$	$O(1)$	5	$w > 16$
Singly Linked List	6	$1.5n$	$1.5n$	$1.5n + 6$	$(4.5n + 12)/4$ $= 1.13n + 3$	$O(n)$	$1.13 \times 10^7 + 3$	$w > 33$
Direct Hashed (with Subtraction Preprocessing)	1 or (3)	2 or (4)	1 or (3)	3 or (7)	$7/4 = 1.75$ or $(17/4 = 4.25)$	$O(1)$	1.75 or (4.25)	$w * l > 16$

(continues)

Table 7.6

Performance of the Balanced Binary Search Tree Structure (m is the number of positions in the key, l is the loading factor, and w is the node width) (continued)

Data Structure	Operation Speed (in memory accesses)							Condition for Density > 0.8
	Insert	Delete	Fetch	Update = Delete + Insert	Average[8]	Big-O Average	Average for $n = 10^7$	
LQ Hashed	$m + 6$	$m + 10$	$m + 10$	$2m + 16$	$(5m + 42)/4 =$ $\leq 1.25m + 11$	$O(1)$	$\leq 1.25m + 11$	$w > 23$
Balanced Binary Search Tree	$11 + 3\,^* \log_2(n + 1)$	$9.3 + 3\,^* \log_2(n + 1)$	$4 + 3\,^* \log_2(n + 1)$	$20.3 + 6\,^* \log_2(n + 1)$	$11.2 + 4\,^* \log_2(n + 1)$	$O(\log_2 n)$	105	$w > 48$
Balanced Binary Search Tree (Array-Based)	$1 + 2\log_2(n + 1)$	not available	$2\log_2(n + 1)$	not available	$0.5 + 2\log_2(n + 1)$	$O(\log_2 n)$	93	$w > 16$

[8]Assumes all operations are equally probable and is therefore calculated as an arithmetic average of the four operation times.

mode. The key can be any type of object, however, the key's class must implement Java's Comparable interface. That is, it must contain a method whose signature is

public int compareTo(KeyObjectType aKey)

that compares two key objects and determines whether invoking object's key is less than (returns a negative integer), equal to (returns zero), or greater than (returns a positive integer) aKey. The String class implements this interface. The other alternative is that the key must have a Comparitor. The wrapper classes for the numeric types (i.e., Byte, Double, Float, Integer, Long, and Short) have Comparitors. Therefore, keys that are instances of Strings or numeric wrappers can be used in TreeMaps without the need to implement an interface.

The class TreeMap has four constructors. The default constructor sorts the nodes into the Red-Black tree according to the key's natural order (i.e., as determined by the key's compareTo method). The following statement declares a TreeMap structure that stores Listing objects in a Red-Black tree named dataBase, which is ordered based on a String key:

```
TreeMap <String, Listing> dataBase = new TreeMap<String, Listing>();
```

This declaration uses the Java 5.0 generic type parameters (i.e., <String, Listing>) to declare the structure dataBase to be a homogeneous structure that can store only Listing objects whose key field is a String object.

The TreeMap class' Insert, Fetch, and Delete operation methods are named put, get, and remove, respectively. The methods get and remove return **null** if the specified key is not in the structure. Descriptions of the other methods in the class are given in the Java online documentation (http://java.sun.com/j2se/1.5.0/docs/api/java/util/TreeMap.html). An application that uses a TreeMap data structure is given in Figure 5.31 with the exception that Line 4 of the application would be changed to the above TreeMap object declaration. The code of the class Listing is presented in Figure 2.16.

The following code outputs the keys (String objects) and the nodes (Listing objects) stored in the TreeMap object dataBase in sorted order based on their key values. The highlighted items are application specific.

```
Set<Map.Entry<String, Listing>> nodes = dataBase.entrySet();
for(Map.Entry<String, Listing> i : nodes)
{   System.out.println(i.getKey() + " ");
    System.out.println(i.getValue() + " ");
}
```

Knowledge Exercises

1. Give an advantage of a binary search tree structure over:
   a. A linked list structure
   b. A stack
   c. An array-based structure
   d. A hashed structure

2. Define the terms:
   a. Root node
   b. Binary tree
   c. Parent
   d. Leaf node
   e. Level 0 of a tree
   f. Highest level of a tree
   g. Balanced tree
   h. Complete tree
   i. Left-balanced

3. What is the *maximum* number of nodes that can be stored in a binary tree with 10 levels?

4. What is the *minimum* number of levels in a binary tree containing 6023 nodes?

5. What is the *maximum* number of levels in a tree containing 6023 nodes?

6. What is the *maximum* number of nodes that can be stored in level 16 of a binary tree?

7. If there are n_l nodes in level l of a balanced binary tree, give an expression for the number of nodes at level $l + 1$ (assuming level $l + 1$ is not the highest level of the tree).

8. True or false:
   a. The highest level of a complete binary tree contains more nodes than all of the other levels combined.
   b. The root node is always at the highest level of the tree.
   c. Level 9 is the highest level in a 10 level tree.

9. State the significance of the word binary in the term binary tree (i.e., why is a *binary* tree called a *binary* tree?).

10. Define the term "binary search tree."

11. Draw the binary search tree resulting from inserting the nodes with the integer key values: 68, 23, 45, 90, 70, 21, and 55 into the tree. Assume key 68 is inserted first, then key 23, etc.

12. The client objects inserted into a Binary Search Tree structure are not actually stored in a binary tree, true or false?

13. Give the data members of the class TreeNode defined in this chapter and state what is stored in each data member.

14. Draw a picture of a binary search tree, implemented using the linked implementation, in its initialized state.

   a. Using the standard tree graphic.

   b. At the implementation level.

15. Under what conditions are the Fetch and Insert operations performed on a binary search tree structure fast?

16. State the three cases of the binary search tree Delete algorithm.

17. The linked implementation is used in the coding of a Binary Search Tree structure. Calculate the structure's density assuming that it contains 200 nodes and:

   a. Each node contains 10 bytes of information.

   b. Each node contains 300 bytes of information.

18. Repeat the above exercise for the array implementation of the Binary Search Tree, assuming it is:

   a. Left balanced.

   b. Skewed to the right.

19. A balanced binary search tree stores 1,000,000 nodes. Assuming a memory access takes one nanosecond, calculate the average time required to fetch a node from the tree for the:

   a. Linked implementation.

   b. Array-based implementation.

20. Give the output produced by an NLR output scan of the tree shown in Figure 7.3f.

21. State the advantage of an AVL tree over a Binary Search Tree Structure.

22. Give the AVL balance factors for each of the nodes in Figure 7.3a.

23. Of the 11 nodes in an AVL tree, 6 of the nodes have balance factors of 1, 4 nodes have balance factors of 0, and 1 node has a balance factor of -1.

   a. Is the tree balanced?

   b. Is the tree complete?

24. An array contains the values 100, 20, 34, 200, 6, 10, and and 31. Element 0 contains 100, element 1 contains 20, etc. Draw the binary tree representation of the array.

25. In the array implementation of a binary tree:

   a. Where is the root node stored?

b. Where is the right child of the node in element 10 stored?

c. How can we determine if the node stored at element 22 does *not* have a left child?

26. True or false, a binary tree containing 20 nodes can always be stored in a 20 element array?

27. Give the size of an array that could store *any* tree containing 10 nodes.

28. Demonstrate that the algorithm used to delete the node referenced by C in Figure 7.18**a** can also be used to delete the node referenced by C in Figure 7.18**b**.

Programming Exercises

29. Write a method to perform an NLR scan on a binary tree. Assume the method will operate on trees implemented as arrays. Provide a driver program to demonstrate that the method functions properly. Use the trees shown in Figure 7.3 as test cases.

30. A database is to be developed to keep track of student information at your college. Their names, identification numbers, and grade point averages will be included. The data set will be accessed in the key field mode, with the student's name being the key field. Code a class named Listing that defines the nodes. The class must comply with the guidelines that permit student information nodes to be stored in the fully encapsulated BinaryTree structure discussed in this chapter. As such, your class should include all the methods in the class shown in Figure 2.16 and include a getKey method. Test it with a progressively developed driver program that demonstrates the functionality of all of its methods.

31. Code an application program that keeps track of student information at your college. Include their names, identification numbers, and grade point averages in a fully encapsulated, homogeneous, linked-based binary search tree. When launched, the user will be presented with the following menu:

    Enter: 1 to i*nsert* a new student's information,

    2 to *fetch* and output a student's information,

    3 to *delete* a student's information,

    4 to *update* a student's information,

    5 to *output* all the student information in descending order, and

    6 to *exit* the program.

32. Do Exercise 31 but use an *array-based* implementation of a binary search tree. Include only user options 1, 2, 5, and 6. Your program should allow the user to specify the minimum density of the structure.

33. Expand the program described in Exercise 32 to allow the user to delete and update nodes.

34. Code the generic version of the linked-based Binary Search Tree using the generic features of Java 5.0, and provide a driver program to demonstrate that the method functions properly. The driver program should declare two binary search tree objects: one to store Listing

objects as defined in Figure 2.16 with a getKey method added to the class, and the other to store Student objects as described in Exercise 30.

35. Redo Exercise 31 using an expanded version of the linked implementation of the binary search tree presented in this chapter that keeps the tree balanced within a client specified tolerance (number of extra levels).

36. Repeat Exercises 31 using an AVL tree.

CHAPTER 8

Sorting

OBJECTIVES

The objectives of this chapter are to familiarize the student with the topic of sorting and the classic sorting algorithms, and to be able to select the best sorting algorithm for a particular application. More specifically, students will be able to

- Explain the motivation for sorting data sets.

- Understand that the speed complexity of a sorting algorithm is dependent on both the number of comparisons it performs and the number of data items it swaps.

- Understand that the theoretical minimum number of comparisons required to sort n items is $n\log_2 n$, and be able to calculate the minimum time required to sort n items.

- Understand, and be able to implement, the classic sorting algorithms: Binary Tree Sort, Bubble Sort, Heap Sort, Merge Sort, and Quicksort, and be able to explain the strengths and weaknesses of each algorithm.

- Determine the speed and space complexity of the classic sorting algorithms (and any other sorting algorithm), and be able to select the best sorting algorithm for a particular application.

- Explain the characteristics of a binary tree that make it a heap, and understand the algorithm that transforms a binary tree into a heap.

- Understand the topic of recursion more fully by examining the recursive parts of the Merge Sort and Quicksort algorithms.

8.1 Sorting

Sorting is the process of ordering a set of items. The two most common orderings are ascending order and descending order. In the context of data structures, it is the process of arranging nodes in an order based on the contents of one of the fields in the nodes. For example, the nodes that comprise a collection of telephone listings are usually sorted in ascending order based on the contents of the name field, while the results of a weight lifting contest would possibly be sorted in descending order based on the contents of the maximum weight lifted field.

Most often, nodes are sorted for one of two reasons:

1. To produce sorted output listings.
2. To improve the speed of a data structure.

Let us first consider sorted output listings. When nodes are output in sorted order, not only are they *more pleasant* to read, but it is also much easier to find a particular listing from among the printed listings. Anyone who has used a phone book would agree that an unsorted phone book would be very difficult to use. The search process would be a time consuming, manual sequential search, instead of the binary search we all intuitively use on a standard sorted phone book.

There is another important reason for outputting nodes in sorted order. Drawing conclusions based on the data presented in sorted order often becomes self-evident. Consider again the output listing of a weight lifting contest that is sorted based on the maximum weight lifted field. It would be obvious who won the competition because the *analysis* necessary to determine the winner is the sorting process itself. Sorted listings can make conclusions self-evident.

Now, let us turn our attention to the second motivation for sorting: to improve the speed of a data structure. Often the speed of the `fetch` method can be improved if the data set is stored in a sorted order. We saw an example of this in Chapter 2 when we studied the Sorted Array structure in which the nodes were stored in sorted order based on their key field. This allowed us to use the binary search algorithm to locate a node which is an efficient, $O(\log_2 n)$, search algorithm. Thus, even if the data set is never output in sorted order, sorting algorithms are important because they can speed up one or more of the basic operations performed on a data set.

Considering the advantages of sorting, the question arises: Why aren't all output listings and data sets sorted? One answer is that sorting takes time. However, through the use of efficient sorting algorithms and good sorting strategies, the additional time needed to sort can be held to acceptable levels.

As an example of a sorting strategy, consider the following scenario. When a data set is to be output in sorted order, two alternatives are available: sort the nodes just prior to outputting them, or store the nodes in the data set in a sorted order. The former approach is attractive if the nodes are rarely output in sorted order, or if the field on which the nodes are sorted often changes. If, however, the nodes are often output in sorted order, then it may be more efficient to store the nodes in sorted order, especially if the contents of the field on which they are sorted rarely changes.

In this chapter, we will study several of the classic sorting algorithms and examine the advantages of each. Some of the algorithms require more memory than others, while some execute faster than others. It can be shown, however, that there is a theoretical minimum number of comparisons required to sort a set of n items, which we will use as a standard for *goodness* when we analyze the performance of the algorithms presented in this chapter. Some data sets exhibit special *characteristics* that allow some sorting algorithms to perform faster than the theoretical minimum. It turns out that these characteristics are not that uncommon, as we shall see. Aside from speed and memory differences, some of the algorithms are much easier to code than others. Thus, the selection of the best sorting algorithm for a particular application is usually based on the speed and memory constraints of the application, the character of the data set being sorted, and the coding skills of the programmer.

For each of the classic sorting algorithms discussed in this chapter, we will:

- Present a pseudocode version of the algorithm.
- Learn how it performs a sort by tracing its execution while sorting a set of integers.
- Determine its performance, space, and time complexity.
- Discuss particular data set characteristics, if any, under which it performs best.
- Enter its performance in a summary chart useful in determining which sorting algorithm to use for a particular application.

Some of the algorithms will be implemented in this chapter, and the remaining implementations will be left as exercises for the student.

Before we proceed to a detailed discussion of the classic sorting algorithms, we will expand our discussion of sorting algorithm performance. As we have previously stated, the measure of a sorting algorithm's performance is based on its memory overhead and its speed. The techniques for determining a sorting algorithm's memory overhead are the same techniques we have used to determine the overhead of the data structures studied in the previous chapters. However, the techniques we used to determine the speed of data structures will require a minor refinement in order to be applied to sorting algorithms.

8.2   Sorting Algorithm Speed

All sorting algorithms have two features in common. Two data items are *compared* in order to determine their relative position in the sorted list, and data items are *swapped* (based on these comparisons). Both of these features require memory accesses that can be counted using the algorithm analysis techniques discussed in the previous chapters. However, in the case of sorting algorithms, it is useful to know not only the total number of memory accesses, but also how many of them were a result of swap operations and how many of them were the result of comparison operations. This more detailed level of analysis allows us to better understand why some algorithms are faster than others. A parameter used in this analysis is *sort effort*, which is defined as:

Sort Effort

Sort Effort = SE = number of *comparisons* required to sort n items.

To illustrate the use of this parameter and our expanded analysis techniques, consider the following code segment extracted from a sorting algorithm. The number of items to be sorted is represented by n.

```
1.    for(int i = 1; i <= n; i++)
2.    {  for(int j = 1; j <= n; j++)
3.       {  if(items[j] > items[i])
4.          {  temp = items[j];
5.             items[j] =  items[i];
6.             items[i] = temp;
7.          } // end of if statement
8.       } // end of inner loop
9.    } // end of outer loop
```

The comparison on Line 3 is executed n times as part of the inner loop (Lines 3–8), and the inner loop is executed n times inside the outer loop (Lines 2–9). Therefore, $n * n$ comparisons are performed by this line of code. Assuming these were the only comparisons performed in the sorting algorithm, its sort effort would be n^2. The variable items[j] is accessed during each of these n^2 comparisons (j changes each pass through the inner loop) and items[i] is accessed n times (i changes every pass through the outer loop). As a result $n^2 + n$ memory accesses are associated with the algorithm's comparisons. Thus, from a Big-O analysis viewpoint, the number of memory accesses and the sort effort are equivalent (both $O(n^2)$). This is typical of sorting algorithms.

To complete the speed analysis, Lines 4–6 perform a data swap operation. If the Boolean expression on Line 3 is always **false**, no swaps are performed. Conversely, if the condition is always **true**, n^2 swaps are performed. The actual number of swaps performed is a function of the data set (and ultimately the rest of the sorting algorithm). For this example we will assume that half the time the Boolean condition is **true**, so $n^2 / 2$ swaps are performed. During each swap items[j] is overwritten. However, an efficient translator would store items[i] in a register during the execution of the inner loop and only write it to memory each of the n times the inner loop ends. Therefore, a total of $n^2 / 2 + n$ memory accesses are performed during the swap operations.

Considering both the comparisons and the swaps performed by this algorithm, its speed is therefore $O(n^2)$. More specifically it is $3/2n^2 + 2n$ ($= n^2 + n$ comparison accesses $+ n^2 / 2 + n$ swap accesses), with the comparison portion of the algorithm contributing $n^2 / 2$ more memory accesses than the swap portion.

8.2.1 Minimum Sort Effort

As previously mentioned, there is an approximate theoretical minimum number of comparisons required to sort n randomly arranged items. This number of comparisons is referred to as the *minimum sort effort*, SE_{min}, and is calculated as:

Minimum Sort Effort

$$SE_{min} = O(n\log_2 n)$$

The derivation of this formula is beyond the scope of this text. However, it is useful to know the minimum effort because it can be used to identify efficient algorithms from a number-of-comparisons viewpoint. For example, consider the algorithm whose sort effort (number of comparisons) is $O(n^2)$. Since the minimum effort is $O(n\log_2 n)$, we know there is considerable room for improvement.

To make the performance difference between an $O(n^2)$ and $O(n\log_2 n)$ sorting algorithm more tangible, and to demonstrate the need for efficient sorting algorithms, let us assume the two algorithms are used to sort 1,000,000 items. In addition, we will assume they are executed on a system that performs a comparison in one nanosecond, and each comparison requires one memory fetch that takes 40 nanoseconds. Then, the time to execute the $O(n^2)$ algorithm would be

$$(10^6 * 10^6) \text{ comparisons} * (41 \times 10^{-9}) \text{ seconds per comparison} = 41 \times 10^3 \text{ seconds}$$
$$\text{or } 11.4 \text{ } hours.$$

However, the time to execute the $O(n\log_2 n)$ algorithm would only be

$$(10^6 \log_2(10^6)) \text{ comparisons} * (41 \times 10^{-9}) \text{ seconds per comparison} = 817 * 10^{-3} \text{ seconds}$$
$$\text{or } 0.8 \text{ } seconds.$$

Clearly, if 1,000,000 items were going to be sorted often, we would not want to use a sort algorithm whose sort effort is n^2. However, we should be sensitive to the fact that even sorting algorithms whose sort effort is equivalent to the theoretical minimum still require a significant amount of computing time when the number of items to be sorted, n, is large. This is illustrated in Figure 8.1, which presents the minimum time required to sort a set of n items. This figure truly presents an overall *minimum* sorting time, since it assumes the sorting algorithm performs $n\log_2 n$ comparisons and no swaps. The figure shows that to sort 300,000,000 social security records would require 5.8 minutes.

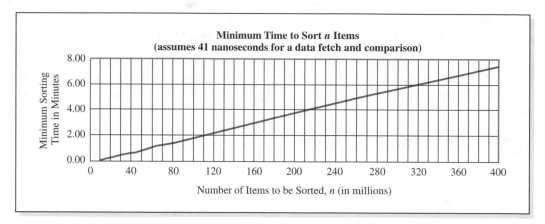

Figure 8.1   Minimum Sort Time

8.2.2 An Implementation Issue Affecting Algorithm Speed

Before we begin our study of the classic sorting algorithms, we will examine an implementation issue common to all sorting algorithms that can greatly affect their speed. As we have discussed, the sorting process involves swap operations. When we are sorting primitives, we simply swap the contents of the two memory cells used to store the primitives. However, when we are sorting nodes, the process of swapping the contents of the memory cells that store the nodes' member data can be very time consuming because (unlike primitives) objects can consist of many data members, each containing a significant number of bytes.

The remedy is to perform a shallow copy of the node objects during the sorting process. Thus, the contents of the reference variables (4 bytes each) that store the location of the nodes are swapped, rather than swapping the contents of the data members of the objects (which contain multiple groupings of 4 bytes per data member). This is always the preferred technique when nodes are being sorted.

Figure 8.2 illustrates the difference between the time-consuming deep copy approach and the more efficient shallow copy approach to positioning nodes C and B in sorted order. The figure assumes the references to the nodes are stored in an array; however, the same advantages will be realized if the node references were stored in a tree structure.

One last introductory comment is in order before we proceed. When the items to be sorted are encapsulated inside a data structure, the sorting algorithm is coded as a member function of the data structure class in order to maintain the encapsulation of the structure.

8.3 Sorting Algorithms

We will now begin our study of the classic sorting algorithms with the Binary Tree Sort algorithm. This is a good starting point, since the algorithm places the items to be sorted in a binary search tree, and we are already familiar with search trees. Therefore, we can focus most of our attention

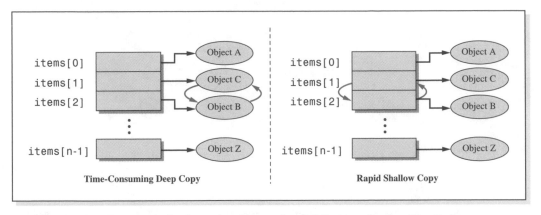

Figure 8.2   Two Techniques for Swapping Objects C and B During a Sorting Algorithm

on the techniques used to evaluate algorithm performance, rather than the development of the algorithm itself.

8.3.1 The Binary Tree Sort

The Binary Tree Sort algorithm is basically the algorithm used in Chapter 7 to insert nodes into a binary search tree. Assuming we are sorting n items, the algorithm is:

Binary Tree Sort Algorithm

1. The first item becomes the root node.
2. For any subsequent item, consider the root node to be a root of a subtree, and start at the root of this subtree.
3. Compare the item to the root of the subtree.
   3.1 **If** the new item is *less than* the subtree's root, then the new subtree is the root's *left* subtree.
   3.2 **Else** the new subtree is the root's *right* subtree.
4. Repeat step 3 until the new subtree is empty. Position the new item as the root of this empty subtree.
5. Repeat steps 2, 3, and 4 for each item to be sorted.

To illustrate the algorithm, let us assume we are to sort a group of 10 integers given in the order: 50, 40, 47, 63, 55, 43, 70, 80, 35, and 68. The integer 50 would become the root node as per Step 1 of the algorithm (see Figure 8.3**a**). The second integer, 40, would then be compared to 50 (Step 3), and since it is less than 50 we would proceed to the left (Step 3.1). Step 4 of the algorithm would cause 47 to be inserted as 50's left child (see Figure 8.3**b**).

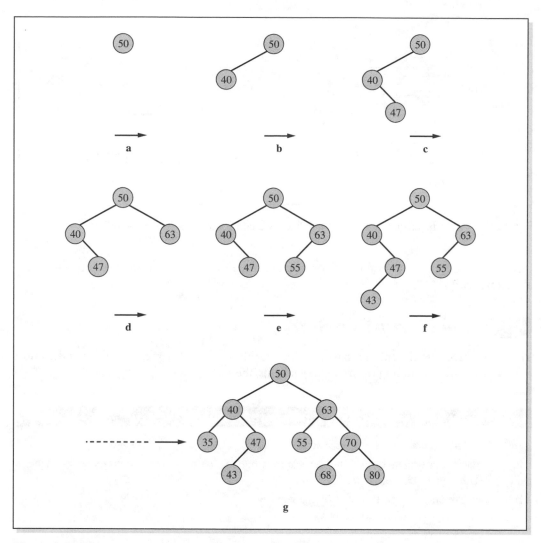

Figure 8.3 Progression of the Binary Tree Sort Algorithm when Sorting the Integers 50, 40, 47, 63, 55, 43, 70, 80, 35, and 68

Next, 47 would be compared to the root value, 50. Again we would proceed to the left since 47 is less than 50 (Step 3.1). Since there is a node to the left of 50, we would compare 47 to that node, 40 (Step 3). Since 47 is greater than 40, this time we would proceed to the right (Step 3.2). Step 4 of the algorithm would cause 47 to be inserted as 40's right child (see Figure 8.3c). The growth of the tree during the sorting of the first six integers is illustrated in Figures 8.3a–f, with the final sorting shown in Figure 8.3g.

Once the items are inserted into the binary tree, they can be listed in either ascending or descending order using the tree traversal algorithms discussed in Chapter 7, Section 7.2.

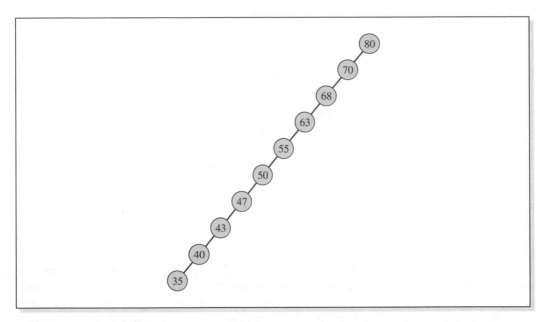

Figure 8.4 The 10-Level Tree Resulting from Sorting the Integers 80, 70, 68, 63, 55, 50, 47, 43, 40, and 35 with the Binary Tree Sort

Speed

Now let us examine the speed of the algorithm. The speed of this algorithm is dependent upon how well the binary tree is balanced, because as the items are inserted into the tree, one comparison is made at each level of the tree (Step 3 of the algorithm). As shown in Chapter 7 (Equation 7.3), a complete binary tree can stores n items in a $\log_2(n + 1)^1$ level tree (see Figure 7.4), while an imbalanced skewed tree stores n items in an n level tree (see Figure 8.4). Whether or not the tree is balanced depends on the order in which the items are processed by the algorithm. If they are processed in a random order, as when Figure 8.3 was generated, the tree will usually be balanced (see Figure 8.3**g**) or close to balanced. However, if the integers are processed in sorted order, the tree will be highly skewed to the right or left (see Figure 8.4).

As a result, the speed of this algorithm varies between the speed required to sort a random set of items (which we will designate SE_{BTmin}) and the speed to sort an already sorted set of items (SE_{BTmax}). Let us begin by determining the performance of the algorithm when sorting a set of items that are already sorted.

When the items to be sorted are already sorted in descending order, the tree is skewed to the left, as shown in Figure 8.4. The sorting process proceeds in the following way. The first item entered

---

[1]If the highest level of the tree is not full, the number of levels should be rounded to the next highest integer: ceil $((\log_2(n + 1))$

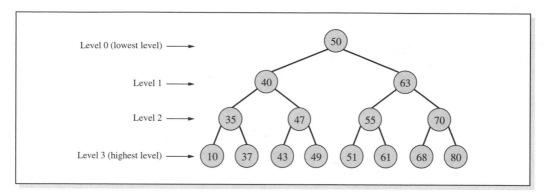

Figure 8.5 A Four-Level Tree Formed by Sorting the 15 Integers: 50, 40, 47, 63, 55, 43, 70, 80, 35, 68, 37, 49, 61, 51, and 10 using the Binary Tree Sort

becomes the root node. The second item is compared to the first item and then inserted into the tree. Thus, one comparison is required to insert the second item. The third item is initially compared to the first item, then compared to the second item, and then inserted into the tree. Thus, two comparisons are required to insert the third item. Continuing in this way, three comparisons are required to insert the fourth item, four comparisons are required to insert the fifth item, etc. Therefore, the total number of comparisons for the skewed tree—which is the maximum sort effort for the Binary Tree Sort—is

$$\text{SE}_{\text{BTmax}} = 0 + 1 + 2 + 3 + \ldots + (n-1) = (n-1)(n) / 2 = n^2/2 - n/2.$$

The minimum sort effort for the Binary Tree Sort, SE_{BTmin} occurs when the items are processed in an order that produces a balanced binary tree. Figure 8.5 presents such a tree, which is the result of processing 15 items in the order shown in the title of the figure.

To derive the minimum sort effort, let us assume that n items are sorted to form a complete binary tree. Then the highest level of the tree contains ½$(n + 1)$ items. Since each level in a balanced complete binary tree contains twice as many items as the level below it, the level just below the highest level contains ½(½$(n + 1)$) = ¼$((n + 1)$ items, the level below that contains ½(¼$(n + 1)$) = ⅛$(n + 1)$ items, etc.

The level number of the highest level of a balanced complete binary tree is $\log_2(n + 1) - 1$, which is also the number of comparisons required to place a single item at that level. To place a single item at one level below the highest level requires one less comparison, or $\log_2(n + 1) - 2$ comparisons; to place an item at the next lower level requires $\log_2(n + 1) - 3$ comparisons; etc.

If N is the number of items at a level of the tree, and C is the number of comparisons required to place a single item at that level, then the total number of comparisons necessary to fill a level of the tree is $N * C$. Therefore, the total number of comparisons required to place all the items in the tree containing n items, T_n, is the sum of $N * C$ for each level of the tree:

$$T_n = \frac{1}{2}(n + 1) * (\log_2(n + 1) - 1) + \frac{1}{4}(n + 1) * (\log_2(n + 1) - 2) + \frac{1}{8}(n + 1) *$$
$$(\log_2(n + 1) - 3) + \ldots$$
$$= (n + 1) \left[\frac{1}{2}(\log_2(n + 1) - 1) + \frac{1}{4}(\log_2(n + 1) - 2) + \frac{1}{8}(\log_2(n + 1) - 3) + \ldots\right]$$
$$= (n + 1) \left[\frac{1}{2}\log_2(n + 1) - \frac{1}{2}) + \frac{1}{4}\log_2(n + 1) - 2/4) + \frac{1}{8}\log_2(n + 1) - \frac{3}{8} + \ldots\right]$$
$$= (n + 1) \left[\log_2(n + 1)(\frac{1}{2} + \frac{1}{4} + \frac{1}{8} \ldots) - (\frac{1}{2} + \frac{2}{4} + \frac{3}{8} + \ldots)\right]$$
$$= (n + 1) \left[\log_2(n + 1)(a) - (b)\right],$$

where

$a = (\frac{1}{2} + \frac{1}{4} + \frac{1}{8} + \ldots)$, and
$b = (\frac{1}{2} + \frac{2}{4} + \frac{3}{8} + \ldots)$.

It can be shown that the series a and b converge to 1 and 2, respectively, as the number of terms in their equations increases. Since there is one term in each series for each level in the tree (except level 0 since no comparisons are necessary to place an item at level 0), and the number of levels in a tree containing n items is $\log_2(n + 1)$, there will be $\log_2(n + 1) - 1$ terms in these two series. For values of n greater than 18,434, both series are within 1% of their terminal values. Therefore, we can approximate T_n as

$$T_n = (n + 1) \left[\log_2(n + 1)(1) - (2)\right]$$
$$= (n + 1) \left[\log_2(n + 1) - 2\right] \text{ with less than a 1\% error for } n > 18,434.$$

Since the total number of comparisons required to sort n items is, by definition, the sort effort, a good approximation of the sort effort of the Binary Tree Sort when sorting n items that produces a balanced complete binary tree would be:

$$SE_{BTmin} = (n + 1) \left[\log_2(n + 1) - 2\right] \text{ with less than a 1\% error for } n > 18,434.$$

Appendix D contains a table of calculations comparing the minimum sort effort calculated using the above approximation and the *actual* minimum sort effort. Aside from demonstrating good agreement, an examination of the numbers presented in the table can aid in the understanding of the minimum sort effort derivation.

Having derived expressions for the minimum and maximum sort efforts of the algorithm, we can express the range of the sort effort as:

Sort Effort of the Binary Tree Sort

$$(n + 1) \left[\log_2(n + 1) - 2\right] < SE_{BT} <= n^2/2 - n/2$$

$$O(n\log_2 n) < SE_{BT} <= O(n^2)$$

The algorithm's speed is close to the theoretical minimum when sorting a random set of items (resulting in a balanced binary tree) and very slow, $O(n^2)$, when sorting an already sorted set of items. However, the speed can be improved when sorting an ordered, or almost ordered, set of items by processing the items through the algorithm in random order.

Memory Overhead

Assuming the linked implementation of a binary tree, the memory overhead required by this algorithm—above that necessary to hold the items being sorted—is the storage required for the reference variables that point to the location of the left and right children. Since there will be n items in the tree, the algorithm requires $2n$ reference variables of additional storage. Assuming each reference variable occupies 4 bytes, the total overhead for the algorithm is $8n$ bytes.

If the binary tree is implemented using an array, and the items to be sorted are primitives, then the primitives can be sorted within the array used to store the items. If the tree is balanced, then there are no unused elements in the array, and the overhead is 0. However, if the tree is skewed, then there will be n levels in the tree and (as we have seen in Chapter 7), $(2^n - 1) - n$ elements of the array will be unoccupied. This is an unacceptably large amount of overhead. For this reason, the linked implementation is used in this sorting algorithm.

Table 8.1 summarizes the performance of the Binary Tree Sort algorithm, its speed, and its memory overhead. As noted in the comments column, this algorithm is fast when the items to be sorted are introduced into it in a random order because the binary tree it produces is balanced. In this case, the sort effort of the algorithm approaches the theoretical minimum, $O(n\log_2 n)$. However, when the items the algorithm processes are already sorted, the algorithm produces a highly skewed tree, and its performance is extremely slow, $O(n^2)$.

As indicated in Table 8.1, the memory overhead of this algorithm is $8n$ bytes (because it normally uses the linked implantation of a binary tree), which is high compared to the other sorting algorithms presented in this chapter.

8.3.2 The Bubble Sort

The Bubble Sort is the simplest sorting algorithm presented in this chapter. For data sets that are already sorted, or close to sorted, it offers good performance. Because of its simplicity, it is easy to code and, therefore, is also used for randomized data sets with few members.

This algorithm, like all sorting algorithms, executes its sorting process inside a loop. In the jargon of sorting, each iteration through this loop is referred to as a "pass through the sorting algorithm." Just as gas bubbles rise to the surface of a liquid, during each "pass" through this algorithm the smaller items rise, or *bubble* upward, toward the top of the array of primitive or reference variables. Thus, the name *Bubble* Sort.

Each pass places one item into its final position in the array. When coded to sort items in ascending order, the first pass places (or bubbles) the smallest item into element 0; the second smallest item is bubbled into element 1 during the second pass; the third smallest item is bubbled into element 2 during the third pass; etc. Figure 8.6 presents the contents of an array of integers after

Table 8.1

The Performance of the Binary Tree Sort Algorithm

Algorithm	Speed		Memory Overhead		Comments
	Range	**Effort**	**Range**	**Bytes**	
Binary Tree	fast/slow $O(n\log_2 n)$ / $O(n^2)$	$(n+1)\,[\log_2(n+1)-2] < SE <= n^2/2 - n/2$	high	$8n$	Fast for random data, slow for already sorted data. High overhead.

Initial Order	End of Pass			
	1	2	3	4
8	1	1	1	1
2	8	2	2	2
6	2	8	3	3
10	6	3	8	6
3	10	6	6	8
1	3	10	9	9
9	9	9	10	10

Figure 8.6 Results of the First Four Passes Through the Bubble Sort when Sorting an Array of Integers

Initial Order	Pass 1					Pass 2					Pass 3				Pass 4			
8	8	8	8	8	8	1	1	1	1	1	1	1	1	1	1	1	1	1
2	2	2	2	2	1	8	8	8	8	8	2	2	2	2	2	2	2	2
6	6	6	6	1	2	2	2	2	2	2	8	8	8	8	3	3	3	3
10	10	10	1	6	6	6	6	6	3	3	3	3	3	3	8	8	8	6
3	3	1	10	10	10	10	10	3	6	6	6	6	6	6	6	6	6	8
1	1	3	3	3	3	3	3	10	10	10	10	9	9	9	9	9	9	9
9	9	9	9	9	9	9	9	9	9	9	9	10	10	10	10	10	10	10

Figure 8.7 Changes to an Array of Integers during the First Four Passes Through the Bubble Sort

the end of each of the first four passes through the algorithm. The shaded cells in the table indicate the integers that have been placed in their sorted position in the array after each pass.

At the beginning of each pass through the algorithm, two integers, b and t, are set to the lowest two indices of the array. For example, when sorting seven items, b would be set to 6 and t would be set to 5. The elements at these indices are then compared. If they are not in sorted order, their positions in the array are swapped or *flipped*. Regardless of whether or not a flip is performed, the integers b and t are decremented (b--, t--), and a comparison is made to determine if the two elements at these incremented indices should be flipped. This process continues until the index stored in t reaches the portion of the array already sorted on previous passes (i.e., t stores the index of the item sorted on the previous passes). As a result, one fewer comparison is made on each successive pass through the algorithm.

This process is depicted in Figure 8.7, which presents the details of the changes to the contents of the array of integers presented in Figure 8.6 during the first four passes through the algorithm.

Moving from left to right as the algorithm proceeds, the shaded cells in each column of the array indicate the two integers that are compared as a pass proceeds. For example, as part of the first pass through the algorithm, 9 and 1 are compared, then 1 and 3 are compared, then 1 and 10 are compared, etc. The comparison of 1 and 3 in the second column of the table initiates the first flip. These two integers are shown in their new positions in the third column of the table.

It turns out that for the initial ordering of the integers presented in Figure 8.6, the entire array is, in fact, sorted after four passes through the algorithm. This is not always the case. As previously stated, the algorithm only guarantees that one item is correctly positioned during each pass. However, for some data sets, several items are swapped into their final positions during a single pass. For example, the integers 10, 9, 8, and 3 were all positioned in their final locations during pass 3.

To take advantage of the fact that sometimes the algorithm completes the sort "early," a Boolean variable flip is set to **false** *before each pass* through the algorithm. Then whenever a flip is performed, the variable flip is set to **true**. If, at the end of a pass, flip is still **true**, no two adjacent elements of the array were out of sorted order, and therefore, the entire array is sorted. At this point the algorithm terminates. Assuming n is the number of items to be sorted, the algorithm is:

The Bubble Sort Algorithm

```
itemsSorted = 0;
do
{ flip = false; // begin a pass
   for (b = n − 1, t = n − 2; t >= itemsSorted; b--, t--;)
      if(items[b] < items[t])   // two adjacent elements are not in sorted order
      { // swap the two elements
         // set flip to true
      }
   itemsSorted++; // one more item is in its final positioning the array
} while (flip == true && itemsSorted != n − 1);
```

We will now consider the speed of the bubble sort algorithm.

Speed

Like the Binary Tree Sort algorithm, there are particular characteristics of the data to be sorted that result in very fast or very slow Bubble Sort speeds. Ironically, one case that was very *slow* for the Binary Tree Sort—when the information to be sorted is initially in ascending order—is very *fast* for the Bubble Sort.

The sort effort for any sorting algorithm is the sum of the number of comparisons performed during each pass of the algorithm. For this algorithm the sum is easily deduced by examining Figure 8.7, in which 7 ($n = 7$) integers were processed through four passes of the algorithm. Since the

Pass Number	Number of Comparisons
1	6 (= n – 1)
2	5 (= n – 2)
3	4 (= n – 3)
4	3 (= n – 4)
5	2 (= n – 5)
6	1 (= n – 6)

Figure 8.8 Number of Comparisons per Pass when Processing $n = 7$ Items Through the Bubble Sort

pairs of shaded cells in the figure represent the comparisons, we simply need to count them to determine the comparisons for each pass and then total these to obtain the sort effort. Pass 1 performed six comparisons; pass 2, five comparisons; pass 3, four comparisons; and pass 4 performed three comparisons.

The number of comparisons for each of the four passes is given in Figure 8.8, which includes an extrapolation out to the sixth pass. Although six passes are not necessary to sort this set of integers, six passes is the maximum number of passes necessary to sort seven items using the algorithm. Intuitively, most students conclude seven passes would be the maximum number of passes necessary to sort seven items. However, the flip performed on the sixth pass (assuming it is necessary) properly positions the next-to-the-largest *and* the largest item in the array.

When the character of the seven items to be sorted are such that six passes through the algorithm are required to complete the sort, then the data presented in Figure 8.8 indicates that the total number of comparisons required to sort the seven items would be $6 + 5 + 4 + 3 + 2 + 1 = 21$, which is the sum of the integers from $7 - 1$ to 1. Alternately, if the character of the items to be sorted were such that only one pass were required to complete the sort, then the data presented in the figure indicates that only 6, or $7 - 1$, comparisons would be require to complete the sort. Generalizing these results for n items, we find the minimum and maximum sort effort for the Bubble Sort to be:

$$SE_{BSmin} = n - 1, \text{ and}$$
$$SE_{BSmax} = n - 1 + n - 2 + n - 1 + \ldots 2 + 1 = (n - 1) * n/2.$$

Thus the range of the sort effort for this algorithm is:

Sort Effort of the Bubble Sort

$$(n - 1) <= SE_{BS} <= n^2/2 - n/2$$

$$O(n) < SE_{BS} <= O(n^2)$$

The minimum sort effort is realized when the items to be sorted are already in ascending order. When this is the case, no flips are performed on the first pass through the algorithm, and the algorithm ends after pass 1. The maximum sort effort is required when the items to be sorted are initially sorted in descending order. When this is the case, $n - 1$ passes are required to complete the algorithm. Thus, from a speed viewpoint, the algorithm performs best when sorting nodes that are close to sorted, or already sorted, in ascending order.

We will make one last point on the speed of this algorithm before turning our attention to its overhead. The algorithm includes swap operations, which require memory accesses. A reasonable assumption would be that, on the average, half of the comparisons result in swaps. Therefore, the number of swaps performed by the algorithm when sorting n items is half the sort effort.

Memory Overhead

When this algorithm is presented with an array of primitive values or an array of object references, the primitive values or the references are swapped within the array. Thus, the only extra storage required to perform the algorithm is one extra memory cell (`temp`), used in the classic swapping algorithm,

```
temp = items[t];
items[t] = items[b];
items[b] = temp;
```

Table 8.2 summarizes the performance of the Bubble Sort algorithm (its speed and memory overhead) and includes the performance of the Binary Tree Sort for comparative purposes. As noted in the comments column, this algorithm is fast when the items to be sorted are already sorted (or close to sorted) in ascending order. In this case, the speed of the algorithm is faster than the theoretical minimum, $n\log_2 n$. However, when the items the algorithm processes are already sorted (or nearly sorted) in descending order, its performance is extremely slow, $O(n^2)$. As indicated in Table 8.2, the memory overhead of this algorithm is 4 bytes, which is the lowest overhead of the sorting algorithms discussed in this chapter.

The sort efforts of the two algorithms we have studied so far are dependent on the character of the data set to be sorted ranging from very fast, $O(n)$, to slow, $O(n^2)$. Still, as we have seen, under the correct circumstances, both algorithms do have their niche. Our familiarity with binary search trees, and the simplicity of the Bubble Sort, made these sorting algorithms a good starting point for our studies. The Heap Sort, which we will study next, is an algorithm whose sort effort is close to the theoretical minimum for *all* data sets.

Table 8.2

The Performance of the Bubble Sort

| Algorithm | Speed | | Memory Overhead | | Comments |
	Range	Effort	Range	Bytes	
Binary Tree	fast/slow $O(n\log_2 n) / O(n^2)$	$(n + 1) [\log_2(n + 1) - 2] < SE <= n^2/2 - n/2$	high	$8n$	Fast for random data, slow for already sorted data. Highest overhead.
Bubble	very fast/slow $O(n) / O(n^2)$	$n - 1 < SE <= n^2/2 - n/2$ $0 <= $ Number of swaps $<= SE / 2$	low	4	Fast for data almost sorted in ascending order. Slow for most data sets. Low overhead. Easy to code.

8.3.3 The Heap Sort

A *heap* is a binary tree in which the nodes exhibit a special relationship to each other. Although only small subsets of all binary trees are heaps, there are some very useful algorithms in computer science that can only be used if the tree they process is a heap. One of them is the Heap Sort algorithm. To understand this algorithm, we must first become familiar with heaps.

> ### A Heap
>
> A heap is *binary tree* in which the value of *each parent* in the tree is
> *greater than both* of its *children's* values.

In the context of heaps that store primitives, the term *value* refers to the value of a primitive, and in the context of heaps that store objects, the term *value* refers to the value of the object's key field. Figure 8.9 presents several examples of binary trees that are heaps. The definition of a heap

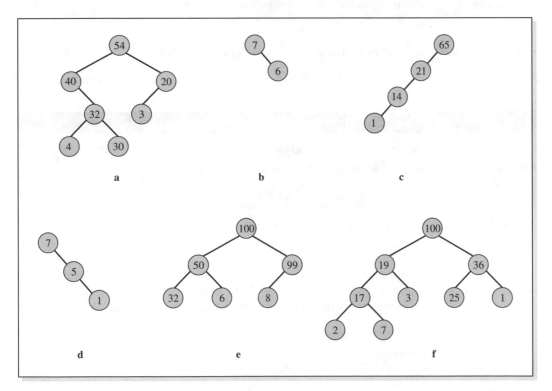

Figure 8.9 Examples of Binary Trees That Are Heaps

excludes them from being binary search trees because in a heap, a node's right child cannot be greater than its parent, which is a necessary condition for a binary search tree.

Examining the trees present in Figure 8.9, we observe that the value of the root node in each tree is the largest value in the tree. This condition is not only true for these heaps, but true for all heaps since, in a heap, the root node must be greater than both of its children, who are greater than both of their children, etc. Thus, the root node being the largest item in the tree is a direct consequence of the definition of a heap and, as we shall see, is an implicit assumption of the Heap Sort algorithm.

Examining the heaps presented in Figure 8.9, another observation can be made. Each subtree in these trees is also a heap. Once again, this condition is not only true for these heaps, but true for all heaps, since, if we start at the subtrees at the highest levels of a heap, the children must be less than their parent, who is less than its parent, etc. Our two observations for any heaps are summarized as follows:

For any heap,

1. The largest node in the heap is the root node.
2. All subtrees in a heap are themselves heaps.

Having gained an understanding of heaps, we will now begin our study of the Heap Sort algorithm.

The Heap Sort algorithm consists of three steps that sort an array of items into ascending order.

The Heap Sort Algorithm

1. Place all the items to be sorted in a left balanced binary tree.
2. Build the initial heap (i.e., reposition the items in the tree to make it a heap).
3. Repeatedly:
   3.1 Swap the root node into its "proper" position, and
   3.2 Rebuild the remaining[2] items into a heap.

If a team of three programmers were each to implement one step of this algorithm, the lucky programmer would be the one assigned Step 1, *place all the items to be sorted in a left balanced binary tree*. The reason is that, as we discovered in Chapter 7, all arrays can be viewed as left balanced

---

[2]The term "remaining items" means the items not yet positioned into their sorted order location (or "proper" position) in the array by Step 3.1 of the algorithm.

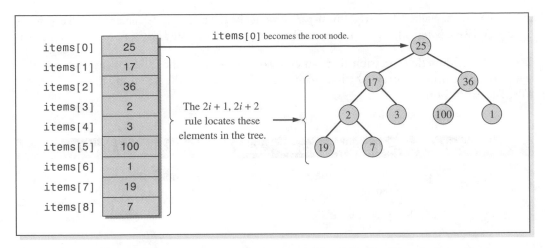

Figure 8.10   Viewing an Array as a Left-Balanced Binary Tree using the "2n + 1, 2n + 2" rule

binary trees using the $2i + 1, 2i + 2$ rule. Therefore, the programmer assigned this step does nothing, which is something most of us are very good at.

Figure 8.10 presents an array of integers and the left balanced binary tree that the array represents when viewed using the $2i + 1, 2i + 2$ rule.

As mentioned in Chapter 7, the easiest way to view the binary tree that represents an array is to index through the array in sequential order starting at element 0, which becomes the tree's root, and then fill in the higher levels of the tree from left to right. Therefore, the array is already a left balanced binary tree, so long as, in Steps 2 and 3 of the algorithm, we use element 0 as the root node and locate the left and right children of element n as elements $2i + 1$ and $2i + 2$, respectively. Nice job, Step 1 programmer; take a break.

It is much easier to understand the remaining two steps of the algorithm if we depict these steps in the binary tree graphical representation of the array. However, it is important to realize that the Heap Sort algorithm simply swaps the items to be sorted between the elements of the array during the sorting process, just as the Bubble Sort algorithm did. Therefore, we will refer to two graphics during the discussion of the algorithm: one graphic will show the changes to the *tree representation* of the array as the algorithm executes (to facilitate an understanding of the algorithm), and the second graphic will show the changes to the *array contents* actually made by the algorithm.

In Step 2 of the algorithm, we *reposition the nodes in the tree to make it a heap.* In Heap Sort jargon, this is referred to as *building the initial heap.* To do this, we examine the highest level of the tree that has parent nodes (level 2 in Figure 8.10). If there are several parent nodes at this level, we locate the level's rightmost parent. This node is referred to as the highest-level-rightmost-parent. Referring to the tree in Figure 8.10, the highest-level-rightmost-parent would be the node whose value is 2. If all the nodes on this level were parents, then the highest-level-rightmost-parent would be the node whose value is 1.

There is an arithmetic expression that can be used to determine the index of the highest-level-rightmost-parent in the array, which is a consequence of viewing the tree using the $2i + 1$, $2i + 2$ rule. The expression is:

Index of the Highest-Level-Rightmost-Parent in a Left Balanced Binary Tree

In a left balanced binary tree with n nodes, the index of the highest-level-rightmost-parent is floor$[(n\ /\ 2) - 1]$.

To demonstrate the validity of the technique, consider the tree depicted in Figure 8.10. There are nine nodes in the tree ($n = 9$) and, therefore, the index of the highest-level-rightmost-parent is calculated to be floor$[(9\ /\ 2) - 1] = 3$. Inspecting the contents of the array and the tree depicted in Figure 8.10, we observe that this index (3) is, in fact, the index of the highest-level-rightmost-parent (the item whose value is 2). If we were to add a tenth node to the tree, it would be added as a child of the node whose value is 3 (to keep the tree left balanced), which is located at index 4 in the array. The numerical technique again yields the correct index, $4 = $ floor$([10\ /\ 2] - 1)$.

Once we have located the highest-level-rightmost-parent we are ready to build the initial heap. The changes to the tree (depicted in Figure 8.10) that occur as the initial heap is built are shown in Figure 8.11, and the corresponding changes to the array contents are shown in Figure 8.12. First, the highest-level-rightmost-parent is compared to both of its children (the shaded nodes in Figure 8.11a and Figure 8.12a). If the parent is larger than both of its children, then no action is taken because it and its children are already a heap. If it is not larger than both of its children (as is the case in Figure 8.11a), it is swapped with the larger of its two children to form a heap with the swapped child becoming the root of the heap (see the lower left side of Figure 8.11b and elements 3 and 7 of Figure 8.12, column b).

This process is repeated for all the other parent nodes decrementing through parents in sequential index order. For the tree depicted in Figure 8.11, the order would be indices 3, 2, 1, and finally, index 0. Thus, the next two parents considered are the nodes whose values are 36 and 17 (the shaded parents in Figure 8.11b and c), which are at indices 2 and 1 of the array (see Figure 8.12, columns b and c). In both cases, a swap is performed.

After swapping the values 17 and 19 (see Figure 8.12d), a situation occurs that has not arisen up to this point in our study of the algorithm. As shown in Figure 8.11d, after the value 17 is moved downward in the tree, it moves into a position in which it is still has children. Since it was smaller than the children's previous parent, 19, it could be smaller than one of its new children (e.g., one of the new children could have the value 18). Therefore, before proceeding to the next higher parent (25), 17 is compared to its *new* children (see the shaded items in Figure 8.11d and Figure 8.12,

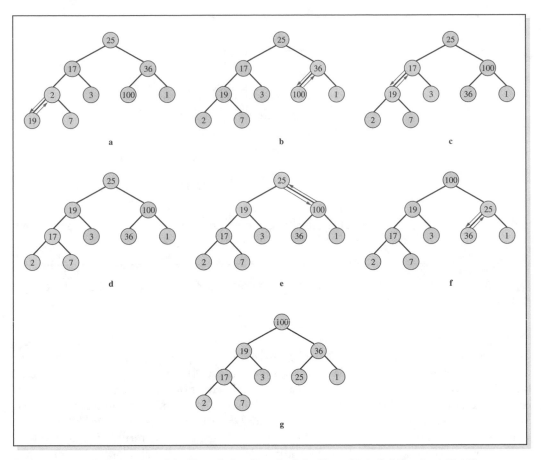

Figure 8.11 Progression of the Tree during Step 2 of the Heap Sort, Building the Initial Heap

column **d**) to see if it should be swapped with either of them (i.e., moved further down the tree). In this case, it remains where it is.

Next, 25 is compared to both of its children (see the shaded nodes in Figure 8.11**e** and Figure 8.12, column **e**) and swapped with 100. Since 25, in its new position, has children, it is compared to them (see the shaded nodes in Figure 8.11**f** and Figure 8.12, column **f**) to determine if it should be moved further down the tree. In this case, it has to be swapped with 36, resulting in the tree shown in Figure 8.11**g** and column **g** of Figure 8.12. Since 25, in its new position, has no children, its path downward is completed.

Since, after considering 25, we have examined all the parent nodes in the tree, Step 2 of the algorithm is complete. The resulting tree, Figure 8.11**g**, is the initial heap, which is equivalent to the ordering of the integers in Figure 8.12, column **g**. By examining this tree, we can verify that each parent in the tree is greater than both of its children, and therefore the array contents shown in Figure 8.12, column **g**, constitute our initial heap.

Index	a	b	c	d	e	f	g
[0]	25	25	25	25	25	100	100
[1]	17	17	17	19	19	19	19
[2]	36	36	100	100	100	25	36
[3]	2	19	19	17	17	17	17
[4]	3	3	3	3	3	3	3
[5]	100	100	36	36	36	36	25
[6]	1	1	1	1	1	1	1
[7]	19	2	2	2	2	2	2
[8]	7	7	7	7	7	7	7

Figure 8.12 Progression of the Array Contents during Step 2 of the Heap Sort, Build the Initial Heap

The process used above to build the initial heap—comparing a parent to each of its children and then moving the parent downward in the tree until it is greater than both of its children—is called the *Reheap Downward* algorithm. It gets its name from the situation that developed when the parent node, 25, was swapped with one of its children (Figure 8.11**e**). The swap caused the subtree it moved into to no longer be a heap, because the root (25) was less than one of its children (36). When this occurs, the subtree is *rebuilt* into a *heap* by moving the node further *downward* in the tree (Figures 8.11**f** and **g**) until it becomes a leaf node, or is greater than both of its children. It is useful to develop the Reheap Downward algorithm separately, since, as we will see, its process is also used in Step 3 of the Heap Sort algorithm.

The Reheap Downward algorithm builds a heap out of any tree whose root, P, is the only node in the tree preventing it from being a heap, As such, the algorithm assumes that all the subtrees in the tree are already heaps. Under this assumption, the pseudocode version of the Reheap Downward algorithm is:

Reheap Downward Algorithm

1. P is the root node of a tree whose subtrees are already heaps
2. **if** (P has no children) **return;**
3. **if** (P > both children) **return;**
4. Swap P with its greatest child;
5. Repeat steps 2, 3, and 4 for the subtree that P is now the root of.

Step 2 of the Heap Sort algorithm is performed by repeatedly applying the Reheap Downward algorithm to each subtree in the tree, beginning with P set to the highest-level-rightmost-parent, and ending with P set to the tree's root node. By working our way up from the bottom of the tree, the subtrees of P have already been transformed into heaps. Therefore, if the tree rooted by P is not a heap, the only node preventing it from being a heap is the root node itself, P. Thus, the assumption of the algorithm is satisfied.

We will now turn our attention to Step 3 of the Heap Sort algorithm:

> "*Repeatedly:*
>
> > *Swap the root node into its proper position, and*
> >
> > *rebuild the remaining items into a heap.*"

Its starting point, the initial heap built in Step 2 of the algorithm is depicted in Figure 8.13**a** and column **a** of Figure 8.14. Remembering the first of the two observations we made about heaps earlier in this chapter, *the largest node in a heap is the root node*, the first part of Step 3, *swap the root node into its "proper" position*, is simple. Since the root (100 in our heap) is the largest item in the tree, and we are sorting in *ascending* order, its *proper* position is at the end of the array. Therefore, it is swapped with the last item in the array (7, as depicted in Figures 8.13**b** and 8.14, column **b**).

Next, we *rebuild the remaining items into a heap*. The phrase *remaining items* refers to all of the items that have not been placed into their proper position in the array. Since 100 is in its proper position it is excluded from the heap, and the remaining $n - 1$ items (array elements 0 through $n - 2$) are rebuilt into a heap. Since only the root (7) of this $n - 1$ node tree has been repositioned, it is the only item that could be preventing this tree of $n - 1$ nodes from being a heap. Therefore, the Reheap Downward algorithm (with item 100 excluded) can be invoked to rebuild this tree into a heap.

The changes to the tree (and to the array it represents) as the heap is rebuilt is shown in Figures 8.13**c–e** and 8.14, columns **c–e**. The arc drawn just above the node 100 in Figures 8.13**b–e**, and the heavy horizontal line drawn just above item 100 in Figure 8.14, columns **b–e** indicate that 100 is no longer considered part of the tree that is being rebuilt into a heap; it has been *carved out* of the tree. Node 7 is first swapped with node 36, and then it is swapped with node 25. Figures 8.13**e** and 8.14, column **e** show the rebuilt heap (excluding node 100). This rebuilding of the heap completes the first pass through Step 3 of the Heap Sort algorithm.

The two parts of Step 3 described above are repeated until all the nodes are in their sorted positions in the array. Each iteration, or pass, through Step 3 operates on a tree containing one less node than the previous pass. Changes to the tree during the second pass through Step 3 are shown in Figures 8.13**f–i** and Figures 8.14, columns **f–i**. The process begins by placing the root of the heap (36) in its proper spot in the array (Figures 8.13**f** and 8.14, column **f**), carving it out of the tree, and then rebuilding the heap (Figures 8.13**g, h,** and **i**). The changes to the contents of the array during the next three passes through Step 3 of the algorithm are shown in Figure 8.14, columns **j** through **t**. The changes to the array during the remaining passes through Step 3 are left as an exercise for the student.

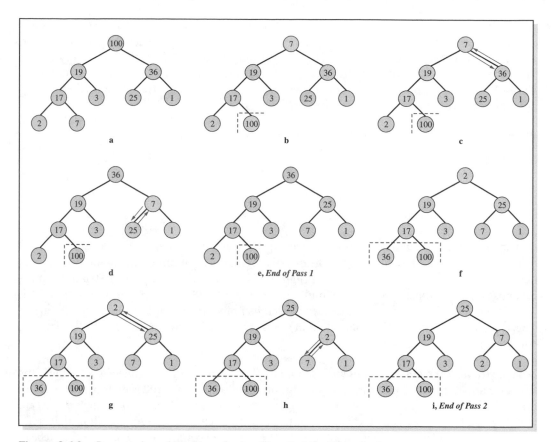

Figure 8.13   Progression of the Heap During Step 3 of the Heap Sort

Speed

Now let us consider the speed complexity of the algorithm by examining its sort effort (the number of comparisons required to sort n items). The total number of comparisons performed by this algorithm is the sum of comparisons performed during the three steps of the algorithm. As previously discussed, nothing is done during Step 1 of the algorithm, since we simply use the $2i + 1$, $2i + 2$ rule to view the array as a binary tree. Thus,

$$SE_{HSstep1} = 0$$

During Step 2 of the Heap Sort, no more than $n / 2$ parent nodes are processed, since $n / 2$ is the maximum number of parent nodes in a balanced binary tree containing n nodes. To decide if a parent node should be moved down a level in the tree, two comparisons are necessary to determine if it is less than either of its children. If it is, it descends a level in the tree. The number of levels a parent can descend through a balanced tree containing n nodes is always less than, or equal to, the

Index	Pass 1					Pass 2				Pass 3				Pass 4				Pass 5		
[0]	100	7	7	36	36	2	2	25	25	1	1	19	19	2	2	17	17	2	2	7
[1]	19	19	19	19	19	19	19	19	19	19	19	1	17	17	17	2	3	3	3	3
[2]	36	36	36	7	25	25	25	2	7	7	7	7	7	7	7	7	7	7	7	2
[3]	17	17	17	17	17	17	17	17	17	17	17	17	1	1	1	1	1	1	1	1
[4]	3	3	3	3	3	3	3	3	3	3	3	3	3	3	3	3	2	17	17	17
[5]	25	25	25	25	7	7	7	7	2	2	2	2	2	19	19	19	19	19	19	19
[6]	1	1	1	1	1	1	1	1	1	25	25	25	25	25	25	25	25	25	25	25
[7]	2	2	2	2	2	36	36	36	36	36	36	36	36	36	36	36	36	36	36	36
[8]	7	100	100	100	100	100	100	100	100	100	100	100	100	100	100	100	100	100	100	100
	a	b	c	d	e	f	g	h	i	j	k	l	m	n	o	p	q	r	s	t

Figure 8.14 Progression of the Array Contents during Step 3 of the Heap Sort

maximum level number in the tree, floor$[\log_2(n)]$. (Actually, only the root node can descend this many levels.) Since a parent is compared to two children, it is reasonable to assume that one-third of the time the parent will be larger than both of its children. Therefore, two-thirds of the $n / 2$ parents descend a maximum of floor$[\log_2(n)]$ levels, making two comparisons at each level and:

$$SE_{HSstep2} < n/2 * 2/3\text{floor}[\log_2(n)] * 2 < n\log_2(n).$$

The analysis of Step 3 of the algorithm is similar to that used in Step 2. During Step 3.2 (rebuilding the heap) *two* comparisons are made to determine if the root node should be moved down a level in the tree. As we have previously stated, the maximum number of levels a node can move down in a balanced binary tree containing n nodes is floor$[\log_2(n)]$. Since Step 3.2 is repeated for each node of the n nodes in the tree, a total of two comparisons are made at most floor$[\log_2(n)]$ times[3] for each of the n nodes in the tree. Thus,

$$SE_{HSstep3} < 2 * \text{floor}[(\log_2(n)] * n < 2n\log_2(n).$$

Adding together the number of comparisons for Steps 1, 2, and 3 of the Heap Sort, we obtain:

$$SE_{HS} = SE_{HSstep1} + SE_{HSstep2} + SE_{HSstep3} < 0 + n\log_2(n) + 2n\log_2(n),$$

or
$$SE_{HS} < 3n\log_2(n).$$

This sort effort is O($n\log_2 n$), which means it approaches the theoretical minimum sort effort and, since the character of the items to be sorted was not considered in its derivation, the Heap Sort algorithm achieves these speeds for all data sets.

---

[3]As nodes are put into their proper place in the tree, the number of levels the root node moves down decreases.

This algorithm includes swap operations, which require memory accesses. Since, in our sort effort analysis for this structure we assumed that two-thirds of the comparisons (a parent compared to both of its children) resulted in a swap, the number of swaps is two-thirds the number of comparisons = 2 / 3 (Sort effort) = $2n\log_2 n$.

Memory Overhead

Like the Bubble Sort, when this algorithm is presented with an array of primitive values or an array of references to objects, the primitive values or the object references are swapped within the array. Thus, the only extra storage required to perform the algorithm is four bytes for the memory cell, temp, in the standard swapping algorithm,

```
temp = items[t];
items[t] = items[b];
items[b] = temp;
```

Table 8.3 summarizes the performance of the Heap Sort algorithm (its speed and memory overhead) and includes the performance of the Binary Tree Sort and Bubble Sort for comparative purposes. As noted in the comments column, this algorithm exhibits the best overall performance of the sorting algorithms presented thus far in this chapter. It is fast for *all* data sets, approaching the theoretical minimum speed, and its memory overhead is as low as the overhead of the Bubble Sort.

8.3.4 The Merge Sort

The Merge Sort is based on the idea that two sorted sublists, A and B, can be merged into one sorted list, T, by comparing the minimum items in each sublist. The smaller of the two items is transferred to list T. This process is continued until either sublist A or sublist B is empty. Then, the remaining items from the nonempty sublist are transferred to T.

Figure 8.15 illustrates the process. The numbers inside the circles indicate the order in which the integers are transferred from the sublists A and B to the list T. First the 3 in sublist A is compared to the 30 in sublist B, and the smaller of the two (3) is copied into list T. Then 21 from sublist A is compared to 30 from sublist B, and the smaller of the two (21) is copied into list T. This process continues until 93 from sublist A is compared to 99 from sublist B and the 93 is copied into list T. At this point all the values in sublist A have been copied into list T, and the remaining values in sublist B (99 and 107) are copied into list T.

The next logical question is: given a list of eight unsorted items how did we sort them into two four item lists (A and B) so that the merge process could be applied to them? The answer is: using the merge process on two sublists of two items each to produce list A, and on two other sublists of two items each to produce list B. Finally, you may ask, given a list of eight unsorted items, how do

Table 8.3

The Performance of the Heap Sort Algorithm

| Algorithm | Speed | | Memory Overhead | | Comments |
	Range	Effort	Range	Bytes	
Binary Tree	fast/slow $O(n\log_2 n) / O(n^2)$	$(n+1)\,[\log_2(n+1) - 2] < SE <= n^2/2 - n/2$	high	$8n$	Fast for random data, slow for already sorted data. Highest overhead.
Bubble	very fast/slow $O(n) / O(n^2)$	$n - 1 < SE <= n^2/2 - n/2$ $0 < $ Number of swaps $ < SE/2$	low	4	Fast for data almost sorted in ascending order. Slow for most data sets. Low overhead. Easy to code.
Heap	fast $O(\log_2 n)$	$SE < 3n\log_2(n)$ Number of swaps $= 2SE/3$	low	4	Fast for all data sets. Low overhead.

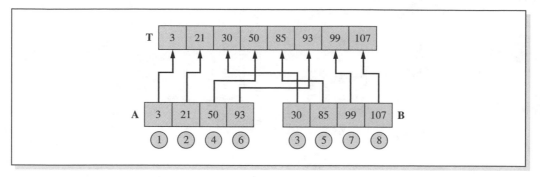

Figure 8.15   The Process of Merging Two Sorted Sublists into a Sorted List

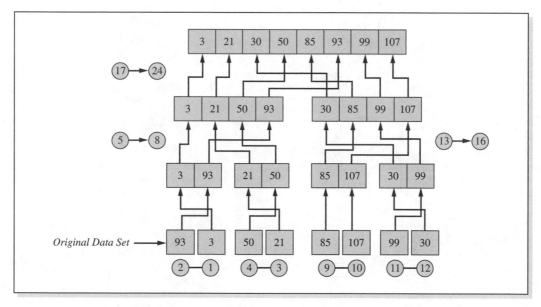

Figure 8.16   Repeated use of the Merge Process to Sort a List of Eight Unsorted Integers

we produce four sublists of two items each? Once again the answer is using the merge process, this time on eight sublists of one item each. If it sounds recursive, your ear is improving, because it is.

Figure 8.16 illustrates the process of sorting the original eight-item list (93, 3, 50, 21, 85, 107, 99, and 30 depicted at the bottom of the figure) using the merge process seven times. In all, 24 items are moved in the order given by the circled numbers, with each of the seven pairs of circled numbers being an application of the merge process. Initially, eight sublists contained one item each, as shown at the bottom of the figure. These eight lists were merged into four lists of two items each.

The four lists of two items were merged into two lists of four items, and the two lists of four items are merged into one list of eight items.

The sublist length always begins at one, because this guarantees that the sublist is sorted, which is a condition of the merge process.

Assuming the original set to be sorted is stored in the array items and that they are copied into the array temp, the array items would be the set of eight numbers at the bottom level of Figure 8.16, and the array temp would be the set of numbers just above it. This means we need two arrays just to produce sublists of length two. To minimize the number of arrays needed to finish the sort, the array temp is copied back into the array items before the next merging of the sublists. Thus, the items are always merged from the array items into the array temp. Just before the sort ends, temp is copied into items one last time so that the sorted list is contained in the original array.

As implied in its description, the Merge Sort algorithm is usually expressed recursively. Using our recursive methodology, we will identify the original problem, the base case, the reduced problem, and the general solution. The original problem is to sort a set of n items stored in the array items, between a left index (leftIndex, initially 0) and a right index (rightIndex, initially $n - 1$), using a temporary array (temp). Stated more succinctly, the original problem is,

```
mergeSort(items, temp, leftIndex, rightIndex)
```

Since the problem involves an integer n, the base case is probably when $n = 0$ or 1. In our case, when $n = 1$, one item is to be sorted and nothing needs to be done. Therefore, we will use $n = 1$ as the base case, in which case the algorithm does nothing and ends.

The reduced problem should be a problem like the original one (sorting n items), but closer to the base case (sorting one item). But how close should it be to the base case? Should it be sorting $n - 1$ items, or $n - 2$ items, or ...? A clue to the answer lies in the top part of Figure 8.16 which actually depicts the general solution. The merge process is applied to two sublists of $n/2$ nodes to produce the solution to the original problem (sorting a list of n items). Therefore, our reduced problem will be to sort a list of $n / 2$ items.

The general solution will use the reduced problem twice. Once to sort the $n / 2$ items in the left half of the original data set, and again to sort the items in the right half of the original data set. Once this is done, the merge process can be used on the two lists of $n / 2$ sorted items to produce the final sorted list. Assuming middleIndex = (rightIndex + leftIndex) / 2 the general solution is:

```
1.  mergeSort(items, temp, leftIndex, middleIndex)
2.  mergeSort(items, temp, middleIndex + 1 rightIndex)
3.  // perform the merge process on the left and right halves of the array items
```

Assuming the arrays are named `items` and `temp`, and the indices of the first and last item to be sorted are `leftIndex` (initially set to 0) and `rightIndex` (initially set to $n - 1$), the recursive pseudocode of the algorithm is:

Merge Sort Algorithm

```
1.   nItems = rightIndex – leftIndex + 1;
2.   if(nItems == 1)                                      // base case, 1 item to be sorted
3.      return;
4.   middleIndex – (rightIndex – leftIndex) / 2;
5.   mergeSort(items, temp, leftIndex, middleIndex);      // reduced problems, sort the left
                                                          // sublist
6.   mergeSort(items, temp, middleIndex + 1 rightIndex);  // sort the right sublist
7.   merge(items, temp, leftIndex, middleIndex, rightIndex); // merge the two sorted  sublists
8.   return;
```

The algorithm of the merge process (Line 7 of the algorithm) is depicted in Figure 8.15.

Implementation

The Java implementation of the Merge Sort pseudocode is given in Figure 8.17, as is the code of the method `merge` that implements the merge process, depicted in Figure 8.15.

Lines 1–11 are the code of the recursive Merge Sort algorithm, and Lines 12–48 are the code of the method `merge` that it invokes on Line 9. Lines 18–43 of the `merge` method moves the items to be sorted from the array `items` to the array `temp`. Lines 18–29 repeatedly move the minimum item from one of the sublists of the array `items` into the array `temp` (Lines 20 and 25) until one sublist is empty. The determination of which sublist contains the minimum item is performed on Line 19. When one of the sublists is empty, Lines 30–43 transfer the remaining items from the non-empty sublist into the array `temp`. The actual data transfer takes place on Lines 32 and 39. The determination of which sublist is not empty is performed on Line 30. Finally, Lines 44–47 copy the contents of the array `temp` into the array `items`.

Speed

Now let us consider the speed complexity of the algorithm by examining its sort effort. The total number of comparisons performed by this algorithm can be expressed as the number of passes through the algorithm times the number of comparisons made during each pass. To find the number of passes, we can simply examine Figure 8.16.

Ignoring the original data set depicted at the bottom level of Figure 8.16, a completion of a pass through this algorithm is depicted as a level in the figure. Thus, three passes through the algorithm

```
1.   public static void mergeSort(int items[], int temp[], int leftIndex,
                                  int rightIndex)
2.   {  int midIndex, nItems;
3.      nItems = rightIndex - leftIndex + 1;
4.      if(nItems == 1) // base case
5.         return;
6.      midIndex = (rightIndex + leftIndex) / 2;
7.      mergeSort(items, temp, leftIndex, midIndex); // first reduced problem
8.      mergeSort(items, temp, midIndex + 1, rightIndex); // second reduced
                                                          // problem
9.      merge(items, temp, leftIndex, midIndex+1, rightIndex); // general solution
10.     return;
11.  } // end of mergeSort method
12.  public static void merge(int items[], int temp[], int leftIndex,
13.                           int midIndex, int rightIndex)
14.  {  int leftEnd, nItems, tempsIndex;
15.     leftEnd = midIndex - 1;
16.     tempsIndex = leftIndex;
17.     nItems = rightIndex - leftIndex + 1;
18.     while ((leftIndex <= leftEnd) && (midIndex <= rightIndex)) // move items
                                                                  // into temp
19.     {  if (items[leftIndex] <= items[midIndex]) // from left sublist
20.        {  temp[tempsIndex] = items[leftIndex];
21.           tempsIndex = tempsIndex + 1;
22.           leftIndex = leftIndex + 1;
23.        }
24.        else // move item from right sublist into temp
25.        {  temp[tempsIndex] = items[midIndex];
26.           tempsIndex = tempsIndex + 1;
27.           midIndex = midIndex + 1;
28.        }
29.     } // end while
30.     if(leftIndex <= leftEnd) // left sublist (LS) is not empty
31.     {  while (leftIndex <= leftEnd) // copy remainder of LS into temp
32.        {  temp[tempsIndex] = items[leftIndex];
33.           leftIndex = leftIndex + 1;
34.           tempsIndex = tempsIndex + 1;
35.        }
36.     } // end if
37.     else // right sublist (RS) is not empty
38.     {  while (midIndex <= rightIndex) // copy reminder of RS into temp
39.        {  temp[tempsIndex] = items[midIndex];
40.           midIndex = midIndex + 1;
41.           tempsIndex = tempsIndex + 1;
42.        }
43.     }
44.     for (int i = 0; i < nItems; i++) // copy array temp into array items
45.     {  items[rightIndex] = temp[rightIndex];
46.        rightIndex = rightIndex - 1;
47.     }
48.  } // end merge method
```

Figure 8.17 The Merge Sort

Table 8.4

Number of Passes through the Merge Sort Algorithm Required to Sort *n* Items

Number of Items Sorted, *n*	Number of Passes, P_{MS}
0	0
2	1
4	2
8	3
16	4
32	5

are required to sort eight items. If we assume that the original data set contained four items (for example the integers 93, 3, 50, and 21, depicted on the left side of the lower level of the figure) then, as shown in the figure, two passes would be required to complete the sort. Finally, if the original data set had contained only two items (for example the integers 93 and 3, shown on the left side of the lower level of the figure) then, (as depicted in the figure) one pass would be required to complete the sort. From these observations, which are tabulated and extrapolated (last two rows) in Table 8.4, we can deduce that the number of passes through this algorithm can be expressed as:

Number of Passes Through the Merge Sort Algorithm

$$P_{MS} = \log_2 n$$

Equation (8.1)

To find the number of comparisons made on each pass through the algorithm, we consider two cases that represent the minimum and maximum number of comparisons per pass.

1. All the items in one sublist are less than all the items in the other sublist.
2. The sublist location of the item written into the array `temp` alternates between the sublists.

An example of the first case would be the sublists 3, 21, 30, 50, and 85, 93, 99, 107. In this example, after $n/2$ comparisons (3 compared to 85, 21 compared to 85, etc.), all of the items in the first sublist would be moved into the array `temp`, and the pass would end after the items in the second list were simply copied into `temp`.

An example of the second case would be the sublists 3, 30, 85, 99 and 21, 50, 93, 107. In this example, after $n - 1$ comparisons (3 compared to 21, 30 compared to 21, 30 compared to 50, 85 compared to 50, 85 compared to 93, etc.), all of the items in both sublists, except 107, would have been moved into the array `temp`, and the pass would end after 107 was copied into `temp`. Since the two cases represent the minimum and maximum number of comparisons performed to complete a pass, to approximate the average number of comparisons for the Merge Sort, C_{Ams}, we will simply average these two extremes.

Approximate Average Number of Comparisons Per Pass Through the Merge Sort

$$C_{Ams} \cong [(n/2) + (n-1)]/2 \cong [(n/2) + (n)]/2 = 3n/4 \quad \boxed{\textbf{Equation (8.2)}}$$

Expressing the sort effort, SE_{MS}, as the number of passes times the average number of comparisons per pass, using Equations 8.1 and 8.2 we obtain:

$$SE_{MS} = P_{MS} * C_{Ams} \cong (3n/4)\log_2 n = (0.75n)\log_2 n.$$

During each pass through the algorithm, all n items are swapped from the array `items` into the array `temp` and back again resulting in $2n$ swaps per pass. Since $\log_2 n$ passes are performed, the total number of swaps is

$$2n\log_2 n = (2 * SE_{MS})/0.75 = 2.67\ SE_{MS}.$$

Memory Overhead

The memory overhead associated with this sorting algorithm is essentially the storage associated with the n element array `temp`. Each element of `temp` stores either a primitive value (the items being sorted) or a reference to the objects being sorted. In either case, each element of the array is 4 bytes wide, resulting in an overhead of $4n$ bytes.

Table 8.5 summarizes the performance of the Merge Sort algorithm, its speed and memory overhead, and includes the performance of the other sort algorithms we have studied for comparative purposes. As noted in the comments column, this algorithm's speed (like the Heap Sort) is fast for all data sets. However, it does require a moderate amount of overhead ($4n$ bytes).

8.3.5 Quicksort

The Quicksort algorithm, if not the most popular sorting algorithm, is certainly the one most written about. A recent search of the internet with a popular browser revealed that there were 3.8 million more hits for information on this algorithm than the combined hits for all the other algorithms discussed in this chapter. Its popularity is based on the simplicity of its recursive implementation (it can be coded in 20 executable Java statements) and its average speed. Still, there are data sets for which the other sorts we have studied far outperform it.

During each pass through this algorithm, the data item in the middle of the unsorted array is chosen to be a *pivot value*. By the end of the pass the item is positioned into its proper sorted place in the array, partitioning it into two parts. In addition, the other items in the array have been positioned such that the values of the items to the left of the pivot value are all less than it, and the values to the right of the pivot are all greater than it. To complete the algorithm, the left and right partitions are considered unsorted arrays, and the algorithm operates each of them (I hope you guessed it) recursively.

Table 8.5

The Performance of the Merge Sort Algorithm

Algorithm	Speed		Memory Overhead		Comments
	Range	Effort	Range	Bytes	
Binary Tree	fast/slow $O(n\log_2 n) / O(n^2)$	$(n + 1)\,[\log_2(n + 1) - 2] < SE <= n^2/2 - n/2$	high	$8n$	Fast for random data, slow for already sorted data. Highest overhead.
Bubble	very fast/slow $O(n) / O(n^2)$	$n - 1 < SE <= n^2/2 - n/2$ $0 < $ Number of swaps $< SE / 2$	low	4	Fast for data almost sorted in ascending order. Slow for most data sets. Low overhead. Easy to code.
Heap	fast $O(n\log_2 n)$	$SE < 3n\log_2(n)$ Number of swaps $= 2SE / 3$	low	4	Fast for all data sets. Low overhead.
Merge Sort	fast $O(n\log_2 n)$	$SE \cong (0.75n)\log_2 n$ Number of swaps $= 2.67SE$	moderate	$4n$	Fast for all data sets. Moderate overhead.

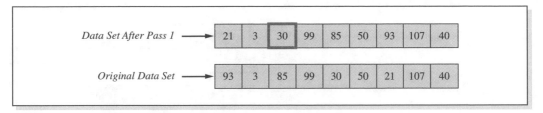

Figure 8.18   Data Set after One Pass Through the Quicksort

Figure 8.18 shows an array of integers before and after the first pass through the algorithm. The integer in the middle of the original data set, 30, was chosen as the pivot value. When the pass is complete, 30 is in its final sorted order position. In addition, the integers 21, 93, and 85 have been relocated so that every integer to the left of 30 (said to be in the *left partition*) is less than it, and every integer that is greater than 30 is to the right of it (said to be in the *right partition*). As mentioned above, the two partitions are then operated on by the algorithm recursively.

The steps required to reposition the items during a pass is illustrated in Figure 8.19 using the set of integers depicted in Figure 8.18. To start a pass through the algorithm, the pivot value is set to the value of the item in the middle of the array, 30. Two variables i and j are set to the highest and lowest index of the array (0 and 8). For convenience, we will refer to i and j as pointers and say that they are set "pointing to" elements of the array. Thus, initially the pointers are set to point to the items stored in the highest and lowest elements of the array.

After their initialization, the pointers are moved toward each other (i is incremented, j is decremented) until each one is pointing to an item in the wrong partition. (In our case, an item is in the wrong partition if it is ≥ 30 and pointed to by i, or ≤ 30 and pointed to by j.) When both pointers have located an item in the wrong partition (93 and 21), the values are swapped. The contents of the array and the position of the pointers just before the first swap are shown at the bottom of Figure 8.19.

After the swap, the pointers are moved toward each other to locate two other items to be swapped. The contents of the array and the position of the pointers just before the second swap are shown in the middle portion Figure 8.19. This process continues until the pointers cross. The top portion of the figure shows that the movement of the pointers has caused them to cross (i to the right of j), which ends the pass.

As we have stated, the algorithm is unusually simple when expressed recursively. Following our recursive methodology, the original problem is to sort the data contained in an array (items) contained between two given indices (leftIndex and rightIndex). Stated more succinctly,

```
quickSort(items, leftIndex, rightIndex)
```

Since the problem involves a given number of items to be sorted (rightIndex - leftIndex +1), the base case once again is when there is only one item to be sorted. In this case nothing is done. The reduced problem is to apply the sorting algorithm to the two partitions. The left boundary of

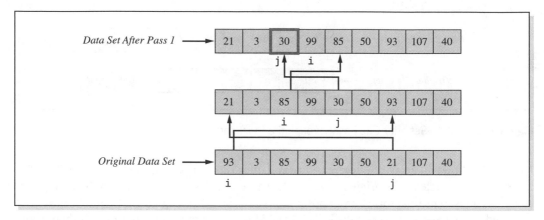

Figure 8.19 The Pointer Locations and Swaps during the First Pass of the Quicksort

the left partition is still `leftIndex`, and the right boundary of the right partition is still `rightIndex`. The two other boundaries of the partitions can be seen in the top part of Figure 8.19. Since the algorithm ends when the pointers have crossed, the right boundary of the left partition is `j`, and the left boundary of the right partition is `i`. Thus, the reduced problems are:

```
quickSort(items, leftIndex,  j)
quickSort(items, rightIndex, i)
```

The general solution is to build the partitions and then invoke the reduced problems. The pseudocode of the algorithm is given below, which assumes the items to be sorted are stored between the indices `leftIndex` and `rightIndex` in the array items.

The Quicksort Algorithm

```
1.    partitionSize = rightIndex − leftIndex + 1;
2.    if(partitionSize <= 1) // base case, one item to be sorted
3.       return;
4.
5.    pivotValue = items[(leftIndex + rightIndex) / 2];
6.    i = leftIndex; // initialize the two partition indices
7.    j = rightIndex;
8.
9.    do
10.   { while (items[i] < pivotValue) // left partition item is in the correct partition
11.        i++;
12.      while (items[j] > pivotValue) // right partition item is in the correct partition
```

```
13.        j--;
14.      if (i <= j) // pointers have not crossed, switch items in wrong partition
15.      { temp = items[i];   items[i] = items[j];   items[j]=temp;
16.        i++;   j--;
17.      }
18.    } while (i <= j); // the pointers have not crossed
19.
20.    quickSort(items, leftIndex, j);      //reduced problems: sort left partition,
21.    quickSort(items, i, rightIndex);     // sort right partition
```

Lines 1–3 of the algorithm are the base case which ends the algorithm (Line 3) when the number of items is <= 1. Lines 5–7 determine the pivot value and initialize the left and right pointers, i and j. Lines 10–18 constitute a loop that continues until the pointers cross (Line 18). The pointers are repositioned on Lines 10–13, and the array elements are swapped on Line 15, assuming the pointers have not crossed (Line 14). Line 16 moves the pointers after a swap. Lines 20 and 21 sort the left and right partitions recursively.

Implementation

The Java implementation of the Quicksort pseudocode is given in Figure 8.20. With the exception of the method heading and the variable declarations on Line 2, it is a line-for-line translation of the pseudocode into Java.

Speed

Now let us consider the speed complexity of the algorithm by examining its sort effort. The total number of comparisons performed by this algorithm can be expressed as the number of passes through the algorithm times the number of comparisons performed during each pass.

When sorting n items, $n + 2$ comparisons are made during each pass though the algorithm. We can see this by examining the first pass shown in Figure 8.19, which is typical of the other passes. The top row of the figure shows the pointers i and j in their final positions. A total of four comparisons were made to position i at 99 (the values 93, 3, 85, and 99 were all compared to the pivot value 30). Similarly, a total of seven comparisons were made to position the pointer j at 30 (the values 40, 107, 21, 50, 30, 99, and 30, were all compared to the pivot value 30). In all, 11 (= 4 + 7) comparisons were made (= $n + 2$ for our nine item list).

The number of passes made depends on the character of the data set. If the data set is such that the pivot values' correct positions are always in the *middle* of the partitions, then the left and right partitions will always be the same size ($\pm$ 1). In this case, one item is positioned on the first pass,

```
1.   public static void quickSort(int [] items, int leftIndex, int rightIndex)
2.   {  int i, j, temp, pivotValue, partitionSize;
3.        partitionSize = rightIndex - leftIndex + 1;
4.        if(partitionSize <= 1) // base case, one item to be sorted
5.           return;
6.
7.        pivotValue = items[(leftIndex + rightIndex) / 2];
8.        i = leftIndex; // initialize the two partition indices
9.        j = rightIndex;
10.   // look for items in wrong partitions and switch them
11.      do
12.      {  while (items[i] < pivotValue) // left item is in correct partition
13.             i++;
14.         while (items[j] > pivotValue) // right item is in correct partition
15.             j--;
16.         if (i <= j) // pointers have not crossed, switch items
17.         {  temp = items[i];    items[i] = items[j];    items[j]=temp;
18.            i++; j--;
19.         }
20.      } while (i <= j); // the pointers have not crossed
21.   // reduced problems
22.      quickSort(items, leftIndex, j); // sort left partition,
23.      quickSort(items, i, rightIndex); // sort right partition
24.   }
```

Figure 8.20 The Quicksort

two additional items (one per partition) are positioned on the second pass (1 + 2 = 3 in total), four additional items (one per partition) are positioned on the third pass (3 + 4 = 7 in total), eight additional items (one per partition) are positioned on the fourth pass (7 + 8 = 15 in total), etc. Assuming that p is the pass number, this means that a total of $2^p - 1$ items are positioned after pass p. Since the sort ends when a total of n items are positioned, the sort ends when $n = 2^p - 1$. Solving this for p we find that $p = \log_2(n - 1)$. Therefore, when the character of the data set is such that the pivot value's correct position is always in the middle of the partitions, $\log_2(n - 1)$ passes are made through the algorithm.

When the character of the data set is such that the pivot values' correct positions are always at one end of the partitions, then one of the partitions will contain one item, and the other will contain all the other items. One item is positioned on the first pass. We will assume it is positioned as the leftmost element of the array, making the length of the left partition one. On the second pass through the algorithm, since the length of the left partition is one, there are no additional items in the left partition to position; therefore, only one additional item (one from the right partition) is positioned on the second pass. Since this is once again positioned at the left end of the partition, the third pass will also position only one item. This one item partition dilemma continues for all subsequent passes through the algorithm. As a result, when the character of the data set is such that the pivot values' correct positions are always at an end of the partition, then n passes are made to complete the sort. Thus the number of passes, p, required by the Quicksort to sort n items is: $\log_2(n - 1) \leq p \leq n$.

There is, however, some good news. Empirical studies show that the average number of passes to sort is $1.45 \log_2 n$, which means that the data set characteristics that produce the one item partitions do not occur very often. Combining this result with the number of comparisons per pass, we find the average sort effort for the Quicksort, SE_{QSAvg}, to be:

$$SE_{QSAvg} = \text{number of comparisons per pass } * \text{ number of passes} = (n + 2) * 1.45 \log_2 n,$$
$$\cong 1.45n\log_2 n,$$

which is $O(n\log_2 n)$.

On average, the sort effort of this algorithm approaches the theoretical minimum. When we consider the swaps performed by the algorithm it is reasonable to assume that, on average, only half of the $n / 2$ items ($n / 4$ items) distributed over the partitions will need to be swapped during each pass through the algorithm. Remembering that the algorithm requires an average of $1.45 \log_2 n$ passes, the total number of swaps is $n/4 * 1.45 \log_2 n = 0.25SE_{QSAvg}$.

Overhead

The overhead associated with this sorting algorithm is the storage required to keep track of the ends of the partitions. Specifically, a pair of the algorithm's pointers (i and j) would be allocated on the runtime stack for each level of recursion the algorithm enters. When the data set is such that the number of passes though the algorithm is $\log_2(n - 1)$, the deepest level of recursion is $\log_2(n - 1)$. Thus, a total of $2 \log_2(n - 1)$ pointers are allocated during the recursive decent to the base case. Adding the two pointers that are allocated before the first recursive invocation, the total number of pointers is $2 + 2 \log_2(n - 1)$. Assuming 4 bytes per pointer variable, the overhead is $8 + 8 \log_2(n - 1)$ bytes, $O(\log_2 n)$.

Table 8.6 summarizes the performance of the Quicksort algorithm, its speed and memory overhead, and includes the performance of the other sorting algorithms studied in this chapter for comparative purposes. As noted in the comments column, this algorithm is the fastest (for most data sets), its overhead is low, and it is easy to code. These attributes account for its popularity. We must remember, however, that for some rare data sets, the speed of this algorithm is $O(n^2)$ and its overhead is 8n.

Subtle but important changes can be made to each of the $O(\log_2 n)$ algorithms to improve their speed. Studies indicate that when these changes are incorporated into the algorithms, the Merge Sort and the Quicksort algorithms emerge as the fastest sorting algorithms with the best performer being dependent on the number of items being sorted and the character of the data set (random, almost sorted, or sorted).

Table 8.6

Performance of the Quicksort Algorithm

Algorithm	Speed		Memory Overhead		Comments
	Range	Effort	Range	Bytes	
Binary Tree	fast/slow $O(n\log_2 n)$ / $O(n^2)$	$(n+1)[\log_2(n+1)-2] < SE <= n^2/2 - n/2$	high	$8n$	Fast for random data, slow for already sorted data. Highest overhead.
Bubble	very fast/slow $O(n)$ / $O(n^2)$	$n - 1 < SE <= n^2/2 - n/2$ $0 <$ Number of swaps $< SE / 2$	lowest	4	Fast for data almost sorted in ascending order. Slow for most data sets. Low overhead. Easy to code.
Heap	fast $O(n\log_2 n)$	$SE < 3n\log_2(n)$ Number of swaps = 2SE / 3	lowest	4	Fast for all data sets. Low overhead.
Merge Sort	fast $O(n\log_2 n)$	$SE \cong (0.75n)\log_2 n$ Number of swaps = 2.67SE	moderate	$4n$	Fast for all data sets. Moderate overhead.
Quicksort	fast/slow	$(n+2)\log_2(n-1) \le SE \le n^2$ Average = 1.45 $n\log_2(n)$ Number of swaps = 0.25SE	low	$8 + 8*\log_2(n-1)$	Fastest for most data sets, but could be $O(n^2)$ for certain data sets. Easy to code. Low overhead.

Knowledge Exercises

1. Define the term "sorting."

2. Give two reasons for sorting a data set.

3. Give a condition under which it would not be advantageous to store a set of nodes in sorted order.

4. Give three factors to be considered in selecting a sorting algorithm for a particular application.

5. Define the term "sort effort."

6. Give an expression for the minimum number of comparisons required to sort n items.

7. My friend has told me that he has discovered an algorithm that performs 5,000,000 comparisons to sort 1,000,000 items, regardless of the character of the data set. Should I believe him, and why?

8. Calculate the time (in minutes and seconds) required to sort 10,000,000 items on a system that performs a comparison in two nanoseconds, assuming the sorting algorithm's sort effort is (don't consider swaps):

   a. n

   b. $n\log_2(n)$

   c. n^2

9. To reposition two nodes into sorted order, is it more desirable to perform a shallow or deep copy of the nodes? Why?

10. Under what conditions is the Binary Tree Sort fast?

11. Calculate the minimum and maximum number of comparisons required to sort 1,000,000 items using the Binary Tree Sort.

12. Give the times, (in minutes and seconds) to perform the sort described in the previous exercise on a machine that performs one comparison in one-half nanosecond (don't consider swaps).

13. The integers 65, 80, 70, 18, 86, 6, and 37 are to be sorted using the Binary Tree Sort. Assume the integers are processed by the algorithm in the order given.

    a.   Show the binary tree that results from sorting.

    b.   As the integers are placed in the tree, count the number of comparisons made. What is the total number of comparisons?

14. Repeat parts (a) and (b) of the previous exercise, but this time process the integers in the order 86, 80, 70, 65, 37, 18, and finally 6.

15. Why is the variable `flip` included in the Bubble Sort algorithm?

16. The integers 65, 80, 70, 18, 86, 6, and 37 are stored sequentially in an array with 65 stored in element 0 and 37 stored in element 6. The Bubble Sort is used to sort them. Trace the execution

EXERCISES

of the sort by constructing a table similar to the one presented in Figure 8.7. Shade the elements being compared.

17. Count the number of comparisons made on each pass through the sort performed in the previous exercise and present the result as a tabulation of pass number vs. number of comparisons.

18. If a Bubble Sort does not end early, how many comparisons are required to sort n items?

19. What is the minimum number of comparisons necessary to sort n items using the Bubble Sort?

20. Give an example of a 10-item data set that would be sorted quickly by the Bubble Sort.

21. True or false? The memory overhead associated with the Binary Tree Sort is less than that of the memory overhead associated with the Bubble Sort.

22. The integers 65, 80, 70, 18, 86, 6, and 37 are stored sequentially in an array with 65 stored in element 0 and 37 stored in element 6. Draw the binary tree represented by the array.

23. Define the term "heap."

24. Is the tree discussed in Exercise 20 a heap? If not, identify the contents of the array that is preventing it from being a heap.

25. How does the Reheap Downward algorithm get its name?

26. The integers 65, 80, 70, 18, 86, 6, and 37 are stored sequentially in an array with 65 stored in element 0, and 37 stored in element 6. The Reheap Downward algorithm is used to arrange the integers into a heap. Trace the execution of the algorithm by drawing a sequence of trees similar to the ones depicted in Figure 8.11. In your figures, shade the elements being compared.

27. Show the changes to the array discussed in the previous exercise in a table similar to the one shown in Figure 8.12.

28. Draw the tree representation of the array shown in column t of Figure 8.14.

29. Show the changes made to the tree drawn in the previous exercise in order to sort the remaining four integers (7, 3, 2, and 1) using the Heap Sort.

30. Show the changes to the array of integers shown in column s of Figure 8.14 that reflect the changes to the trees drawn in the previous exercise. Produce a table similar to the one shown in Figure 8.14.

31. A 16 element array stores the integers 81, 16, 2, 89, 54, 23, 76, 25, 37, 107, 1, 74, 45, 16, 31, and 58 in elements 0 through 15, respectively. They are to be sorted using the merge sort.

    a. How many passes will be performed to complete the sort?

    b. Show the contents of the array at the beginning of the sort and after each pass.

    c. Count the number of comparisons that were made to sort the 16 items.

    d. Count the number of swaps made to complete the sort of the 16 items.

e. Compare your answers in parts (c) and (d) of this question to results obtained when the formulas presented in Table 8.6 are used.

32. What characteristic of a data set makes the Quicksort slow?

33. The array described in Exercise 31 is to be sorted using the Quicksort.

    a. How many passes will be performed to complete the sort?

    b. Show the contents of the array at the beginning of the sort and after the first two passes.

    c. How many partitions will there be after pass three?

    d. Give the total number of comparisons and swaps performed by the algorithm using the formulas presented in Table 8.6.

Programming Exercises

34. Code the Bubble Sort in a static method whose parameter is an array of integers to be sorted. Provide a driver program to demonstrate that the method functions properly.

35. Modify the method described in the above exercise so that it counts and outputs the number of comparisons and swaps performed during each pass through the algorithm.

36. Code the Reheap Downward algorithm in a static method and code a driver program to demonstrate that it functions properly. The array to be built into a heap should be passed to the method. Use the tree shown in Figure 8.13b and e (less item 100) as test data for your driver program.

37. Modify the Reheap Downward method coded in the previous exercise so that the index of the root node of the tree and the size of the array are passed to the method as parameters: reheapDown(int[] array, int root, int size). Provide a driver program to demonstrate that the method functions properly. Use the arrays shown in Figure 8.12c and Figures 8.14b and f as test data for your method. In each case, output the contents of the array before and after the method is invoked. The invocations for the three test cases should be:

```
reheapDown(array, 1, 9);
reheapDown(array, 0, 8);
reheapDown(array, 0, 7); respectively.
```

38. Code the Heap Sort algorithm and provide a driver program to demonstrate that it functions properly. (Hint: complete the previous exercise first.)

39. Code the Merge Sort in such a way that it outputs the number of comparisons and the number of swaps performed when sorting a random set of items. Then use it to sort 1000, 5000, 10,000, and 100,000 integers. Tabulate the results and compare it to the number of comparisons and swaps calculated using the formulas given in Table 8.6.

40. Repeat Exercise 39 for the Quicksort.

EXERCISES

41. Write a GUI application that demonstrates the changes to a six-element array of integers as it is sorted by the Bubble Sort (see Figure 8.7). The user should be able to enter the initial data set and be able to interact with the program using GUI buttons to perform the follow functions:

    a. Initiate the sort from the beginning of any pass to completion.

    b. Step through the sort, one comparison at a time, from the beginning of any pass to the sort's completion.

    c. Reset the sort to its initial condition.

42. Write a GUI application that demonstrates the changes to an eight-element array of integers as it is sorted by the Heap Sort (see Figures 8.12 and 8.14). The changes to the heap tree should also be depicted (see Figures 8.11 and 8.13). The user should be able to enter the initial data set and be able to interact with the program using GUI buttons to perform the follow functions:

    a. Initiate the sort from the beginning of any pass to completion.

    b. Step through the sort, one comparison at a time, from the beginning of any pass to the sort's completion.

    c. Reset the sort to its initial condition.

43. Write a GUI application that demonstrates the changes to a sixteen-element array of integers (and the temporary array) as the integers are sorted by the Merge Sort (see Figure 8.16). The user should be able to enter the initial data set and be able to interact with the program using GUI buttons to perform the follow functions:

    a. Initiate the sort from the beginning of any pass to completion.

    b. Step through the sort, one comparison at a time, from the beginning of any pass to the sort's completion.

    c. Reset the sort to its initial condition.

44. Write a GUI application that demonstrates the changes to an eight-element array of integers as it is sorted by the Quicksort (see Figure 8.19). The user should be able to enter the initial data set and be able to interact with the program using GUI buttons to perform the follow functions:

    a. Initiate the sort from the beginning of any pass to completion.

    b. Step through the sort, one comparison at a time, from the beginning of any pass to the sort's completion.

    c. Reset the sort to its initial condition.

45. Implement a Priority Queue structure using a heap. Provide an application that demonstrates your structure functions properly.

CHAPTER 9

Graphs

OBJECTIVES

The objective of this chapter is to familiarize the student with the features, implementation, and uses of graph structures. More specifically, the student will be able to

- Understand that trees and linked lists are subsets of graphs, and understand the characteristics of trees and linked lists that restrict them to subsets.

- Understand the standard graphics used to depict graphs, the terminology of graphs, and the mathematics of graphs.

- Understand the array-based, linked, and hybrid memory models programmers use to represent graph structures, and the advantages and disadvantages of these representations.

- Be able to determine the best representation for a particular graph.

- Understand the differences between digraphs and undirected graphs, weighted and unweighted graphs, and their uses in problem modeling.

- Understand the modes used to access nodes stored in graphs and the basic operations performed on graphs, including depth-first and breadth-first traversals.

- Implement a fully encapsulated version of a graph structure that includes a traversal operation, and use the implementation in an application program.

- Understand, and be able to explain, the concepts related to graph connectivity and path (including spanning trees and minimum spanning trees), and be familiar with a set of problems that involve these concepts.

- Understand and be able to implement the classic graph algorithms related to connectivity and path (Warshall's algorithm, spanning and minimum spanning tree algorithms, Dijkstra's algorithm, and Floyd's algorithm), and be able to identify applications of these algorithms.

9.1   Introduction

To put the material of this chapter into the context of what we have discussed so far in this text, graphs are very similar to trees and linked lists. In fact, trees and linked lists are subsets of the broader topic, graphs.

Like trees and linked lists, graphs are composed of a collection of nodes, which are called *vertices* in graph theory. Vertices, like the nodes of trees and linked lists, store information. In trees and linked lists there is an ordering to the nodes that implies certain nodes are adjacent to other nodes. For example, in a tree, the adjacency relationship is expressed as a parent–child relationship, while in linked lists, the adjacency relationship is a *predecessor–next* relationship. The vertices of a graph also have an ordering to them, and the relationship is called *adjacency*. If two nodes that are positioned in a tree as parent and child were to appear in a graph, they would be said to be *adjacent vertices*. In the case of trees and linked lists, adjacent nodes are depicted with lines or arrows drawn between them. Similarly, depictions of graphs use lines and arrows between adjacent vertices. In graphs, these lines and arrows are called *edges*.

Where graphs differ from trees and linked lists has to do with the graph's edges. As we will see, in a graph there are no restrictions on which vertices can be adjacent. An edge can connect any two distinct vertices in the graph.[1] That was not the case for trees and linked lists. For example, two siblings in a tree could not be adjacent (have an edge between them), and at least one of the nodes in a tree had to have no children (be a leaf node). In addition, the edges in a graph can also contain a piece of information, called the edge weighting, that is not relevant to a tree or a linked list.

To illustrate the similarities and differences between graphs, trees, and linked lists consider the six graphs depicted in Figure 9.1. Figure 9.1**a** depicts a graph that is also a tree and a linked list. Viewing it as a tree, its root node would be node A, and B would be A's left child. Viewing it as a linked list, we could consider A to be the first node in the list, and B the last node in the list. Figure 9.1**b** adds another edge and another vertex, C, to the graph. This graph is no longer a linked list since there are now two nodes after node A. However, it is still a tree with vertex A being the parent of

---

[1]This implies the edge does not begin and end at the same vertex.

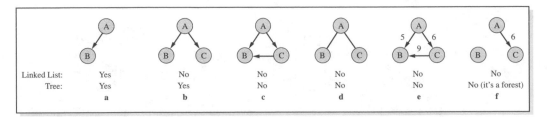

Figure 9.1   Six Graphs, Two Trees, and One Linked List

vertices B and C. Figure 9.1**c** depicts the graph with another edge added to it between vertices B and C. This graph is no longer a tree because B does not have a unique predecessor. For example, we can reach B from A or C. However, in a graph, an edge can connect any two nodes, so connecting B and C is valid.

Figures 9.1**d, e,** and **f** depict three more valid graphs in which the edges possess features that cannot be present in trees or linked lists. In Figure 9.1**d,** the arrows representing the edges have been replaced with lines. Although this looks like a tree, it is not, because a line connecting two vertices in a graph eliminates the parent–child relationship essential to all trees.[2] Node A can no longer be considered a parent node. Figure 9.1**e** illustrates the concept of an *edge weighting*, which is not a concept used in trees or linked lists. In this graph, the edge between C and B carries more weight then the other two edges in the graph (i.e., 9 > 5 and 6). Finally, in Figure 9.1**f** the edge between vertices A and B, and the edge between vertices B and C have been eliminated. In a graph, unlike a tree or a linked list, a vertex need not have an adjacent vertex.

Of the problems in computer science whose solutions use graphs, many do not need the additional edge properties that are not available in trees and linked lists. We have seen examples of these problems in the preceding chapters that discussed these structures. However, there is a set of very interesting and important problems whose solutions are greatly simplified when they are modeled using these additional properties. For example, a GPS navigation system uses graphs in the algorithm that determines the shortest route to a destination. The road intersections are represented as the graph's vertices, and its edges represent the roads between the intersections. The distances between the intersections are the weightings. A similar problem is the determination of the cheapest way to fly from Indianapolis to Miami. In this problem, the hub airports would be represented by the graph's vertices, the edges would represent the flights between them, and the edge weightings would be the cost of the flights.

In the 18th century, the mathematician Leonard Euler examined one of the earliest problems involving graph theory. In this problem, known as the Bridges of Koningsberg, the residents of the town wanted to know if there was a way to stroll across all seven bridges that connected an island to the rest of the town, and return to the starting point, without crossing the same bridge twice

---

[2]It is only for graphical convenience that standard tree graphics (like those presented in Chapter 7) do not use arrows. Rather, the parent–child relationship between two nodes is implied by their relative position in the graphic.

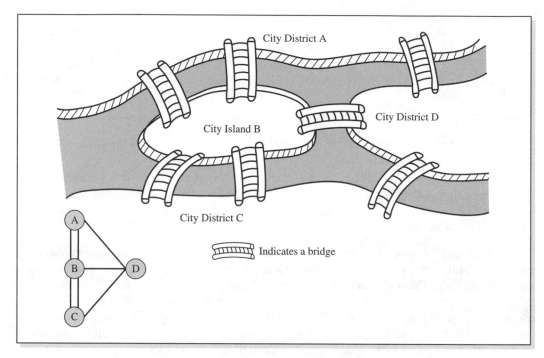

Figure 9.2   The Seven Bridges of Koningsberg and its Graphical Representation

(see Figure 9.2). Euler modeled the problem using the graph shown in the left portion of Figure 9.2, using the vertices to represent the land masses and the graph's edges to represent the bridges. Then, using graph theory, Euler was able to prove that because of the arrangement of the bridges and the land masses, the stroll was impossible. In fact, he produced a more general solution that states that a stroll like this is possible if and only if the number of edges incident on (leading to) each vertex is even. Since an inspection of the graphical representation of the problem shown in the left portion of Figure 9.2 reveals that this is not the case (e.g., the number of edges incident on vertex D is 3), the Koningsberg stroll is impossible.

Before proceeding to a discussion of how graphs are represented in memory and the algorithms used to operate on them, it is necessary to gain an understanding of the depictions and terminology of graphs, and also two mathematical implications of the terminology.

9.1.1 Graphics and Terminology of Graphs

Standard Depiction of a Graph

In the standard depiction of a graph the vertices are represented by circles and the edges are represented by either lines or arrows drawn between two vertices. Figures 9.1 and 9.2 present examples of the standard graph depictions, which typically contain either all arrows or all lines to represent the graph's edges. Arrows and lines are never mixed in a depiction of a graph. Arrows are used to indicate the allowed *one way* direction of travel between the two vertices the edge connects. Lines indicate that *bidirectional* travel is allowed along the edge.

Graph

A graph is a set of vertices and a set of edges that connect pairs of vertices.

Undirected Graph

An undirected graph is a graph in which all edges permit bidirectional travel. In these graphs the edges are depicted as lines (not arrows). The graphs shown in Figures 9.1**d** and Figure 9.2 are examples of undirected graphs. The wires and solder joints on a printed circuit board form an undirected graph (the solder joints being the graph's vertices and the wires being the graph's edges) because electricity can flow between the solder joints in either direction.

Directed Graphs (Digraphs)

A directed graph, also known as a *digraph*, is a graph in which all of the graph's edges permit travel in only one direction. To depict the direction of travel, the edges of a digraph are drawn as arrows in their graphical representation. With the exception of Figure 9.1**c**, all of the graphs shown in Figure 9.1 are examples of directed graphs. The one-way grid of streets in a large city would be an example of a digraph with each street being an edge of the graph and the intersections being its vertices. It could be the case that travel is permitted in both directions between two vertices in a digraph. When this is the case, the vertices are considered to have two distinct edges represented by two opposite-facing arrows in their graphical depiction. An example of this would be a large city in which some of the streets were two-way streets. In much of the literature, the undirected graphs are referred to simply as graphs, and directed graphs are referred to as digraphs.

Weighted Graphs

A weighted graph is a directed or undirected graph in which each edge has a weighting factor assigned to it. The graph depicted in Figure 9.1**e** is a weighted graph. The weighting factors could be used to represent the lengths of the interstate highways between the points at which they intersect.

Adjacent Vertices

Two vertices are said to be adjacent if there is an edge between them. All of the vertices in the graphs depicted in Figures 9.1**a–e** have at least one adjacent vertex. However, vertices B and C in Figures 9.1**b** and 9.1**d** are not adjacent, nor are the vertices A and B, or vertices B and C in the graph depicted in Figure 9.1**f**.

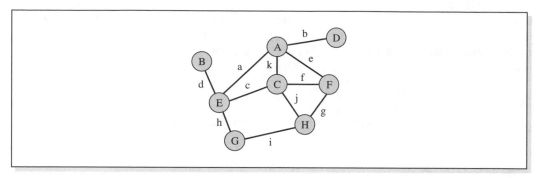

Figure 9.3   An Undirected Graph

Path

A path is a sequence of edges that connects two vertices in a graph. Referring to the undirected graph depicted in Figure 9.3 whose eleven edges have been named *a, b, c, d, e, f, g, h, i, j*, and *k*, the edges *c,f,g* are a path from vertex E to vertex H, as are the edges *c,k,e,f,j*.

Simple Path

A path in which all vertices encountered along the path, except possibly the first and last vertices, are *distinct*. Referring to Figure 9.3, the path *c,f,g* is a simple path, as is the path *a,h,i,j,k*. However, the path *c,k,e,f,j* is not a simple path because the vertex C is encountered twice.

Cycle

A cycle is a path in which the first and last vertex is the same. The path *a,h,i,j,k* in Figure 9.3 is a cycle, beginning and ending with vertex A, as is the path *a,c,f,g,j,k*.

Simple Cycle

A simple cycle is a simple path in which the first and last vertex is the same. The path *a,h,i,j,k* in Figure 9.3 is a simple cycle beginning and ending with vertex A. However, the path *a,c,f,g,j,k* is not a simple cycle because the path is not simple (vertex C is encountered twice).

Path Length

In an *unweighted* graph, path length is the *number of edges* that make up a path. Referring to Figure 9.3, the path length of the path *a,c,j,i* is 4. In a weighted graph, path length is the *sum of the weighting factors* of the edges that make up a path. Referring to Figure 9.1**e**, the path length from vertex A to vertex B is either 5 or 15 depending on whether we go through C to reach B.

Connected Vertices

Two vertices are said to be connected if there is at least one path between them. All pairs of vertices in the graphs depicted in Figure 9.1 are connected, except for vertices B and C in Figure 9.1**b**, **d**, and **f**, and vertices A and B in Figure 9.1**f**. All pairs of vertices in the graph depicted in Figure 9.3 are connected.

A Connected Graph

A graph is a connected graph if, given any two of its vertices v_i and v_j, there is a path between them. The graphs depicted in Figure 9.2 and 9.3 are connected, as are the graphs shown in Figure 9.1, except for the graph shown in Figure 9.1**f**.

A Complete Graph

A graph is said to be complete if the path length between any two distinct vertices is 1. The graph in Figure 9.3 is not complete because there is no edge connecting vertex A to B, H to B, etc. The two graphs depicted in Figure 9.4, are complete. Stated another way, for an undirected graph to be complete there must be an edge connecting every vertex to every other vertex. For a directed graph to be complete there must be two edges connecting every vertex to every other vertex, so that the path length from vertex v_i to v_j is 1, and the path length from v_j to v_i is also 1. Thus, a complete digraph with n vertices will have twice as many edges as a complete undirected graph with n vertices. Both of these situations are depicted in Figure 9.4.

To derive an expression for the number of edges in a complete undirected graph with n vertices, we simply draw all the edges and count them. Beginning our count at any vertex (call it vertex A), we count $n - 1$ edges emanating from it to make its path length 1 to each of the other $n - 1$ vertices. Moving to any other vertex, B, and ignoring the edge between A and B which has already been counted, we would count another $n - 2$ distinct edges connecting it to the other $n - 2$ vertices. Continuing in this way, and only counting edges that have not been already counted, the sum of the

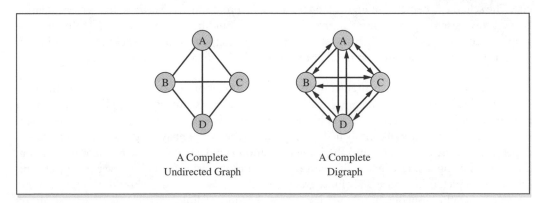

A Complete
Undirected Graph

A Complete
Digraph

Figure 9.4 Complete Graphs

edges would be $(n-1) + (n-2) + (n-3) + \ldots\ 1 = n(n-1)/2$. Therefore, in a complete undirected graph containing n vertices, there are $n(n-1)/2$ edges. Since (as we have already observed) a complete digraph with n vertices will have twice as many edges as a complete undirected graph with n vertices, a complete graph must contain $n(n-1)$ edges (= $2 * n(n-1)/2$). Thus we have:

The Number of Edges in a Complete Graph

The number of edges in a complete *undirected* graph with n vertices is $n(n-1)/2$	**Equation (9.1)**
The number of edges in a complete *digraph* with n vertices is $n(n-1)$	**Equation (9.2)**

These equations can be verified for $n = 4$ by counting the edges in the graphs depicted in Figure 9.4. The directed graph in the figure has six edges (= $4(4-1)/2$), and the digraph has 12 edges (= $4(4-1)$).

9.2   Representing Graphs

As we have discussed, a graph is composed of vertices and edges that are incident on the vertices. Stated a bit more formally, a graph G is a set of vertices V, and a set of edges, E. Thus, to represent (or store) the graph in memory we must store the set of vertices and the set of edges.

9.2.1   Representing Vertices

The set of vertices are often stored as an array of reference variables each pointing to a vertex object. The vertex object stores the information contained in the vertex. For example, if the vertices represent cities, the vertex objects could be `String` objects each containing the name of a city. The scheme is depicted in Figure 9.5**a** for a graph containing five vertices that represent cities. Being array-based, the maximum number of vertices would have to be specified at the time the graph structure is created. When the structure is implemented in the key field mode, an integer variable `next` is included to keep track of the next place to add a new vertex.

If it is impossible to accurately predict the maximum number of vertices the graph will contain, or if the number of vertices in the graph varies over a wide range during the application, the array can be expanded dynamically as the application proceeds. As discussed in Section 2.4, the expansion is most efficiently accomplished in Java with the API `arraycopy` method. Sometimes, depending on the application and the implementation language, it is more efficient to represent the vertices using a singly linked list with each node in the list referencing a vertex object. This scheme is depicted in Figure 9.5**b** for a graph containing five nodes. It should be kept in mind, however, that the noncontiguous memory representation of linked list-based structures always makes their Fetch and Delete operations slower than array-based structures.

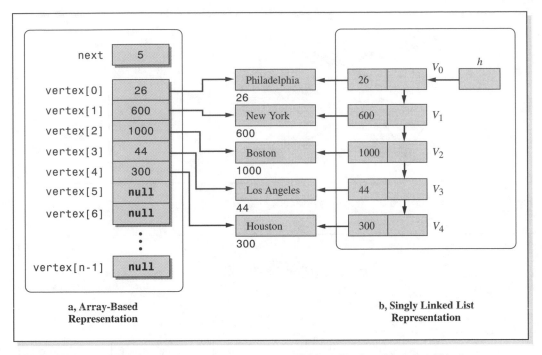

Figure 9.5 Array-Based and Linked Representations of Graph Vertices (That Are Cities)

9.2.2 Representing Edges

The edges of a graph are represented using two different schemes. The choice of which representation is used often depends on the operations that will be performed on the graph. One scheme is called an *adjacency matrix*, and the other scheme is called an *adjacency list*. We will examine them separately starting with the adjacency matrix.

Adjacency Matrix

An adjacency matrix is a square matrix in which each element stores one edge of the graph. The matrix is represented in memory as a two-dimensional array consisting of *n* rows and *n* columns, where *n* is the number of vertices in the graph. This scheme can be used when the vertices are represented using an array, as in Figure 9.5a, but is not used when the vertices are represented using a linked list as in Figure 9.5b. The rows of the adjacency array are considered parallel to the vertex array in that all of the edges that *emanate from* the vertex stored in element 0 of the vertex array, are stored in row 0 of the adjacency array. The column numbers are the vertex numbers that the edges are *incident on*. Thus, the element in row 3, column 5 of the adjacency array stores the information for the edge going from vertex 3 to vertex 5. Since a vertex in a graph cannot have an edge to itself, the elements along the diagonal from element [0][0] to element [n-1][n-1] are not used. An entry of 1 in element [i][j] of the matrix indicates that the edge from vertex i to vertex

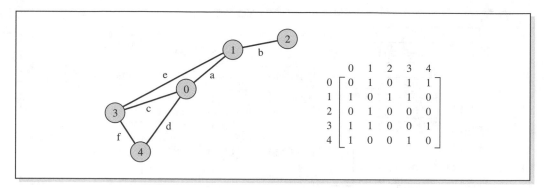

Figure 9.6   An Undirected Graph and its Adjacency Matrix

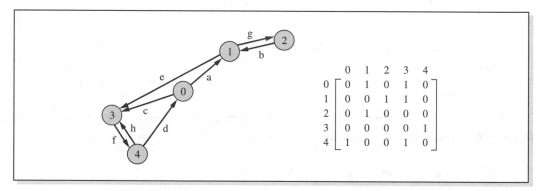

Figure 9.7   A Digraph and its Adjacency Matrix

j is present in the graph. Otherwise, the element is set to 0. Figure 9.6 depicts a five vertex graph and its corresponding adjacency matrix.

Since, in an undirected graph, the travel along the edges is bidirectional, if element `[i][j]` is 1, element `[j][i]` is also 1. Consequently, the adjacency matrix for an undirected graph is always symmetric (see Figure 9.6). This fact can save some time in algorithms that process undirected graphs because only half the array elements need to be fetched from memory. The values of the other half of the elements can be determined from those by reversing the indices (i.e., `edge [i][j] = edge [j][i]`).

Travel along the edges of a digraph is *not* bidirectional and, therefore, the adjacency matrix of a directed graph is usually not symmetric. The matrix of a digraph is symmetric only when there are two edges between pairs of vertices. Figure 9.7 depicts a digraph and its adjacency matrix.

The combination of a graph's vertex array and its adjacency matrix would be a complete representation of the graph. The complete representation of the graph depicted in Figure 9.6 is shown in Figure 9.8. The variable *edge* stores a reference to the two-dimensional edge array.

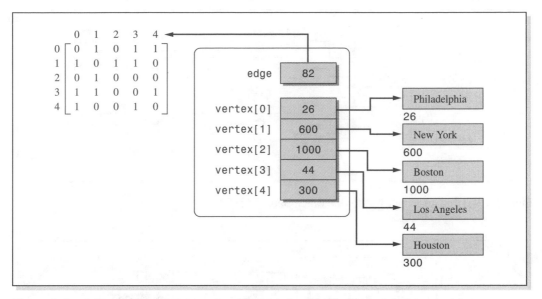

Figure 9.8 A Graph Object Representing the Graph Depicted in Figure 9.6 Using an Adjacency Matrix to Represent the Edges

Adjacency List

Aside from the four basic operations (Insert, Fetch, Delete, and Update) a common operation performed on graphs is to determine which vertices are adjacent to a given vertex, for example, vertex v_i. To accomplish this in an undirected graph, we simply examine the elements of row i of the adjacency matrix.[3] If there is a nonzero entry stored in element [i][j] of the array, then the graph contains an edge from v_i to v_j, and the two vertices are adjacent. Although the algorithm is straightforward, it does perform n memory accesses for a graph with n vertices; the algorithm is $O(n)$. Thus, even if there were only one edge emanating from a vertex in a graph that contained 1000 vertices, the algorithm would perform 1000 memory accesses to locate the adjacent vertex.

From a space complexity viewpoint an adjacency matrix can be an inefficient way to represent a graph. Consider the case when each of the 1000 vertices in a directed graph has two adjacent edges. In this case only 2000 of the 1,000,000 elements of the matrix would contain a 1. The remaining 998,000 elements would store a 0. A matrix such as this, in which most of its elements contain a default value (in our case 0, to represent no edge) is called a *sparse matrix*. From a space (and time) complexity viewpoint, sparse matrices are better represented as a set of linked lists. Enter the adjacency list.

An adjacency list is a set of n linked lists, one list per vertex, which are considered parallel to the vertex array. The first linked list stores the edges emanating from vertex 0, the second linked list

---

[3]In a directed graph, the elements in column i would also have to be examined.

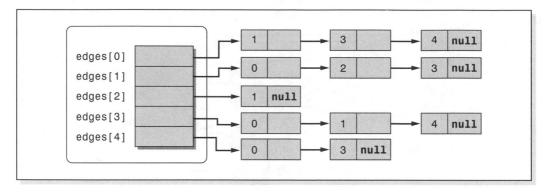

Figure 9.9   The Adjacency List for the Graph Depicted in Figure 9.6

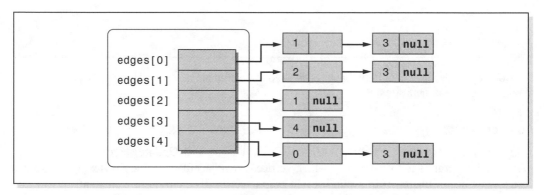

Figure 9.10   The Adjacency List for the Digraph Depicted in Figure 9.7

stores edges emanating from vertex 1, etc. Each node on the linked list contains at least two pieces of information, the vertex number of the edge it is incident upon and, of course, the location of the next node in the linked list. Figure 9.9 shows the adjacency list for the undirected graph depicted in Figure 9.6, and Figure 9.10 shows the adjacency list for the directed graph depicted in Figure 9.7.

To determine which vertices are adjacent to a given vertex under this representation of the edges, we simply traverse the vertex's linked list. Two memory accesses are required at each node in the linked list, one to fetch the adjacent vertex number and one to fetch the location of the next node in the list. Assuming there are an average of n_l vertices adjacent to each vertex in the graph, the linked lists will contain (on the average) n_l nodes; therefore, $2n_l$ memory accesses are required to determine the adjacent vertices. Since the adjacency matrix scheme requires n memory accesses to locate adjacent vertices, the speed of the two schemes are equivalent when $n = 2n_l$ or $n_l = n / 2$. Thus, for values of $n_l < n / 2$ the adjacency list scheme provides better speed performance.

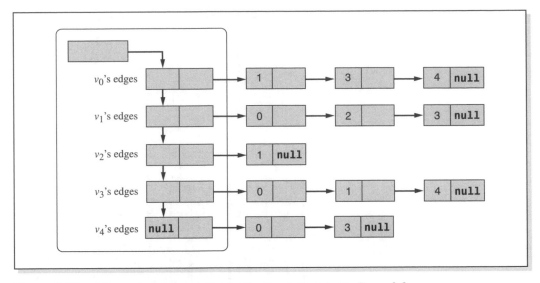

Figure 9.11   A Dynamic Adjacency List for the Graph Depicted in Figure 9.9

In a complete graph that contains n vertices, n_l would be equal to $n - 1$ (each vertex would be adjacent to the other $n - 1$ vertices). In this case, $n_l = n - 1 > n / 2$ and the adjacency matrix scheme would be the better scheme. However, since most graphs are far from complete, n_l is usually significantly less than $n / 2$ and the adjacency list is, therefore, usually the favored scheme.

When the vertices of a graph are represented using a singly linked list as depicted in Figure 9.5b, the edges are always represented using an adjacency list. Consistent with the conditions that dictate the choice of a linked representation of the vertices, the array edges, depicted in Figures 9.9 and 9.10, are replaced with a singly linked list. This allows the number of adjacency lists to grow dynamically as the number of vertices grows. Figure 9.11 shows the linked version of the adjacency list depicted in Figure 9.9. The linked list used to store the headers of the adjacency lists is considered parallel to the linked list used to represent the vertices, in that the nth node in both linked lists is dedicated to vertex n.

Figure 9.12 summarizes the three combinations of vertex and edge representations most often used to represent graphs. The two schemes on the left side of the figure use arrays that must be expanded at run-time if the maximum number of vertices in the graph cannot be accurately predicted. Of these two schemes, the lower scheme is preferred when the average number of adjacent vertices in an n vertex graph is less than $n / 2$. When the maximum number of vertices in the graph cannot be accurately predicted and the implementation language does not support a fast array copy operation, the dynamic structure on the right side of Figure 9.12 is used to represent the graph.

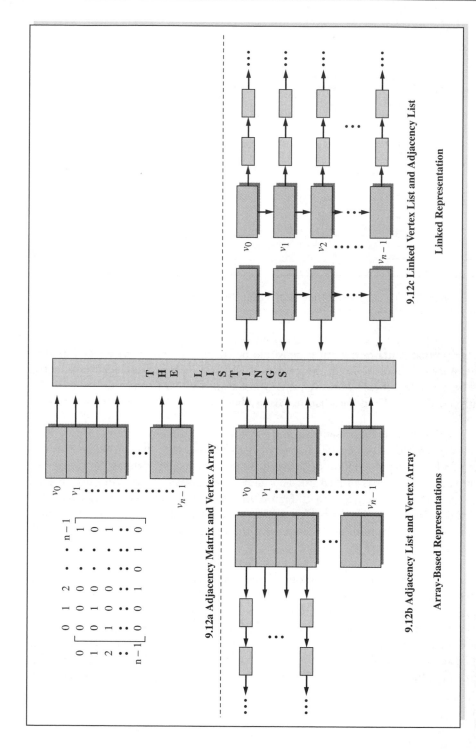

Figure 9.12   Array-Based and Linked Representations of a Graph's Vertices and Edges

9.3 Operations Performed on Graphs

The operations performed on graphs expand the basic operation set performed on the previous structures we have studied. The reason for expanding the operation set is that, not only do the nodes hold information (i.e., client listings) but, as we have discussed, the edges also hold information. Typical information held "in" the edges include which vertices they connect, which direction of travel is allowed, and the weighting factor of the edge. In addition, the ability to traverse a graph is so fundamental to many graph applications that it is usually considered a basic operation. A typical set of fundamental operations, therefore, provides the ability to operate on both vertices and edges, and to perform a traversal operation.

Turning our attention first to *vertex* operations, the functionality of the Insert, Fetch, and Update operations is the same as that of the previous structures presented in this text. They are used to add a vertex to the structure and store information in it (Insert), retrieve the information stored in a vertex (Fetch), and modify the information stored in a vertex (Update). The Delete operation, however, extends the functionality of the previous structures, in that, when we delete a vertex from a graph, the edges emanating from it, and incident upon it, must also be deleted. Edges must connect *two* vertices.

The operations performed on the *edges* of a graph typically include an Insert operation that adds an edge between two existing vertices, a Delete operation that eliminates an edge that connects two vertices, and a Fetch operation that returns the edge's weighting factor. The Update operation is used to change the value of an edge's weighting factor.

As far as access modes are concerned, graphs can be accessed in the key field mode or in the node number mode. Generally speaking, when the node number mode is used, the client specifies the number of the node to be operated on. In the case of a graph, the vertex number would be specified, and we will refer to this mode as the *vertex number* mode. A typical client invocation to insert the `Listing` object P into the graph g as vertex 2 would be g.insertVertex(2, P), and the client's statement g.fetchVertex(2) would be used to fetch back a reference to the information. Many applications that utilize graph structures lend themselves to node number mode access. Alternately, if the key field mode is used, the invocations become g.insertVertex(P) and g.fetchVertex(targetKey), assuming targetKey is the contents of the key field of the information to be retrieved.

To begin with, we will develop and implement the pseudocode of just the Insert operation on the vertices and edges in the vertex number mode. The graph will be assumed to be an unweighted digraph. Then we will expand the set of operations to include a traversal operation. The implementations that include the remaining operations, access in the key field mode, and a dynamic expansion of the structure is left as an exercise for the student.

In the interest of simplicity, the vertices will be represented as a one-dimensional array and we will store the edges in an adjacency matrix (see Figure 9.12**a**). Assuming the vertex and edge arrays are named vertex and edge, respectively, and that the graph can initially store a maximum of five vertices, Figure 9.13 is a depiction of a graph object after it is initialized.

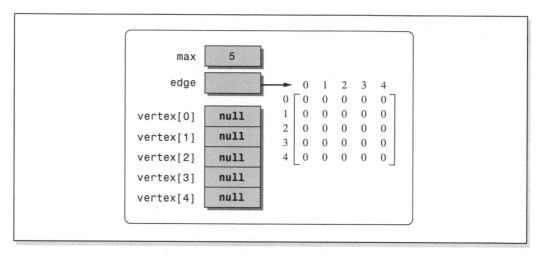

Figure 9.13 A Graph Object that can Contain Five Vertices in its Initialized State

To insert a vertex into the structure we simply set a reference to a deep copy of the information into the vertex array. Assuming the vertex number specified by the client is *v* and the listing to be inserted is referenced by newListing, the pseudocode is simply:

The Insert Vertex Algorithm (Assumes a Figure 9.13 graph representation)

1. **if**(v >= max) // the graph is full
2.   **return false;**
3. vertex[v] = newListing.deepCopy(); // insert the node
4.   **return true;**

Assuming the graph is a directed graph and its edges are unweighted, the pseudocode to insert an edge from vertex *from*, to vertex *to* is simply:

The Insert Edge Algorithm for an Unweighted Digraph
(Assumes a Figure 9.13 graph representation)

1. **if**(vertex(from) == **null** || vertex(to) == **null**) // vertex not in the structure
2.   **return false;**
3. edge[from][to] = 1 ;
4.   **return true;**

If the graph was an undirected graph, the statement edge[to][from] = 1 would be added to the algorithm after Line 3.

9.4 Implementing Graphs in the Vertex Number Mode

Figure 9.14 presents a class called SimpleGraph, which is the Java implementation of the graph representation scheme depicted in Figure 9.12a and the previous pseudocode insert algorithms. The code initializes the graph to the state shown in Figure 9.13; however, the maximum number of vertices the graph will contain is specified by the client and a data member, numberOfVertices,

```
1.    class SimpleGraph // a directed graph, (digraph)
2.    {   Listing vertex[];   // the reference to the vertex array
3.        int edge[][];   // reference to the adjacency matrix array
4.        int max, numberOfVertices;
5.        public SimpleGraph(int n)
6.        {   vertex = new Listing[n]; // allocation of the vertex array
7.            edge = new int[n][n];    // adjacency matrix initialized to zeros
8.            max = n;   numberOfVertices = 0;
9.        }
10.       public boolean insertVertex(int vertexNumber, Listing newListing)
11.       {   if(vertexNumber >= max)   // the graph is full
12.               return false;
13.           vertex[vertexNumber] = newListing.deepCopy();   numberOfVertices++;
14.           return true;
15.       } // end insertVertex method
16.       public boolean insertEdge(int fromVertex, int toVertex)
17.       {   if(vertex[fromVertex] == null || vertex[toVertex] == null)
18.               return false; // nonexistent vertex
19.           edge[fromVertex][toVertex] = 1;
20.           return true;
21.       } // end insertEdge method
22.       public void showVertex(int vertexNumber)
23.       {   System.out.println(vertex[vertexNumber]);
24.       } // end showVertex method
25.       public void showEdges(int vertexNumber) // emanating from vertexNumber
26.       {   for(int column = 0; column < numberOfVertices; column++)
27.           {   if(edge[vertexNumber][column] == 1) // an edge found
28.                   System.out.println(vertexNumber + "," + column);
29.           }
30.       } end showEdges method
31. } // end of class SimpleGraph
```

Figure 9.14 The Implementation of a Simple Directed Graph in the Vertex Number Mode

has been added to keep track of the number of vertices the graph contains. In addition, the class includes methods to output the information stored in a vertex and to output the incident vertex numbers of all of a vertex's edges.

The class SimpleGraph is a fully encapsulated data structure whose vertices store objects in a class named Listing. When a graph object is created, the client passes the maximum number of vertices the graph will contain into the class' constructor, Line 5. Lines 6, 7, and 8 then allocate and initialize the vertex array, the adjacency matrix array, the vertex count, and save the maximum number of vertices. The methods insertVertex and insertEdge, that begin on Lines 10 and 16, respectively, are the Java equivalent of the pseudocode versions of these algorithms previously discussed, except that Line 13 of the insertVertex method increments the vertex count.

The vertex and edge output methods (showVertex and showEdges) are coded as Lines 22–24 and Lines 25–30, respectively. The vertex method outputs the contents of a Listing object (a vertex) by implicitly invoking the toString method (Line 23) of the Listing class. The edge output method indexes its way across the columns of a given vertex's row in the adjacency matrix (Line 26) outputting the incident vertex number (the adjacency matrix column number) on Line 28 whenever a 1 is encountered in the row.

An airline hub application that demonstrates the use of the class SimpleGraph is presented in Figure 9.15 and the output it generates in shown in Figure 9.16. The application uses the graph's vertices to represent the airline's hub cities, and the connections between the cities are represented by the graph's edges. The airline's routes are given in Figure 9.7, with hubs in Philadelphia (vertex 0), New York (vertex 1), Boston (vertex 2), Los Angeles (vertex 3), and Houston (vertex 4). Consistent with the coding of the class SimpleGraph, the definition of the hub city objects stored in the vertices is given in a class named Listing (presented as Figure 9.17). The Listing class has one String data member used to store the hub city's name.

Lines 4–21 of the application loads the hub airport names and routes into the SimpleGraph object flyUS declared on Line 3. Lines 22–27 output the hubs and the routes that originate from them.

9.5 Traversing Graphs

In general, traversing a data structure is the process of performing a processing operation on each item in the structure, once and only once. When we perform the processing operation on an item, we are said to have *visited* the item. Typical processing operations are to modify the contents of a particular field, output all the fields, or to count the items to determine how many are in the structure.

```
1.   public class MainSimpleGraph
2.   {  public static void main(String[] args)
3.      {  SimpleGraph flyUS = new SimpleGraph(5);
4.         Listing v0 = new Listing("Philadelphia");
5.         Listing v1 = new Listing("New York");
6.         Listing v2 = new Listing("Boston");
7.         Listing v3 = new Listing("Los Angeles");
8.         Listing v4 = new Listing("Houston");
           // add the hub cities to the graph as vertices
9.         flyUS.insertVertex(0, v0);
10.        flyUS.insertVertex(1, v1);
11.        flyUS.insertVertex(2, v2);
12.        flyUS.insertVertex(3, v3);
13.        flyUS.insertVertex(4, v4);
           // add the routes to the graph as edges
14.        flyUS.insertEdge(0,1);
15.        flyUS.insertEdge(0,3);
16.        flyUS.insertEdge(1,2);
17.        flyUS.insertEdge(1,3);
18.        flyUS.insertEdge(2,1);
19.        flyUS.insertEdge(3,4);
20.        flyUS.insertEdge(4,0);
21.        flyUS.insertEdge(4,3);
           // output the hubs and the routes stored in the graph
22.        for(int i = 0; i < 5; i++)
23.        {  System.out.print("hub " + i + "\'s ");
24.           flyUS.showVertex(i);
25.           System.out.println("its routes are: ");
26.           flyUS.showEdges(i);
27.        } // end the output loop
28.     } // end of main method
29.  } // end class MainSimpleGraph
```

Figure 9.15   An Airline Hub Application That Uses a `SimpleGraph` Object to Store the Hub Cities and Routes

Of the structures we have examined in previous chapters, array-based structures and linked list structures are the simplest to traverse. The linear nature of these data structures allow us to traverse them using a loop construct that sequentially indexes through the elements of the array, or that moves through the members of a linked list until a **null** reference is found. As we have seen in Chapter 7, the algorithm for traversing a binary tree structure is not as simplistic because a binary tree is, generally speaking, not a linear structure. Most often, there is more than one node, or subtree, succeeding a node. Therefore, after visiting a node in a tree, a decision has to be made as to which subtree to enter next. In the case of the NLR traversal, the left subtree is entered next, while in the case of the NRL traversal the right subtree is entered next.

```
hub 0's Name is Philadelphia
its routes are:
0,1
0,3
hub 1's Name is New York
its routes are:
1,2
1,3
hub 2's Name is Boston
its routes are:
2,1
hub 3's Name is Los Angeles
its routes are:
3,4
hub 4's Name is Houston
its routes are:
4,0
4,3
```

Figure 9.16   The Output generated by the Airline Hub Application Shown in Figure 9.15

```
1.   // definition of a hub city (a vertex)
2.   public class Listing
3.   {  private String name;
4.      public Listing(String n)
5.      {  name = n;
6.      }
7.      public String toString()
8.      {  return("Name is " + name);
9.      }
10.     public Listing deepCopy()
11.     {  Listing clone = new Listing(name);
12.        return clone;
13.     } // end of deepCopy method
14.  } // end class Listing
```

Figure 9.17   The Class Listing for the Airline Hub Application Shown in Figure 9.15

When we traverse graphs, the decision process is more complicated because in a graph that contains n vertices there could be as many as $n - 1$ edges emanating from each vertex. The two most common traversal techniques for graphs are the depth-first traversal (DFT) and the breadth-first traversal (BFT). In both of these traversals any one of the graph's vertices can be designated to be visited first. Then, in a depth-first traversal for each vertex visited, all of its adjacent vertices (its *descendents*) are visited *before* any of its *siblings* are visited. In the context of graph traversals, siblings are vertices that have an edge from a common vertex, assuming the common vertex was the

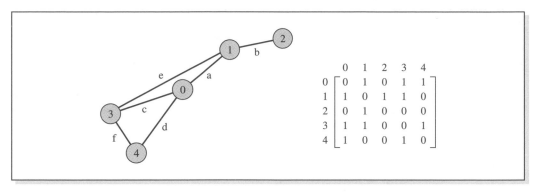

Figure 9.18   An Undirected Graph and its Adjacency Matrix

vertex previously visited.[4] Thus, if vertex 0 in Figure 9.18 has just been visited, then vertex 1's siblings would be vertices 3 and 4. Conversely, in a breadth-first traversal all of a visited vertices' siblings are visited before any of its decedents are visited.

9.5.1 Depth-First Traversal

To illustrate the depth-first traversal process, consider the tree depicted in Figure 9.18 (which also shows its adjacency matrix). We will assume that vertex 3 (V_3) was arbitrarily selected to be visited first. Its descendents are its adjacent vertices V_0, V_1, and V_4, easily determined by indexing our way through row 3 of the adjacency matrix. One of these vertices will be visited next. Although the choice is arbitrary, in the interest of speed and to simplify the coding process, the one chosen is usually the vertex with the *highest* vertex number, in our case V_4.[5]

To see why this vertex is selected we must recall that the decedents of the selected vertex (V_4) will be visited before any its siblings (V_1, V_0) are visited, which necessitates "remembering" these unvisited siblings while we visit V_4's descendents. In the case of a DFT, for reasons we will mention later, a stack is used to remember the *unvisited* siblings. As we index our way across row 3 of the adjacency matrix, we push all the siblings onto the stack in the order encountered: first V_0, then V_1, and finally V_4. Then, to determine the next vertex visited we simply pop the stack, and since V_4 is at the top of the stack, it is visited next.

The reason a stack is used in this algorithm is that if V_4 has descendents (adjacent nodes that are not siblings), in a DFT they must be visited *before* V_4's siblings (V_0 and V_1). Adding them to a stack

---

[4]This implies that the first vertex visited has no siblings unless the graph is a forest (see Figure 9.1f).

[5]When an adjacency list is used to represent the vertices, the next node visited is usually the *last* vertex along the visited vertex's adjacency list.

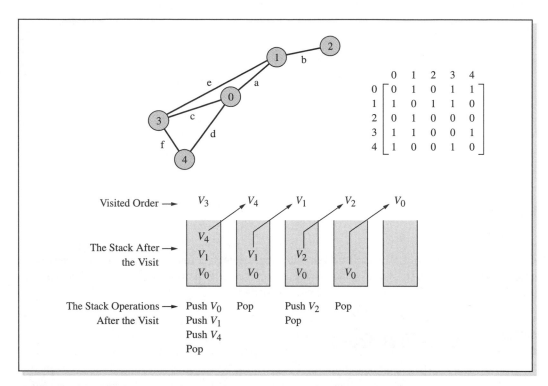

Figure 9.19 A Depth-First Traversal of A Graph Beginning at Vertex V_3

guarantees that they will be visited before V_0 and V_1 since they are pushed onto the stack after V_0 and V_1, and the vertices are visited as they are popped from the stack. For example, if V_4 had two more adjacent vertices that were not adjacent to any other vertex in the graph, these vertices would be visited before V_0 and V_1.

Figure 9.19 presents the order in which the vertices of the graph presented in Figure 9.18 are visited, using the depth-first traversal process, assuming vertex 3 is the first vertex visited. It also shows the progression of the stack as the traversal takes place, and the operations performed on the stack after a vertex is visited.

First V_3 is visited and row 3 of the adjacency matrix is examined to determine V_3's descendents, found to be V_0, V_1, and V_4. These vertex numbers are pushed onto the stack. Next, V_4 is popped off the stack and visited, and row 4 is examined to determine V_4's descendents. However, V_4's descendents, V_0 and V_3, are either already on the stack (V_0) or already visited (V_3). When this is the case, the descendent vertices are *not* pushed onto the stack because we do not want to visit a vertex twice.

Next, V_1 is popped off the stack and visited, and row 1 is examined to determine V_1's descendents. The only descendent of V_1 that has not been already pushed onto the stack (or not already visited) is V_2, so it is added to the stack. Then V_2 is popped off the stack and visited. V_2's descendent, V_1, has already been visited so it is not pushed onto the stack. Finally, V_0 is popped from the stack and visited. Since all of V_0's descendents (V_1, V_3, and V_4) have been visited, nothing is pushed onto the stack. The stack is now empty, which signals the end of the algorithm.

The pseudocode version of this process follows. For convenience, the first node to be visited is pushed onto the stack before it is visited. It is assumed that the graph is represented, as shown in Figure 9.12a, using arrays named vertex and edge. Also, each vertex has the ability to store a record of whether or not it has been pushed onto the stack in a Boolean data member named pushed (see Line 2 of the algorithm). The name of the stack object used in the algorithm is stack and the number of the first vertex visited is stored in the variable firstVertex. When reading the algorithm it is helpful to remember that the row and column numbers of the adjacency matrix, edge, represent vertex numbers.

The Depth-First Traversal Algorithm for Graphs Represented as Shown in Figure 9.12a

```
1.   stack.push(firstVertex); // add the number of the  first vertex to be visited to the stack
2.   vertex[firstVertex].setPushed(true);  // mark the vertex as pushed
3.   while(!stack.isEmpty) // continue the traversal
4.   { v = stack.pop();
5.      vertex[v].visit(); // visit a vertex
6.      for(int column = 0; column<n; i++) // look for descendents of vertex v
7.      { if(edge[v][column] == 1 && !vertex[column].getPushed()) // unpushed descendent
                                                       // found
8.         { stack.push(column); // add it to the stack (note: column == vertex number)
9.            vertex[column].setPushed(true);
10.        } // end if
11.     } // end for
12.  } // end while
```

The time complexity of the above algorithm is $O(n^2)$ because the inner and outer loops on Lines 6 and 3 each execute n times.

Implementation

Figure 9.20 presents the implementation of a class SimpleGraphDFT, which is the code of the class SimpleGraph presented in Figure 9.14, expanded (see Lines 11–32) to include a method DFT that performs the depth-first traversal. On Line 13, the DFT method declares an object stack that is an instance of the class Stack defined the package java.util (see Line 1). This generic class implements a traditional stack (LIFO) structure.

Lines 15–18 set the data member pushed (of all the Listing objects the vertices represent) to **false**. This data member, and the methods that set and fetch its value, are part of the client's class Listing2, which is presented in Figure 9.21 (see Lines 4, 15, and 18). This class is an expanded version of the class Listing, shown in Figure 9.17, that also includes a method visit() to perform the client defined operation on the vertex being visited (Line 21). In this case, the Listing2 object stored at the vertex is simply output.

```
1.    import java.util.Stack;
2.    class SimpleGraphDFT // adds a method DFT to the class in Figure 9.14
3.    {  Listing2 vertex[];   // the reference to the vertex array
4.       int edge[][];    // reference to the adjacency matrix array
5.       int max, numberOfVertices;
6.       public SimpleGraphDFT(int n)
7.       {  vertex = new Listing2[n]; // allocation of the vertex array
8.          edge = new int[n][n]; // adjacency matrix with elements set to 0
9.          max = n;   numberOfVertices = 0;
10.      }
11.      public void DFT(int firstVertex)
12.      {  int v;
13.         Stack<Integer> stack = new Stack(); // uses Java Stack class
14.         // initialize all vertices to not visited
15.         for (int i = 0; i < numberOfVertices; i++)
16.         {  if(vertex[i] != null)
17.               vertex[i].setPushed(false); // mark all vertices unvisited
18.         }
19.         stack.push(firstVertex); // visit the first vertex
20.         vertex[firstVertex].setPushed(true);
21.         // visit all the decedents
22.         while (!stack.empty())
23.         {  v = stack.pop();
24.            vertex[v].visit(); // visit a vertex
25.            for (int column = 0; column < numberOfVertices; column++)
26.            {  if(edge[v][column] == 1 && !vertex[column].getPushed())
27.               {  stack.push(column);
28.                  vertex[column].setPushed(true);
29.               } // end if
30.            } // end for
31.         } // end while
32.      } // end DFT method
33.      public boolean insertVertex(int vertexNumber, Listing2 newListing)
```

(continues)

Figure 9.20   The Extension of the Class SimpleGraph (Presented in Figure 9.14 to Include a Depth-First Traversal Operation

```
34.     {  if(vertexNumber >= max) // the graph is full
35.            return false;
36.        vertex[vertexNumber] = newListing.deepCopy();    numberOfVertices++;
37.        return true;
38.     }
39.     public boolean insertEdge(int fromVertex, int toVertex)
40.     {  if(vertex[fromVertex] == null || vertex[toVertex] == null)
41.            return false; // nonexistent vertex
42.        edge[fromVertex][toVertex] = 1;
43.        return true;
44.     }
45.     public void showVertex(int vertexNumber)
46.     {  System.out.println(vertex[vertexNumber]);
47.     }
48.     public void showEdges(int vertexNumber) // edges from vertexNumber
49.     {  for(int column = 0; column < numberOfVertices; column++)
50.        {  if(edge[vertexNumber][column] == 1) // there is an edge
51.               System.out.println(vertexNumber + "," + column);
52.        }
53.     } // end showEdges method
54. } // end class SimpleGraphDFT
```

Figure 9.20   The Extension of the Class `SimpleGraph` (Presented in Figure 9.14 to Include a Depth-First Traversal Operation *(continued)*

```
1.     import javax.swing.JOptionPane;
2.     public class Listing2
3.     {  private String name;
4.        boolean pushed;
5.        public Listing2(String n)
6.        {  name = n;
7.        }
8.        public String toString()
9.        {  return ("Name is " + name);
10.       } // end of toString method
11.       public Listing2 deepCopy()
12.       {  Listing2 clone = new Listing2(name);
13.          return clone;
14.       } // end of deepCopy method
15.       public boolean getPushed()
16.       {  return pushed;
17.       } // end of getPushed method
18.       public void setPushed(boolean value)
19.       {  pushed = value;
20.       } // end of setPushed method
21.       public void visit()
22.       {  System.out.println(this);
23.       } // end of visit method
24. } // end class Listing2
```

Figure 9.21   An Expansion of the Class `Listing` Presented in Figure 9.17 to Include a Data Member and Methods Necessary to the DFT Method of the Class `SimpleGraphDFT`

The remainder of the code of the DFT method (Lines 19 through 32) is the Java equivalent of the pseudocode version of the depth-first traversal presented above. The first vertex to be visited is passed to the method DFT as an argument (Line 11).

An application that demonstrates the use of the method and the output it produces is presented in Figure 9.22. The graph used in the application is the graph presented in Figure 9.19. It performs a traversal of the graph starting at vertex 3 (Line 30).

```
1.   public class MainSimpleGraphDFT
2.   {  public static void main(String[] args)
3.      {  SimpleGraphDFT flyUS = new SimpleGraphDFT(5);
4.         Listing2 v0 = new Listing2("V0");
5.         Listing2 v1 = new Listing2("V1");
6.         Listing2 v2 = new Listing2("V2");
7.         Listing2 v3 = new Listing2("V3");
8.         Listing2 v4 = new Listing2("V4");
9.
10.        flyUS.insertVertex(0, v0);
11.        flyUS.insertVertex(1, v1);
12.        flyUS.insertVertex(2, v2);
13.        flyUS.insertVertex(3, v3);
14.        flyUS.insertVertex(4, v4);
15.
16.        flyUS.insertEdge(0,1);
17.        flyUS.insertEdge(0,3);
18.        flyUS.insertEdge(0,4);
19.        flyUS.insertEdge(1,0);
20.        flyUS.insertEdge(1,2);
21.        flyUS.insertEdge(1,3);
22.        flyUS.insertEdge(2,1);
23.        flyUS.insertEdge(3,0);
24.        flyUS.insertEdge(3,1);
25.        flyUS.insertEdge(3,4);
26.        flyUS.insertEdge(4,0);
27.        flyUS.insertEdge(4,3);
28.
29.        System.out.println("DFT of the graph in Figure 9.19 starting " +
                             "at Vertex 3, \"V3\"");
30.        flyUS.DFT(3);
31.     } // end main method
32.  } // end class MainSimpleGraphDFT
```

Output

DFT of the graph in Figure 9.19 starting at Vertex 3, "V3"
Name is V3
Name is V4
Name is V1
Name is V2

Figure 9.22 An Application that Performs a Depth-First Output Traversal and its Output

It should be noted that `SimpleGraphDFT` is coded in a generic way, in that it can perform any client defined operation on the nodes stored in the graph during its traversal operation as long as the node definition class, `Listing2`:

- Contains a Boolean data member, and the methods `setPushed`, and `getPushed` to set and return its value.
- Contains a method `visit` that carries out the operation to be performed on each vertex during the traversal.

9.5.2 Breadth-First Traversal

In a breadth-first traversal, for each vertex visited all of its siblings are visited before any of its adjacent vertices (descendents) are visited. In the contexts of graph traversals, siblings are vertices that have an edge from a common vertex, assuming the common vertex has just been visited.[6]

To demonstrate this traversal technique, we will use the graph depicted in Figure 9.23 and assume the traversal starts at vertex V_3. V_3 is visited, and since V_3 has no siblings (no other node has been visited), we move to its descendents V_0, V_1, and V_4. One of these will be visited next and the others will be remembered on a to-be-visited list and visited later. Let us assume that V_0 will be visited next and that V_1 and V_4 are remembered by placing them on the to-be-visited list. After V_0 is visited, its descendents must be remembered since they will be visited *after* V_0's siblings (V_1 and V_4) are visited. To insure the correct order of visitation (siblings before descendents) the descendents of the visited vertex must be placed on the to-be-visited list *after* the siblings. This is easily done if the list is a *queue*. Therefore, a breadth-first traversal replaces the stack used in a depth-first traversal with a queue. Otherwise, the two algorithms are identical.

Figure 9.23 presents the order in which the vertices of the graph presented in Figure 9.19 are visited using the breadth-first traversal process, assuming vertex 3 is the first vertex visited. It also shows the progression of the queue as the traversal takes place and the operations performed on the queue after a vertex is visited.

The implementation of a breadth-first traversal is left as an exercise for the student.

9.6 Connectivity and Paths

Two vertices in a graph are said to be connected if there is a way of reaching one from the other by traveling along the graph's edges. The sequence of edges we travel along from one vertex to another is called a *path*. Vertices 2 and 4 in the directed graph presented in Figure 9.24a are

---

[6]This implies that the first vertex visited has no siblings unless the graph is a forest (see Figure 9.1f).

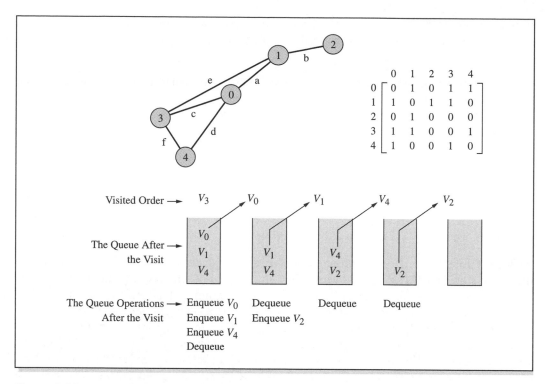

Figure 9.23 A Breadth-First Traversal of a Graph Beginning at Vertex V_3

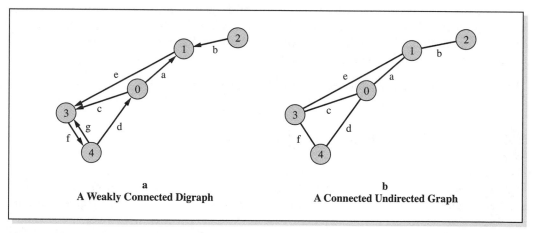

a
A Weakly Connected Digraph

b
A Connected Undirected Graph

Figure 9.24 A Directed and an Undirected Version of a Graph

connected by path *b,e,f*. In the graph presented in Figure 9.24**b**, these two vertices are connected by several paths, e.g., edges *b,e,f*; edges *b,a,d*; and edges *b,a,c,f*.

An undirected graph, and a directed graph whose *edge directions are ignored*, is said to be *connected* if, given any two vertices, there is a way of reaching one from the other by traveling along the graph's edges. The graph shown in Figure 9.24**a** and 9.24**b** are both connected graphs. If a graph is not connected it is said to be *disjoint*. The graph shown in Figure 9.1**f** is disjoint.

A directed graph is said to be *strongly connected* if, considering the direction of its edges, and given any two vertices, there is a way of reaching one from the other by traveling along the graph's edges. The directed graph show in Figure 9.24**a** is not strongly connected because, when we consider the direction of the edge between vertex 2 and 1, there is no way to reach vertex 2 from vertex 1 (or from any other vertex in the graph). This type of connected digraph is said to be *weakly connected*. If we were to delete vertex 2 from the graph, then it would be strongly connected.

In an unweighted graph, the path *length* is the number of edges that make up the path connecting two vertices. The length of the path from vertex 2 to 4 in Figure 9.24**a** is 3. In a weighted graph, the path length is the sum of the weighting factors of the edges that make up the path. The path length between vertex A and B in the graph depicted in Figure 9.1**e** is either 5 or 15 depending on which path is taken to reach vertex B.

Many interesting problems involve the consideration of connectivity and path. For example, suppose we are building roads between towns in an isolated area. Once constructed, we may ask:

- "Can any town be reached from any other town?" (The Connected Undirected Graph problem.)
- "Can we still reach every town if some of the roads are changed to one way streets?" (The Strongly Connected Directed Graph problem.)
- "Which roads can be closed for repair such that travelers will still be able to reach every town?" (The Spanning Tree problem.)
- "Which roads can be closed for repair such that every town can be reached and the total road mileage is minimized?" (The Minimum Spanning tree problem.)
- "What is the route that minimizes the mileage traveled between two towns?" (The Shortest Path problem.)
- "What is the route that minimizes the number of roads traveled?"
- "Is there a route we can travel such that we pass through each town once but never visit a town twice?" (The Hamiltonian Path problem.)
- "Are there routes that travel across all the roads just once, and is there one of these routes that will return to the starting point?" (The Bridges of Koningsberg problem.)
- And finally, "what is the shortest route to visit all towns once and return back to the starting town?" (The Traveling Salesman problem.)

These problems are not only applicable to roads connecting towns but also to a variety of other problems in electronics, computer science, operations research, and many other fields.

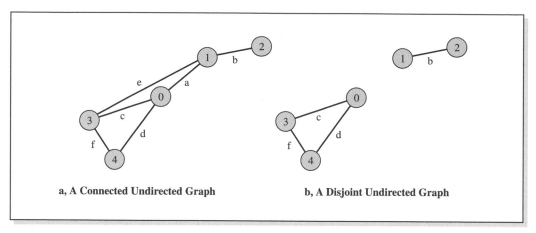

a, A Connected Undirected Graph   b, A Disjoint Undirected Graph

Figure 9.25   A Connected and a Disjoint Undirected Graph

9.6.1 Connectivity of Undirected Graphs

Let us begin our study of connectivity and paths by considering the first problem in our list of questions, the problem of determining if any town can be reached from any other town by traveling along *bidirectional* roads that connect the towns. If the towns are represented by the vertices of an undirected graph, and the roads by its edges, then the problem becomes one of determining if the directed graph formed by the vertices and edges is connected. If it is, then any town can be reached from any other town. We can determine if an undirected graph is connected by simply traversing the graph (using either a DFT or a BFT) starting at any of the graph's vertices, and if all the graph's vertices have been visited, the graph is connected. Otherwise, the traversal identifies the vertices that are connected.

Consider the two graphs shown in Figure 9.25. A simple inspection reveals that any of the "towns" represented by the vertices of the connected graph on the left, can be reached from any other, but that is not the case for the towns represented by the disjoint graph on the right side of the figure (e.g., Towns 1 and 2 cannot be reached from Towns 0, 3, and 4, and vice versa). The depth-first traversal of the graph on the left side of the figure that begins (arbitrarily) at vertex 1, visits the vertices 1, 3, 4, 0, and finally, 2. Since this list includes all the vertices, the graph is connected. However, the depth-first traversal of the graph on the right side of the figure that begins (again arbitrarily) at vertex 1, visits the vertices 1, then 2. Since vertices 0, 3, and 4 are not on the "visited" list, the graph is not connected (disjoint).

9.6.2 Connectivity of Directed Graphs

Now let us consider the case where the roads connecting our towns are one-way streets. Again, the towns will be represented as vertices of a graph and the roads will be represented as the graph's edges. Since the direction of travel along the roads is *not* bidirectional, the vertices and edges form

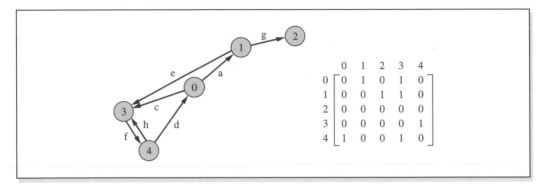

Figure 9.26   A Weakly Connected Digraph and its Adjacency Matrix

a digraph and, therefore, any town can be reached from any other town if and only if the graph is *strongly* connected. To determine if the graph is strongly connected, it is not sufficient to perform a DFT (or a BFT) beginning at *any* vertex and then checking to see if all the vertices are visited. This is easily demonstrated by performing a depth-first traversal on the graph shown in Figure 9.26 beginning at vertex 1. The traversal visits all the vertices in the order, vertex 1 followed by vertex 3, 4, 0, and finally, vertex 2. Yet there is no way to travel from vertex 2 to another vertex in the graph. Therefore, a DFT beginning at any vertex is not sufficient to determine if a digraph is strongly connected.

There is hope, however. If a traversal is initiated at *every* vertex in a directed graph and each of these traversals visit every vertex in the graph, then the digraph is strongly connected. For the graph depicted in Figure 9.26, the DFT initiated at vertex 2 would only visit vertex 2 demonstrating that the graph is not strongly connected. For a graph containing n vertices, the speed of an algorithm that performs n depth-first traversals is $O(n^3)$ since the traversal algorithm is itself $O(n^2)$. In addition, as we have discussed, each of the n traversals must be examined to determine if all n vertices were visited, which is an $O(n^2)$ operation.

Warshall's Algorithm

Warshall's Algorithm presents an alternative method for determining if a directed graph is strongly connected and, if it is not, also affords a rapid way of determining which vertices have paths connecting them. The algorithm begins by copying the array that represents the graph's adjacency matrix into another array, t. Then, it modifies t by placing a 1 in column j of row i if there is a path from vertex i to vertex j. The path could be a single edge (a path length of 1, which would already be present in the adjacency matrix) or the path could consist of a sequence of edges (a path length > 1 which would not appear in the adjacency matrix). The resulting modified version of the matrix t is called the *transitive closure* or *reachability* matrix. A 1 in row i, column j of the adjacency matrix indicates that there is an *edge* between vertices v_i and v_j, however, a 1 in the corresponding element in the transitive closure matrix indicates that there is a *path* from vertex v_i to vertex v_j.

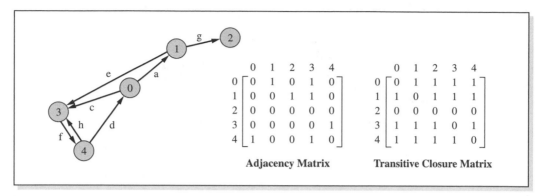

Figure 9.27 A Directed Graph's Adjacency and Transitive Closure Matrices

For example, the transitive closure matrix for the graph depicted in Figure 9.26 is shown in Figure 9.27, along with its adjacency matrix and the graph itself. Warshall's Algorithm has changed the 0 in columns 2 and 4 of row 0 of the adjacency matrix (which indicates that there is no *edge* from vertex 0 to vertex 2 or 4), to a 1 in the transitive closure matrix (which indicates that there is a *path* from vertex 0 to vertex 2, and a *path* from vertex 0 to vertex 4). Other rows of the transitive closure matrix reflect similar changes. The only row unchanged is row 2, since there are no paths from it to any other vertex in the graph.

After generating the transitive closure matrix for a graph, we can determine if the graph is strongly connected by examining its elements. If all the elements of the matrix are 1, except for the elements along the main (upper-left-to-lower-right) diagonal, then the graph is strongly connected. In addition, if the graph is not strongly connected, we can rapidly determine if there is a path from vertex i to vertex j by simply testing t[i][j] to determine if it is 1. If so, a path exists between the two vertices.

The basis of Warshall's Algorithm is the transitive property in mathematics: if $a = b$ and $b = c$, then $a = c$. The algorithm reasons that if there is a path from vertex v_b to vertex v_c then there is a path to v_c from every vertex that can reach v_b. Consistent with this reasoning, the algorithm examines each element of the adjacency matrix working its way across the columns beginning with row 0. When it finds an element with a value of 1, (e.g., vertex[b][c] = 1, indicating a path exists from vertex v_b to vertex v_c), it indexes its way down column b of the matrix to find the vertices with a path to v_b; e.g., vertex[a][b] = 1, indicating that there is a path from v_a to v_b. If this is the case, there must be a path from v_a to v_c (through vertex v_b) so vertex[a][c] is set to 1. Provisions are made in the algorithm to not place a 1 along the main diagonal of the matrix.

Figure 9.28 presents the code of the method transitiveClosure which implements Warshall's Algorithm. It returns the transitive closure of the array *adjacency* passed to it as a parameter (Line 2). The parameter *n* is the number of rows (and columns) in the adjacency matrix. Lines 4–6 copy the adjacency matrix into the transitive closure matrix, t. Lines 8–19 is the coding of Warshall's Algorithm. Line 8 indexes through each vertex in the graph. For each vertex, *b*, Lines 9–10 find a

```
1.   public class TransitiveClosure {
2.   public static int[][] transitiveClosure(int n, int adjacency[][])
3.   {  int t[][] = new int[n][n];
4.      for(int row=0; row<n; row++) // set t to the adjacency matrix
5.         for (int col = 0; col < n; col++)
6.            t[row][col] = adjacency[row][col];
7.      // Warshall's Algorithm
8.      for (int b = 0; b < n; b ++) // for each vertex, b
9.      {  for(int c = 0; c < n; c++) // locate the paths from vertex b to c
10.        {  if(t[b][c] == 1) // a path from vertex b to some vertex c found
11.           {  for(int a = 0; a < n; a++) // find the paths to b
12.              {  if(t[a][b] == 1  &&  a != c) // a path to b from a found
13.                    t[a][c] = 1; // mark path from vertex a to c
14.              } // end for
15.           } // end if
16.        } // end for
17.      } // end for
18.      return t;
19.   } // end transitiveClosure method
20.   } // end class TransitiveClosure
```

Figure 9.28   A Method that Determines the Transitive Closure Matrix of a Given Matrix

vertex, c, it is connected to. Then Lines 11–13 locate all the vertices, a, connected to b, and mark a path in the transitive closure matrix from a to c.

Figure 9.29 presents an application that determines the transitive closure matrix of the graph depicted in Figure 9.27. The program output (shown at the bottom of the figure) is the returned transitive closure matrix, t (which is also shown in Figure 9.27).

The three nested loops on Lines 8, 9, and 11 of Figure 9.28 make the speed complexity of Warshall's Algorithm no better than performing n depth-first traversals to determine if a directed graph is strongly connected. However, Warshall's Algorithm provides an additional piece of information: a permanent record of all the possible paths via the transitive closure matrix.

9.6.3 Spanning Trees

A simple cycle is a simple path in a graph that begins and ends at the same vertex. The paths a,c,e; c,d,f; and d,f,e,a in Figure 9.30a are simple cycles. A tree is a connected graph that does not contain simple cycles. Eliminating the edges c and f from the graph depicted in Figure 9.30a make it a tree because it is still connected and has no simple cycles. For simplicity, we will refer to simple cycles as cycles.

A graph's spanning tree is a tree that contains all of the vertices of the graph connected by a subset of the graph's edges. The edges are chosen such that is there is a path from each vertex to

```
1.   public class MainTransitiveClosure {
2.   public static void main(String[] args)
3.   {   int a[][] = new int[5][5]; // adjacency matrix
4.       int t[][] = new int[5][5]; // transitive closure matrix
5.       a[0][1] = 1; // set adjacency matrix to matrix shown in Figure 9.27
6.       a[0][3] = 1;
7.       a[1][2] = 1;
8.       a[1][3] = 1;
9.       a[3][4] = 1;
10.      a[4][0] = 1;
11.      a[4][3] = 1;
12.      t = TransitiveClosure.transitiveClosure(5, a); // compute transitive
                                                        // closure matrix
13.      for(int row = 0; row < 5; row++) // output transitive closure matrix
14.      {   System.out.println();
15.          for(int col = 0; col < 5; col++)
16.              System.out.print(t[row][col] + " ");
17.  } // end main method
18.  } // end class MainTransitiveClosure


Program output: (the transitive closure matrix, t)

0 1 1 1 1
1 0 1 1 1
0 0 0 0 0
1 1 1 0 1
1 1 1 1 0
```

Figure 9.29   A Program to Demonstrate the Use of the Method `transitiveClosure`

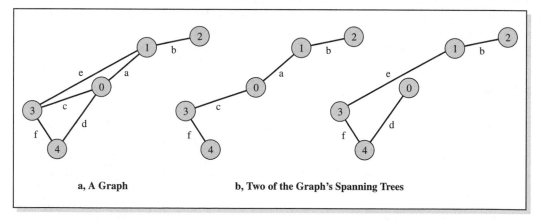

a, A Graph   b, Two of the Graph's Spanning Trees

Figure 9.30   An Undirected Connected Graph and Two of its Spanning Trees

every other vertex, and (since it is a tree) there are no cycles. Most graphs have more than one spanning tree. Two of the spanning trees for the graph shown in Figure 9.30**a** are shown in Figure 9.30**b**.

There is always one, and most often more than one, spanning tree for every connected undirected graph. Since there are no cycles in a spanning tree, or trees in general, they always contain one less edge than the number of vertices in the graph. Thus, the spanning tree of an undirected connected graph is a subgraph that contains the minimum number of the graph's edges and still allows a path from any vertex to any other.

These characteristics give spanning trees an important role in many applications. Consider the problem of deciding which bidirectional roads connecting towns to plow first after a major snowstorm so that all of the towns could be reached. If the towns are represented as the vertices of a graph and the roads its edges, then any spanning tree of the graph presents a solution. For this problem, a more interesting solution would be the spanning tree that offers the shortest plow route. As we will see, a spanning tree exhibiting this characteristic is called a *minimum spanning tree*. In the remainder of this section, we will examine the techniques for determining a graph's spanning trees and its minimum spanning trees.

To find a spanning tree of a connected undirected graph we can simply use a depth-first traversal and record the edge between each node visited and its descendents as the descendents are pushed onto the algorithm's stack. Since the vertices are only pushed onto the stack once, only one edge to each vertex will be recorded, and since all the vertices are pushed onto the stack, the edges will include an edge to each vertex. These edges will be the edges of the spanning tree. Alternately, a breadth-first traversal could be used and then we would record the edge to each vertex added to the queue used by the BFT algorithm. Since, when building a spanning tree, we don't actually operate on the nodes, we eliminate the code that visits the nodes from the DFT and BFT traversals.

The pseudocode to find a subset of a graph's edges that are included in one of its spanning trees follows. It is a modification of the DFT pseudocode presented earlier in this chapter, which assumed that the graph is represented using a vertex array named `vertex` and an adjacency matrix named `edge` (see Figure 9.13). These, as well as the starting vertex number, `firstVertex`, are supplied to the algorithm. It produces an adjacency matrix, `st`, that represents the edges of the spanning tree. The modifications to the DFT algorithm are to eliminate the traversal's visit of a node (Line 5 of the DFT algorithm) and to add two lines (the following Lines 9 and 10), which place the edge to a descendent vertex into the spanning tree's adjacency matrix, `st`.

Algorithm to Produce a Spanning Tree from a Connected Undirected Graph

```
1.  stack.push(firstVertex);  // add the first vertex to the stack
2.  vertex[firstVertex].setPushed(true);
3.  while(!stack.isEmpty)
4.  { v = stack.pop();
5.    for(int column = 0; column<n; i++) // look at descendents of vertex v
```

```
6.    { if(edge[v][column] ==1 && !vertex[column].getPushed()) // unpushed descendent
                                                               // found
7.         { stack.push(column); // add it to the stack
8.          vertex[column].setPushed(true);  // mark it pushed so it will not be pushed again
9.          st[v][column] = 1;  // place the edge to the descendent into the tree's adjacency
                                // matrix
10.         st [column][v] = 1; // make the adjacency matrix symmetric (its edges are
                                // undirected)
11.        } // end if
12.     } // end for
13. } // end while
```

The implementation of the spanning tree algorithm is left as an exercise for the student. As presented, it, like the implementation of the DFT algorithm, would be coded as an operation method in a class that defines a graph object. The most efficient way of doing this would be to extend the class SimpleGraphDFT (shown in Figure 9.20). The new class would support both depth-first traversals and the generation of spanning trees.

Minimum Spanning Trees

Minimum spanning trees are spanning trees that consider an additional piece of information associated with the edges of a connected undirected graph. That piece of information is called an *edge weighting*. For example, consider the graph whose vertices represent towns and whose edges represent the roads between the towns. A typical edge weighting could be the length of the roads. Other edge weightings could be the toll charged to travel along the roads, or the amount of snow on the roads. A graph whose edges carry weightings is called a *weighted graph*.

In the typical depiction of a weighted graph (see Figure 9.31), the values of the weighting factors are shown along the graph's edges. In this graphical depiction, no attempt is made to make the relative length of the edges correspond to their relative weights. For example, the edge with the highest weight that connects vertex 3 and 0 is not the longest edge in the graph. As shown in Figure 9.31, the weights are stored in a matrix using the same row and column assignment scheme used in the adjacency matrix. That is, the weight of the edge from vertex v_i to vertex v_j is stored in row i, column j of the weight matrix. Nonexistent edges (e.g., between vertex 0 and 2) are represented by an impossibly low or impossibly high value of the weighting factor depending on the application. Most programming languages provide a predefined constant that can be used (e.g., Java's Integer.MIN_VALUE and or Integer.MAX_VALUE). For convenience, the impossibly low value of the weight for the graph depicted in Figure 9.31 is 0.

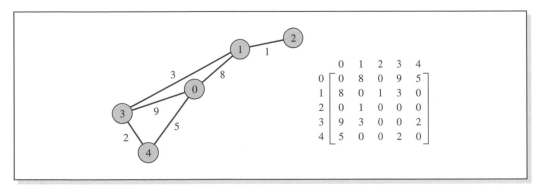

Figure 9.31 A Weighted Graph and its Weight Matrix

A *minimum* spanning tree is the spanning tree whose edges are selected to minimize the sum of the weighting factors of the edges that make up the tree. It can be shown that, if there are no two edges in a weighted graph with the same weighting factor, then there is only one minimum spanning tree for the graph.

To find a minimum spanning tree of a connected undirected graph, we begin by placing vertex 0 in the tree. Then we consider all the vertices currently in the tree (initially only vertex 0), and select the edge emanating from them with the minimum weight. This edge, and its incident vertex, is added to the tree and the process is repeated until all the vertices are added. During the process, an edge to a vertex already in the tree is not considered. Figure 9.32 illustrates the process of generating the minimum spanning tree for the graph depicted in Figure 9.31. The vertices that have been added to the tree are shown as gray circles, and the edges added to the tree are shown as colored lines.

First, vertex 0 would be added to the tree (Figure 9.32**a**). Then the edges emanating from vertex 0 would be considered (dashed edges in Figure 9.32**b**) and the edge with weight 5 (the minimum of weights 8, 9, and 5) would be selected. It and its incident vertex, vertex 4, would be added to the tree. Next, the edges emanating from vertices 0 and 4 would be considered (dashed edges in Figure 9.32**c**), and the edge with weight 2 (the minimum of weights 8, 9, and 2, with 5 not considered since it is a weighting of an edge to a vertex already in the tree) would be selected. It and its incident vertex, vertex 3, would be added to the tree. Then, the edges emanating from vertices 0, 4, and 3 would be considered (dashed edges in Figure 9.32**d**) and the edge with weight 3 (the minimum of weights 8 and 3 with 9, 2, and 5 not considered since they are weightings of edges to vertices already in the tree) would be selected. It and its incident vertex, vertex 1, would be added to the tree. Finally, the edge emanating from vertices 0, 4, 3, and 1 would be considered (dashed edge in Figure 9.32**e**) and the edge with weight 1 would be selected (the edges with weights 2, 3, 5, 8, and 9 are not considered since they are the weightings to vertices already in the tree).

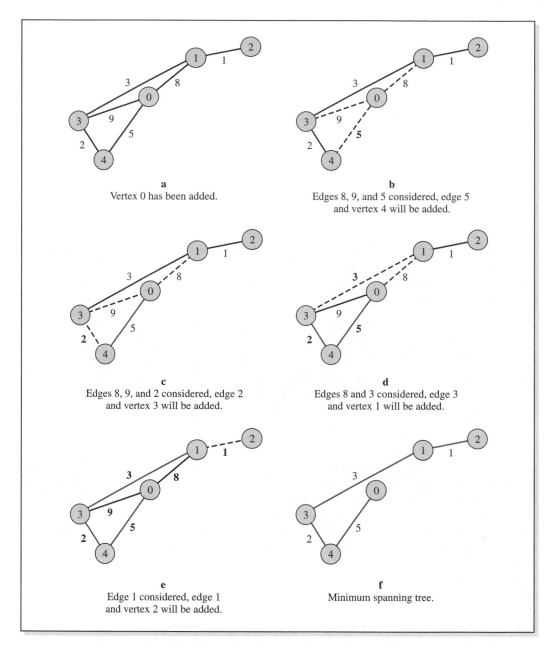

a
Vertex 0 has been added.

b
Edges 8, 9, and 5 considered, edge 5
and vertex 4 will be added.

c
Edges 8, 9, and 2 considered, edge 2
and vertex 3 will be added.

d
Edges 8 and 3 considered, edge 3
and vertex 1 will be added.

e
Edge 1 considered, edge 1
and vertex 2 will be added.

f
Minimum spanning tree.

Figure 9.32   Process of Building a Minimum Spanning Tree

Having added all the vertices to the tree, the algorithm ends. The minimum spanning tree it generated is shown in the lower right portion of Figure 9.32. The sum of the weightings of the edges of the tree is 11. This means that if the edge weights represented the length of the roads connecting five towns, the shortest plow route to make all the towns accessible after a snow storm would be the 11 mile route shown in Figure 9.32f. In addition, the best place to locate a snow plow garage would be town 0 or town 2.

The pseudocode version of the process that generates a minimum spanning tree follows. It uses three arrays. One array, verticesIncluded, stores the vertices of the graph added to the tree as the algorithm proceeds; another array aCopy is assumed to be initialized to the graph's weight matrix; the third array mst is the product of the algorithm, the weight matrix of the graph's minimum spanning tree; noEdge is an impossible high weighting value.

Minimum Spanning Tree Algorithm

```
1.   verticesIncluded[0] = 0;  // add vertex 0 to the tree;
2.   numVerticesIncluded = 1;  // one vertex has been added to the tree
3.   for (int i = 0; i < numberOfVertices; i++) // eliminate the edges to vertex 0
4.      aCopy[i][0] = noEdge;
5.   while (numVerticesIncluded < numberOfVertices) // all vertices are not in the tree
6.   { findMinWeightEdge(numberOfVertices, aCopy, verticesIncluded, numVerticesIncluded,
7.                          rowMin, colMin, weightMin)
8.      for (int i = 0; i < numberOfVertices; i++) // eliminate edges to the included vertex
9.      {  aCopy[i][colMin] = noEdge;
10.     }
11.     mst[rowMin][colMin] =minWeight; // add min. weighted edge to tree
12.     mst[colMin][rowMin] =minWeight;
13.     verticesIncluded[numVerticesIncluded] = colMin;  // add the vertex to the included list
14.     numVerticesIncluded++;
15.  } // end while
16.  return mst;
```

Lines 1–4 of the pseudocode perform an initialization. Vertex 0 is added to the tree (Line 1), and then the variable numVerticesIncluded is set to 1 (Line 2) to indicate that one vertex has been added to the tree. Lines 3–4 eliminate all the edges to Vertex 0 by setting their entry in the array aCopy to noEdge, a value selected to be *higher* than any of the edge weightings in the graph. The edges to a vertex are eliminated from the array aCopy when a vertex is added to the minimum spanning tree because once a vertex is added to the tree, we no longer have to consider edges that lead to the vertex; it is already part of the tree. Figure 9.33 shows the contents of the arrays verticesIncluded and aCopy after the initialization performed by Lines 1–4 is complete.

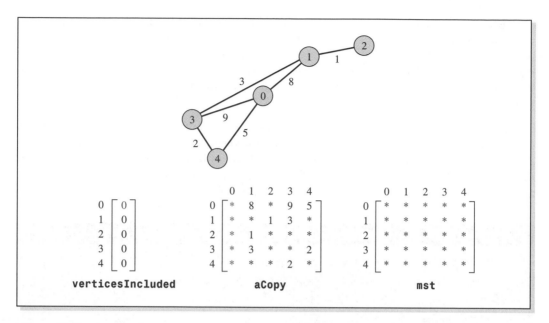

Figure 9.33 Arrays of the Minimum Spanning Tree Algorithm in their Initialized State (* is the impossibly high edge weight)

It also shows the array mst in its initial state. In the figure, an asterisk in an element of a matrix indicates that the element has been set to the impossibly high value of the weighting factor, noEdge.

Line 5 begins a **while** loop that terminates on Line 15 after all the vertices have been added to the tree. Figure 9.34 shows the changes to the contents of the arrays as the loop executes. The progression of the array aCopy is shown in the center portion of the figure with the arrays mst and verticesIncluded on the right and left. The first row of arrays in the figure depicts the array contents during the first pass through the **while** loop, with subsequent passes shown sequentially in the rows below it. The status of the array, verticesIncluded, before each pass through the loop begins, is shown on the left side of each row.

During each pass through the loop, a vertex and an edge is added to the minimum spanning tree. Line 6 uses a method findMinWeightedEdge (assumed to exist) to locate the minimum weighted edge emanating from those vertices currently included in the tree (initially just vertex 0), and returns the row (rowMin) and column (colMin) of that edge's weighting in the array aCopy. It also returns the value of the edge's weighting factor (weightMin).

The rows of aCopy searched each time through the loop by the method appear in color in the leftmost depiction of the array in Figure 9.34, and the minimum weighted edge located by the method each time through the loop is colored in the center depiction of aCopy. Lines 8–10 eliminate the minimum weighted edge, and all the other edges leading to the vertex added to the

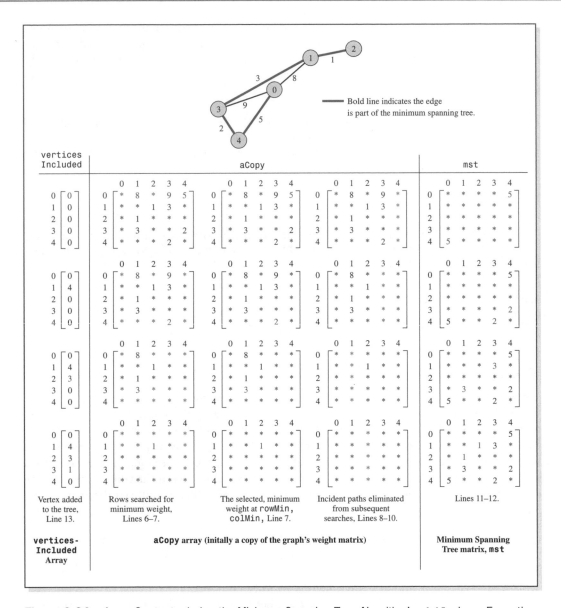

Figure 9.34 Array Contents during the Minimum Spanning Tree Algorithm's **while** Loop Execution (* is an impossibly high edge weight)

tree from the array aCopy. It does this by setting the vertex's column of the array to the value noEdge (see the colored column of the rightmost depiction of the array aCopy in Figure 9.34). As stated above, all these edges are eliminated because once a vertex is added to the tree we no longer have to consider edges that lead to the vertex; it is already part of the tree.

Before the loop ends, Lines 11–12 include the minimum weighted edge in the minimum spanning tree's weight matrix, mst, (as shown on the right side of Figure 9.34). Then, Line 13 adds the vertex's number the edge is incident upon, to the list of vertex numbers included in the tree (see the left side of the next row of Figure 9.34). Finally, Line 14 increments the number of vertices included in the tree.

The coding of the minimum spanning tree algorithm and the method findMinWeightEdge is left as an exercise for the student. Both methods could be added to the class SimpleGraph presented in Figure 9.14. Assuming the name of the method that implements the minimum spanning tree algorithm is minSpanningTree its signature would be:

```
public int[][] minSpanningTree()
```

The returned two-dimensional array would be the weight matrix of the minimum spanning tree. Thus, the client invocation to determine the minimum spanning tree of a SimpleGraph object g would be:

```
minTree = g.minSpanningTree();
```

where minTree is a two-dimensional integer array reference.

9.6.4 Shortest Paths

There are many applications in which we would like to know the shortest path length from one vertex of a graph to another. For example, suppose the vertices of the graph shown in Figure 9.33 represent cities and we want to know the shortest trip between the two cities represented by vertex 0 and vertex 1. Assuming the graph's edges represent the roads connecting the cities and the edge weightings represent the miles between them, the shortest trip would be along the eight mile road connecting the two cities. On the other hand, the shortest trip between the cities represented by vertex 0 and vertex 3 would be the indirect trip of seven miles that would pass through the city represented by vertex 4.

Often, when students are introduced to the problem of determining the shortest path between two vertices, they believe the solution is to travel along the edges of the graph's minimum spanning tree; especially if they have just concluded a study of minimum spanning trees (ring any bells?). However, the minimum spanning tree algorithm produces the shortest route connecting *all* cities, which may not include the shortest route between two cities. For example, the minimum spanning tree for the graph presented in Figure 9.33 is the tree whose edges are represented by the bold lines in Figure 9.34. The roads included in it are the roads from vertex 0 to 4, vertex 4 to 3, vertex 3 to 1, and, finally, from vertex 1 to 2. Therefore, the trip from vertex 0 to 1 would be a 10 mile trip passing through vertices 4 and 3 before arriving at vertex 1. However, as we have previously discussed, it is clear that the shortest trip from vertex 0 to 1 is the eight mile trip along the edge connecting them. Since this edge is not included in the minimum spanning tree, it is apparent that we will need another algorithm to determine the shortest path between any two vertices.

Enter Edsger Dijkstra. In 1959, Edsger Dijkstra discovered an algorithm that determines the shortest path between any two vertices in a connected undirected graph or a connected digraph. The algorithm is aptly named the Dijkstra Shortest Path algorithm. As we will see, the algorithm not only determines the shortest path from any vertex A to any other vertex B, but it also determines the shortest path from vertex A to all the other vertices in the graph, and the path lengths along these paths. The tree comprised of all the vertices of the graph and the edges that form the shortest path from vertex A to all the other vertices, is called the shortest path tree from vertex A.

Dijkstra's Algorithm

Dijkstra's Shortest Path algorithm is very similar to the minimum spanning tree algorithm. They both begin by placing the starting vertex into the tree. Then they consider all the vertices currently in the tree (initially only the starting vertex), and select an edge emanating from them based on a "consideration" of the edge weightings. The selected edge, and its incident vertex are then added to the tree and the process is repeated until all the vertices are added. During the process, an edge to a vertex already in the tree is not considered.

Where the algorithms differ is in the consideration of the edge weightings used to determine which edge to add to the tree. As we have seen, to build a minimum spanning tree, the edges emanating from the vertices currently in the tree *with the minimum weighting* is selected. In the Shortest Path algorithm the edge emanating from the vertices currently in the tree *that produces the shortest path length to the vertex it is incident upon* is selected.

For example, suppose we are to build a minimum spanning tree (MST) starting at vertex 0, and a shortest path tree (SPT) from vertex 0 for the graph depicted in Figure 9.32**a**. Let us assume that the vertices 0, 3, and 4 and the edges 5 and 2 have been added to both trees as shown in Figure 9.32**d**. The next edges to consider for both trees are the edges not already in the tree, emanating from these three vertices that are incident upon vertices not already in the tree. Thus, as depicted in Figure 9.32**d**, the edges with weightings 3 and 8 would be considered (because vertex 1 is not in the tree) and the edges with weightings 2, 5, and 9 would not be considered (because vertices 0, 3, and 4 are already in the tree).

Now things get different. In the case of the minimum spanning tree, the edge with *minimum weighting*, 3, is selected for inclusion in the tree. In the case of the shortest path tree the edge with weighting 8 would be selected, because if 3 were selected the path length from the starting vertex (0) to vertex 1 would be larger than 8, i.e., $10 = 5 + 2 + 3$. Figure 9.35 shows the graph depicted in Figure 9.32**a** along with its minimum spanning tree and the shortest path tree from vertex 0.

The complete process of building the shortest path tree from vertex 0 for the graph depicted in Figure 9.35 is illustrated in Figure 9.36. The vertices that have been added to the tree are depicted as gray circles, and the edges added to the tree as colored lines. The dotted lines are edges under consideration for inclusion into the tree.

First, vertex 0 (the starting vertex) is added to the tree (see Figure 9.36**a**). Then the edges emanating from vertex 0 would be considered (the dashed edges in Figure 9.35**b**) and the edge with weight 5

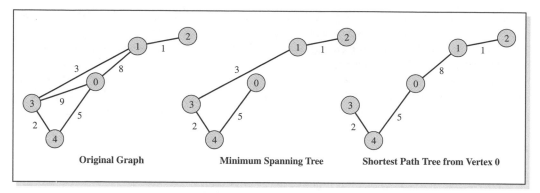

Figure 9.35 A Graph's MST and SPT (from Vertex 0)

(the minimum path length of the paths from vertex 0 to vertices 1, 3, and 4) would be selected. It and its incident vertex, vertex 4, would be added to the tree. Next, the edges emanating from vertex 0 and 4 that are incident upon vertices not yet in the tree (vertices 1 and 3) would be considered (see Figure 9.35**c**). The edge with weight 2 would be selected because it would complete a path from vertex 0 to vertex 3 whose length is 7, which is shorter than the direct path length 9 to vertex 3, or 8 to vertex 1. Thus, the edge with weight 2 and its incident vertex, vertex 3, would be added to the tree. Next, the edges emanating from the tree's vertices 0, 4, and 3 that are incident upon vertices not yet in the tree (vertex 1) would be considered (see Figure 9.32**d**). The edge with weight 8 would be selected because it gives a path length from vertex 0 to vertex 1 of 8 which is shorter than 10 (= 5 + 2 + 3 the path from vertex 0 to 4 to 3 to 1). It and its incident vertex, vertex 1, would be added to the tree. Finally, the edges emanating from vertex 0, 4, 3, and 1 that are incident upon vertices not yet in the tree (vertex 2) would be considered (see Figure 9.32**e**). The edge with weight 1 would be selected (the edges with weights 2, 3, 5, 8, and 9 are not considered because they are either already in the tree or incident upon vertices already in the tree). Having added all the vertices to the tree, the algorithm ends.

The shortest path tree from vertex 0 generated by the algorithm is shown in Figure 9.35**f**. The tree gives the minimum paths from vertex 0 to any other vertex in the tree. This means that if the edge weights represent the length of the roads connecting five towns, the roads included in the graph would be the shortest routes to any town from the starting point (the town represented by vertex 0).

The pseudocode version of the algorithm, which is a modification of the pseudocode version of the minimum spanning tree algorithm, is presented below. The algorithm not only determines the shortest path tree, but also the path lengths of the shortest paths between the starting vertex and each of the tree's other vertices. It uses four arrays. Three of these arrays serve the same function as in the minimum spanning tree algorithm. The array `verticesIncluded` stores the vertices of the graph added to the shortest path tree as the algorithm proceeds; the array `aCopy` is initialized to the graph's weight matrix, and the array `spt` (named `mst` in the minimum spanning tree algorithm) is the weight matrix of the shortest path tree produced by the algorithm.

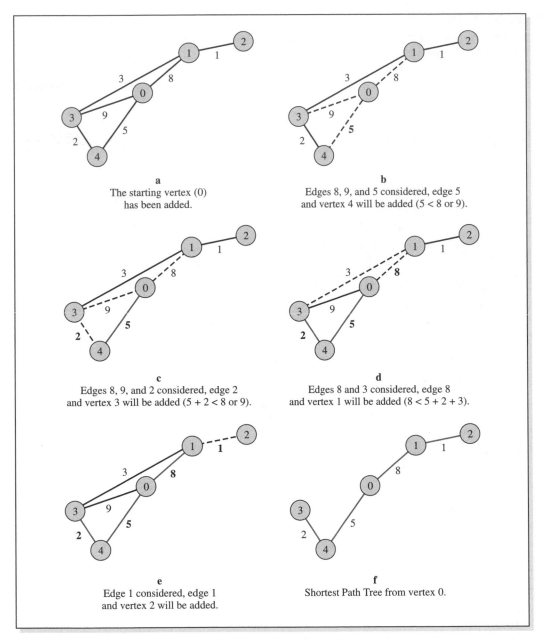

a
The starting vertex (0)
has been added.

b
Edges 8, 9, and 5 considered, edge 5
and vertex 4 will be added (5 < 8 or 9).

c
Edges 8, 9, and 2 considered, edge 2
and vertex 3 will be added (5 + 2 < 8 or 9).

d
Edges 8 and 3 considered, edge 8
and vertex 1 will be added (8 < 5 + 2 + 3).

e
Edge 1 considered, edge 1
and vertex 2 will be added.

f
Shortest Path Tree from vertex 0.

Figure 9.36 The Process of Building a Shortest Path Tree from Vertex 0

The fourth array, `minPathLengths`, has been added to the algorithm to store the path lengths of the shortest paths between the starting vertex and each of the tree's other vertices as these path lengths are generated by the algorithm. The path lengths in this array are initialized to an impossibly high value, `noPath`. When the algorithm ends, the shortest path length from the starting vertex to vertex 0 will be in element 0 of the array, the shortest path length from the starting vertex to vertex 1 will be in element 1, etc.

Dijkstra's Shortest Path Algorithm

```
1.   verticesIncluded[0] = startVertex; // add the starting vertex to the tree;
2.   numVerticesIncluded = 1; // one vertex has been added to the tree
3.   for (int i = 0; i < numberOfVertices; i++) // eliminate edges to the starting vertex
4.   {  minPathLengths[i] = noPath
5.      aCopy[i][startVertex] = noEdge;
6.   }
7.   minPathlengths[startVertex] = 0 // set its path length from the starting vertex to 0
8.   while (numVerticesIncluded < numberOfVertices) // all vertices are not in the tree
9.   { findMinPath(numberOfVertices, aCopy, verticesIncluded, numVerticesIncluded,
10.                  minPathLengths, rowMin, colMin, minWeight, minPath)
11.      for (int i = 0; i < numberOfVertices; i++) // eliminate edges to the included vertex
12.      {  aCopy[i][colMin] = noEdge;
13.      }
14.      spt[rowMin][colMin] =minWeight; // add min. weighted edge to tree
15.      spt[colMin][rowMin] =minWeight;
16.      minPathlengths[colMin] = minPath; // add path length to list of min path lengths
17.      verticesIncluded[numVerticiesIncluded] = colMin; // add vertex to the included list
18.      numVerticesIncluded++; // update the count of vertices included in the tree
19.   } // end while
20.   return spt;
```

Lines 1 to 7 of the pseudocode generalize the initializations performed by the minimum spanning tree algorithm so that any vertex, whose vertex number is contained in the variable `startVertex`, could be the starting vertex. Line 1 adds the starting vertex to the list of vertex numbers included in the tree, and then Line 2 sets `numVerticesIncluded` to 1 to indicate that one vertex has been added to the tree. Lines 3 to 6 is a loop that initializes the path lengths, (Line 4), to an impossible value (`noPath`), and eliminates all the edges to the starting vertex (Line 5) by setting their entry in the array `aCopy` to `noEdge`, an impossible value of the of the edge weightings. The edges to a vertex are eliminated from the array `aCopy` when a vertex is added to the shortest path tree because once a vertex is added to the tree we no longer have to consider edges that lead to the vertex; it is already

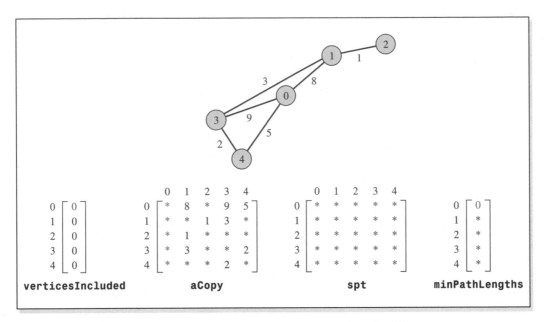

Figure 9.37 Arrays of the Shortest Path Tree Algorithm in their Initialized State

part of the tree. Line 7 completes the initialization process by setting the path length to the starting vertex (from the starting vertex) stored in the array minPathlengths to 0. The four arrays verticesIncluded, aCopy, spt, and minPathlengths are shown in their initialized state in Figure 9.37. The figure depicts the values of noPath and noEdge as an as asterisk, and vertex 0 is assumed to be the starting vertex.

Line 8 of the algorithm begins a **while** loop that terminates on Line 19 after all the graph's vertices have been added to the tree. During each pass through the **while** loop, a vertex and an edge is added to the shortest path tree. Figure 9.38 shows the changes to the contents of the arrays as the loop executes. The first row of arrays in the figure depicts the array contents during the first pass through the loop, with subsequent passes shown sequentially in the rows below it. The status of the array verticesIncluded before each pass through the loop begins, is shown on the left side of each row.

Line 9 of the algorithm uses a method findMinPath (assumed to exist) to determine the minimum of the path length from the starting vertex to the vertices adjacent to those vertices currently included in the tree (initially just vertex 0). It returns the location in the array aCopy (rowMin and colMin) of the edge that completes the minimum of these paths. It also returns the value of the edge's weighting factor (weightMin) and the minimum path length (minPath) from the starting vertex to the incident vertex (colMin).

The rows of aCopy searched by the method each time through the loop appear in color in the leftmost depiction of the array aCopy in Figure 9.38. These are the rows that store the edge weightings

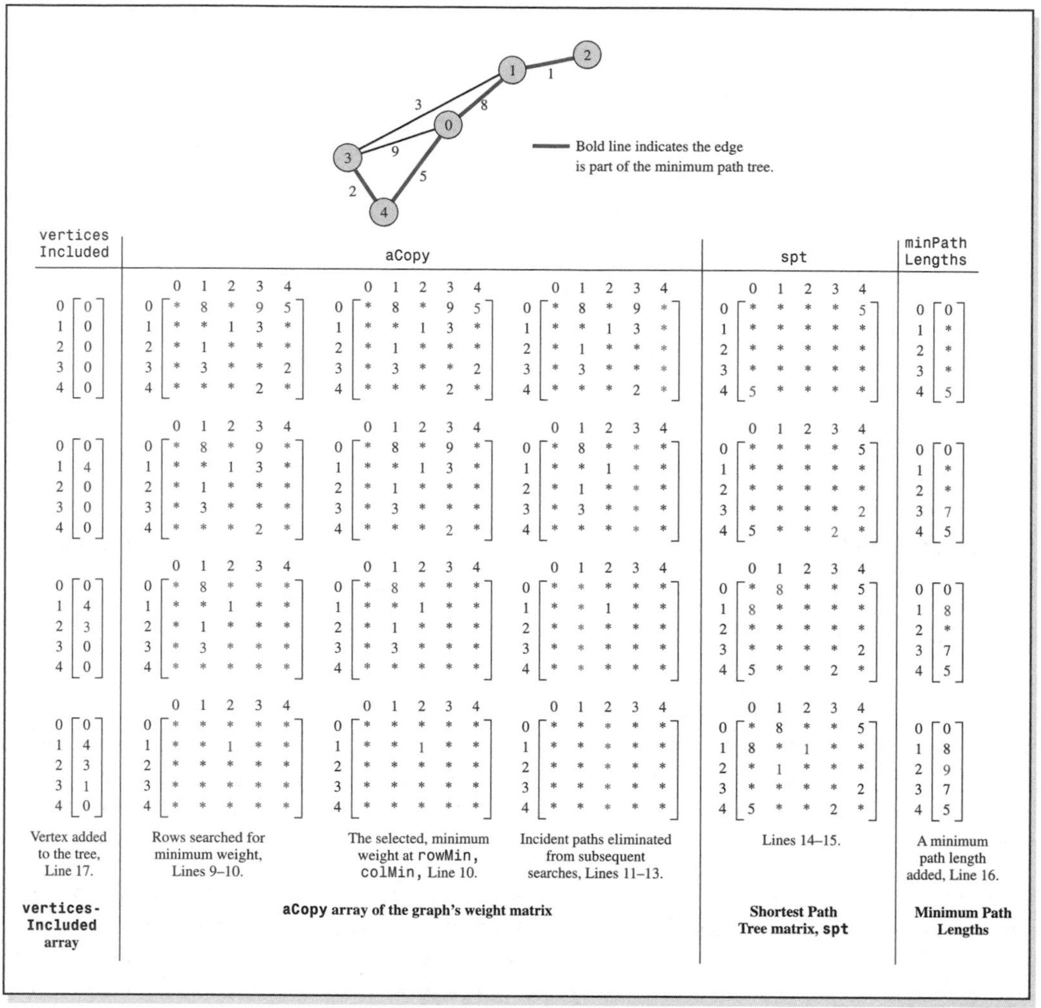

Figure 9.38 Array Contents during the Shortest Path Tree Algorithm's **while** Loop Execution (* is an impossibly high edge weight or is an impossibly high path length)

from the vertices already included in the tree. The minimum of the sum of each of these edge weightings and the path length to each vertex (stored in the corresponding row of the array minPathLengths and intialized to noPath) determines which edge is added to the tree each pass through the loop. The weighting of the edge added to the tree is colored in the center depiction of the array aCopy.

Lines 11–13 eliminate all the edges leading to the vertex included in the tree from the array aCopy. It does this by setting the vertex's column in the array to the value noEdge (see the colored column of the rightmost depiction of the array aCopy in Figure 9.38). As stated, all of these edges are eliminated because once a vertex is added to the tree we no longer have to consider edges that lead to the vertex; it is already part of the tree.

Lines 14 and 15 add an edge to the tree by writing its weighting into the tree's weight matrix, spt, (as shown on the right side of Figure 9.38). Line 16 places the path length to the vertex added to the tree during this pass through the **while** loop into the minPathLength array (see the colored entry on the far right of Figure 9.37).

Finally, Line 17 adds the incident vertex to the tree by writing its vertex number into the list of the tree's vertices (see the left side of the next row of Figure 9.38), and Line 18 increments the number of vertices included in the tree.

The coding of the shortest path algorithm and the method findMinPath is left as an exercise for the student. Both methods could be added to the class SimpleGraph presented in Figure 9.14. Assuming the name of the method that implements the shortest path algorithm is shortestPath, its signature would be:

```
public int[][]shortestPath(int startVertex, int minPathLengths[]).
```

The returned two-dimensional array would be the weight matrix of the shortest path tree containing the edges that produce the shortest paths from the starting vertex. The first parameter would be used by the client to specify the starting vertex number. The second parameter returns the shortest path lengths from that vertex to all the other vertices after the method completes its execution. Thus, the client invocation to determine the shortest path tree from vertex 1 of a SimpleGraph object g would be:

```
shortestPathTree = g.shortestPath(1, minPathLengths);
```

where shortestPathTree is a two-dimensional integer array reference and minPathLength is a one-dimensional integer array reference.

Floyd's Algorithm

As we have seen, Dijkstra's algorithm determines the shortest path from one vertex to all the other vertices in the graph. During the period from 1959 to 1962, Bernard Roy and Robert Floyd developed a remarkably simple algorithm that took the determination of the shortest paths in a graph to a higher level, in that the algorithm determines the shortest path between *all* the pairs of vertices in a directed weighted graph. In addition, its speed is equivalent to the speed of Dijkstra's algorithm.

The algorithm is most commonly known as Floyd's Algorithm, although it is also referred to as the Roy-Floyd Algorithm, or the All-Pairs Shortest Path Algorithm. While it is true that Floyd's Algorithm does not determine the weight matrix that describes the edges involved in the shortest path as Dijkstra's Algorithm does, its ability to treat every vertex as a starting vertex in one pass through the algorithm makes it a very useful algorithm for many applications.

The basis of the algorithm is the idea that the shortest path length from vertex A to C is the shortest of the following two path lengths:

1. The path length from A to C;
2. The path length from A to B plus the path length from B to C, *for all B*.

In other words, the algorithm looks for an intermediate vertex, B, to travel through on its way to C, such that the sum of the path lengths from A to B, and B to C, is shorter than the path length from A to C.

As an example, consider the graph shown in Figure 9.38 and suppose we want to find the shortest path from vertex 0 to 3. The edge connecting them has a path length of 9. If we consider the intermediate vertex to be vertex 1, the total path length would be 11 (= 8 + 3) which is longer than 9, and so vertex 1 would not be accepted as an intermediate vertex for the trip from 0 to 3. However, when vertex 4 is considered the intermediate vertex, the path length is 7 (= 5 + 2) so the algorithm would, from this point forward, consider the path length from vertex 0 to vertex 3 to be 7. The 9 in row 0, column 3 of the weight matrix would be overwritten with a 7.

Proceeding in this way, the algorithm considers each vertex to be a candidate intermediate vertex for every possible point-to-point trip. When a path length that includes an intermediate vertex B is found to be shorter than the entry in the weight matrix for the path length between vertices A and C, the shorter path length is written into the Ath row and Cth column of the weight matrix. This process eventually transforms the weight matrix into the all-points shortest path matrix.

Figure 9.39 shows a weighted graph, its weight matrix, and the all-points shortest paths matrix generated by Floyd's Algorithm. This algorithm once again uses an impossibly large value of an edge weight to indicate the nonexistence of an edge between two vertices (e.g., Java's `Integer.MAX_VALUE`). In the interest of simplicity, Figure 9.39 uses an * symbol as the impossibly large value. The entries in the shortest paths matrix, the product of the algorithm, are the shortest

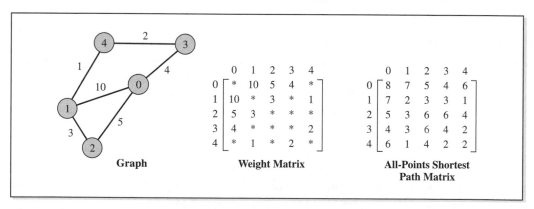

Figure 9.39 A Graph and its All-Pairs Shortest Path Matrix (* is an Impossibly High Edge Weight)

paths between each pair of vertices in the graph. For example, the shortest path between vertex 3 and vertex 2 is 6 (the colored element of the matrix). The path is from vertex 3, to 4, to 1, to 2 (although this path is not produced by Floyd's Algorithm).

The generation of the all-pairs shortest paths matrix for the graph depicted in Figure 9.39 is illustrated in Table 9.1. The leftmost column of each row of the table contains the number of the intermediate vertex, B, that was used for the point-to-point paths identified in the other 16 cells of the row.[7] For example, the first intermediate-vertex considered is vertex 0, and the first point-to-point path examined is the path from vertex 1 to vertex 1 (denoted as $1 \rightarrow 1$ in the table's first row and second column). In some cells of the table there is a number below the path entry. This indicates that the path between the two vertices that included the intermediate vertex was shorter than the path between the two vertices currently stored in the weight matrix. The value in the cell is the path length between the two vertices that includes the intermediate vertex. The current (longer) path length stored in the weight matrix is overwritten with this value.

Let us again consider the trip indicated in the first row and second column of the table, from vertex 1 to vertex 1 with vertex 0 as the intermediate vertex. This is the first case processed by Floyd's Algorithm, and so the weight matrix is in its initialized state as depicted in Figure 9.39. Since the path length for this trip (from A = 1 to C = 1) in the weight matrix is initially impossibly high (* in row 1, column 1 of the weight matrix) and the trip through the intermediate vertex (B = 0) is 20 (the path length from vertex 1 to 0 is 10, and the path from vertex 0 to 1 is 10), the * in the weight matrix is overwritten with the shorter path length 20. The 20 in the first row and second column of the table reflects the overwriting process. The 20 is highlighted in the table, to indicate that it is also overwritten later in the algorithm, first in row 3, column 7, and then again in row 5, column 7.

Next the algorithm considers the trip from vertex 1 to vertex 2, with vertex 0 as an intermediate vertex (see the first row, third column of the table). Examining the weight matrix, the path length from vertex 1 to 2 is currently 3. For the alternate trip, the trip that travels through the intermediate vertex 0, the path length of the trip from 1 to 0 and 0 to 2 is 15 (= 10 + 5). Since this is greater than the current value of the path length stored in the weight matrix (3 in row 1, column 2) the value is not overwritten. Thus, there is no path length entry in the second row, third column of the table.

---

[7]For a five-vertex graph there are a total of 25 point-to-point trips: 0 to 0, 0 to 1, 0 to 2, 0 to 3, 0 to 4, 1 to 0, 1 to 1, etc. Only 16 of these are shown in each row of Table 9.1 because for the trips that begin or end with the intermediate vertex, the indirect trip can only be longer than the direct trip. For example, consider the trip from 0 to 1 with 0 as the intermediate vertex. The trip from 0 to 0 plus the trip from 0 to 1 must be longer than the trip from 0 to 1. Similarly, consider the trip from 1 to 0 with 0 as the intermediate vertex. The trip from 1 to 0 plus the trip from 0 to 0 must be longer than the trip from 1 to 0. Thus, the following 9 trips can be eliminated from the search for an indirect shorter trip when vertex 0 is the intermediate vertex (row 1 of the table): 0 to 0, 0 to 1, 0 to 2, 0 to 3, 0 to 4, 1 to 0, 2 to 0, 3 to 0, and 4 to 0.

Table 9.1

A Trace of Floyds Algorithm Indicating the Changes Made to the Weight Matrix

B	Trip from Vertex A to Vertex C (Denoted A → C)															
0	1→1 **20**	1→2	1→3 **14**	1→4	2→1	2→2 **10**	2→3 **9**	2→4	3→1 **14**	3→2 **9**	3→3 **8**	3→4	4→1	4→2	4→3	4→4
1	0→0 20	0→2	0→3	0→4 **11**	2→0	2→2 6	2→3	2→4 4	3→0	3→2	3→3	3→4	4→0 **11**	4→2 4	4→3	4→4 2
2	0→0 10	0→1 **8**	0→3	0→4 **9**	1→0 **8**	1→1 **6**	1→3 **12**	1→4	3→0	3→1 **12**	3→3	3→4	4→0 **9**	4→1	4→3	4→4
3	0→0 8	0→1	0→2	0→4 6	1→0	1→1	1→2	1→4	2→0	2→1	2→2	2→4	4→0 6	4→1	4→2	4→4
4	0→0 7	0→1 7	0→2	0→3	1→0	1→1 2	1→2	1→3 3	2→0	2→1	2→2	2→3 6	3→0	3→1 3	3→2 6	3→3 4

2→3 ··· Denotes a trip from vertex 2 to vertex 3.

20 ··· Denotes that the path length 20 of the trip that included the intermediate vertex, B, was written into row 2, column 3 of the weight matrix because that trip was shorter than the current path length from vertex 2 to 3 stored in the matrix. The shading indicates a shorter trip from vertex 2 to 3 was eventually found.

In total, 33 new path length values are written into the weight matrix, with 18 of them overwritten (see the 18 highlighted path lengths in the table) by shorter path lengths as the algorithm proceeds.

One of the attractive things about Floyd's Algorithm is that it is amazingly simple to code. For an intermediate vertex, B, the algorithm simply compares the path length from A to C, for all A and C, to the path length from A to B to C. The minimum of these two path lengths is written into the weight matrix as the (shortest) path from A to C. This process is repeated with B set to each vertex in the graph. The pseudocode of the algorithm, including the initialization of a copy of the weight matrix, aCopy, is given below. When the algorithm ends, the shortest path between all pairs of vertices is stored in the weight matrix, aCopy.

Floyd's Algorithm to Find the All-Pairs Shortest Paths

```
1.   for (int b = O; b < numberOfVertices; b++) // all vertices considered as intermediates, B
2.   { for (int a = O; a < numberOfVertices; a++) // all starting vertices, A
3.       { for (int c = O; c < numberOfVertices; c++) // all destination vertices, C
4.           { if (aCopy[a][c] > (aCopy[a][b] + aCopy[b][c])) // A to C > A to B to C
5.                 aCopy[a][c] = aCopy[a][b] + aCopy[b][c]; // store the indirect path length
6.           }                                             // in the weight matrix
7.       }
8.   }
9.   return aCopy;
```

Line 1 generates all possible intermediate vertices, b. Lines 2 and 3 generate all starting vertices, a, and all destination vertices, c. Line 4 compares the path length currently stored in the weight matrix aCopy from vertex A to C to the path length from vertex A to B to C. When the latter path length is shorter, Line 5 stores it in the array aCopy. The coding of the algorithm is left as an exercise for the student.

It should be noted that Floyd's Algorithm can be used to find the all-pairs shortest paths in an undirected or in a directed graph. In a directed graph, it could be the case that a path does not exist between two vertices. The directed graph shown in Figure 9.40 illustrates this point in that there is no way of reaching vertex 2 from any other vertex in the graph, and vertex 3 can only be reached from vertex 2. In addition, none of the vertices can be reached from vertex 3. When a path does not exist between two vertices in a directed graph, Floyd's Algorithm leaves the impossibly high value of the weighting factor in the shortest paths matrix, as indicated by the colored elements of the matrix on the right side of Figure 9.40.

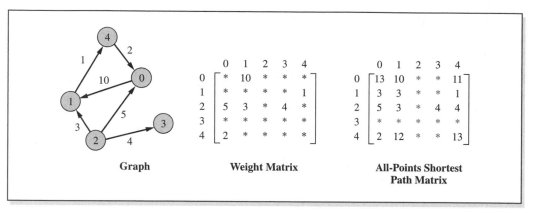

Figure 9.40 A Directed Graph and All-Pairs its Shortest Path Matrix (* is an impossibly high edge weight or path length)

Knowledge Exercises

1. Draw a binary tree that contains six nodes. Then modify the figure so that it is no longer a tree but it is:

   a. A connected graph.

   b. A disjoint (unconnected) graph.

2. Draw a singly linked list that contains four nodes. Then modify the figure so that it is no longer a singly linked list but it is:

   a. A connected graph.

   b. A disjoint (unconnected) graph.

3. Define the terms:

   a. Graph

   b. Undirected graph

   c. Directed graph

   d. Path

   e. Path length

   f. Unconnected (disjoint) graph

   g. Cycle

   h. Complete graph

   i. Simple path

   j. Strongly connected digraph

EXERCISES

4. Calculate the number of edges in a complete graph containing five vertices, and then draw the graph and count the edges to verify your calculation assuming the graph is:

   a. An undirected graph.

   b. A digraph.

5. Give the adjacency matrix for the graphs A and B shown below.

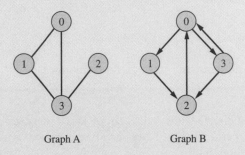

Graph A   Graph B

6. Give the adjacency list representation of the graphs A and B, shown above, assuming:

   a. The number of vertices is fixed.

   b. The number of vertices can expand to a potentially large value and expanding arrays is a slow operation.

7. Draw the graph whose edges are represented by the following matrices. Assume the vertices are named V_0 through V_4.

	0	1	2	3	4
0	0	1	0	1	1
1	0	0	0	0	1
2	0	1	0	1	0
3	1	0	0	0	0
4	0	1	0	1	0

	0	1	2	3	4
0	0	5	0	0	9
1	3	0	0	1	0
2	0	0	0	0	0
3	0	0	4	0	0
4	0	0	0	7	0

	0	1	2	3	4
0	0	1	0	1	1
1	1	0	1	0	0
2	0	1	0	0	0
3	1	0	0	0	0
4	1	0	0	0	0

8. Consider the graphs in the previous exercise. Which of them are:

   a. Disjoint?

   b. Directed?

   c. Weighted?

   d. Undirected?

9. The number of vertices and edges for two undirected and two directed graphs are given in the following table. Fill in the last column of the table to indicate which representation presented

EXERCISES

in Figure 9.12 would be the best performing representation for each graph from a time-complexity viewpoint. Assume array expansion is slow.

Type of graph	Maximum Number of Vertices in the Graph	Maximum Number of Edges in the Graph	Best Representation Figure 9.12a, 9.12b, or 9.12c?
Undirected	10	35	
Undirected	10	16	
Directed	10	35	
Directed	unknown	unknown	

10. Assuming that an undirected, unweighted graph is represented as shown in Figure 9.12**a** and that operations are performed in the vertex number mode, give the signature and describe the actions of a method that:

   a. Deletes an edge from the graph.

   b. Deletes a vertex from the graph.

   c. Updates an edge in the graph.

11. Repeat the previous exercise assuming the graph is:

   a. Directed and unweighted.

   b. Undirected and weighted.

12. Assume a graph is represented as shown in Figure 9.13 and that operations are performed in the vertex number mode. Give the errors that could occur during:

   a. An insert vertex operation.

   b. An insert edge operation.

   c. A show vertex operation.

13. Give the changes to the code presented in Figure 9.14 so that it could store a digraph rather than an undirected graph.

14. Is an NLR traversal of a binary tree a depth-first or breadth-first traversal?

15. Which traversal algorithm uses a queue, breadth-first, or depth-first, and why?

16. Assuming vertex 1 in graph A of Exercise 5 is visited first, give the order in which the vertices of the graph are visited if the traverse is a:

   a. Depth-first traversal.

   b. Breadth-first traversal.

17. In a connected undirected graph, there is always a path from vertex A to B, for all A and B. True or false?

18. In a connected digraph, there is always a path from vertex A to B, for all A and B. True or false?

19. Identify an algorithm for determining if an undirected graph is connected.

20. Identify an algorithm for determining if a digraph is strongly connected.

21. Given a digraph's transitive closure matrix, how can we determine if there is a path from vertex v_i to v_j, and a path from vertex v_j to v_i?

22. State the difference between a spanning tree and a minimum spanning tree.

23. It is possible to have more than one minimum spanning tree for a graph, true or false?

24. What does Dijkstra's Algorithm do that Floyds Algorithm cannot do?

25. What does Floyd's Algorithm do that Dijkstra's Algorithm cannot do?

26. Dijkstra's Algorithm is to operate on a graph containing n vertices. Using Big-O notation, give the speed of the algorithm.

27. Floyd's Algorithm is to operate on a graph containing n vertices. Using Big-O notation, give the speed of the algorithm.

28. Draw the graph obtained when Dijkstra's Algorithm operates on the following graph, assuming vertex 4 is the starting vertex.

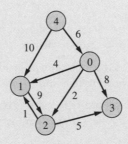

29. Give the contents of the returned array when Floyd's Algorithm operates on the graph shown in Exercise 28.

30. True or false, Floyd's Algorithm can only operate on directed graphs?

31. Of the algorithms we studied, which would be used to determine the two-way roads to close a connecting group of towns, and still allow access to all towns?

32. Of the algorithms we studied, which would be used to determine the toll roads to travel to minimize the tolls when traveling from a given town to all other towns?

33. Of the algorithms we studied, which would be used to determine if there is a way to pass through all towns connected by one-way streets?

34. Of the algorithms we studied, which would be used to determine the cheapest fares between all the cities that an airline flies to?

Programming Exercises

35. Extend the class SimpleGraph, shown in Figure 9.14, so that it expands the size of the arrays whenever necessary. Write a simple application to demonstrate it functions properly.

36. We wish to expand the class SimpleGraph, shown in Figure 9.14, to include methods to delete a vertex, delete an edge, fetch a vertex, fetch an edge, update an edge, update a vertex.

    a. Give the pseudocode of the methods' algorithms.

    b. Extend the code of the class SimpleGraph, to include the new methods and write a simple application to demonstrate they function properly.

37. Modify the class SimpleGraph so that it can store a weighted graph and expand its methods to include those mentioned in Exercise 36.

38. Change the class SimpleGraph, shown in Figure 9.14 so that the access mode of the revised class is the key field mode. Write a simple application to demonstrate it functions properly.

39. Revise the class SimpleGraph, shown in Figure 9.14, so that it represents a graph using the scheme depicted in Figure 9.12b. Write a simple application to demonstrate it functions properly.

40. Revise the class SimpleGraph, shown in Figure 9.14, so that it represents a graph using the scheme depicted in Figure 9.12c. Write a simple application to demonstrate it functions properly.

41. Add a method to the class SimpleGraphDFT, shown in Figure 9.20, that performs a breadth-first traversal. Write a simple application to demonstrate it functions properly.

42. Add a method to the class SimpleGraph, shown in Figure 9.14, that implements Warshall's Algorithm. Write a simple application to demonstrate it functions properly.

43. Modify the spanning tree method presented in this chapter so that the client can specify the starting vertex. Write a simple application to demonstrate it functions properly.

44. Add a method to the SimpleGraph, shown in Figure 9.14, that implements the minimum spanning tree algorithm. Write a simple application to demonstrate it functions properly.

45. Implement the minimum spanning tree algorithm for the graph representation depicted in Figure 9.12b. Write a simple application to demonstrate it functions properly.

46. Implement Dijkstra's Algorithm for the graph representations shown in Figures:

    a. 9.12a

    b. 9.12b

    c. 9.12c

    Write a simple application to demonstrate your implementation(s) function properly.

47. Implement Floyd's Algorithm for the graph representations shown in Figures:

    a. 9.12a

   b.   9.12**b**

   c.   9.12**c**

Write a simple application to demonstrate your implementation(s) function properly.

48. We wish to supply water to a group of *n* villages. Given the distances that separate each village from every other village, write a program that determines the minimum total length of water pipe that can be run between the villages, such that each village will be supplied water.

49. A set of roads connect towns with multiple routes available from each town to the others. Write a program that determines the minimum plowing time necessary to clear the roads after a snowstorm so that any of the area residents will be able to travel to all towns. The snow plow travels 20 miles an hour, less 1 mile per hour for each 6 inches of snow on the road. The number of towns, the roads that connect them, the distance between the towns, and the amount of snow (in inches) on the roads will input to the program. You may assume that the residents will stay off the roads until the roads are plowed.

50. Given the flight times for a set of connecting flights between *n* cities, write a program to determine and output the *maximum* flight times between all pairs of cities.

ASCII Table

(First 127 Unicode characters)

(ASCII = *A*merican *S*tandard *C*ode for *I*nformation *I*nterchange)

Decimal	Octal	Hex	Binary	Value	
000	000	000	00000000	NUL	(Null char.)
001	001	001	00000001	SOH	(Start of Header)
002	002	002	00000010	STX	(Start of Text)
003	003	003	00000011	ETX	(End of Text)
004	004	004	00000100	EOT	(End of Transmission)
005	005	005	00000101	ENQ	(Enquiry)
006	006	006	00000110	ACK	(Acknowledgment)
007	007	007	00000111	BEL	(Bell)
008	010	008	00001000	BS	(Backspace)
009	011	009	00001001	HT	(Horizontal Tab)
010	012	00A	00001010	LF	(Line Feed)
011	013	00B	00001011	VT	(Vertical Tab)
012	014	00C	00001100	FF	(Form Feed)
013	015	00D	00001101	CR	(Carriage Return)
014	016	00E	00001110	SO	(Shift Out)
015	017	00F	00001111	SI	(Shift In)
016	020	010	00010000	DLE	(Data Link Escape)
017	021	011	00010001	DC1	(XON) (Device Control 1)
018	022	012	00010010	DC2	(Device Control 2)
019	023	013	00010011	DC3	(XOFF)(Device Control 3)
020	024	014	00010100	DC4	(Device Control 4)
021	025	015	00010101	NAK	(Negative Acknowledgment)
022	026	016	00010110	SYN	(Synchronous Idle)
023	027	017	00010111	ETB	(End of Trans. Block)
024	030	018	00011000	CAN	(Cancel)
025	031	019	00011001	EM	(End of Medium)
026	032	01A	00011010	SUB	(Substitute)
027	033	01B	00011011	ESC	(Escape)
028	034	01C	00011100	FS	(File Separator)
029	035	01D	00011101	GS	(Group Separator)
030	036	01E	00011110	RS	(Request to Send)
031	037	01F	00011111	US	(Unit Separator)
032	040	020	00100000	SP	(Space)
033	041	021	00100001	!	
034	042	022	00100010	"	
035	043	023	00100011	#	
036	044	024	00100100	$	
037	045	025	00100101	%	
038	046	026	00100110	&	
039	047	027	00100111	'	
040	050	028	00101000	(	
041	051	029	00101001	)	
042	052	02A	00101010	*	
043	053	02B	00101011	+	
044	054	02C	00101100	,	

Decimal	Octal	Hex	Binary	Value
045	055	02D	00101101	-
046	056	02E	00101110	.
047	057	02F	00101111	/
048	060	030	00110000	0
049	061	031	00110001	1
050	062	032	00110010	2
051	063	033	00110011	3
052	064	034	00110100	4
053	065	035	00110101	5
054	066	036	00110110	6
055	067	037	00110111	7
056	070	038	00111000	8
057	071	039	00111001	9
058	072	03A	00111010	:
059	073	03B	00111011	;
060	074	03C	00111100	<
061	075	03D	00111101	=
062	076	03E	00111110	>
063	077	03F	00111111	?
064	100	040	01000000	@
065	101	041	01000001	A
066	102	042	01000010	B
067	103	043	01000011	C
068	104	044	01000100	D
069	105	045	01000101	E
070	106	046	01000110	F
071	107	047	01000111	G
072	110	048	01001000	H
073	111	049	01001001	I
074	112	04A	01001010	J
075	113	04B	01001011	K
076	114	04C	01001100	L
077	115	04D	01001101	M
078	116	04E	01001110	N
079	117	04F	01001111	O
080	120	050	01010000	P
081	121	051	01010001	Q
082	122	052	01010010	R
083	123	053	01010011	S
084	124	054	01010100	T
085	125	055	01010101	U
086	126	056	01010110	V
087	127	057	01010111	W
088	130	058	01011000	X
089	131	059	01011001	Y

Decimal	Octal	Hex	Binary	Value	
090	132	05A	01011010	Z	
091	133	05B	01011011	[	
092	134	05C	01011100	\	
093	135	05D	01011101	]	
094	136	05E	01011110	^	
095	137	05F	01011111	_	(underscore)
096	140	060	01100000	`	
097	141	061	01100001	a	
098	142	062	01100010	b	
099	143	063	01100011	c	
100	144	064	01100100	d	
101	145	065	01100101	e	
102	146	066	01100110	f	
103	147	067	01100111	g	
104	150	068	01101000	h	
105	151	069	01101001	i	
106	152	06A	01101010	j	
107	153	06B	01101011	k	
108	154	06C	01101100	l	
109	155	06D	01101101	m	
110	156	06E	01101110	n	
111	157	06F	01101111	o	
112	160	070	01110000	p	
113	161	071	01110001	q	
114	162	072	01110010	r	
115	163	073	01110011	s	
116	164	074	01110100	t	
117	165	075	01110101	u	
118	166	076	01110110	v	
119	167	077	01110111	w	
120	170	078	01111000	x	
121	171	079	01111001	y	
122	172	07A	01111010	z	
123	173	07B	01111011	{	
124	174	07C	01111100			
125	175	07D	01111101	}	
126	176	07E	01111110	~	(tilde)
127	177	07F	01111111	DEL	(delete)

Derivation of the Average Search Length of a Nondirect Hashed Data Structure

The derivation will be based on the following assumptions:

- There are n nodes in the structure, and the size of the primary storage area is N.
- All N primary storage area locations are equally probable to be generated each pass through the collision algorithm.

The easiest way to present the derivation for average search length is to consider the search for an unused location in which to perform an Insert operation. By our first assumption, n of the N locations are used. Therefore, the probability of hashing into an occupied location is n/N. For example, if there are 700 nodes in the structure, and the size of the primary storage area array is 1000, then n/N is 0.70, meaning there is a 70% chance that we will hash into an occupied location. Under our second assumption, every probe into the primary storage area has the same probability, n/N, of hashing into an occupied location. This implies that the previously hashed location is just as likely as any other to be hashed into.

As an aside, if the collision algorithm were sophisticated enough to *not* revisit a location after it was found to be occupied (as some are), then the probability of a collision would decrease after each pass through the collision algorithm. The collision probability of the first pass would still be n/N, but since the location probed would no longer be considered, the total number of remaining occupied spots would be one less, and the total of the primary storage area would also be one less. Therefore, the probability of a collision on probe two would be $(n - 1)/(N - 1)$, on the third pass $(n - 2)/(N - 2)$, and on the ith pass $(n - i - 1)/N - i - 1)$. Since N is greater than n, this expression approaches zero as i increases.

Under our second assumption however, the probability of the hashing and collision algorithms calculating an occupied location is n/N, for every probe into the primary storage area. Since a location can only be occupied or not occupied, the sum of the probability of finding the location occupied, p_o, and unoccupied, p_u, must be equal to 1. Thus $p_o + p_u = 1$, or $p_u = 1 - p_o$. Therefore, the probability of finding an unoccupied location on any probe is $(1 - n/N)$. Returning to our example, if the probability of a collision is 0.70 (70%), then the probability of finding an unused location (a noncollision) is 0.30 (30%).

The probability of finding an empty spot by the ith probe, means that the first $i - 1$ probes resulted in a collision, while the ith probe resulted in a noncollision. The probability of the first $i - 1$ probes resulting a collision is $(n/N)_{probe1} * (n/N)_{probe2} * \ldots * (n/N)_{probe i-1} = (n/N)^{i-1}$.

The probability of finding an empty spot on the ith probe is therefore:

$$P_i = (n/N)^{i-1} * (1 - n/N)$$

which is the probability of $i - 1$ collisions, followed by a noncollision. Returning to our example again, the probability of finding an open spot on the fourth probe is:

$$(0.70)^{4-1} * 0.30 = 0.70 * 0.70 * 0.70 * 0.3 = 0.1029 \text{ or approximately 10\%.}$$

The average search length, for a group of operations, is the total number of memory accesses to perform the operations divided by the number of operations. To determine a formula for the average search length, it is useful to consider a case where 10 Insert operations are performed. Three of these find an empty spot with no collisions, and so the number of memory accesses for each of these operations is one. Four inserts resulted in one collision each, and so the number of memory accesses for each of these inserts is two. Finally, three inserts resulted in two collisions, and so they each take three memory accesses. The average search length, L_{avg}, per operation is:

L_{avg} = total access/number of operations

$$= \frac{(1 \text{ access} * 3 \text{ inserts}) + (2 \text{ accesses} * 4 \text{ inserts}) + (3 \text{ accesses} * 3 \text{ inserts})}{10 \text{ operations}}$$

$$= (1 * 3/10) + (2 * 4/10) + (3 * 3/10)$$

Examining the above equation, we observe for this example:

3/10 is the probability of finding an open location on the first probe,
4/10 is the probability of finding an open location on the second probe,
3/10 is the probability of finding an open location on the third probe,

and that the multiplier of these probabilities are the probe numbers. Generalizing this observation we have:

$$L_{avg} = 1 * P_1 + 2 * P_2 + 3 * P_3$$

or, in general,

$$L_{avg} = 1 * P_1 + 2 * P_2 + 3 * P_3 + \ldots + N * P_N,$$

where: P_1 is the probability of finding an empty spot on the first probe

P_2 is the probability of finding an empty spot on the second probe, etc.

From our earlier result, $P_i = (n/N)^{i-1} * (1 - n/N)$, and so the above can be written as:

$$L_{avg} = 1 * (n/N)^0 * (1 - n/N) + 2 * (n/N)^1 * (1 - n/N)$$

$$+ 3 * (n/N)^2 * (1 - n/N) + \ldots + N * (n/N)^{N-1} * (1 - n/N)$$

$$= \left(\sum_{i=1}^{N} i * (n/N)^{i-1} \right) * (1 - n/N).$$

But since $i * (n/N)^{i-1}$ is positive, extending the summation from zero to infinity will produce a larger result. Therefore,

$$L_{avg} \leq \left(\sum_{i=0}^{\infty} i * (n/N)^{i-1} \right) * (1 - n/N).$$

Since the summation in the above equation can be shown to be[1] equal to $1/(1 - n/N)^2$ the average search length is:

$$L_{avg} <= 1/(1 - n/N)^2 * (1 - n/N) = 1/(1 - n/N).$$

---

[1] In the absence of a proof, use an Excel® spreadsheet to calculate $\sum_{i=0}^{50} i * (n/N)^{i-1}$ and compare it to $1/(1 - n/N)^2$ for any $n < N$.

Here's the proof (thanks to David Holtzman of St. Joseph's College, New York):

Let $n/N = x$. Note that the right-hand side becomes $1/(1 - 2x + x^2)$. Let us cross-multiply the infinite sum on the left by the quadratic denominator on the right with the hope of getting 1. This would prove the identity.

Now

$$\left(1 - 2x + x^2 * \sum_{i=1}^{\infty} i * (x)^{i-1} = \sum_{i=1}^{\infty} i * (x)^{i-1} + (-2x) \sum_{i=1}^{\infty} i * (x)^{i-1} + x^2 \sum_{i=1}^{\infty} i * (x)^{(i-1)} \right)$$

$$= 1 + \sum_{i=1}^{\infty} (i + (-2(i + 1)) + (i + 2))x^{i+1}$$

Here we have just collected the coefficients of each power of x from 2 up to infinity. (Note that the linear terms of $2x$ and $-2x$ cancel out.)

Now observe that $i - 2i - 2 + i + 2 = 0$. Thus, we end up with 1, as desired.

Proof That If an Integer, *P*, Is Not Evenly Divisible by an Integer Less Than the Square Root of *P*, It Is a Prime Number

546

Appendix C: Proof That If an Integer, *P*, Is Not Evenly Divisible by an Integer Less Than the Square Root of *P*, It Is a Prime Number

Preliminary Proof

Given:

R = the square root of P.

Prove:

If $P = H * L$, either $H = L$ = the square root of P, or H or L is $< R$ and the other is $> R$.

Proof:

If both were $> R$, then their product would be greater then P, and if both were less than R, their product would be less than P.

Desired Proof

Given:

There are no integers less than R (the square root of P) that divide evenly into P.

Prove:

There are no integers greater than R that divide evenly into P.

Proof:

Assume: H is an integer $> R$ and that H divides evenly into.

Then: Define L as $L = P / H$.

L is an integer, since $L = P / H$ and H divides evenly into P

L must divide evenly into P since H is an integer and $H = P / L$.

Since $P = H * L$ and $H > R$, then $L < R$ (as per preliminary proof).

The assumption implies L is an integer that divides evenly into P and is less than R, which contradicts the given fact. Therefore, the assumption cannot be true.

Calculations to Show That $(n + 1) (\log_2(n + 1) - 2)$ Is the Minimum Sort Effort for the Binary Tree Sort

Appendix D: Calculations to Show That $(n + 1)(\log_2(n + 1) - 2)$ Is the Minimum Sort Effort for the Binary Tree Sort

Calculated Sort Effort $(n + 1)*$ $(\log_2(n + 1) - 2)$	level	Number of Nodes		Actual Sort Effort (Number of Comparisons)	
		at this level	in the tree, n	to fill this level	to fill the tree
0	0	1	1	0	0
0	1	2	3	2	2
8	2	4	7	8	10
32	3	8	15	24	34
96	4	16	31	64	98
256	5	32	63	160	258
640	6	64	127	384	642
1536	7	128	255	896	1538
3584	8	256	511	2048	3586
8192	9	512	1023	4608	8194
18,432	10	1024	2047	10,240	18,434
40,960	11	2048	4095	22,528	40,962
90,112	12	4096	8191	49,152	90,114
196,608	13	8192	16,383	106,496	196,610
425,984	14	16,384	32,767	229,376	425,986
917,504	15	32,768	65,535	491,520	917,506
1,966,080	16	65,536	131,071	1,048,576	1,966,082
4,194,304	17	131,072	262,143	2,228,224	4,194,306
8,912,896	18	262,144	524,287	4,718,592	8,912,898
18,874,368	19	524,288	1,048,575	9,961,472	18,874,370
39,845,888	20	1,048,576	2,097,151	20,971,520	39,845,890
83,886,080	21	2,097,152	4,194,303	44,040,192	83,886,082
176,160,768	22	4,194,304	8,388,607	92,274,688	176,160,770
369,098,752	23	8,388,608	16,777,215	192,937,984	369,098,754
771,751,936	24	16,777,216	33,554,431	402,653,184	771,751,938
1,610,612,736	25	33,554,432	67,108,863	838,860,800	1,610,612,738
3,355,443,200	26	67,108,864	134,217,727	1,744,830,464	3,355,443,202
6,979,321,856	27	134,217,728	268,435,455	3,623,878,656	6,979,321,858
14,495,514,624	28	268,435,456	536,870,911	7,516,192,768	14,495,514,626
30,064,771,072	29	536,870,912	1,073,741,823	15,569,256,448	30,064,771,074
62,277,025,792	30	1,073,741,824	2,147,483,647	32,212,254,720	62,277,025,794
128,849,018,880	31	2,147,483,648	4,294,967,295	66,571,993,088	128,849,018,882
266,287,972,352	32	4,294,967,296	8,589,934,591	137,438,953,472	266,287,972,354
549,755,813,888	33	8,589,934,592	17,179,869,183	283,467,841,536	549,755,813,890
1,133,871,366,144	34	17,179,869,184	34,359,738,367	584,115,552,256	1,133,871,366,146
2,336,462,209,024	35	34,359,738,368	68,719,476,735	1,202,590,842,880	2,336,462,209,026
4,810,363,371,520	36	68,719,476,736	137,438,953,471	2,473,901,162,496	4,810,363,371,522
9,895,604,649,984	37	137,438,953,472	274,877,906,943	5,085,241,278,464	9,895,604,649,986
20,340,965,113,856	38	274,877,906,944	549,755,813,887	10,445,360,463,872	20,340,965,113,858

Glossary

A

Abstract data type   A set of data and the operations that can be performed on the data.

Abstraction   The idea of knowing how to use something without the underlying knowledge of how it functions.

Access specifier   A key word in a language that determines the scope of an entity.

Access mode   See key field mode or node number mode.

Adjacency list   A set of linked lists, one list associated with each vertex in a graph, in which each one of the nodes in a list stores information about one of the edges emanating from the vertex it is associated with. The information includes the adjacent vertex number and, in a weighted graph, the edge's weight.

Adjacent vertices   The vertices in a graph that have an edge between them, or in the case of a digraph, two edges between them (one from vertex a to b, and another from vertex b to a).

Adjacency matrix   A square matrix in which each element stores one edge of the graph.

ADT   *Abstract Data Type* (see data abstraction).

Algorithm   A step-by-step solution to a problem that a computer can execute.

Algorithm complexity   A measure of the efficiency of an algorithm. See time and space complexity.

Ancestor   In a tree, a node's ancestor is any of the nodes encountered in moving from the root to the node, including the root node.

Ancestor class   See parent class.

Application code   In the context of data structures, it is the code that declares an object in the data structure class.

Arc   A directed edge in a graph.

Argument   A piece of information passed to a method.

Array   A technique for naming groups of memory cells that share a common first name and a unique last name. In Java, the unique last name, called an index, must be a literal integer or a variable that stores an integer. From a data structures perspective, an array is a data structure whose major design goal was speed. It is stored in contiguous memory, accessed in the node number mode, and supports the Fetch and Delete operations.

Array-based structures   Those data structures that utilize an array as their underlying structure (at their lowest level).

ASCII   *American Standard Code for Information Interchange.* ASCII is a table of characters and the bit patterns that represent them.

AVL tree   A self-balancing binary search tree that is always balanced to within one level.

B

Balanced binary tree   A binary tree in which all the levels of the tree below the highest level are filled.

Base case   The base case is the known portion of a recursive problem solution. It is often called the escape clause.

Base class   See parent class.

BFT   See breadth-first traversal.

Big-O analysis   An analysis technique that approximates the upper bound of a function. It is used to determine the complexity of an algorithm.

Big-O notation $O(n^2)$ is read as order n^2.

Binary search   A search technique used on a sorted list of n data items in which the middle item is accessed, half the list is discarded, and the list is replaced with the remaining half of the list.

This process is repeated until the item being searched for is found. Its speed complexity is $O(\log_2 n)$.

Binary search tree   A binary tree in which the nodes are arranged such that, for every node in the tree, all the keys in a node's left subtree are less than its key, and all the keys in a node's right subtree are greater than its key.

Binary tree   A tree in which every node in the tree has, at most, two children.

Bit   Binary digit. A single on-off switch of storage, which, when on is designated 1, and when off is designated 0.

Boolean   A variable type that can assume one of two values, true or false.

Breadth-first traversal   A graph traversal technique; for each vertex visited all of its siblings are visited before any of its descendents are visited. In a graph, siblings are vertices that have an edge from a common vertex, assuming the common vertex has already been visited.

Bubble sort   A sorting technique that compares adjacent items in a list and exchanges them when they are not in their proper sorted position relative to each other. During each pass through the algorithm at least one item is positioned in its final sorted position in the list.

Bucket   Elements of the primary storage area in a hashed structure that are not used to store references to a single node, but rather to multiple nodes. For example, they are used as a header of a singly linked list of nodes or a reference to an array of nodes.

Built-in data type   A data type that is defined as part of a language standard.

Byte   Eight contiguous bits of storage.

C

Ceiling x Rounding a floating point value x up to the next highest integer.

Child class   A class that inherits from (or is derived from) another class.

Child node   A child node is a node that comes directly after a node in a tree. Any node in a tree that is not the root node.

Circuit   A cycle that passes through every vertex of a graph once.

Circular doubly linked list   A doubly linked list in which the forward link field of the last node references the first node, and the back link field of the first node references the last node.

Circular singly linked list   A singly linked list in which the forward link field of the last node references the first node.

Class   A programming construct that permits the programmer to define a type consisting of data definitions and the methods that operate on that data. A template for an object.

Client code   The code that declares an instance of an ADT, or invokes a method.

Clone   A newly created object whose data fields contain the same values as an existing object.

Clustering   The tendency of nodes in a hashed data structure not to be randomly distributed over the primary storage area.

Collision   When two keys map into the same position in the primary storage area of a hashed structure.

Collision resolution   The process of finding an alternate position in a hashed structure after a collision has occurred.

Compile time   That point in time when the correctness of a program's syntax and semantics is verified and, if correct, the program is translated into a lower-level language.

Complete tree   A tree that contains the maximum number of nodes for its height.

Complete graph   A graph is said to be complete if the path length between any two distinct vertices is 1.

Complexity   See algorithm complexity.

Connected graph   A graph is a connected graph if, given any two of its vertices v_i and v_j, there is a path from v_i to v_j, ignoring the direction of the edge.

Constructor   A method in a class that has the same name as the class and is used by a client to create an object.

Contiguous   Adjacent; side-by-side.

Cycle   A path in a graph that begins and ends with the same vertex.

D

Data   Information.

Data abstraction   The idea that we need not know the details of how data is stored in order to access it.

Data encapsulation   Utilizing compiler-enforced protocols to restrict access to the data that a program processes.

Data member   A variable definition that is part of a class. Each instance of the class will be allocated storage for the variable.

Data structure   A data structure is an organization of information, usually in memory, for better algorithm efficiency.

Data type   A name that defines a set of values and the operations that can be performed on them.

Descendent class   See child class.

Deep copy   The process of copying the contents of all of the data members of one object into the data members of a second object.

Default constructor   A constructor with no parameters that sets a newly created object's data members to default values.

Delete A fundamental operation performed on data structures that removes a node from the structure.

Depth-first traversal A graph traversal technique in which for each vertex visited all of its adjacent vertices (its *descendents*) are visited before any of its siblings are visited. In a graph, siblings are vertices that have an edge from a common vertex, assuming the common vertex has already been visited.

Dequeue An operation performed on a queue that fetches and deletes the node that has been in the queue the longest amount of time.

Derived class See descendent class.

Descendent class A class that inherits from another class.

Descendent of a node A node encountered in a path from the node.

Digraph A graph for which the direction of travel along the graph's edges is specified.

Directed edge An edge for which the direction of travel is specified.

Directed graph See digraph.

Disjoint graph A graph that is not connected.

Division Hashing function A hashing function in which the key is divided by an integer and the remainder is used as the key's home address.

Doubly-linked list A linear linked list in which each node contains the address of its successor node and its predecessor node.

Dummy node A node in a data structure that will not be used to store client information.

Dynamic memory allocation The allocation of storage for variables at run-time.

Dynamic structure A data structure that can expand or contract at run-time via dynamic memory allocation.

E

Edge A bidirectional path between two vertices in a graph.

Edge weight A value assigned to an edge in a weighted graph.

Encapsulation The concept of combining data and the operations that operate on the data as one entity. Access to the data is restricted, normally by compiler-enforced protocols, to the use of the encapsulated operations.

Enqueue An operation performed on a queue that inserts a node at the end of the queue.

Exponential complexity Algorithm complexity that is a function of the power of the number of items (n) being processed, denoted $O(c^n)$.

Exception An out-of-the-ordinary event that occurs during the execution of a program.

F

Factorial of *n*   The product of the integers from *n* to 1 . Denoted *n*!.

Factorial complexity   Algorithm complexity that is a function of the factorial of the number of items (n) being processed, denoted $O(n!)$.

Fetch   A fundamental operation performed on data structures that returns a node from the structure.

Fibonacci sequence   A sequence in which each term's value is the sum of the values of the two terms before it, with the exception of the first two terms whose values are 1.

Floor *x*   Rounding a floating point value *x* down to the next lowest integer.

Field   An indivisible piece of data.

First-in-first-out (FIFO)   The idea that the first item added to a data structure will be the first item fetched from the data structure.

Flag   A variable used by a program to indicate that an event has occurred.

Floating point number   A number with a fractional part; a real number.

Flowchart   A graphical representation of an algorithm aimed at depicting execution path.

Folding   The process of dividing a key into groups of bits and then arithmetically adding the groups to produce a pseudokey.

Fold shifting   A folding algorithm.

Four-k-plus-three prime   A prime number that, when reduced by 3 and then divided by 4, produces an integer value.

Front of a queue   The position of the next item to be fetched (and deleted) from a queue.

Function   A method that returns a value via a return statement.

G

Garbage collection   The process of returning memory assigned to a program, or to a data structure, that is no longer in use to an available memory pool.

General solution   The part of a recursive algorithm that uses the reduced problem to solve the original problem.

H

Hashed structure   A data structure that uses a hashing algorithm to locate a node.

Hashing   A process in which a node's key is used to determine the node's probable location in a data structure without searching through memory.

Hashing function   A function that maps keys into node locations.

Header   The reference variable that stores the location of the first node in a linked list.

Heap   A binary tree in which the key of each node in the tree is larger than the keys of both of its children.

Heap sort   A sorting algorithm that transforms a list of items to be sorted into a heap. Then it repeatedly swaps the root into its correct sorted position and rebuilds the heap out of the remaining items.

Height balanced   See balanced binary tree.

Height of a tree   The number of nodes in the longest path from the root to any of the leaf nodes.

Home address   The location produced by preprocessing and hashing a key.

I

Indegree   The number of directed edges incident upon a vertex of a graph (or node of a tree).

Index   An item (an integer in Java) used to specify a particular element of an array.

Infix notation   A technique used for writing mathematical expressions in which the operator is placed between the two operands it operates on.

Inheritance   The object-oriented concept of incorporating all of the member data and methods of an existing class into a new class. The new class can add additional methods and data.

Inline function   The inclusion of a copy of the executable code of a method into a program's executable module wherever the method is invoked (as opposed to transferring the execution to a single copy of the method at run-time).

Inner class   A class that is defined inside of another class.

Inorder traversal   A binary tree traversal technique in which a node's entire left subtree is visited before the node, then the node is visited, and then the node's entire right subtree is visited recursively.

Insert   A fundamental operation performed on data structures that adds a node to the structure.

Integer   A number without a fractional part.

Interface   A Java construct that specifies the signatures of methods, not their code. It is a "promise" to the translator that methods with these signatures will be written in the future. Once the interface is defined, the methods can be invoked on instances of the interface without a compile error, and an instance of a class that codes the methods can be referenced by an interface reference.

Instance of a class   An object in a class (created with the new operator in Java).

Instantiation   The process of creating an object.

Iteration   A single pass through a loop construct.

Iterative solution   An algorithm whose solution involves loop(s), not recursion.

Iterator   An item that moves sequentially through a linear list and retains its position between moves.

J

Java   An object-oriented language whose design goal was platform independence.

K

Key field   A designated field in a node whose contents is used to identify the node.

Key field mode   An access mode in which the contents of the key field is used to specify which node in a data structure is to be operated on.

L

Last-in-first-out (LIFO)   The idea that the last item added to a data structure will be the first item fetched from the data structure.

Leaf   A node in a tree that has no children.

Left child   In the standard depiction of a binary tree, the node that is below and to the left of a node.

Left subtree   In the standard depiction of a binary tree, all of the nodes in a binary tree below and to the left of a node.

Level of a node   The number of nodes in the path from the root to the node (not counting the node).

Level of recursion   The number of times a recursive method has invoked itself.

Linear collision algorithm   A collision algorithm that adds 1 to the current primary storage area location to determine the next location to be examined (usually using modulo arithmetic).

Linear list   A set of nodes in which there is a unique first and last node, and every other node has a unique predecessor and successor.

Linear Quotient collision algorithm   A collision algorithm that adds the quotient obtained by dividing the key by the size of the primary storage area to the current primary storage area location to determine the next location to be examined (usually using modulo arithmetic). When the quotient is an even multiple of the size of the primary storage area, a predetermined $4k + 3$ prime is used in place of the quotient.

Link field   A field in a node that stores the address of (reference to) another node in the structure.

Linked list   A linear list in which each node contains at least one reference to another node in the list.

List   An ordered set of nodes.

LNR traversal   See inorder traversal.

Loading factor   The ratio of the number of nodes in a hashed structure to the size of the primary storage area.

Logarithmic complexity   Algorithm complexity that is a function of the base-two logarithm of the number of items (n) being processed, denoted $O(\log_2 n)$.

M

Member method   A method that is coded inside the definition of a class.

Merge sort   A sorting technique that divides a list into two halves, sorts each half, and then merges the two sorted lists into one sorted list. The merge is performed by indexing through each list, comparing their members, and copying the smaller member into the sorted list. Each half of the list is sorted the same way.

Method A programming language construct (or subprogram) that consists of a sequence of instructions to perform a specific task (or set of tasks). The transfer of the execution path to and from it, and the transfer of the information shared between it and the invoking code, is provided for by the compiler.

Minimum Spanning Tree A spanning tree of a weighted graph whose edges are chosen such that the sum of their weightings is minimized.

Modulo operator An operator that determines the remainder of division.

N

NLR traversal Stands for *node-left* subtree-*right* subtree. See preorder traversal.

Node A collection of related fields.

Node number mode An access mode in which the number of a node is used to specify which node in a data structure is to be operated on. A node's number usually corresponds to its position in a linear structure.

Null The value stored in a reference variable when it does not reference an object.

O

Object A particular occurrence of a class. The memory allocated for the data members and the associated methods of the class.

Open Addressing collision algorithm A collision algorithm that resolves collisions by producing an alternate position in the primary storage area (as opposed to a position in a linked list, or an index into an array referenced by the primary storage area).

Operand The item in an expression on which an operation will be performed.

Operator The item in an expression that specifies the action to be performed on one or more of the operands in the expression.

Outdegree The number of directed edges emanating from a vertex of a graph (or node of a tree).

Outer class A class that has another class (an inner class) defined inside it.

Overflow The error that occurs when an attempt is made to insert an item into a full restricted structure.

P

Package access The default Java access specifier (i.e., public, private, or protected is not specifically declared) for a class' member data and methods. Their scope is the code of any class in the same package.

Parameter The type of a piece of shared information and the name used to refer to the information while a method (subprogram) is in execution.

Parent class   A class that is inherited from.

Parent of a node   A node's unique predecessor in a tree.

Path   A sequence of edges that connect two vertices in a graph.

Perfect Hashed structure   A hashed structure that uses a Perfect Hashing function.

Perfect Hashing function   A hashing function that maps each key, or pseudokey, into a unique location in the primary storage area.

Pivot value   The item in a list of items to be sorted by the Quicksort algorithm, which will divide the partitions used by the algorithm.

Pointer   Another name for a reference variable (used in C and C++).

Polynomic complexity   Algorithm complexity that is a function of the number of items processed, n, raised to a power (e.g., $O(n^2)$, $O(n^3)$, ...).

Pop   An operation performed on a stack that fetches and deletes the node that has been in it the shortest amount of time.

Postfix notation   A technique used for writing mathematical expressions in which the operator is placed after the two operands it operates on.

Postorder traversal   A binary tree traversal technique in which a node's entire left subtree and then its entire right subtree is visited before the node is visited, recursively.

Predecessor node   Generally speaking, the node that comes before a node in a structure. In a linked list, the node that contains the address of a node is its predecessor. In a directed graph, the vertex whose directed edge is incident upon a vertex is its predecessor.

Prefix notation   A technique used for writing mathematical expressions in which the operator is placed before the two operands it operates on.

Preorder traversal   A binary tree traversal technique in which a node is visited, and then its entire left subtree is visited, and then its entire right subtree is visited, recursively.

Preprocessing   The action performed on a key in a hashed data structure to convert it to the type of the hashing function's independent variable, or to more evenly distribute nodes over the primary storage area, or both.

Prime number   A number that is only evenly divisible by 1 and itself.

Private access   Limiting the scope of a class' data members or methods to code of the class' methods.

Primary clustering   In a hashed structure, when the nodes that map into the same home address are located in close proximity to the home address.

Primary storage area   In a hashed data structure, the storage indexed by the home address generated by the hashing function. The storage is usually implemented as an array, and often it is referred to a hash list or a hash table.

Primitive data type   In Java, the built-in types `boolean`, `byte`, `short`, `int`, `long`, `char`, `float`, and `double`.

Primitive variable   A named memory cell that stores the value of a primitive data type.

Priority queue   A restricted data structure that fetches (and deletes) nodes in an order based on a priority assigned to each node.

Probe   In a hashed structure, one "look" into the structure.

Procedural abstraction   The concept of knowing how to use a method (subprogram) without knowing the underlying algorithm or implementation.

Programmer defined data type   A data type whose definition is specified as part of a program (as opposed to a built-in data type).

Pseudocode   A sequence of statements used to specify an algorithm that resembles a programming language but exhibits less precise syntax.

Pseudokey   The result of processing a key through a preprocessing algorithm.

Pseudorandom preprocessing   A preprocessing algorithm that attempts to introduce more randomness into the keys before they are processed by a hashing function. The objective is to reduce clustering and thereby reduce the search length.

Public access   Setting the scope of a class' member method or data to the code of any method in a program.

Push   An operation performed on a stack that inserts a node into the stack.

Q

Quadratic collision algorithm   A collision algorithm that adds the square of the probe number to the current primary storage area location to determine the next location to be examined (usually using modulo arithmetic).

Quadratic complexity   Algorithm complexity that is a function of the number of items processed (n) squared, denoted $O(n^2)$.

Query   An inquiry.

Queue   A restricted data structure that operates on a first-in-first-out basis.

QuickSort   A sorting technique in which a list of items is partitioned into two sublists divided by a pivot item. Then, the items in the left and right sublists are repositioned such that each of the items in the left and right partitions are less than and greater than the pivot value, respectively. This process is applied to each of the partitions recursively.

R

Random number   A number chosen from a set of numbers under the condition that each number in the set has an equal probability of being chosen.

Real number   A number with a fractional part.

Real-time   Processing events at the time they occur, usually so rapidly that the processing appears to be instantaneous.

Rear of a queue   The position in a queue where the next node inserted will be placed.

Recursion   Defining the solution to a problem, at least partially, in terms of similar problems that are closer to a known solution.

Recursive method   A method x is a recursive method if it invokes itself, or if it invokes a method that eventually leads to an invocation of method x.

Recycle   See garbage collection.

Recurrence relation   An algorithm for generating the terms of a sequence by using the terms previously determined. See the Fibonacci sequence.

Reduced problem   In a recursive algorithm, a problem similar to a problem to be solved that is closer to the base case and eventually becomes the base case.

Red-Black tree   A self-balancing binary search tree that assigns a color (red or black) to each node in the tree as part of its balancing algorithm.

Reference variable   A variable that stores a memory address.

Restricted structure   A set of data structures whose operations and access modes are severely restricted. Among other restrictions, the Fetch and Delete operations are combined, key field mode access and Update are not allowed, and node number mode is restricted.

Return   A programming language statement that terminates the execution of a nonvoid method and returns a value to the invoking method.

Right child   In the standard depiction of a binary tree, the node below and to the right of a node.

Right subtree   In the standard depiction of a binary tree, all of the nodes below and to the right of a node.

Root   The unique first node in a tree (that has no predecessor).

Rotation   A repositioning of nodes performed by AVL and Red-Black trees as part their balancing algorithms.

Run-time   The time during which a program is in execution.

S

Scope of an item   That part of a program in which the item can be accessed.

Search tree   A tree whose nodes are positioned to facilitate the operations performed on them (e.g., binary search trees, AVL trees, Red-Black trees).

Secondary clustering   In a hashed structure, when nodes with the same home address (although scattered throughout the primary storage area) generate the same sequence of collision addresses.

Sentinel   A signal.

Sentinel value   An unrealistic value of a data item.

Sentinel loop   A loop that terminates when a sentinel value is detected.

Sequential search   A search technique in which the items of a linear list are searched in item number order.

Shallow copy   The process of copying the address of an object from one reference variable to another. Both variables then refer to the same object. A new object is not created.

Shortest path   The path between two vertices in a directed graph that the minimizes the sum of the edge weights.

Siblings   In a tree, nodes with the same parents. In a graph, siblings are vertices that have an edge from a common vertex, assuming the common vertex has already been visited.

Simple cycle   A simple path in which the first and last vertex is the same.

Simple path   A path in which all vertices encountered along the path, except possibly the first and last vertices, are distinct.

Singly linked list   A linked list in which each node in the list contains one link field.

Software engineering   A branch of computer science that deals with the techniques of developing software products that are fault free, within budget, delivered on time, and satisfy the clients' needs now and in the future.

Software engineer   A programmer that utilizes the techniques of software engineering to develop a software product.

Space complexity   The efficiency of an algorithm from a memory overhead viewpoint.

Spanning tree   The set consisting of a graph's vertices and a subset of its edges chosen such that each vertex can be reached from every other vertex and there are no cycles.

Stack   A restricted data structure that operates on a last-in-first-out basis.

Stack frame   The collection of information on a stack maintained by an operating system that is particular to a specific invocation of a method (subprogram).

Strongly connected digraph   Given any two vertices in a digraph there is a way of reaching one from the other by traveling along the graph's edges, considering the direction of the edges.

Subclass   See child class.

Subtree of a node   All of the nodes in a tree whose root is a child of the node.

Successor   Generally speaking, the node that comes after a node in a structure. In a linked list, a node's successor is the node whose address is stored in its link field. In a directed graph, vertex a is vertex b's successor if there is a directed edge from vertex b to vertex a.

Super class   See parent class.

Symmetric matrix   A matrix, in which, for every pair of elements a_{ij} and a_{ji}, $a_{ij} = a_{ji}$.

Synonym   Two keys that map into the same home address of a hashed structure's primary storage area.

T

Time complexity   The efficiency of an algorithm from an execution speed viewpoint.

Token   An item in a string delimited by white space.

Top of a stack   The position in a stack were the next pop will be performed.

Traversal   The process of locating and visiting each node in a structure once and only once.

Tree   A connected graph with no cycles.

U

Underflow   The error that occurs when an attempt is made to fetch (and delete) an item from an empty restricted structure.

Undirected graph   A graph in which bidirectional travel is permitted along its edges.

Update   A fundamental operation performed on data structures that changes the contents of the fields of a node stored in the structure.

User   The person interacting with a program while it is executing.

Unicode   A table of characters and the 16 bit patterns that represent them. The ASCII characters are the first 128 entries in the Unicode table with eight zero's added to the high order side of the ASCII bit representations. Java represents characters internally (i.e., in storage) using the Unicode table.

V

Variable   A named memory cell that stores a specific type of information, and whose contents can change during the execution of a program.

Vertex   A node in a graph.

Visiting a node   The process of performing an operation on a node in a data structure.

Void method   In Java, a method that does not return a value. In other programming languages, a method that does not return a value by way of a return statement.

W

Wall time   The passage of time as measured by a clock (on the wall).

Weakly connected graph   A connected digraph that is not strongly connected.

Weighted graph   A graph whose edges are each assigned a value.

Weight of an edge   See edge weighting.

Index

A

absolute speed, 22–23, 26–29
  case study, 28–29
  methodology, 29
abstract data type (ADT), 17
abstraction, 17
access function, 233
access modes, 13
  key field, 13
  node number, 13
access modifiers, 35, 39
adjacency list, 487
  vs. adjacency matrix, 487–489
adjacency matrix, 485–486
adjacent vertex, 481, 487, 488
ADT. *See* abstract data type
algorithm complexity
  functions, 21
  space, 20 (*see also* density)
  time (absolute speed,
    relative speed), 19
algorithm speed, 19, 22–23

absolute 23, 26–29
relative, 23–26
algorithms
  Dijkstra's, 519–525
  Floyd's, 525–530
  Warshall's, 507–509
all-pairs shortest path
    algorithm. *See* Floyd's
    algorithm
API classes
  `ArrayList`, 118–119
  `Hashtable`, 291–292
  `LinkedList`, 223–225
  `ListIterator`, 223–225
  `Stack`, 168–169, 500
  `System`, 105
  `TreeMap`, 412, 423–426
application code, 6
  array based structures,
    99, 117
  generic data structure
    application, 115

application code, (*Continued*)
  graph structures, 504, 510
  hashed structures, 293
  iterators, 216, 222, 224
  linked structures, 199, 216, 222, 224
  queue, 162
  stack, 142
  trees, 399, 426
application programmer interface, 6.
    See also API classes
array, 15, 17, 60
  access mode, 13, 65
  abstraction, 15, 17
  base address, 61
  column-major order, 63
  declaration of, 33, 44
  design goals, 60
  expanding, 35, 105–106
  index, 15, 17, 63
  Java syntax, 33–35, 44–45, 63
  mapping function, 62, 63
  memory model, 61–64
  multidimensional, 63
  of objects, 44–45
  of primitives, 33–35
  one-dimensional mapping function, 62
  operations allowed, 60, 63
  row-major order, 63
  subscript, 60, 63–64
  two-dimensional mapping function, 64–65
  two dimensional syntax, 63
  viewed as a binary tree, 413
  viewed as a data structure, 60, 65
array-based structures, 65–66
  binary tree (*see* binary search tree array-based)
  errors, 66, 84
  graphs (*see* graphs)
  hashed structures (*see* direct hashed structures;
    LQHashed structure)
  performance comparison, 82, 425
  sorted array, 73
  unsorted array, 66 (*see also* unsorted
    array-based structures)
  unsorted-optimized array, 79 (*see also* unsorted-
    optimized array-based structures)
ArrayList class, 118
ASCII, 259
  table, 537

AVL trees, 364, 407–412
  balance factor, 408, 413
  delete algorithm, 407–409, 412
  extent of imbalance, 409
  fetch algorithm, 408, 412
  insert algorithm, 408
  performance vs. red-black, 413
  rotations, 409–412
  update algorithm, 408, 412

B
backtracking, 328
  application of methodology, 336–342
  decision points, 329
  decision trees, 331–333
  generalized backtracking algorithm,
    333–335
  Knights Tour problem, 329
  Knights Tour solution, 343
  maze example, 331
  methodology, 335–336
  Queens Eight problem, 328, 342–346
  recursion (use of), 332
  summary of methodology
    adaptation, 345
balanced trees, 357, 363–364, 380
  advantage of, 363
  AVL trees, 364, 407
  parent-child node distribution,
    785–786
  red-black trees, 364, 412
  search trees, 364, 406
base case, 307, 313–314, 316, 318
  for several problems, 324
basic operations, 14
  action of, 15
  standard signatures, 16
belongs-to relationship, 12
BFT. *See* breath-first-traversal
Big-O, 20
  algorithm complexity, 21
  analysis, 20–23
  notation, 21
Big-Omega (Ω), 22
Big-Theta (Θ), 22
binary search, 24, 66
  performance, 25–26
  use of, 73–75

binary search trees. *See also* AVL; red-black trees
  advantages of, 361
  array-based, 413 (*see* binary search tree
    array-based)
  balancing, 406–407
  client code, 399, 426
  definition of, 361
  delete algorithm, 372–380, 384–385
  density, 391–392
  example of, 360–361
  fetch algorithm, 371, 383
  findNode algorithm, 367–370, 381–382
  implementation (linked), 392
  initialization, 366 –, 367, 417
  insert algorithm, 367, 371, 383, 417, 419
  node representation, 363
  operation algorithms (linked), 367–380
  performance, 380–393
  performance comparison, 393, 425
  positioning nodes in, 362
  showAll method, 398, 406
  skewing, 363, 406, 418–421,
  speed complexity, 380–391
  traversal, 398, 406
  TreeNode class, 365, 396
  TreeNodeWrapper class, 396, 397
binary search tree array-based, 413
  children's index rule $(2i + 1, 2i + 2)$, 413
  compared to linked implementation,
    421, 425
  delete algorithm, 416, 423
  density, 420
  density if balanced, 421
  density if imbalance, 421–423
  fetch algorithm, 418
  imbalance (tolerance for), 419, 421
  initialization, 416–417
  insert algorithm, 416
  performance, 419
  performance comparison, 425
  root node index, 413
  size of the array, 419
  speed complexity, 419
  update algorithm, 71
binary trees. *See also* binary search trees
  density (linked), 391
  definitions and terms, 352
  mathematics of, 358

standard graphics, 355, 356
  traversal (*see* binary tree traversal)
binary tree representations
  array, 413
  linked, 365
binary tree sort, 437
  algorithm, 437
  overhead, 422
  performance, 439
  performance comparison, 472
  sort effort, 441
  sorting process, 437–438, 439
  speed complexity, 439–442
binary tree traversal
  definition of, 355
  examples of, 405
  LNR traversal, 401, 402, 406
  standard traversals, 398, 400–401
  trace of LNR, 403–405
  visiting a node, 355, 398
breadth-first traversal (BFT), 400, 503
  algorithm, 504
  example of, 504
  visitation order, 503
  queue use, 503
Bridges of Koningsberg, 479–480
bubble sort, 442
  algorithm, 445
  early termination, 445
  overhead, 447
  performance, 445
  performance comparison, 448, 472
  sort effort, 447
  sorting process, 442–445
  speed complexity, 445
  swap effort, 447
bucket hashing, 292. *See also* linked
    hashed structures
built-in
  structure, 4
  types, 33
burdened labor rates, 9

C

child and parent references, 47–48
child class, 46
circuits. *See* cycles
circular singly linked list, 202

class
    naming convention, 36
    data members, 34–35
    definition of, 34
    definition code, 35
    method naming convention, 40–41
    methods, 35–36
classes
    BinaryTree, 394
    Factorial, 308
    FactorialTrace, 310
    GenericStack, 166
    Listing, 89, 141,
    Listing2, 202, 501
    LqHashed, 280
    NewNode, 219
    Node, 102, 190
    Person, 36
    PersonGeneric, 35
    PhoneListing, 116
    Queue, 160
    SimpleGraph, 493
    SimpleGraphDFT, 500
    SinglyLinkedList, 189
    SinglyLinkedListIterator, 213
    SllIterator, 219
    SllExternalIterator, 220
    Stack, 140
    TreeNode, 396
    TreeNodeWrapper, 396
    UnsortedOptimizedArray, 91
    UOA (generic), 113
    UOAUtilities, 103
    WeightLossClass, 45
classes in the API. *See* API Classes
client code, 39, 90. *See also* application code
    error detection, 93
    generic data structure application, 115
client side code. *See* client code
clock pulse, 27
clone. *See* deep copy
clustering, 266
    primary clustering, 266–268, 273
    secondary clustering, 266, 268–269, 270, 273
collision, 235, 250. *See also* non-perfect hashing
collision algorithms, 236, 263. *See also* non-perfect
        hashed structures
    clustering, 266, 266–269, 270, 273
    linear, 264, 266

    linear-quotient, 269–270
    multiple accesses, 266, 271
    non-open addressing, 263–264
    open addressing, 263
    primary clustering, 266–268, 273
    problems with, 250, 252
    quadratic, 264, 266
    secondary clustering, 266, 268–269,
        270, 273
column-major order, 62–64
Comparable interface, 426
Complexity, 22. *See also* algorithm complexity
    complexity functions
compareTo method, 89, 141
complete trees, 9, 11, 40, 75, 91
connected graph, 483, 503, 505
connectivity, 503, 505
    determination of, 507
    speed complexity, 507
constant complexity, 21
constructor, 36
containership, 45–46
    memory model, 45
contiguous, 18, 33, 174–175
copies. *See* shallow copy; deep copy
current loading factor, 252
C++, 5, 12
CPU register, 29
cycles, 482, 509, 511

D
data, 2–3
data abstraction, 17
data encapsulation, 18
data structure, 5
    basic operations, 14–15
    client side declaration, 91
    client side error checking, 92–93
    design process, 9–11
    error checking, 84
    generic guidelines, 16–17 (*see also* generic data
        structures)
    implementation class, 16
    implementation of, 16
    memory, 4
    selection process, 5–11
    speed, 4, 29
    standard for goodness, 5
    terminology, 11–13

data structure performance
  calculation of, 8
  comparison of, 425
  frequency weighted average, 30–31
  importance of, 3, 8
data structures. *See also* array-based structures
  built-in, 5 (*see also* graphs; hashed structures;
    linked implementation of)
  programmer defined, 5–6
  performance comparison, 8, 425 (*see also* queue;
    stack; trees)
decision points, 329
decision trees, 331–333
deep copy
  in data structures, 69–70, 93
  methods, 43–44
  syntax, 44
  water analogy, 42–43
default constructor, 80, 105, 118, 141
default prime, 270–272, 284
delete operation, 14
delete problem, 274
  solution, 276
deleting edges, 491
deleting nodes
  array-based structures, 68, 74, 80
  binary search trees
  graphs, 484, 487, 491
  hashed structures, 242, 243, 274, 279
  linked structures, 186
  queues, 127, 150, 154
  stacks, 127, 131, 134
deleting vertices, 491
density
  constant vs. variable overhead, 32–33
  definition of, 32
  examples, 32–33
  formula for, 31–32
density vs. node width
  array-based structures, 84
  binary tree (array-based), 422, 423
  binary tree (linked), 392
  doubly linked list, 207, 210
  hashed structures (array-based), 246,
    255, 287
  hashed structures (linked), 296
  multi-linked list 210
  queue, 138, 159 (*see also* density vs. node
    width, stack)

singly linked list, 194, 207
stack, 138
depth first traversal (DFT), 400, 497
  algorithm, 499
  client side code, 502
  example of, 498
  implementation, 500
  stack use, 497–498
dequeue
  algorithm, 154
  method, 160
derived class. *See* child class
descendent
  class, 47
  node, 7–5
  vertex, 497
design process. *See* trade-off
DFT. *See* depth first traversal
digit extraction preprocessing, 262
Dijkstra's shortest path algorithm, 519
  algorithm process, 521
  application of, 518
  client side use of, 525
  example of, 520
  implementation guidelines, 925
  pseudocode, 522
  speed complexity, 525
  trace, 524
  vs. Floyd's algorithm, 525
  vs. minimum spanning tree, 519–520
directed edge, 481
directed graph, 481
direct hashed structure, 238
  delete algorithm, 242
  density, 244
  encapsulation, 241
  fetch algorithm, 242
  garbage collection, 242
  hashing function, 240
  initialized state, 239–240
  insert algorithm, 240
  loading factor, 245–46
  overhead, 245
  performance, 243, 247
  primary storage area, 239
  speed, 246
  string preprocessing, 238
  subtraction preprocessing, 238
  update algorithm, 243

direct recursion, 308
directed tree, 353
disjoint graph, 505, 506
division hashing function, 233, 276
dominate terms, 21–22
dot operator (.), 38
doubly linked list, 205
dummy nodes
    in hashed structures, 275, 277, 284, 286, 292, 295
    in linked structures, 181
duplicate definition error, 35
dynamic hashed structures, 290
dynamic memory allocation, 175
dynamic programming, 327
    advantage of, 291
    Hashtable class (*see* API classes)
    hybrid approach, 290–291, 296
    memory model, 290
dynamic structures
    array-based, 105
    binary tree, 365
    hashed, 290
    linked, 175

E
edges
    definition of, 478
    information stored in, 491
    insert algorithm, 492–493
    operations performed on, 491
    representation of, 485–498
    weighs, 479, 491
edge array. *See* adjacency matrix
encapsulation, 23
    advantages of, 19
    data, 18
    demonstration of, 97
    in classes, 90
enqueue
    algorithm, 153
    method, 160
error handling
    in applications, 91
errors
    client side detection of, 92–93
    demonstration of, 98
    detection of (*see* specific data structure)
    in basic operations, 84
    out-of-bounds, 266

queue overflow and underflow, 149
stack overflow and underflow, 129
system memory, 90
expanding arrays at run time, 35, 105–106
    algorithm, 105
    speed, 106
exponential complexity, 21–22
extending classes, 47, 212, 500
extends key word, 47

F
factorial, 306
factorial complexity, 21–22
factorial methods
    iterative, 327
    recursive, 307
fetch operation, 13–14
fetching nodes
    array-based structures, 69, 74, 79, 86
    binary search trees, 371, 383, 418
    graphs, 492
    hashed structures, 242, 278, 282, 284, 286
    linked structures, 184
    queues, 149, 154
    stacks, 129, 130
Fibonacci sequence, 320
field, 11
FIFO, 148
findNode method, 396
first-in-first-out (FIFO), 148
Floyd's algorithm, 525
    basis of algorithm, 526
    pseudocode, 529
    shortest path matrix, 526, 530
    speed complexity, 525
    trace, 527–528
    vs. Dijkstra's algorithm, 525
folding preprocessing, 258–261, 262, 276
    speed complexity, 285
four-k-plus-three prime (4k + 3), 255, 257, 270, 284
frequency weighted average time, 30–31
front of a queue, 148–149

G
garbage, 68
garbage collection, 68
    hashed structure, 242
    Java memory manager, 42

linked list, 187
   queue structure, 143, 156
   sorted array-based structure, 74
   unsorted array-based structure, 68
   unsorted-optimized array-based structure, 80
general solution, 313, 315, 316, 317–318
   for several problems, 330
generic classes, 51
generic data structures. *See also* generics
   advantages of, 106
   application code, 117
   array-based structure conversion, 109
   class GenericStack, 166
   class UOA, 113
   client side, 110, 115, 167
   coding guidelines, 16–17
   conversion methodology, 164
   conversion to, 109
   design considerations, 106
   hashed, 289–290,
   heterogeneous data set, 117
   interfaces, 110–111, 165–166
   node definition, 116
   stack, 165
generic methods, 50–51
GenericNode interface, 166
generics. *See also* generic data structures
   classes, 51–52
   Java features, 49
   methods, 50–51
   object declaration, 50–51
   parameters, 50–51
   primitive arguments, 52
   type placeholders, 49, 109
GenericStack class, 166
get prefix, 40–41
get methods
   getAge, 40
   getKey, 283, 284, 289, 290
graph access modes
   vertex number, 491
   key field, 491
graph connectivity, 503
   definitions of, 503, 505
   in directed graphs, 481, 483, 484, 486–488, 493,
     503–505, 509, 525
   minimum spanning tree, 512
   shortest paths (*see* Dijkstra's algorithm; Floyd's
     algorithm;)

   spanning trees, 509
   in undirected graphs, 481–484, 486–488, 493,
     497, 504–506, 510, 512, 513, 519, 529
   Warshall's algorithm, 507
graph operations, 491
   insert algorithms, 492
   methods, 493
   on edges, 491
   on vertices, 491
graph representations, 484
   adjacency list, 487
   adjacency matrix, 485
   edges, 485
   impact on performance, 487–489
   selection criteria (summary), 489
   vertices, 484, 490
graph terminology, 481–483
   adjacency, 478, 481
   complete, 483
   connected graph, 503, 505
   connected vertex, 503
   cycle, 482
   directed (digraph), 481
   disjoint, 505, 506
   edges, 478
   path, 482
   path length, 482
   shortest path, 518
   simple path, 482
   strongly connected graph, 505
   undirected graph, 481
   vertex, 478
   weakly connected graph, 505
   weighted, 481
   weights, 479
graph traversals, 494
   BFT (breadth first traversal), 497
   DFT (depth first traversal), 503
   visitation, 494
graphs
   adjacency, 478, 481
   adjacency lists, 485, 487–489
   adjacency matrix, 485–487
   all-pairs shortest path, 525
   applications of, 479, 505
   Bridges of Koningsberg, 479
   breadth-first traversal, 503
   client side code, 495, 502, 510
   compared to trees and linked lists, 478–479

graphs (*Continued*)
    connectivity (*see* graph connectivity)
    definition of, 481, 484
    depiction of, 480
    depth-first traversal, 497
    implementation using arrays, 493, 500
    maximum number of edges, 483–484
    minimum spanning tree, 512
    operations (*see* graph operations)
    representing edges (*see* graph representations)
    representing vertices (*see* graph representations)
    shortest path, 518 (*see also* Dijkstra's and Floyd's
        algorithms)
    spanning tree, 509
    terminology (*see* graph terminology)
    transitive closure matrix, 508
        (*see also* Warshall's algorithm)
    traversing (*see* traversing graphs)

H
hashed structures. *See also* direct hashed structure
    and LQHashed structure
    advantages of, 232
    direct hashed, 238
    dynamic (*see* dynamic hashed structures)
    LQHashed structure, 276
    non-perfect LQHashed structure, 237, 246 (*see
        also* non-perfect hashed structures)
operation algorithms, 240–242, 277–279
    perfect, 237 (*see also* perfect hashed structures)
    performance of, 243, 250, 285
    primary storage area, 233,
    primary storage area size, 236, 257
    schemes, 233
hashcode method, 259, 289, 290, 291
hashing. *See also* non-perfect hashed structures
    access function, 233
    alphanumeric keys (*see* preprocessing algorithms)
    buckets, 292
    collisions (*see* collision resolution algorithms)
    current loading factor, 252
    linear probing (*see* collision algorithms)
    linear quotient probing (*see* collision
        algorithms)
    loading factor, 234, 236, 245–246, 252–253, 276,
        287, 291, 295–296
    maximum loading factor, 234, 252
    numeric keys (*see* preprocessing)

    open addressing (*see* collisions)
    perfect, 236–237 (*see also* perfect hashed struc-
        tures and direct hashed structure)
    preprocessing (*see* preprocessing)
    process, 233–234
    quadratic probing (*see* collision algorithms)
hashing access functions, 232
    direct, 233, 235
    division, 233, 235
    perfect, 236
Hashtable class, 291
    client code, 293
    constructors, 291
    encapsulation (lack of), 292
    equals method, 291
    generic nature of, 292–293
    hashCode method, 291
    key types, 291
    methods, 291–292
    use of, 293
hasNext method, 211, 214
header
heap, 449
    array representation, 456, 457
    definition of, 449
    examples, 449
    implications of, 450
heap sort, 449
    algorithm, 450
    definition of a heap, 449
    highest-level right-most parent, 452
    initial heap, 450–454
    initial heap process, 452–454
    overhead, 458
    performance, 456
    performance comparison, 459, 472
    re-heap down algorithm, 454
    sort effort, 457
    sorting the heap, 455
    sorting the heap process, 455–457
    speed complexity, 456–457
    swap effort, 458
hashed structures, 232, 240, 246
height of a tree, 355, 407–408
heterogeneous data set, 106
    in a generic structure, 117, 118
high probability of access ordering, 79
homogeneous data set, 11, 15, 106

homogeneous structure, 59
    and generics, 116, 118

I

imbalanced trees, 407–408, 410–411, 418–419, 422
implementations
    binary search tree, 394
    graph, 493, 500
    generic optimized array, 113
    generic stack, 166
    hashed structure, 280
    iterator, 214, 219
    optimized array, 103
    queue, 160
    singly linked list, 189
    stack, 140
implements key word, 111, 116, 166
index, 34
indirect recursion, 308
information bytes, 31
inheritance, 47, 212
initial heap, 450–454
initialization of structures
    array-based, 67
    binary trees, 366–367
    graphs, 491–492
    hashed structures, 239
    linked list, 182–183
    queues, 151
    stacks, 132
inner classes, 190, 240, 212, 214, 218, 397–397
inorder traversal, 410
input method, 99, 102
insert operation, 14
inserting edges, 492
inserting nodes, 14
    array-based structures, 67, 76, 79
    binary search trees, 367
    graphs, 492
    hashed structures, 240, 277
    linked structures, 183
    queues, 152
    stacks, 132–133
interfaces
    Comparable, 426
    KeyMode, 111, 115
    GenericNode, 166
interface, 111, 166

iterative solutions, 305, 306, 327
iterator, 209
    advantages of, 210
    client side multiple iterators, 218, 222
    client side single iterator, 211, 216
    external, 212, 219, 221
    implementation of multiple iterators,
        217–219
    implementation of single iterator, 212–214
    internal type, 212, 214
    Java's ListIterator class, 223
    methods, 211
    multiple iterators, 217
    objects, 210
    operations, 211
    performance improvements, 210
    singly linked list iterator classes, 213, 220

J

Java API data structure classes. *See* API classes
Java built in types, 33
Java character representations, 259
Java code. *See also* methods and classes
    array-based structure, 91, 103, 113
    binary search tree structure, 394
    deep copy, 42–44
    depth-first traversal, 500
    factorial, 307, 327
    Fibonacci sequence, 321
    graph structure, 493, 500
    hashed structure, 280
    initial data base loading, 99
    merge sort, 463
    node definition classes, 89, 102, 116, 141, 202,
        219, 396, 501
    queue, 160
    Quicksort, 470
    shallow copy, 41–42
    singly linked list node class, 102
    singly linked list structure, 189
    singly linked list structure with Iterator,
        213, 220
    stack, 140, 166
Java generic typing, 109.
        See also Java review-generics
Java Interface construct, 111, 116, 166
Java memory manager
    garbage collection, 42, 242

Java methods
  arraycopy, 105
  in ArrayList class, 119
  compareTo, 90
  in Hashtable class, 291, 293
  hasMoreTokens, 170
  length, 105
  in LinkedList class, 223
  in ListIterator class, 224
  nextToken, 170
  in Stack class, 168
  in TreeMap class, 426
Java primitive types, 33
Java review, 33
  arrays of objects, 44
  arrays of primitives, 45
  classes, 35
  clones (*see* deep copy)
  containership, 45
  deep copies, 42
  generics, 49
  get methods, 40–41
  inheritance, 47
  input method, 41
  method naming prefixes, 40
  objects, 37
  return, 40
  set methods, 40–41
  void and non-void methods, 40

K

key, 12
key field, 12
key mode access, 13
Knights Tour problem, 329

L

last-in-first-out (LIFO), 129
leaf, 354
  deletion of, 372
left subtree, 357
length of an array, 105
levels of a binary tree, 355
levels of recursion, 305, 307, 309, 326, 327
LIFO. *See* last-in-first-out
linear collision algorithm, 264, 266
linear complexity, 21
linear list, 13
  access function, 61

linear logarithmic complexity, 21
linear probing. *See* linear collision algorithm
linear-quotient collision algorithm, 269
  default prime, 270
  example of, 272
  multiple accesses, 271
  primary clustering, 273
  secondary clustering, 273
  speed complexity, 285
link field, 176
linked hashed structures, 292
  buckets, 292
  collision resolution, 292
  density, 294–296
  hybrid, 296
  performance, 294–296
  performance comparison, 297, 425
  primary storage area size, 294
  speed considerations, 295–96
linked implementation of
  graphs, 484, 487, 490
  hashed structures, 292
  queues, 204
  singly linked list, 188
  stacks, 194
  trees, 392
linked list nodes. *See* singly linked list
linked lists, 175
  algorithm discovery methodology,
    178–180
  circular singly linked, 202
  double ended singly linked, 202
  doubly linked, 205
  iterators (*see* iterators)
  multi-linked, 44
  non-contiguous memory, 174
  performance of, 191, 194–195, 206–207,
    209–210
  singly linked (*see* singly linked list)
  sorted singly linked, 204
linked representation of trees, 365
linked structures
  advantages of, 174–175
LinkedList class, 223
  client side, 224
list iterator. *See also* iterators
  advantages of, 210
Listing class, 89, 141
Listing2 class, 215

ListIterator class, 223
  client side, 225
LNR, 401, 405, 406
loading factor, 234, 236, 245–246, 252–253, 276,
    287, 291, 295–296
  direct hashed structures, 236, 245–246
  LQHashed structure, 252–253, 276, 287
  optimum, 253–254
logarithmic complexity, 21–22, 26
LQHashed structure, 278
  alphanumeric key preprocessing, 276,
    283, 285
  collision resolution algorithm, 270, 285
  default prime, 284
  delete algorithm, 279, 281, 284, 286
  density, 287, 289
  use of dummy node, 273, 276, 284
  fetch algorithm, 278, 281, 284, 286
  generic considerations, 289–290
  getKey method, 283, 284, 289, 290
  hashing algorithm, 276
  insert algorithm, 277, 280, 284, 285
  implementation, 280
  implementation restrictions, 283
  loading factor, 276, 285
  operation algorithms, 277–279
  performance, 285
  performance comparison, 288, 425
  performance degradation, 586
  preprocessing, 276, 283
  primary storage area sizing, 257, 284
  ShowAll method, 284
  speed complexity, 285
  update method, 282
LRN, 401, 405

M

macro level of a program, 3
maximum loading factor, 234, 252
memory fragmentation, 174
memory model
  arrays, 61–65
  array of objects, 45
  array of primitives, 34
  containership, 46
  deep copy, 43
  dynamic hashed structures, 290–291
  objects, 36, 38
  shallow copy, 42

merge sort, 458
  algorithm, 462
  implementation, 463
  merging process, 459, 460
  overhead, 465
  performance, 462
  performance comparison, 466, 472
  speed complexity, 462–465
  sort effort, 465
  sorting process, 459–461
  swap effort, 465
merging sorted sublists, 459, 460
method naming conventions, 36
  prefixes, 40
methods
  arrayCopy
  compareTo, 89, 90
  deepCopy, 43, 44, 89–90
  fourKplus3 prime generator,
    258, 282
  fibonacci, 321
  findNode, 396
  getAge, 40
  getKey, 283
  getPushed, 501
  Hanoi, 325
  hashCode, 291
  input, 102
  LNRoutputTraversal, 406
  mergeSort, 463
  nFactorial, 308
  outputIntegerArray, 50
  outputNumericArray (generic), 50
  quickSort, 470
  setAddress, 89, 93, 142
  setPushed, 501
  setWeight, 40
  showAll, 104, 141, 406
  showEdges, 501
  showVertex, 501
  stringReverse, 323
  stringToInt, 261, 283
  toString, 36, 48, 89
  transitiveClosure (Warshall's
    algorithm), 509
  xToN, 320
minimum spanning tree, 512
  algorithm, 515
  algorithm process, 513–515

minimum spanning tree, (*continued*)
    algorithm trace, 517
    application of, 505, 512
    client side code, 518
    definition of, 513
modularization, 19
modulo arithmetic, 266, 269, 270
multiple access problem, 266, 271

N

n factorial, 306
    friends analogy, 306
    iterative method, 327
    non-recursive definition, 306
    performance, 327–328
    recursive definition, 306
    recursive method, 308
    trace of method, 308
nanosecond, 27
new operator, 37
    action of, 37
next field, 181, 182
nextToken method, 170
$n\log_2 n$ complexity, 21
NLR, 401, 405
node, 12
    in binary tree, 365–366
    child, 354
    depiction of, 12
    in doubly linked list, 205
    dummy, 182, 205, 275
    leaf, 354
    parent, 354
    reference, 67
    root, 353
    in singly linked list, 182
    visiting, 154, 271, 285, 355, 494
Node class, 102, 190
node deletion. *See* deleting nodes
node fetch. *See* fetching nodes
node insertion. *See* inserting nodes
node update. *See* updating nodes
node width, 33
non-access instruction, 28
non-open addressing, 263, 264
non-perfect hashed structures.
        See also LQHashed structure

alphanumeric keys, 259
collisions, 248
collision resolution algorithms, 263
the delete problem, 274
density, 254–255
general flow, 248
hashing functions, 262
implementation of, 276
    (*see also* LQHashed structure)
optimum loading factor, 253–254
preprocessing algorithms, 259
primary storage area optimum sizing
    rule, 257
primary storage area sizing issues,
    232, 233
prime number generator, 258
search length, 252, 253
use of prime numbers in, 254, 270
non-void methods, 40
null reference, 16, 34, 37
    in error detection, 16, 86, 92, 98

O

object
    accessing (. operator), 39
    arrays of, 44
    and classes, 37
    creating, 37, 38
    deep copy of, 43
    memory allocation, 37, 38
    reference to, 37
    shallow copy of, 42
    sorting, 436–437
    speed vs. primitives, 38
Object class, 109
open addressing, 263
    linear probing, 264–267
    linear quotient probing, 269
    problems with, 266
    quadratic probing, 264–266, 268–269
operators
    dot (.), 39
    new, 37
optimized array-based structure. *See* Unsorted-
    Optimized array-based structure
optimizing compiler, 29, 138, 243
optimum loading factor, 253–254
order of magnitude analysis. *See* Big-O

overhead, 5
   calculation of, 32
   definition of, 32
   example, 32, 33
   fixed vs. variable, 32
overflow, 129

P

package access, 35, 219, 221
parameters, 36, 40
parent
   class, 47
   node, 354
parent and child object references, 48
parsing strings, 170
   StringTokenizer class, 170
partition pointers, 467
partitions, 465
path
peek operation, 127, 131, 148, 150, 163, 168
perfect hashed structures.
      See also direct hashed structure
   definition of, 237
   overhead, 236, 238
perfect hashing, 236
   minimum hashing function, 236, 238
   static key set, 236, 237
   and subtraction preprocessing, 238
   unique mapping, 236, 237
performance, 425. *See also* data structure
      performance; algorithm complexity
pivot value, 465
pointer, 34
polynomial complexity, 21
pop operation, 129. *See also* stack array-based;
      stack linked based
post-fixed notation, 144
   evaluation algorithm, 145–147
post-order traversal, 401, 405
preorder traversal, 401, 405
preprocessing, 234
preprocessing algorithms
   alphanumeric key method, 261
   digit extraction, 262
   fold shifting, 259–261, 285
   pseudorandom, 261
   subtraction, 238
primary clustering. *See* clustering

primary storage area, 239
   schemes, 233
primary storage area sizing
   direct hashed structure, 236
   LQHashed structure, 257
   non-perfect hashed structures, 257
prime numbers, 254
   four-k-plus-3 (4k + 3), 255
   generator algorithm, 257–258
   generator method, 258
   table of, 256
   use in hashed structures, 257, 254, 270
primitive data types, 33. *See also* built-in
   arrays of
priority queue, 166–167
private access, 34, 90
probability of operations, 31
procedural abstraction, 17
program
   standard for goodness, 5
pseudo key, 234
pseudo loading factor, 296
pseudorandom preprocessing, 261
public access, 34, 39
push operation, 129. *See also* stack array-based;
      stack linked based

Q

quadratic complexity, 21
quadratic probing, 264–267
   clustering, 268
   multiple accesses, 266
   short comings, 266
Queens Eight problem, 328, 342–346
queue, 148
   analogy, 148
   applications of, 161
   array based, 151
   in breadth-first traversals, 503–504
   circular, 153
   dequeue, 149, 154,
   empty, 149, 153
   enqueue, 149, 153
   expanded features, 162
   FIFO, 148
   front, 148, 151
   full, 149, 153

queue (*Continued*)
   link based, 204
   operations and errors, 149
   overflow, 149
   performance, 156
   performance comparison, 159, 425
   peek operation, 150, 163
   priority queue, 166
   rear, 149, 151
   representation of, 149
   vs. stack, 127–128, 159
queue array-based
   client code, 162
   density, 158
   dequeue algorithm, 154
   encapsulation, 154, 156
   enqueue algorithm, 153
   front, 149, 151
   garbage collection (recycling), 155
   implementation, 160
   initialized state, 151
   memory model, 151, 152
   numOfNodes, 151
   overflow condition, 153
   performance, 156
   rear, 149, 151
   size, 151
   speed, 156, 159
   underflow condition, 154
Queue class, 160
Quicksort, 465
   algorithm, 468
   implementation, 470
   overhead, 471
   partition pointers, 467
   partitions, 465
   performance, 469
   performance comparison, 472
   pivot value, 465
   popularity of, 465
   speed complexity, 469–471
   sort effort, 471
   sorting process, 467
   swap effort, 471

R
reachability matrix. *See* transitive closure matrix
record, 4
recurrence relation, 304

recursion, 303
   base case, 313, 314, 315–316, 318
   binary search tree traversal, 402
   definition, 305
   domino analogy, 312
   direct, 308
   dynamic programming, 327
   flow chart of, 315
   formulating recursive algorithms, 313
   general solution, 313, 314, 315, 317, 318
   indirect, 308
   iterative alternative, 305, 323, 327
   levels of, 305, 307, 309, 326, 327
   merge sort, 462, 463
   methodology, 614
   n factorial, 306, 314, 315–316, 327
   performance considerations, 325–327
   performance comparison vs. iteration, 327
   practice problems, 319
   problems with, 325
   quicksort, 365, 368, 370
   reduced problem, 314, 315, 316, 317, 318
   run-time stack implications, 326–327
   Towers of Hanoi, 323
recursion practice problems, 317
   Fibonacci sequence, 320
   reverse a string of length n, 321
   table of problems, 319
   table of solutions, 330
   Towers of Hanoi, 323
   x^n, 318
recursive algorithms
   backtracking, 334
   Fibonacci sequence, 321
   findNode, 369
   merge sort, 462
   n factorial, 308
   quicksort, 468
   reverse a string of length n, 323
   Towers of Hanoi, 323
   tree traversal, 402
   x^n, 320
red-black trees, 412
   deletions, 413
   extent of imbalance, 412
   fetch algorithm (*see* binary search tree insert)
   inserts, 413
   maximum number of levels, 412
   ordering conditions of nodes, 412

performance vs. AVL, 413
   re-balancing condition, 413
   rotations, 413
reduced problem, 314, 315, 316, 317, 318
   for several problems, 330
reference variables, 34
   null references, 34
re-heap down algorithm, 454
re-initialize operation, 146, 162
relative speed, 22
   case study, 23, 29
   methodology, 24
representing graphs. *See* graph representations
requirements phase, 10
restricted structures, 125
   application subset, 126
   difference in the fetch-delete
      operation, 128
   queue (*see* queue)
   restrictions on operations, 127
   restrictions on access, 127
   stacks (*see* stack)
retrieve operation. *See* fetch operation
return statement, 40
right child, 357
right subtree, 357
root
   of a heap, 450
   of a tree, 353
rotations
   in AVL trees, 409–412
   in red-black trees, 413
row-major order, 64
run-time stack, 326

S
searching
   arrays, 66, 67, 70, 232, 234, 236
   binary trees, 361–362, 368
   binary search, 24, 66
   graphs (*see* sequential search; linked lists;
      traversing graphs)
   linked lists, 184–186
   sequentially, 5, 65, 67, 69, 71, 176, 191, 204
search length, 250
   linear quotient collision algorithm, 285
   at optimum loading factor, 253
secondary clustering. *See* clustering
seed value, 3

self-balancing trees
   AVL trees, 364
   red-black trees, 412
sequential search, 5, 65, 67, 69, 71, 176,
      191, 204
   performance of, 82
setAddress method, 37, 89, 93, 99, 142
set prefix, 40
shallow copy, 41
   in a data structure, 93
   syntax, 42
   water analogy, 42
shortest path. *See* Dijkstra's shortest path
      algorithm; Floyd's algorithm
showAll method, 99, 104, 140, 141, 190, 282, 284,
      398, 404
sibling
   node (children of same parent), 54
   vertex, 496–497
singly linked list
   algorithm discovery methodology, 178–181
   client side, 191
   defined, 177
   delete algorithm, 186
   delete traversal, 187
   density, 193
   dummy node, 181
   fetch algorithm, 184
   fetch traversal, 184–185
   header, 177
   implementation, 188
   implementation level graphic, 182
   initialization, 181
   insert algorithm, 182
   l field, 181–182
   linked Nodes, 181–182
   next field, 181–182
   Node (inner) class, 190
   Node objects, 181–182
   operation algorithms, 178
   overhead, 193
   performance, 191
   performance comparison, 195, 207, 426
   showAll method, 190
   speed complexity, 191
   stack, 194–200, 201
   standard graphic, 178–179
   traversals, 179, 184–185, 186–187
   update algorithm, 188

skewed tree, 363, 407
  problems with, 407
  remedies, 407–409
software cost, 8, 10
software engineering, 8, 10
sorted array. *See also* sorted array-based structure
  binary search, 24, 66
Sorted array-based structure, 73
  binary search, 73, 74 (*see also* binary search)
  delete algorithm, 74
  density, 83
  encapsulation of, 75
  errors, 84
  fetch algorithm, 74
  garbage collection, 74
  initialization, 66
  insert algorithm, 76
  operation algorithms, 73
  performance, 77, 78, 82
  speed complexity, 77
  update algorithm, 73
sorted linked list, 204
sorting. *See also* sorting algorithms
  comparisons, 434
  minimum sort effort, 435
  minimum time to sort *n* items, 435, 436
  motivation for, 432
  performance, 433
  sort effort, 434
  sorting objects, 436–437
  swaps, 434–435
sorting algorithms
  Binary Tree, 437 (*see also* binary tree sort)
  Bubble, 442 (*see also* bubble sort)
  Heap, 449 (*see also* heap sort)
  Merge, 458 (*see also* merge sort)
  performance comparison, 472
  Quicksort, 465 (*see also* quicksort)
sorting algorithm performance, 472
sorting the heap, 455
space complexity, 19, 30
spanning tree, 509. *See also* minimum spanning tree
  algorithm, 511
  application of, 505
  definition of, 505–506
  determination of, 511
  examples of, 510
  implementation guidelines, 512

sparse matrix, 487
Stack class, 140
stack
  applications, 144
  analogy, 129
  array-based, 130
  expanded features, 130, 146, 147
  frame, 326
  in depth-first traversals, 497–498
  last-in-first-out, 129
  LIFO, 129
  operations and errors, 129
  overflow, 129, 133, 327
  peek operation, 131, 148
  performance, 136
  performance comparison, 139, 425
  pop operation, 129, 130
  push operation, 129–130
  in post-fixed evaluation, 144–145, 147
  vs. queue, 128
  use in recursion, 325–327
  run-time, 326
  top, 129, 131
  underflow, 129, 132
stack array-based, 130
  client code, 142
  density, 137
  encapsulation, 133, 136
  garbage collection, 133, 136
  generic implementation, 164–166
  implementation, 140
  initialized state, 132
  memory model, 131, 132
  overflow condition, 132
  performance, 136
  pop algorithm, 134
  push algorithm, 133
  speed, 136
  top, 131
  size, 131
  underflow condition, 133
Stack class, 140
  generic implementation, 166
  Java's API class, 167, 500
stack link based, 131, 194–201
  as singly linked list, 194–197
  using SinglyLinkedList class, 196–201
Standard abstract data, 17

Standard Template Library, 6
state of the machine, 326
static methods, 39
String class, 38
string preprocessing, 238, 259, 261, 289
StringTokenizer class, 170
subarray, 25
subscripted variables, 60
subtraction preprocessing, 238–239
subtree, 357
super class. *See* parent
super key word, 46
swapping, 447
    in fetch algorithms, 79
    in sorting algorithms, 436–437, 472
System class, 105

T
telephone information request case study, 88
    node description, 88
time complexity, 19
token, 145
top, 129
toSting method, 36, 48
total bytes, 32
Towers of Hanoi, 323
trade-off process, 9
    criteria, 9 (*see also* density vs. node width)
    factors, 9
    speed, 425
transitive closure matrix, 507–508.
        See also Warshall's algorithm
traversing graphs, 494
    breadth-first, 503
    depth-first, 497
    use in determining connectivity, 506–507
traversing lists, 177
traversing trees. *See* binary tree traversals
TreeMap class, 412, 423
    client side, 426
    Comparable interface, 426
trees. *See also* binary trees; binary search trees
    advantages of, 352
    array based representation, 413
    AVL, 407
    balanced (*see* binary trees)
    binary tree, 356
    binary tree traversals, 398

directed, 353
graphical depiction, 353
height of, 355, 407–408
implementation of, 392
levels, 355
linked representation, 365,
    operation algorithms, 366–380, 416–418, 423
red-black, 412
skewed, 363–364, 406–407, 418–421
terminology, 353–355
triangular series, 319, 330
$2i + 1, 2i + 2$ rule, 413
type place holders, 51

U
unbalanced trees. *See* imbalanced trees
underflow, 129, 133, 154
undirected graphs, 481. *See also* graphs
Unicode, 259, 262
    ASCII subset, 259, 537
Unsorted array-based structure, 66
    delete algorithm, 67
    density, 84
    encapsulation of, 66, 70
    errors, 66
    expansion of, 105
    fetch algorithm, 69
    garbage collection, 68
    initialization, 66
    insert algorithm, 66
    operation algorithms, 66–70
    performance, 70, 72, 82, 84
    speed complexity, 70
    update algorithm, 71
Unsorted-Optimized array-based structure, 79
    client code, 99
    delete algorithm, 81
    delete optimization, 80, 87
    density, 82, 83
    encapsulation of, 79
    errors, 84
    expansion of, 105
    fetch algorithm, 79, 86
    fetch optimization, 79
    garbage collection, 80
    implementation (baseline), 91
    implementation (with utilities), 103
    initialization, 66

Unsorted-Optimized array-based structure
    (*Continued*)
    insert algorithm, 67, 85
    operation algorithms, 79
    performance, 85
    showAll method, 101, 104
    sorted on probability of being fetched, 79
    speed complexity, 81
    update algorithm, 71, 87
    utility methods, 99
updating nodes, 14, 71

V
vertex
    adjacent, 478
    descendent, 497
    insert, 491–492
    operations on, 491
    representing, 484, 490
    siblings, 496–497, 503

visiting
    vertices, 494–497
        (*see also* traversing graphs)
    visiting a node, 355, 398
        (*see also* traversing graphs)
void (vs. non-void) methods, 40

W
Warshall's algorithm, 507
    algorithm, 508
    client side code, 510
    implementation, 509
    speed complexity, 509
    transitive closure matrix, 507, 508
    transitive property in
        mathematics, 508
weighted edges, 479, 491
weighted graphs, 481
wrapper classes, 397
    implementation of, 396